THE
EASTERN
EUROPE
COLLECTION

AUSTRIA IN 1848-49

Volumes I & II

William H. Stiles

ARNO PRESS & THE NEW YORK TIMES

New York - 1971

Reprint Edition 1971 by Arno Press Inc.

LC# 75-135834

ISBN 0-405-02776-1

The Eastern Europe Collection
ISBN for complete set: 0-405-02730-3

Manufactured in the United States of America

AUSTRIA IN 1848–49

AUSTRIA IN 1848–49:

BEING A HISTORY OF THE

LATE POLITICAL MOVEMENTS

IN

VIENNA, MILAN, VENICE, AND PRAGUE;

WITH

DETAILS OF THE CAMPAIGNS OF LOMBARDY AND NOVARA;
A FULL ACCOUNT OF THE

REVOLUTION IN HUNGARY;

AND HISTORICAL SKETCHES OF THE AUSTRIAN GOVERNMENT AND THE
PROVINCES OF THE EMPIRE.

BY WILLIAM H. STILES,

LATE CHARGÉ D'AFFAIRES OF THE UNITED STATES AT THE COURT OF VIENNA.

WITH

Portraits of the Emperor, Metternich, Radetzky, Jellacic, and Kossuth.

IN TWO VOLUMES.

VOL. I.

NEW YORK:

HARPER & BROTHERS, PUBLISHERS,

329 & 331 PEARL STREET,

FRANKLIN SQUARE.

1852.

PREFACE.

In the following pages the aim has been to afford the reader a just, however inadequate knowledge of one of the most important series of events which have occurred *in our own times*. Such an attempt is always perilous to the reputation of a writer for impartiality, and in the present instance this is especially liable to be the case, since the events recorded have given rise to many conflicting opinions. Admonished by such considerations of the difficulty and delicacy of the task, the author has been encouraged to undertake it, on account of the favorable opportunities he has enjoyed, both for accurate observation and candid judgment. Honored with the office of representative of the United States government in Austria, he witnessed the rise, progress, and final catastrophe of the revolution. He embraced the means which his official residence in Vienna afforded to collect materials from all sources to illustrate the general history of the times. By constant reference to official documents, some of which were only to be found in the imperial archives, as well as to more public authorities, and by means of his own personal observation, he has endeavored to present a faithful picture of the eventful struggles in Vienna, in Milan, in Venice, and in Prague, as well as full details of the campaigns in Lombardy, in Piedmont, and in Hungary.

To understand the causes, as well as to appreciate the facts of the recent political convulsions in Austria, the author has conceived it essential to present some preliminary considerations on the condition of the empire prior to the revolution. He has, therefore, reviewed at some length the history of the races which inhabit the provinces now composing Austria, the manner in which they became subject to the sway of a common sovereign, as well as considered the wholly different circumstances through which they have respectively developed ; subjects little understood, yet indispensable to a correct appreciation of subsequent events. No one who has not had occasion to investigate the obscure early history of the various races of Eastern Europe, or who has not attempted to reconcile the contradictory statements of those whose sole aim, in relating more recent events, appears to have been that of ex-. tolling one party and ascribing the worst motives and the foulest crimes to their opponents, can have an adequate idea of the obstacles in the way of arriving at truth. In tracing the past history of the Austrian empire, he has relied on the standard authorities ; and in reference to events comparatively recent, he has labored, by a full investigation of a vast amount of conflicting evidence, to educe from the confused mass a clear and, as he believes, a reliable statement of facts ; while his own views, in many cases, are modified by ample citations from the leading reviews and journals of the day, as well as the most approved works of late travelers and historians. His object has been to give the reader all the facts, and at the same time intimate frankly the various phases of public sentiment. In his comments on the actions of individuals, the reader must bear in mind that three parties are distinctly recognized, the government party, or Monarchists ; the Radicals, or reckless agitators ; and the intelligent or moderate reformers. It is important that the movements and opinions of each should be distinctly appreciated. The intention has been to report all parties fairly, and to elicit truth from a careful survey of authentic facts. To the author, the examination of these subjects has been replete with interest and instruction, and he ventures to hope that his labors will be favorably regarded by those who follow with interest the general tendency of events in Europe. To such he commends them, with the sincere conviction that no partisan spirit has dictated the views advanced; while, as an American, he could not be indifferent, first, to the joyful burst of acclamation which hailed the advent of an era of liberty, nor, afterward, to the mournful fate to which the constitutional system in Austria seemed doomed; yet, taught by the duties of his position to regard the moment-ous events which transpired in such rapid succession around him with the calm reflection which should characterize official station, he has been guided by the same impartial spirit in recounting them.

If, in the elucidation of truth, the author has found it necessary to allude to the errors of all parties, the unpleasant duty has been attempted for that object only, and under the hope that, while interest would be excited by a relation of events in which they were conspicuous, lessons of practical wisdom might at the same time be learned from their exposure.

No 55 Broadway, New York.

CONTENTS OF VOL. I.

BOOK I.

CHAPTER I.

HISTORICAL INTRODUCTION.

CHAPTER II.

HISTORICAL INTRODUCTION—*Continued.*

BOOK II.

CHAPTER I.

CHAPTER II.

CHAPTER III.

CHAPTER IV.

AUTHORITIES.

The following standard works, official documents, private memoirs, and public journals have been examined during the preparation of the following volumes, and, while the author most gratefully acknowledges the great assistance they have rendered him, he relies upon them confidently to establish the authenticity of his statements.

Coxe's History of the House of Austria.

Menzel's History of Germany.

Pölitz, Geschichte des Oesterreichischen Kaiserstaates.

Sigismond Calles, Annales Austriæ ab ultimæ ætatis memoria, ad Habsburgicæ gentis Principes deducti.

Franz Ferdinand Schrötter, Versuch einer Oesterreichischen Staatsgeschichte von dem Ursprunge Oesterreich bis nach dessen Erhöhung in ein Herzogthum.

Lünig's Reichs-Archiv.

Mailath, Oesterreichischen Kaiserstaates.

Palacky's History of Bohemia.

Melch. Goldasti, Commentarius de Bohemiæ regno.

F. A. Fessler's Geschichten der Ungarn.

Heeren's Historical Researches.

Allgemeine Congress-Acte (9 Juni, 1815).

Staats Lexikon, von Carl von Rottech und Carl Welcher.

Adrian Rauch, Rerum Austriacarum Scriptores, etc., ex authenticis bibl. Vindob. codicibus ustis et Diplomaticis instrumentis.

Kasp. Lehmann, Versuch einer Geschichte Oesterreichischen Regenten.

Ferrand, Histoire des Démembrements de la Pologne.

Von Raumer, Polens Untergang.

Sanctio Pragmatica.

Wheaton's Digest of the Laws of Nations.

Europe after the Congress of Aix-la-Chapelle, by M. De Pradt.

Congrès de Vienne, par M. Capefigue.

Alison's History of Europe.

Turnbull's Austria.

Kohl's Austria.

Thompson's Austria.

Wilde's Austria.

Fürst Clemens von Metternich und sein Zeitalter, von Josef Binder.

Tablettes Autrichiennes.

Germany, Bohemia, and Hungary, by G. R. Gleig.

Daru's History of Venice.

Sketches of Venetian History, from the Family Library.

Hallam's Middle Ages.

Der Oesterreichischen Universal-Kalender für das Jahr 1849. 1 Gang, Richtung der Wiener-Revolution von 13 März bis 6 Oct., 1848, von Dr. F. C. Weidmann. 2. Wien und Buda-Pesth im Herbste 1848, von Joh. Moshamer.

Dunder's Wiener Revolution.

Paget's Hungary.

Klapka s War oi Hungary.
Schlessinger's War in Hungary.
Pragay's Hungarian Struggle for Freedom.
Scenes of the Civil War in Hungary.
Memoirs of a Hungarian Lady, by T. Pulszky.
History of Slavic Literature.
Demain's Tableau de la Hongrie.
De l'Esprit publique en Hongrie, par A. Degerando.
Encyclopædia Americana.
British Encyclopedia.
Hormayer's Franz und Metternich.
Franz der Erste, Kaiser von Oesterreich, und sein Zeitalter.
A Voice from the Danube.
Blue Book of the English Parliament.
Biography of Manin.
Williston's Campaign of Lombardy.
Custoza.
Campagne de Novara, par l'Auteur de Custoza.
Le Spectateur Militaire.
La Hongrie en 1848, par J. Boldényi.
La Hongrie, par Emile Marguérin.
Lettres sur la Hongrie, par Ladislas Szalay.
The Case of Hungary stated by Count Ladislas Teleki.
Question Austro-Hongroise et l'Intervention Russe.
De l'Intervention Russe, par le Comte Ladislas Teleki.
Parallels between the Constitutions of England and Hungary, by J. T. Smith.
Correspondence relative to the Affairs of Hungary, 1847–49, presented to both Houses of Parliament by Order of Her Majesty.
Events in the Austrian Empire in 1848–49, by Baron Pillersdorf.
Count Hartig on the Events of 1848.
Edinburgh, Quarterly, Westminster, and North British Reviews; Blackwood's Magazine; Allgemeine Zeitung, Wiener Zeitung, Lloyd's Gazette, Gazzetta di Milano, Gazzetta di Venezia, Piedmontese Gazette, Galignani's Messenger, La Presse, London Times, Chronicle, Examiner, North American Review, Christian Examiner, &c.

AUSTRIA IN 1848 AND 1849.

BOOK I.

CHAPTER I.

HISTORICAL INTRODUCTION.

AUSTRIA AND ITS PROVINCES.—ACCOUNT OF THEIR ORIGIN, AND HISTORY OF THEIR CONNECTION WITH THE EMPIRE, TO THE TREATY OF VIENNA IN 1815.

THE present Empire of Austria, with its two hundred and fifty-six thousand square miles, and thirty-eight millions of inhabitants, was, at the period when its name became first known, literally, as it has been described in a recent state paper, " but as a patch on the earth's surface."*

When the " barbarian irruptions" of the fourth, fifth, and sixth centuries, which overwhelmed the Roman provinces, obliterating the boundaries of Vindelicia, Noricum, Pannonia, Illyricum, and Rhætia, had subsided, the River Enns† was found to constitute the eastern limit of civilization in Central Europe.

On the left bank of this river were established the Bavarians, or Bajoarii, descending from the Boii; and the right bank was inhabited by the Avars, a wild Tatar race.

While the former remained stationary, and lived under their own dukes—recognizing, however, the supremacy of the Frankish kings, by the performance of feudal military service —the latter continued, during the short period of their historical existence, mere lawless invaders and wandering plunderers. After the incorporation of Bavaria with the Frankish empire, Charlemagne marched against the Avars, and sub-

---

* Letter of Mr. Webster, U. S. Secretary of State, to Chevalier Hülsemann, Dec. 21, 1850.

† The Enns, a small river emptying into the Danube on its right bank, a little below Linz.

A

dued them, in 791–799. Ten thousand of these barbarians
were drowned in the Danube, and the remainder were driven
beyond the River Raab, which then became the eastern boundary of the empire.

The territory between the Enns and the Raab, thus vacated
by the expulsion of the Avars, known as Avaria, was subsequently called Austria. It was also designated *Marca Ori-
entalis*, or the Eastern Frontier, and the administration and
defense of this newly-created fief were committed to margraves. The name given by the Germans to this recently-con-
quered country was Ostirrichi (Ostirrich, Osterreich, and finally
Oesterreich), signifying domain of the East, and appeared
for the first time, in the year 996, in an imperial document.

Suabian and Bavarian families, who colonized the country,
introduced the first germs of civilization; and the territory,
thus limited in extent, formed the nucleus around which, during
the lapse of centuries, there have been gathered sixteen great
states, besides numerous small principalities, inhabited by four
of the seven different races of Europe, among whom are spoken
twelve distinct languages and countless dialects, and between
whom the only bond of union has been the sway of a common
sovereign. What were the different countries that formed this
empire—what was the period, and what the manner of their
acquisition—whether by conquest, election, succession, or marriage,* the following brief chronological account will make
manifest; while, at the same time, it will render more intelligible, if not more interesting, the events and considerations
hereafter disclosed.

ARCHDUCHY OF AUSTRIA.

The new margraviate of Austria had existed but a brief
period, when it was invaded by the fierce and invincible Magyars (Hungarians, abandoning their homes on the northern

---

* A great portion of Austria was acquired by marriage with princesses who
were heiresses to these kingdoms and principalities. It was thus that Hungary,
Bohemia, and the Tyrol were acquired. Hence the lines:

> " Bella gerant alii : tu felix Austria, nube;
> Nam quæ Mars aliis, dat tibi regna Venus."

> You, Austria, wed as others wage their wars,
> And crowns to Venus owe, as they to Mars.

coasts of the Black Sea, wandered in the plains of the Danube), who, by their victorious arms, acquired the largest portion of this territory.

The empire of the Franks had by this time, on the death of Charlemagne, been divided between France, Italy, and Germany; and Austria, from its geographical position, had fallen to Germany. Louis, "the child"* who then sat on the German throne, terrified by the disasters which encompassed him, consented to the payment of a ten years' tribute to the Magyars, and made Mölk the eastern boundary of the Austrian margraviate. To mark the spot, a royal castle was erected by the Hungarians, on the commanding hill overlooking the Danube, on which now stands the splendid monastery of Mölk, to challenge the admiration of every traveler who descends the waters of that picturesque stream. Margraves of different houses, under the appointment of the emperor, succeeded to the Austrian fief, until 983, when it became hereditary in the family of Babenberg. Leopold von Babenberg having saved the life of Otho the First, of Germany, in a boar hunt, the emperor presented to him the margraviate of Austria as a reward for this service.

After the victory of Otho the First on the Lechfeld (955), the original boundaries of the margraviate were nearly re-established, and the Magyars, driven from Mölk, were compelled to confine themselves within the limits of modern Hungary.

The family of Babenberg ruled in Austria from 982 to 1246, although the succession was not regulated by primogeniture, but solely by the will of the German emperor. The fiefs were, at first, held for a term of years, afterward for life, and finally they became hereditary.

During this period Austria extended its frontiers on the east to the Leitha, which formed for a long time her boundary with the Hungarians; while on the west, in consequence of the struggles between the Hohenstaufen—the reigning family of Germany—and the Welfs—the dukes of Saxony and Bavaria—she gained the country above the Enns, belonging

---

* "Woe to the land whose king is a child," then preached in Germany, is now repeated by the Hungarians; but the *youth* of the emperor, which then favored the Hungarians, is now regarded as their greatest misfortune.

to Bavaria, and which was taken from the Welfs and conferred by the emperor on his kinsmen, the margraves of Austria, for their highly-esteemed services and fidelity in 1156.

Both territories, that above as well as that below the Enns, were then united, and this enlarged territory was afterward created by Barbarossa—the Emperor Frederick the First—a duchy, and was acknowledged an hereditary fief, with the right to leave it by testament, after the expiration of the male line, to the female posterity.

Besides this, many rights and liberties were granted to the new duchy,* so that Austria may be considered from this period as an established state in the German Confederacy.

STYRIA.

The first accession of territory to the Duchy of Austria was the annexation of Styria, the limits of which, during the reign of Conrad the First, had been gradually extended from the fortress of Steyer on every side.

After the victory of the emperor, Otho the First, over the Hungarians, this territory was added, in 955, to the German empire; and in 1180, Ottocar the Sixth, obtaining the title and powers of duke, disposed of the duchy in favor of his father-in-law, Leopold the Sixth of Austria.

The German feudatories had already become sufficiently powerful to compel the monarchs to respect such testamentary dispositions as they might make of their fiefs; and already had Lothar the Third established a law that fiefs rendered vacant by the extinction of the family of the incumbents should, instead of lapsing to the crown, fall to the next of kin.† Thus the Duke of Austria, in 1192, became legally and rightfully invested with the possession and control of Styria.

---

* This new duchy was smaller than the present "Austria above and below the Enns," as the southern boundaries were not yet extended to the Semmering Mountain; while, as far as the Piesting River, all belonged to the Carenthanian, and on the east only, as now, the Leitha continued to remain the frontier. After the political organization of Carinthia, Styria belonged to the Marchia Carenthana; but the proprietors of the castle and city of Steyer soon obtained the title of margrave. Leopold the Brave, son of Ottocar of Styria, acquired the largest portion of this marchia by purchase, inheritance, and investiture. From his time the name of his dynasty became attached to the land itself.

† Menzel.

Lands of the Ecclesiastical Principality of Freisingen, in
Carniola.

In 1229, Leopold the Seventh purchased of the Ecclesiastical Principality of Freisingen certain lands in Carniola, and
prepared the way, by this purchase, for the future connection
of Carniola with Austria.

Leopold the Seventh, or the Glorious, as he was called, excelled in the administration of internal affairs. He built the
palace in Vienna, in which the emperors still reside, and, with
the ransom paid by England's king, Richard Cœur de Lion, is
said to have constructed the walls which surround the capital. To his brilliant court the most renowned embassadors
were dispatched, and Austria shone forth in the highest splendor of the Middle Ages. But, amid all this magnificence, the
useful sciences were neglected, and the worthy duke absolutely died for want of a surgeon to amputate a fractured limb.
Having fractured his leg by a fall from his horse, he seized an
ax, and, placing its edge on the broken limb, ordered his attendant to strike upon it with a mallet; and thus was his
leg severed from his body.

With the ·death of Frederick the Warrior, son of Leopold,
in 1246, the male line of the house of Babenberg became extinct. Austria and Styria were then declared vacant fiefs,
and provisionally governed by imperial stadtholders. The period from 1246 to 1282, and styled the Austrian interregnum,
proved disastrous to the union of both countries. The German emperor was placed under ban by the Pope, and the anti-
emperor and the kings of Hungary and Bohemia were enjoined
by the pontiff to take possession of the Austrian lands.

The Estates or Diets of Austria and Styria at length elected Ottocar, son of the King of Bohemia, to the office of duke.
His father, King Wenzel, having bribed the Austrian deputy,
as he passed through Prague on his errand to tender the dukedom to Henry von Meissen, and having also succeeded in inducing the Estates to make choice of his son.

Ottocar having soon after ascended the throne of Bohemia,
and having been invested by Richard of Cornwall, the aspi-
rant to the German throne, with the vacant fiefs of Austria

and Styria, and having reduced under his authority the Duchy of Carinthia, and the largest portion of Carniola, with Friul and Istria (bequeathed to him by the Duke Ulrich von Ostenburg, who died without issue), became the most powerful prince of Europe.

Too confident of his power, Ottocar refused to acknowledge the election of the Count Rhodolph of Habsburg as Emperor of Germany (1273), and entered into war with him. On the March-field opposite Vienna, on the same plain where nearly six centuries afterward occurred the famous battles of Aspern and Wagram between the Archduke Charles and Napoleon, Ottocar was totally defeated and slain; and his son, to preserve his hereditary states, was obliged to renounce all claim to the Austrian possessions.

All the lands of Ottocar, except his hereditary states, were now conferred by the emperor on his sons Albert and Rhodolph; but Carinthia, at their request, was reserved by the emperor, and bestowed on Meinhard of Tyrol, father-in-law of Albert, in reward for his services during the war with Ottocar. At the solicitation of the Estates, the emperor (1283) declared Austria and Styria an inalienable and indivisible domain, with their former ancient rights and privileges, vesting the sole administration in Albert, and assigning a specific revenue to Rhodolph and his heirs. From that period the successors of Rhodolph assumed to themselves the title of " Princes of Austria." Indeed, the chief object of Rhodolph seemed to be the confirmation of the Austrian possessions in his family.*

CARINTHIA.

A new accession of territory followed in 1336, upon the death of the Duke of Carinthia. After the invasion of Noricum by the Slavi, and the invaders had retired, Carinthia, a portion of that territory, was occupied by the Carnians (Carantani). From the seventh century they had existed under their own princes, but at the same time acknowledged some dependence upon Bavaria.

---

* Not content with this, he was also desirous of making the imperial crown hereditary, and of naming his son Albert his successor to the throne. But the refusal of the prince hastened his death, which occurred in 1291.

After the death of Carlman, son of Louis the German, in 880, his illegitimate son Arnulf became Margrave of Carinthia.

In 926 it was separated from Bavaria, by the Emperor Otho the Second, and elected its own dukes.

The last duke of the house of Sponheim, in 1269, declared the King of Bohemia heir of Carinthia, to which belonged also the largest portion of Carniola, with the Friul and Istria.

After the fatal war between the emperor and Ottocar, those lands were transferred to Albert and Rhodolph, sons of the emperor ; but, at their request, were resumed by the emperor, and conferred on the Count of Tyrol, who possessed them until 1336. During this year the last Count of Tyrol died, and Carinthia, with all its appendages, reverted to the Dukes of Austria.

This title, however, did not consist so much in the former possession of the land as in the new investiture bestowed upon them by the emperor, who feared the increasing power of the Luxemburgs in Bohemia, and against whom they were now united. The emperor even revoked, on this occasion, the declaration of succession to Carinthia and Tyrol, which he had previously made, in favor of the kings of Bohemia. But the triumph of the King of Bohemia and his allies prevented, then, the transfer of the Tyrol, and Carinthia was, consequently, the sole accession which Austria at that time received.

TYROL.

A still further acquisition took place in 1364. Tyrol, a name derived from the ancient Roman Teriolis, formed a part of Rhætia, and, with the exception of some portions afterward added to Carinthia, had, ever since the sixth century, belonged to Bavaria. The southern part remained occupied by the Longobards. When Henry the Lion was put under the imperial ban, Tyrol was divided, and bishops and counts formed of it separate and independent states.

The most conspicuous of these new masters were the counts of Andecks, who received from the emperor, Frederick the First, the title of dukes. In 1248, the dukes of Meran Andecks, who guarded, according to Hormayer, the frontier of the empire, as far as the shores of the Adriatic (hence their name

Meer-an), becoming extinct on the death of Otho, their possessions fell to their cousin Albert, count of Tyrol, whose
daughter Adelheid brought them afterward, in dower, to her
husband, Meinhard the First, count of Göritz.

Meinhard left two sons, Meinhard the Second, who inherited
the Tyrol, and obtained the investiture of Carinthia from the
emperor; and Albert, who succeeded to Göritz.   In 1310 the
inheritance of Tyrol fell to Henry the Second, father of the famous Margaret, called Maultasch—a name derived, as some
authors say, from her pouting lips; or, according to others,
from her castle of Maultasch.   She procured from the Emperor
Louis a decree, recognizing Carinthia and Tyrol as feminine
fiefs—a document which he afterward found it expedient to
annul, when he chose to invest the dukes of Austria with Carinthia and Tyrol.

After a war between Margaret's adherents and the Austrian
princes, Carinthia, together with Carniola, which was attached
to it, remained in possession of the latter, and Tyrol was assigned to Margaret.

The marriage of Margaret Maultasch, heiress of the Tyrol,
with Louis of Bavaria, not having been confirmed by the Pope,
her son Meinhard was branded as illegitimate.   Through the
exertions of Rhodolph the Fourth, duke of Austria, the pontiff
was induced to sanction the marriage, and to establish the legitimacy of Meinhard, on whom he then bestowed the hand
of his sister Margaret.   In gratitude for these favors, Margaret Maultasch gave the reversion of the Tyrol to the dukes of
Austria, should her husband and son die without issue.

After the death of her husband in 1361, and that of her son
in 1363, Rhodolph, fearful lest the Bavarian princes should
obtain possession of the Tyrol by virtue of the marriage contract of Margaret with Louis, which secured the reversion of
that province, in failure of his issue, to the house of Lower
Bavaria, crossed the Alps, with great difficulty and danger, in
the depth of winter, and prevailed on Margaret to ratify the
former grant, and to yield to him immediate possession of the
Tyrol.   But a far greater difficulty yet remained, that of obtaining the sanction of the emperor to the arrangement; for,
notwithstanding the tie of Rodolph's marriage with Catha-

rine, the daughter of the Emperor Charles, the natural jealousies of the houses of Austria and Luxemburg had occasioned frequent contests between them. At this juncture, Rhodolph and his three brothers united in a league with the kings of Hungary and Poland against the emperor as king of Bohemia.

Fortunately, however, Catharine was enabled to effect a reconciliation between her father and husband, and in 1364 a meeting took place at Brünn between Charles and the Austrian princes, when Charles confirmed the donation of Margaret, invested Rhodolph with the Tyrol, and even entered into a family compact with the Austrian princes for the reciprocal reversion—in failure of male issue—of their respective territories.*

In the same year (1364) Rhodolph and his brothers concluded a compact with Albert the Fourth, count of Göritz, a collateral branch of the house of Tyrol, which opened the way to the subsequent acquisition, by the Austrian house, of the counties of Göritz, and of Gradisca and Mittenburg.

Feldkirch.

In 1375, Leopold the Third purchased the claims of the Count of Feldkirch for 36,000 gold guldens, and this beautiful country was added to the Duchy of Austria. With Feldkirch was also purchased a portion of the county of Bregenz, called the Innerwald.†

Trieste.

In 1382 the territory of Trieste was acquired. This was originally a Roman colony, and from the time of the visit of Constantine the Great to Italy, after the defeat of Maxentius, became attached to the Occidental empire, and remained subject to the exarchat of Ravenna, until the contest between the Pope Virgilius and the Bishop of Aquileia in the sixth century. It afterward fell to the dukes of the Friul; and in 973 be-

---

* Coxe's House of Austria.

The same Rhodolph, provoked by the article of the Golden Bull, which gave the electors precedence over all other princes, assumed the title of Archduke Palatine; but the title was dropped by his successors, until confirmed by the Emperor Frederick the Third, 1453.

† Jos. Bergmann.

came subject to the Patriarch of Aquileia, and soon afterward
to the Count of Göritz.   In 1202, the city placed herself under the protection of Venice.   During the Venetian wars, the
inhabitants, dissatisfied with the government of Venice, rebelled, and surrendered themselves to the confederate forces,
and the sovereignty of the city was again transferred to the
Patriarch of Aquileia.   But the people, harassed with intes-
tine commotions, and finding the new sovereign too weak to
protect them against their former rulers, whose dominion they
dreaded, offered their submission to Leopold the Second of Austria.   He acceded to their overtures, promised to respect their
privileges and preserve their municipal government, appointed
a captain or prefect in the city, and thus secured to the house
of Austria this most important port of the Adriatic.*

PLUDENTZ, WITH THE VALLEY OF MONTAVON

In 1394 the Duke Leopold the Second, who equaled his
ancestors in his eagerness to increase his possessions, pur-

---

* It should here be remarked that the Austrian possessions became divided in
1379 between the two brothers Albert and Leopold; that by this division two
lines were formed—the Austrian and the Styrian. The possessions of the last of
the Austrian line (of Albert) devolved on the Styrian line in 1457; and the lands
became again divided between the members of this line, until the year 1496, when
Maximilian the First reunited the Austrian possessions.

Not only had the family compact, but the imperial investiture, established the
indivisibility of the Austrian territories, and vested the administration in the eldest
brother, but the discordant characters of the two Austrian princes proved fatal to
the family union; and Leopold applied for and obtained the consent of the emperor to the division, who, in readily yielding his sanction, Charles remarked,
"We have long labored in vain to humble the house of Austria, and now the dukes
of Austria have humbled themselves."   The rapid development of the European
states during this age, together with the political and religious disturbances, required a strong head and powerful arm for the occupant of the German throne;
and as, in these respects, the German princes were inferior to the Austrian, it was
very natural that selections should be made for that post from the latter house.

With the election of the reserved Albert the Fifth to the German throne, in
1438, who died the following year, began the unbroken chain of German emperors elected from the Austrian house.   Thus began, in the Middle Ages, the connection of Austria with Germany by the union of the crown in the person of the
same monarch.   This connection continued until August 1st, 1806, when, upon
the *fiat* of Napoleon, and the construction of the Confederation of the Rhine, the
empire was dissolved.   In consequence, Austria laid aside the imperial crown of
Germany, adopting, instead, the imperial crown of Austria, and Francis the Second of Germany became Francis the First of Austria.

chased from the Count Albert of Werdenberg the county of Pludentz, with the valley of Montavon.*

Castria.

This Estate, now in the province of Illyria, was purchased in 1400.

The "Vorderwald" of the county of Bregenz.

The remainder of the former county of Bregenz, called "The Vorderwald," was sold by Elizabeth, wife of the margrave, William of Hochberg, to the Archduke Sigismund of Austria, in 1451.

Sonnenberg.

The county of Sonnenberg, in Tyrol, was bought by the Archduke Sigismund for 34,000 gold guldens, in 1474.

Göritz, Gradisca, Mittenberg, and the Pusterthal.

In 1500 the counties of Göritz, Gradisca, Mittenberg, and the Pusterthal were escheated to the princes of Austria. These lands constituted an important acquisition from their extent and their local situation, as they joined the frontiers of Carinthia and Carniola, and connected those countries with the territory of Trieste. The Counts of Göritz and those of Tyrol were probably of the same descent. The first mention of the Counts of Göritz is found under the Emperor Henry the Fifth.

In 1362, Albert the Fourth, Count of Göritz, concluded a compact with Rodolph, Duke of Austria, by virtue of which his possessions were to fall to Austria on the extinction of the male succession. In 1500 the male line ceased, upon the death of Count Leonard, and his three counties fell to Maximilian of Austria.

Subsequently to this acquisition, Gradisca was bestowed by Ferdinand the Third, in 1641, on the princes of Eggenberg; but in 1717 it fell back again to Austria, after that line became extinct.

---

* Jos. Bergmann's Früheste Kunde über den Bregenzerwald, &c.

BOHEMIA, MORAVIA, AND AUSTRIAN SILESIA.

A most important acquisition of territory was made by Austria in the annexation of Bohemia, together with Moravia and Silesia.

Bohemia was, as Tacitus relates, inhabited by the Boji, who, one hundred years (P. C. U.) were driven from it by the Marcomanni. After the irruptions of the Huns, Goths, and Lombards, the Marcomanni were, in turn, expelled, and their places supplied by a new people from the East, called Czecks, of whom the earliest accounts are fabulous and obscure.

In the eighth century, Crocus reigned in Bohemia. His daughter and successor was the prophetess Libussa,* and her husband the peasant Przemisl, the Bohemian Cincinnatus, who was called from the plow to the highest office of state.

As among the Slavian nations generally, so with the Czecks, the first elements of their political constitution were patriarchal and democratic. Their chiefs afterward obtained the title of dukes, and, still later, that of kings.

After the treaty of Verdun, in 843, when the country had been subdued by the Franks, under Charlemagne, Bohemia was added to the German empire, although the dukes had been indefatigable in their efforts to preserve its independence.†

The sovereignty of the country, however, always rested with their own princes. They, in conjunction with the Estates, made the laws, declared war, concluded treaties, &c., without the sanction of the German emperor.

The Duke Wratislaus was the first who received the royal dignity. It was in 1086; at which time, also, Moravia was declared a margraviate. With Wenzel the Third, who was slain in 1306, terminated the race of native Bohemian kings, and the Estates elected, in 1309, John of Luxemburg, son of the German emperor, to the vacant throne.

The last king of the line of Luxemburg in Bohemia was

---

* After the death of Libussa broke out "the War of the Maid-servants," under the celebrated Wlasta. This war of the Bohemian Amazons is replete with wild and picturesque legends.

† The tribute imposed on the conquered Bohemians was only one hundred and twenty fattened oxen.

Sigismond, who died in 1437, after having recommended to the principal nobles of Bohemia and Hungary (for he was also king of the latter country) his son-in-law, Albert the Fifth of Austria, who had rendered him essential service in the Hussite war, as his successor.   Sigismond wept on this occasion, and concluded his address to the Estates as follows: "I beseech you by these tears, comfort my soul, which is departing to God, by confirming my choice and fulfilling my will."   Though repeated compacts had been made between the Bohemian and Austrian sovereigns, they had been ineffectual in transferring the crown, so long as the Estates continued to reserve to themselves the right of election.   Albert died in 1439, and many contests between the various pretenders took place, until George Podiebrad, a simple, but true and resolute nobleman, was raised to the throne, and which he occupied until his death, in 1471.

The Estates then made choice of Wladislaus, a Polish prince of the house of Jaghello; and upon the death of his son Louis, who lost his young and vagabond life in the battle of Mohatz, in 1526, the crowns of Bohemia and Hungary, rendered vacant by his death, were then claimed by Ferdinand of Austria, under a double title: one derived from family compacts, which secured the reversion to the house of Austria in failure of male issue to the reigning family; the other through his wife, the only sister of the deceased monarch, to whom the Estates of Bohemia once promised the crown, in case Louis should die without nearer successors.   The Bohemians and Hungarians would neither respect these compacts nor acknowledge his claims as husband of the princess, and Ferdinand, prudently waving these pretensions, offered himself according to the usual mode of election.   On the 26th of October, 1526, he was elected by a committee of twenty persons, appointed by the Estates to choose a king to succeed Louis; and on the 4th of February, 1527, Ferdinand was duly crowned, with his wife Anne, in the cathedral at Prague.

Since this period Bohemia has remained united with Austria.   Ferdinand the Second, who soon succeeded to the throne, having abolished all the rights and privileges of the Estates, which he had sworn to observe, rendered the throne of Bohemia hereditary in the house of Austria.

Moravia, which fell together with Bohemia to Ferdinand the First, formed, in the eighth century, a Slavic kingdom. The king, Samoslaw, was defeated by Charlemagne, and Moravia became subject to his successors. The German margraves placed over them Wilhelm and Engelschalk, who treated the Moravians so arbitrarily that they rebelled. Swatopluk,* the nephew of the Moravian Prince Rastiz, left his honorable confinement at Ratisbon, under pretext of appearing against them, but in truth to make common cause with them. The armies sent into Moravia against them were defeated, but Swatopluk was victorious on the Danube, and laid the country waste until the weak and despicable "Charles the Thick" appeared, in 884, in person, to sue for peace. Swatopluk not only preserved, but extended his dominion. After the death of Swatopluk, the kingdom of Moravia was divided, and portions of it fell to Germany, to Poland, and to Hungary. That part of it which lay next to Bohemia placed itself under the protection of the Bohemian Duke Wratislaus the First, who defeated the Hungarians and annexed this portion of Moravia to his possessions. The Bohemian Duke Udalrich, and after him Brzetislaus, acquired still more of the dissolved kingdom, so that, in 1026, Moravia embraced about the same extent of country that it does at this day.

The dukes and kings of Bohemia left Moravia at different times as a fief to their sons or successors. Since the dissolution of the kingdom, the Moravian territory has remained constantly annexed to Bohemia, and its affairs administered, from the eleventh to the seventeenth century, by relatives of the Bohemian kings.

With Bohemia and Moravia there also fell to Austria that portion of Silesia which, after the wars of Austria and Prussia, was continued in possession of Austria by the treaties of 1742, 1745, and 1763, and embrace at this time but two small circles. This province was in the tenth century subdued by the dukes of Poland, and in 1163 was divided into three parts, and assigned to their own princes. In the thirteenth century the whole territory was divided into so many portions that a de-

---

* Zwentibald.

fense against the Mongols could only be effected by successive submissions to the Bohemian kings.   Charles the Fourth declared Silesia a fief of Bohemia, and incorporated it with Germany.   After the second half of the seventeenth century, the last Silesian Piast died, and the whole of Silesia was then united to Bohemia as an *accessorium*.

Principalities of Gurk, Lekau, and Lavant.

In the year 1521, there existed within the limits of Austria, lying mostly in her own provinces, three petty but independent principalities, viz., those of the bishops of Gurk, of Lekau, and of Lavant, which in the course of time were either purchased or merely secularized, and submitted to the authority of the house of Habsburg.

Hungary and Croatia.

The disastrous and untimely death of King Louis of Hungary resulted in the annexation of this country to Austria. The territory now known as Hungary was formerly embraced in the Roman province called Pannonia, and a part of that of Dacia.   Afterward it was successively occupied by the Huns, Goths, and Gepidæ, between the years 489 and 526; by the Lombards until 568; and later by the Avars.

In the year 889, the Magyar,* an Asiatic tribe, driven from their homes beyond the Ural Mountains by the Petchenegues, under their leader Arpad, invaded Hungary, then parceled out among several petty lords and princes, who formed a kind of federal aristocracy, or union of clans, owing a limited obedience to a superior or chief.

The Magyars, under Arpad and his posterity, overran, plundered, and left desolate a large portion of the Continent, particularly the centre of Europe.

These formidable enemies, whose active cavalry it was almost useless to attack, and who at this early period displayed great strategic skill, were first defeated by Henry the First, emperor of Germany, at Merseberg, in 933.   Their last in-

---

* A name derived, as M. De Besse says, from the Tatar *Madjar*, meaning a long car or wagon, still in common use in Hungary.

cursion into Bavaria, in 954 and 955, terminated in their complete overthrow on the Lech, by Otho the First of Germany. They gradually learned from the Slavonians and Germans, whom they conquered, the arts of peace, and, dropping their migratory habits, became settled in the valleys of the Danube and Theiss, and devoted themselves to agriculture.

Stephen, the son of Geysa (third in descent from Arpad, and who was the first to embrace Christianity), attained the dukedom in the year 1000. For the services rendered to Christianity "in extirpating the heathen," he was raised by Pope Sylvester the Second to the dignity of king, with the approval of the German emperor, Otho the Third. The monarchy was elective, but the legitimate heir was generally the individual elevated by election to the throne. Stephen, during his reign, added Transylvania to the Hungarian kingdom. Under the succeeding reign in 1077, Croatia and Slavonia were also annexed to the Hungarian crown.

The male descendants of the house of Arpad sat upon the throne of Hungary four hundred years, but with Andrew the Third the male line became extinct in 1301.

The unsettled state of the succession to the crown, and the consequent interference of the neighboring princes and of the Roman court in the domestic concerns of Hungary; the inveterate hatred of the Magyars to all foreigners (a characteristic they still retain, and which proved so fatal to them in the late revolution); the arrogance of the clergy and nobility; the crusades; and the steady advance of the Mongul hordes on Eastern Europe, long retarded the prosperity of the country.

The crown next passed, by election of the Diet, to the house of Anjou, whose princes claimed their descent from Arpad through the female line. Under the princes of this house Hungary attained the summit of its power. The dominion of the Hungarian throne extended from the Baltic Sea to the Adriatic; the University of Buda was founded, and the court of Hungary became the resort of men of learning and science from all parts of Europe.

In 1526, on the invasion of the Turks, and the death of the youthful King Louis without heirs, in the disastrous battle of Mohatz, the crown of Hungary became again vacant.

Ferdinand of Austria, brother of the Emperor Charles the Fifth, who had married his cousin Anne, daughter of Ladislaus and sister of Louis, the late king of Hungary and Bohemia, presented himself as a candidate for the vacant throne. His personal character, his connection with the royal family of Hungary, and the assistance he might be expected to obtain from his brother, the emperor, in the war against the Turks, prevailed over the national antipathy to Austria, and he was, though not without much difficulty, elected to the throne.

In 1505 an attempt was made by Count Zapolya, a powerful magnate, for the passage of an act to revive an ancient law, to the effect that, in the event of a failure of the royal line, the choice of a sovereign should be limited to *natives* of Hungary. On the death of Louis, the party which had supported Zapolya declared in favor of his succession to the throne. A civil war ensued, in which Ferdinand was at length successful, and in 1547 he was regularly installed in the regal office, which has ever since been filled by his descendants, the emperors of Germany and Austria, as kings of Hungary.

The Emperor of Germany surrendered to Ferdinand the crown of Austria; and thus were the three crowns of Hungary, Bohemia, and Austria, for the first time, united in a prince of the house of Habsburg.*

The monarchy of Hungary continued to be elective, and the nation continued to give a preference to the heirs of the late monarch. The princes of the house of Habsburg, who succeeded to the throne of Austria, and were thus successively elected to that of Hungary, were separately crowned in the latter kingdom, according to its ancient customs, and at their coronation took the same oath to support the laws, Constitution, rights, and privileges of the Hungarians which Ferdinand the First had taken. In 1687, the Diet of Hungary decreed that the throne, which had hitherto been elective, should thenceforward be hereditary in the *male* heirs of the house of Habsburg; and in 1723, the Diet, by assenting to the Pragmatic Sanction of Charles the Third of Hungary (Charles the Sixth of Germa-

---

* These states were altogether independent of each other, and had no other bond of connection than the accidental union of the crowns in one person.

B

ny), extended the right of succession to the *female* descendants of that prince.*

By these steps has Hungary, with its dependencies, become
permanently attached to the Austrian dominions.

The mode of annexation with Hungary was precisely similar to that of Bohemia. In both instances the connection commenced by the acts of their respective Diets in electing members of the Habsburg family to the throne, and ended in the
foul intrigues and usurpations by which the descendants of
the same family succeeded in crushing the liberties of the
people, and converting those free and elective monarchies into
their own enslaved and hereditary kingdoms.

Of all the *partes annexæ regni Hungariæ*, Croatia alone
formed a considerable part of Hungary, the remainder having
been seized in the several invasions of the Turks.

Croatia, in the time of Augustus, belonged to Illyria, which,
by the division of the Roman empire, passed to the Greek emperors.

After the downfall of the Western Roman empire, the Avars
became masters of the country, but were expelled from it in
the seventh century, by the Chrobati (Horvati†), a Slavian
tribe, who descended upon them from the Northern Mountains. They remained under their own chiefs (zupans), who
were at first dependent upon the Frankish, and later upon the
Greek emperors, and finally became, for a short period, altogether independent. Their first king was called Dircesla.
After the extinction of his house, about the end of the eleventh
century, the Croatians, as their historians maintain, submitted themselves to the Hungarians.

The indivisibility of the hereditary provinces of the house
of Habsburg passed into a law in 1621.

Transylvania.

Although Transylvania became united with Hungary in the
year 1002, and so remained until 1526, it became in that year
separated from Hungary, under its own voyvod, John Zapolya,

---

* For the influence exercised in effecting these changes, see book ii., chap. vi.

† Horvati, from Hora, a mountain.

and his heirs, until 1699, when it was again annexed to Hungary and the Austrian dominions.

This country was the Dacia Mediterranea of the Romans, and for one hundred and seventy years formed a province of that empire, until subdued by the barbarians, when the Romans abandoned the country. The names of Trajan, who conquered the country; of Constantine,* who sent back their prisoners handless; and of Aurelius, who carried away the legions and left the country to the invaders, are still familiar to the inhabitants of Transylvania. After the Romans, this country was successively invaded by Goths, Huns, Gepidæ, and Avars, until the Gyla, a race of the Petchenegues, the early settlers of the country, together with the remnants of the Roman descendants, were conquered by the Magyars in the year 1002.

The Magyars called it Sylvana Regio, the land of woods; and, from its location on the southeastern extremity of Hungary, gave to this Dacia Mediterranea the name of Ultra or Transylvania.

In the twelfth century, Geysa the Second, king of Hungary, probably with a view of protecting his southern frontiers, and at the same time of introducing the arts of civilization among his rude subjects, encouraged the emigration of Saxon settlers in Transylvania. In 1160 they founded Hermanstadt, and have to the present day preserved their native language, customs, and privileges. In 1222, Andrew the Second granted to them more extensive privileges. They remained separate as a Saxon nation; paid merely a small tax, which they themselves were allowed to fix; elected a count of their own nation, who, in recognition of his newly-received rank, was honored with the present of a banner, a sabre, and a club. The Szecklers, another nation in Transylvania, entered the country about the same time with the Magyars, and are supposed to be a branch of the same race.

After the death of Louis, king of Hungary, in the battle of Mohacs, Transylvania fell to John Zapolya, the opponent of Ferdinand the First of Austria, and voyvod of Transylvania, who was protected by the Sultan of the Osmans. Transylva-

---

* See the handless Dacians on Constantine's Arch, at Rome.

nia was then governed by elective princes, but tributary to the Porte. The Austrian princes, however, could never forget that rich country, and its former annexation to the Hungarian crown.

After a long and bloody contest between the Turks and the princes of Transylvania and Austria, Michel Apafi, a native prince, resigned in favor of Austria, and the whole country, at a later day, passed as a princedom to Austria; and this compact was duly recognized by the Turks, in the treaty of Carlowitz, in 1699, concluded with Austria after their defeat at Zenta, in 1697.

SLAVONIA.

By the treaty of Carlowitz, the Austrian princes also acquired a part of Slavonia. The first inhabitants of this land had been the Scortisci, after whom followed the Pannonians. After it was subdued by the Romans, it received the name of Pannonia Savia. During the great migration of nations, the Avars took possession of this land, but they were subsequently conquered by Pepin, the son of Charlemagne. The land was then laid waste and completely deserted, and Slavonians were called in from Dalmatia, by the Germans, to settle it. Slavonians lived under their own princes as early as the time of Louis the Pious.

In 1079, the country was conquered by the Magyars; in 1524, by the Turks, who created there a paschalic; and finally by Leopold the First of Austria, to whom it was then ceded by the Turks, in the treaty of Carlowitz, 1699.

MANTUA.

In the year 1708, the house of Austria made its first acquisition in Italy—it was the Duchy of Mantua. Mantua belonged first to the Longobardian union of cities, and preserved its authority and privileges even during the long and atrocious contest with the German emperors. As in other parts of Italy, so in Lombardy, the power and influence of certain families arose to such a pitch that it resulted in their obtaining hereditary possession of those cities or districts.

From the year 1328 Mantua was governed by her own

princes, the Gonzagas, whose memory is still dear to the Man-
tuans. The emperor, Charles the Fourth, recognized the dignity of the Gonzagas as vicars of the state of Mantua. The
Emperor Sigismond erected it into a margraviate ; and Charles
the Fifth made it a duchy. But when, in the Spanish War
of Succession, the Duke of Mantua, Charles the Fourth (from
the house of Nevers), whose hatred against the Austrians
was so great as to induce him to take part against Joseph
the First ; the latter put him under the ban, and executed
it by appropriating Mantua in 1707.

MILAN.

A still further addition of Italian territory followed in 1714,
by the annexation of the Duchy of Milan. This country, now
known as Lombardy, derived its name from the Lombards or
Longobardi, with their long beards,* who first occupied the
districts in Pannonia which the Ostrogoths had abandoned.
Their king, Alboin, who drank from the skull of the king
whom he had conquered, had been invited by the valiant eu-
nuch and rebel, Narses, to assist him in the invasion of Italy.
Milan was taken, and sacked by him and his Longobardi. The
Lombards took possession of the upper part, and Pavia became
their capital. Lombardy formed, in the eighth century, a part
of the Frankish empire, having been conquered by Pepin, son
of Charles Martel. After the dissolution of the Frankish empire, Milan, though called an imperial city, was still independent.

The Emperor Barbarossa, irritated by the insolence of its inhabitants, or instigated by the neighboring rival cities, razed
it to the ground, and, if some historians are to be credited,
tore up its foundations, and passed the plowshare over its
ruins.

These cities of Lombardy with their territories, in the thirteenth century, formed numerous independent republics. All
became more or less opulent and powerful, but they were harassed by external and internal discord, and, before the end of
the thirteenth century, Milan was under the rule of Signori.

* Their name has also been derived from the word Hellebard, a halbert.—
MENZEL.

Next ruled the Torreani, and then the Visconti, whose pastors, like the Roman pontiffs, after having long been the benefactors and fathers of their flocks, at length became their sovereigns. The most distinguished of these, both by his military talents and the useful institutions which he introduced, was John Galleazzo Visconti, who purchased of the Roman emperor Wenzel, in 1395, the ducal dignity for 100,000 gold guldens. The dynasty of Visconti becoming extinct in 1447, the Milanese then elected the natural daughter of the last duke, Bianca Maria, whose husband was Francisco Sforza. But the family of the Visconti, having formed matrimonial connections with the royal dynasty of France, this dynasty, on the extinction of the Visconti, laid claim to their territories, and made repeated attempts, with various success, to take possession of them. These attempts at length terminated in the decisive battle of Pavia, which broke the French power in Italy, when Milan was declared a fief of the Roman-German empire. Upon the extinction of the last Sforza in 1535, the Emperor Charles the Fifth invested his son Philip, afterward King of Spain, with Milan, which then remained attached to the Spanish crown until 1700, when, on the death of Charles the Second, the Habsburg family became extinct in Spain. The destinies of the duchy followed the Spanish War of Succession, which ended with the treaty of Baden in 1714, and by which Milan was taken possession of by the Emperor Charles the Sixth, and by him added to the dominions of Austria.

BANAT AND CITY OF TEMESWAR, AND THE TURKISH POSSESSIONS ON THE LEFT BANK OF THE SAVA RIVER.

The remainder of Hungary and of the parts annexed, which, after the treaty of Carlowitz, continued still under the dominion of the Turks, viz., the Banat and city of Temeswar, and the Turkish possessions on the left bank of the River Sava, were acquired by Austria in 1718, by the treaty of Passarovitz.

With the death of Charles the Sixth, the *male* line of the Habsburgs became extinct. He was succeeded by his daughter, Maria Theresa, whose husband was Francis, duke of Lorraine. The Pragmatic Sanction by which Charles would assure the female succession in Germany, produced long and serious wars among the European powers. The electoral votes were finally cast, in 1745, for Francis of Lorraine, who opened a new line, which reigned in Germany for fifty-nine years, and rules in Austria at this day.

HOHENEMBS.

In 1759 the county of Hohenembs, in Tyrol, was rendered a vacant imperial fief by the death of Count Francis William Maximilian, and, by the conclusion of the imperial court council in 1765, bestowed upon the house of Austria, to which it remained, even after the dissolution of the German empire.

CASTIGLIONE.

In 1773, the small principality of Castiglione, west of the lake of Garda, in Italy, was purchased by Austria for 200,000 florins.

BUKOWINA.

In 1777, Bukowina was acquired from Turkey by a treaty of boundaries.

This province belonged originally to Transylvania, and subsequently to 1482 to Moldavia.

In 1774 it was conquered by Russia, and delivered over to Austria, a transfer which the Porte recognized in the above-mentioned treaty.

POLAND.

During the whole geographical development of Austria, from the time of the first Babenberg until the latter part of the eighteenth century, no acquisition of territory occurs which could not be defended or justified under some legitimate, or, at all events, specious title; but such is far from being the case with Poland, whose divisions between the three great powers is without excuse or justification, as it is without a parallel in the history of civilized nations.

Poland was settled by a Slavic tribe, and acquired its name from a Slavic word, signifying a plain, from the level character of the country, which is one of the most extensive plains in Europe.

Until the reign of the family of Piasts, and the introduction of Christianity, which occurred about a century after, the early accounts of Poland are too intimately blended with the fabulous to be relied on.

The family of Piasts, who came to the throne in the year 830, preserved their authority, with some interruption, until 1386, when that dynasty became extinct by the death of Casimir the Great, and that of the Jaghellos commences.   The Jaghellos reigned until 1572, when the constitution of Poland underwent a great change, and the crown became elective.

The period following the extinction of the Jaghellos seemed to prepare the way for the eventual downfall of the country. The arbitrary power of the nobility, the absurd right of the *liberum veto*,* the luxury and licentiousness produced by the sudden acquirement of liberty, undermined the moral and physical power of the people, and rendered them supple instruments in their own destruction.

"With the interference of Russia in the regal elections, commences," says Rotteck, "the history of the passion of Poland, and opens the most gloomy drama in modern history."

August the Third ascended the throne of Poland by the will of Russia, and through his whole reign proved himself rather a Russian officer than a Polish king.

After the death of August, in 1763, the Diet assembled, surrounded by Russian troops.   Its first endeavor was to amend the Constitution, and to abolish the fatal veto ; but the Prussian and Russian embassadors would not consent, nor permit them to pass any laws except a few of an unimportant character on the subject of subsistence, &c.

On the 6th of September, 1764, the members finally made choice of Stanislaus Poniatowsky, whose election was altogether owing to the fact of his being one of the favorites of the Empress Catharine—the northern Clytemnestra—who then sat upon the throne of her murdered husband.

The animosities between the Catholics and the dissidents, who contended for equality of rights, were fomented by Cath-

---

* *Liberum veto* was the right by which every representative (nuntius terrestris) at the " Free Diet" could defeat with his own vote a law, and even dismiss the whole assembly, as it happened in 1652.

arine, and her troops behaved with the utmost insolence. A civil war and a struggle against the Russian intruders agitated the unhappy country. Futile old claims were trumped up against Poland, and the king and people both invoked justice, but in vain, for the fatal hour of Poland's doom had come. The conscience of the Austrian princess was relieved by her confessor (a Jesuit, who undertook to intercede for her at Rome), and by the purchased opinions of hireling jurists; the Russian empress had no conscience to relieve; and the Prussian king expressed his readiness to share the booty and shame; and thus the definitive treaty between Austria and Russia and Prussia was concluded in 1772, and Poland dismembered.

Austria's portion of the spoils was consolidated and annexed to the Austrian territories, under the ancient appellation of the kingdoms of Galicia and Lodomeria. A third part of the Polish kingdom was thus divided among the royal plunderers.

To add insult to injury, a Diet was convoked under the influence of the great powers, to legalize this outrage, by giving their sanction to the dismemberment of their country, after possession had already been taken. A majority of six votes in the senate, and one in the assembly of nuncios, sanctioned this base act in 1773.

After a period of ever-varying destinies, Poland once more attempted to assume the attitude of a sovereign state. By a change of the Constitution in 1791, Poland became a hereditary instead of an elective monarchy. The Elector of Saxony was declared the successor, the throne made hereditary in his house, and the king, with the Council of State, invested with the executive power. The Diet was to continue in two chambers, with the abrogation of the *liberum veto;* all the privileges of the nobility were confirmed, though some favors were accorded to the citizens and peasants.

To these proceedings on the part of Poland, Catharine, involved in a war with the Turks, observed an intentional and ominous silence; but as soon as the peace of Jassy left her free, Poland was again divided between Russia and Prussia, and lost all but a third of her former territory in 1793, and Russian bayonets again compelled the indignant Diet to acquiesce in this dismemberment of their country. The remnant of Poland was now under Russian guardianship.

The heroic Kosciusko, unable to submit quietly to this degradation, became the head of the confederates of Cracow in 1794, and in the holy contest for their country, Warsaw and Wilna were liberated. The battle of Raclawice, and the relief of Warsaw, besieged by a Prussian army in 1794, are the most glorious periods of Polish history. But it was too late. Without fortresses, discipline, allies, or even arms, surrounded by Russians, Austrians, and Prussians, the convulsive efforts of national despair were unavailing, and "this barrier and outwork of Brandenburg," as Frederick the Great called it, against the barbarians of the North, was broken down. In the third partition of Poland, Austria obtained West Galicia ; Russia and Prussia received their respective shares; and there remained to the unhappy Poles nothing but wounded feelings and national pride, a bitter hate against Russians and Germans, and fruitless appeals for French aid and public sympathy.

CIRCLE OF THE INN.

Within the periods embraced by the two acquisitions of Polish territory, Austria obtained the province of the Inn or Innkreis. Joseph the Second, then at the head of the Austrian dominions, on the death of Maximilian Joseph, Elector of Bavaria, without issue, in 1777, persuaded the next heir, Charles Theodore, to cede Lower Bavaria to Austria. The so-called Potato War ensued.

Frederick the Second of Prussia espoused the cause of Maria Anna, the talented widow of Duke Clement Charles, Theodore's sister-in-law, who placed herself at the head of the Bavarians. Neither party seemed in earnest. Frederick was old and infirm, and Maria Theresa, who conducted the negotiations without the knowledge of her son, too timid for efficient action. A compromise was finally effected by the treaty of Teschen in 1779, in which Austria agreed to accept the province of Inn, and to relinquish the remainder of the disputed territories to Bavaria.

Venice, Dalmatia, and Istria.

In 1797 the Austrian dominions received a most important addition by the acquisition of two thirds of the republic of Venice, including Dalmatia, its islands, the Venetian part of Istria, and the Bocca di Cattaro.   The origin of this republic dates from the time of Attila, the leader of the Huns, who, invited* by Honoria, the sister of the Roman emperor Valentinian, crossed the Alps into Italy in 452.   Desolation, rapine, and slaughter marked the progress of this self-styled " Scourge of God."   On the extreme western point of the Adriatic Sea dwelt the Veneti, whose territories, called Venetia, formed a part of Cis-Alpine Gaul.   Many of the inhabitants of this region, on the approach of the Huns, fled for refuge to the small marshy islands of the Adriatic, at the mouth of the Brenta, on which they built the town of Riva Alta—high banks—afterward called Venice.   Sheltered by their position and their poverty, they continued gradually to increase, so that, by the end of the seventh century, they occupied not less than seventy-two islands.

The maritime situation of Venice rendered the inhabitants expert in navigation ; her commerce increased, and power extended.   She was the recipient of all the treasures of the East, and at length became not only " Queen of the Adriatic," but mistress of the Mediterranean.

The provinces of Istria and Dalmatia, exposed to the ravages of pirates, a prey to civil dissensions, and unsupported by the dying Greek empire, threw themselves under the protection and dominion of Venice.

Vicenza, Verona, Bassano, Feltre, Belluno, and Padua, with their territories, fell to Venice in 1402, and Friuli in 1421.

Venice, after an independent existence of more than thirteen hundred years, submitted without a blow, on the demand of Napoleon, to be blotted from the list of nations.   " Lost in stupor for a century," says Heeren, " this republic had resorted, in the conflict of the more powerful, to neutrality, the usual defense of weak states.   She had long outlived herself ;

---

* By the offer of her hand in marriage.

but her fall first disclosed her utter weakness. She was not only without energy, but without counsel. She fell, the victim of convenience and the desire of contiguity of possessions. But, apart from this, how could a constitution exist which stood in the most direct contradiction to the prevailing maxims of the age."*

By the treaty of Campo Formio (1797) Austria renounced all its claims to the Netherlands in favor of France, but obtained, in lieu thereof, the territory of Venice, from the Adige River to the Adriatic; the city of Venice itself; the Venetian Istria, Dalmatia, with the islands, and Bocca di Cattaro.

Dalmatia, now a province of Austria, receives its name, according to Strabo, from the town of Dalmium or Delmium. The inhabitants of this country, who were conquered by Octavius, were a union of different tribes, mostly pirates, and utter barbarians. The latter Roman emperors enriched the land with cities and palaces, and Diocletian exchanged even the throne of Rome for the gardens of the proud Salona. After the death of Honorius, Dalmatia was united to the Byzantine empire, and formed a part of Illyricum.

The inhabitants who appeared upon the soil after the barbarian invasions of Alaric, Attila, and the Ostrogoths, were of the Slavic race, and they still populate the country, while the towns are mostly made up of Italians.

As was the case with the Western Roman Empire, so also with the Eastern, the distant boundaries of the empire were left unprotected, and the Franks were enabled to extend their limits to the Sava River.

Following the example of the Croats, a part of the Dalmatian cities submitted to the dominion of Charlemagne. But the Frankish supremacy lasted only fifty years. The Greeks again took possession of the country at the end of the ninth century, and permitted all the cities and inhabitants on the coast to be subject to the princes of Croatia, in order to obtain protection against the Saracens, and the Narentini, who were the pirates of their own country.

But as perfect and complete protection to commerce at that

---

* Heeren's Historical Researches.

period could only be obtained from the Venetians, they submitted themselves to the city of the Lagunes, and remained under their dominion until the peace of Campo Formio.

The first inhabitants of Istria were probably emigrants from the city of Istrianopolis, at the mouth of the Ister, or Danube, though several derive them from Jason, or his persecutors at Colchis. The Istrians harassed the Roman merchants on the Adriatic, and the Roman consul* sent to demand satisfaction. Having by his insolence provoked their queen, Penta, she ordered him to be put to death. The murder of the Roman embassador led to a long and bloody war. The Istrians, according to Livy, fought with great bravery ; but their metropolis, Nexantrium—where women and children were destroyed by their own husbands and parents, to prevent them from falling into the hands of the enemy—fell, and was replaced by Roman colonies.

Istria flourished in the time of the Emperor Augustus. The splendid ruins of Pola, its amphitheatre, the Temple of Augustus, the Porta Aurea, &c., still in a state of excellent preservation, serve to exhibit the ancient importance of this country. The Romans, agreeably to Pompeius Festus and Plutarch, first derived a knowledge of theatrical representations from the Istrians, and from this circumstance arises the name *histriones*, given to actors.

The province of Istria was administered by a Roman consul till 452, when Attila visited the country with his terrible devastation. In 500 the Ostrogoths became masters of Istria, in 535 the Lombards, and in 789 the Franks. The Slavians afterward overran the land, and the inhabitants could find an asylum only in the fortified cities and castles. Istria fell afterward under the Dukes of Bavaria, who bore the titles of Marchiones Istriæ. In 1208, Istria was ceded to the Patriarchs of Acquileia, and in 1308 to the Venetians, who retained it until their own fall in 1797.

TRIENT AND BRIXEN.

In 1803 the archbishoprics of Trient and Brixen were secu-

---

* Lucius Coruncanius.

larized and delivered to Austria.   Before that time both archbishops were independent German princes, entitled to seats
and votes in the German Diet.

SALZBURG.

In 1805, Austria became possessed of that part of the modern
Austrian archduchy known as Salzburg.

It formed at one time a part of the bishopric of Salzburg,
whose head was also primate of Germany.   Salzburg was, by
the treaty of Luneville, secularized, and in the peace of Pressburg in 1805, conferred on Austria, more in ridicule than by
way of indemnification for the loss of the large and valuable
territories which she had sustained.

Although the wars following the French Revolution at the
commencement of the present century produced a great change
in the hereditary possessions of the Austrian emperor, by deci-
mating their extent, the Congress of Vienna, in 1814 and 1815,
restored all which the ruthless hand of Napoleon had torn from
the princes of Habsburg.

The simple declaration made by Napoleon to the German
Diet, that he no longer recognized the empire, was sufficient to
subvert the structure of a thousand years.   In consequence,
Austria voluntarily laid aside the imperial crown of Germany
in 1806, having adopted instead the hereditary imperial crown
of Austria on the 11th of August, 1804.   From that time Austria formed a monarchy in the proper sense of the word.

BRESCIA, BERGAMO, CREMA, &c.

By the treaty of Vienna in 1815 the Emperor of Austria obtained, in full sovereignty for himself and his successors, the
territories between the Ticino, the Po, and the Adige, which
formerly belonged to the Venetian Republic, as Brescia, Bergamo, Crema, &c.

THE VALLEYS OF THE VELTLINE, OF BORMIO, AND OF CHIAVENNA.

By the same treaty of Vienna in 1815 fell to Austria the valleys of the Veltline, of Bormio, and of Chiavenna, which belonged, before the formation of the Cisalpine Republic and the
Italian kingdom, to the bishopric of Chur.

Republic of Ragusa.

A further acquisition of territory made by the treaty of Vienna in 1815 was the Republic of Ragusa.

This republic dates its existence from the thirteenth century, and remained independent (though, since the year 1357, first under Hungarian and afterward under Venetian protection) till the year 1807, when it was conquered by France, and by the above-mentioned treaty delivered to Austria.

Sabionetta.

By the treaty of Vienna, Austria finally received the small territory of Sabionetta (now in the delegation of Mantua), which belonged previously to the Duchy of Guastalla, and was separated from it to arrange the boundaries of Austria more advantageously.

Present Divisions of the Austrian Empire, and their Character and Administration.

Out of these many portions, acquired up to 1815, at thirty different epochs, the following division, for their administration, was then adopted, and existed in force until 1848.

I. Bohemia: two thirds Slavi, the remainder Germans, Jews, and Gipseys, under one governor.

II. Moravia and Silesia: two thirds Slavi, the remainder Germans and Jews, under one governor.

III. Galicia and Lodomeria: four fifths Slavi, the remainder Wallachians, Magyars, Germans, and Jews, under one governor.

IV. Austria, below the Enns River: Germans, under one governor.

V. Austria, above the Enns: Germans, under one governor.

VI. Tyrol: five eighths Germans, the remainder Italians, under one governor.

VII. Styria: two thirds Germans, the remainder Slavi, under one governor.

VIII. Carniola and Carinthia: two thirds Slavi, the remainder Germans, under one governor.

IX. The province of Trieste: one half Slavi, the remainder Italians and Germans, under one governor.

X. Dalmatia: five eighths Slavi, the remainder Italians, under one governor.

XI. Lombardy: Italians, under one governor.

XII. Province of Venice: Italians, under one governor.

XIII. Hungary, Slavonia, and Croatia: two fifths Magyars, the remainder Slavi, Wallachians, Germans, Greeks, Jews, Gipseys, under the Palatine and the Ban.

XIV. Transylvania: one third Magyars, the remainder Saxons, Wallachians, Bulgarians, Gipseys, etc., under one governor.

XV. The military frontier along the boundaries of Turkey: three fourths Slavi, the remainder Wallachians, Magyars, Germans, under entirely military rule.

CHAPTER II.

HISTORICAL INTRODUCTION—*Continued*.

FOREIGN POLICY AND INTERNAL ADMINISTRATION OF THE AUSTRIAN EMPIRE, FROM THE TREATY OF VIENNA IN 1815, TO THE VIENNA REVOLUTION IN MARCH, 1848.

WHEN Napoleon, in his victorious march in 1813, had completed the tour of Europe, and planted his triumphant standard in every great capital of the Continent, from the Tuileries to the Kremlin, the princes, who had every where fled at his approach, appealed to the fidelity as well as to the interest of their subjects, to " save their thrones from overthrow, and the national liberty from the destruction of a foreign despot."

In this war of " Liberation," as it was most ingeniously miscalled, all Europe was summoned to arms, and the call was answered by the people with an enthusiasm equaled only by the embarrassment of their sovereigns.

" Every one," says a German author, "that could bear arms, seized them; the plow and work-shops were abandoned, the lecture-rooms and counting-houses were deserted; even young females, dissembling their sex, hastened in arms to the ranks of the combatants, while matrons, undismayed at contagion or death, nursed the sick and the wounded." But the history of the time is nowhere more correctly described than in the following proclamation of the King of Prussia.

"When, in time of danger, I called my people to arms, to combat for the *freedom and independence of the country*, the whole mass of the youth, glowing with emulation, thronged around the standards, to bear with joyful self-denial unusual hardships, and resolved to brave death itself. Then the best strength of the people intrepidly joined the ranks of my brave soldiers, and my generals led with me into battle a host of heroes, who have shown themselves worthy of the name of their fathers, and heirs of their glory. Thus we and our allies, attended by victory, conquered the capital of our enemy. Our banners waved in Paris. Napoleon abdicated his authority. *Liberty was restored to Germany*, security to thrones, and to the world the hope of a durable peace."

Thus the foreign despotic power was broken, and the duty of organizing German liberty devolved upon the Congress of Vienna.

The enemy once subdued, the people, credulous as brave, waited in confident reliance on the promises of the monarchs. From Vienna, where the latter were assembled or represented, was expected the realization of those laws and institutions which were to repay all sacrifices, meet all wishes, and close the bloody arena so long occupied by contests for personal aggrandizements.

However strange it may appear, it is undoubtedly true that, on the first assembling of this Congress, the spirit of the allied powers was sincerely liberal. The efforts of the people, stimulated by the promises of their rulers, had produced the expulsion of the French armies, and it was apparently not more in acknowledgment of the debt they owed them, than for the promotion of their own honest designs, that the monarchs in their turn felt disposed to make some concessions to the people.

Austria, in the person of the President of the Congress, declared that "the subjects of every German state under the ancient empire possessed rights against their sovereign which had of late been disregarded, but that such disregard must be rendered impossible for the future." Prussia deliberately proposed a scheme of almost the same Constitution, which thirty-two years after was revived by the present king.   Russia was naturally called upon for very little exertion as regarded her unawakened provinces; but her propositions in behalf of Poland, and which were in part actually realized, were so remarkably liberal as to excite serious apprehensions in her western neighbors.   While Hanover insisted upon the declaration as the fundamental law of the alliance, that Constitutional Estates should be created wherever they did not already exist; and all three of these powers, viz., Austria, Prussia, and Hanover, placed on record a note (November 16, 1814), in which was maintained the necessity of introducing universal Constitutional Estates,* and giving to them a voice in questions of "taxation, public expenditure, the redress of public grievances, and general legislation."

The plan for a German Confederation originally proposed by Prince Metternich declared that its object should be the maintenance of the internal and external security of Germany, and of the independence and inviolability of the confederated states, "as well as that of the rights of each class of the nation." These last words were especially objected to on the part of the King of Wurtemberg, at that time engaged in a dispute with his subjects respecting their constitutional rights, in which he was joined by the King of Bavaria.†

The conferences on this point had been broken off in November, 1814, when the King of Wurtemberg abruptly quitted Vienna.   Scarcely had they been resumed in 1815, when tidings of the return of Napoleon from Elba arrived, and all other questions became of secondary importance to the aim of uniting entire Germany in arms against the usurper, who was declared, by a special act of that body, "the enemy of nations, and to have forfeited the protection of the laws."   Wurtemberg, on this occasion, was absent.   Bavaria, however, was represented, and she contested, from the same point of view as Wurtemberg, the thirteenth Article of that Confederation, which guaranteed a representative Constitution to each of the states; while, on the opposite side, Stein and his friends were

---

* Diets or Parliaments.   † Wheaton, 473.

anxious to pledge the Confederation to the establishment of a popular representation in each state.

A medium course was at last adopted, after a discussion of four weeks, chiefly through the influence of Austria, and the result was the concise expression of the thirteenth Article, viz., "a representative Constitution, to be adopted in all the federative states," which, like the Delphic oracle, committed its authors to no very definite result, and of which the true meaning has been to this day a subject of dispute.*

The occurrence of the Hundred Days must ever be a subject of deep regret to Germany, by reason of its having precipitated the settlement of this and other important internal questions.†
All hopes of the union of Germany were just on the point of being abandoned, when a higher destiny, confirming the tardy resolutions of the princes by an appeal to their fears, revived them, and, owing to a concurrence of other favorable circumstances, the act of the German Confederation was at length brought to a successful issue.

The wars of the French emperor had not only destroyed the former metes and bounds of empires, but left scarcely a state in Europe whose territorial relations were not in an embarrassed condition.

Upon the reassembling of the Congress in the following year, it was the territorial distribution and international organization between the states, and not the political rights or social condition of the people, that now exclusively occupied the attention of the sovereigns. Only the limitation of France to its ancient boundaries by the treaties of Paris, in consequence of which so many important countries on that side of the Rhine and the Alps were placed at the disposal of the allies, could render adjustment or restoration possible. But a complete restoration could not, it was thought, be effected without greater injustice than had been previously inflicted.

As to territorial arrangements, the Congress took little heed of nationality, of race, of natural sentiments, of historical traditions, or of popular predilections. The number of inhabitants and square miles, and the amount of revenues, were the

---

* Quarterly Review, March, 1849.
† For the Act of Confederation, see Heeren.

general, and, in many instances, the only criterion of adjustment.   They treated states and principalities as so many unconscious and lifeless parts of a huge machine.   They marshaled provinces and people like squadrons and battalions in
a line of battle, calculated by the individual decisions of a commander.   They did even more.   They carried their distribu-
tive powers beyond any pretended compulsion of necessity, and
partitioned populations to satisfy ministerial crotchets or royal greed.   There was a formal *partage d'ames.*   Claims to
so many millions of souls, founded on previous bargains, pre-
sumptions, or services, were put in and recognized, at the cost
of all national feelings, and in councils over which no requisite geographical or historical knowledge is said to have presided.*

Although this repartition of territory by the Congress was
a measure of great importance, it was quite as remarkable
when it is considered that the professed object for which this
body assembled was the *peace* of Europe ; and yet that, in
their efforts to accomplish this, they exhibited, by their *partage d'ames,* the utmost contempt both for personal rights and
national feeling.

It is, indeed, wonderful that it should never have occurred
to them that satisfaction among the people, and protection of
their just rights, was more essential to the tranquillity of Europe than the gratification of the ambitious lusts of monarchs;
and that a peace violated in this manner would probably give
rise to a war, not merely between the states of Germany, but
a war of opinion that might extend its influence beyond the
country, and even beyond the age in which it originated.

As soon as the new formation of states had been effected,
the great powers of Austria and Prussia, notwithstanding the
liberality at first exhibited, retained for their own dominions
the system of absolutism, a form of government totally unsuited to the age ; and the influence of that system, pursued
with blind obstinacy, exercised upon the German confederated
Diet, paralyzed all the efforts of the other princes, who had
made partial concessions to the times by adopting the consti-

---

* Edinburgh Review, Oct., 1848.

tutional system, the necessity of which the wants of the age amply demonstrated.*   It is to this period and to these transactions that we must look for the germs of those revolutionary ideas by which all governments are at this time threatened.†   The people had made, with great enthusiasm, the dearest sacrifices, and they were entitled to expect a reward for them.   This they confidently anticipated in obtaining those institutions by which a just degree of liberty should be assured them, based on the natural rights of humanity; in short, by the possession and enjoyment of a constitutional monarchy. This just as well as reasonable demand, sustained by a wellfounded claim, was not regarded.   The Vienna Congress, by which Europe was reorganized, zealously protected the rights of the dynasties; but the rights of the people were almost totally neglected.   The appeals of the latter against such a condition of things, being unheeded, could not but produce reaction.   The obstinate course of the rulers, sustained by no legal grounds, but directed solely by their own arbitrary will, soon created a bitterness in the hearts of the people, which became more injurious and demoralizing in proportion as the attempt was made to repress it.   A deep and painful breach had taken place in the confidence between the people and their princes. Threatening symptoms of the existence of that bitter hostility soon manifested themselves.   In the hour of need, as it was sufficiently proved, the yoke of the foreign oppressor, becoming more and more insupportable, could not be thrown off except by a general and armed rising of the people; no means, therefore, were spared to accomplish this result, and to awaken the German people to a consciousness of their power. It was by eloquent appeals, by watch-words,‡ songs, and heroic deeds, that the people of Germany had been inspired with an ardent desire for liberty.   Impressed with this hope, they rushed into the contest and achieved the victory; but it was without fruits for them.

---

* Constitutions were formed in Bavaria, Wurtemberg, Hanover, Baden, Grand Duchy of Hesse, Brunswick, Nassau, Mecklenberg, Saxe-Weimar, &c.   Amer. Encyc., art. "Constitutions," p. 473; Engl. Encyc., art. "Constitutions," p. 469 Heeren, 485.

† History of Vienna Revolution, Almanac, 1849.   ‡ Ibid.

The system of absolutism, as created by the treaties of 1815, founded upon a basis alike adverse to national and liberal ideas, grew intolerable as the people became aware that their noblest feelings of patriotism had been fraudulently converted into instruments of their own thraldom. Dissatisfaction and excitement, therefore, increased among the people throughout Germany. They began to discover to what extent they had been deceived; instead of the restoration of a powerful empire, they were to accept the mere phantom of a Constitution; instead of the promised liberty, new fetters were forged, which, by diplomatic shrewdness, were concealed for a time under the Act of Confederation. The beautiful dreams of a German empire, with but one man at its head, and the revival of its ancient splendor, had been dissipated. Germany had delivered herself from the bonds of the powerful Corsican, only to put on the more disgraceful chains of a German Congress. It was natural that a feeling of shame should stir the German nation, and with it the desire to throw off the yoke, and to acquire those sacred rights and privileges to obtain which had cost the blood of thousands. On every side the people rose, and demanded the accomplishment of the thirteenth Article of the Confederation, "In all the states of the Confederation will be given a representative Constitution;" became louder and louder; the people knocked at the doors of the princes, and summoned them to fulfill their promises. To meet this tergiversation of the courts, all the modifications of *Carbonarism*, and its traditionary details, were now put into operation; and every state in Central Europe had its secret societies for the prosecution of its peculiar object.

This indignation was naturally strongest in the hearts of the students, from the baffled enthusiasm of youth. Secret associations were formed in the universities, and the first manifestation of that excitement occurred at the Wartzburg festivity, so well known.* The governments did not hesitate to employ coercive measures to suppress this spirit. It was, however, far too widely extended to be overcome by such means. Excited to fanaticism, these youthful demagogues did not scorn

---

* Occurred 18th October, 1817. See Menzel's Germany

any means, not even assassination, to effect a revolution, the
object of which was the overthrow of all thrones, as they considered the wearers of the crowns the only obstacles in the
way to the accomplishment of the end at which they aimed,
viz., German freedom accordant with their ideas.   By one of
these misled youths, Kotzebue fell, and this assassination—
permitted, no doubt—suggests to what extremes this party
was ready to go.   The united measures of the German governments succeeded, however, at that time, in preventing any
further outbreak; but the revolutionary spirit was only suppressed, not extinguished.

It was distinctly known that not Germany alone had become
the seat of revolutionary ideas and plans, but that, since the
fall of Napoleon, a revolutionary propaganda had been formed,
the seat of which was involved in impenetrable obscurity, un-
discovered by the whole police of the European powers; and
that this association was indefatigable, and furnished with
powerful means to effect the overthrow of all thrones, and to
transform the countries of Europe into republican states.*

These movements upon the part of the people very naturally led to movements on the part of the monarchs; and the
common danger, with which they were all equally threatened,
was not long in producing a union among the crowned heads.
It is a remarkable fact which the history of Congresses discloses, that never, previous to the year 1814, had monarchs

---

* These secret societies of students were aroused during the war of the liberation; their motives were at first strictly social and patriotic (they had the special approval of their sovereigns), but they afterward became political.   They
served as excellent auxiliaries in the war of liberation; but even at that time the
enlightened statesmen of Germany could not but tremble at the power which
had been evoked.   They felt that the mind of Germany was making giant strides
in advance of the body, and threatened, if it pursued its course without a check,
to part company from it.   With the conclusion of the war, the secret societies,
instead of dissolving themselves or contracting their sphere of action, assumed a
much wider development.   It was attempted, accordingly, in 1816, to put them
down by a royal edict.   In the following year the fraternization of the Burschenschaft took place at Wartzburg, in Saxe-Weimar, when the students of Jena welcomed the students of twelve other universities, and an association of the Burschen
of Germany was formed under an established directory.[1]   The next year saw
the union still more effectively organized, with its leaders and its banners, the flag
of the ancient empire, black, red, and gold.

[1] Quarterly Review, March, 1849.

agreed so well and acted so much in concert, because, since
that date, they have felt the necessity of making common
cause against liberty. Never before were so many Congresses
held in the same space of time ; the constant instances of insubordination required frequent consultation ; and the uneasy
state of the monarchs at home made it particularly desirable
for them to meet in Congresses abroad.* The first Congress
of the sovereigns, having for its object the suppression of all
liberal sentiments, and riveting more closely the chains of the
people, was that of

AIX LA CHAPELLE.

At this Congress, which met on the 13th of November, 1818,
no measures were openly concerted for suppressing the liberal
movements ; yet the apprehensions excited, especially in Germany, by these popular manifestations, had been chiefly influential in provoking the conference ; and it was there determined to retract or suspend those concessions of constitutional
privileges which had been originally promised.

CONGRESS OF CARLSBAD.

The next Congress of the crowned heads which followed
was that held at Carlsbad, in Bohemia, and commenced its
sittings on the 29th of September, 1819 ; the objects and conclusions of which can not be better explained than they are in
the address presented to them, on assembling, by Prince Metternich, the presiding officer of that body.

" The imperial royal presiding embassador has received
from his exalted court the most high order to make to the
federal Diet the following communication :

" His imperial majesty believes that he expresses, the same
time with his own, the desire of all the members of the confederacy, on summoning the confederated Diet, to direct, before its adjournment, its whole attention to the troublesome
movements and fermentation of the spirits throughout a great
portion of Germany ; to examine studiously the causes of the
serious appearances which have disclosed themselves for the

---

* Americana Encyclopedia.

last few years, becoming daily more perceptible, but at last manifesting itself in undisguisable symptoms, by pamphlets preaching insurrection, by widely-extended unlawful unions, and even by repeated crimes; and to take into consideration all means by which order and peace, respect for the laws, confidence in the governments, general satisfaction, the undisturbed enjoyments of all those benefits which will be conferred on the German nation under the protection of peace, may, by the hands of the princes, be secured and strengthened for the future. The sources of this evil (to stop the further advance of which must be, at present, the most sacred duty of all German governments) are to be found partly in the present condition of affairs, upon which no government is enabled to exert an influence direct or momentary, and partly they are connected with certain indigenous errors and abuses, and which can only be corrected by a happy agreement and well-considered measures.

" Among those points which require the earliest and most careful consideration, the following are predominant:

" 1st. The uncertainty, and consequently the false interpretation as to the sense and meaning of the thirteenth Article of the Act of Confederation.

" 2d. Incorrect ideas as to the rights of the confederated Diet, and the insufficiency of the means to exercise those rights.

" 3d. The faults of the schools and the system of instruction.

" 4th. The abuse of the press, and particularly mischief carried on by newspapers and pamphlets."

In conclusion, the prince says, " It is the most ardent desire of his majesty that the confederated Diet may occupy itself without delay in these important matters, and the presiding embassador is therefore ordered to communicate suitable projects for conclusion upon these four points, and upon the nomination of a Central Commission, the efficacy of which will be more detailed in the course of these deliberations."[*]

The results of this Congress were that laws were passed for

---

* The eighteenth Article of Confederation guarantees liberty of the press. Wheaton, 454.

the establishment of a stricter police in the universities, which since that time have been brought into closer contact with the governments, and officers appointed to watch over the conduct of the students. Periodical works, and such as contain less than twenty sheets, were put for five years under a severe censorship; and the Diet was to have the right to suppress any books which disturbed the peace or attacked the dignity of any member of the Confederation, or tended so to do. For the detection and prosecution of secret political societies throughout Germany, and the checking of demagogic tendencies, a central police was commissioned and organized.*

SECOND CONGRESS OF VIENNA, 1820.†

The second Congress of Vienna immediately followed, May 15th, 1820, which produced the final act of the Confederation, a heterogeneous composition, the design of which was to annul by interpretation the spirit, while it kept within the letter of the act of 1815. No one of its articles in favor of popular rights had ever been enforced, but all those against them had been executed ostentatiously, and were now paraded anew in the protocol before the house.

From this it was learned that the Diet was offended at the journals and pamphlets which inundated the country, and with the abuse of liberty of speech in the legislative chambers. It invoked the eighteenth Article of the Federal Act of 1815, which declared that uniform laws should be established to secure liberty of the press, and, at the same time, stated that, until all the governments should concur in establishing such laws, the decree of Carlsbad (September 20th, 1819), abolishing the liberty of the press, should continue to be rigorously executed throughout the Confederation. If after this the Diet should be enabled to sustain itself, it was well; "but if not, Austria and Prussia would, at the invitation of one of the confederated states, employ every means at their disposal for the maintenance and execution of the Federal Constitution, its important execution," etc.‡ The important point to be observed is the attitude gradually assumed by the allied powers, and its

---

* Americana Encyclopedia.

† Congress of Vienna, 1820; see Wheaton, 455.   ‡ Wheaton, 476

remarkable influence upon the public policy of Europe. The contracting parties represented themselves as charged with the general superintendence of tranquillity, and characterized their combination against the " revolutionary" spirit of Europe as the natural continuation of that alliance, which, by overwhelming the power of Napoleon, had restored the peace of the world. The result was a perpetual league of crowned heads, which, if originally directed against license, was soon made available against liberty. The principle now promulgated was this— that if any disturbance of the " tranquillity" constituted and prescribed by the dispensing powers should occur at any place in Europe, the entire force of the alliance should be immediately employed to suppress it. In this manner the political system as usually organized between sovereign and independent states, was to be superseded by a kind of confederation, which would have transformed the governments of Europe into a Diet, of which Austria or Russia would have seized the presidency. Forms of government were put in the same category with configurations of frontiers, and the mutual guarantee was extended from integrity of territory to integrity of absolutism. Intervention upon these principles, in the internal affairs of an independent state, was proclaimed a duty incumbent upon the allied governors of the world ; and so strict was the union thus contracted, and so hearty the concurrence of purpose, that it was hoped wars and tumults would never again be found afflicting nations or dethroning kings.*

By this Congress, the extent of the powers conferred on the Diet by the Federal Act of 1815, was more fully defined by an additional act (composed of one hundred articles), signed May 15th, 1820, and ratified by the Diet at Frankfort on the 8th of June of the same year.

Congress of Troppau.

In Germany the insurrectionary spirit took the disgraceful form of assassination ; in the Italian and Spanish peninsulas the more dangerous guise of military revolts. In this Congress, which took place from October to December, 1820, the

---

* Edinburgh Review, October, 1848.

assembled monarchs, the Emperors of Austria and Russia, and the King of Prussia announced the principle of *armed intervention*. The revolutions of Spain, Portugal, and Naples, more especially, gave occasion to this Congress. The object of the deliberations was also to effect a compact between the great powers, that they would not acknowledge any Constitution which should deviate from the legitimate monarchical standard. England and France endeavored to establish the system of neutrality. Great Britain expressed her unwillingness to take part in any measures of violence against Naples ; and France would join the league only upon certain conditions, which were, however, refused by Austria, Russia, and Prussia, as these powers were resolved to use force to put down the insurrectionary spirit. It was further resolved, at Troppau, that in case a war should actually break out with Naples, Austria should carry it on alone ; while Russia and Prussia pledged themselves to keep watch on the rest of Europe, and guaranteed the security of the Austrian states.

CONGRESS OF LAYBACH.

The Congress of Laybach was held from the 26th of January, 1821, to May of the same year. This assembly forms a conspicuous epoch in the history of European politics, as it was here that the right of *armed intervention*, agreed upon at Troppau, was *regularly proclaimed and diplomatically admitted into the international code* of the European continental powers. The consequences of this Congress, from whence the allied powers issued a proclamation against Naples, were the occupation of Naples, Sicily, and Piedmont by Austrian armies ; the abolition of the Spanish Constitution in these countries, and the restoration of the old order of things. Such armed interventions arose from the fellow-feeling of sovereigns, who claimed the right of assisting each other against their subjects, and directly to contravene the right of independent development which belongs to the character of a nation.

It was a natural consequence of the Holy Alliance, and the Congresses of rulers or their representatives assembled, only, to prop the pillars of despotism. Such a step not only contravened the rights of other neutral nations, but was in direct violation of the Second Article of the German Confederation, as established by the Congress of Vienna in 1815, which guarantees "the independence and inviolability of each of the German states." It is the instrument always used to suppress liberty, and of which we have recently had a striking illustration in the inhuman intervention of Russia in aid of Austria against Hungary, and the Republic of France to crush the liberties and extinguish the Republic of Rome, which presented a more striking example of order and greater prospect of stability than France itself.

Congress of Verona.

The two emperors had determined, at Laybach, to hold a new Congress, in 1822, at Florence. Verona was afterward substituted for Florence, and a Congress was held there, from October to December, 1822, on account of Spain and Portugal, and the political state of Greece. The war of France against Spain, in 1823, was a consequence of this Congress, as the powers permitted France to re-establish the ancient monarchy in Spain by force of arms, and promised assistance, if it should be necessary, to put down the Cortes and suppress the Constitution of that country. Measures were also here taken for the suppression of secret societies.

What were the circumstances which at this time strengthened the power of absolute monarchy? The first, undoubtedly, was the intimate union formed among the monarchs for mutual support, the discovery they had made that it was better for them to fight together against the liberties of their people, than to fight with each other for the mere enlargement of their dominions. The detestable conspiracy into which they had entered, under the blasphemous name of the *Holy Alliance*, was the great means of sustaining more tyrannical measures, upon which each now thought he might safely proceed to administer his government; and, so long as they look upon increase of personal power and security in practical tyranny as of more value than mere increase of territory or of foreign influence, so long it is not impossible that this unhallowed confederacy may continue. Another great source of the strength and immediate safety of these governments was the general diffusion of improvements in the art of war, and the maintenance and equipment of armies, by means of which a much smaller force was capable of keeping in awe a larger population, and, at the same time, a limited revenue enabled to maintain more numerous forces. These were the immediate and occasional causes of the confidence and apparent security with which arbitrary power has since been proclaimed as the only legitimate spring of European government.*

But there was another and a more ominous cause, which has only begun to operate of late years, to exercise influence in support of the same system, and this was the improved knowledge and policy of absolute governments themselves, and their gradual correction of many of the abuses which did not tend to maintain their despotism.

Tyrannical governments had before been singularly ignorant and prejudiced, and more than one half of the abuses which made them odious in the eyes of their subjects, had no immediate connection with political rights or institutions, and might have been safely redressed without at all improving the Constitution, or increasing the political consequence of their subjects.

Their great danger was the superior intelligence of the people, with whom the policy of their rulers had usually been a subject of contempt as well as of resentment, and who, in their plans of reform or resistance, had uniformly possessed a most mortifying advantage in point of contrivance, combination, address, and prudence. A new era, however, began as to all these particulars; the eyes of the rulers were at last opened to their own nakedness and weakness, and great efforts were made, and are still making to secure to the cause of tyranny some part of those advantages which the spread of intelligence and general increase of ability had conferred on all other institutions.* They employed better casuists and more ingenious sophists to defend their proceedings; they sought spies of more activity and intelligence, and agents of corruption more crafty and acute, than they had previously thought it necessary to retain

---

* Edinburgh Review, 1824   † Idem.

in their service.   But, above all, they endeavored to rectify those gross errors in their internal administration which had been a source at once of weakness and discontent, and by the correction of which they did infallibly extend and multiply their resources, while they cut off one fruitful spring of disaffection.   They continued to seek, therefore, not only to improve the economical part of their government, and to amend the laws and usages by which the wealth and industry of the people were affected, but endeavored to conciliate their goodwill, by mitigating all those grievances from which they themselves derived no advantage, and which might be redressed without at all advancing the people in their *pretensions to the character of freemen.*

They constructed roads and canals, encouraged agriculture and manufactures, and reformed the laws of trade, abolished local and subordinate oppressions, endowed seminaries of education, inculcated a reverence for religion, and patronized academies of arts ; and all this good they did not hesitate to perform at the instigation of that more enlightened, but more determined hostility to popular rights,* by which they have ever been professedly actuated, and with a view merely to these two plain consequences.   In the first place, that, by increasing the wealth and population of their subjects, they might be enabled to draw from them larger taxes and supplies, and to recruit greater armies to uphold their tyrannical pretensions ; and in the second place, that, by keeping the body of the people, in other respects, in a comfortable condition, they might have a better opportunity of reconciling them to the privations of political rights, and not be annoyed by the discontents which arise from distress, and be forced to combat, at the same time, those which arise from injustice.†

During this period and the following years, the attention of the allied powers was sufficiently occupied in directing the movements during the revolutionary outbreaks in Spain, Naples, and Sicily, occasioned by the struggles of those countries against the absolutism which, under the pretense of a constitutional system, was enforced among them.

---

* Edinburgh Review.   † Ibid.

In the mean time, the dissatisfaction of the people of the German states continued to increase, not only on account of the total disregard by the sovereigns of all their rights, but from the obnoxious measures which the Diet of Frankfort, from time to time, thought proper to adopt. In the protocol of that assembly, the final act of 1820 was made responsible for all these new enactments of the Diet. But the article first cited for this purpose was unfortunate. It declared that "the sovereign can not be bound to admit the co-operation of the Estates, except in the exercise of rights especially determined." But in many states the co-operation of the Diet in granting and appropriating taxes was already specially determined, and, in order to escape from the effect of this provision, it was stated that the internal constitution of the confederated states could not be so construed as to prejudice the objects of the Confederation, and especially so as to defeat the supplies of money which each state was bound to contribute for the common defense. The protocol also repeated the provision of the final act of 1820, that, if any state, in case of internal troubles, was prevented from applying for the assistance of the Confederation, the Diet was bound, though not called on, to interfere; so that the Diet, or, rather, Prussia and Austria, were left the sole judges of the necessity of such interference; and the protocol finally concluded with a sweeping clause, that the Diet should be, in all cases of doubt, the ultimate judges of the extent of their own powers, which thus completed the annihilation of the chartered liberties of Germany.

The fermentation continued to increase the spirit of fellowship created in the wars of the Revolution, and which resulted in the liberation of Germany from foreign oppression, imparted to them the ideas of unity and nationality, which have ever since distinguished them, and which, thirty years after, they attempted to embody in some palpable form. Such of the constitutions as, agreeably to the thirteenth Article of the Confederation, had been bestowed, were, by the repressive measures on the part of the separate powers, or of the Frankfort Diet, either completely withheld, or rendered, by those measures, totally void, and inadequate for the satisfaction of the people. In 1827 the Burschenschaft was revived, with a more definite object, and which was the unity and freedom of Germany, at all hazards.

From this period until the events of July, 1830, in France, which again constituted a new era for Germany, years glided on in profound peace ; but the deep feeling of popular indignation was working its silent and sullen way. No period of the world's annals contains such an instance as this of rulers owing so much to those they governed, yet refusing, with perfidious breach of faith, the payment of their debt of gratitude, and persecuting those who had fought and bled in their service, for making use of the very words and phrases which those same princes had so profusely lavished when entreating the assistance of the people. Every one who raised the voice of patriotism was put under the ban ; imprisonment, confiscation, and exile were the lot of all who dared to whisper that the bloody battles which had been fought and won had any objects beyond the re-establishment of absolute power and aristocratic prerogative.

As an act in the general movement of the people, and of that excitement in the public mind which prevailed every where, the Revolution of July, 1830, then occurred. He who, upon the fall of Napoleon, proclaimed to the people of France " the triumph of liberty, the reign of the laws," was found violating (with his unpopular ministry) the charter which he had sworn to support, and by the people hurled from power, and Louis Philippe of Orleans called to the throne. By the election of the king, the calculations of the Republican party were disappointed for a moment, yet the throne of a popular king, surrounded by such democratic forms, was certainly an advance in the condition of things, and the destiny of the people seemed already ameliorated. The interval between the original pacification and the late convulsions of Europe is divided into two nearly equal portions by the French Revolution of 1830, which conveniently separates one period from another, and constitutes an important epoch in the history of human rights. Previous to that year, the policy of the allied powers, described above, had almost undisputed sway, and the incidents of European history, during the fifteen years which intervened, were mainly confined to such manifestations of its force as were supplied.

D

by the successive suppression of liberal movements in Germany, as well as in Naples, Piedmont, Portugal, and Spain. But the Revolution of July gave a new aspect to affairs. Not only was France, a leading power, transformed into a real constitutional* monarchy, and transferred in the balance of political principles from the side of the Allies of Laybach and Verona to the side of Great Britain and its reformed Parliament, but the effect of this metamorphosis was most sensibly felt in the several revolutions which followed then, as now, in the train of Parisian catastrophies.†

The insurrections in Belgium and Poland were the immediate, if not the legitimate successors of the Paris Revolution. The first ended with the separation or overthrow of the kingdom of the Netherlands, the handiwork of the Congress of 1815, and the entire independence of Belgium; the second with the complete defeat of the Poles by the Russians under Paskiewitch. In Italy, too, revolution had raised its head, but was again overpowered by an Austrian army entering the states of the Church. In Germany, also, matters did not remain untroubled: the people of Brunswick drove away its Duke Charles. The Hessians forced their sovereign to grant a Constitution. The desire of the people was also acceded to, and the king then granted a Constitution, on the 4th of September, 1831. In several small duchies the example was followed, but every where prevailed the utmost dissatisfaction.‡ This movement

---

* Edinburgh Review, October, 1848.   † Ibid.

‡ The following is a list of the sovereigns who complied with the letter of their promise, by granting Constitutions to their subjects:

Sovereigns.	Date of Constitutions.
King of Bavaria	May 26, 1828.
King of Wurtemberg	September 25, 1819.
King of Hanover	December 7, 1819.
King of Saxony	March 1, 1831.
Grand Duke of Baden	August 28, 1828.
Grand Duke of Hesse Darmstadt	December 17, 1820.
Elector of Hesse	January 1, 1831.
Grand Duke of Luxemburg	August 24, 1815.
Duke of Brunswick	April 2, 1820.
Duke of Nassau	September 2, 1814.
Duke of Saxe-Weimar	May 1, 1816.
Duke of Saxe-Meiningen Hilburghausen	August 23, 1829.
Duke of Saxe-Coburg Gotha	August 8, 1821.

was not confined to a blind and fanatical party, but prudent. and well-disposed, and high-minded men (like Rottech and Welcher) declared themselves openly and decisively in favor of the imperious necessity that concessions should be made to the claims of an advanced age, to the full exercise of constitutional institutions, that a legal and reasonable* liberty should be granted upon a reconciliation between prince and people, and upon the re-establishment of reciprocal confidence between them.†

The effects of the French Revolution of 1830, in its reaction upon the public mind throughout Europe, manifested themselves in Germany in popular commotions, which were followed by various reforms in the local constitutions of several states, such as Saxony, Electoral Hesse, and Hanover. In the states of Germany which had already obtained, by

Duke of Swarzburg Rudolstadt .... January 8, 1816.
Prince of Lechtenstein .... November 9, 1818.
Prince of Waldeck .... April 15, 1816.

The following is a list of those who violated their pledge, both in its letter and spirit, by refusing Constitutions:
Emperor of Austria.
King of Prussia.
Grand Duke of Mecklenberg Schwerin.
Grand Duke of Mecklenberg Strelitz.
Grand Duke of Oldenberg.
Duke of Holstein.
Duke of Saxe-Altenberg.
Duke of Anhalt Dessau.
Duke of Anhalt Bernberg.
Duke of Anhalt Coethen.
Prince of Hohenzollern Heckingen.
Prince of Hohenzollern Sigmaringen.
Prince of Reuss, Senior Branch.
Prince of Reuss, Junior Branch.
Prince of Lippe,   } who offered the mockery of a Constitution,
Prince of Lippe Schaumberg, }   which the people rejected.
Prince of Swarzenberg Sonderhausen.
Landgrave of Hesse Hamberg.

* German Almanac.

† On the 27th of May, 1832, the Hambacher festival took place, the confused effusion of all vague ideas of German demagogism, and this unfortunate meeting gave a pretext to the Diet of the Confederation, a month after, to decree a still stricter repression of constitutional liberty, and which had been previously determined on.[1]

---

[1] German Almanac.

the voluntary concessions of their sovereigns, representative
constitutions more or less corresponding to the wants and
wishes of the people, the legislative chambers assumed an attitude and a tone of discussion which had been unknown since
the repressive measures adopted under the additional powers
given to the Diet by the final Act of the Confederation in 1820.*
The liberty of the press, which was still tolerated, to a certain
extent, in some of the minor states, was freely used to arraign
the German governments before the tribunal of public opinion,
to demand further concessions in favor of popular rights—in
some instances to excite popular commotions. The Diet at
first contented itself with exercising its acknowledged powers,
by specific measures for suppressing the publication of certain
offensive newspapers. But these measures proving insufficient, in the opinion of the Austrian and Prussian cabinets, to
check the rapid progress of the revolutionary spirit, a decree
was adopted by the Diet on the 28th of June, 1832, on the motion of Austria, seconded by Prussia, by which very important
modifications were introduced into the fundamental laws of
the Confederation established in 1815 and 1820.†

The motives for adopting the decree were stated by the presiding officer, and delegate from Austria, Count Münch Bel-
linghausen; and after reading a communication to the same
effect, to the Diet of the Confederation, from the Emperor of
Austria, the propositions contained therein were converted into
a law of the Confederation by an act of the Diet, dated the
28th of June, 1832.‡

Besides this resolution of the Frankfort Diet of 1832, "a
similar object (says Binder, the biographer of Metternich), together with the completion and clearer explanation of some
points of the Treaty of Federation, occupied the great Congress
of ministers assembled, at the desire of Prince Metternich, at
Vienna, from the 13th of January to the 13th of June, 1834,
some of whose resolutions have been published by the Diet."

The purport of these resolutions, which so palpably infringed
that clause of the treaty of Vienna of 1815, which guaranteed
internal independence to every state of Germany, was the in-

---

* Wheaton, p. 460.   † Ibid., 460–461.   ‡ See Appendix, No. 1.

stitution of a Board of Control or Arbitration, named by the territorial sovereigns of Germany, which, as the highest court of appeal, were to watch over the proceedings of the States-General or Assemblies, and to decide all disputes which might arise between them and their respective governments.   The sittings of the assemblies or chambers in the different states were ordered to be held with closed doors, and the official publication of their proceedings, which had been adopted voluntarily by several, among others by Hanover, was prohibited. Other points related to restrictions of the press, regulations at the universities, and systems of education.

The people, through their respective assemblies, protested against that decree, but, notwithstanding, it was enforced. The last warning voice passed unheeded by the rulers.   It really seemed as if they intended to suppress such an intellectual movement by brute force.   How had they mistaken the time !   In the year 1815,* and even in the year 1830, it would have been an easy task to have effected a reconciliation by yielding to the public desires, which, until that time, had always been respectfully proposed to the crown.   The moderate party then formed an immense majority of the German people.   With gratitude and joy, concessions would have been received at that time, which would not have limited the rights of the crown, but only its abuses.   Faithfully the grateful people would have rallied around the throne, and their breasts would have proved the safest buckler against the criminal designs of the revolutionary propagandism.   By the course adopted, the people were exposed to demoralization, which afterward brought forth its dreadful fruits.   The disheartening conviction now took root, that it was no longer possible to expect a settlement in a legal way, and that only by force or revolution could the resistance be overcome which blind or culpable ministers opposed to the wishes of the people.

The revolutionary propaganda was not idle in taking advantage of this excited state of the public mind, and in applying the match.†

Moral fidelity and obedience to law became, among a great

---

* Coxe's House of Austria.   † German Almanac.

part of the German people, undermined by systematic and continued suggestions.

Increased poverty and proletarianism, strangers of all principles and manners, furnished numerous elements to the criminal (demagogical) stratagems of the revolutionary party, and the communistic principles and ideas infused a quantity of poison into the body of the people.

From this time the tendencies of German liberalism took another direction and wider scope. The exclusively German and purely national ideas of 1812 to 1815, yielded to a perception that the condition of the continent indicated that the constitutional bond must be an universal one to insure success, and this idea gave rise to the party commonly called Young Germany. Many sections of the old exclusive national party, as it was called, could not forget their accustomed hue-and-cry against France; while Young Germany contended that, now she had recovered her constitutional liberty, she deserved to be considered as a sister nation. Young Germany gained many adherents by the truth of its suggestions; and as the antipathy to France subsided, public opinion was more and more employed in scrutinizing domestic grievances, and the melancholy fate of Poland indicated the dangers that awaited their own country.*

The exertions of the advanced liberal party were not only directed against that rotten body, the Frankfort Diet, but against the whole compact of the treaties of 1815, by virtue of which Russia and Austria held Poland and Italy chained, like Prometheus, to the rock of absolutism, and the impassioned strictures which had hitherto been directed against France, were now applied to St. Petersburg and Vienna.

Thus the idea of German unity assumed a more general and efficient character, being associated with the literature of Italy and Poland; and the people looked to England for the rescue of the former, and of the latter to France. The policy of Louis Philippe soon disenchanted the friends of liberty, as it became apparent that he preferred making concessions to his brother sovereigns, to forming such an alliance with England

---

* Westminster Review.

as might have compelled them to pursue a constitutional course. Meanwhile, the general and ardent thirst for constitutional liberty, far from being checked by disappointment, followed the general law of natural desires, and was increased by the obstacles which opposed it. The German sovereigns acknowledged the mutual-responsibility principles of Young Germany, by taking care that their own subjects should always pay for the folly of their trans-Rhenish neighbors. Every *émeute* in Paris was followed by wholesale imprisonments in Berlin and Vienna; and every attempt on the life of Louis Philippe formed an excuse for fresh measures of coercion at home; and, after the subjugation of Poland, the *triad* of the Holy Alliance—Russia, Austria, and Prussia—might be seen walking hand in hand, and dragging their subjects through the old dreary by-ways of absolutism and treachery.

These stringent measures on the part of the sovereigns were attended with no popular outbreak, not because absolutism had become more palatable, or the feeling of the necessity of radical reform less vehement, but from the fact that a belief seemed now to have taken possession of all minds that a great change was at hand, and could not possibly be long deferred. This change was expected to take place at the deaths of Louis Philippe and Metternich,* who were regarded as the pillars of the existing system. The people looked to these events like a spendthrift heir, who expects, with Christian patience happily tempered with certainty, the decease of a rich but indifferent relative. Metternich seemed to share the general belief, but hoped that he should be allowed to enjoy his glory for the term of his natural life; he bespoke peace and quiet for himself, but bequeathed a deluge to his successors.

The events of 1848 were foreseen, nay expected, and yet they took the world by surprise. No party was sufficiently prepared either for attack or defense. Governments, secure in stupid blindness, actively accelerated the convulsion they had so long been anxious to avert, while the people had not the

---

* The four sponsors of the peace of Europe, as was thought a few years since, were Louis Philippe, Prince Metternich, Mehemet Ali, and the Duke of Wellington. Two are now deceased, one driven from power, and the other perhaps too advanced in age for efficient service.

slightest idea of a sanguinary revolution.   They thought that
the two obnoxious men were growing old, and would enjoy their
last days in peace; and that, when they disappeared from the
stage, constitutional liberty would achieve a bloodless triumph.
Such an expectation was far less unpractical than might seem,
for as all parties were agreed upon the main principle of constitutional liberty, all other questions promised an easy solution, as soon as the chief abettor of division, the great apostle
of *divide et impera*, should be gathered to his fathers.   The
question was simply one of time.   The death of Louis Philippe
or of Metternich was variously assigned as the moment beyond
which a general outbreak could not be deferred.   Events have
been somewhat precipitated, but the outbreak was inevitable,
as another will be, if grievances are merely compromised for
the moment, and no provisions made to give security to the
political fabric of Europe.

Foreign Policy of Austria.

A brief reference to the foreign policy, as well as the internal
administration of the empire, will not fail to indicate that the
causes for popular dissatisfaction existed, in a still more striking degree than in other parts of Germany, within the empire
of Austria, and that there, so far at least as oppression and discontent are considered, the people were ready for the events
of 1848.

The foreign policy of Austria since 1815 is so intimately
blended with, and, in fact, inseparable from, the character of
her great statesman, that the biography of the one naturally
embraces the history of the other.   Prince Metternich has long
held, by common consent, the rank of the most distinguished
statesman of Europe.   Two conditions are essential to the highest renown in public life, the possession of great qualities and
great opportunities for their exercise; and with both he was
sufficiently provided.   The career of the prince has been the
longest, the most difficult, and (for his own principles) the
most triumphant in the annals of modern diplomacy.   He has
been now before the world for near half a century.   During
the former part of his public life he was engaged in sustaining the fallen strength of Austria, and during the latter half

in the scarcely less difficult task of securing her established power. The fortunes and policy of the imperial house of Austria have been more than once identified with the characters of those supreme servants of state, whose ministerial functions have been extended to the utmost limit of absolute power, and protracted beyond the ordinary duration of human life. But of these illustrious ministers, who have lived in the long and secure administration of one of the greatest empires of the earth, none ever retained that high and responsible position amid events of such infinite magnitude and variety, or with so unlimited control, as Clement, prince of Metternich.*

Prince Metternich was born at Coblentz on the 15th of May, 1773. The son of an able Austrian minister, of ancient and noble family, he was educated for diplomacy, and after studying the national law of Europe at Strasburg, and going through the admirable course of education appointed for the *élèves* of the foreign office, he entered early into the service, and was one of the masters of ceremony at the coronation of Leopold the Second, in 1792. He afterward continued his studies at Mentz until 1794. In 1795 he was sent as Austrian minister to the Hague. The first Congress which he attended was that of Radstadt, in 1797; in 1801 he was sent minister to Dresden; afterward to Berlin, where he represented also the court of Westphalia; and he rose with such rapidity,† that in 1806, after the peace of Pressburg, he was selected for the important post of embassador in Paris. Austria, like Prussia, had suffered excessively in her conflict with France.

Both were undergoing terrible retaliation by the sword of the French emperor, for the feebleness of their assault on the French Republic, and both, by their calamities, were exhibiting the most direct moral of the hazards of national insincerity, of timidity in council, and of slackness in the field. At length, both powers, with all their strength mowed down, and their sovereignty plowed and harrowed by the power of France, were forced wholly to abandon dependence on themselves, and to

---

* Galignani's Messenger.

† Was the chief agent in uniting Austria, Prussia, and Russia, by tne treaty of Potsdam in 1805, for which he received the Grand Cross of the order of St. Stephen.

wait for the chances of time and the course of things to reno-
vate the moral soil.   Diplomacy was now the only instrument
by which Austria could hope to preserve even the semblance
of an independent government; and it is a signal proof of the
talents of young Metternich, that he was selected for that most
important of all missions, the embassy to France; for it is in
times of national distress that court favoritism and imperial
folly lose their power of perverting the national choice, and the
claim of superior abilities establishes its right to distinction.
On his arrival at Paris, Count Metternich, although only thirty
years of age, yet, by his noble and engaging physiognomy, his
easy and graceful manners, his refined and cultivated mind,
descendant of the old and aristocratic family, and representing a great and ancient monarchy, soon became distinguished
above all others, and gained for himself an easy access to the
favor and consideration of the French emperor.*   Napoleon
never treated him with roughness, but seemed rather pleased
with his society; and Metternich embraced the opportunity to
prove to him the necessity of a union between France and Austria.   The policy of Metternich was to conceal from the emperor
all thoughts of the intended breach; and, with that dissimulation of which he was a perfect master, continued his assurances
of amity, while Austria armed herself for the coming contest.

Upon the declaration of war by Austria against France, Metternich returned to the imperial dominions, and joined the Emperor Francis, who had taken refuge in the fortress of Comorn,
in Hungary.   Three days after the memorable defeat of Wagram, Count Stadion retired from the office of minister of foreign affairs, and Count Metternich was selected to succeed him.
His first effort, upon his elevation to that station, was to conduct the negotiations with the French minister Champagny,
and to gain a respite for his bleeding country at the price of
an archduchess.   The reasons assigned by Prince Metternich
for this step were, that he found the finances of the country

---

* Napoleon at this time had relaxed his policy toward the French noblesse,
and was, in consequence, surrounded by a mass of the ancient nobility, with whom
Metternich soon ingratiated himself with the insinuating address and graceful manners which he so eminently possessed.   He was not long in penetrating the secrets and scandals about the court of the Tuileries, and in captivating and obtaining the favor of the principal personages, and even of Napoleon himself.

embarrassed ; its military strength weakened; its public spirit crushed by misfortune ; and he hoped by this measure to raise his country from the abyss into which it had fallen, as well as to recover back such portions of the empire as Napoleon had wrested from it.   But if any thing can aggravate the humiliation of that transaction, it is the conviction, which the court of Austria must then have had, that this sacrifice was made in vain.

The time approached when the great scourge of the Continent was at length to be trampled under foot, and France to feel a portion of the evils which she had inflicted upon Europe. The march to Moscow was the phrensy of conquest; the delay at Moscow was the infatuation of a power which thought itself irresistible ; the retreat from Moscow was the infliction of a punishment long ripening for the crimes of the empire.   On the return of the French armies into the field, the murderous battles of Bautzen and Lutzen gave formidable demonstration to the French emperor that he had taught his enemies to fight, and that his European supremacy could no longer be maintained by the sword.   Diplomacy was now to decide the question of empire, and the fate of the war depended upon Austria.

In the interval of dubious peace which had uneasily followed the treaty of Schönbrunn, the Austrian government, under the control of Metternich, had applied itself unostentatiously, but indefatigably to the arrangement of its finances ; the restoration of its army, and to all the means by which national vigor is to be infused once more into a fallen country. Within the four years from the defeat in 1809 to 1813, Austria had made prodigious advances in the renovation of her power.   The great object of the allies was to obtain her connection; the great object of Napoleon was to secure her neutrality.   On this occasion, Austria proposed herself as mediator, and Russia, Prussia, and France acknowledged her armed mediation ; and Napoleon found the former embassador now the organ of a voice which was virtually to decide his fate.   Metternich met him in perhaps the most momentous conference that ever was held in the field.   His first proposal was peace, but the conditions were the surrender of the French conquests in Germany.   Napoleon, with an infatuation only equaled by his attempts to negotiate at Moscow, spurned the idea, and even went to the length of charging the prince with receiving the money of England.*   An insult of this stamp, put an end to the interview, which had lasted till near midnight, and was carried on at times in tones of passion so violent as to be over-heard by the attendants.   The alliance of Austria decided Napoleon's fate.   The 10th of August, 1813, had been assigned as the period within which France might accede to the proposals of the three powers.   That fatal hour passed by, and Count Metternich drew up on that night the declaration of war on the part of Austria against France; and on the morning of the 11th, the Russian and Prussian troops marched over the Bohemian and Silesian frontier.   A month later, the grand alliance was signed at Toeplitz; and on the eve of the battle of Leipsic, the Emperor Francis conferred on Metternich and his heirs the dignity of a prince of the empire.   In the conferences and negotiations at Frankfort, Friburg, Basle, Langres, and Chaumont, which accompanied the invasion of France, Prince Metternich took a prominent and active part.   He directed the negotiations of the Congress of Chatillon, signed the convention of Fontainebleau with Napoleon, and subsequently that of the first and second peace of Paris, in 1814 and 1815.   Subsequently he presided, as has been seen, at the several Congresses of the allied powers at Vienna, Carlsbad, Troppau, Laybach, and Verona; and has, without exception, received all the highest orders of distinction which the different monarchs of Europe could bestow.

Prince Metternich in person is rather below the ordinary size, has a well-formed head, nose large and aristocratic, eyes blue and expressive, a mouth well shaped, and with a smile ever at command.   His whole person, countenance, and demeanor, are indicative of high station, superior intellect, and finished elegance.   He was not remarkable for his native genius or subsequent acquirements, but his distinguishing traits were his knowledge and perception of character, and the arts by which he bent them to his own purpose. . He could enter tain a circle of fifty persons with ease and amiability, without

---

* Alison's Europe.

resorting to ordinary resources. He would participate in the dissipation and the follies of his superiors and equals; but he would, at the same time, be searching the means by which he could turn them to profit. It was impossible to know better than he how to discover the weak sides of those around him, and, what is still more difficult, to render himself necessary to their frailties.*

The mode of execution which Metternich employs is truly singular. To a perfect knowledge of the principal persons with whom he has transactions, he joins an address not less astonishing in the choice of his instruments. He has formed for himself a gallery of living Metternichs, from whence he draws forth his embassadors and agents. With a gigantic mind he spread his toils over the whole Continent—had his spies in all the capitals of Europe: in Portugal he was with the Miguels; in Spain, France, and in Italy, with the aristocrats and priests; and at Constantinople most intimate with the sultan. It was by these means that he held for so long a time the destinies of Europe in his hands.

Metternich was never the sanguinary tyrant that some have supposed; he was averse to all extreme measures, and particularly opposed to shedding human blood. No political executions ever took place at his instance. Those which occurred upon the tumults in the empire, which followed the French Revolution of 1830, occurred by the express orders of the Emperor Francis. Metternich's disposition is more truly exem-

---

* L'Empéreur de Russie, commençant à se fatiguer des bacchanales nocturnes qui se succédaient pendant la durée du Congrès de Vienne, et Metternich craignant de se voir privé de sa présence et de perdre tout le fruit de ses belles combinaisons, imagina de nouveaux passe-temps plus analogues aux goûts de son nouveau maître. Les magnifiques tournois, les bals, et les diners, furent tout à coup remplacés par de *petites soirées* données par Metternich, et auxquelles présidait, en qualité de *souveraine*, la belle Princesse de S. née Princesse de C. La famille de cette dame, ne voulait point se prêter à ce manège, fit manquer le plan projeté, et cette dernière quitta Vienne incognito pour se rendre à F——g, où Alexandre la suivit. La belle fugitive fut encore obligée de se dérober aux poursuites de celui qui voulait absolument faire sa conquête; mais Metternich, dans cet intérim sut profiter des circonstances; et c'est principalement par la vertu des charmes transcendans de ce talisman, qu'il attira successivement Alexandre aux ennuyeux Congrès de Troppau et de Laybach.—*Tablettes Autrichiennes.*

plified by the general amnesty for all political offenders throughout the empire, with which commenced the reign of the imbecile Ferdinand, and during whose term Metternich was "indeed the state."*

As a legislator, Prince Metternich's capacities have ever been regarded as moderate; as a financier, the bankruptcy of Austria during his administration certainly furnishes no recommendation; but as a skillful diplomatist or an adroit courtier, it can not be denied that he has ever stood unrivaled.

The first great secret of his success was, that by the qualities described he ingratiated himself into favor with Napoleon, and, during his residence at that court, occupied himself in acquiring a profound knowledge of the character of the French emperor, and in devising his plans and preparing himself for performing, in after years, the principal part in the political drama of Dresden and Prague. The principal object in procuring the marriage between Napoleon and the Austrian archduchess, was not so much to restore the fallen fortunes of his country, as by this means to obtain a still more perfect knowledge of even the private life of Napoleon, and to acquire such influence over him as to make it, in after years, an easy task to hold the conqueror of Europe in suspense, during the Congress of Dresden, the invasion, armistice, and Congress of Prague, until the Austrian armies should have been sufficiently recruited and prepared to enter the contest.

The art with which Metternich passed from the alliance with Napoleon to neutrality, from neutrality to mediation, and from mediation to the coalition against him, will in every age be considered a master-piece of diplomacy.

The great principles in the foreign policy of Austria which Metternich seems, during his whole career, to have kept steadily in view, are:

1st. To preserve the principles of legitimacy throughout all governments.

2d. To maintain peace, and secure the balance of power in Europe.

The term legitimacy is a modern device in the politics of

---

* Francis himself was heard to say, "In forgiving and pardoning I am a bad Christian; it is too difficult for me; Metternich is much more compassionate."

Europe. When the allies dethroned Napoleon and his brothers, they wanted something to oppose to the claims which he derived from his election by the people. A phantom was consequently created at the Congress of Vienna, called *legitimacy*, and since that time has been constantly used, but never defined, as indeed it would be difficult to do, since the facts before the world are too stubborn for this theory of the hereditary descent of nations, like property. The Legitimists of Europe, par excellence, and they who are especially known by that name, are the Elder Bourbons, the oldest house except that of the Guelphs, and one which has supplied one hundred and twenty sovereigns to Europe, *originated with a usurper*. But it is generally used to denote the lawfulness of the government in a hereditary monarchy, where the supreme dignity and power pass by law from one regent to another, according to the right of primogeniture.

In the support of this system, nations and their rights became as chattels in his hands, which he disposed of at pleasure, where he could effect the greatest advantage. He sacrificed the Greeks to the Turks, the Poles to Russia, and the Italians to their oppressors. He aided, in France, the restoration of the ancient absolutism, and favored the bigotry of Spain.

But his principles are best explained by himself.

When the Neapolitans, in 1820, heard that the Austrians intended interfering to suppress the Constitution they had extorted from their king, Prince Cimitilé was sent to Vienna to deprecate the intervention, and to give assurances of the wish of his government to conform as much as possible to the desires of the Austrians. The answer given by Prince Metternich, at a personal interview, is stated as follows: "The present Neapolitan revolution is the work of a profligate sect, the work of surprise and force. Were the courts to grant it any countenance, even by silently looking on, it would be equivalent to scattering the seeds of rebellion in lands where they have never yet taken root.*

"The first duty, and the highest interest of the powers required them to crush it in the beginning. As to the readiness

---

* *Fürst Clemens von Metternich und sein Zeitalter*, von Dr. W. Binder.

of the Neapolitan government to endeavor to prevent the extension of the propaganda, even if it be really able to do so, it
merits but little gratitude for that which we shall require
from it as a duty.   The recognition of the new order of things
in that kingdom would both shake the foundation of our own
state, and deprive Naples of the only means she now possesses
of opposing the terrors of anarchy.   These means are, order
and the support of those principles on which alone the tranquillity of states is grounded ; and these principles will conquer as
soon as the government is resolved to maintain its former institutions against the attacks of innovators and party spirit."
When the embassador, not a little astonished at these remarks
upon the true state of things, inquired "if a peaceable arrangement was quite out of the question," the prince continued as
follows : "Here arrangement is not the object in view.   We
must apply a cure.   Use your endeavors to cause all the well-
disposed men in your country to request the king to reassume
the reins of government ; to annul every act since the 5th of
July ; to punish the individuals who have brought their country to the brink of destruction ; and, finally, to adopt measures
likely to ensure the happiness and prosperity of the people.
Then will Austria, all Europe, support you in this praiseworthy undertaking."*

On Cimitilé's expressing his doubts that any one could be
found, in the actual state of things at Naples, to hold such language, the prince replied, with noble confidence, "If you do
not find such, his majesty, my emperor and master, will assuredly supply them.   He, the ruler of men who avow these principles, and who have power sufficient to effect the good I have
pointed out to you, will come to your aid.   *Dispose of eighty
thousand, or, if needful, one hundred thousand Austrian troops,
which shall advance at your first requisition, and conduct you
to Naples as conqueror of the rebels.*"

Prince Cimitilé expressed, with bitter feeling, his regret
that, having come to prevent measures of violence and bloodshed, the Austrian cabinet should devote itself wholly to such
extreme measures.   "Yes," continued Prince Metternich, and

---

* Binder.

concluded the interview, "blood must flow, but it will fall upon the heads of those who have sacrificed the honor and happiness of their country to the suggestions of selfish ambition. As for me, I throw off all responsibility, for I only act as the interests of my nation make it incumbent for me to do."

This principle of legitimacy owes its origin more properly to that aristocracy among the powers of Europe which was commenced by the Quadruple Alliance, for twenty years, of Austria, Russia, England, and Prussia, made at Chaumont in 1814, confirmed by the form of negociations at Vienna, and finally perfected by the accession of France, at the Congress of Aix la Chapelle.

It is remarkable that a principle so totally at variance with the rights of man, should have its origin in a convention which could make the following declaration : " The sovereigns recognize as the fundamental principle of the high compact now existing between them the unalterable resolution, neither in their own reciprocal concerns nor in their relations with other powers, to depart from *the strictest obedience to the maxims of popular right ;* because the constant application of these maxims to a permanent state of peace, affords the only effectual guarantee for the independence of each separate power and the security of the whole Confederation."

To maintain the Peace and preserve the Balance of Power in Europe.

It is the complacent boast of his biographer that Metternich had maintained the peace of Europe for twenty years; and, in fact, the great monument which the prince has raised for himself, after near half a century of public service, is that of richly meriting a title which Louis Philippe arrogantly assumed, "the Napoleon of peace." In the first place, the position which the Austrian empire occupies in relation to Europe rendered the pacific policy, with her, more a matter of necessity than it was an exhibition of virtue. By reason of its geographical location, occupying a middle place between the east and the west, between the north and the south of the European continent, the empire is called upon to discharge the functions of ballast in the European ship of state; and as

E

the shock of every disturbance, in whatever quarter of Europe
it might occur, must vibrate through her, the readjustment of
the European equilibrium, on such occasions, becomes to her
a matter of vital interest.

While such have been the leading motives or inducements
to such a course, "the line of policy adopted by the Austrian
court to keep at a distance from the destructive movements
of the times," as he terms it, is explained by the biographer
of Metternich to have existed, not in the measures of internal
policy alone, but in endeavors to effect a restriction of the press
in Germany; in the direct interference to suppress the Revolution of Naples; and in the indirect intervention, by urging
an obsequious ally* to undertake the crushing of the revolutionary party in Spain.

To avoid "the destructive movements of the times," he afterward occupied the states of the Church with Austrian armies
upon the slightest disturbance.   Even as late as two years before he surrendered his power, he extinguished the Republic
of Cracow, the only foot of soil left of an empire that once extended from the Baltic to the Black Sea, and the last refuge
of Polish nationality; and the very last year of his more than
imperial sway, opposed the liberal party of Switzerland, and
supported their opponents, the Sonderbund, as is said, by the
"material aid" of a million of dollars.   The twenty years of
peace so boastfully alluded to, have witnessed not fewer changes
than the period which preceded them, the sole difference being
that it will probably require more time and more bloodshed to
correct much of the evil accomplished in them.   Such a peace
is not the peace of satisfaction and content; it is the peace of
the grave, and which follows the extinction of all vitality and
energy among the people.

A lasting peace on the European continent can not be expected until such a modification of the existing governments
takes place as shall cause the rights of individual citizens to
be respected under all circumstances, at home and abroad.
The system of crushing, by armed interference, the demands
which must, by turns, be made in every country for an enlarge-

---

* France.

ment of popular rights, can only be justified by the supposition that no progressive mental improvement takes place among the people which would entitle them to what they claim; and as no government has hitherto gone the length of attempting to prove that civilization is stationary in any part of the world, these demands will not end, the pretext for encroaching on the rights of the weaker states not cease; but these commotions and troubles continue to increase in frequency and virulence, so long as the present system of opposition prevails on the part of the stronger governments.

SUBSERVIENCY TO RUSSIA.

While Austria, in the furtherance of her pacific policy, has extended her influence over her neighbors on three sides, a totally different policy has been pursued toward the powerful and encroaching nation that joins her eastern frontier, and to which she seems to have endeavored, of late years, by every means to render herself subservient.

Had the Austrian monarchy been justly governed, the interest of the people properly regarded, the resources of the country wisely developed, it might at this day have stood at the head of all the powers of Europe.

The inexhaustible resources of every province, each large enough to form a separate kingdom, combined with the varieties of mental capacity displayed in the inhabitants, constitute materials for the creation of an unconquerable power. The agricultural profusion and mineral wealth of the Hungarian and Polish provinces; the manufacturing spirit of the inhabitants of Bohemia and its agricultural wealth; the mines of Styria and Carinthia, and the unsurpassed fertility of Lombardy, united, offer a mass of internal wealth unrivaled by any other European state. Large navigable rivers traverse the country in all directions, and afford means of communication to commercial enterprise, to which the possession of no unimportant extent of sea-coast likewise invites. In the population such varied elements combine as might be expected to turn these means to the best advantage. The skillful, industrious Lombard, the wily Illyrian, the hardy Hungarian, the meditative German, the patient, persevering Bohemian, and the fiery but versatile Pole, form a mixture of energies admirably calculated to assist and correct each other. With these advantages, added to those of her geographical position in the centre of Europe, and holding the supremacy of the German Confederation, it is not a little mysterious that Metternich should have suffered, if not assisted to promote, Austria's subserviency to Russia.

The policy of Austria has been characterized for ages by an insatiable thirst for the extension of territory, and by the oppression of every country which she has held in subjection. What has become of her former ambition, as boundless as that of ancient Rome, and which dictated the device of the five vowels graven on her earliest monuments, A. E. I. O. U.? (Austriæ est imperare orbi universo.) She could repel the French from Italy in 1831, and restore the ancient regime, but she does not oppose the ever-increasing influence of Russia in Poland, Persia, Turkey, and even allowed her great outlet, the mouth of the Danube, to be guarded by Russian bayonets. Since the days of Catharine the First, Russia has augmented the religious ties which exist between the Russian and the Turkish provinces of Moldavia, Wallachia, Bosnia, Bulgaria, and of Turkish Croatia and Dalmatia, and striven to detach them gradually from the Ottoman Porte. They are now almost entirely governed by Russian consuls, and that influence increases the more from its being unobserved, as it were, in the shade; and the inhabitants are, even at this day, more Russian than Turk. Sooner or later these provinces will be attached to the colossal power of Russia, and they will become, with Greece, the natural allies of Russia (the same religious tie binding them), and form one boulevard, which will surround Austria, and bid defiance to all Europe, while she controls the waters of the Mediterranean.*

In later years Austria has placed herself under obligations to Russia, from the influence of which she will never be able to escape; in the first place, by pecuniary relief which Russia afforded her, in 1847, by a loan of 50,000,000 florins, a sum which has since been increased rather than diminished; and,

---

* Tablettes Autrichiennes.

In the second, by the incalculable debt of armed intervention, in saving for the Austrian crown the important province of Hungary, which, without the aid of the autocrat, would have been lost to the empire.

Internal Administration of the Austrian Empire.

Throughout the empire the form of government is monarchical, though in some provinces the power of the sovereign is absolute, in others limited; in some he has always been hereditary, in others he was formerly elective.*

In the hereditary or German states of Austria the power of the emperor has long been absolute. These are under the direct control of the imperial chancery at Vienna, and are all governed by one and the same code of laws, civil and criminal. The Italian states are governed by a viceroy, and have a jurisprudence of their own. Hungary is a distinct kingdom, under a palatine, in the selection of whom they have a voice, with an independent Constitution. Transylvania, except that it is but a principality, stands on nearly the same footing as Hungary. Throughout the empire (with the exception, perhaps, of Hungary), the whole *legislative* power is vested in the emperor, who proceeds either by original edict or by rescript, which is a reply to some public body or person empowered to make application to the crown.†

The edicts and rescripts are forwarded to the various functionaries, and copies are printed annually for general use.

No approval, adoption, or registration of any sort is required to give efficacy to an edict or rescript, except on the subject of finance; but a money bill must be submitted to the Stände or State, meaning a kind of Diet, by which the right of apportioning the taxes is exercised.

---

* The empire of Austria is not, as is frequently supposed, a pure monarchy; it is rather a cluster of monarchies, some of which are pure, others mixed; some parliamentary and constitutional, others not. Accordingly, the system of government which has hitherto been pursued has endeavored to accommodate itself, as much as possible, to the peculiarities of each monarchy; and, while the *executive* functions have been exercised by the emperor alone, or by his officers, the *administrative* functions have been exercised by him conjointly with the respective Estates or Parliaments.[1] † Quarterly Review.

[1] Eight kingdoms, one grand duchy, four duchies, one principality, one sovereign earldom, and one margravate.—*Thompson's Austria.*

These Stände, which exist in the German, Illyrian, Bohemian, Galician, and Tyrolian provinces, are composed of four classes : 1st, the clergy ; 2d, the nobility ; 3d, knights or inferior nobility ; and, 4th, the citizens or deputies of the royal towns.   The members who represent the clergy and the nobles, sit, some in their own right as individuals, and some as deputies for the rest; the burghers or citizens are elected by the corporations of their respective towns.   The States meet once a year or oftener ; they form a single chamber ; the governor of the province or royal commissioner presides, and resolutions are decided by a majority of votes.   The deliberations of the States extend only to subjects relating to the internal regulation of the provinces and legal apportionment of the taxes. The land-tax, which it has been resolved on to raise, is consequently announced to them by the government in the form of a postulate, and they have the right, in their legal assemblies, to present remonstrances to the emperor or provincial government.*   Possessed of no power, they have dwindled down into mere agricultural societies ; the whole system is a mockery, as no member, for years, has been found hardy enough to allude to subjects not contained in the postulate.

In the Lombardo-Venetian kingdom, a somewhat more popular system prevails.   Each of the two provinces has its Assembly, with attributes and powers similar to those of the German Stände, but their internal composition is wholly different. They have neither ecclesiastical members nor nobles sitting in right of birth or property, nor deputies of close corporations. The members are all elected ; but through the medium of a double, or, rather, a triple stage of election.   The two great classes of Contadinni, the proprietors of land, and Cittadinni, the inhabitants of towns, are the primary electors, the suffrage dependent upon the payment of a certain sum in annual taxes. Those primary electors choose by ballot, from their general body, a Council of Election, the members of which must possess a still higher property qualification than is requisite for the primary elector himself.   The Council of Election nominates by vote, from the members of its own body, a certain

---

* Turnbull's Austria.

number of candidates, and from these candidates the crown
selects those who shall act as members of the Provincial Assembly; with the power, however, in its discretion, of rejecting them all, or of ordering a new selection.*

In Hungary and Transylvania the diets or parliaments, previous to 1848, were purely aristocratical bodies, which have
been hitherto omnipotent in maintaining for the nobles their
feudal privileges and their exemption from all direct taxation.
They consist of two chambers—a chamber of hereditary magnates, and an elective chamber of deputies from the counties,
the free towns, the higher clergy, the magnates, and the widows of magnates.†

But of these deputies, the country members, who are themselves all noble, and are chosen by nobles, have alone the privilege of voting; the deputies of the free towns, contrary to the
spirit of the ancient Constitution, being merely allowed by the
nobles to sit and speak, on the ground that, being under the
immediate protection of the crown, they might be obsequious
instruments in its hands.‡ The *executive* or sovereign acts
through central councils or boards, each of which has its chancellor or president, communicating below with the provincial
councils, and. above with the cabinet, which surrounds the
emperor. The cabinet, for many years, in Austria, and down
to the outbreak of the late Revolution, consisted of the Archduke Louis, uncle of the late emperor; the Archduke Francis Charles, the brother; Prince Metternich, and Count Kolowrath. Nominally, the Home or Interior Department was
under the charge of Count Kolowrath, and the Foreign Department under Prince Metternich; but the prince was the
animating spirit of the whole.

The policy of Francis (or, rather, the policy of Metternich),
which has governed Austria for the last fifty years, was, in a
measure, decided by the remarkable course of his uncle, the
Emperor Joseph, who almost immediately preceded. The
Emperor Leopold succeeded Joseph; but his reign, which
lasted but two years, was not distinguished by any particular

---

* Turnbull's Austria. † Ibid.

‧ Quarterly Review, 1849.

stroke of policy, other than an attempt to efface, as rapidly as possible, the reforms of Joseph.

Joseph no sooner became sole sovereign than he began a multitude of reforms. With headlong enthusiasm he at once attempted to uproot every ancient abuse, and to force upon his subjects liberty and enlightenment for which they were totally unfitted.* Abolishing, without hesitation, the customs of the different countries which he undertook to reform, he required all to surrender the portion of good they possessed, and to receive at his hands what he imagined to be a fuller measure of the means of acquiring prosperity.† With an abundance of excellent intentions, but with a total want of practical sense, he pulled down the edifice of the state in order to construct a huge scaffolding, which broke under its own weight. He established liberty of the press, a tolerance of all religions, relieved the peasants from vassalage, emancipated the Jews, abolished torture and capital punishment, also the begging orders, closed all nunneries, and six hundred and twenty-four monasteries, humbled the hierarchy and the nobility, and attempted to give unity to the state by establishing uniform laws and a uniform administration throughout his empire. But these reforms, although commendable of themselves, were so injudiciously applied, and the people so unprepared for their reception, that they were unattended with any beneficial effects; but all tended to his own injury and final destruction, and the latter part of his reign was devoted to revoking his most important reforms, in order to avoid the necessity of resorting to extreme measures. The liberty of the press, which he granted, was by the Jesuits employed mostly against himself. In his abasement of the nobility‡ and clergy, he created for himself a host of implacable enemies, who harassed him to his latest hour. His attempts at reform in Transylvania excited a revolt of the peasantry against the nobility, which he quelled only by the severest measures. Despite his abolishment of capital punishment, the leaders of the' revolt were condemned to

---

* Menzel's Germany.   † Quarterly Review, 1837.
‡ Colonel Szekuly to exposure in the pillory for swindling, and Prince Podtsat-sky Lichtenstein, for forging bank-notes, to sweep the streets.—3 Menzel, 90.

the wheel, and one hundred and fifty others impaled alive.*
The Hungarians rebelled; and so intense and general was the
feeling against him, that, to the astonishment of all Europe,
he revoked all the acts of his government in that country.
Against his tax law of 1789, both nobility and peasantry rose,
and gave the signal for a general revolt. His attempts to govern Belgium by laws suited to the Austrian empire created
an outbreak in that distant province. On hearing that even
the peasantry, on whom he had attempted to bestow such immense benefits, had arisen against him, he exclaimed, "I shall
die! I must be made of wood, if this does not kill me!"

Broken-hearted and dejected, he died in three weeks, leaving behind him the following lines, which will serve as his ep-
itaph: "I know my own heart; I am convinced of the sincerity of my motives; and I trust that, when I shall no longer
exist, posterity will judge more justly and more impartially
of my exertions for the welfare of my people."

It is, no doubt, comparatively easy for us, who have the experience of half a century, the most fertile in historical results
that any age of history affords, to form a clear judgment of
the true course which the Emperor Francis ought to have pursued, on his accession to the throne, to consolidate his power,
and insure the prosperity of his people, than it was for him at
the time, bewildered as his view must have been by the failure of the well-meant, but inconsiderate changes attempted
by his uncle Joseph. Had any enlightened friend been at his
side, who could have pointed out where the real faults of Joseph's policy lay, it is probable that the unsophisticated mind
of the young emperor, which raised the hopes of his subjects
to a high pitch, would have comprehended the truth; and the
firmness which he sufficiently displayed in after-life must have
secured his success in acting up to it.† As it was, nothing
could be more natural than that he should deem the people
incapable of appreciating efforts made for their good, and consider his uncle as the victim of the basest ingratitude. It was,
probably, the experience thus gathered, strengthened by the
terror and disgust which the disgraceful scenes of the French

---

* 3 Menzel, 85.   † Quarterly Review, 1837.

Revolution at that time were calculated to awaken, which brought the conviction into the mind of the Emperor Francis, that an unlimited power in the chief governor. of a nation is the surest pledge of its prosperity; and that, as all popular reforms tend to limit that power, they must be opposed, as the sources of all evil. He also looked upon this high prerogative as an inherent right in his family—one holier and less disputable than any other; and the line of conduct which he pursued aimed at first procuring its acknowledgment by all his subjects, and then at securing it against all attacks.

As the policy of Joseph and of Francis were totally antagonistical, the first step of Francis was to annul all the popular reforms of Joseph. The policy pursued by Joseph was to depress the nobility and elevate the people; the earliest efforts of Francis were directed to the prosecution of opposite measures.

In order to keep the people in check, the privileged classes were raised, conciliated, and supported. It was laid down as a settled principle, that the preservation of the *status quo* should be the unchangeable rule for the future; that the inviolability of their property and of their full rights should be guaranteed to the possessors of estates; that no further invasion of their rights and possessions should be made by the state; and that thenceforth the privileges of the lords of the soil should be the foundation of all rules of government, and its guide in the protection of national rights. From this period the state became nothing more than a guardian institution for the benefit of the titles, privileges, and possessions of the great landholders; and on this the system of legislation was settled, and its political course adopted.* The nobles by descent now acquired a greater degree of personal freedom than they had ever before enjoyed; at the same time, they secured the valuable prerogative of filling exclusively the different offices of the state, and thus appropriated to themselves the first posts in every branch of the administration.

Leagued with the clergy, they constituted themselves the especial guardians and supporters of the throne, against which,

---

* Thompson's Austria.

as they imagined and pretended, the people were hostile, and meditated mischief.

Both the nobles and clergy were decreed to be inviolable from all strictures of the press, an indulgence as ill-advised as it was injurious; for, in the absence of all restriction in responsibility, the nobles became overbearing, and the clergy negligent of their duties. The people, who had been raised, by the humane and philanthropic consideration of Joseph, from a condition of slavish dependence to a state of freedom, and were permitted to aspire to the highest honors, alarmed and intimidated at this sudden change of principles in the state, submitted in silence to the yoke again imposed on them. They were required to observe a demeanor passive toward the government, placing a blind and unlimited confidence in its wisdom, and submitting to its commands with prompt and patient obedience.*

The most striking contrast between the policy of Joseph and Francis, consisted in the fact that the former attempted to reign through the unity, the latter through the division of the different nationalities of the empire. Joseph's great effort was to give unity to the state, to establish uniform laws and a uniform administration. In the plenitude of arrogant power, and in the confidence of delegated wisdom, he planned laws from the midst of a distant and enervated capital for the citizens of Belgium, for the nobility of a Slavonic, and the rude and haughty freemen of a Tatar nation; but all his efforts were contravened by the diverse nationalities, and by the different degrees of civilization of the various provinces beneath his rule.

The fact that the Austrian Empire is composed of such heterogeneous parts of different races, varying in interests, language, and civilization; all bound up at different epochs to a whole, actuated by a centrifugal tendency, and having no other bond to connect them than the identity of a common sovereign, would, to a superficial observer, appear to constitute a great source of weakness, and the opinion would be unhesitatingly advanced that such an empire could not possibly be held together. But, under Metternich, this very circumstance proved

---

* Thompson's Austria.

the great pillar of its strength; by exciting the national an-
tipathies, and successfully arraying one race against another—
German against Bohemian, Austrian against Italian, Croat
against Magyar, Serb against Szeckler, and Wallach against
Saxon, he managed to hold the whole in check, and thus preserve, by the exercise of his favorite policy, *divide et impera*,
the unity of the empire.

The subjects of the empire, divided by differences of race,
language, religion, and sentiment, were incapable of combining against the monarch; and, however solicitous each people
might be to preserve their own liberties and privileges, they
were not prepared to resist encroachments on those of a neighboring people, for whom they had no friendly feeling.   Thus
the disunion, which was a source of weakness to the empire,
was a source of strength to the emperor.

The leading feature in the administration of Francis, and
which Metternich continued until the day of his abdication,
was the so-called *Conservative* system.   It was only by maintaining the existing order of things, which he held to be the
only safe course, that Francis believed it possible to secure his
subjects from being led astray by speculative ideas, and from
entertaining notions of a constitutional form of government.
The practice of adhering firmly to a principle because it exists,
and is therefore presumed to be founded in justice, presup-
poses perfection in government, and that no improvement can
be made.   The result was, that all progress and advancement
in every art and liberal science, in every calling, employment,
and business of life, was impeded by the timidity of his cabinet, and the empire of Austria became stupid, stagnant, and
torpid.

But this was not conservatism or statesmanship; for the
magic of true conservatism and statesmanship consists in lop-
ping off what is bad or decayed, in repairing what is old or
broken, and, if necessary, in adapting the state to altogether
new or different machinery.

The great effect of such a system was not only to arrest the
onward movement of society, prevent the development of national characteristics, but its obvious tendency was to limit the
freedom of exertion in the people; and this was the grand cause

of their dissatisfaction with the government.   And what rendered it still worse was, that this state of things, with the pledges made by the government, was unalterable, since every indulgence granted to the people, every improvement made in their condition, every extension of their freedom, would have been an invasion of the guaranteed *status quo.*

The impediment to change which this conservative system presents under such circumstances, becomes, therefore, the necessary apology for inactivity when policy requires exertion; while this plea is advanced to excuse an injustice, which causes actual injury to individual as well as general interests.

Such being the policy determined on by the government, all the means at its disposal were marshaled in its support.

Bureaucratic System.

1. The first source of influence brought by the government to the support of this policy, after that of elevating the nobility, was the " Bureaucratic system."

It is said to be a part of the plan of government in every German state, to employ one half of the nation to govern the other half; and the paternal care of the sovereign is studious to prevent the number of *employés,* who live at the expense, and, as they doubtless imagine, for the benefit of their fellow-subjects, from being diminished.*   Besides, the number of those whose appointments are either of too low a rank, or of too secret a nature to be introduced in company with the first men of the country, may amount to as many more.   Imagine these civil officers, dependent solely on the crown, dispersed through a nation which contains so many jarring elements, and where much loyalty can not, it seems, be presumed to exist; follow each of these as he enters into society, anticipating defection in all out of office, and necessarily disposed to vindicate the authority which gives him consequence; add to

---

* It was reported to the government several years since, by Count Radetsky (in his efforts to obtain an increase of the army), that the civil officers of the empire (not including Hungary and Transylvania), both open and secret, were one fourth larger than the army.   The army at that time exceeded three hundred thousand; it has since been augmented to seven hundred and fifty thousand; and if the civil officers have borne any thing like a proportionate increase, some idea may be formed of the number of these officials at the present day.

these the number of fifteen thousand officers and non-commissioned officers of the staff and commissariat departments, all of which are to be found within the empire at the head of an army of seven hundred thousand,* including the peace establishment, together with the landwehr or reserve, and we shall see that the government has monopolized, by means of these individuals and their families, a powerful number of defenders in every social circle.† When it is recollected that the secrecy observed in all transactions, and especially in the administration of justice, screens every individual from the share ·of responsibility which every public officer ought to incur toward the public, some idea may be formed of the fearful power thus created, and of the abuses to which it must be subject. If it be considered that these officials, civil and military, require a rather superior degree of education to enable them to fulfill their respective functions, it must be evident that an immense mass of talent is abstracted from the middle classes of

---

* To which may be added, also, three hundred thousand custom-house officers throughout the whole empire, and at least fifty thousand grentzers. It is the middle classes which are possessed with a mania for entering the bureaus.

† The following rough calculation, drawn from the official statistics of the empire, will afford some idea of the means at the disposal of the government to secure its influence and support.

Those interested or employed in the support of government are as follows, viz. :

1st. Clergy whose revenues are protected by government...	70,000
2d. Nobility whose privileges exist only through government.	800,000
3d. The industry and commerce, " " "	784,000
4th. Civil officers, servants, and overseers in public offices ..	400,000
5th. Pensioned individuals..............................	100,000
6th. Army	600,000
7th. Proprietors of houses in cities, at least...............	400,000
	3,154,000

Of the thirty-eight millions of inhabitants in the empire, twenty-six millions, it is calculated, are cultivators of the soil, unenlightened and removed from the stage of political action. This leaves but twelve millions to embarrass the government; of these, one half, it may be calculated, are females; of the other half, viz., six millions, three millions one hundred and fifty-four thousand are, as has been shown above, interested in the support of the government. Of the remainder, viz., two millions eight hundred and forty-six thousand, one third, viz., nine hundred and forty-eight thousand, may be presumed to be young boys or imbecile old men, incapable of mischief, leaving, out of thirty-eight millions of inhabitants, but one million eight hundred and ninety-eight thousand who may be opposed to the government, or just about one half the number of its hired servants and interested agents.

the nation, which, in the pursuit of science, agriculture, commerce, or the fine arts, could not be otherwise than productive of the greatest benefits.

Monopoly in Trade.

2. Another source of influence to the government in the support of its policy is the system of monopoly in trade. A fact that the history of the last fifty years has sufficiently proved is, that popular tumults seldom originate among the peasantry of a country, and that the great problem of internal police is to keep the inhabitants of the towns satisfied and tranquil. To this end every city in Austria, beginning with the metropolis, is allowed to grant the freedom of trade to only a limited number of individuals; so that the mere fact of an apprentice having served his time by no means warrants his setting up in business.* Strangers who come into a city must either show that they are provided with means of support, or that they can procure employment, otherwise they are at once expelled. In return for this privilege of exemption from much competition, the merchant or tradesman pays a tax of no trifling amount, bearing the candid designation of earnings or income-tax.† In this manner the whole industrial class in Austria, being in some measure dependent on the government, which possesses the power to introduce a system of competition at will, are not dissatisfied with a state of things which assures to it a certain competence; and thus, apparently on easy terms, their support is gained for the present system.‡

Patronage of the Church.

3. Another source of influence to the government arises from the extensive patronage of the Church. The superior dignities are stated to consist, including those in Hungary, of twelve Catholic archbishoprics, fifty-nine Catholic bishoprics,

---

* Quarterly Review.　　　　　　　　† Erwerb. Steuer.

‡ It does not seem that any exact compact exists between the trading classes and the state, as to the number of privileged individuals in every branch; the butchers, however, form an exception, their number being fixed. This immunity is purchased by an extra tax, called the Slaughtering tax.

one hundred and fifty-one abbots and deans, with domains and revenues, beside an innumerable host of canons, deacons, archdeacons, and heads of convents. The monasteries have been reduced to the number sufficient for the service of the churches and the care of education ; but, still the number of the clergy is immense, as may be inferred from the above enumeration of the hierarchy : in addition to which, the United Greek Church has five bishoprics ; the Armenian Catholics, one archbishopric ; the Schismatic Greeks, one archbishopric and ten bishops, besides inferior dignities, all of which (together with the nomination of all parish *curés*) are either presented by the crown or under its influence. These charges are also well provided for. The revenue of the Archbishop of Gran, primate of Hungary, is generally computed at one million of florins. The archbishoprics of Prague, Olmütz, and Vienna are proportionably well endowed ; and, indeed, the revenues of the Church, including the tithes, when compared with the price of necessaries in so productive a land, may be said to exceed in amount those of the clergy in any of the great states of Europe.*

The remainder of the population, who are neither directly or indirectly under the influence of the government, are operated upon and kept in check by the following repressive measures of the government.

EDUCATION.

1. The Emperor Francis, at the Congress of Laybach, in an address to the professors of a public seminary, enjoined them to be careful not to teach their pupils too much ; he did not want learned or scientific men, but obedient subjects ;† and the various scholastic institutions are so regulated as to teach the several classes what is necessary for their respective callings, and, at the same time, to inculcate the precepts of religion and the duties of morality. With this view, the general supervision of the schools is vested in the clergy.

---

* For table of bishops and archbishops, also monasteries, see Appendix, note 2.

† " Leading principles of education to consist in guarding the mind against the danger of entertaining political errors, instead of encouraging its full development by free exercise of the faculties and well-regulated self-dependence."

Austria has exhibited a certain degree of determination and vigor in her plans of national education, which is the more remarkable when we take into consideration the difficulty she must have met with in organizing a scheme embracing the whole of her vast empire, with its variety in language, religion, and nationalities.

Education is under the direction of the *Hof-Studien Commission* in Vienna, *i. e.*, a commission to superintend studies appointed for the empire, whose duty it is to examine and report on every point connected with instruction, profane or sacred, civil or military; but they have no legislative authority of any kind, and even the substitution of one grammar for another can not be effected without the sanction of an imperial edict.* Education is gratuitous, but compulsory : it is not left to the option of parents whether they will or will not have their children instructed ; they are compelled to send them, when of a certain age, to the national school of their parish. Besides, the disadvantages under which the uneducated labor are too many, and the laws too strictly enforced against them, even in the most distant country districts, to permit of general ignorance.† All children, both males and females, from the ages of five to thirteen, come under what is called the school age ; and, as the description of education they are to receive is strictly defined, all, from the child of the simple peasant to that of the highest university professor, must pursue the path of instruction in the manner marked out by the state.

Public instruction is divided into the popular or national, the intermediate, and the superior. The popular consists of that afforded at the elementary national schools (Trivial-Schulen), the superior primary schools (Haupt-Schulen), and the (Wiederholungs-Schulen) repetition schools, for persons above the age of twelve years, analogous to the *Ecoles de perfectionnement* in France. Between this last and the next class there are a number of very admirably appointed seminaries, for the

---

* Thompson's Austria.

† Not only does neglect operate as a perpetual disqualification for employment, public or private, but the parish priest is forbidden to marry any not provided with a certificate of education.— *Quarterly Review*, 1839.

F

purpose of teaching the useful arts, and of giving special instruction in particular trades, being the schools of utility (Real-
Schulen). The intermediate instruction is acquired in the
gymnasiums, lyceums, and faculties or academies of different
kinds, and the superior education is that attained in the universities.*

All the elementary and primary schools are under the direction and control of the clergy, the masters being the church-
wardens of the parish. Besides these primary schools, gymnasiums, and lyceums, there are nine universities, normal
schools for the education of teachers, and one establishment
unique of its kind and extraordinarily emblematical of the
character of the government. It is the Theresanium, a college
founded by the empress whose name it bears, for the purpose
of affording the youth of the aristocracy an education fitting
them for the posts of *employés* and of general officers throughout the empire. The effects of this are manifold. All the
scholars in the institution must be of the rank of *von* or baron,
at the least, and, as the great majority of the pupils are pen-
sioners on the government, which thus provides for a number
of the children of poorer nobles, it links the high-born with
the state, and creates a bond of union, which it is the interest
of both parties to preserve. By keeping these young men distinct and separate from the lyceums and universities, it assists
to preserve that line of demarcation between the noble and the
class below him, which it has ever (with the exception of Joseph the Second's reign) been the policy of Austria to maintain.
It affords to the students an early diplomatic education, and
furnishes to the state a sufficiency of men versed in the theory
of Austrian politics, to fill every office of emolument and trust
under the crown ; thus precluding the middle classes from rising to a share, however humble, in the administration of affairs. When the effects of this system are considered, it offers some clew to the means by which this vast empire has not
only been preserved in tranquillity, but also in civil and political ignorance for so long a period, while the nations which
surround it have labored under convulsions that have either

---

* Thompson's Austria.

threatened, or ended in, revolution, long before even a silent and unnoticed undercurrent was setting in that direction in Austria.*

In fact, throughout all the institutions of the Austrian empire, the system of studies prescribed by the state is in perfect keeping with its principles of government, acting always on the defensive, and jealous lest any thing should intrude itself opposed to the prerogatives of the civil authority, the laws of the country, or the rights of the sovereign.   With respect to instruction in ecclesiastical law, the broadest distinction is made between the spiritual and temporal authorities, and that all controversies as to the independence of the temporal over the spiritual power, as to the immunities belonging to the ecclesiastical order, as to the rights of the sovereign to decree laws of mortmain, and to fix the age of vows, etc., are forbidden; such discussions belonging, it is alleged, properly to former ages, and not to the present time.

This excuse is a vail thrown over the governing principle of the empire, a vain attempt to conceal its jealous fear of having its principles touched upon, or an inquiry made into its rights. But, clearly as this vail is seen through, it shrouds the empire like a pall, which, corpse-like, rests beneath it.†

The University of Vienna, and, indeed, those of Austria generally, are held in little estimation in other parts of Europe.‡ But few professors of distinction, or works of celebrity, have thrown a lustre over them.   A reference to the book catalogues of the Leipsic Easter fairs will present a state of facts which require no comment, that, in the year 1839, out of three thousand one hundred and twenty-seven German publications, only one hundred and eighty were Austrian.§   Such a state of facts is clearly attributable, not to the character of the country itself, but to the spirit of the government, which fetters the exertion of the human intellect, by coercing its energies, and by its Procrustean policy of attempting to mold every capacity after the same model.   The system of education in Austria is unique in the history of mankind.   The government monopo-

---

* Thompson's Austria.   † Ibid.
‡ For the number of universities, schools, etc., see Appendix, note 3.
§ Quarterly Review, 1839.

lizes the charge; no one dares to instruct youth who has not
received an authorization to that effect; the books employed
must be those written by agents appointed to the task, and
every word that falls from a professor's mouth is a subject of
inquiry and interest for the council of state.

CENSORSHIP.

2. The next restrictive measure of the government is the
Censorship.

Soon after the invention of printing, when the authority of
the Church had been assailed, and was tottering under the
load of its abuses, the popes of Rome resorted to the expedient
of establishing this institution, in order to prevent the diffusion of knowledge, so injurious to the course which they were
pursuing. They endeavored, therefore, to prohibit, first, the
reading; and, secondly, the printing of certain literary works.
They enforced the ancient decrees of the Church against the
reading of heretical books, and introduced an ecclesiastical
superintendency of the press in 1479 and 1496, which was
more completely established by a bull of Leo the Tenth in
1515. As the papal decree could not be carried into effect in
all countries, on account of the Reformation, the Council of
Trent, in 1546, not only renewed the censorship, but prepared
an index of books,* which nobody was to read under penalty
of the censure of the Church. The censorship was soon after
adopted by secular authority, particularly by the German Diet,
from 1541 to 1577. At the peace of Westphalia, 1648, the
institution was further not only sustained and sanctioned, but
the emperors, in their elective capitulations, promised to watch
strictly over the fulfillment of this Article.† In the capitulations of the Emperor Leopold the Second of Austria, in 1790,
and of Francis the Second, it was further added (Article VI.,
§ 8), "that no work should be printed which could not be reconciled with the hyperbolical books of both Catholics and Protestants, and with good morals, or which might produce the
ruin of the existing Constitution or the disturbance of public peace." Since then the censorship of the press has been

---

* *Index librorum prohibitorum.*   † Americana Encyclopedia.

upheld in all the nations of Europe (except England, where it was abolished in 1694), as one of the most important machines of government.*

In accordance with the decrees of the Carlsbad Congress, 1819, and the resolutions of the German Diet sustaining them, September 20, 1819, the censorship in all the states of the German Confederation became one of the conditions of union.

In Vienna twelve censors are established, to some of whom every book published within the empire, whether original or reprinted, every article which appears in the newspapers, even to an advertisement, must be submitted. The censor having received the manuscript, exercises his own taste and judgment in erasure or alteration of such passages as he disapproves; and being generally some phlegmatic personage, well imbued with the genius of the government, one great object of his care is to exclude all expressions which might appeal to the imagination or the passions of the reader. It is not permitted even to elucidate the actually-established political system, the dreaded discovery of whose weakness is carefully guarded against by purging the language of common usage from all such dangerous words and expressions as " popular rights," " popular opinion," " public spirit," and " nationality."

Their corrections are sometimes exceedingly ludicrous, as appears from the following example of a work treating of conflicts quite unconnected with the Austrian empire, where the expression " heroic champions" was cut down to " brave soldiers ;" and " a band of youthful heroes, who flocked around the glorious standard of their country," became " a considerable number of young men who voluntarily enlisted themselves for the public service."† The effect of this institution upon the literature of Austria has been already hinted at. Chilled by the restrictions of the censorship, more vigorous and stringent than in any other of the German states, in fact, than in any other state of Europe except Russia, the literature of Austria possesses no character, and hardly a name. An Academy of Sciences, such as exists in all the other capitals of Eui ·pe, uniting men remarkable for their capacity and

---

* Americana Incyclopedia.   † Turnbull's Austria.

merit, and stimulating by encouragement their emulation, was never attempted in Vienna before the year 1847, and then was likely to prove a failure, because, notwithstanding all the exertions of Baron von Hammer Purgstall, its most zealous as well as distinguished supporter, they were unable to procure for their efforts an exemption from the strictures of the censors. If the refining process was limited in its operations, and works of an exceptionable character alone excluded from circulation, an excuse might readily be found for the maintenance of the system; but when a tyrannical and meddling authority is exercised, descending even to puerilities, genius revolts from the rule, and, rather than be controlled by official ignorance, narrow-minded prejudice and intolerance, it refrains from the exercise of its powers, and sinks into apathy.

ESPIONAGE.

3. The next repressive measure of the government is through the system of *espionage*.

The institution of a secret police—if we do not consider the informers which every tyrant, from the earliest ages, probably, has had—may be said to have originated in France, under the Marquis d'Argenson, the lieutenant of police from 1697 to 1718, during the reign of Louis the Fourteenth. The prevailing licentiousness of those times had occasioned innumerable outrages, and D'Argenson, called, by his contemporaries, Rhadamanthus, hunted out crime in its deepest recesses, and brought it to light, whatever was the rank of the offender. The Austrian government, doubtless, copied a good deal from the French in this respect, as Lenoire, the chief of the police of Paris from 1774 to 1784, at the request of the Empress Maria Theresa, wrote a work for her on the subject of police regulations.* The secret police consists of a body of people of all classes, needy men and women of rank, mistresses, &c., down to the waiters in coffee-houses, and the lowest visitors of taverns and brothels, who report whatever they hear against the government.† The deplorable consequences of an institu-

---

* *Détail sur quelques établissmens de la ville de Paris, demandé par S. M. I. la reine de Hongrie.*   † Americana Encyclopedia.

tion so destructive to all confidence and sense of security are obvious, especially when we consider that these spies are the most worthless part of the community, and who may often invent stories to make themselves important, or serve some diabolical end.   On the reports of such miscreants men's lives, liberty, and property depend; and the charges being kept secret, no means are afforded of refuting them.   The more absolute a government is, and the more it strives to be the sole moving and regulating principle of society, to the destruction of individual freedom, the more will the police be developed; while, on the other hand, the freer a country is, and the more it follows the principle that every thing which can possibly be left to take care of itself should be so left, the more strictly is the police confined to mere matters of municipal regulation.   In free countries, like the United States, the place of a secret police is, in a great measure, supplied by public opinion and the liberty of the press; and it is curious to observe how the most secret transactions or correspondence will, by degrees, come to light.   In fact, a politician needs to be quite as much on his guard in the statements which he makes as in absolute governments, since the danger of their reaching the press is as great as that of their detection by the secret police.*   In no country of Europe—without, perhaps, it be Russia—is the secret police more thoroughly organized, and its inquisition more vexatious and oppressive, than in the Austrian empire.   Besides the regular corps of spies, who have no other occupation or means of subsistence, almost every other man you meet with is under the pay of the police—the man with whom you transact business in the city, the servants who attend upon your wants at home, and often even the companion who enjoys your hospitality, and to whom you confide your inmost thoughts, leaves you, and repairs to the police office to report your unguarded expressions.

The great object, however, of the system of espionage is not so much the information the spies are enabled to collect, which is generally not worth the cost of collection, but it is to keep down public opinion—to exercise a terrorism over the

---

* Americana Encyclopedia.

people, and thus effectually stifle the utterance of any liberal, and consequently deemed injurious sentiments.

It is well known that in no city of Europe, perhaps, is society so divided into little cliques as in Vienna; and this had its origin in the persecutions of the police, which forced a great portion of the community to withdraw altogether from general social intercourse, and to restrict its communications exclusively to its own set and connections; and even there, as well as elsewhere, the interchange of ideas was limited to such topics as the theatre, the fashions, and the light literature of the day. But these restrictions upon intercourse and conversation were among the least of the evils of this system.

To avoid the dungeons of Spielburg for life, there existed no other safeguard than either the maintenance of the most profound silence on all political and social questions, or the exercise of subserviency to the hypocritical extent of acquiescing in or extolling whatever was permitted to be seen, said, and believed by the community, or ordered to be received with demonstrations of satisfaction. In establishing the fundamental principle that the people should exercise no opinion, the natural consequence that they would be reduced to the point of possessing no temperament at all was lost sight of. The worldly direction given to the desires of the whole community, its estrangement from all intellectual pursuits, and its narrow-mindedness, founded on the most selfish struggles after money and possessions, produced by degrees so powerful an influence on the moral feelings, as well as on the social habits of the nation, that the grossest materialism and the most unblushing sensuality predominated universally.* The natural consequence of this state of things is easily foreseen; for man, consisting both of body and soul, feels as much the necessities of one as the other. As the existing systems rendered nugatory all attempts to satisfy the higher aspirations of his nature, his whole being became absorbed in the acquisition of wealth and substance, and the enjoyment of sensual indulgences; and, being blunted to all feelings of intellectual refinement, he sunk into a state of demoralization and effeminacy.†

---

* Thompson's Austria.   † Ibid.

An institution ever open to receive impeachments, but closed to all vindication, which encourages information against the simplest expressions of opinion and the slightest objections of a political tendency, which even intrudes into the most insignificant domestic and social concerns, affords unbounded scope for the indulgence of hatred, revenge, and defamation; and, letting loose the evil passions of bad and depraved spirits, places in their hands weapons more dangerous to the well-disposed than the sword itself.   By offering facilities to the evil to blast with a lie the most valuable rights of man—his liberty, honor, and good name—and thus to ruin the prosperity of one family, and destroy the happiness of others, the whole foundation of public morality is undermined, and the very institutions which should be its support and protection, become the vehicles of terror and dismay.

Nor did this institution confine itself to the capital, or even the cities, but in its ramifications it extended throughout the empire, and, Briareus-like, held it all in its vast embrace.

Examination of Letters.

4. Another check of the government upon the acts and conduct of the people consists in the examination of all the letters which pass through the Austrian post-offices.

The people of Austria have long been obliged to submit in silence to this heartless invasion of the sanctity of private correspondence.   Even as early as the Smalkaldian war, this "devilish art," as the historian* terms it, was introduced into Germany by Spaniards and Jesuits.

The first regular post established in Central Europe, that of the "Thurn and Taxis," was distinguished by such a system of espionage.   The knowledge of the affairs of other governments, which the examination of the correspondence between princes and generals afforded, most naturally suggested the importance of such an engine in matters of internal police; and in the Flemish intrigues and the Milan conspiracies, in the time of Joseph the Second, it already appeared in full and successful operation.

---

* Hormayer, *Franz und Metternich.*

The " Thurn and Taxis" post, which had its central bureau
at Vienna, was presided over, at first, by a "plenipotentiary
secret counselor;" and under the reign of Joseph the Second,
was connected with the police of the city, and with the most
secret cabinet of the emperor, and its operations brought to
great perfection by his prime minister, Kaunitz.

Later, it was called the "*Chiffre Cabinet,*" and had its bureau in the Imperial Palace, in that portion of the building
fronting the Joseph's Place, known as the " Stallburg."   The
principal post in Vienna closed in the evening, most punctual-
ly, at seven o'clock, and the letter-bags, apparently, started off;
but they were with great rapidity conveyed to the Chiffre Cabinet, in the Stallburg.

Here, by the assistance of a large number of clerks (who,
composed of two sets, worked both night and day), the correspondence of embassadors, bankers, foreign agents, and any
letters calculated to excite suspicion, were quickly selected
from the mass, and, with great circumspection, opened, examined, and copied—a proceeding which lasted usually until midnight, but frequently until daylight, when the mail at length
started, in truth, upon its destination.

The lives of the officers and clerks in this department must
have been truly deplorable.   Although well remunerated, they
were, indeed, but little better than state prisoners.   They
were so strictly watched by the police, that the minutest matters of private conduct and character were familiarly known.
How they lived, what they expended, where they went, who
visited them and their families ; in short, all that they said or
did, were matters with which the police was at all times perfectly cognizant.

By the intense application necessary to the unraveling of
diplomatic ciphers, and which was carried on with great success, many of their principal adepts lost their minds.   But the
most serious ills under which they labored, says the historian,
were the injuries to conscience in the commission of perjury
and forgery, which, in the course of their duties, they were
not unfrequently compelled to undergo.   Hormayer, the able
historian of Austria, and for a long time keeper of the Imperial Archives at Vienna, after a quarrel with the Austrian offi-

cials, entered, in the same capacity, the service of Bavaria; and there, in his last works, written but a few years since, he exposes all the details of this iniquitous procedure; which, but for that circumstance, might have remained to this day undivulged.

A correspondence, he relates, was carried on for the space of fourteen years, by the Chiffre Cabinet, with a person in Bohemia, whose letters had afforded grounds for suspecting his loyalty. Assuming the name and imitating the handwriting of his correspondent in Vienna, they pretended to approve his designs, encouraged him to a full disclosure of his plans, as well as accomplices, and when these were sufficiently divulged, which it seems it took fourteen years to accomplish, the whole party were immediately seized and committed for trial.

The letters were opened, and the seals instantly imitated with a skill which defied detection.* The copies of all such correspondence, whose importance warranted the labor necessary in transcribing them, were, by order of the Emperor Francis, laid upon his table each day at seven o'clock, by which hour he returned from the morning mass, and the perusal of these documents, together with the reports of the secret police upon the subject of the foreign embassadors and ministers, their indulgences, expenses, connections, and transactions in the city, and which were also presented at the same hour, constituted, it is said, by far the most agreeable portion of his matinal exercises.†

What at first gave great importance to this proceeding—the examination of the mails—was the extent of the system, that it embraced the entire bounds of the German empire, and extended even to the Baltic Sea and Ostend, limits within which no state or family secrets could possibly remain sacred. By it all the intrigues carried on in relation to the Spanish, Polish, and Swedish crowns were fully disclosed; but, owing to the very importance and extent of these discoveries, they could not

---

* The impression of the seal was first taken with wax, and then, by some chemical process, this wax was immediately hardened, and constituted, in a moment, another similar seal.

† A curious document appeared in the London papers in the fall of 1851. It was the order of General Gergowski, imperial officer now in command of Venice, in which he invites information respecting every officer under his command.

long remain concealed, and the correspondence between Russia and Prussia, in regard to Poland, in 1772, coming to light in this manner, led to the establishment of separate government mails and private couriers. To this day, no foreign embassador or minister in Vienna thinks for a moment of committing his dispatches to an Austrian post, but private couriers take charge of and convey their entire correspondence.

But even these, as Hormayer discloses, can not be implicitly relied on. The Prussian couriers, he relates, as early as the reign of Joseph the Second, were bribed for life. At the first post station near Pirna, upon the frontiers of Saxony and Austria, from its retired position being a suitable location, a small house was erected, and there a branch of the Vienna Chiffre Cabinet was located. Upon the expected arrival of the Berlin couriers, they, with their dispatches, were taken charge of by these Austrian agents, conveyed in their own post-chaises, and during the most rapid driving they always managed to take full copies of all the important communications. In this way they continued their journey together to the last post station before Vienna (Langenzers Dorf), where the dispatch-bag was returned to the courier, and he and the Austrian agents separated, the one directing his way to the Prussian embassy, the other to the Foreign Office in the *Ballhaus Platz ;* and, at the same moment that Count Keller, the Prussian embassador, was examining the original dispatches, Prince Kaunitz, imperial prime minister, would be occupied in reading the copies.

HABITUAL CONFESSION.

5. Still another check of the government upon the acts and conduct of the people is supposed to arise through the *confession* which the Catholic religion enjoins, and which, by the Jesuitical portion of the priests (who have ever been the instruments of state), especially in secrets of a political character, is not regarded as a sacred service. The introduction of the Jesuits into Austria by the government is not only coeval with the accession of the house of Habsburg to the throne, but the most efficient support at all times afforded that class by the state evinces the importance which has ever been attached to their services.

The mutual support of Church and Court has ever been re

garded as equally indispensable to both parties; and while the monarchs have never failed to put them forward on all occasions, the clergy, on their part, have not been remiss in faithfully preaching and teaching the enjoined doctrines of non-resistance and passive obedience. It is not, however, by means of preaching and teaching alone that they have been regarded so powerful an arm toward resisting the innovations of the age, but it is especially by the powerful hold they have over the community, through the practice of habitual *confession*.

Every true Catholic at stated periods, either weekly or monthly, discloses most fully to his priest every crime or indiscretion of which he may have been guilty; and although in other countries, where the clergy are more independent of the government than in Austria, such confidence may not be betrayed; yet, under the relations between Church and state which exist in the imperial dominions, it would be taxing credulity rather too heavily to suppose that any important disclosure of a political character is not, by the Jesuits at least, immediately conveyed to the ear of power.

Standing Army.

6. Another and most powerful check upon the acts and conduct of the people, and by which all attempts against the authority of the government are immediately suppressed, is the *Standing Army*.

All the disclosures, however important, obtained through means of the system of espionage, the violation of the secrecy of private correspondence, or that of habitual confession to priests, would be of no avail, without an armed and government-supported soldiery to crush insurrection in the bud, and suppress revolt wherever it may venture to raise its head. Austria possesses an army which, under the peace establishment, numbers five hundred and fifty thousand, and which was increased in 1848 to seven hundred and fifty thousand.*

A body of troops, in ordinary times, is quartered in every capital and in every town in the empire, the number in each

---

* For rates of pay in the army, see Appendix, Note 4.

being regulated by the size and character of the population. Infinite care, too, is taken in the disposition of these troops, which is always made with reference to the different nationalities. Agreeably to the "divide and conquer" principles of Metternich, no troops were permitted to remain at home, or in those provinces where they were enlisted and belonged, but invariably transferred to another and more distant nation, where they could not speak the language, had no sympathy with the people, and where they were ready, at any moment, to shoot them down with as little compunction as they would a foreign enemy whom they had never before seen. Bohemians, for instance, were quartered upon the Hungarians; Hungarians upon the Austrians; Austrians upon the Poles; Poles upon the Italians; and Italians upon the Croatians, &c.

Another most admirable arrangement for carrying out the same principle, and strengthening the empire at the expense of the provinces, consisted in the arrangement of the army, and by which each nation of the empire was instructed only in a single arm. The Bohemians, for example, were mostly infantry; the Hungarians, cavalry; the Austrians, artillery; the Tyrolese, riflemen; the Poles, lancers. The whole, therefore, when united under imperial command, constituted a powerful and efficient force; but divided, no province, in case of revolt, was possessed of a complete and formidable army.

Since 1830, the attention of the sovereigns and cabinets of Europe has been chiefly directed to military organizations, to defenses, to fortifications. Millions of money, and the highest orders of intellect in each country, have been devoted to armies, their discipline, implements, and organization, and this avowedly for the purpose of making the army serve as *internal police* as well as for external force.

Actuated by such principles, and aided by such measures, the enormous mass of machinery which pervaded the empire, and held in subjection the heterogeneous and discordant nations of which it was composed, was kept in continued and successful operation.

Though the form of government was despotic, yet in administration it was mild, and not personally oppressive. If there was the hand of lead, there was, at least, the glove of silk to

cover it.   The government took care that the mass of the people were possessed of all animal comforts and enjoyments;
that they were provided with work when well, and taken care
of when sick; that the price of amusements was by law made
so low that none need be deprived of their enjoyment; while
the easy and happy temper of the people, and a long habit of
obedience and submission to constituted authority, rendered
them kindly disposed and easily governed.

But yet the people were far from being satisfied.   Man
has *intellectual* as well as *material* wants, and the former
had always been totally disregarded.   In fact, the principal
cause of complaint with the people was that the government
did too much for them, took too good care of them, provided
too solicitously for their visible and material welfare; so that
when that government was overthrown, they were in the condition of helpless infants, totally unable to take care of themselves.

Prince Metternich had forgotten, in his old age, that all
Europe had been, during the last quarter of a century, in a
state of progression, and that even in Austria, so still and stagnant, it was necessary to keep some pace, if only in a German
jog-trot, with the rapid progress of other countries.   Twenty
years ago, Vienna was ten or twelve days' journey from Paris,
and fifteen or sixteen days' journey from London.   Now the
Austrian capital may be reached in three or four days from
either, and for every single traveler in 1830, from France or
England, there are now fifty and a hundred pouring into the
Leopold Stadt and the Stephen's Platz.

Travelers propagate ideas and notions as quickly, and possibly more successfully than newspapers.   Although the newspapers in Vienna, before the Revolution, did not exceed the
three which existed twenty years previous, still the great lines
of German rail-roads had been completed, and these had done
more to open the minds and awaken the intelligence of this
Bœotia of Germany.   During the latter part of Prince Metternich's administration, too, the various provinces of the empire,
which had neither been drawn together by closer ties to the
hereditary states, after the policy of Joseph, nor gratified by
local administrations and reforms in accordance with their

usages, tneir language, and their laws, began to exhibit all the national tendencies which he labored so strenuously to extirpate or control; and the Magyar, the Czeck, the Pole, and the Lombard spoke in their several tongues the same language of independence.

To the prince, whose long experience, vigilant sagacity, and native instinct enabled him to pierce below the surface of society, and discern all that was feeble in its seeming strength; all that was unreal in its superficial prosperity; all that was boiling beneath its smooth tranquillity, a suspicion of the truth did not fail to present itself. Still, he struggled on. For a while he trusted that the deluge of democracy, which he had long foreseen, could be stayed during the term of his natural life; but latterly even this hope deserted him.

In the winter of 1848, his daughter remarked to a member of the diplomatic corps, at the court of Vienna, that her father had "never seen, during the long period of his public career, so dark a future, such sombre clouds," as then lowered over the political horizon. And, still later, the prince himself said, to a Prussian diplomatist,* "I am no prophet, and I know not what will happen; but I am an old practitioner, and I know how to discriminate between curable and fatal diseases. This one is fatal; here we hold as long as we can; but I despair of the issue."

Such was the condition of Europe in general, and of the Austrian empire in particular, when the French Revolution of 1848 fell like a bomb amid the states and kingdoms of the Continent; and, like reluctant debtors threatened with legal terrors, the various monarchs hastened to pay their subjects the constitutions which they owed them.

---

* M. von Usedom.

BOOK II.

CHAPTER I.

THE REVOLUTION IN VIENNA ON THE THIRTEENTH OF MARCH, 1848.—THE TRI-
UMPH OF THE PEOPLE, AND FALL OF METTERNICH.—SUBSEQUENT ESCAPE
OF THE EMPEROR FROM VIENNA, AND REIGN OF TERROR WHICH FOLLOWED.

THE commencement of the year 1848 was tranquil throughout Europe; and the European statesmen, particularly those
of England, thought less of revolution than of projects of universal peace; and it was even contemplated that the several
powers of the Continent should disband the vast armies gathered around their respective thrones, and convert their swords
into plowshares. Yet, scarcely six weeks afterward, the dissatisfaction which had long pervaded France began to assume
a threatening aspect.

Throughout the realm of Louis Philippe there was a suspicion abroad, which, though of slow growth, had ripened to a
conviction that the king was false to the people; that a system of enormous corruption and extravagance was undermin-
ing the integrity of the country and absorbing its finances;
that the interests of France, at home and abroad, were sacrificed to those of the Orleans dynasty; that a disguised, but
not less real despotism, occupied the throne; indeed, that every advantage which had been gained by two revolutions was
in danger of being repudiated; and that all this was not an
accidental or an evanescent state of things, but the result of a
policy deeply planned and relentlessly pursued—the development of an elaborate system, which had been matured even
before its author was raised to the position whence it was to
be put in practice.* The distrust of the king was almost universal.

Not a session of the Chambers had taken place for fifteen
years without a demand for electoral reform; yet reform was

---

* North British Review, 1848.

G

far from being a popular desire until after the elections of 1846.
At that election the Guizot ministry obtained an immense
majority, as it was believed, by means of every kind of corruption and undue influence. Among its supporters were
more than half a million of functionaries, most of whom were
liable to removal by the will of a body of little more than four
hundred and fifty deputies (three hundred of whom were themselves functionaries), and which did not represent the opinions
and feelings of the people. This gave to the reform movement
a vitality and energy which it had never before possessed.

In the stormy session of 1847, distinct and specific charges
of corruption were made against the ministry. The trial of
M. Teste and General Cubieres showed, at least, that there
was good reason for inquiry; and the subsequent affair of M.
Pettit, when the scandal was carried on within the cabinet of
the incorruptible Guizot himself, has since indicated that the
suspicions then existing were not wholly without foundation.
The ministry refused any inquiry whatever. Trusting to its
numerical strength, it took what may be called a vote of confidence; and, a great majority having declared themselves satisfied with their conduct, the ministry considered their triumph
complete. This ill-advised step produced a disastrous effect
upon the country. If the ministry, it was said, succeeded in
packing the Chamber by corruption, who could expect that the
corrupted would be otherwise than satisfied with the corrupt-
ers? The result was, that, instead of regaining the confidence
of the nation in themselves, they impaired the confidence of
the nation in the Constitution; for if, under it, such things
could exist, men would reason that the instrument itself must
be defective, as "the tree is known by its fruits."

The Constitution, however, they were still unwilling to attack. In electoral reform they continued to place great hope.
To promote it, the Opposition resolved to appeal from the Chamber to the country.* Agitation was to be their weapon; and
this was to be carried on through a series of banquets. Several
banquets were held, in various parts of the kingdom; but at
length they were forbidden by the government. The Opposi-

---

* North British Review, 1848.

tion disregarded the interdiction; and, in the attempt to suppress the one proposed to be given by the electors of the twelfth *arrondissement* of Paris, on the 20th of February, the Revolution commenced.*

Then followed the struggles between the populace and the troops; the attack by the mob on the Chamber of Deputies; the fatal fire in front of the hotel of Foreign Affairs; the construction of barricades; the defection of the National Guard and the line; the abdication of Louis Philippe; the establishment of a provisional government; and the declaration of a republic.

The Provisional Government was proclaimed at Paris on the 24th of February. Scarcely had the French provinces accepted the revolution, when revolutionary movements were commenced throughout the southwestern states of Germany. On the 28th of February, a public meeting at Stuttgardt resolved to petition the King of Wurtemberg to aid in promoting the representation of all his German people in the Frankfort Diet, and for the emancipation of the press throughout Germany. A meeting of the members of the Chamber of Deputies, held simultaneously, expressed sympathy with this petition. A few days later, a liberal ministry was appointed, and a liberal envoy to the Frankfort Diet named to replace the conservative who had filled that office. On the same day, a similar motion was made in the Darmstadt Chamber of Deputies by Henry von Gagern; and on the following day, a large public meeting, held in Mayence, under the eyes of the Austrian and Prussian garrison, addressed a petition to the Darmstadt government embodying the sense of Von Gagern's motion.†

On the same day—the 29th—a deputation waited on the Grand Duke of Baden at Carlsruhe, and demanded liberty of the press, a burgher guard, and trial by jury. The grand duke acceded to their demands, and summoned M. Welcher, the leader of the constitutional opposition, to his council.‡ On the 1st of March similar scenes were witnessed at Hanau, where the Elector of Hesse-Cassel followed the example of the grand duke. On the 3d, Cologne, in the Rhenish provinces;

---

* M. Odillon Barrot's speech, and reply of Duchatel.
  † North British Review, 1848.   ‡ Quarterly Review, 1848.

on the 4th, Wiesbaden, in Nassau, and Frankfort; on the 5th, Dusseldorf, made similar demonstrations. On the 6th, a revolution took place at Munich; and Saxony and Saxe-Weimar followed in the train. The same demands were every where made for the abolition of the laws of 1819 and 1832 against the press. In the mean time, the Diet at Frankfort attempted to keep in advance of the movement. On the 3d, it resolved to abandon the idea of a uniform censorship of the press for all Germany, and to allow the several states to exercise a discretionary power, subject to certain guarantees. The torrent, however, moved on with an impetus that the Diet could neither check nor overtake. The citizens of Frankfort assembled on the 4th, and demanded the repeal of all exceptional laws since 1819; unconditional liberty of the press; trial by jury; a burgher guard; a general German Parliament, etc. At Leipsic, a public meeting of citizens, held on the 1st of March, petitioned the King of Saxony to lend his aid in promoting the representation of the German people in the Diet, and the establishment of the liberty of the press throughout Germany.* The next day the same measure was adopted by the university. The king attempted to evade the delegates who presented the petition by fair words, but yielded at last to renewed representations, sustained by petitions from various Saxon towns and villages.

Bavaria did not remain inactive; simultaneous meetings, held in Munich and Nuremberg on the 3d of March, adopted the usual petitions for representation in the Diet of the Confederation, and for liberty of the press. On the 7th, a royal proclamation was issued, pledging the king to use his utmost efforts for the accomplishment of these objects. On the 21st, the king abdicated in favor of his son. At Brunswick the movement began on the 5th of March, and in Hanover a few days later.

By the middle of March all the secondary German powers, Bavaria, Wurtemberg, Baden, the Hesses, ducal and electoral, Saxony, Brunswick, and Hanover, had yielded to the popular will. The movement was equally triumphant in the smaller

---

* North British Review, 1848.

states.   The Dukes of Weimar and Gotha surrendered unconditionally on the 8th of March, and Henry, the seventy-second
of Reuss, on the 16th.

Meanwhile, the Austrian empire was not tranquil ;* in the
north, Galicia, since the Polish revolt of 1846, and the political
extinction of Cracow, had been kept in subjection only by the
strong arm of military power.   In the east, Hungary was making violent efforts to regain the many rights assured to her by
her Constitution, but of which the Austrian rule had gradually
deprived her ; and in the south, the Italian provinces at that
moment presented by far the most threatening aspect in their
desperate struggles for independence.   The German provinces
of the empire were at this period calm ; and little apprehension was entertained that their peace would be disturbed,
owing to the fact that the people, as it was thought, were the
most tame, material, and anti-revolutionary in Europe.   Their
immobility had been proved on so many occasions during the
last half century, that if an intelligent observer were asked to
point out a European capital where there was the least prospect
of disturbance or revolution, he would confidently have designated Vienna.   The inhabitants, appreciating the value and
uses of money not less than their continental neighbors, were
passive and immovable under the great monetary revolution
of 1811, when, by an imperial decree, in a moment the *Schuld-
scheine,* or government notes, were reduced two fifths in value.†
Yet a measure inflicting ruin on thousands was neither resisted nor complained of by the *burghers* of Vienna, but was submitted to almost as cheerfully as if it brought " healing on its
wings."

Revolutions in other countries seemed, eighteen years previous, to produce as little effect on the inhabitants of the Kai-
serstadt as this disastrous interference with their domestic currency.   The French Revolution of 1830, although it profoundly agitated sections of Northern and Southern Germany, fell
altogether without effect on Vienna.   Not a citizen was taint-
ed with French revolutionary principles, not a student looked
otherwise than with disrelish on the tricolor.   Nor was this

---

* Metternich had just arrived at the conviction of Louis the Sixteenth, that he
must have his States-General.   † Galignani's Messenger.

very wonderful. The tradesmen and inhabitants of Austria were, in comparison with other European countries, neither highly taxed nor grievously oppressed, and no change was deemed practicable as long as the present incumbents held the reins of government.

The first intelligence of the new revolutionary movement in France came upon Vienna like a thunder-bolt from a clear sky, and caused a shock which vibrated through every nerve of her political system. The public funds, the unfailing barometer of the public weal, immediately fell thirty per cent. The imperial family, panic-stricken by the tempest which threatened, were closeted in deep consultation; while the people, collected in groups throughout the streets, in the *cafés*, and reading-rooms, expressed themselves with a freedom and an earnestness altogether foreign to the habits of the calm and phlegmatic Germans. In the most public manner the people of Vienna sympathized with the revolutionists of Paris, loudly complaining of their own oppressions, and even, against their own interests, sustaining these opinions by acts, as in the case of the unanimous refusal of the medical students of the university to accept the situations of surgeons in the Austrian army, which, under other circumstances, they would have been so anxious to obtain. The authors and publishers had previously addressed a petition to the government for a modification of the censorship. This petition was unanswered and disregarded, and the petitioners felt themselves aggrieved by such an exhibition of ministerial haughtiness, as it was known that the emperor, from his kindness of heart, always felt inclined to gratify the wishes of his people. At the same time, among the trading and working classes, the demand for a more liberal government had become daily more vehement. At the meeting of the royal family and imperial cabinet alluded to, it was reported that all its members, with the exception of the Archduke Louis and Prince Metternich, were in favor of making immediate concessions to the people, as the only means of retaining the provinces, if not of preserving the throne. The Archduke Louis, uncle of the emperor, advanced in years, and still more antiquated in his opinions and policy, is said to have declared that, so long as he retained his situation in the cabi-

net, he would administer the government agreeably to the principles of his brother, the late Emperor Francis, by whom he
was originally invested with the charge, and who, on his death-
bed, had exacted of him a promise to this effect; but he added that, as his views were not in accordance with those of the
other members of the imperial family, he would willingly resign his situation in the cabinet, and thus present no obstacle
to the adoption of an opposite course.   Prince Metternich, it is
also said, declared his willingness to withdraw, but, not being
able to dispense with his services, the imperial family and cabinet would not listen to his proposal.   He, therefore, consented
to retain his post, on condition of being, as hitherto, unob-
structed in his administration of the government.   Notwithstanding the number and skill of his spies, Prince Metternich
was not at this time aware of the precise tone of public feeling in Vienna, but formed an erroneous opinion of it from the
partial and sycophantic reports of his flatterers; or, if he was
aware of what was actually transpiring in the city, he felt so
confident in his own power, as to treat the development with
contemptuous indifference.*   That he foresaw the storm which
threatened is evident, not only from the expression attributed
to him, but from the frequent meetings of the cabinet and the
anxious concern therein manifested.   But how a man possessed
of the superior intelligence, unexampled experience, and remarkable foresight for which the prince is so justly celebrated,
should have taken no measures whatever to avoid or to meet
the threatened catastrophe, is almost incomprehensible, and
can only be accounted for, like the fall of Louis Philippe, on
the ground of an overweening self-confidence.   Had he, but a
few months, or even a few weeks earlier, made some concessions to the people, they would have been content with much
less than they now demanded, and he would have held in his
own hands the control over them.   The empire would then
have been saved from danger, and he would have lived and
died in honor in his own land, instead of being driven from it
in disgrace in his declining years, and after half a century's
unremitting labor in its service.

---

* If he foresaw, why did he not guard against the catastrophe?   See book i.,
chapter ii.

The meeting of the Landstände, or Diet of Lower Austria, was fixed for the 13th of March. Among different classes of the people, petitions had been prepared asking for reforms, which it was designed to present, through the Stände, to the throne. The liberal character of the Land-marshal, or President of the Stände, Count Monticuculli, encouraged the hope that these movements would not be fruitless.

Especial activity in these preparatory measures was manifested by the *Politische Juridishe Lese Verein*, a reading-club, composed of lawyers and others friendly to liberal principles ; and among them were the students of the university, who, like their brethren in other parts of Germany, were thoroughly inspired by the spirit of progress. On the 12th, at a meeting in the university, it was resolved to present, on the next day, to the Stände, a petition prepared by one of the professors,* humbly soliciting an extension of political freedom, and in which the students exhibited a degree of boldness and energy which struck great terror to the hearts of their more prudent and timid instructors. Accordingly, on the following day, the 13th of March, between ten and eleven o'clock in the morning, the procession of students, headed by two professors, left the university and proceeded toward the *Landhaus*, in the *Herrengasse*, where were held the meetings of the Stände, the body to whom they designed to present their petition. Vienna had been engrossed with the subject for some days previous, and all were anxious to witness the result of so extraordinary and bold a proceeding : many laughed at it, and all considered its failure certain. A large number of the students, fearing that their names would be inscribed in the "black book," refused to join the procession, which was mainly composed of the more reckless portions, and presented a novel sight for Vienna as it moved along the streets, shouting for liberty, and terrifying the assembled crowds through which it passed. Having assembled in the court of the *Landhaus*, and in front of the building, many of the students, raised upon the shoulders of their brethren, or mounting the winter covering of the fountain in the centre of the

---

* Professor Hye.

court, which they used as a rostrum, and, pale with terror at
their own daring, addressed short but significant speeches to
the crowd, while the members of the Stände collected to receive them.* At an early hour the whole of the Herrengasse
and the neighboring streets were filled with the populace.
The crowd continued to increase; the shops were closed; and
the affair began to assume a serious aspect, when the Archduke Albert† thought proper to ride through the Herrengasse,
where he was received with acclamations. He urged the
people to disperse, assuring them that their wishes should be
taken into consideration; but they insisted on remaining until the result of their application to the emperor had been ascertained. His attempts at persuasion proved fruitless with
the people, who by this time began to relish an excitement
hitherto unknown in Vienna. The city gates were ordered to
be closed, and the military called out. By this time, the Land-
marshal having made his appearance, a deputation of the students advanced into the great saloon to present their petition.
Not meeting with the favorable reception which they had anticipated, and thinking their personal liberty endangered, they
raised the windows and cried out to their comrades in the
yard below that they had been "entrapped in a snare." With
a furious cry the young men rushed forward to the relief of their
friends, demolishing the doors and windows which obstructed
their progress; the excitement communicated itself to the
crowd in the street, and the confusion and disorder became so
great as to justify, in the eyes of the Archduke Albert, the
intervention of the military. A company of grenadiers was
then marched to the scene, when the archduke peremptorily
ordered the people to disperse; but, being disobeyed, he directed the soldiers to fire. The troops, although of unshaken
loyalty, could not at first conceive the necessity of an order to
fire on an unarmed crowd, which could easily have been dispersed with the bayonet, and they hesitated. The hesitation
was but for a moment; the order was soon repeated; the soldiers fired, and many victims fell. That moment—although

---

* Kossuth's able speech on the 4th of March, in the Diet of Pressburg, was
read, and the effect upon the crowd was very impressive.

† Son of the late Archduke Charles, and general of the Austrian army.

without action—was the most important one that Austria has ever witnessed. In that moment the Revolution was assured, the fall of Metternich accomplished, and the unlimited power of the house of Habsburg, which they had enjoyed for centuries, struck to the earth. That hesitation on the part of the troops, though but for the briefest space of time, was long enough to shake the implicit confidence reposed in the imperial army.

The people now became enraged, and attempted to drag the archduke from his horse, which was only prevented by the courage of his troops.* The excitement was fearful, and grew more portentous as the news of this ill-judged measure spread like wild-fire through the city. The cavalry were then ordered to disperse the people; and in the great square, *Am Hof*, where they had assembled in large numbers, near the civic arsenal, another man was killed and several wounded. In the *Ball Platz*, where the palace† occupied by Prince Metternich stands, many inflammatory speeches were delivered, particularly against the prince, interrupted a thousand times by the cry of "Down with Metternich!" The military here again interposed; an orator, mounted on the shoulders of his comrades, was shot; and several others shared a similar fate. Military interference occurred about the same time in other parts of the city, and the people were thereby aroused to an indescribable pitch of excitement. To increase the agitation, a wounded student was mounted on horseback, and paraded through the streets, to exhibit to the outraged people his gaping wounds.

Intelligence of these disasters having been communicated to the emperor, by his orders the firing ceased, the city gates were closed, and the military were withdrawn to the most commanding positions of the city. The cries of the people for arms became more and more vehement; for, until that moment, axes, iron bars, and sticks, were the only weapons with which they could provide themselves. The utmost anxiety was felt to ascertain the conduct of the *Burgher* Guard, or armed militia, a kind of intermediate power between the

---

* German Almanac.   † The Bureau of Foreign Affairs.

troops and the people. Would they side with the throne which had armed them, and become, at its bidding, the executioners of their fellow-citizens ? or, would they defend the people against the hirelings of a monarch who had ordered them shot, because they asked for salutary reforms ? Scarcely a moiety of this corps, harassed by conflicting duty, could be observed in the streets, in obedience to the summons which had been issued to secure the order of the city; but an accident, which shortly after occurred, soon decided that question, and with it the fate of the Revolution.

After nightfall, the mob made an attack upon the police office, the source of many of their sufferings. The policemen defended themselves and the building by firing upon the crowd that gathered in front of it. In one of these discharges, a ball, aimed at another individual, killed a *Burgher* Guard; the whole corps then immediately united with the students and populace; and opening to them the Civic Arsenal, over which they had control, all soon furnished themselves with arms.

In the afternoon, about five o'clock, the students again met in the university, and, after consultation, dispatched a deputation to the emperor, headed by the rector, to represent to his majesty the alarming condition of the city, and the necessity for preventing the further effusion of blood. Deputations from other corporations appeared, at the same time, before the assembled princes of the imperial house; and the emperor and his ministers were then besought and requested to accede to the wishes of the people for the salutary reforms which they had asked, and particularly for the removal of Prince Metternich and Count Sedlnitzky.*

The prince, who was present at that interview, with all the grace of the courtier, for which he has long been so highly distinguished, instantly tendered his resignation, stating that he "desired not to hold office one moment after he had survived the confidence of the people." The emperor immediately accepted his resignation, and expressed himself with energy against the employment of military force for the suppression of the insurrection. The several deputations returned in triumph to

---

* The chief of the police, and who was exceedingly unpopular.

their fellow-citizens, and an illumination was immediately commenced in honor of the partial victory.

During the night, numerous bands of ruffians, armed with clubs, perambulated the streets, breaking windows, and committing other acts of violence; but in the city proper they were prevented from the perpetration of any serious injury by the newly-armed citizens, who formed themselves into corps of patrols; yet in the more distant faubourgs, and particularly at their extremities, where the guard could not reach, the ravages were excessive in the plunder of stores, burning of dwellings, and total destruction of factories.

The next morning, the 14th, the triumph of the people seemed almost complete; and an order was issued, at eight o'clock, for the withdrawal of all the regular troops from the city, and for arming the citizens as a civic guard, in their place. The enlistment of men and formation of companies then commenced; and the students, and citizens generally, thus armed, and commanded by the officers of the *Burgher* Guard, now paraded the streets in an orderly manner, and preserved the tranquillity of the city. The proclamation of the emperor, permitting the arming of students and citizens, appeared in the *Wiener Zeitung* of the same morning; but, although gratified at the concession, the people did not relish the concluding sentence, which threatened a resort to force, in case tranquillity was not restored. This portion of the proclamation was openly and energetically denounced. The people expressed a determination not to suffer themselves to be intimidated, but to represent to his majesty the absolute necessity of granting the concessions demanded by the advanced spirit of the age.

The principal concessions demanded of the government by the people, in their petitions, were the following: 1st. The arming of the citizens as a National Guard; 2d. The abolition of the censorship, or freedom of the press; 3d. A budget or publicity as to the disbursements of the public revenue; 4th. Responsibility of the ministry; 5th. The assurance of a Constitution.

The following is a chronological statement of the leading events which followed the successful efforts of the people:

On the second day, the emperor granted the National Guard, and forty thousand citizens immediately enrolled their names, and were furnished with arms. On the afternoon of the same day, two proclamations were issued by the government; one announcing that the censorship would be discontinued, and laws prepared, as soon as possible, for the regulation of the press; and the other declaring that the emperor would convene a deputation, or "Central Congregation of the German, Slavonian, and Lombardo-Venetian provinces, on the third day of July next, to give their counsel upon such questions of legislation and administration as might be submitted to them." These two proclamations, although pleasing to many, were not satisfactory to the leading and determined spirits of the Revolution, and were immediately met by counter-petitions—one from the booksellers and printers, and others from the citizens generally—complaining that the concessions in regard to the press were not sufficiently explicit, and that the delay in the convention of the Assembly for the formation of the Constitution was unnecessarily long. No fighting occurred on this day; but the citizens, provided with arms, and in full possession of power, awaited, with equal patience and determination, the compliance, on the part of the government, with the additional demands they had made. The National Guard. to preserve the public tranquillity, and to protect private property from the ravages of the mob, continued to parade the city, with great order and decorum, during the entire day and night, marching through all the streets, except those immediately around the imperial palace, where strong guards of the regular troops were still posted, to defend every avenue to its approach. It was strongly in contemplation, about this time, to force through the powerful guard that surrounded the imperial residence, and when access had thus been obtained to the presence of the emperor, to demand, and perhaps insist on receiving, the Constitution. Fearing such an event, the guard at every point was that night doubled; but no attempt of the kind, on the part of the citizens, was at any time made. Throughout the whole struggle, the citizens every where exhibited that remarkable patience and coolness for which the Germans are so distinguished. An illumination, however, again took place on the evening of the second day, in honor of its results.

The third day (the 15th of March) appeared, and with it was to conclude the glorious struggle. In the morning, the population were still in a state of feverish excitement. Doubts were yet entertained whether they could fully depend on a peaceful settlement of the great questions of the day. The minds of many wavered between hope and fear. It was understood that the emperor had no objections to granting the two next reforms demanded, viz., a budget, and the responsibility of the ministry ; but, as yet, the Constitution, the principal object of their wishes and efforts, remained unmentioned. About the same time appeared notices of resignations of several high officers, both civil and military, whose acts had rendered them obnoxious to the people. Among these were the Archduke Albert, commander of the Austrian army ; Count Appony, the high chancellor of Hungary ; Count Sedlnitzky, the detested minister of the Secret Police. Their stations were immediately filled by persons of acknowledged popularity.

After these repeated manifestations of obedience to the public will, the emperor, with a view to allay the public excitement, or to ascertain the effect of his concessions on the public mind, appeared, in an open carriage, in the streets, in his usual unostentatious manner. This mark of confidence on the part of the monarch was duly appreciated, and did not fail to call forth that love and devotion to a kind sovereign which they had ever entertained, and which the events of the last two days had not impaired. His appearance was the signal for joyful acclamations, which rent the air wherever he passed, and his carriage was at length beset by the enthusiastic crowd, who detached the horses from it and drew it themselves to the palace.

These exhibitions of loyalty and devotion excited the nervous temperament of the feeble monarch, and agitated him even to tears, as he exclaimed, " Why did you not communicate your wishes to me sooner ?" It needed but this remark to prove that he had been a passive instrument in the hands of a *Camarilla*,* who, however successful in curbing the free prog-

---

* A Spanish word, meaning a little chamber, but applied in Europe to a secret and not recognized cabinet, and generally composed of the relations of the prince,

ress of the people, had not succeeded in impairing their loyalty.   On his return to the palace (whether his majesty was so
deeply penetrated with the manifestations of fidelity and attachment on the part of his subjects, or alarmed by the placards of the morning calling for a rally at three o'clock of all
those who were not satisfied with his concessions, is a mooted
point), appeared the proclamation granting to the people all
that they had asked, in the most full and ample manner—not
only a National Guard, and freedom of the press in more explicit terms than had as yet been given, but a convocation of
deputies from each of the provinces, in which all classes were
to be represented, with the least possible delay, *for the purpose of framing a Constitution for the empire.*

The publication of this proclamation, expressive of the emperor's entire compliance with the demands of the people,
awakened among his subjects joy amounting almost to frenzy.
Every doubt was now removed, every care dissipated.   Deputation after deputation, from every class of the population,
wound its way to the imperial residence, to express to his majesty the heartfelt gratitude which his concessions had awakened.   On the appearance of the emperor on the balcony of
the palace, acclamation followed acclamation, until it seemed
there would be no end to the plaudits of the people, when an
agreeable turn was suddenly given to the enthusiasm of the
occasion by striking up, with ten thousand voices, the national
air of Austria.   Tears of emotion and delight filled every eye
of that vast and motley group, and every heart seemed penetrated with the importance of that sacred hour which witnessed
the dawn of their liberty.   On the same evening, amid the
jubilees and illuminations in honor of the promised Constitution, a deputation arrived from the Hungarian Diet, then sitting at Pressburg, consisting of one hundred and fifty members, headed by Kossuth.   The object of their visit to Vienna
was to ask a Constitution for the whole empire, as well as a
separate and independent ministry for the kingdom of Hungary.   In the first request, they were anticipated by the previous movements in Vienna ; and the second, after much urg-

---

priests, intriguing women, etc.   " A power behind the throne, greater than the
throne itself."

ent solicitation, and even, it is said, violent altercation, in
which the Hungarians were aided by their palatine (the Archduke Stephen, the emperor at length yielded to their demands,
and appointed Count Louis Batthyányi as prime minister,
with authority to form such a ministry.

On the fourth morning, the first period of the Revolution having passed, and the task of the people for the present terminated, the occasion was devoted to rejoicings and celebrations
over the victory which had been achieved.   Triumphal processions, in every direction, promenaded the streets.   The emper-
or and empress appearing in public, the horses were detached
from their carriage, and the sovereigns were drawn through the
streets by their grateful subjects, while brilliant illuminations
and torch-light processions closed the ceremonies of this memorable occasion.

In Vienna the whole aspect of things seemed changed, as it
were, by a magician's wand.   The people appeared to have
passed at a bound from Egyptian darkness to " marvelous
light."   The secret police had entirely disappeared from the
streets; the windows of book-stores were now crowded with
forbidden works, which, like condemned criminals, had long
been withdrawn from the light of day; boys hawked throughout
the city addresses, poems, and engravings, illustrative of the
Revolution—the first issues of an unshackled press; while the
newly-armed citizens formed into a National Guard, marched
shoulder to shoulder with the regular military, and maintained
in unison with them, at every point, the public tranquillity.

Thus Austria, from being the farthest in the rear, had, by
a single step, taken the advance of all Germany in the path
of freedom; and nothing could have prevented her from realizing the splendid future which then dawned upon her political horizon, had her people only possessed the wisdom to improve the occasion, and profit by the victories which had been
gained in the cause of enlightened government.

It is a prevalent doctrine that the desire for a constitutional
government on the part of a people is evidence of their fitness
to enjoy it; but whether this doctrine is universally true, or
whether there should not be an exception to it, when that desire is not spontaneous, and where the people are incited by

the example of a neighboring state, by the feebleness of their own sovereign, or some other accident in the political atmosphere, the following history of events in Austria may possibly demonstrate.

No revolution—in examples of which the continent of Europe has, within the past few years, abounded—was more pure in its origin, honorable in its proceedings, stained with less blood, or disgraced by fewer outrages, than the March Revolution in Vienna, and which will ever remain a bright page in the annals of Austria.

The proclamation of the emperor, granting a Constitution to the empire, was received, except in her Italian possessions, with the utmost favor and joy, throughout all the provinces of Austria. With the exception of the highest aristocracy, to whom the late movements were a severe blow, universal exultation seemed to pervade all ranks and professions of the people. The educated, who were aware of the nature and benefits of a Constitution, duly appreciated the concession, while the ignorant were even more enthusiastic, regarding it as a panacea for all ills, or of the same nature with the measure which the English parliamentary candidate promised the people at the hustings; it was " to bring every thing to every body." They probably had as faint a conception of the meaning of the word *Constitution* as the Russians, who, during the rebellion which took place about the time the present monarch came to the throne, actually understood by the cry for a *Constitution* then made, to refer to the wife of Constantine, the elder brother who had been supplanted by the elevation of Nicolas.*

The government, by immediately commencing the necessary preparations for meeting the great change in the administration which had been decreed, manifested a sincere desire to pursue the course marked out for the ship of state upon its constitutional tack. The state of siege declared over the city by the military and civil governor, Prince Windischgrätz, during the first days of the Revolution, was soon raised, and the emperor granted a general amnesty to all persons throughout

---

* An Austrian peasant being asked what a Constitution was, replied, "Not to pay the Robbot." Cry of workmen in Vienna was, "A republic with an emperor."

H

the realm convicted or charged with political offenses. The prison doors were thrown open to all political offenders, not only to those engaged in the late struggle, but to those committed on all former occasions.

On the 17th of March, a new and responsible ministry was appointed by the emperor, of which Count Kolowrath became the President, Count Fiquelmont Minister of Foreign Affairs, and Baron Pillersdorf Minister of the Interior. It also embraced a Minister of Public Instruction, an office previously unknown in Austria. All the members of the ministry were regarded as men possessed of liberal and enlightened views.

On the 29th, the imperial police-office was entirely reorganized, the whole system of *espionage* abolished, and such portions of the department as it became necessary to retain were placed under the superintendence and control of the minister of the interior.

On the 4th of April, the *Staatsrath*, or Council of State—a bureau or department whose duty it was to regulate, at the capital, the affairs of all the provinces of the empire—was discontinued; as under the reform, the affairs of the provinces were to be regulated by their own officers at home, instead of by a bureau of strangers in Vienna. On the following day occurred the dissolution of the emperor's private cabinet. This imperial council being irresponsible to the people, and differing in its views and policy from the ministry beneath them, which it controlled, impeded most seriously all its movements and operations. But the most essential point gained by this measure was the consequent repudiation of the controlling influence of the Archduke Louis, who was at the head of the board, and the most obstinate and uncompromising advocate of the Metternich policy.

On the 7th of April, official intelligence was communicated to the public, that the Archduke Francis Charles, brother of the emperor, and heir-apparent to the throne, a man of moderate capacity, but amiable and liberal, and consequently a favorite with the people, was called upon to share with his brother the imperial labors, and in that capacity to preside over the council of ministers. On the same day occurred the resignations from the ministry of Count Kolowrath and Baron Kübeck, the only members of the former cabinet that were retained in the first ministry, but who had been notoriously distinguished for the liberality of their views, and consequent opposition to Prince Metternich. Their places were filled by the substitution of Barons Wessenberg and Krauss, the former a statesman of note, who had been for many years an exile from Austria, on account of his opposition to the policy of the late administration of the empire.

On the 11th of April, the Emperor of Austria, by a *manifesto*,* released all tenants upon *soccage* lands from the payment and performance of such tithes and labor as they had been previously subject to, the decree to take effect after the expiration of the year 1848, and, in the mean time, they were allowed to become immediately free, upon satisfactory compensation to the proprietor for the intervening time.

By another decree, bearing date the 25th of March, the emperor ordered that the sanctity of private letters should no longer be violated, and that no communications passing through the post-offices of the government should be subject to inspection as formerly.

All these, it will be perceived, were liberal measures, and manifested a sincere desire, as well as effort, on the part of the government, to fulfill its promises and carry out the reforms projected.

Notwithstanding these favorable movements of the government, however, the situation of the empire was at this time imminently critical. Like the case of a patient who had just passed the crisis of a severe and dangerous disease, the utmost skill and judgment were requisite to avoid a relapse, which, in such an exhausted state of the system, was more to be dreaded than the original attack.

The following were some of the difficulties and dangers to which the empire was at that period exposed.

1st. It was composed of such a heterogeneous mass of races, differing from each other as much in character and civilization, as the countries in which they dwelt did in climate and production; and among several of whom no more similarity was

---

* Wiener Zeitung.

to be found than existed between the barren and snow-clad hills of Galicia and the fertile and sunny plains of Lombardy, and where, consequently, the nature of their wants and requirements must be totally dissimilar, and each probably would be dissatisfied with the boon granted to another.

2d. The sudden transition from an unlimited to a constitutional government; the want of sufficient preparation on the part of the people for such a change; and the danger that they would be inclined to demand too much, while the government might be disposed to grant too little.

3d. The fact that the concessions recently made were extorted by the people from the government, and not freely granted by it; and, consequently, the limit to those concessions being determined by the people, and not by the government, the danger to be apprehended was, that they would not agree in relation to their extent.

4th. The want on the part of the government of an able, independent, and popular ministry, which the crisis imperiously demanded. That body was composed, not only of few men adapted to the crisis, but none who were prepared even to undertake the duties of the station. The high aristocracy were the only persons in Austria educated for ministerial stations, and they were so obnoxious to the people as to render their appointment impossible.

It might have been expected that the people, duly acknowledging the important concessions granted them by the crown, would have rendered all the aid in their power toward carrying out the reforms which it had promised, and which it exhibited every disposition faithfully to fulfill. Such, however, was far from being the case. The gratitude which they felt, though almost unbounded at first, was but of short duration; and, in a very few days, every effort on the part of the people was made to increase those embarrassments, already nearly insurmountable.

Even the students of the university, whose important and laudable efforts had contributed so much to the success of the Revolution, became perfectly intoxicated by the glory which they had acquired, and the praise and homage bestowed upon them from every quarter, and soon conducted themselves in a

manner, not only to tarnish the fair fame which they had acquired, but to cover themselves with disgrace.

As soon as it became known throughout Europe that Austria had joined the progressive movement of the times, emissaries from different parts of the Continent, particularly from
France and Northern Germany, flocked to Vienna, and, by their
acuteness and activity, soon discovered the elements upon
which to base their operations.   The students of the university, ardent, inexperienced, and untiring, became admirable instruments in the hands of the unprincipled propagandists, whose
great effort seemed every where to break down all government,
destroy all the bonds of society, and to produce, as rapidly as
possible, a Pandemonium on earth.   So artfully did they flatter the vanity, and minister to the pride of the inexperienced
youths, that they found it but an easy task to convince them
of their fitness to perform the first parts in the drama before
them, and to utter the leading voice in the reorganization of the
state ; and there was, consequently, from that period, no measure of the government which they did not feel themselves called
upon to consider, and universally to condemn.

Another element for the action of these emissaries consisted
in the numerous *proletaria*, or rabble, in and around the city,
consisting of a large number of *ouvriers*, or workmen, in the
different factories with which the faubourgs and neighborhood of Vienna abound, together with the thousands of idle
and criminal beings that exist in every large capital, who, becoming easy converts to the Communist principles, diligently
circulated among them, proved sources of great embarrassment
to the government.

Still another obstacle to its efficacy was the abuse by the
press of the concessions which had been made to that interest,
under favor of which it filled the rabble with Socialism and
other fatal doctrines.

In a few weeks Vienna was flooded with a most shameful
literature.   At every corner of the streets, and in all the public places, placards were stuck up for the perusal of those passing by, while boys and old men hawked about the streets the
most licentious prints and pamphlets.   These outrageous productions soon exercised the most baneful influence over the

ignorant and already corrupt mob, instilling into them a poison, which they swallowed with the greater avidity, because it
had so long been forbidden. The most unwarranted attacks
were made upon the imperial family ; the most high and honorable statesmen were, in placards, exposed to the vilest abuse,
and the nobility and clergy to the utmost insult. The sanctity of private life and character was most shamelessly invaded.
Private differences became matters of public discussion, and
the most solemn secrets of domestic life were published to the
world. Every villain embraced the opportunity to inflict a
stab in the dark, as it were, upon the man of irreproachable
character, because he happened to be his enemy. In short,
this liberty was soon changed into licentiousness, and this blessing into a curse.

Many new newspapers appeared, which soon increased the
number from three to one hundred : these were the weapons
with which the designing operated. By these means the students were excited to a still greater degree of intolerance and
madness ; the *proletaria* were corrupted, and the citizens eulogized as the van-guard of liberty throughout the Continent,
became, for the most part, bewildered and extravagant both
in their opinions and designs. The people, by these means,
being thoroughly demoralized, violations of law and order soon
commenced.

On the 1st of April appeared the provisional law for the
regulation of the press. Although defective in many of its
provisions, it was calculated to restrain, in some measure, the
abuses of the press, which had become so rank and glaring.
But, for this very reason, it did not accord with the views
and plans of the agitators ; and therefore, in the open contempt for its provisions, occurred the first palpable resistance
to the law and authority. The university led the movement
with its usual arrogance, and the provisional law of the press
was publicly burned in front of that institution. Every one,
excited by these agitators, was opposed to this enactment ;
and the government, instead of enforcing its observance, yielded obedience to the clamor, and withdrew the law.

A new and wider field was now afforded for the activity of
the press. On the 2d of April, a decisive step was taken to-

ward a closer union with revolutionary Germany. The German tricolored banner, black, red, and gold, was hoisted by the students upon the tower of the cathedral of St. Stephen.*

The people, ignorant of the object of these demonstrations, and believing, as they were told, that it was merely an expression of sympathy for a closer union with the German Confederation, hailed the manifestation with great joy.

Even the emperor, not dreaming that the adoption of that flag betokened an incorporation with the Republics† of Germany, and, consequently, the overthrow and destruction of his monarchy, accepted a banner, when insidiously presented to him by a procession of students, who had proceeded with that object to the palace; with his own hands he waved the standard before them, and then ordered it to be hung from the windows of his palace. A united Germany now became the watch-word of the day, and as laws at this time issued from the university instead of the palace, every house in Vienna, in obedience to directions from that institution, was surmounted by a German national flag. The students not only marched under German banners, but paraded the streets decorated with German cockades and ribbons. It was remarkable how all, with one consent, gave up at once their own national standard. To be an Austrian had already become a reproach, and the venerable " *Schwartz-Gelb*,"‡ black and yellow, the only acknowledged colors of the imperial monarchy, the standard which had led the armies of the empire to victory under Maria Theresa, Wurmser, and the Archduke Charles, was by these new lights totally proscribed. In fact, so odious had the name of *Schwartz-Gelb* become, that no one had the courage to assume it; it was applied by the mob to the aristocracy, and was intended to signify every thing that was inimical to human rights, and deserved the universal execration of mankind.

The agitators now found a new means to gratify their licentiousness, and, at the same time, maintain the excitement so necessary to the prosecution of their plans, and that was the creation of *tumults* in the streets. The first exhibition of the

---

* German Almanac, "Austria," 1849.

† It was contemplated by the Radicals to convert Germany into six republics.

‡ Black and yellow, the Austrian national colors.

kind occurred on the 5th of April, in giving to the venerable archbishop of the city a mock serenade, and, at the same time, destroying his windows, under the pretext that he, and the clergy generally, were opposed to the new order of things; or, as was also alleged, because he declined to pronounce a blessing on the crown and *regalia* of the German empire, which, since the abdication of the Emperor Francis, the last monarch of that expired empire, had been kept in the imperial treasury at Vienna, but which the Emperor of Austria now proposed to send back to Frankfort by the newly-elected deputies.*

On the same day, a similar insulting serenade was given to the monasteries, the Liguorian or Redemptorists, and the Armenian Mechitarist's congregation.

On the following day, the Liguorians were lawlessly expelled from the city by a tumultuous mob, headed by the students and National Guard. These monks had been brought to Vienna by the state, to assist in the management and control of the people. The government of Austria, at that time, possessed neither force enough to save its friends or prevent this outrage.

It is true that the members of this order, from their connection with the Jesuits, were exceedingly unpopular among the people, and especially on account of their interference in the domestic affairs of different families. They had been pronounced guilty by the tribunal of history. A constitutional state afforded no place for their concealment, or field for the prosecution of their dark designs; but they should have been 'expelled by law, or the act of government, and not by the arbitrary violence of the mob. Later, by an imperial edict, this order of monks was dissolved; thus virtually giving the sanction and approval of government to the palpable violation of law and order which had occurred.† As might have been expected, after this public countenance by the government of such conduct, these tumults continued; and on the 8th of April, the mansions of the Pope's nuncio, of Prince Lichtenstein, the convent of Scottish monks, and the residence of the Minister of Justice (Count Taafe), were similarly assailed.

---

* German Almanac, "Austria," 1849.   † Wiener Zeitung.

On the 20th of April, the magistrates of the city, on account
of the repeated disturbances which were occurring, published
a proclamation enjoining order, which was received, like every
other legal communication at the time, with scorn.   No one
thought for a moment of regarding it.*   All legal authority
had ceased, and the Reign of Terror commenced.

The ministry were incapable of any energetic interference,
and stood by silent and idle spectators of such scenes, without
one effort to suppress them, and without endeavoring, by other means, to attract the attention and allay the excitement of
the people.   No effort was made either to enforce order or to
preserve the integrity of the empire.   At this very time a foreign enemy had invaded her soil; but, with the exception of
a few additional regiments ordered into Lombardy, no measures were taken, and no patriotic appeals made to urge the
people to the defense of the nation and the honor of the government.   A gross violation of European treaties, and a total
destruction of the balance of power adjusted by them, was in
the act of consummation; and yet, so far as could be known,
the ministry did not seek to ascertain whether these acts, on
the part of the invading powers, met the approbation or disap-
proval of the other contracting rulers.   When, in short, the
empire was obliged to encounter both invasion from without
and insurrection from within; when the emergency required
vast concessions to the tributary kingdoms, and an energetic
concentration of all the resources of the empire; when, indeed,
it appeared that nothing could save the ship of state but heroic
resolution and dictatorial power, the government of Austria
was as inactive as if not a cloud had obscured the political
horizon.

The ministry were, at this time, as far removed from the
people as they ever were in the palmiest days of the ancient
monarchy—too far to witness their sufferings or hear their
complaints; while, unlike their predecessors, they were deprived of the aid of the secret police, and therefore had no
knowledge of either the conspiracies or movements of the mob.
They labored, also, under other embarrassments; they had no

---

* German Almanac.

public press to sustain their views and acts, while the columns of all the journals were open to attacks upon them. By the late changes, also, the aristocracy were rendered powerless, and could afford no support to the throne, while the people had no enlightened leader, to direct their movements or restrain the licentiousness of the mob; and it was, even at this time, greatly feared that, unless the ministry should awaken to their duties, and to the interests of the empire, these insurrectionary movements would become, at length, so insupportable, that the government would be obliged to quell the disorders by military force; and that this would give rise to a struggle which might result in the dethronement of the emperor and the proclamation of a republic—a form of government that the people, unfitted, as they were, even for a constitutional monarchy, would have found one of the greatest evils to which they could possibly have been subjected.

The students began now to cultivate a most cordial intimacy with the lowest classes of the population.* Declaring war against the nobility, clergy, military, and court; criticising and censuring whatever of character and respectability existed among these classes of society, they became the flatterers of the mob; talked to the *proletaria* of their sacred rights, and of the liberty, equality, and fraternity of all classes of society; and, with the breath of adulation, instilled into their minds the poison of corruption. For the advancement of their purposes, and to give more extensive circulation to their baneful influence, numerous clubs were now formed. Like that of the Jacobins at Paris, these clubs were the rendezvous of all the agitators. Here the masses received the first beams of enlightenment, and heard for the first time such words as liberty and sovereignty of the people; or, rather, were first taught practical definitions of those terms; that of the first, licentiousness; and of the second, anarchy. By a republic, they understood a total absence of all government. Each one, under such an administration, being a sovereign—the equal, in all respects, to the emperor; and their commands, whatever they might be, entitled equally to implicit obedience. Re-

---

* German Almanac.

spect for the authority of the laws was a lesson which they
were never taught.

It was impossible that such seed could produce other than
corresponding fruit, which soon began to manifest itself. Upon
the principle that the government must support the people instead of the people the government, the employment of workmen at the expense of the state now commenced. Having
nothing for them to do, but feeling obliged to afford them employment, the Minister of Public Works was forced (through
the exertions of their friends of the university) to engage the
proletaria at some unnecessary occupation, such as turning
the course of a little dirty stream which runs through the
glacis or common surrounding the interior city. The government had no one to overlook them; for the very idea of masters
or overseers for sovereigns was an absurdity in terms, and they
labored or not, as best suited their inclinations.

To continue to increase and to disseminate more widely the
public excitement, *Popular Assemblies* were now resorted to.
On the 14th of April, the first meeting of the kind took place
in the Odeon, the largest room in the world, about five hundred feet in length and two hundred in width. Students, National Guards, and citizens, amounting to the number of six
thousand, were in attendance. Discussions commenced, and
the principal speaker was a Dr. Schütte, a foreign adventurer,
well known throughout Germany from his active co-operation
in all the revolutions of the time. He had the assurance to
attempt to teach the citizens what their duties were in the
present emergency; he told them that they should forthwith
present to the emperor a *Sturm Petition* (a storm petition, or
memorial to be accompanied by preparations for the use of
force), which document, already printed, he drew from his
pocket, and in which the desires of the people were expressed,
viz., the opening of the Diet on the 25th of April, and the
adoption of the same basis for the coming elections as had
been followed when the committee of fifty for Frankfort had
been elected. But at this time the people were not sufficiently ripe for such movements, and the proposal was declined.
But a resolution that the present ministry of Austria (Baron
Pillersdorf excepted) was unpopular, that particularly Counts

Fiquelmont and Taafe should be replaced by more acceptable men, and that Count Hoyos should be dismissed from the command of the National Guard—as a civic man should alone command civic guards ; and, finally, that a proper electoral ticket should be issued, was passed amid tremendous enthusiasm.*

Such meetings were now of frequent occurrence, and every where Schütte was conspicuous for the violence of his speeches. On the 18th of April, he was arrested by the police, and expelled from the city. Upon this occurrence great stress was laid, and the excitement increased. The expulsion of this dangerous agitator, for which the government, in the maintenance of internal peace, would have been perfectly justified, took place in an improper and illegal manner. It seemed to be the fate of the executive authorities of that period either to do nothing at all or to do what they attempted in an improper manner. The arrest of Schütte made him a martyr, and aggravated the people by causing them to suppose that through him all their most sacred rights had been violated.

The agitation of the city became daily more visible, and only increased as the period for the publication of the Constitution approached. Its provisions began to be discussed even before the document appeared ; the election law was openly condemned, and the propriety of one chamber instead of two in the legislative branch, warmly advocated.

Finally, on the 25th of April, his majesty's birth-day, when a great military display took place, forty thousand troops parading in honor of the occasion, the emperor embraced the opportunity to present to the empire his promised Constitution,† which in every essential particular corresponded with the desires and reasonable demands of his subjects, conferring on them as much freedom as was enjoyed under any Constitution in Europe, excepting that of Great Britain, and in one important particular excelling that, in its granting to *all* the provinces of his empire separate Legislatures for the management and government of their internal interests.

With the exception of the radicals previously described, who

---

* German Almanac.

† It was an alteration of the Belgian Constitution, to suit the state of affairs in Austria. The only objection urged against it was that it was too aristocratical.

had no precise idea what they wanted, and would not have been satisfied under any circumstances; the new Constitution seemed to have given general satisfaction; and in the evening, in token of the common joy, the city was brilliantly illuminated, and an immense torch-light procession paraded the streets and serenaded with patriotic songs the emperor and the ministry.

Despite the excitement kept up during several days, the efforts of the agitators were inadequate to suppress the prevalent indications of satisfaction produced by the final realization of the monarch's promise, in which fact the people recognized his determination to advance in the progressive course.

But the charter granted by the emperor did not accord with the views of the agitators. It was now criticised, and rendered odious in all the clubs and public meetings, and by means of placards and pamphlets. In this way the public mind was gradually prepared for the demonstration which was to take place on the 15th of May. Complaints of the reactionary stratagems of the Camarilla became more and more numerous and impudent. The press opened all its batteries upon the court, the nobility, and the clergy; and no step whatever was taken by the ministry to restrain its licentiousness.

Count Hoyos, being unable to endure longer the insults and annoyances to which his position as commander of the National Guard exposed him, the emperor with reluctance accepted his resignation, and appointed in his place F. M. L.* Chevalier von Hesse. The National Guard (who, during the whole period of its existence, had never attained a just conception either of their duties, their rights, or even the purposes of their existence) now demanded of Count Hoyos to resume the command which they had, by repeated insults, provoked him to resign. This noble and truly patriotic man responded to the call; and this sacrifice on his part was received, for the moment, with great joy; but scarcely had a fortnight elapsed, before their base ingratitude forced him a second time to relinquish the command.

On the 30th of April, the minister of war, Zanini, resigned

---

* F. M. L., Field-marshal-lieutenant, corresponding to the rank of General.

his office, and Count Latour, who succeeded him, entered upon his duties with great vigor, and issued an order to the army characterized by energy and point. He soon filled up the thin ranks of the army in Lombardy, which Count Radetzky shortly after led, with so much honor, to victory.

At this time another means of keeping up the excitement and agitation among the citizens was discovered. This was the celebration of what were called *"fraternal festivities."* They were base imitations of the French banquets, not, like them, intended to ascertain public feeling, but only to array the refractory spirit of the people against any and every measure of the government.

The city of Vienna, from being one of the most quiet and orderly in Europe, became now daily a scene of the utmost anarchy. On the 4th of May, a party of students entered the office of the Minister of the Interior, and demanded the documents on file there relative to the Liguorians (Jesuitical monks), who had a few weeks before been expelled from the city, and for whose return it was understood that a number of citizens had petitioned the government. This petition, which was the principal object of their search, as well as the communication of the archbishop praying the government to make some provision for the support of the Liguorians out of the property of which they had been divested, together with the reply of the minister that the government would endeavor to take some measures for their relief, were thus forcibly extracted from the department, and immediately published. On the night succeeding that day, the students and National Guards, leading a mob of workmen from the faubourgs, numbering in all about ten thousand, appeared before the hotel of the Minister of Foreign Affairs, and saluted him with the usual mock serenade.

After calling in vain for the minister to appear, against the remonstrances of the servants, who assured them the minister was not at home, they invaded the sanctity of his dwelling, and, penetrating his apartment, demanded of his terrified family where the count was. The countess replied, " At the Foreign Office." A deputation was immediately despatched to that bureau, while the great mass remained about the minister's hotel. The deputation sent to the Foreign Office, after some resistance on the part of the domestics, gained access to the minister, and told him that the object of their visit was to communicate the will of the people, which was, that he should immediately resign his office. Count Fiquelmont, instead of ordering the insolent intruders from his presence—an act not only justifiable, but one which might reasonably have been expected from a veteran general of the army—proceeded to inquire of the committee what unpopular measures he had been guilty of that could have provoked the displeasure of the people. The deputation replied, that they had not come to debate any questions with him, or to pronounce any judgment upon his official conduct, but simply to advise him that his own personal safety, as well as the tranquillity of the city, depended upon his immediate compliance with the demands of the people. After a few moments, the count replied, that he would not only resign his office, but leave the city, if the public tranquillity demanded it. As this declaration was not sufficiently definite to suit the mob, they demanded further to be informed of the *exact* time when he proposed to carry his determination into effect. At this moment another deputation from the crowd entered the apartment, and assured the minister of the very great danger which would probably attend any delay on his part in offering his resignation, as the masses were increasing and pressing on his hotel. Count Fiquelmont then pledged himself to resign within twenty-four hours, and, in the interim, not to affix his signature to another official document. Satisfied with this assurance, the deputation escorted the minister to his hotel, where one of them, from a veranda, harangued the multitude, informing them of the accomplishment of their object; and, after compelling the count to make his appearance, and to reassure them of the fact, they withdrew. On the following day, agreeably to the pledge which he had given (although under duress), Count Fiquelmont tendered his resignation of the bureau of Foreign Affairs.

The details of this disgraceful affair are given, not only to afford a more correct idea of the state of anarchy which then prevailed in the city, but also to illustrate the remarkable fact that a government, which a few weeks before had been, physically speaking, one of the most powerful in Europe, from the gross mismanagement with which its affairs had been conducted, had become so weak as to be unable to protect the highest officer of state from the insults and indignities of the rabble.

On the day following this outrage, the emperor issued an earnest and touching exhortation to his people, to keep within the bounds of law, as the only means of insuring the progress of the ameliorations they desired. The agitation, however, so far from subsiding, continued daily to increase.

For some time there had been in Vienna a self-constituted committee, called "the Central Political Committee of the National Guards." This association, aided by the students of the university, had been, from time to time, discussing in the public prints the propriety of the different measures of the government, and directing all the political movements which had recently taken place; while, on the other hand, the ministry, instead of suppressing, on its very first appearance, this unconstitutional body, or controlling its movements; instead, even, of defending, by the aid of reason, its own measures, or combating the arguments advanced against them, at length arrived at the determination to issue an order for abolishing instantly this central political committee; and, upon the injudicious and absurd ground, that, having become now a part of the *military* power of the *country*, the members were, consequently, excluded from all participation in *civil* affairs, or from engaging in political movements, and the discussion of political subjects.

The next day (the 14th) a petition was forwarded to the ministry, remonstrating against the order of the previous day, and stating that, although they had taken up arms for the maintenance of order and tranquillity in the city, they were not, by that act, to be disfranchised, and that they would never blindly lend their aid to sustain measures of the government which did not meet their own approval; and they consequently demanded the immediate revocation of the order against the committee. They also took occasion, at this time, to ask that the Legislative Assembly, as proposed by the emperor, in his programme of a Constitution, should consist of one instead of

two Chambers; that certain alterations should be made in the
law provided for the elections to this Chamber; that the city
gates and imperial palace should be guarded equally by regular military, National Guards, and the Academical Legion; and
that the military should not interfere in preserving order in the
city, except under the most pressing circumstances, and then
at the request of the National Guard. The National Guard
and students combined having sent in this petition, and threatening violence in the event of its rejection, the community became more agitated than ever. The National Guard paraded
the streets during the night, while the regular military remained under arms on the *glacis*. On the following day the
excitement increased; and in the afternoon, when no answer
appeared to their petition, the students resolved upon what
they termed their *Sturm Petition*, or carrying the petition by
storm. Having loaded their fire-arms, they marched against
the palace, where they expected to be joined by the National
Guard, and a large number of workmen, whom they had summoned from the faubourgs. In the mean time, by order of
government, the gates of the city were closed, and a strong
guard of regular military stationed in every direction around
the palace, with cannons loaded with grape-shot, and torches
ready lighted. Night came on; the students and National
Guard were pressing, on all sides, upon the palace, while
workmen by thousands, armed with scythes and axes, thundered for admission at the city gates. No answer had yet
been given to the petition. The government, from all appearances, had determined on resistance, and a dreadful collision
was momentarily expected. Nothing occurred, however, until just before eleven o'clock, the time fixed on by the students for the termination of their forbearance, when the government, intimidated by the formidable display made against
it—though a single discharge of grape or charge of cavalry
into the densely-thronged masses would have mowed down all
opposition—yielded, and issued a proclamation revoking the
order for the suppression of the committee, and directing that
the Legislative Assembly should consist of one instead of two
houses; granting, in short, all the points mentioned in the
Storm Petition in the most ample and satisfactory manner.

I

Appeased by this proclamation, the students, National Guard, workmen, and citizens all retired quietly to their homes.

The next morning the entire ministry tendered their resignations to the emperor, as the events of the previous night fully demonstrated that the means under their control were so crippled as to enable them to furnish no support to the throne. At the request of his majesty, they consented, however, to retain their places until others could be selected.

Scarcely forty hours of quiet passed by, when the city was, on the morning of the 17th, again thrown into the utmost consternation by a proclamation of the ministry, advising the people that the emperor (with the imperial family) had left the capital the evening before, without affording them the slightest intimation of his intention.

On the 16th, his majesty and family had left the summer palace of Schönbrunn, about five' o'clock in the afternoon, as if to take their usual drive, and, proceeding on the road to Innspruck, had not returned. The secrecy which attended the movement, and the stratagem resorted to, made the escape amount almost to a *flight*.* The cause of the emperor's departure at this time was generally believed to be intimidation, resulting from the late disorderly conduct of the students and rabble, together with his dislike at being surrounded by the Academical Legion and National Guard as his body-troops. He also cherished the hope that a short absence from the capital would tend to restore the citizens to order and subordination. But the experiment, at that time, in the excited and disordered state of the city, as well as during the rapid advance of republicanism throughout the Continent, was a most dangerous—indeed, a desperate one. The official journal, of the morning of the 17th of May, contained an article written on the evening previous, and before the departure of the emperor was generally known, in which, after commenting on the late demonstration in the city, and answering some rumors in

* The late concessions of the emperor having inflicted, as was supposed, a death-blow on the aristocracy (as it was to dispose of this class that the single Legislative Chamber and the change in the electoral law were required), as well as the example set by the court. produced a general flight among the nobility, no less than eighty families having left in one day, among them the Princes Litchtenstein and Schwartzenburg.

relation to his majesty's proposed departure from his capital, states: "The emperor has no more safe asylum than Vienna; nowhere will he be better guarded than by the faithful citizens of the capital; therefore we conjure him, and all those to whom the throne is precious, not to listen to the syren voice which would allure them from the home of their ancestors. Let us speak freely, for the time is past for tame words or half-way measures. The emperor's departure would be looked upon in the same light as the flight of Louis the Sixteenth; and the last day of his residence here would be the first day of the republic."

If the past affords any index of the future, if conduct furnishes any clew to motive, an observer of the events occurring about this time, in the Austrian capital, would unhesitatingly have declared that a republic would soon be proclaimed. Unwilling to rest longer under the despotism by which they were oppressed, the people had broken the proud crest of the monarch, and wrested from his hands the unlimited power which in one unbroken chain had descended to him from his fathers. Not satisfied with the provisions of the Constitution which he proposed to them, they had forced him to make alteration after alteration, until he had destroyed the aristocracy, the supporters of the throne, and completely crippled his own power. Not content with these, they had continued to persecute him until, for his own personal security, he was compelled to seek safety in flight. Self-government, and nothing less, it would seem, could gratify their wishes; and now, when all power in the ministry was annihilated, when the military were removed, when the emperor had fled, when, in short, all power was centred in their own hands, what did they do? Establish a provisional government? declare a republic? No. They were terrified and confounded at the vast accumulation of responsibility with which they had suddenly become burdened, and but one idea occupied their minds, and that was, how they could relieve themselves from the weight of this power, how they could procure the emperor's return. In bewildering excitement, they had wandered upon an unexplored path, and suddenly found themselves, as it were, on the very brink of a precipice, that yawned before them, the depths of which they were unable to fathom, and whence they retreated in horror. All things in a moment took a retrograde movement. Every one who had the rashness to breathe the name of a republic was instantly seized and cast into prison. Under this charge about twenty persons were arrested, among them two females and eight editors of newspapers.*

The "Political Central Committee of the National Guard," the attempt to destroy which had induced the crisis, now dissolved of their own accord. The National Guard and Academical Legion, who had required that the regular military should be under them, now placed themselves under the military. The law regulating the press, and which the ministry were afraid to publish before, now appeared in the morning's print. The editor, who had written the spirited article of yesterday, makes an humble apology in the journal of to-day. The proclamations of the ministry against disorder, formerly not noticed at all, or, if noticed, simply to be destroyed, are now attentively read, and receive the universal and hearty approbation of the reader. In fact, the departure of the emperor, so sudden and unexpected, seemed to have roused all classes of the agitators from the dreams in which they indulged, and to have restored them again to the possession of their senses. The more prudent and sensible citizens now saw and felt that the masses were not sufficiently enlightened for self-government; the capitalists and landlords discovered that the removal of the court from Vienna would be the destruction of the city; while the students acknowledged that they lacked the power which they supposed they possessed over the more respectable and unofficious inhabitants; and all were consequently engaged and united in restoring order and maintaining the peace of the city.

But one idea seemed now to occupy the minds of the people, and that was the emperor's return. Deputation after deputation, from every class of the population and from both sexes,† were now dispatched upon this object to Innspruck.

---

* The author saw the crowd in Vienna dragging a man through the street, and crying, "To the lamp-post with him!" And, on inquiring what great offense he had committed, was told that "he had been conversing with a friend about a republic."

† One deputation of ladies, among them two princesses, who, it is said, went down on their knees to the empress.

Petitions, signed in one instance by more than eighty thousand of the inhabitants, expressive of the deep regret at the departure of the imperial family, earnestly invoking their immediate return, and avowing the most sincere attachment to his majesty and loyalty to his government, were dispatched from Vienna. The better class of citizens were, doubtless, honest in their demonstrations. They were peaceably disposed, lovers of order, and, as the best means of securing it, fervently desired the return of the emperor. They naturally hoped, also, that the ignorant masses and fanatical youth had learned wisdom by experience ; and that, if the old order of things was restored, and the most requisite privileges retained, tranquillity would succeed. But this hope, rational as it was, proved a delusion. The baffled agitators gained fresh boldness from this interval of repose, and soon renewed their reckless schemes. The vulgarity and impudence of their attacks upon the Camarilla, the nobility, and the clergy, exceeded all former vituperation. It was the Camarilla, they alleged, that had carried off the emperor from his faithful subjects—it was the Camarilla, now at Innspruck, that would influence the court to reactionary measures ; and they finally declared, that the Camarilla and nobility must first be destroyed before any enduring liberty could be expected.

So palpable a misrepresentation of the reasons which drove the emperor from his capital could impose on no intelligent and well-disposed citizen. It was evident that no intrigues or seductions were necessary to induce the emperor to leave Vienna. The cause of his departure was ascribable alone to the disgraceful events of the 15th of May, the folly and errors of which could not be denied. The emperor was deeply and justly grieved at the unkind and insolent manner in which these concessions had been obtained. He had become a slave in his opinions, and a prisoner in his palace. Where were these outrages to end ? Who would say that the Storm Petition was to terminate the designs of the agitators, or whether a second would not soon be presented (and which is said to have been actually prepared, to demand the surrender of Italy and Poland) ? And that a third would not soon have followed, if, by that time, such an one had been necessary, to require the emperor to abandon his throne and country. It is evident, under such circumstances, that no efforts of a Camarilla were necessary to induce a feeble and timid monarch to relieve himself from such embarrassment by exchanging, temporarily, his residence to another of his capitals, and to one amid the romantic scenery of the Tyrol, and among a people for centuries distinguished, above all others of the empire, for unwavering loyalty and attachment to the house of Habsburg.

The tranquillity of the city was but brief. One week only of quiet was suffered to elapse, when a most hasty and injudicious proceeding on the part of the ministry produced a scene of far greater excitement than had been as yet witnessed in Vienna. Whether they were influenced by the favorable disposition of the people toward order recently manifested, or by the present indications of anarchy; whether, at length persuaded that it would be impossible to maintain the tranquillity of the city without it; or that, if not the most favorable, the present was the only time to effect it, is indeed questionable. On the 25th, however, the ill-advised order that the Academical Legion should be dissolved, and the university closed within twenty-four hours, and that, if resisted by the students, it should be enforced by the military, was promulgated. The students were on the same day addressed by their commander, Count Colloredo Mansfeld, who conjured them to lay down their arms, which they declined; and issued a placard, in which it was declared that the Academical Legion would under no circumstances dissolve; that, on the contrary, they considered it a holy duty to contribute as hitherto to the preservation of the constitutional acquisitions, and to co-operate in the maintenance of order and tranquillity. Although a great portion of the citizens perceived the destructive ends to which the course of the students tended, and, in consequence, warmly expressed their disapprobation; yet their influence was contravened by other manifestations of a different character, and that emboldened the students to adhere to their resolution. To add to their encouragement, the faubourg Wieden addressed the university a vote of thanks on account of its conduct on the 15th of May; and nearly all the companies of the National Guards of the suburbs of Schottenfeld, Gumpen dorf, and Neudorf, dispatched deputies to the Aula* assuring it of their sympathies. The Guards of the ninth section, second company, issued summons to all National Guards not to abandon the students in that trying hour ; and the temper of the people, a few days before apparently so tranquilly inclined and well disposed, had become already altogether changed. On the morning of the 26th, by order of the ministry, the regular military were called out at an early hour, and stationed at different points throughout the city, with a view, doubtless, of carrying the recent order into effect. At seven o'clock, Count Colloredo Mansfeld, at the head of a body of National Guards, appeared before the university, and summoned its inmates to surrender their arms, and to leave the institution. The students refused to obey. Subsequently, Count Montecuculli, the governor president, and General Sardagna, commander of the city, visited the university for the same purpose, and were attended with no better success ; the students protesting against the order, and threatening to hold Montecuculli and Sardagna responsible for any blood that might be shed on the occasion. A battalion of the regular infantry were then advanced to the spot, and surrounded the building. The students, not intimidated by these demonstrations, saluted the troops with fraternal shouts as they appeared ; and the mass of people, attracted to the spot by the noise, as well as by curiosity to witness the closing of the university, increasing from moment to moment, and impeding any operation of the troops, it was deemed advisable by the commanders that they should be withdrawn. The excitement increases, the *rappel* is beaten, the tocsin sounded, and thirty thousand workmen from the faubourgs, at the summons of the students, armed with axes, spades, and iron bars, rush to the spot ; the city gates are occupied by the regular military, and partly closed ; the laborers forcing their way through the *Rothenthurm* door, the military fire, and one man is killed, and several wounded. The report spreads like lightning through the city, the excitement becomes intense, and the construction of barricades, hitherto unseen in Vienna, commences. The alarm is beaten through the

---

* University.

streets, and every one summoned to arms to defend the threatened liberty ; the mounted National Guard announces that the
Academic Legion must be sustained ; the workmen receive the
news with enthusiasm, and prosecute their labor at the barricades.* The pavement of Vienna, beyond all comparison the
most cleanly and beautiful of any city in Europe, composed
of blocks of granite a foot square, is torn up ; and with these
stones, together with articles of furniture of every description,
carts, and carriages, barricades are soon constructed through
the whole interior city at all the intersections of the streets,
and rising as high, in many places, as the second stories of the
houses. In the course of a couple of hours, the inhabitants
are completely blockaded in their own houses. The immense
paving stones, carried to the upper stories, together with quantities of boiling water, are prepared, in case of an attack, to be
thrown on the troops below. Where the paving stones were
not employed in making barricades, every other stone was torn
up and placed on the one which remained stationary, making
a succession of pitfalls, or such an uneven surface as totally to
obstruct the movement of cavalry.

It was terrible to behold a city in the process of transformation from the abode of peace, the mart of trade, or the seat of
pleasure, into a fortress and battle-field. It was impressive
to watch the excited faces and brawny arms of the workmen,
as, with pick-axes, they ripped up the substantial pavement,
and tore down the railings and wood-work, while the women
conveyed these materials to the rising barricade. In some
places, where these barricades were completed, covered with
mattresses, behind which the combatants were to crouch as
they fired upon the charging troops, students in their grotesque uniforms addressed the populace, and inveighed against
the Camarilla and their reactionary measures; while over
them waved either the red or black flag, those certain emblems of blood and death.† While these events were trans-

---

* In the houses behind the barricades well-dressed females engaged in arrang-
ing the paving stones ; others engaged in addressing the people, and encouraging
them to action ; while others carry baskets of bread and wine to those who defend the barricades.

† On a sign-board at the university is written, " What we demand. The garri-

piring, the soldiers were withdrawn to the public squares, and there awaited, with loaded arms and burning impatience, the order to charge the barricades.   During the whole morning a desperate conflict was momentarily expected; for it was not supposed that the ministry, however weak and wavering their previous conduct had proved them, could have been guilty of so gross an absurdity as to have issued an order without knowing whether they possessed either the moral or physical courage necessary to carry it into effect; but such, however irreconcilable with our ideas of good sense, and particularly with the caution and prudence peculiar to the German character, was nevertheless the case.   If order and tranquillity were to be restored to the city, the measure determined on, to disarm the Academical Legion, had become absolutely necessary (in fact, it was the grossest error, in the first instance, ever to have furnished with arms a large body of undisciplined and agitated students, who needed no other supply than proper books).   The slight preparation made by the ministry, however, for effecting their object, together with their base timidity, will ever be a matter of severe and unqualified reproach.

The manifestations on the part of the students, National Guard, and mob, toward noon, became so threatening that the intimidated ministry issued a proclamation revoking the order of the previous day for disarming the students and closing the university, and directing the immediate withdrawal of all the regular troops from the city.   The proud Roman legions, stripped of their arms, and almost of their clothing, and forced by the Samnites to pass under the yoke at the Caudine Forks, could not have felt more chagrin than did those brave troops, compelled now, for a third time, to march out and leave the city to a party of insolent youths and unarmed workmen.   It was enough to have broken the spirit of any soldiers; and they did, unanimously and immediately, petition the ministry to be removed to some other field of action.

As soon as the news that the ministry had yielded was conveyed by guards to the barricades, the students in command received the intelligence with scorn; and, seizing the procla-

son shall leave the town within twenty-four hours, and the ministry shall guarantee the acquisitions of the 16th of May.

mation of the government, they tore it to pieces before the assembled crowds, contemptuously trampling its fragments under foot. About two o'clock the House of Judicature, on the *Hohen Markt*, was stormed by the students, because one of their speakers had been arrested, and was confined in the building. All the windows were demolished, the iron railings torn down, and the statue of Justice, ornamenting the front, mutilated The building was finally entered, the guard of security disarmed, and compelled to leave under the most violent threats. Those who, on the 18th of May, had been incarcerated for breathing the word "republic," and some of whom had, in the interim, undergone trial, and been sentenced for years to imprisonment in fortresses, were now relieved, and, like martyrs in a great cause, paraded in triumph through the city.

But at this point the difficulty was far from being at an end. The students, as was quite natural, availing themselves of the advantage they had acquired, thought it had now come to their turn to demand, and required that the concessions granted them on the 15th of March and 15th of May, and which they chose to think the government, by the late movements, were disposed to take away, should be reassured to them; that the regular troops should all be confined to their respective barracks; that the entire control of the city and of its gates should be surrendered into their hands; and that the *ouvriers* should be furnished with work; all of which the ministry, by several proclamations, which appeared during the afternoon, fully conceded.

Although it was evident that nothing was to be feared from the military, the alarming report was repeatedly raised during the afternoon that regiments were advancing to storm the barricades, and bodies of workmen and National Guards were dispatched to the Northern Rail-road and to the bridges over the Danube, to repel Prince Windischgrätz, who, it was said, advanced with four companies against the city.

During the whole night, the students, National Guard, and workmen remained upon the barricades.   Fires were made in the middle of the streets; students with their Calabrian hat and feathers, National Guards with their helmeted caps, *ouvriers* without coats, and peasant women without bonnets, seated on paving stones around the bright blaze, indulged in coarse jokes and laughter, or in songs.

It was a strange and painful sight to see these camps in the heart of a city; yet the motley groups by the dusky light of the watch-fires, with the houses high and dark for a background, were picturesque in the extreme.

About midnight, a rumor being circulated that Prince Windischgrätz was actually approaching with a large military force to retake the city, the alarm became excessive. The tocsin was again sounded, guns were fired, the inhabitants aroused from their beds, and forced, even before they were dressed, to commence work and engage in taking up into the third and fourth stories quantities of the immense paving stones, to be thrown upon the heads of the invaders. A great destruction of property ensued, by tearing down columns and wrenching out iron railings to strengthen the barricades and furnish arms to the mob. These acts of violence caused great damage to the city, and terror among the inhabitants; and, after all the mischief had been accomplished, the alarm, as was discovered, proceeded from a band of students arriving by steamer from Pressburg, who had come simply to join their comrades of the barricades, and to participate in the exciting scenes which they had learned were transpiring in Vienna. The next day a document appeared, signed by the ministry, and confiding to the charge of the students and National Guard, all the property of the government, the public institutions, the safety of the inhabitants, and the tranquillity of the city. They, of course, readily undertook the charge; but immediately demanded cannon for the better execution of the important trust with which they had been invested. The ministry did not hesitate, but complied at once with the demand, and even made the delivery of the twelve cannons which they consigned to the students an occasion of pomp and ceremony. The guns were covered with garlands of roses, and were received by the students, paraded as important trophies through the streets, and then deposited very carefully, subject to their control, in the Civic Arsenal. This was an inexplicable act certainly, on the part of men who had not notoriously lost either their wits or their virtue—to commit the government property with which they were intrusted into the hands of those whose sole objects had been to wrest it from them — to intrust the safety of the inhabitants and the tranquillity of the city to those by whom alone the former had been endangered or the latter disturbed!

History nowhere affords so striking an example of reckless confidence; or was it a piece of unheard-of magnanimity, a master-stroke of policy, to surrender every thing into the hands of the enemy, make a virtue of necessity, yield with grace what could not be retained, and look to implacable foes for mercy ?*

The empire of Austria, shaken to its foundation by the Revolution of March, had now reached the second act in the eventful drama of its political regeneration. The time had arrived when the promises, vouchsafed by the sovereign in the hour of alarm and danger, were to be fulfilled, and the concessions so obtained to be finally accepted by the people. The time had arrived when the temporary connection between the friends of free government and the enemies of all government had to be dissolved, if the results of the Revolution were ever to assume the shape of regular institutions and established laws. The time, in short, had arrived when a reaction must take place, not in favor of the old and extinct order of things, but in favor of real freedom, and against anarchy. Upon the issue of this struggle the fate of Austria now depended. The imperial government, at the outset, had been surprised and overcome, and now lay prostrate, paralyzed, and incapable, for the moment, of any action whatever. That authority was now as entirely removed from the scene of action as though it had never been in existence; and the struggle was to take place between the friends of rational liberty on the one hand, and

---

* The proclamation[1] of the ministry, dated the 27th of May, is the most extraordinary document that was ever signed. The ministry surrender Count Hoyos to the students, as a guarantee for the concessions of the emperor, on the 15th and 16th of May. What, we may inquire, in the name of common sense, had Count Hoyos to do with the emperor or his concessions? If any one should have guaranteed the concessions of the emperor, it was surely the ministry, who alone had the power of regulating affairs. In the next place, the ministry say that those who caused the disturbances of the 26th of May should be brought to trial. Who caused those disturbances but the ministry themselves, by their order for closing the university?

[1] Wiener Zeitung.

the anarchists on the other. Should the former prevail, there was reason to hope that the first united and legitimate effort would not be in vain; and that the concessions in the cause of freedom and governmental reform, which they had obtained, would be carried out in good faith, and result in the liberation and prosperity of their country; but, on the other hand, were the supporters of anarchy to succeed, there was no alternative for the people but to submit, for a time, to that most unreasonable, exacting, and cruel of tyrants, a tyrant mob; until the former government, aroused to its self-possession by the atrocities of the rabble, should interfere, and, in so doing, crush the liberty which had been gained, and restore the former institutions.

As soon as they were installed in power, the students resolved that the emperor should either return himself to Vienna, or send in his place one of the royal princes; and a deputation was forthwith dispatched to Innspruck for the delivery of the message. Orders were then issued for the arrest of all those who had been instrumental in introducing the troops into the city on the 26th of May.

Count Hoyos, the former commander of the National Guard, who had just returned from Innspruck, whither he had been sent by the ministry in quest of the emperor, was taken; and Count Maurice Ditchrichstein, the imperial chamberlain, one of the most inoffensive and worthy gentlemen of the city, was seized in his palace, at night, and dragged to the university, where they were both imprisoned for several days; but when it was discovered that they had no knowledge of the introduction of the troops into the city, they were discharged.

Count Colloredo Mansfeld, the former popular commander of the Academic Legion; Count Montecuculli, the liberal Landmarshal, or presiding officer of the Diet, on whom their hopes so strongly rested on the 13th of March; and Count Breüner, the great supporter of the petition in the Diet, and who was subsequently the bearer of it to his majesty, and its bold advocate in the imperial presence, fled from Vienna to escape the arrests, as well as summary vengeance with which they were now threatened.

Even their own two favorite and most liberal professors,

they who had acted on all their deputations to the court, and who with them were the first to seize arms in defense of liberty, one escaped arrest by flight; the other, after enduring imprisonment for some time, was, by strong intercessions in his behalf, released.   These individuals, who, six weeks previous, were regarded, even by the students themselves, as the most liberal men of their class, as men attached to real progress, were now denounced as traitors.

The students, proceeding with youthful rapidity, had found themselves far in advance of their cautious professors.   The latter, it was declared, did not keep up with the age; they had become too conservative, and they were seized and tried for no offense in the world, except that they had not kept pace in extravagance and crime with the warm blood and light heads of their pupils.   Time moved rapidly, and a few days was quite sufficient to convert Liberals into either Radicals or Conservatives.   It seemed impossible to stand still, and it was therefore necessary either to advance or retrograde.   The most formidable enemies of the new liberal Constitution were those who, but a few weeks before, were its most strenuous partisans; for they were the first to denounce the very concessions which they had been the first to demand.

To the Liberals, or friends of free government, there was now a double conflict opened: first, that of the people against the old form of government; secondly, that of the new form of government against the Radicals, or enemies of all government.

It was greatly to be feared that they would not justly appreciate the delicate situation in which they were then placed; that they would see only the single conflict between the old form of government and the Radicals, and between the choice of evils, select the former as the least; on the principle that a bad government was preferable to no government at all.

After these extraordinary proceedings, it was not to be wondered at that the disorders and disturbances increased in the city.   The ministry having become tools of the mob, the Liberals or friends of good government offering no resistance, and every one who could, escaping as rapidly as possible, for fear of becoming a victim, Vienna was given up to perfect anarchy.   Meetings were held to consider the propriety of making

landlords diminish the rents of houses, and to determine that
the proper time of payment was subsequent, and not, as formerly, previous to occupation.   Processions of workmen promenaded the streets, striking for wages, and determined not to
work until assurances were received that their pay would be
increased and hours of labor diminished; requisitions fatal to
contractors, and a serious inconvenience to builders.

The tailors held a great assembly; the grievance to be rem-
edied with them was that the women had appropriated certain
work, such as making ladies' habits and mantillas, which they
asserted belonged more properly to them.*   Breaking into the
establishment of the most fashionable French milliner in the
city, they destroyed the greater part of her goods and carried
off the remainder.

Two offices or booths, erected on the glacis for the purpose
of receiving enrollments for the army of Italy, openly and at
mid-day were attacked by the mob, and torn to pieces in the
presence of the National Guard, who made no attempt at interference; the object being to prevent the departure of any able-
bodied men from the city at that time.

The students established among themselves a legion known
as the Death's-head Legion, and bearing on their caps, as em-
blematic ornaments, a skull and cross-bones; and boys of fourteen and sixteen years, with such devices to their Calabrian
hats, exhibited their enthusiasm for liberty, and expressed
their determination neither to yield or accept pardon in the
struggle for it.   No one could now walk the streets of Vienna
without the fear of injury.   Every where appeared placards
of menace and violence.   It was quite usual for creditors to
penetrate the houses of their debtors, insulting them when unwilling or unable to respond to their unreasonable demands.
Any one who disapproved of such disorders was visited with
summary vengeance; and if one desired to gratify his long-
indulged hate, it was only necessary to hint to the mob that
the unhappy victim had expressed a sentiment or performed an
act favorable to order or good government.   There was no personal security, for any well-attired individual was liable to in-

---

* In Vienna ladies' dresses are always made by men—*Damen Schneidern*, as
they are called.

sult while quietly promenading the streets.   Every one dreaded what the next day might develop, and despondency increased
from hour to hour throughout the city.   In this exigency, the
police acknowledged its inefficiency; the National Guard shrug-
ged their shoulders; and the ministry, terror-stricken, sought
refuge either in flight or obscurity, upon the first symptoms
of danger.

In such a condition of affairs national bankruptcy and individual ruin seemed inevitable.   The government was obliged
to borrow large sums of money, mortgaging the valuable salt
mines of Gmünden as security, and this was chiefly expended
in useless works of internal improvements, to give employment
to the people.   The aristocracy were ruined by the repudiation
of the labor and tithes formerly yielded by the peasantry;
merchants could effect no sales, for there was no money wherewith to make purchases.

Even freedom of the press, to obtain which was a principal
object of the previous agitation, now existed no longer; for no
one dared to publish any thing reflecting, in the slightest degree, upon the patriotism, wisdom, or moderation of the students.   Although it was the unanimous wish of the middle
classes to free the community of the students, who were the
primary cause of the existent difficulties, a petition to that effect, extensively circulated, was not signed by six individuals,
such was the alarm which the young fanatics inspired.   The
programme adopted by the extreme left at the Diet at Frankfort now became known, and this was to form in Germany a
great confederation of republican states; and the partisans of
this object in Vienna now urged upon Austria to join the league.

For this purpose, German ribbons were only worn, and German patriotic songs alone sung; Radical papers even dated
their news, not from Vienna, but from " the United States of
Germany."   The question of an Austrian monarchy no longer
existed.   It was universally said that the Constituent Assembly
would determine a form of government for Austria; and it was
openly suggested that certain rights should be permitted, and
others taken from, the emperor.*   It was no longer allowed to
speak of the privileges of the crown and of the monarch.   It

---

* The *Radical.*

was only the sovereign people to whom remained any rights whatever..

To hint at the compatibility of the public desires with the rights of the crown was an insult to the sovereign people. By the clubs, the Democratic meetings, and the Radical press, the population were constantly imbued with these views.

Schütte, the agitator, admits, in his journal since published, that the object of the Democratic leaders at Vienna was the establishment of a republic.

"What Paris," he says, "had employed some tens of years to accomplish, the people of Vienna thought to obtain in a few months, and then to be able proudly to proclaim, 'Behold, the Viennese are the leading free people of the world; in one year they have overthrown absolute monarchy, obtained a constitutional monarchy, and gloriously won a republic.'" The Radical party, although at this time possessed of full power, so far as the city of Vienna was concerned, to carry their desires and intentions into effect, did not entertain this purpose, or consider it advisable to urge things to extremities; their policy seemed rather to await the action of the Central Diet at Frankfort, to keep affairs at Vienna in the same unsettled and disordered state, and to be ready to adopt any plan that might be proposed by the central power.

Alarmed by the critical situation of his capital, the emperor, by a manifesto, bearing date the 16th of June, appointed the Archduke John as his representative in opening the Diet, and in the other affairs of government. On the 24th, the archduke, a favorite with the people of the empire (not only on account of the gentleness and suavity of his demeanor, but from his unostentatious manner of life, and particularly on account of his having married, not among the courts, but among the people),* arrived in Vienna.

He was most cordially received, and all parties expressed their high respect for him. At two o'clock at night, a grand torch-light procession took place in honor of him, and thousands of citizens, National Guards, and students, exhibited the utmost enthusiasm in his favor. On the next morning, he received, in the name of the emperor, the ministry, the National

---

* He married the daughter of a country postmaster.

K

Guard, the garrison, the magistrates, committees of security, and the municipality.

This was by far the most judicious move that the emperor could have made, as, owing to his universal popularity, the Archduke John was more likely to exact obedience than any other member of the imperial family. The Committee of Students and National Guard, who had assumed all authority in the city, proposed to the archduke, it was said, to relinquish all their powers; but he committed the great error of saying to them, that, *as they had been enabled to preserve order in the city* for some weeks past, they might still retain their stations, until other arrangements could be made by the Assembly which was shortly to convene in Vienna.

The assembly or convention for the formation of the Constitution, the convocation of which had been fixed for the 26th of June, had not as yet taken place, owing to a delay in the elections, which were still proceeding in some of the provinces. Many deputies, however, from those portions of the empire where the elections had already occurred, had reached Vienna, viz., from Galicia, Croatia, and other Slavonian provinces; and, of about sixty who had made their appearance, not one spoke or understood a word of German. Notwithstanding all the assurances of loyalty, attachment, and devotedness to the crown, which exhibited itself on the appearance of the Archduke John, the efforts of the agitators were continued with daily increasing zeal.

On the 24th, the very day of the archduke's arrival, discussions were opened in the Radical papers upon the question, whether, after the events of the months of March and May, the emperor should bear the title, " By the grace of God."*

On the 29th the archduke was elected, by the National Assembly of Frankfort, as Regent of the German empire, and a deputation immediately dispatched by that body to Vienna to inform his imperial highness of his election, and to request his acceptance of the station. The deputation arrived in Vienna on the 4th of July, and was received on the 5th by the archduke in solemn audience. Upon the proposal of the deputation, the archduke declared himself ready to accept the offered

---

* *Demokrat.*

dignity. The Regent of the Empire appeared on the balcony
of the palace, hand-in-hand with the deputation, and there addressed the assembled crowd in a brief but animated speech,
which was received with great enthusiasm; the firing of cannon, playing the German national hymn, and shouts of an excited populace continued; while the diplomatic corps, the ministry, and the National Guard, tendered their felicitations. Although it must have been gratifying to the hearts of the Viennese to witness the honor conferred on a member of the imperial house, yet the appointment of the Archduke John at that
time, when he had just undertaken a similar task in Austria,
and when he was the only man who inspired confidence, was
particularly unfortunate for the empire. Serenades and torch-
light processions concluded, on that night, the ceremonies in
honor of the deputies, the archduke, and the occasion.

As indicative of the public feeling abroad at this time in
Germany, it may not be unimportant to notice the proceedings of a visit, paid the next day, by two of the deputies to
the university. After an address made them by one of the
most self-important of the youths, and which was strongly
tinctured with Republicanism, Hecksher replied, that he was
from Hamburg, and a Republican himself, but that he was
fully persuaded that the German people were not yet prepared
for a republic, and that it could not be introduced without anarchy and bloodshed; that he, consequently, had taken his
seat on the *right* side at Frankfort. After this rebuff to the
young Republicans of the Aula, Hecksher adroitly returned to
the German question, declaring his willingness to make any
sacrifice for the liberty of Germany; and finally concluded his
remarks by reminding the audience, that he, too, had shouldered his musket, and battled against the tyranny of Napoleon; but that, the conflict over, he had returned again to his
studies. "Therefore," said he, "I take the liberty to remind
you, my dear young friends, that you may now more properly
continue your exploits upon the field of science." Such wholesome advice was not relished by the students, in fact, would
have been altogether unendurable, had it not been followed by
a speech from the Radical deputy, Raveaux, who was attached
to the *extreme left* of the Frankfort Assembly. He directed

the attention of the students to the fact, that the commission of the Archduke John contained neither the words "inviolable," nor "by the grace of God;" that the latter expression in connection with sovereigns was obsolete, and that the people alone were "by the grace of God;" and that Archduke John (or, as he would rather say, citizen John) had also adopted these principles.

It was a great gratincation, indeeu, a triumph to the Radicals, to use or listen to such language with impunity then, which indulgence in less than six months previously would have cost them their heads.

About this time the excitement against Baron Pillersdorf, Minister of the Interior, became very great. He was the object of attack in all-the papers, and his withdrawal from the ministry vehemently demanded. Reports of revolutionary outbreaks in contemplation were diligently disseminated. The "Democratic Union," which now began to exhibit itself more confidently than ever, dispatched a deputation to the archduke, demanding the immediate dismissal of Pillersdorf. The Committee of Security did the same. Pillersdorf, notwithstanding he had been a pliant tool through whom they had effected much mischief, was not, in all respects, satisfactory to the Radicals, or fitted, perhaps for the ends which they then had in contemplation. The Committee of Students, headed by M. Fraulich, addressed the archduke, after which he replied: "I am an old Austrian—an old German. I wish to dedicate the last days of my life to the good of my country. My intentions are good. He who directs the destinies of the universe will judge me. You, my young friends of the university, have done much; act for the general interest; I have the utmost confidence in you." These remarks alone, if other and abundant proof were not at hand, show that the Archduke John was not the man for the crisis.*

On the 8th of July, Baron Pillersdorf surrendered his portfolio into the hands of his imperial highness, the representa-

---

* On the same evening, the archduke (in company with the deputation) took his departure for Frankfort, after having issued a proclamation announcing his intention to return by the 19th instant, to represent the emperor at the opening of the Diet.

tive of the emperor.   His resignation was accepted, and Baron Dobblhof was charged with the formation of a new ministry.*   By this step the Radical party made an important advance.

Owing to the inexperience of the people in the conduct of elections, together with the indolence manifested on the occasion, the Radical party, by their stratagems and zeal, succeeded in electing to the Assembly some of the most violent Revolutionists ; who, with their adherents, formed the left side of the Austrian Diet, and who sanctioned, if they did not instigate, the dreadful occurrences of the 6th of October.

On the 17th of July, the Archduke John, in conformity with his promise, returned to Vienna, in order to officiate, in place of the emperor, at the opening of the Diet.   On the 19th was published, in the official gazette, a list of the new ministry, which did not, however, meet the general approbation.   Particular objections were made to the Minister of Public Works. His character, together with the manner in which he had procured his nomination, were by no means satisfactory.   And even the appointment of Dobblhof, demanded as it was by the "Democratic Union" and the " Committee of Security," rested under a cloud of suspicion ; but, the most incomprehensible part of the transaction was, that the archduke, in the dissolution of the old ministry, should have thought proper to yield obedience to such a demand, and from such a source.   Such a ministry could not be otherwise than suspicious.   A ministry under a constitutional, as well as a republican government, should be formed in accordance with the public will ; but the mistake committed here, throughout the entire struggle, was that of considering a mere faction the people.   And that this faction was flattered, instead of being opposed ; courted, instead of being suppressed, was the error committed both by Pillersdorf and Dobblhof—the rock upon which both their administrations were wrecked.

To continue the excitement, a deputation now arrived from Paris, bringing a flag and an address of thanks to the students of Vienna.   Warm debates took place in the sessions of

---

* For a list of the Austrian ministry during the years 1848 and 1849, and which, in point of numbers, exceeded any thing before known, see Appendix, Note 5.

the Committee of Security, upon the question whether, now that the Diet was about to commence its sittings, the committee should or should not be dissolved. That such a self-constituted and revolutionary body should exist in opposition to the legally-elected and regularly-constituted Diet would not admit of a moment's doubt, even had it not been so expressly determined at its installation. It was evident, therefore, that all the debates were instituted with no other object than to impose on the people, produce an excitement in their favor, and thus prolong their authority; and this object was attained.

The Baroness Brandhof, the wife of the Archduke John, and born neither of imperial, royal, or even noble parents, but belonging originally to the ranks of the people, arrived, on the 18th, in Vienna. The occasion was improved by the Radicals to indulge in great ceremonies and festivals in her honor; to make to her addresses, welcoming her as a sister who, "amid a poisoned atmosphere, had preserved a simple, honest mind," etc. To such a degree had their impudence on the one hand, and stupidity on the other, increased, that such insults, in the very face of the archduke, to whom so much devotedness and attachment had been feigned, were received with acclamations by the crowd. No occasion, indeed, was ever lost to undermine the court in the minds of the people.

About this time the first meeting took place of the Union of Journeymen and Workmen, established by the Democratic Union, to promote the corruption of that class, and to instill into them the principles of communism.

On the 22d of July, the opening of the Constituent Assembly took place, under the auspices of the Archduke John, empowered by the emperor to represent him on that occasion.

The powerful element which formed the left side of the house, excited already from the commencement dread in the minds of the more prudent citizens, as to the influence which that party would one day exercise. These forebodings were but too soon justified.

The address delivered by his highness on the occasion was appropriate and interesting, so far as it touched cursorily upon the affairs of the government; the desire of the emperor for the full equality of rights to all the nations of the empire, and their voluntary annexation with Germany, as well as the intention of the government to conduct with vigor the war in Italy, and to look only to the force of arms for an honorable peace.

The first days of the session were appropriately enough devoted to an examination of the election returns of the members, and deliberations upon the subject of rules for the government of the Assembly; but their entire ignorance of all parliamentary proceedings was extremely ridiculous.

Not a week had expired after they met before operations were commenced to entrap the right side. By a concert of action between the left side and those revolutionary bodies of the city, the Democratic Union and the Committee of Security—in fact, the most violent members of the left side were also members of those associations—an invitation was addressed to the Diet to join in a funeral ceremony, to take place in honor of those who had fallen in the March Revolution; and, without suspicion of the design, the invitation was accepted by the Diet with applause. The municipality, the dignities of the university, all the various committees, and 40,000 National Guards, in all upward of 100,000 persons, took part in the ceremonies which were conducted with great pomp. They purported to be merely the religious service of mass for the souls of the fallen; but, in truth, were a political maneuver of great depth, to obtain not only a confirmation of the legal existence of the "Revolutionary Committee of Security," but to compromise the Diet, and to force its members to recognize the principles contended for on that occasion, and in this way to sanction all the acts of lawless violence since committed as legitimate parts of one and the same transaction.

The ministers Dobblhof, Bach, Hornbostel, and Kraus, were present in the uniform of the National Guard; whether they were honest dupes, or *participes criminis*, it would be a waste of labor to ascertain.

As the Archduke John was now obliged to leave Vienna for a length of time, the return of the emperor became not only a matter of importance, but of loud and animated discussion. All classes seemed to unite in one desire for his return, although the motives which actuated them were, doubtless,

widely different. The well-disposed, influenced by sincere loyalty to the throne and dynasty, desired it from the hopes which
they entertained that the imperial presence would tend to tran-
quilize, the public mind, and restore life, prosperity, and happiness to the city. But those who drove him off, desired him
back that they might obtain more concessions, or subject him
to further humiliations; while they felt confident that such a
"petrified effigy of extinct authority" could not, in the slightest degree, defeat their plans or embarrass their operations.

As the deputations previously sent to the emperor had been
unsuccessful in procuring his return, a new deputation, of one
member from each of the provinces, was appointed by the
Diet to bear him an address.

An address was prepared, in which it was stated that not
only the interests of the empire required his presence at the
capital, but that the fate of the dynasty depended on it. This
address was considered too tame to suit the views of the Radical party, and they sought to introduce into it the word "*demand*," in connection with the emperor's return. Count Stadion, of the right side, proposed as a substitute the word "*entreat*," when he was hissed by a great portion of the House.
The former, after a stormy debate, was accordingly introduced,
and, as one deputy remarked in his speech, it was the only
word in the address that came up to his ideas, and met his approbation.

The Democratic monarchy (*Democratische Monarchie*),
however absurd and contradictory the expression, became now
the watch-word. A throne, with democratic institutions upon
the widest basis; clearly defined, in other words, a republic
with a hereditary president—with an imperial title, but without imperial rights. The word *republic* was studiously avoided, while the institution itself was most clearly recognized.

The session of the Diet of the 29th of July was remarkable
for developing the boldness of the Radicals. One deputy expressed himself favorable to the return of the emperor, but
stated that he was to be warned of the danger of irresponsible
counselors. The Revolution has been acknowledged; therefore, the National Guard must constitute the guards of the
throne, and the Committee of Public Security must be sustain-

ed.   Another member, with the insolent arrogance peculiar
to him, arose and said, " I rise in the name of the aggrieved
Austrian people—the people who have exhibited an attachment unparalleled in history ; who have shown a patience,
during those intrigues by which the emperor has been carried
off, never before manifested ; who have sent deputation after
deputation to Innspruck, begging him to return.   I declare
there will be a time when people will cease to beg.   Had
they but spoken more energetically at first, we would not be
obliged to-day to use such language.   The people are deeply
afflicted by the mortification they have suffered.   Had such
an occurrence happened to another nation, what would have
become of the dynasty ?   Look to the history of Charles the
First, James the Second, Louis the Sixteenth !"

To continue the excitement, and keep up the tumults, constant spectacles, processions, consecrations of flags, festivities
of fraternity, reception and dispatch of deputies between the
provincial towns and the capital, to present reciprocal sympathies, daily took place.   The increasing frantic tendencies of
the Democratic and other unions, the noise of the placard and
newspaper sellers during the day, and *charivaris** at night,
not unfrequently accompanied with destruction of property—
excesses against which the most earnest representations were
made by the ministry, but to no effect—increased the agitation.

Such events had produced a sad change in Vienna.   The
ancient splendor of the imperial city passed away.   All the
style and magnificence of the court and of the nobility disappeared.   From twenty to thirty millions of florins withdrawn
from circulation, injuriously affected all trades and professions.
Commerce and manufactures were crippled, and poverty prevailed to a most threatening degree.   The old serenity and
joyfulness of Vienna were supplanted by the riotous festivities
of the students and National Guard.   At all the public places
they took the lead, with revolting arrogance, and banished all
true enjoyment.   A demon of discord separated families, interrupted the friendships of years, and spread distrust among all
classes of the population.   Instead of the wealthy and respectable stranger, once attracted to the city by its gayety and

---

* Mock serenades.

splendor; adventurers, agitators, demagogues, in short, the rabble from all parts of the monarchy and the Continent, rushed
to Vienna to re-enforce the ranks of their comrades.   Instead
of the well-dressed persons that usually thronged the streets,
beggars of every description, suspicious-looking figures, never
before seen, met the eye at every turn.   Among the male population, scarcely a civil costume was to be seen.   Every one
wore a military uniform or Calabrian hat.   During the whole
day an uninterrupted sound of the clanking of long swords
upon the stone pavement was audible, while a great many of
the creatures to whom they were attached seemed themselves
rather appendages to the unmanageable sabre.

Every one felt that the tide of revolution was on the rise.
Every one saw that the ministry, so far from raising a dam to
stop the angry current, themselves joyfully plunged in and
were swept away by a torrent that they could not stem.   In
the minds of all prudent and reflecting persons, the conviction
was irresistible that such a state of things could only be of
short duration, and that there was no other end than in some
dread catastrophe.

Not a day, in these excited times, passed without being
marked by a ceremony for which all the daily pursuits of life
were abandoned, and the people only craved excitement, which
had now become as necessary to their moral, as food to their
corporeal existence.   The 6th of August was distinguished by
the ceremony of the adoption of the German colors, by the
German regiments at Vienna, in obedience to the decree of the
Frankfort Diet.   By an order of the 16th of July, the Minister
of War of the German empire notified the ministers of war of
the various German nations, that the Archduke John, elected
Regent of the Empire, had taken command of all the armed
power of Germany, and that accordingly they were required
to parade all troops of the German Confederation attached to
their respective garrisons on Sunday, the 6th of August, to
announce to them, by the reading of the proclamation, that
fact, and to order, as an expression of homage, three cheers for
the Regent of the Empire; and, when circumstances would
permit, to be accompanied by three salutes; and from that
day, all troops, where it had not already been done, should

adopt the German colors, by wearing the German cockade in their caps, and the German ribbons on their flags.

The deputation dispatched by the Diet to the emperor had an interview with his majesty at Innspruck, on the 5th of August; and, upon their presentation of the address, the emperor said, "I am glad to receive the deputies of the Constituent Diet. Anxious only for the welfare of my states, I will, under the circumstances mentioned, comply with the request contained in the address you bear me, and return among you. As my health is not yet fully re-established, I shall not be able to commence my journey before the 8th of the present month, when I shall return to my faithful Austrians. I am happy to receive the assurances of your loyal dispositions."

On the day last mentioned, agreeably to advices received, a proclamation was issued by the ministry of Vienna, informing the inhabitants of the capital that their "most beloved emperor" would arrive in Vienna on the 12th of August, by the steamer from Linz, accompanied by her majesty the empress, and his imperial highness the Archduke Francis Charles, and his son the Archduke Francis Joseph. That the other members of the high court at Innspruck, viz., her imperial highness the Archduchess Sophia and family, would arrive one day later; and that the Minister of the Interior hastened to bring to the public knowledge this highly agreeable intelligence.*

The joyful news of the emperor's intended return having rapidly spread through the city, all minds became immediately occupied in preparations for his reception. At 5 o'clock on the morning of the 12th, the commission of the commune, deputations of magistrates from the university, the garrison, and several public bodies, started by steamer for Stein, about forty miles up the Danube, in order to meet their majesties, who arrived there at noon, and were received with great respect. The deputations, with M. Dobblhof, Minister of the Interior, at their head, were presented to the emperor, and congratulatory speeches delivered, expressing sentiments of profound devotedness to the emperor and to the constitutional monarchy. The emperor replied in suitable terms, and frequently declared that he was

* Wiener Zeitung.

delighted to return to Vienna. Having reached Nussdorf (the
landing-place of the steamers from the Upper Danube), their
majesties were greeted by the acclamations of the assembled
people, and passed to their carriages through rows of young
girls tastefully dressed, who strewed their path with flowers.
At several points triumphal arches were erected, through which
the imperial family drove, where a number of children were
stationed with branches of olive and bouquets of flowers. The
National Guard were assembled with their muskets decorated
with flowers. Houses were dressed out with flags and garlands. On the Place of St. Stephen, the emperor was received by the ministry, the staff, and detachments of the Hungarian and Italian Noble Guards. A *Te Deum* was performed
in the cathedral, in the presence of the court and the National
Assembly. The emperor and empress subsequently proceeded
to the palace amid an immense assemblage, while the balconies
of every house were occupied by ladies, who waved their handkerchiefs and scattered flowers. At the palace, the public authorities, and many members of the National Assembly, were
in waiting; and there an address was made the emperor, by
Dr. Smidt, President of the Diet, who, in the name of the National Assembly, and in the name of all the free people represented by it, greeted with loyalty his majesty's return to the
palace of his ancestors. In short, all the preparations and arrangements made, to give a joyous welcome to the imperial
family, were carried out with that exquisite taste peculiar to
the people of Vienna; while the joy and enthusiasm on the
occasion were unbounded.

Although the disappearance of the emperor from his capital,
in the secrecy with which it was effected, bore a strong resemblance to the departure of Louis the Sixteenth from Paris,
yet his return presented the most striking contrast to that of
the unfortunate French monarch, detected by the likeness on
his own coin, and, brought back a prisoner under a guard of
the Assembly, treated with the utmost contumely, the crowds
who flocked to see him as he passed, heaping upon himself and
family every sort of indignity and insult. Whereas, with the
Austrian monarch, from Nussdorf to Vienna, and through the
city to Schönbrunn, the summer palace, a distance of not less

than six miles, by the road he passed, there was but one uninterrupted and solid wall of happy beings. On either side
stands had been erected, and rented at enormous rates, and
there the people patiently waited, under a scorching August
sun, from early morning until evening, for the momentary gratification of a single glance at the dear monarch whom, only six
weeks before, their conduct had driven from his capital and his
throne. The day succeeding that of the emperor's return to
Vienna, he issued a proclamation to the citizens, characterized
by judgment and taste, expressing gratification at their reception, and the hope that peace and unanimity would now prevail, and trusting that, in conjunction with his ministers, the
Diet might be enabled to carry on to completion the Constitution of the empire.

Notwithstanding these joyous manifestations, the satisfaction, which appeared every where on the surface, was of little
depth. The students, to counteract the pacific and salutary
effects which the emperor's return to the city, or that of the
news of the victorious entry of the imperial troops into Milan,
which had just arrived, were calculated to produce, seemed to
redouble their energies in the exercise of that injurious influence which they held over the capital. To the aid of their
cause, the notorious Schütte, who, on account of his baneful
activity, as has been seen, was expelled from the city in the
spring, again appeared, and was most joyfully welcomed by his
partisans of the university. Having, in the interim, traversed
Germany in the service of the Propaganda, and met with many
adventures, he returned now to communicate the result of his
labors, and to stir up the Radicals of Vienna to increased activity; while the ministry, as inefficient as their predecessors,
dared not, in opposition to the university, take any steps for
his removal or the prevention of disturbance. Every day he
delivered one of his inflammatory addresses, some of which are
too characteristic of the times—too expressive of the history
of the period, to be omitted.

On the 17th of August, in the Aula, before a crowded audience, Dr. Schütte arose and said: "Carried off three months
ago, I return once more among you. Having traveled over the
whole of Europe, I am familiar with the general political con-

dition of all countries ; and I return now with the strong conviction that Vienna is the greatest city of liberty.   Vienna has
accomplished things never before done in France, in Belgium,
or any where else.   In Paris, the press is far more restrained.
In Frankfort, the number of those who keep to the side of freedom is small, and therefore overwhelmed.   In Berlin, they are
under military rule, which most brutally suppresses every free
movement.   There they refused, on the 6th of August, to execute the decree of the National Assembly, and to pay homage
to the Regent of the German Empire.   In Vienna, I find a
more numerous National Guard than exists in any other city.
I find the old spirit of the March days still in existence.   Yesterday the Aula ventured to rise* up for its acquisitions ; and,
if liberty is threatened in Paris, Berlin, or Frankfort, Vienna
will offer her a strong-hold.   But your merits are every where
acknowledged ; every German heart palpitates at the sight of
a Viennese ; and I myself traveled as a Viennese, as I am
dearly attached to Vienna.   In Mayence, I was carried off
with some Viennese students from the hotel, as the citizens
there considered it an honor to offer hospitality to a Viennese.
The same occurred at Cologne, in Paris, and in the Department of the Sorbonne, when I loudly expressed the sympathy
of the Viennese for France ; and for their admiration and love
of the population of Vienna, the flag over my head is a guarantee !   The especial object of my visit at this time to Vienna is
important.   In Frankfort, a struggle is now going on between
the men of stability and the men of progress ; the latter are in
a minority, and not only have protests been entered against
them, but the right side have joined in oppressing them.   It
is, therefore, necessary for Vienna to give a sign of life, a cry
of terror to the right side, and of sympathy for the left, to
which also the Viennese deputies belong.   I will read over
again the address, and desire that it may become, by a resolution of this Assembly, an Address of the Aula."   The address
was then read and unanimously adopted.

---

* A shameful affair which occurred on the night of the 16th, in trying to relieve
by force the editors of the "Students' Courier," arrested for a violation of the
laws of the press.   The caution-money was afterward paid, and the difficulty
ended.

Some idea may be formed of the excitement that existed at that period among the masses, as well as of the grade of their political intelligence, by the fact that such a speech was considered as "electrifying eloquence." But this circumstance affords but a partial insight into the history of the times, as thus illustrated. This brief harangue of Schütte's, as the attentive observer will not fail to discover, exposes the whole plan of operations, and demonstrates how, in the remarkable year of 1848, public opinion was first produced, afterward exported, then manufactured into maxims and principles, and finally restored to its original source. How excitement of the population by the agitators commenced; how by sympathy it was communicated, from point to point, and by reaction continued from month to month, until almost all Europe became involved. How few the instigators, and how untiring their industry, may be inferred from the orator's performances, when he completed the tour of Europe, and ascertained the political condition of the people, as he says, in three months. How they operated upon the feelings of the masses, may be judged of by the fulsome flattery in which he indulges toward the Viennese, calling them the champions of liberty, telling them that they had accomplished things never before done in France, Belgium, or any where else, and that their merits were every where acknowledged.

But by far the most important disclosure which this effort presents, is the fact of how small a part the people took in the origin of all the measures by which the excitement was prolonged, and how completely they rendered themselves servile instruments to further the ends of designing agitators. The very acts by which Vienna acquired the appellation of the greatest city of liberty on the Continent, were the destruction of the ministry and storming of the emperor's palace, on the 15th of May; and these, it will be recollected, were the results of Schütte's own recommendation, when, after his speech in the Odeon, on the 14th of April, he drew from his pocket the *Sturm Petition*, which inevitably produced those events. And "the especial object of his visit" to Vienna at this time, as he has the candor to acknowledge in the conclusion of his address, was to manufacture for the inhabitants of that capital some further opinions, to serve as a "terror to the right, and sympathy for the left" of the Frankfort Assembly.

About this time, a new element was introduced into the political arena, to swell, if possible, the already overflowing excitement. It was the agitation of the new religion, termed the German Catholic, a kind of compromise between the Roman Catholic and the Protestant, and of which Ronge, if not the author, was at least the chief disciple. Several very crowded meetings took place. The religion, however, found but few converts; but the object in view, and which was openly avowed, was advanced, viz., to continue the excitement, to undermine the established religion of the country, and increase the demoralization of the people.

The 21st of August was marked by a tumult with the workmen. The students, by fraternizing with this class, and calling upon them for co-operation in their efforts against the government, brought the proletaria to a knowledge of their physical strength, and thus shook the foundations of social order. They had let loose a power which they found themselves unable to control. A single hand, they forgot, might unbar the cage and let the grim lion out; but, when out, how many and what force would it not require again to confine him?

The Minister of Public Works, perceiving that no labor was performed, resorted to the expedient of giving out the work by contract, or, rather, of remunerating their services, not by the day, but by the quantity of work which had been accomplished. The terms offered were liberal, and the measure could not have affected injuriously the industrious, but only the indolent; yet this measure was deemed such an interference with the rights of the sovereign people as could not be submitted to with patience. Accordingly, on the 21st of August, the day on which this new arrangement was to go into operation, crowds of workmen assembled with flags before the convent of the Liguorians (which, since the expulsion of that body, had been converted into an office for the Committee on Public Works), and before the bureau of the magistracy, to demand the revocation of the obnoxious order. As the authorities would not yield to the demand, and the fermentation became more serious, the Guard of Security,* and some divisions of the National Guard, were called out to disperse the crowd with the utmost forbearance. No obedience was yielded to the mild measures taken to disperse them; but, on the contrary, they grossly insulted the guards, and the street was finally cleared by a division of the National Guard. The same took place on the *Hohen Markt* and the *Tuchlaben.* The repeatedly uttered threats of the workmen that they would go back for their tools, and thus enforce their rights, induced the city council, for the maintenance of the public tranquillity, to cause the *rappel* for the National Guard to be beaten, the gates of the city to be closed, and the bastions surmounted with cannon. Toward evening, however, the crowds of *ouvriers* had been dispersed, and completely expelled from the city, and no further dist/.bance occurred on that day

On the 22d of August all was apparently quiet; but soon it was discovered that the workmen had come to a resolution among themselves, that, on the following day, they would be prepared to sustain their demand more energetically. Accordingly, on the next afternoon, between two and three o'clock, several thousand workmen, collected in one of the faubourgs known as the *Leopoldstadt*, were engaged in representing a mock funeral of the Minister of Public Works (who, it was represented, had been choked to death by the kreutzers abstracted from the workmen), and a body of Municipal and National Guards, endeavoring to disperse them, met with resistance. In the excited state in which both parties were, a conflict ensued, several of the Guards were killed and many wounded; and among the workmen, as nearly as could be ascertained, about one hundred were either killed or wounded.† The Municipal Guard acting with intrepidity, and the National Guard with more proper energy than they had ever previously evinced, a few hours were quite sufficient to subdue all opposition, and with the shades of night tranquillity was again restored.

The next morning the city was quiet, and all immediate

---

* A new municipal guard which had been established.

† The authorities published ten killed and seventy wounded. **Many of the** wounded subsequently died in the hospital.

danger to the public peace removed. The vigor with which the workmen had been attacked by the National Guard; their failure in receiving that support which they had expected from the students, for whom, when similarly situated, they had rushed to the rescue; and then the fact of their having no arms themselves to continue the conflict, and no enlightened heads to direct their movements, brought them reluctantly to the conclusion that peace was their wisest policy.

The energy which the National Guard had displayed on this occasion having given the hope that, when necessity required, they were ready to fire upon the rioters, and might, consequently, be depended on in future emergencies, so encouraged the ministry, that they summoned, for the moment, energy sufficient to issue an order, having for effect the dissolution of the revolutionary Committee of Security, which had of late usurped all the powers of the ministry.

On the 24th, the ministry issued two proclamations, to the effect that they would again assume all power to themselves in the preservation of order, and that the National Guard, as well as all other organs, should in future be subservient to their orders alone.

This unlooked-for boldness and resolution on the part of the ministry confounded the revolutionary party, and staggered for a moment their proud dreams of usefulness and inviolability. The fury of the demagogues, of which that committee consisted, was boundless. For the moment, however, feeling too weak for open resistance, they contented themselves with abusing, through the prints and in placards, the National Guard, who had acted with energy on the previous day, denouncing them as "murderers, fratricides, traitors to the majesty of the people, and instruments of reaction." At a meeting of the committee called that evening, the only measure resolved on by way of opposition was to send rather a threatening communication to the ministry, "challenging them to perform openly and by publication that which they had done only by implication, and, not only to do so, but to do it at once—if possible, that very day."* When they had sent this

---

* German Almanac.

communication to the ministry, and were still in session, they received from them a note, bearing date the day previous, inclosing them a copy of their proclamation, and stating that they had considered the measure necessary. The deputation dispatched to the ministry soon returned with the written intimation of the dissolution of the committee. The ministry preserved firmness sufficient to adhere to its resolution, but lacked the boldness to assert the true causes which had impelled them to such a course, and, in fact, dishonored themselves by an apology, as degrading to their self-respect as it was inconsistent with truth—stating that "the mission of that committee, accomplished with so much resignation and courage, and crowned with so much success, was at an end." "The ministry consider it a sacred duty to express to the honorable members of that committee its warmest thanks and full esteem for their successful activity for the city and state during the most threatening moments." That, "in retiring into private life, the committee would carry with them the consoling reflection of a conscientious and honorable discharge of their duty as citizens," etc.

If these fulsome compliments to a revolutionary committee, who had usurped all the powers of the government, and had contributed chiefly to the disturbance of the capital, had been characterized by truth, they should never have been dissolved. Efforts for the tranquillity of the city, discharged with so much courage, and attended with so much success, during the severest trials to which the city and state were exposed, certainly merited a better fate than a dissolution of such a body. Certainly a singular way to express thanks, and manifest esteem for an association, to order its immediate annihilation. But prevarication and inconsistency were among the slightest charges to which the conduct of the ministry in this affair was amenable.

By the dissolution of that committee, the ministry had performed, if not the only, certainly the most important and praiseworthy act of their whole administration. They had reassumed the reins of government, which had been snatched from them by a self-constituted and unauthorized body; but by the very document in which they communicate that measure, they basely surrender all the advantages which they had gained. They had not only manifested the fear they entertained of the committee itself, as well as of its friends throughout the city, but, as it were, put into their hands the very weapons by which that act could be reversed, and the ministry themselves destroyed, since it would require no further evidence than their own statements to convince the public that a committee whose laudable efforts had been attended with so much success ought, at least, to be sustained; while it was equally clear, that a ministry who could have been guilty of the rashness to decree their dissolution were worthy themselves of instant dismissal.

During that sitting of the committee, a beautiful and most enthusiastic lady rushed into the apartment, and implored the committee not to dissolve. "To whom shall the people now address itself in its hour of need," said she, "if you retire?" "Do not give way to reaction! It only desires your dissolution! Vienna is in a troubled state; all minds are excited; parties oppose each other with hostility; how will all these difficulties end?"

Despite this extraordinary solicitation, the president pronounces a valedictory address to the committee, and declares them dissolved; but immediately the members of that committee form another association, to be composed of the same members, for the prosecution of the same objects, only to be distinguished by a different name. Instead of a committee, it was to be called a club; instead of being composed of National Guards, students, and citizens, it was to consist of citizens, National Guards, and students; instead of having for its object the public security, it was to confine itself to the preservation of the public order.

The first meeting of that club, on the 28th of August, was distinguished as the last meeting of its predecessor, by an address from females; and, what was another remarkable feature in the matter, the address, signed by fifteen females, was not a congratulation to the new, but a vote of thanks merely to the old committee—another evidence, if it were needed, of the identity of the two bodies.

Meanwhile, the unfortunate occurrences of the 23d of August had been profitably embraced by the Propagandists to create dissatisfaction in all directions. The Aula became furious; and notwithstanding the audacity manifested in attacking its militia (the *proletaria*), as it dared not undertake openly its defense, became more active in secret intrigues. The example set was by no means flattering or consolatory; for who could undertake to say that the National Guard, brought to a sense of their duty, and convinced of their own strength, would not next be brought to operate against those other disturbers of the public peace—the Academical Legion. No means were spared which could be effectual in creating prejudice against the National Guard, who had been in service on the 23d, the Municipal Guard, and the ministry.

From that day the destruction of the ministry was resolved on. The animosity of the public was particularly concentrated on Latour, Dobblhof, Bach, and Schwarzer. The first had incurred their displeasure on account of the ability and fidelity with which he devoted himself to his duties, the restoration and strengthening of the army, which he regarded as the sheet-anchor of the monarchy. Dobblhof and Bach had offended by their suddenly-changed positions; and Schwarzer by his measures against the workmen.

On the 28th of August, the first measures were taken toward the formation of a society of Democratic women. An anonymous female writer called, through the newspapers, a meeting of all " German women," to take place on a certain day, in the *Volksgarten*, where all favorable to the cause were to appear with German-colored ribbons. The assembly was numerous, but they were much annoyed by the men, who also appeared in great numbers as spectators. That they were the miserable dupes of designing agitators, was evident from the very first motion made by one of these female politicians; which was, that a collection should be taken up for the poor wounded workmen and their families, and to request the ministry to increase their wages. This was the first entrance of the female sex into the political arena. Their subsequent advance, incorporation into a regiment, fighting upon the barricades, and disgraceful exit, will appear in the October Revolution.

On the 3d of September, the Democratic Union, indefatigable in its efforts to maintain and increase the public excitement, had prepared a solemn funeral procession in honor of the workmen killed on the 23d of August.

These misguided *proletaria*, who, at that time, in attempting to enforce their insolent demand for higher wages by a most culpable demonstration, and who finally, by a most willful provocation of the National Guard, met their deaths, were now eulogized and honored as martyrs of liberty and victims of arbitrary power. This willful demonstration against the ministry and the National Guard was participated in by thousands of the latter, to the great astonishment and grief of the well-disposed. All Democratic and Radical clubs, as well as the new society of women, took part in the proceedings. The whole Academical Legion, and the Union of Workmen were present. The endless procession, with vailed banners, marched from the glacis in front of the *Schottenthor* to the *Währinger* church-yard. With peculiar gravity, the Democratic Union headed the column, not one of the Radical leaders being absent. The procession having reached the church-yard, the graves of the fallen workmen were, with much ceremony, decorated with flowers; after which, they proceeded to a large meadow adjoining, where hymns were sung and revolutionary speeches made. One of the speakers then called on the audience to take the solemn oath that they would "struggle and die for liberty;" when they all, with one voice, exclaimed, "We swear it!" A preparatory step toward the awful 6th of October was thus taken; but, as the ministry now prudently determined not to notice any insurrectionary conduct which they had not the courage to put down, no further disturbance resulted from this demonstration.*

---

* On the 5th of September, a meeting was held at the Hotel of the Roman Emperor, at the instance of Dr. Vivenot, at which it was proposed that all those who were in favor of the maintenance of the constitutional monarchical system should form a powerful union, to counteract the ruinous tendencies of the Radical and Republican party. The suggestion met with unbounded applause. The necessity of such a union could no longer be denied; it should have been formed long previously. In less than eight days, more than twenty-five thousand members had signed. The best effect was expected from the efficacy of that union, which was to have been extended to the provincial cities. But, tardy as the Ger-

From the want of energy displayed by the ministry on this occasion, the disorders of the city now daily increased. On one day, torch-light processions took place, and exciting speeches were delivered in honor of a deputy who had very suddenly turned from the *right* to the *left* side. On the next, an attack was made by the mob on the office of a paper called the *Geisel* (Scourge), the editor of which had been so imprudent as to raise the Austrian flag from his windows. It might have been supposed that, in a city where so many harangues were heard in favor of liberty, a person might have enjoyed the privilege of raising on his house the national standard of his country—that which had been for centuries the banner of the empire. But no; the appearance of that flag was the signal for his immolation. The office of the *Geisel* was attacked, the black and yellow flag was torn down and carried by the students, as a trophy, to the university. The windows were all broken, and the papers found in the office torn to pieces and scattered through the streets. Such was their idea of the inviolability of private property, the sacredness of private dwellings. What a contrast to the household freedom of England, which Chatham so eloquently and poetically describes, when he says, "An Englishman's house is his castle. Its roof may be of straw, the winds may whistle around, the snow and the rain may enter it, but the king can not, he dare not!"

On the 11th, the city was again thrown into a state of great agitation, in consequence of a demonstration made by the mob, and which was produced in the following manner. It appears that a financial measure was proposed by some designing individuals, ostensibly for the relief of the tradesmen of Vienna during these distracted times, but in reality for the advancement of their own pecuniary interest; and the emperor, in the benevolence of his heart, having contributed ten thousand florins toward the relief of the public necessities, this circumstance was seized upon by the intriguing speculators as a pretext for insisting that the government should guarantee the validity of the paper or stock issued by them; and to obtain

mans generally are, the society had scarcely become organized, when the 6th of October arrived, and the society was dissolved.

the connivance of all the tradesmen, who had become involved in the project, was an easy task.

On the afternoon of the 11th, the shareholders, students, and mob marched upon the bureau of the Minister of the Interior, and demanded that the minister should guarantee the stock, and, in case of refusal, threatened to find means to reimburse themselves by force. The minister, alarmed at the increase of the tumult, finally gave the assurance, to a deputation which had forced its way into his apartments, that an answer should be given to their demands the next morning. The mob, satisfied with this reply, for the moment retired from the spot; but other outrages were committed before the bureau of the municipality, which was broken into during the night.

On the morning of the 12th, the place or square before the bureau of the Minister of the Interior was crowded with people. The ministry issued a proclamation declaring that the stock company established by Swoboda* was but a private enterprise, and of which the ministry could, under no circumstances, undertake the guarantee; but, in order that the poor tradesmen might not endure a serious loss by these shares, the ministry would appoint a commission whose business it should be strictly to examine into the matter, and prevent any further frauds on the part of that company; and they further urged that all this could only be effected by the practice of moderation on the part of the people, and a respect for the public tranquillity; and they declared against any tumultuous demand or illegal usurpation, the most severe measures would be employed. Such language at this time was singularly offensive to the ears of the sovereign people. To obtain any thing in a legal manner had become unfashionable since the Storm Petition of the 15th of May; while popular tumults had become not only more agreeable and exciting, but vastly more efficacious. Insults and threats were immediately made use of; the word "*severity*" was cut out of the proclamation, and loud voices cried, "A decision must be given instantly, or we will interfere with '*severity*.' Our money we demand; the ministry must guarantee the shares."

---

* The author of the project, and a man of very ambiguous character.

The disorder increased, and the crowd at length broke into
the bureau in search of the minister, to force him to yield.
His life was threatened. The bureau was occupied by only
a few National Guards. The advancing mob, destroying all
windows and doors on their way, reached, finally, the apartment of the minister; but, fortunately, he had escaped. The
tumult became alarming. Toward noon the city was aroused,
and the National Guard called out. Later, the faubourgs became agitated. The watch-posts at the gates were re-enforced
by guards. At one o'clock the regular military entered the
city, and took positions on the *Hof* and *Juden Platz*. The
Academical Legion was also under arms, at the university.
No conflict took place, although every thing betokened a
dreadful struggle; when (on the 13th) the Diet undertook
a discussion of the matter, and concluded to appropriate a
million of florins* toward the immediate relief of those who
had suffered by that fraudulent speculation, and two millions,
besides, for the sustenance of all unemployed tradesmen of the
city. The publication of that measure, the compliance with
their unjust demand, should have been sufficient, it might
have been supposed, to satisfy the desires of the most unreasonable; but such was not the case; the excitement thus
produced was taken advantage of by the students and Radicals generally, and a plot commenced, having for its object to
crush the ministry, dissolve the Diet, and re-establish the late-
ly-suppressed "Committee of Security." Inflammatory addresses were made to the people. Every one favorable to the
movement wore upon his hat a placard bearing the inscription,
"Citizens of Vienna, the reinstallation of the Committee of
Security alone will save you!" From what the citizens were
to be saved, or by what they were threatened, no one stopped
to inquire; while a deputation of students, National Guards,
and citizens were dispatched to the ministry, to demand the immediate reinstallation of the committee. The ministry, on
this occasion, remained firm, and refused to receive the deputation. The Minister of War had that morning announced to
the Diet that he had been furnished with proof of the conspir-

---

* An Austrian florin is about forty-eight cents.

acy which was on foot in the city; that he had been advised, by some of the captains of the National Guard, that their men had refused obedience to the *rappel*, and would not appear unless sustained by the regular military; and he requested, therefore, permission of the Diet to call in the military to the support of the Guard, and the mutual defense of the city. The permission sought was accorded. The Diet forthwith pronounced itself in permanent session. The military were introduced, and took up threatening positions. The support of the workmen, owing to the lesson they had received on the 23d of August, was wanting. The summons to erect barricades met with no response; and the Legion and the agitators could not avoid the conviction that their plans had, this time at least, failed. The quiet of the city was restored without the loss of blood, except on the part of a grenadier, who was shot at and wounded as the troops were marching out of the gates, and returning to their barracks. The assassin escaped under cover of the night.

The shameful tumult of the 13th of September passed uninvestigated and unnoticed. The demagogues, who could not deny their defeat, were not at all discouraged. On the contrary, they proceeded with their task, but with increased boldness and activity, perceiving that their audacity had met with no more serious check. Insurrection now appeared without disguise. Hitherto it had been like the "pestilence which walketh in darkness;" but now it stalked abroad under the light of a meridian sun.

Manifestations which, under any well-organized government, would never have occurred, or, if attempted, have been instantly suppressed, now took place daily, under the eyes of imperial authority, without exciting the slightest attention.

The disaffected National Guard from the various faubourgs, and the workmen of the neighborhood, now dispatched deputation after deputation to the students, assuring them that they were "ready at any hour to sacrifice their lives for the Academical Legion."

Those Austrians, who, with more spirit than their fellows, provoked by the insults offered to the imperial flag, purposely adopted cockades of those colors, were pursued, attacked, and beaten by the Radicals each day in the streets, without being able to obtain from the authorities either redress for the past or security for the future.

A deputation arriving from Hungary is received at the landing-place of the steamer with tumultuous shouts, and conducted through the city with uninterrupted *eljens*.* Honored by the Democratic Union, the students, and National Guard, with a torch-light procession, the most inflammatory speeches were delivered on the occasion, in which it was declared that "the Austrians would share with the Hungarians liberty or death;" that "the Pragmatic Sanction had ceased to exist;" and that "the Hungarian and Austrian people alone were sovereign."

But a single step remained to be taken before the final blow, viz., to secure the co-operation of the peasantry; and this was accomplished, on the 24th of September, in the following manner. On that day occurred a meeting of all the various unions of the city, to be followed by a torch-light procession, in honor of a deputy named Küdlich, who had been successful in carrying through the Diet a bill for the relief of the peasantry, in having them emancipated from the serf-labor to which they had been subject. Although the emperor had recommended such a project as early as the month of April, the deputy Küdlich was, in the eyes of the Radicals, entitled to all the credit, and a thousand peasants joined the procession to do homage to their great benefactor. The mass addressed by Küdlich, and several other deputies of the left side, were openly summoned to resistance, and to a violation of all order and authority. The orators expressly avowed that a time might come when the liberal representatives of the country would need the assistance and support of the *Landsturm*,† and the peasantry were directly interrogated to *know* whether, in such an emergency, they could be relied on.

The news of the outbreak in Frankfort, which occurred on the 17th and 18th of September, now reached Vienna, to add fuel to the flame. The attempt to storm the Assembly, and to proclaim a republic, failed through the intervention of Austrian and Prussian troops from Mayence; but two distinguish-

---

* Hungarian *vivats*. † Peasant soldiers.

ed deputies and members of the government were brutally assassinated. The affair was extolled in the "Radical," edited by the ill-fated Dr. Becher,* as a noble act of the public will, barbarously suppressed by military despotism; and the hope was expressed that, Antæus-like, the German people would rise with renewed energies to the struggle, and that the inhabitants of Vienna would not be slow in imitating so laudable an example. This open summons to rebellion passed, however, unnoticed by the government.

Affairs were rapidly approaching a climax. On the 22d and 25th of September, the emperor issued, in Schönbrunn, proclamations in relation to Hungarian affairs, and in which he expresses his determination to oppose the movements in progress in that kingdom with all possible energy. But, strange to say, despite these manifestoes, in which he characterized the conduct of the Hungarians as insurrectionary, volunteer corps were formed in Vienna, in the actual presence of all his authorities, for the purpose of rendering aid to the Hungarian cause. The Aula entered most enthusiastically into the movement, and formed a corps which was dispatched to the relief of their Hungarian brethren. Amid the acclamations of the people, several divisions of volunteer corps, with that from the Academical Legion, left Vienna, toward the end of the month, for Pesth; and it was by one of these volunteers that the High Commissioner of his majesty, Count Lamburg, was recognized after his arrival at Pesth, and there inhumanly murdered.

A dark cloud overhung the city. It daily grew more ominous. All saw and felt that it must soon burst upon their devoted heads, and yet, spell-bound, no one attempted to avert or prevent the catastrophe. All authority was paralyzed; the peaceable and well-disposed were disheartened; the agitators alone, joyful and active, like storm-birds of the ocean, seemed to welcome the approaching tempest, and to be inspired by a war of the elements, which strews death and desolation on its path.

All was now prepared for carrying their projects into effect; for striking a blow at the head of imperial authority in the capital which would extinguish the remaining symptoms of vitali-

---

* Shot upon the taking of Vienna, after the October Revolution.

ty that still lingered in the paralyzed body, and emancipate, as they thought, not only the capital, but the provinces from all submission to the imperial sceptre. That event occurred on the 6th of October; and with it those awful scenes so memorable in the annals of Austria, and to which will be devoted the pages of a succeeding chapter.

The origin, development, and conclusion of the March Revolution in Vienna are full of instruction. Nothing could have been more laudable than the first efforts of the people, if not to rid themselves of the oppression under which they labored, at least to acquire those essential ingredients of freedom enjoyed by other enlightened nations, and loudly demanded by the advanced spirit of the age. Their first demands, viz., for freedom of the press, liberty to bear arms, and a Constitution, were just and reasonable; the entire body of the people united in the application; the appeal could not be resisted, and the monarch yielded to the popular will. The wisdom, however, which enables its possessor to use political power, and not abuse it, is one of the rarest acquisitions of mankind, and can be gained only by many ages of well-regulated industry and experienced freedom. Such privileges, therefore, can not with safety be extended to the population where the nation is just emerging from the fetters of servitude, where they have never before enjoyed any political advantages, and have always lived under a despotism in ignorance of their rights. It would seem to be the intention of Nature, that the power of the people should increase as society advances; but it is not her will that this increase should take place in such manner as to convulse the state, and ultimately extinguish the freedom of the people. All improvements that are really beneficial, all changes which are destined to be lasting, are gradual in their progress.*

---

* "It is by suddenly increasing the powers of the lower orders that the frame of society is frequently endangered, because the immediate effect of such a change is to unsettle men's minds, and bring into full play the most visionary and extravagant ideas of the most desperate and ambitious men. If there be any one conviction which has united the suffrage of all the greatest statesmen and most profound political reasoners—of Aristotle, Bacon, Montesquieu, and Burke—it is that all great political changes should be gradual and continuous, wrought out so as not to supersede, but to harmonize with preceding institutions, and so that there

The privileges conceded by the sovereign, although containing many defects in their terms, as was most natural to inexperienced legislators, were found, nevertheless, to include more freedom than the people were prepared for, and, like deadly weapons in the hands of the unskillful, facilitated their destruction instead of contributing to their defense.* The law relative to the press, though objectionable in the unreasonable amount of "caution-money" demanded, and the superior guards it threw around the members of the imperial family, nevertheless allowed too much freedom for those who had always written and read under a censorship that supervised even the most trivial advertisement; the columns of their numerous prints, therefore, instead of being devoted to the cause of legal order, were prostituted to the most incendiary and abusive attacks both of the government and the people, and excited constant rebellion and outrage.† The important right to bear arms, not only for their own personal defense, but the high privilege of being themselves the defenders of the state in the hour of peril, which would have enabled the government to dispense with a hireling soldiery, whose arms might at any moment have been turned against their own defenseless bosoms; and the immense amount of taxes of which they would thus have been relieved by constituting themselves the bulwark of the country, were considerations entirely lost sight of; and those very arms confided to them by the government for its own defense, were, on the very first occasion they were used, turned against constituted authority.

The idea once prevailed that anarchy was little to be apprehended when the armed body reckoned soldiers in every house, and on every floor in the peasant's hut, as well as the rich man's *château;* but experience has dispelled the delusion, and proved that an immense mass of armed men often become a prey to disturbing passions, and, instead of suppress-

---

shall not only be no solution of continuity in the series of political developments, but even no visible danger of it."—*Alison.*

* Solon, when asked if he had given the best laws to Athens, remarked, the best it could bear.

† Many of the new prints, instead of touching political subjects, did nothing but attack private character, and that often of the most unobtrusive and estimable citizens.

ing disorder and violence, are themselves its frequent promoters.

There is no instance on record where a National Guard, established upon the close of a Revolution, has remained entirely true and loyal to the government by which it was armed. The only situation in which a citizen soldier becomes of any efficiency to the country is where (as is the case of the militia in the United States) he is a part of the government, and so identified with the institutions of the country that their destruction would inevitably involve his own ruin. These Guards, moreover, have seldom proved efficacious in opposing the violence of the rabble. In the last century, in Paris, they were the passive spectators of the cruelties daily enacted before their eyes; and in February, 1848, they stood aloof, neither making, resisting, nor even directing the Revolution, but only paralyzing the regular army, to which they owed their escape from instant annihilation.

The Constitution granted to the Austrian people contained many of the elements of freedom. The ministers were to be responsible; the emperor could dissolve the Diet; but, in such case, must convoke a new one in ninety days; the private citizens were guaranteed individual liberty, freedom of worship and of the press, the right of association, of petition, and of emigration; liberty of trade, open courts of justice, and trial by jury. The document was indisputably loose and defective; but, it should be recollected, it was merely an *outline*.* Objections might fairly be made to the composition of the Upper Chamber, which was to consist of princes of the blood and an indefinite number of counselors, some elected by the people, others nominated by the crown. But it was expressly understood that the whole scheme was to be subject to revision by the assembled representatives of the nation, and for their judgment it should have been reserved. Once promulgated, it should have been adhered to, until the sentiments of the people could be ascertained in a fair and legitimate way. Instead of that, it was virtually abandoned by the excision of its princi-

---

* The instrument possessed all the advantages of a *charte octroyée* and an ordinary and popular Constitution; since, though given by the sovereign, it was to be revised and corrected by the people.

pal features at the command of a mob of fanatical youths. An attempt at intimidation, which it was the bounden duty of the government to treat as a riot, and to put down at any cost, was submitted to as an expression of the paramount will of the people.

This was a fatal error on the part of the government; it was not the impulse of enlightened patriotism. "The love of real freedom," says Alison, "may always be distinguished from the passion for popular power. The one is directed to objects of practical importance and the redress of experienced wrongs, and the other aims at visionary improvements and the increase of popular influence. The one complains of what has been felt, the other anticipates what may be gained; disturbances arising from the first subside, when the evils from which they spring are removed; troubles, originating in the second, magnify with every victory which is achieved. The experience of evil is the cause of agitation from the first; the love of power the source of convulsions from the last."

It was a profound remark of Sir James Macintosh, that "political constitutions are *not made, but grow.*"

Had the people been content to try the Constitution offered them by the emperor, they might, after witnessing it in practical operation, judge better of its defects; while their increasing experience in legislation would have enabled them to make sound and wholesome amendments.

The people, in short, were not prepared for so great and sudden a change. "It is necessary," says Montesquieu, "that people's minds should be prepared for the reception even of the best laws." The evils latent in the most promising contrivances can only be discerned upon trial, and are best provided for as they arise. Rapid and extensive innovations, suddenly effected, even though, abstractly, for the better, change too rapidly the habits and associations of the national mind in relation to its institutions. The sudden introduction of even a better Constitution is not sure to carry with it that great element of political excellence, *stability;* and the reason is, that such stability is founded less upon ideas of theoretical perfection than upon association and habit.*

* Edinburgh Review.

Not only was the change too sudden a one, but the people themselves were not adapted for it, either in education or habit. A population thus place-ridden and police-governed, where the people were looked upon as an animal mass, created for the will and pleasure of the state, it may readily be conceived, was totally unfitted for self-government. In our ardent enthusiasm in the cause of liberty, we are apt, in the United States, to assimilate the late revolutions in Europe with our own struggle for independence, and to think that there, as with us, it is only necessary to throw off the yoke of the tyrant, and the people would be found perfectly prepared for the enjoyment of all the rights of freedom; but a greater error never was committed. Such opinions are held by persons who forget that our ancestors sprang from the most free country in the world—a country that had existed for near two centuries under a Constitution guaranteeing to them the *Habeas Corpus*, trial by jury, and all the other essential elements of freedom. Our ancestors, also, could not bear even the restraints of this government; which was considered, on that side of the water, as a perfect prodigy of freedom; and hence they fled to this Western wilderness, to avoid the restraints which they found insupportable there. It is a fact, too, the truth of which subsequent events fully corroborate, that our ancestors left their homes beyond the water with the settled plan and fixed determination to establish, on the soil of America, a separate government—a government which, while it should embrace all the liberal portions of the British Constitution, should still be free from the unjust restraints and oppressive features of that instrument.

Civil independence was as truly the object of our ancestors in emigrating to America as religious liberty. At any rate, that the one was considered the essential means of securing the other, was evident from the fact that, in the early charters which they brought with them, for the original government of the colonies, *independence* was most dextrously grafted.* It can, then, be easily conceived that, with a people thus accustomed to the enjoyment of liberty—thus familiar with all

---

* Charter of the Colony of Massachusetts Bay.

M

the rights of man—it was only necessary to throw off the yoke of Great Britain, and they were quite prepared for the enjoyment of rational liberty, quite able to undertake the difficult task of self-government. But how widely different is the situation of the unfortunate people in Europe who have always existed under the iron sceptre of despotism; where the only law is the tyrant's will; where the education of the people, so far as they enjoyed any instruction at all, was so carefully guarded by the government, that not one ray of liberty ever penetrated their benighted minds; where they could not even define the word; and where their only conception of it was *licentiousness*, or the freedom to do any thing and every thing which inclination or interest might dictate.

One of the most talented of the Radical leaders in Vienna—one who afterward paid the forfeit of his life for the extravagance of his opinions—was heard to say to an American,* " We wish no such republic as you have in the United States; we wish something original; we wish a government where there shall not only be an equality of rights and of rank, but an equality of property, and an equality of every thing." Another influential Radical, one of the celebrated Council of Fifty-two, to whom, for a season, was committed all the affairs of the German Confederation, remarked to the same gentleman, " Sir, the only course left to us is, to raise the *guillotine*, and to keep it in constant and active operation; our only watchword should be, *Blood! blood! blood!* and the more blood that flows, the sooner shall we attain our liberties!" Such sentiments were not only freely promulgated, but even published. The *Reich Zeitung*, edited by two members of the Diet at Frankfort, in the number which appeared on the 24th of November, 1848, contains the following awful idea: " The destroying angel of the Revolution will pass over the world, and the word of mercy will become paralyzed upon the lips of the triumphant people!"

And that such ideas were not confined to words, the brutal murders of Prince Lichnowsky and Count Auerswald, at Frankfort; Count Latour, at Vienna; Count Lamburg, at

---

* The author.

Pesth; and Count Rossi, at Rome, will attest. Such atrocities were uncalled for, unsuited to the cause, and destructive of the very ends they were intended to accomplish. How different was the conduct of the people of the United States, when placed under similar circumstances! When the English colonies in America declared their independence of the mother-country, and dissolved "all connection between them and the crown of Great Britain," there were royal governors presiding, "in the name and by the authority" of the King of England, over each of the colonies. Were these mercenaries of a sovereign—these instruments of royalty—brutally murdered? their bodies hung up to lamp-posts, or dragged, perhaps, through the streets of a capital? Was even a hair of their heads touched? No! they were suffered to depart in peace; they were considered but the minions of power; and had the Americans descended so far as to soil their hands in their blood, it might not only have defeated the ends at which they aimed, but would have proved them unworthy of the blessing to which they aspired.

It is a fact which can not be contradicted, that there exists in every country in Europe a certain party more remarkable for its daring and its violence than for its numbers, which is the avowed enemy of all government, and of society itself. The free institutions of England, or the Republican novelties of France, are just as obnoxious to their animosity as the despotism of Austria or the autocracy of Russia. Alike under all forms of government, they deny the stringency of rights and the authority of law. To buy off their hostility by concessions, is but a sign of weakness. Instead of appearing before them at the window of the Tuileries, with the red cap of liberty on his head, as Louis the Sixteenth did, such fiends are rather to be treated in the manner suggested by the youth who witnessed the humiliating spectacle—"they should cut down the first five hundred with grape-shot, and the remainder would soon take to flight"—and who lived to put his principles in practice on the very spot. It was Napoleon Bonaparte. Whether living under a monarchy or a republic, society must defend itself against such men, either by the penal code or the cannon. The great bane of all European governments is that class of population inseparable from most European capitals ; who feel not a particle of interest either in the government or its institutions ; to whom any political change, as it could not be for the worse, must be for the better, and who consequently are ever ready, at the call of a foreign emissary or a domestic agitator, to take up arms against the government. Destitute alike of property, education, and morals, they become the most willing and efficient instruments of destruction.* Had the students of Vienna not held at their beck and call a troop of fifty thousand, at least, of such *proletaria*, they could never have created those disturbances, wrested from the government all its authority, and kept the city in a state of continued and alarming excitement. The government is, in a great measure, to blame for this evil, in the ignorance in which the masses are kept, and in their deprivation of the means of a more honorable and independent existence, where they are not allowed to pursue any trade, however humble, without leave of the government ; and until there is a change of policy on the part of the rulers, one can hardly be expected on the part of the subjects.

One of the principal causes of the failure of the Revolution was the destruction of that over-ruling power so necessary for the preservation of order in all governments—the failure to enforce upon the people the adoption of those salutary measures indispensable to their existence. This sentiment was expressed by General Washington just before the meeting of the Convention, at Philadelphia, that formed the Constitution : " We have probably had too good an opinion of human nature

---

* Had there been no such population in London or Paris, the Chartist demonstration in the former, however feeble, or the insurrection of June in the latter, however terrible, would not have occurred. Fortunately for the United States, they are free from such a danger ; for, according to the principles of our political system, every man is a part of the government, and its destruction would involve his own ruin. All that he possesses, be it more or less, he holds by no other tenure than that of the permanency of the institutions under which he lives. We have not, and never can have, as long as our present form of government endures, one class of inhabitants who will have less interest in its institutions than another. And we have not, and never can have, for centuries, the class of population who are the bane of Europe, with such an ocean-bound continent as we possess. The Mississippi Valley alone, it is computed, will contain a population of seventy-five millions, when it becomes as thickly settled as England.

in forming our *Confederation*. Experience has taught us
that men will not adopt and carry into execution measures
the best calculated for their own good without the intervention of a coercive power." But the great body of the Republicans of Europe are as remote from the principles of the great
founder of the American commonwealth as they are from the
purity of his personal character. This coercive power, in the
shape either of monarchy or of executive government, is precisely what the Revolution overthrew; and, until it is restored, by a resuscitation of imperial authority as in Vienna,
or a substitution of another power as in France, no advances
could be made toward order and government.

Another cause which impeded the success of the movement
party was the total inefficiency of the National Assemblies.
Nowhere did they seem to understand, with any precision, the
nature of their duties or the limits of their powers. Where
they were *constituent* assemblies, they encroached on the province of permanent legislation; where they were *legislative*
bodies, they endeavored to assume the functions of the executive. Their whole history was one pertinacious effort to concentrate, in their own hands, all the powers of the state; and,
in the course of their attacks on the executive, they contrived
often, by demands which no rulers with the least comprehension of, or respect for their own position, could dream of
conceding, to put themselves so completely in the wrong, that
public sympathy had deserted them long before their fall. Another mistake, committed by the friends of freedom in 1848,
was the mixing up of two objects, wholly distinct in themselves, and of which the desirableness was by no means equally
clear—constitutional rights and national unity. Both in Italy
and Germany, instead of concentrating their efforts on the attainment of free institutions for each separate state, they complicated their cause, and distracted and weakened their party,
by raising the standard of freedom and that of unity at the
same time.* The two objects united were hopeless, for each
of itself was gigantic. Representative assemblies, a free press,
an open administration of justice, were boons which every one
could appreciate, and which every one was willing to fight for.

* North British Review.

The creation of a great state out of the various nationalities of Italy and Germany respectively was a dream of enthusiastic theorists; and, however important or beneficial it might ultimately have proved, was not universally desired, and it was surrounded by difficulties which, if not insuperable, demanded at least a peaceful era and patient toil for their solution.

In every country the friends of movement committed precisely the same series of blunders. They had not yet learned the lesson, now taught them, alike by the successes and the failures of that memorable year, that concessions wrung from sovereigns form the surest basis of a nation's freedom; that it is only by making the most of these, by consolidating and using them, not by pushing them to excess, that constitutional liberty is secured; and that to press victory so far as to drive away the sovereign, is, in nine cases out of ten, to resign themselves, bound hand and foot, to the dictation of the mob. They became excited, instead of contented by the vast concessions they had won; they grasped at more, instead of employing and securing that which they had gained.

They showed by their attitude, their proposals, and their language, that they were neither intellectually nor morally *masters of their position;* they were not educated up to the requirements of their new station; their minds could not rise to a full comprehension of its duties, nor their consciences to a clear comprehension of its responsibilities; they alarmed where they should have soothed; disgusted where they should have conciliated; dared where they should have shrunk; and, like "fools, rushed in where angels fear to tread."*

They did not understand the business, nature, and limits of constitutional freedom. They committed the fatal error. in their position so difficult to avoid, of tolerating, and encouraging even, rather than suppressing popular turbulence and mob dictation; of relaxing the arm of the law at the very moment when its strength and its sternness required to be most plainly felt. By these errors and deficiencies, they signed the death-warrant of their own ascendency, by convincing the wise and patriotic that liberty was not safe with them; the proprietary body that property was not secure in their hands; and

* North British Review.

the commercial classes that credit was insecure under their guardianship.

It is impossible, however, that so many experiments should have been tried, so many mistakes made, so many failures incurred, so many catastrophes brought about, without leaving behind many sad but salutary convictions. The great lesson which, it may be hoped, the friends of liberty and progress will have learned from the events of 1848 is this—that constitutional freedom must be gained by degrees, not by one desperate and sudden effort. The people must be content to conquer their political and civil rights step by step, as not only the easiest and surest, but, in the end, the speediest way. Their true and safe policy is to accept and make the most of all concessions which either a sense of danger or a sense of justice may dictate to their rulers; to remember that these, small though they may seem to one party, doubtless appear great to the other, and may have cost much self-sacrifice; and that, at all events, they are bound to use them diligently but soberly, to grow familiar with them, become masters of them; to acquire by practice dexterity in their use, and thus consolidate and secure their possession. Let them gradually, as opportunity shall serve, use these concessions as the stepping-stone to more; but never, save in the last extremity, supersede the executive authority, or call in the mob. Any attempt on the part of the people to snatch, in the hour of victory, more than they know how to wield, more than they can use well, is a retrograde and fatally false step; it is, in fact, playing the game of their opponents. If they employ their newly-acquired rights and institutions in such a manner as to show that they do not understand them and can not manage them, and that, therefore, public tranquillity and social security are likely to be endangered by mistakes growing out of their excitement and inexperience—the great body of sober and peaceful citizens are quick to take alarm, and to carry back the material and moral weight of their sympathies to the side of the old system, however despotic may have been its character. The just and true views, when expressed in the language of a principle, are simply these: all wise and educated people will prefer a free to a despotic government, *ceteris paribus*, i. e., order and security being the bases in both cases; but the worst theoretical government which assures these essential predicates will be, and ought to be, preferred to the best theoretical government which endangers them. The majority of the sober and influential classes will always be found on the side of that party which best understands *the practical act of administration,* however defective or erroneous may be its fundamental principles, however medieval may be its name. If the year 1848 has taught this truth to the movement party, the cause of rational freedom will have gained incalculably by its first disasters.

CHAPTER II.

SINCE the fall of Napoleon, the power of Austria over Italy has been predominant.

In 1816, the King of Naples was prohibited, by an engagement with Austria, from granting a Constitution to his subjects. Austria, shortly after, exacted a treaty to the same effect from the King of Sardinia, and from every prince in Italy. The Neapolitans having, notwithstanding, established a Constitution in 1820, Austria immediately suppressed it by force of arms. She interfered, in 1821, in Piedmont. In 1831, and again in 1832, for the same object, and to realize a similar purpose, she bore down upon the Papal States. The native governments, every where enslaved and trammeled by Austrian agents, Italy became little less than a Cis-Alpine Austria. On the 14th of June, 1846, Cardinal Mastai was elected to fill the pontifical chair, and assumed the appellation of Pius the Ninth. The Pope, a plain, upright man, who could not foresee the consequences of his bounty, immediately commenced the work of reform and regeneration, with a view to relieve Italy from the foreign domination and bad government under which she labored. The sovereigns of two of the best administered of the Italian states determined on following the example of the pontiff. They wisely resolved that there should be no room for invidious comparisons between the condition of their own subjects and that of their Italian neighbors.

Austria put herself, as of old, at the head of the stationary faction, in which she was joined by the King of Naples, and the Dukes of Modena and Parma.

No part of the Italian people were more keenly alive to the difference between a national and improving government, and a foreign despotic oppression, than the inhabitants of Lombardy and Venice, who were immediately subject to Austria. While they themselves were left under the galling yoke of the Viennese bureaucracy, they had now only to look over their border and behold the Swiss on one side free; the subjects of the Pope, of the King of Sardinia, and of the Grand Duke of Tuscany on the other, governed by native Italians, and rapidly advancing in their political condition.   The grievances of which the Lombards particularly complained, and which it is necessary to understand before contemplating the struggle, appeared in a manifesto issued to the European nations after the expulsion of the Austrians from Milan.   It is as follows :

" The Austrian government levied immoderate taxes on our property, on our persons, and on necessary articles ; it extorted from us the means by which alone it was saved from that bankruptcy, to the brink of which it was brought by its bad and dishonestly administered financial system ; it forced on us shoals of foreigners, avowed functionaries and secret spies, eating our substance, administering our affairs, judging our rights, without knowing either our language or our customs ; it imposed on us foreign laws, inextricable from their multiplicity, and an intricate, endless system of proceeding in criminal cases, in which there was nothing either true or solemn except the prison and the pillory, the executioner and the gallows ; it spread round us ensnaring nets of civil and ecclesiastical, military and judicial regulations, all converging to Vienna, which alone engrossed the monopoly of thought, of will, and of judgment ; it forbade the development of our commerce and our industry, to favor the interests of other provinces, and of government manufactures, the speculations of Viennese oligarchs ; it submitted our municipal institutions, the boast of our country and the proof of national good sense, to a petty, harassing control, conceived for fiscal purposes, and tending only to fetter us ; it enslaved religion, and even public benevolence of its free course, making it subject to administrative interference, and turning it to an engine of government.   It was after endless difficulties, and only after having recourse to the lowest precautions, that private individuals were permitted to help the public wants, and preserve from contagion and corruption the poor abandoned to themselves in the streets, in their hovels, or in prison. It seized the property of minors, by forcing guardians to invest it in public securities, which were to be dealt with arbitrarily and mysteriously by secret agents of the government; it subjected the liberal arts to the most vexatious restraints; it persecuted native knowledge; it raised the most ridiculous objections and the most odious difficulties against printing or importing printed foreign books; it persecuted and entrapped our most distinguished men, and raised to honor slavish understandings; it systematized the sale of conscience, and organized an army of spies; it encouraged secret informations, and made suspicions the rule of its proceedings; it gave the police full power over liberty, life, and property, and threw the patriot into the same prison with the assassin."

The first public indication* of unanimity on the part of the Lombards, subsequent to the declared division of the rulers of Italy into those who were in favor of, and those who were opposed to reform, openly appeared when the new Archbishop of Milan took possession of his see, early in September, 1847. On this occasion the armed police were let loose on the people, who had given no other provocation than by singing hymns in praise of Pius the Ninth. The course pursued by the new Pope had revived the ancient spirit of nationality throughout the entire peninsula; and the imprudent step of the entry of the imperial troops into one of the Italian cities called that feeling into active operation, and the occupation of Ferrara was the signal for a general rising, not only in Rome, but also in Florence, Bologna, Leghorn, Lucca, and Genoa, without regard to their distinct governments, against the Emperor of Austria, and in favor of the sovereign pontiff.

The population of the Lombard and Venetian provinces were not behind hand in this national movement. Some time previous, the students at the University of Pavia and Padua had become particular objects of dislike to the Austrian officers, who attacked and murdered them in a cowardly manner. Meanwhile, the authorities of every description addressed pe-

---

* That of Ferrara had occurred a short time previous.

titions to the government, from which it should have taken seasonable warning.   On the contrary, it continued to irritate as well as to oppress the people; and even wearing a hat of a singular shape, or a waistcoat of a peculiar cut, or dressing the hair or the beard in a certain manner, reduced the police to despair.   The moment an edict was published against any remarkable fashion, another was universally adopted, equally remarkable and absurd.   These, it is true, were trifles; yet the tacit agreement on both sides, by the nation and the government, not to consider them as trifles, but as symbols of grave import, ought to have opened the eyes of the Austrians, and shown them their true position.*   The unanimous feeling of the Milanese was soon exhibited in a more alarming form.

Next to Rome, Milan, perhaps, is the most important city of Italy; more abundant in beautiful public buildings than Munich, and, on occasions, as animated as Paris.   The circuit of its line of ramparts is nearly ten miles.   Its situation is admirable for the interior commerce of Italy, communicating by canals with the Lakes Como and Maggiore, and with the River Po.   One of the most striking architectural entrances to any European city is the *Arco della Pace*, on the Simplon road.   One of the most superb cathedrals in the world is the well-known *Duomo*, with its hundred spires and three thousand statues, covering its exterior of florid Gothic with a marble army of saints.   The *La Scala*, with one exception only, the largest theatre in Europe; the *Circo*, the most complete and stately arena; the *Corso di Porta Orientale*, the noblest promenade in Italy, or rivaled alone by the *Corso* of Naples, and then only from the view it commands of the bay.   Milan abounds in charitable institutions, lyceums, and other places of education; and last, though by no means least, it possesses the celebrated Ambrosian Library.   Since the peace of 1815, the population of Milan has rapidly increased, perhaps doubled, and it now exceeds 150,000.

In their opposition to the Austrian government, and with a view to diminish the revenues of the imperial treasury, the citizens of Milan determined on abstaining from all use of tobac-

---

* Edinburgh Review.

co. At first a circular was distributed, in which the people were reminded that the Americans, as a prelude to the war of Independence, had refused to make use of tea brought them by the English, and, in accordance with that example, all good citizens were enjoined to discard tobacco, that article being a monopoly of the Austrian government. After this resolution, not content with simply abstaining from tobacco themselves, the populace attempted to suppress its use altogether, by treating with indignity and violence all persons found smoking.

On the 3d of January, an Austrian soldier encountering such treatment, a cigar being rudely snatched from his lips while quietly promenading the streets, he instantly returned and reported at the military quarters the circumstance which had occurred. The soldiers, incensed, immediately started forth in squads (some allege that they were sent out by their commanders), and paraded the streets with cigars in their mouths, with a view, doubtless, of inducing a repetition of the insult. One of these groups had not proceeded far when they encountered the mob, and met with the treatment which they had expected; whereupon, drawing their side-arms (which alone, fortunately, they had been permitted to wear) and charging the crowd, they killed eight persons and wounded about fifty.* Nothing serious afterward transpired, though several proclamations, issued both by the emperor and the viceroy, proved ineffectual in restoring the public tranquillity.

On the 6th of February, a grand fête took place in honor of the success of the Sicilians and Neapolitans, in having exacted of their monarch a Constitution.

Upon the frequent recurrence of these popular manifestations, the police demanded of the government the *jugement statuaire*,† or immediate judgment; that is, the power to try and to hang, without delay, all in the space of *two hours*. This regulation went into effect on Shrove Tuesday, at the commencement of the Ambrosian Carnival, which, prolonged

---

* Agreeably to some accounts, as many as sixty-one persons were killed; six of whom were under eighteen years, five over sixty years, and one (a counselor in the Court of Appeals) seventy-four years.

† The Judicium Statuarium was signed by the emperor on the 14th of November, 1847, and not put in force until the 22d of February, 1848.

four days, constituted at Milan a brilliant fête, and made the
city a rendezvous for many of the highest families of Lombardy and Piedmont.   Radetzky caused the chateau to be
fortified ; and, under his advice, Count Spaur, the governor,
and the viceroy, with his family, quitted Milan, on the 16th
of March, escorted by five hundred hussars (he had previously
removed all his property and effects).   Terror seized the unfortunate city.   Females trembled, for the situation of things
became terrible ; still no one dreamed of flying, as the order
had been given to remain.   At the same time, all the tidings
which reached them from abroad tended to excite the imagination of the inhabitants.   On one day it was reported that
Palermo had arisen ; on another, that Naples, Florence, and
Turin had proclaimed a Constitution ; then came the news of
the Revolution in Paris.   It was evident that the day of combat rapidly approached.   The Austrian authorities taking no
steps to repress them, the disorders daily increased.   The may-
or, Casati, presented himself, accompanied by a large number
of respectable inhabitants, to Count Fiquelmont (the nobleman
who afterward, for a short time, filled Prince Metternich's
place), and "remonstrated against these abominations."   Fiquelmont, who had been sent to Milan from Vienna on a special
mission to soothe the Italians, told the mayor that he had only
power to propose arrangements, but not to order them, and
that the utmost that he and the governor, who was present at
the interview, could undertake to do, was to lay the matter
before Radetzky.   On calling upon Radetzky, and presenting
the subject to his consideration, he replied to Fiquelmont and
the others, " The *injured* troops can not be restrained.   If
the municipal authorities will answer for the tranquillity of
the inhabitants, I will keep the soldiers in their barracks for
eight days."   It might have been expected that the government would have taken measures to prevent such occurrences,
and to protect its unarmed citizens from the violence of its
troops ; but such was not the case.   The emperor was made
to sign a letter to the Viceroy of Lombardy, the pith of which
admitted of no mistake.   " I perceive that there is in the
Lombardo-Venetian kingdom a faction inclined to overthrow
the political state of the *country*.   I have done all that was

necessary for the happiness and satisfaction of my Italian provinces. I am not inclined to do more. I rely on the known bravery and fidelity of my army."

This was, in so many words, approving what had happened, threatening worse for the future, and taking away all hope. It is never wise to drive a nation to extremities.

After the publication of the letter of the emperor to the viceroy, the Austrian police, at Milan, arrested a great number of persons, banished several, and obliged others to flee the country. The course of the government was impolitic in the extreme. To discover who the disaffected were, they resorted to the expedient of encouraging the citizens to petition the government against any grievance under which they might labor; and such as had the independence to do it were immediately subjected to the severe *surveillance* of the police.* Others, whose disaffection could not be proved, but whom it was thought necessary to destroy, were disposed of in the following manner, suggested by the director of the police: publications were made in foreign prints, in which it was obscurely hinted that the individual was an Austrian spy, whose endeavor it was to compromise his friends, and sell them to Austria.† At the point to which things had now advanced, the only remaining question with the people was one of expediency and time; that of right they regarded as settled. It was their right, they considered, to free themselves from a government which not only failed to protect the people under its rule, but was their greatest enemy.

The proclamation of a republic in France hastened the crisis, which the departure of the viceroy and governor, leaving the city to the tender mercies of the police and military, still more accelerated; and by the unexpected tidings of the Revolution in Vienna, the climax was precipitated.

On the evening of the 17th, a dispatch was received by the vice-governor, giving intelligence of the first outbreak in Vienna, and the excitement in Milan became intense. By daylight the next morning, placards were printed, and pasted on the corners of the streets, apprising the people of the occur-

---

* Nassani, deputy from the city of Bergamo to the government of Milan.
† M. Cesare Cautri, an author well known in Italy by his writings.

rences in the capital, and the concessions which had been made
by the emperor.   On the morning of the 18th, the *municipium*
and the *congregations* (or municipal authorities), headed by
the mayor, Casati, and accompanied by the Archbishop of Milan, presented to the organs of the government, assembled in
the palace, petitions praying the installation of a political magistracy, under the direction of the *municipium*, the annulling of
some severe laws, the liberation of political prisoners, the election of deputies, and the establishment of a National Guard.

The petitions were refused; and the excited masses stormed,
upon that news, the palace of the government.

The guard on duty at the palace, alarmed at the violence
of the crowd, fired one charge, as some assert, above the heads
of, and not at the people.   In fact, no one was wounded; but
such an impression made, that, had the discharge been repeated, the multitude would have been dispersed; but, at the moment of wavering, a courageous youth, not more than sixteen,
drew out a pistol and fired at the soldiery, exclaiming, at the
same time, *Viva l'Italia!*   The shot and the cry had a magic-
al effect; the crowd rushed forward, and in one moment the
guard was overpowered, O'Donnell made prisoner, and the tricolor banner placed on the balcony of the hotel.   O'Donnell,
being convinced that further opposition was useless, drew up
an order of the day establishing a National Guard, and agreed
to accompany the *podesta* and the people to the municipality,
for the purpose of having it countersigned and published by
that body.   No sooner, however, had he and the *podesta* left
the hotel, than a strong patrol-guard of Croats was seen advancing, who, without one word of explanation, discharged
their pieces, and killed several persons.   The crowd did not
fly; but, every person rushing into the houses at each side of
the street, flew to the upper windows and roofs, and in one instant a storm of tiles, pokers, tables, and every missile that
could be laid hold of, fell on the heads of the devoted Croats.
The effect, as described by an eye-witness, must have been
ludicrous.   No sooner did these savage troops, who, in regular
array, would face a battery, feel the weight of the falling tiles,
than they broke, abandoned their ranks, and rapidly dispersed.

The rest of the story has been told.   Radetzky hesitated;

and, instead of sending all his force to clear the streets, withdrew his men within their respective barracks; and by the time he had made up his mind, the affair was decided, the city barricaded, and it was impossible to retake it without a bombardment.

In order to appease the assailing mass, some printed placards had been issued, but no effect was produced, until a proclamation, hastily published, without legal form, was circulated, in which the establishment of a provisional government and the abolition of the police were declared. The rest of the day, and the night between the 18th and 19th, was principally devoted to the construction of barricades throughout the city, in which the first and richest citizens of Milan were engaged, giving advice, and distributing money and provisions among the lower classes, and fanning the glimmering spark into a flame. The enthusiasm was universal. Those who had no fire-arms to defend the barricades with, provided themselves with all sorts of missiles to throw on the soldiers from the roofs of the houses. Alarmed by the tocsin, which sounded from all parts, occupied, at the same time, with the necessary task of keeping open their communications, and especially of saving the residences of the officers in the city, as well as the families of German *employées*, the Austrian army could not accomplish all that the exigency required. Many important objects were overlooked; and two millions of francs in silver, deposited in the military chests of different bureaus, were forgotten. Even the venerable Radetzky, in the utmost haste, scarcely saved himself, leaving behind his waistcoat and his sword, which had served in so many battles. The chateau, or castle, became his refuge. This massive square building formed the centre of an ancient fortress, of which Napoleon had razed the exterior polygon, so that it now remained separated from the town by a vast esplanade. From thence, and by the bastions which commanded the city and the neighboring country, Radetzky surrounded Milan with the two wings of his army. At each barrier he had placed a mass of troops and of artillery, and advanced his men by the largest and most direct streets to the heart of the city, where he held possession, for three days, of the Cathedral, the Royal Palace, the Palace of Justice, of Marine, the Police, the Hôtel

N

de Ville, and many of the military barracks. The Tyrolian riflemen, posted upon the marble needles of the Cathedral, amused
themselves in shooting, at hazard, the men and women as they
passed in the streets, and even in the interior of the houses
which they thus overlooked.

The parts of the city where the insurrection had made the
greatest progress were not at all in communication with each
other—that which, by mere chance, contained the head-quarters of the mayor, having the form of a horse-shoe, extended
by the two streets of Monte and Durino; from thence they developed themselves in all directions, and, being wide and thin-
ly-populated streets, difficult to barricade and to defend, were
consequently commanded by the fire of the troops.   During
the first night the head-quarters were not protected on the side
of the Porta Nuova, except by two feeble barricades and by
about sixty young men, who formed themselves into five sections, and who underwent the drill during the whole night to
prepare themselves for the combat of the ensuing day, scarcely
half of them having ever fired a gun.   It was calculated that,
during the first night, there was not in line more than from
three to four hundred guns of every description, many families
having previously sent their arms into the country, to avoid delivering them up to the police.   At eight o'clock in the evening,
Radetzky summoned the municipality to disarm the National
Guard.   "Unless this is done," said he, "to-morrow I will
resort to bombardment, sack, and all the other means of reducing a rebellious city, having at my disposition a drilled
army of one hundred thousand men and two hundred pieces
of cannon."

He also ordered General Wohlgemuth, who commanded the
troops of that circle, to take the barricades by storm, whereupon the government palace was reoccupied.   Meanwhile the
engagement had begun throughout the city.   From all the
windows the inhabitants commenced firing upon the troops,
and throwing upon them all sorts of projectiles from the roofs
of the houses.   General Rath, who proceeded to the interior
of the city to occupy the *Place* and the main government offices, had to fight for every barricade.   The troops, however,
took them all, and arrived at their different destinations.   The

evening approached, the fight in the streets, or rather, as Marshal Radetzky said, "the firing upon our troops had already continued for six hours," when the field-marshal concluded to take the building of the municipality at all hazards, and to destroy, if possible, the principal nerve of the revolt by seizing the provisional government.   The engagement continued four hours, as the position was defended with great obstinacy by the people.   At length, the carpenters ordered to destroy the gates of the building being killed or wounded as fast as they approached, Marshal Radetzky determined to force the gates by means of twelve-pounders, in which he succeeded, carrying off two hundred and fifty prisoners, among them many persons of the highest rank, who had gone there to enlist.   The prisoners and arms found in the building were forwarded to the castle.   After the capture of the Hôtel de Ville, at ten o'clock, the streets were cleared of people, and tranquillity restored for the night.   Sincerely concerned on account of the feeble means of defense with which the city was provided, and especially the exposed situation of the mansion Vidiserti, now become the head-quarters of the provisional government, and whose members might, like the persons who had gone to the *Hôtel de Ville* to enlist, be taken prisoners, the quarters of the government were changed to the mansion of Count Charles Taverna, a house sufficiently large, and not distant from that of Vidiserti.   To reach it one had only to cross the Bigli, a street narrow and winding, and which could be easily barricaded.   The garden of this mansion communicated with many other gardens, and the front of it being surrounded, there would be time sufficient, in case of danger, to escape to another point.

The key of the grating which opened opposite to the house of Manzoni was obtained, and a hole constructed in the wall of the garden of Belgiojoso, and sentinels placed upon the walls of the other gardens.   The mansion Vidiserti became thence a kind of advanced redoubt, behind which were traced many successive lines of defense, with sure points of retreat. These dispositions were taken a few moments before the first rays of day appeared.   A moment after, the sound of the tocsin was heard, followed by the cry " To arms !"

It was apprehended by the leaders of the insurgents that the reflections of the night might chill the ardor and dampen the spirits of the people, but these apprehensions were soon dispelled, as they were now seen rushing with enthusiasm to the barricades.

Sunday, 19*th March.* — In conformity with the phrase, " There are no Sabbaths in revolutions," the next morning the firing was renewed on both sides with the greatest obstinacy. The feebly-armed citizens had a severe task in opposing, with any effect, the regular troops, who still occupied the castle, the barracks, archducal palace, and other important positions, from whence was maintained a well-directed fire against the opposite houses ; while the artillery, placed at the head of the several leading *corsos*, and keeping up a heavy discharge, endeavored to batter down the formidable barriers constructed across every street. Fortunately, however, for the people, the communication was maintained by the insurgents in the whole interior of the city, and the sharp-shooters, creeping from house to house, got eventually within reach of the soldiers who served the guns, and brought them down one after another. It was quite remarkable to see the intelligence and ingenuity evinced by those brave sportsmen in mastering the fire of disciplined Austrian troops. The narrowest door-way afforded cover, a few fagots concealed an advance, until the troops were driven back, not knowing from whence they were attacked, and on the ground they retired from, a barricade was immediately thrown up ; the most costly furniture, bureaus, damask sofas, and even pianos, which the enthusiastic ladies most liberally contributed for the purpose, were employed in their construction, and the same system of annoyance again established.

As the ardor of the people increased, the moral courage of the troops became weakened, and at several points important posts were carried almost without combat. The general enthusiasm effected wonders. All houses were opened to receive the wounded, and to afford assistance to the struggling inhabitants. Even women and children labored in bearing to the tops of their houses stones, tiles, and other projectiles, to be thrown from thence on the heads of the devoted troops. The defense was conducted on the principle of mere instinct, and the people fought for the whole of that day as they had done on the preceding—without leaders, without direction—by a common accord in what each said, "He can not do wrong who brings down an Austrian." In the evening, general joy seemed to prevail on account of the successful resistance of the inhabitants; but, the city being again threatened with a bombardment, the Consul General of France assembled the other consuls, and, after a brief deliberation, addressed to Marshal Radetzky a "protest," in the names of their respective governments "against an act of such unnecessary violence."

20th March.—On the 20th the fighting was continued with unabated fury, and on both sides many victims fell. About two thousand barricades arose in different parts of the city. Carriages, omnibuses, and post-chaises upset; tables, boards, boxes filled with earth; large flagstones; in short, all things that could be used to form a barrier, were amassed together, and strong traces and heavy chains placed before them. And, as all these bulwarks were instantly manned by the brave people, whose blood was now thoroughly excited, the idea of the city's being obliged to capitulate to the force possessed by Radetzky seemed now at an end. The marshal continued to fire from the castle, and several people were killed by the cannonade; in like manner, the fire was kept up from the gates of the city, still occupied by the troops. By a glance at the plan of the city, it will be observed that an open space exists within the walls as well as outside. By that space the Imperial Generals Wohlgemuth and Clamm (unable longer to retain their posts in the interior of the city) kept up their communications; but their men were constantly picked off by the people, who fired from under cover of houses within, and from behind hedges and ditches without the walls. All the efforts of the people to get possession of the gates having as yet proved abortive, they were unable to receive any external assistance. The correspondence with the country was, however, kept up in an ingenious manner, by means of little balloons: letters and proclamations were dispatched in these aerial messengers, with entreaties to the persons among whom the balloons fell to see to their delivery. As the letters were sure to fall into friendly

hands, whichever way the wind carried the balloons, the commissions were faithfully executed. By these means, the people of the environs were invoked to take up arms, and to come
to the relief of the city. They were enjoined, also, to destroy
the roads leading to Verona and Mantua, so as to prevent the
arrival of re-enforcements, which Marshal Radetzky might call
for. Warned in this manner, the people flocked from all sides ;
if they were not strong enough to force the gates, kept up a
constant fire on the patrols and soldiers who appeared on the
bastions, and rendered the continuation of Radetzky's system
impossible.

On this day, Marshal Radetzky replied to the protest of the
foreign consuls, in substance, that the troops under his command had been attacked by the citizens without any notice or
provocation whatever ; that the people, by breaking into and
sacking the *Hôtel de Ville* and *du Gouvernement*, exacted of
the official chief (after killing the feeble guard placed there for
his protection) what it was not in his power to subscribe to,
and which alone were the attributes of the government. "It
depends, gentlemen," said the marshal, "on your influence
with the chiefs of the revolutionary government, to induce
them to abstain from any further acts of hostility ; for, as long
as I am attacked and my soldiers killed under my eyes, I shall
defend myself with the courage which is mainly inspired by
the manner in which we have been attacked, and by a proper
sentiment of duty to my troops. Nevertheless, out of respect
to the several governments, of which you are the organs, I am
willing to suspend the execution of the rigorous measures
which I mean to take against Milan until to-morrow, the 21st,
on condition that the same reserve will be exercised by the
opposite party. I await the result of your intervention before
I commence the renewal of my operations."

From this reply, it seemed evident that, as early as the
20th, after only two days' fighting, Radetzky would gladly have
come to any arrangement which would have been consistent
with his reputation ; and the consuls felt their position was
changed, and that, instead of asking favors from the marshal,
that they were called on by him to use their influence, for his
sake, with the leaders of the revolt. The consuls accordingly

addressed Radetzky a dispatch, at eight o'clock in the evening, informing him that they had consulted the municipal authorities, and requested an interview with the marshal, to communicate the results of their negotiations.   To which Radetzky replied by a communication, dated two A.M., and affixing an interview for seven o'clock the next morning.

21st March.—In consequence of this note, the consuls went to the castle, but they did so at the risk of their lives, as several shots were fired at them through mistake.   The Consul General of France, as spokesman, explained, at some length, that the troops, and not the people, at the Hôtel de Ville first commenced the firing; and then, after going into the immediate object of their visit, the interview was closed by a proposition of Marshal Radetzky, of an armistice of three days, provided the heads of the movement acceded to the arrangement.

The consuls next visited the Provisional Government (which had by this time been formed), and though at first the leaders were inclined to accept the armistice, yet, on a remark being made that a revolution once commenced should never be interrupted until full success was obtained, the proposal was definitely rejected, and the consuls communicated the result to the marshal in a note of that day.   When it was known that the armistice was refused, the inhabitants of Milan began to fear for their houses and property, and something like depression was visible; but in a few hours the gloom cleared off, every one hurried to his post, with gun, sword, stick, or any offensive weapon he could procure; and, from that hour, the favorable termination of the struggle was assured.   The people soon, by a vigorous assault, possessed themselves of the palace of the viceroy and the Duomo, on which they hoisted the Italian tricolor.   The general Prefecture of Police fell into the hands of the people, who pillaged it.   The family of the Director General, Torresani, and the famous Count Bolza, so abhorred by the Milanese, were captured in that hotel, but their persons were respected, and they were conducted as hostages to the Boromeo Palace.   At that time, the only public edifice still held by the troops was the hotel of the commander-in-chief,

which, owing to the brisk cannonading, all the efforts of the
people to take possession of it had proved fruitless.

22d March.—Again, on the morning of the 22d, the fight
was renewed more vigorously than ever. The Milanese, seconded by the people from the country, who had hastened to
their assistance, attacked the gates; but a formidable artillery baffled all their efforts. The troops, having been always
masters of the gates, had cut off all provisions from the city.
Beef was already fifty cents per pound. The walls were, however, escaladed by emissaries, who informed the Milanese that
Pavia and Bergamo were in full insurrection, and that the son
of the viceroy had been captured. At length, on the evening
of the fifth day's fighting, the citizens, protected by the ingenious contrivance of a movable barricade, advanced deliberately
on one of the gates, the Porta Tosa. A set of brave young
fellows made up bundles of fascines, which they rolled before
them, firing from the shelter thus afforded, while a flanking
fire, from the houses on each side, covered their advance. In
this way, after long-protracted efforts, the artillerymen were
picked off one by one, until, at last, a dash was made, and, all
sorts of combustibles being prepared, the gate and the houses
covering it were set fire to, and in a moment all were enveloped in flames. Several ladies, from a distant balcony, witnessed this advance; and it was said that each time an Austrian was brought down they clapped their hands as at the theatre, and gave *vivas* for the lucky marksman; but when the
aim was wrong, and no mischief done, they saluted the failure with a general hiss. A communication with the country
was now opened. Another gate was soon carried—that of
Como—by armed peasants from Lecco, and the main body
of the troops driven, from all points, into the castle. Intelligence was received, from the persons who now poured into the
city, that the Piedmontese forces on the Ticino were increasing, had crossed the river at several points, and that, from the
Swiss frontier, particularly from the Valteline, armed peasants,
amounting to ten thousand, invaded the country, and that the
whole Lombardian territory was in open insurrection. Radetzky had thought to draw all the detached garrisons to Milan,
and to attack the city on every side; but all communications

were interrupted ; single couriers were shot, and greater divisions met with overwhelming difficulties on the roads, and in the
towns through which they attempted to pass.   He ordered up
the brigade Mauer, stationed in Magenta, and that of Strasaldo,
from Sarano (with which points the communications were still
open), to join his forces in Milan.   This order was effected ; but,
while the embarrassments of his situation increased with every moment that transpired, the veteran marshal continued the
struggle with redoubled energy.   The generals, Wohlgemuth
and Clamm, still protected their communications by destroying with artillery all the buildings touching the ramparts.
" The troops," said Marshal Radetzky, in his official report;
" fought well ; they are really admirable ; they effect more
than possibilities, and are in fine spirits, although they have
had no rest for four days, and part of the time encountered the
most dreadful weather."

On the evening of the 22d, the marshal—in consequence of
the highly excited state of the population in the city, the volunteers flocking in from all quarters, the disastrous news from
Padua, Venice, and other points, evincing that the whole country was in a state of revolt, especially that a considerable
force was approaching from Switzerland, and that the King of
Piedmont, with a most formidable army, had already crossed
the frontier—came to the conclusion that it would be impossible for him to retain any longer his position in that city.   It
was to the Austrian army a dreadful resolution ; but there was
no alternative : Milan must be evacuated.   Accordingly, on that
night the following order was issued, signed by the field-marshal.   " Soldiers ! the treachery of our allies, the fury of an
enraged people, and the scarcity of provisions, oblige me to
abandon this city of Milan, for the purpose of taking position
on another line, from which, at your head, I can return to victory."   As soon as it grew dark, all the troops were concentrated on the *Place d'Armes*, and immediate preparations for
departure made.   The march through the gates and over the
ramparts of the city, amid the terrible cross-fire of the enemy,
it was anticipated would be perilous in the extreme.   In fact,
the Milanese suspecting the contemplated retreat of Radetzky,
every nook and corner on both sides of the way, on the line

of his exit, were filled by sharp-shooters, who, from their safe and unsuspected retreats, could direct their deadly aim upon the troops. Every cellar, window, and roof of each house in the town, was crowded with marksmen, and through the suburbs and outskirts every tree was occupied by armed peasants.

To protect his retreat, Radetzky ordered the constant discharge of his sixty cannons, by which many dwellings were set fire to in the extremities of the city. The burning houses spread a lurid light over the dark horizon. Suddenly, an immense volume of smoke issued from the midst of the castle. The Austrians had set fire to large quantities of straw, hay, wagons, and furniture; not, as some of the Milanese supposed, to consume their dead, but, more probably, for the purpose of distracting attention from their retreat. While the noise of the cannonade, and the light of the conflagration, were absorbing the attention of the population, the troops, with their flanks protected by numerous *tirailleurs*, abandoned the castle and began to defile through the narrow passages of the bastions. The march through the ramparts was accomplished in good order, as quickly as possible, but under the greatest obstacles. Carrying, as Radetzky was obliged to do, all his artillery and ammunition, his wounded, more than three hundred families of Austrian officers and *employées*, the unfortunate prisoners whom he had taken as hostages, and some thousands of Italian soldiers whose fidelity he mistrusted, eight hours were necessary to disengage his troops from the double-circle fire, which was, during every moment of the time, discharged upon them.

The Italian regiments had behaved well during the engagement, but now exhibited some reluctance at quitting their country under the lead of "foreigners." In difficult passages, where their desertion was feared, cannons were directed against them, and, at the smallest sign of hesitation, the officers in command cried out the terrible words, "March on, or you are dead men!" To excite the inhabitants and intimidate the troops the alarm-bells were sounded from the sixty steeples of Milan. On several occasions, when too heavily pressed, the troops, fell into confusion, they stopped and reformed their columns amid the most terrific fire. At the Porta Comasina it was attempted to prevent their passage; but the troops, by a desperate effort, overwhelmed all resistance. As they passed the Porta Tosa the environs were one uninterrupted sea of fire. It was long after midnight when the rear-guard evacuated its position on the ramparts, from which it had protected the egress of the troops. The retreat succeeded completely; and, in comparison with the danger and difficulty of the task, the loss was small. It was one of the sad master-strokes of the art of war, in which the energy of the general and the unsubdued courage of his troops can not but be admired.

After the terrible fighting for five days, the number of killed was incredibly small. As reported by the Milanese Ministry of Foreign Affairs, the loss on the part of the Austrians was seven hundred, that of the Italians, two hundred and fifty. Some Italian writers place Radetzky's loss in killed and wounded as high as four thousand.* The loss of the troops was vastly greater than that of the Milanese, owing to the exposed position of the former, and the protected points occupied by the latter. The loss of property was considerable. Besides the destruction of isolated buildings at various points, and the extensive conflagration at the extremities of the city, two streets, from the windows of which the enraged citizens were pouring down boiling oil and pitch upon the troops, were so completely demolished as to present one uninterrupted mass of ruins.†

---

* Author of "Custoza."

† Many instances of cruelty are said to have been perpetrated by the Croats during the struggle. Women, it was said, were violated, men cut down, and houses set on fire. A poor child was nailed to the door of a house where the entrance of the soldiers was at first resisted. In one place, the bodies of five women, half burned, were found; and even in a house near the castle, the corpses of women, with their faces horribly disfigured, were exposed. The hand of a lady, with several rings on it, was hid in the pocket of a Croat prisoner; and limbs of women, separated from the bodies, which had been burned or buried, were discovered near the gates. Even Radetzky himself, though incapable of countenancing these horrors, is not quite guiltless of acts of perfidy which entailed a great deal of personal suffering on his victims, and caused the despair of several noble families, in having seized as prisoners at the *Hôtel de Ville*, on the 18th, the hundred and fifty gentlemen who went there to enroll themselves as National Guards under the proclamation of O'Donnell and the podesta. These prisoners suffered every privation for four days, and at last seventeen of them were carried off. The Milanese, on the other hand, are said to have treated their prisoners with all imaginable lenity. O'Donnell, Balza (the detested instrument of the police),

Having with great difficulty accomplished his retreat from Milan, Marshal Radetzky determined to retire to Lodi; but in this his progress was slow, as barricades had been thrown up, and the road dug away in a number of places, which with difficulty the van-guard succeeded in restoring before the arrival of the main body. On reaching Molignano in the course of the day (23d), that insignificant town had the assurance to order the troops to lay down their arms, and actually seized and imprisoned the interpreting officer, Colonel Count Wratislaw. The bridge over the Lambro being also destroyed, this handful of men kept the Austrian army in check for an entire day. As soon as the bridge was restored, Marshal Radetzky, approaching within shot of the town, immediately ordered its bombardment; and, amid a general conflagration, stormed the village, and rescued the imprisoned imperial officer. No further resistance was offered the army; the severe chastisement inflicted on the presumptuous little town of Molignano prevented the recurrence of similar attempts. The Archduke Ernest had succeeded in keeping Lodi in submission, and the field-marshal, having reached that city, there paused to give repose to his exhausted troops.

INVASION OF CHARLES ALBERT.

It was the maxim of one of the early princes of the house of Savoy, and constantly held in view by his descendants, that Lombardy ought to be considered as an artichoke, to be eaten leaf by leaf; but it was the fancy of Charles Albert that he had an appetite sufficient to devour the whole plant at once. Lombardy has been under the dominion of the house of Austria for three centuries (from the death of Charles the Fifth); and, since the peace of Utrecht, has been positively assured to that dynasty by all Europe, and therefore is not a dominion which the King of Sardinia could regard as usurped by the house of Austria. Lombardy, too, had been confirmed to Aus-

---

the wife of Torresani (the intendant of the police), Count Thun, nephew of Count Fiquelmont, and a large body of counselors, against whom the people had many complaints, were lodged in the first palaces of the city, and most strictly and honorably attended to.[1]

---

[1] Correspondent of the London Times.

tria, by the treaty of Vienna, in 1815; by which compact the
King of Sardinia holds a large portion of his own possessions;
a treaty by which Genoa was stripped of her independence,
her republic extinguished, and her territory placed under the
rule of the house of Savoy. In a note dispatched on the 8th
of February, 1848, by the Minister of Foreign Affairs at Turin, to the imperial embassador at that court, announcing that
the King of Sardinia had determined to grant a constitution
to his subjects, appears the following passage: "The king is
desirous that his majesty, the Emperor of Austria, will accept the assurance that the maintenance of treaties shall be
in the future, as it has been in the past, the basis of his policy; and that, in calling his subjects to take part in the internal government of the kingdom, far from rendering his relations with foreign powers more difficult, it will only bind more
closely the ties of friendship between the two states." The
official declarations of the Sardinian government, on other occasions, and even as late as the 22d of March, were marked
by the same sentiments. It seems astonishing, however, that
the royal censorship should have allowed journals not only to
make the most violent attacks against Austria, but even direct
appeals, and excitations to revolt, addressed to the inhabitants
of the Lombardo-Venetian kingdom. The multiplied remonstrances of the imperial government obtained only sterile expressions of regret, fresh assurances of friendship, and excuses
founded on the difficulties arising from the pressure of circumstances. During the time when the continual armaments
of Sardinia were the more calculated to call the attention of
the imperial government to the fact, the Sardinian authorities
replied that they were caused by the fermentation of all Italy,
and of Sardinia itself; and that they absolutely had no offensive character.

Scarcely had the news of the glorious events which had occurred at Milan on the 18th reached Turin, when some Milanese, who had previously fled to that city, hastened to his majesty, the King of Sardinia, and invoked his assistance, which,
as they urged, they had a right to expect, " as Italians, from
their Italian brethren, and from the heroic intrepidity of their
revolt against the common enemy of all Italy." To this en-

treaty of the Milanese patriots an answer was given, "that it was impossible for the government of his majesty to undertake the initiative of a military subsidy in Lombardy without a direct demand on the part of the people of Milan." This intelligence, notwithstanding the many difficulties and dangers which impeded entrance to the city, was immediately conveyed to, and reached Milan on the morning of the 21st.* The satisfaction with which it was accepted by the provisional government may easily be imagined; and a mission was immediately organized for the purpose of conveying to the King of Piedmont the sense of gratitude which was felt, and the expression of a fervent hope that he would not delay in coming to their aid. Previously, however, to the arrival of this mission, a corps of volunteers for the invasion of Lombardy had been decreed at Turin, and into which foreigners were to be admitted. The Austrian embassador at Turin considered it his duty to demand, without delay, whether the subjects of his master, the emperor, were also to be permitted to enlist. To this interrogatory the Sardinian minister, the Marquis Pareto, returned an evasive and insufficient answer, but concluded as follows: " The undersigned, after having answered the note of Count Bual, hastens to add, that he will do all that depends upon him to insure the relations of amity and good neighborhood between the two states." Such was the tone of the official organ of the Sardinian government on the 22d of March.

On the same, or, at furthest, on the succeeding day, King Charles Albert convoked a cabinet council, to consider the expediency of marching an armed force to the assistance of the Milanese; and the following proclamation, issued on the 23d (just a day after the amicable assurances above stated), was the result of their deliberations:

" Charles Albert, by the grace of God, King of Sardinia Cyprus, and Jerusalem. People of Lombardy and Venice The destinies of Italy are maturing; a happier fate awaits the intrepid defenders of inculcated rights. From affinity of race,

---

* Proclamation of the Provisional Government of Milan to the inhabitants of Lombardy.

from intelligence of the age, from community of feeling, we, the first, have joined in that unanimous admiration which Italy manifests toward you.   People of Lombardy and Venice ! Our arms, which were already concentrated on your frontier when you anticipated the liberation of glorious Milan, now come to offer you, in your further trials, that aid which a brother expects from a brother—a friend from a friend.   We will second your just desires, confiding in the aid of that God who is visibly with us—of that God who has given to Italy a Pius IX.—of that God who, by such wonderful impulse, has given to Italy the power of acting alone.   And, that the sentiment of the Italian union may be further demonstrated, we command that our troops, on entering the territory of Lombardy and Venice, shall bear the escutcheon of Savoy on the tricolored flag of Italy.   CHARLES ALBERT."

Upon these developments, the imperial embassador at Turin immediately demanded and obtained his passports ; and, as soon as the tidings of these occurrences reached Vienna, the Sardinian minister at that court left the Austrian capital.*

The King of Sardinia, in a council of ministers, had previously decided to call out immediately the two classes of recruits necessary for filling up the ranks of the army, in active service ; to send to the frontier all the regiments of infantry, cavalry, and artillery ; to accept the generous offers of individuals, of horses for transport, and voluntary contributions for the victualing of the army ; to order the army of reserve to hold itself in readiness to march at the first notice ; and to open a voluntary but temporary loan, at five per cent., for immediate expenses.

On the 26th, a portion of the Piedmontese troops, under General Bes (five thousand in number), entered Milan.   Another division of the same army (the advance-guard, eight thousand in number), under General Trotti, penetrating Lombardy at a point lower down, passed through Lodi on the 28th, and established themselves at Crema ; while the king, Charles

---

* According to official information, the Austrian coat-of-arms were torn down by the populace from the residence of the embassador at Turin, as well as of the consul at Genoa.

Albert, with the main body of the army (forty thousand strong), following the course of the Po, passed through Pavia on the 29th, and reached Lodi on the 30th, where he issued a proclamation to his army, " congratulating them on having marched one hundred and ten miles in seventy-two hours, and expressing his joy that Lombardy and Venice had called on him to expel the Austrians from their territory."

On the 26th, the Provisional Government of Milan published a proclamation, announcing a convention concluded with the Piedmontese government, in virtue of which the Piedmontese troops will act in concert with the Milanese as their faithful allies, the expense of provisions to be at the charge of Milan, and the pay of the troops to be at the charge of the Sardinian government. Ten thousand Roman and seven thousand Tuscans were at this time marching to the Po, by Bologna and Ferrara. The Neapolitan government, about the same time, dispatched fifteen thousand men to the scene of action, twelve thousand to be conveyed by sea to Ancona, and three thousand to cross the Pope's dominions, and join the others on the frontiers of Lombardy.

" It is not a little remarkable that these Italian powers should so readily have committed themselves," to use the language of Lord Aberdeen, "in having violated the public law of Europe, and entering the territory of a neighboring, a friendly, and an allied power, without the slightest pretext of grievance, without any provocation, without any complaint or any reason assigned whatsoever, and in direct violation of engagements by which they were bound ;" especially when their efforts, if successful, would end in their own downfall. But the truth was, these monarchs were doubly forced into the positions which they found themselves compelled to assume. In the first place, they were driven to it by their own subjects ; ever since the struggle commenced between the Lombardians and the imperial government, the people throughout all Italy had urged their respective monarchs in vain to the assistance of the insurgents ; and when the tidings of the success of the Milanese and their repulse of the imperial troops arrived, their demands became irresistible, and the immediate compliance on the part of these monarchs became as necessary as the preservation of their own thrones. In the next place, the Italian monarchs felt themselves forced to this step in defense of the constitutional governments which they had recently established, and their own position at the head of them, by the conviction that, unless they afforded assistance to the struggling Lombardians, there would be no alternative left the insurgents but to proclaim a republic and throw themselves into the arms of France, and that government, it was thought, would not have hesitated to consider, agreeably to the address of Lamartine, that the time for the reconstruction of this oppressed nationality had arrived; and, with Lombardy a republic, it would have followed, "as surely as the day to night," that all Italy would have become republican also, and have hurled these monarchs from their thrones.

In the mean time, the whole Lombardo-Venitian kingdom and its vicinity seemed to be in open rebellion : in the language of the proclamation of the Grand Duke of Tuscany, " the period for the regeneration of all Italy had arrived."

Venice, the proud city of the Lagoons, upon the receipt of the news of the revolution in Vienna, immediately threw off imperial authority, and declared a republic. In Parma and Modena, the dukes had fled, and the governments given up or consigned to the hands of the people. Throughout all the towns of the Lombardo-Venitian kingdom, with the exception of Verona, Mantua, and Peschiera (where were formidable Austrian fortresses, and where the troops, by retiring into the citadels, preserved their positions), the power fell into the hands of the people, and the imperial troops were either suffered to depart or were taken prisoners. At Brescia, the Austrian garrison, after the arrest of General Shoubals, two colonels, and fifty-three officers of different grades, were compelled to leave the place ; but the route of their departure not having been indicated, they marched and joined Radetzky at Crema. At Bergamo, the eight hundred Austrians stationed there retired, on the outbreak, to their barracks, and prepared to defend themselves ; a deputation of citizens, calling on them to deliver up their arms on being granted an unmolested retreat, were seized and imprisoned ; and the citizens, from regard to the deputation, were obliged to compromise for their release by suffering the

O

soldiers to depart *with* their arms. At Como (a provisional government was formed, which published a proclamation, dated
23d March, ordering all functionaries to be retained in their respective óffices, but the arms of Austria and the title of "imperial and royal" to be every where effaced) all the barracks,
with one exception, were in the hands of the people, twelve
thousand men were disarmed, and their weapons distributed
among the people, who hurried to the assistance of the Milanese.
In Varese, the troops wished to withdraw without resistance,
when the insurrection commenced, but the people would not
permit it, and two hundred Croats and a detachment of huz-
zars were compelled to surrender. At Lodi and Cremona, sanguinary combats took place, which resulted in the triumph of
the people. Similar occurrences took place at Pavia and De-
zensano. At Pizzighettone, the garrison surrendered, and the
fortress and ten pieces of cannon were taken. The garrison
at Piacenza was compelled to evacuate the castle. In the
towns of Udine, Treviso, and Padua, in the Venetian kingdom,
the imperial troops were permitted to leave under capitulations.

PROCEEDINGS IN MILAN.

All fears of Field-marshal Radetzky's return being at an end,
a superior and disciplined force now pursuing him, all the barricades in Milan were rapidly removed,* and the city began to
resume once more its former prosperous aspect. While the
Provisional Government was actively engaged in issuing proclamations to arouse the inhabitants, raising levies, and dis-

---

* "The barriers are being actively demolished, and, while nobles at one end
claim their magnificent carriages, a good housewife at the other asks for the
kitchen table, which she contributed for the same patriotic purpose. The mana-
gers of the *Scala*, and the other theatres, are looking for their benches, and the
malle-poste and diligence owners are entreating that the heaps of straw and ma-
nure stuffed in at their doors and windows shall be removed. In one place, a
crowd of honest women are disputing the right of ownership to several mattresses
and feather beds which had been exposed, in the common cause of the country,
to the last week's rain; and, in another, the green-grocer and the oil-man, alternately laying hold of a counter which the cloth-dealer finally carries off. The only
things unclaimed were the sentry-boxes of the Austrians, which, in these strange
days, had been employed to exclude the very men they were constructed to shelter."[1]

[1] London Times.

patching them as rapidly as possible in pursuit of the fleeing
enemy, the people were engaged in the more solemn occupation of paying the last sad honors to their fallen countrymen.   The funeral service for the "victims of the five days,"
is represented as one of the most sublime and splendid ceremonies ever witnessed ; and those who are familiar with the
magnificent interior of the Duomo, and with the magnitude of
the open space before it, will admit that a more suitable *locale*
for a festival of that nature can scarcely be found.   The whole
interior of the cathedral was hung in black, a mourning pile
being raised in the centre, on which numerous inscriptions
appeared, commemorating the death of the victims, and insuring immortality to their names.   A profusion of wax lights
rendered "the darkness visible," and brought into full view
the innumerable banners which were pendant from the columns and from every part of the roof.   The floor of the temple was covered with green cloth, and seats were placed for the
use of the privileged classes ; but the whole body of the building was thronged with people of all ranks, who took part in the
proceedings with that order and propriety which distinguishes
the Milanese.   The effect was grand, when the solemn sound
of the colossal organ was heard united with the voices of a
hundred choristers, and when the people outside took up the
hymn, and made the *plaza*, as well as the church, re-echo to
the strain.   A procession of the archbishops and a long train
of ecclesiastics also had a fine effect; and the ceremony was
rendered still more awful by the appearance in the deepest
mourning of the relatives of the deceased, and by the sobs which
seemed to burst against their will from the bosoms of the most
afflicted.   The Provisional Government, all the newly-appoint-
ed authorities, and the foreign consuls, preceded by a long
flight of banners, were introduced with similar forms, as well
as a procession of charitable ladies, who were employed in raising a subscription for the families of those who had fallen in
the patriotic cause.   However grand the ceremony within the
church, aided as it was by the effect of the solemn draperies,
the immense columns, the arched roof, the stained windows,
the monumental sculpture, all brought into relief by the flame
of a thousand wax-lights—it was not to be compared to the

exhibition offered in the *plaza* before the Duomo, where the whole population of Milan appeared, as if by a miracle, to have found room. A mourning pyramid, with suitable inscriptions, had been raised in the centre, and a proper space about it was preserved by the National Guard, who, dressed in their becoming costume of black velvet, with Tyrolese hats, performed public duty for the first time. All the houses of the square, the windows and balconies, were hung with black, and every spot where human forms could be introduced was filled with ladies clad in mourning, whose picturesque appearance, all in sable vails, instead of bonnets, as is their custom in Milan, rendered them by no means the least attractive part of the ceremony. From every window streamed the tricolor ribbon, and the contrast between these gay tints and the deep mourning in which the houses and the people were arrayed, was most striking and impressive. The solemn enthusiasm of the people of Milan on this occasion can not be justly described. No language can do justice to the religious sentiment which appeared to dictate all they said and did. Persons of rank, and those of the humblest life, were equally elevated in feeling, and the fervor of the popular voice was tempered with a devotional gravity worthy of the best days of ancient Rome.

MOVEMENTS OF RADETZKY.

The original plan of Field-marshal Radetzky was to take position behind the Adda, to concentrate there all disposable troops, to open communications with the great fortresses of Mantua, Peschiera, and Verona in his rear, and then to march back and retake Milan; but the general insurrections which had occurred in all the towns of the Lombardo-Venetian provinces, together with extensive desertions of Italian troops[*] at various posts, caused this plan to be abandoned. Accordingly, Radetzky left Lodi, and marched to Crema, and there, on the 25th of March, issued the following proclamation:

" The events of Milan and other towns have induced me to concentrate my forces, and to draw nearer to the focus of my

---

[*] The regiment Albert and the third Ceccopieri deserted at Cremona, and the regiment Haugwitz in Brescia

military operations and of my resources. The peaceful inhabitants have nothing to dread, and will meet with protection
for their persons and property; they are warned, however, not
to offer any opposition to the march of the imperial and royal
troops. I shall cause the severest discipline to be observed;
whoever is taken with arms in his hands shall be judged by a
military commission, and, upon conviction, be immediately
shot. The tried fidelity of the army I command, and the numerous troops that compose it, will answer for the fulfillment
of my present declarations."

From thence, retreating across the Adda, he proceeded with
his forces to Orcinuovo and Laucino, and there, on the 30th of
March, halted on the banks of the Oglio. From want of provisions in the fortress, the Austrians were obliged to abandon
the intention, subsequently entertained, of throwing themselves into Mantua, with the exception of a portion under
General Walmoden.

The Piedmontese general, Bes, captured about this time, it
is said, a detached corps of Austrians at Chiari, a small town
one day's march from Brescia, on the road to Milan.

General Ancioni arrived at Brescia on the 30th of March,
at the head of a column of Milanese, to re-enforce General
Monti, who had preceded him to that point. The Piedmontese column under Bes also directed its movements to the same
point. The first legion of Lombardy left Milan on the same
day for Antignate.*

On the night of the 4th, the Austrians evacuated Monte
Chiaro, Castiglione delle Steviere, and Lonato, and took the

---

* On entering the territory of Lombardy, the King of Piedmont declared that
he was actuated by no other ambition than a desire to aid the independence of
Italy. He found the population in a strange temper: they received the Piedmontese as brothers, and loaded them with praises, but appeared to regard their
intervention as a matter of slight utility, after the retreat of Radetzky. The deputies from Milan, who came to salute him at Pavia, on his entrance into Lombardy, represented that the Austrian troops were in full flight, and incapable of
the slightest resistance; that they had crossed the Alps; and vauntingly spoke of
pursuing him there, and conquering Illyria, Istria, and Dalmatia, the ancient possessions of Italy. But on passing through Lodi, and coming up with their van-
guard at Crema, on the 1st of April, they discovered, on the contrary, that Radetzky's army, in good order, had concentrated, and occupied the plain of Monte
Chiaro.

roads to Verona and Mantua.   On the same day that the Austrians were crossing the Mincio, the Sardinian army crossed the Oglio.   On the 5th its head-quarters were at Pozzolo and the first corps at Marcaria.

On the 6th, the commander of the fortress of Mantua, upon the order of Radetzky, directed a reconnoitre against the Piedmontese van-guard at Marcaria.   Colonel Benedek, charged with that reconnoitre, intended to have surprised the enemy; but the execution of the plan failed, owing to a shot fired by a peasant.   Entering Marcaria, however, they took ten dragoons and thirteen horses of the regiment of Genoa, stormed those houses whence the troops had been fired upon, and drove the Piedmontese back over the Oglio.

The idea of Radetzky at this time seemed to be to withdraw his forces between the fortresses of Peschiera, Verona,* and Mantua, and to defend the line of the Mincio; but circumstances, perhaps, induced him to change his plan of operations, for by refusing battle, the whole line of the Mincio was abandoned; and his object appeared confined to the possession of Peschiera and Verona, and to the maintenance of the line of the Adige north of Verona, and leading to Roveredo and Trient.

Charles Albert's plan† seemed clearly to be, to secure, in the first place, the passages of the Mincio, to place large bodies of men between Peschiera and Verona, and to cut off the line of the Upper Adige, by gaining Pontone, where the only bridge over that river is placed.   Should he be successful in these movements, he could not fail to reduce Peschiera, isolate Verona, and thus bar Radetzky's retreat, or cut off the arrival of re-enforcements from Vienna.

The occupation of the important fortresses of Mantua, Verona, and Peschiera changed altogether the prospect of affairs, and the fate of Lombardy now depended on the degree of power possessed by the government of Vienna, and its willingness or unwillingness to attempt the recovery of this kingdom.   The independence of Lombardy, which a few days before appeared

---

* On reaching Verona, Radetzky published an order of the day to his troops, containing the expressive words, "On military grounds, and in my capacity as commander, I say you have retired before the enemy; you have not been conquered."   † Evening Mail.

within the grasp of the Provisional Government, seemed now to be indefinitely postponed;. and however anxious France might be to acknowledge it, she could not get rid of the obvious consideration that the country, while the Austrian troops held possession of the three great fortresses in its very centre, was still subject to Austrian rule.*   This untoward state of things was mainly owing to the over-cautious military proceedings of the King of Sardinia, and the military inexperience of the persons at Milan charged with the direction of affairs.   Had Charles Albert but made two or three forced marches with the large army that he commanded, he might have prevented the concentration of Radetzky's forces.   The Provisional Government of Milan are also censurable for having rejected a plan laid down by experienced men, and by which the defeat of the Austrians was assured.

The Milanese, however, elated by their success in casting off from their city the incubus under which it labored—the imposition of imperial troops—were unable to realize the danger of their situation, as no immediate attack on the city was threatened, and they remained undisturbed by passing events. They considered the result of the war as predestined, and they left it in the hands of their too willing ally the King of Piedmont, and the Sardinian, Tuscan, Roman, and Neapolitan troops, who, without any *casus belli*, or declaration of war, were flocking in every direction for the purpose of expelling the stranger from Italian soil.

On the morning of the 8th, at seven o'clock, the Piedmontese, who to this time were on the right bank of the Mincio, the head-quarters of the king being at Castiglione delle Steviere, and the Austrians on the left (the great body of them having retired to Verona), the former with from eight to ten thousand men, coming down from Marcaria, appeared before Goito.   That place was occupied by a single Austrian company of the fourth battalion of riflemen, under the command of Captain Knezick; the rest of the brigade Wohlgemuth was on the left shore of the Mincio.

A lively fire, between the *tirailleurs*, on both sides was kept

---

* Evening Mail.

up for several hours, in which the company of Austrians sustained themselves with great credit; but, being unable to
stand up before three to four thousand of the enemy* who were
said to be engaged, General Wohlgemuth withdrew the company, partially destroyed the bridge, and placed but two guns
to bear upon its passage. But the Sardinian light troops, from
the houses on the right bank, which had been abandoned to
them, killed off the gunners serving the pieces; and so sharp
was the fire, with cross batteries from the shelter which they
occupied, that the Austrians were forced to retire; and the
Piedmontese, crossing in triumph, remained masters of the passage of the Mincio.†

While this success was attending the Piedmontese arms, a
similar struggle, on the same day, but at another point, occurred, which proved favorable to the Austrians. Numerous undisciplined crowds of insurgents had made their appearance at
Montebello. The field-marshal dispatched the brigade Lichtenstein to San Bonifacio, to undertake from there a reconnoitre
of Montebello. Leaving Verona on the morning of the 7th,
they slept that night in San Bonifacio, and executed on the 8th
the order. The roads had been rendered impracticable by barricades, but the Austrian pioneers soon removed all obstructions. A strong resistance was only met with in Sono, which
was strongly barricaded, and defended by a thousand men.
Sono was carried by storm, fifty of its defenders were killed
on the spot, thirty or forty taken prisoners, and two ship cannons captured. While this was going on on the heights, Colonel Martini, with a column, stormed the bridge of Montebello,
took two sea cannons, and caused the complete evacuation of
the place.

As soon as the passage of the Mincio was effected by his
troops, Charles Albert removed from Castiglione delle Steviere,
passing through Valeggio, invested Peschiera, and carried his
head-quarters to Somma Campagna, the enemy retiring at his
approach; from thence he attacked and drove back a column
of two thousand men, sent from Verona for the purpose of for-
aging, or of re-enforcing the garrison of Peschiera. The Croats

---

* Radetzky's Dispatch.   † Evening Mail.

fought well; but there was a far superior force against them, and they were driven successively from all the positions which they occupied; and, their retreat being cut off by a spirited advance of the right of the Piedmontese toward Verona, they were obliged to abandon Busolongo, and to fall back to Pontone on the Adige. This affair was no battle, but simply the resolute advance of a superior force against a weaker, and the abandonment of all their positions by the latter, after some brave but ineffectual attempts to maintain their ground.* The position occupied at this time by this portion of the Piedmontese army can be easily understood. On the right bank of the Mincio, from Peschiera to Valeggio, there is a chain of hills, bounded by a heath of four or five miles, and gradually sinking to the vast plains in which Villa-Franca and Verona stand. The same chain is (across the Mincio) continued northward to Pontone, whence the Adige, that has flowed nearly due south from Trient and Roveredo, takes suddenly an eastern direction, and winds through the vale of Verona to that city, situated on the extreme verge of the plain, with gentle hills above it, similar to those that skirt the left bank of the Mincio. The Piedmontese army was encamped at the base of the chain of hills above described, occupying all the villages between Valeggio and Busolongo, where the royal head-quarters were at this time located, with its right at Villa-Franca in the plain, and its left on the banks of the Lake of Garda, where the line of the blockade of Peschiera begins.

Upon learning the affair of the Bridge of Goito, the forcing of the Mincio at that point, as well as at Monzanbano, Marshal Radetzky, supposing that his enemy's object was to give battle, advanced all the troops that he could dispose of at Verona as far as Villa-Franca, where, on the evening of the 8th, eighteen to twenty thousand men, exclusive of the garrison of Mantua, were united. But, contrary to all expectation, on the morning of the 9th, the Piedmontese, as Marshal Radetzky writes, had disappeared without making any hostile demonstration. The first army corps of the Austrians being concentrated around Villa-Franca, and the second occupying Verona,

---

* Galignani's Messenger.

and being ready at any moment to turn toward a threatened point.

The spot occupied at this time by the hostile armies is especially familiar to the reader of history, from the immortal campaigns of Prince Eugene of Savoy, in 1701, and of Bonaparte in 1796. At this period, however, the natural strength of the lines of the Mincio and the Adige had not received all the improvements which modern science has added to them. Verona, Mantua, and Peschiera now form almost an equilateral triangle of impregnable fortresses, within which no army ought to be forced, and there Radetzky seemed to be waiting, either for the direct attack of the enemy, or for re-enforcements which would enable him to resume the offensive.

The position of Charles Albert and the Piedmontese army is very nearly that occupied by Napoleon on the 1st of August, 1796,* when he extricated himself from a position of great peril, in six wonderful days, by gaining successively the battles of Lonato and Castiglione, thus overcoming the different Austrian corps which were advancing on both sides of the Lake of Garda.

Afterward Radetzky thought it expedient to unite the whole first army corps before Verona, in order to effect a better concentration of his forces and secure a more free use of the facilities which offered. On the side of the Piedmontese, detachments are pushed close to the walls of Verona, while the troops scour the whole plain between that city and the villages of Villa-Franca, Somma Campagna, and Busolongo ; so that, in reality, the Austrians seemed almost inclosed within the city of Verona and the line of the Adige to the northwest, leading to the Tyrol.

On the 10th of April the fortress of Peschiera was summoned by a Piedmontese *Parliamentiare* to surrender, but the proposal was rejected by the commander of the fortress. In the afternoon, at two o'clock, appeared two hostile engineer officers in the environs of Trassine, followed by columns of infantry, which brought forth a battery at Laghetto, and extended up to Ponti. A lively but useless fire was opened against the fort

---

* Galignani's Messenger, 1848.

† The scenery at this point, and particularly at such an hour, was full of beauty.

Salvi (one of the fore posts of Peschiera). After six o'clock the firing ceased.† On the 11th, a band of Piedmontese and Milanese volunteers having crossed the Lake of Garda, and landed at Cazine, advanced as far as the villages of Cavalca-selle and Castel Novo, on the road from Peschiera to Verona. Whereupon Radetzky dispatched two battalions, two squad-rons, and one battery, under the command of General Prince Taxis, to that point. The roads were barricaded and defend-ed by peasants, who were soon driven into the towns that were found also strongly barricaded. These were soon carried by storm one after another, and the defenders driven back in wild confusion to Cazine.

The Piedmontese army, in the locations above described, be-tween the Mincio and the Adige, extending from Busolongo on the north, through Villa Franca, Somma Campagna, down to Goito on the south, and approaching within a few miles of Verona, remained in a state of unaccountable inactivity.

Tuscan, Roman, and Neapolitan troops continued to arrive, and swell Charles Albert's forces. His army consisted, from all accounts, of from forty to fifty thousand disciplined troops, and twenty-four thousand Roman, Tuscan, and Neapolitan

---

The far west is before you, the gentle hills burning under the expiring rays of the summer's sun. On the one side the towers of Ponti, Manzanbano, and the distant castle of Valeggio appear in full relief; at their feet the Mincio gliding in silvery stream. On the other, the broad expanse of the Lake of Garda is display-ed, reflecting in its still bosom the numerous hills and mountains that bound it on every side, and showing the white sails of some tiny bark returning to Dezensa-no, or winding its way to the many little ports that communicate with the Tyrol. At the extremity of the lake are seen the Alps, their summits still covered with the last remains of the winter's snow, and their sides in the clear atmosphere re-vealing the clefts, and chasms, and fantastic shapes, which some great natural convulsion has produced. Turning to the east, the landscape is quite changed. The church spires of Cavalcassali, Castel Novo, San Giorgio, and of other villages, protrude, dotting at intervals a vast amphitheatre, broken into pasture grounds, vineyards, or plantations of mulberry-trees, rising and falling into a succession of hills and dales—presenting, not only in its general features, but by the coloring given by the dewy mist risen just after the bright light of day has closed, the strongest possible contrast to the bold features of the western landscape: while the sun's rays still crown the vast sheet of water in the lake, and the mountains of the Tyrol and of Verona. It was exciting, at such an hour, to overlook the siege, to hear the crash of exploding shells, to mark the flashes from the contend-ing batteries, the circle of smoke which rises over the spot where a bomb has fallen, and the vast cloud in which the fortress and batteries are at all times en-veloped.

soldiers arrived and advancing to re-enforce him. The Italian army was likely, therefore, soon to amount to nearly one hundred thousand men. To oppose this force, Radetzky had an army of forty thousand strong under the walls of Verona; and General Welden, with ten thousand men, from the Tyrol; and General Count Nugent, with thirty thousand men, from the Friul, to co-operate with him. These forces were independent of strong garrisons in Mantua, Peschiera, and other important towns. The policy of the Austrian commander, at this time, was delay. With his troops inclosed within the line of formidable fortresses, he was quietly awaiting re-enforcements, to the approach of which there was apparently no impediment.

Verona is the most important of the four places which defend the double line of the Mincio and the Adige. Built on both banks of the Adige, at the point where it issues from the mountains to flow through the plain, it commands the course of the river, and covers the routes through the Tyrol.

The part on the left bank, situated on the declivity of a hill which forms the last swell of the Alps, is defended by the fortified heights which overhang the town. That on the right bank, lying on the skirts of an immense plain, extending from these mountains to the Apennines, is surrounded by an intrenched camp, and other works to guard the approaches.

Besides the strength of this position, Radetzky, if defeated, could either fall back on the Tyrol, or seek shelter within the fortresses; whereas, should Charles Albert be unsuccessful, he might find it impossible to retreat with any order across the Mincio, in his rear.

But the most unaccountable portion of Charles Albert's conduct at this time was his failure to strike before the different wings of his enemy's army should have united. That he should have been, as Radetzky, in his official dispatch at this time, represents, "inactive at all points, and seeming to have neither the courage or the power to act upon the offensive;" thus throwing away the golden opportunity which circumstances afforded him of destroying the Austrian army in detail, rather than wait until they should have united, and become invincible.*

---

* Evening Mail.

Slight engagements took place almost daily between the advanced posts of either army, attended with alternate success; but the King of Sardinia never attempted to bring on a general battle.   He was, perhaps, satisfied with the success of his skirmishes, which his sycophantic and vain-glorious followers magnified into important victories; or, perplexed by the firm front presented by the Austrians, he regarded them with a feeling of despair.   At all events, the previous chance was lost. Time, so important under any circumstances, and on all occasions, but vital in military operations, he seemed to regard with indifference.   On the other hand, the Austrian marshal keeps his troops in close quarters; and, while he quietly awaits the re-enforcements which are on their march to join him, suffers none of his designs to transpire.   Wherever the Sardinian troops move, they receive a check.   They besiege Peschiera, and find it impregnable; they make a *reconnaissance*, and see nothing but mounted cannon or bristling bayonets; they hazard a skirmish, and are cut down or captured.   Charles Albert makes flourishing bulletins of what he has not done, and magniloquently covers his troops with glory for taking possession of deserted villages and abandoned posts.

While matters were in this situation, the opposing armies, in hostile array, experience that stillness which precedes the tempest and the shock of war.   The Emperor of Austria, loth to part with the richest jewel of his crown, the fertile province of Lombardy, dispatches a commission, at the head of which is the Count de Hartig, who had formerly held an official station in Italy, to repair to the scene of operations, and to induce, if possible, the people to return to their allegiance to Austria. Accompanying the army of Count Nugent, he published a proclamation, in which he states, in the name of the emperor, that if the Italians would remain connected with Austria, their nationality should be recognized, and they should have all the political and other advantages and privileges which they had demanded before the Revolution, with a free press, and every kind of liberty.   In conclusion, the count asks, " Would it not be an imprudence to attempt to gain by arms what would be granted you without the horrors of war ?"

While the armies are thus face to face, time for consideration, for conference, for arrangement is afforded to the contending parties. Milan has been a fief of the German empire for a thousand years,* and acknowledged allegiance to the emperor even in the time of the Visconti. Had there been any men of prudence and sagacity among the members of her existing government, it behooved them to weigh well the inconveniences of either a Piedmontese or of a French invasion against the objections of a treaty with Austria, though it should involve a nominal submission to the empire. It was scarcely possible that the cabinet of Vienna would be at that time inaccessible to reason. Lombardy, west of the Adige, has been a source of weakness more often than of strength to Austria; has involved her in wars, and wasted those resources which, applied to her own dominions, would have been of the highest value in strengthening, improving, and consolidating them. If her sense of honor be consulted in some new adjustment of the Lombardo-Venetian territory, she will be little inclined to quarrel with the terms. It was even understood that the mediation of England and France had been invoked, and that Austria was favorable to a division of the country by the Mincio, retaining the fortresses of Peschiera and Mantua, provided the Lombardians would assume their portion of the public debt.

But neither of these questions, however, seemed to enter into their deliberations; but a third and totally different one occupied all their thoughts. It was that of the immediate adhesion of Lombardy to Piedmont; and in order to determine this question, registers were opened to receive the votes of the inhabitants.

The Provisional Government of Lombardy published a proclamation, dated the 12th of May, in which, after a succinct *exposé* of the critical state of the affairs of Lombardy, it recommends the immediate junction of that country with Piedmont, under the constitutional sceptre of the house of Savoy, and, at the same time, orders lists to be opened in different parts of the state to record the votes of the citizens in favor of or against the measure; these lists to be definitively closed on the 29th, the anniversary of the battle of Legnano, which ended

---

* Britannia.

in the defeat of Frederic Barbarossa in the twelfth century.*
The lists to contain the votes *against* the measure to be headed
by a declaration that the decision of the future destiny of Lombardy ought to be postponed until after the war.   Those of the
opposite opinion to be headed by a declaration that the supreme
necessity of liberating Italy from the Austrians obliges Lombardy to proclaim her immediate fusion with the Sardinian
States, on the condition of convoking a Constituent Assembly
on the principle of universal suffrage, to decide upon the form
of a constitutional monarchy under the dynasty of Savoy.

While these things were transpiring, the King of Sardinia,
the " descendant of the glorious Eugene of Savoy," meets with
a severe repulse before Verona—an affair in which he made the
attack, which was unnecessary, without an object, and tended,
doubtless, to the depression of his men by the consciousness
of defeat.   The affair is thus described by Field-marshal Radetzky in his official report to the Minister of War.   " I have
to inform you that I was attacked this morning, 6th of May, a
little before nine o'clock, in my position on the rideau before
Verona, and especially on the left wing at St. Lucia, while,
at the same time, the enemy opened the engagement with
a heavy cannonade in the direction of St. Massimo, Croce Bianca, and Chiemo, and made a feint of attacking them.   They
directed all their force against St. Lucia, which was defended
only by the weak brigade Strassaldo.   The conflict lasted altogether fully eight hours.   The brigade fought with the courage of lions.   Never have I heard so well-sustained a fire as
that which the enemy opened at this point.   Only one short
pause intervened during the engagement, in which time the
enemy attacked St. Massimo, and made continual demonstrations against the centre and right wing, consisting of the brigades Gyulai, Lichtenstein, and Taxis, but was here forced
to retire."   The Piedmontese fought well, but they failed in
all their attacks.   The marshal thus states the results of the
conflict :

"The retreat of the enemy from St. Lucia had rather the
appearance of a flight, as many military accoutrements, drums,
knapsacks, etc., were found there.   The engagement lasted

---

* Galignani's Messenger.

from nine in the morning until five in the afternoon. The ground being much broken, did not admit of our pursuing the enemy effectively with our cavalry, and we were therefore not in a position to make many prisoners ; but a great number of wounded, whom the enemy were not able to carry off, fell into our hands."*

The situation of the battle-field of St. Lucia is represented by military writers as one of the most favorable which can be offered for a defensive battle. A thick forest of mulberry-trees conceals from the attacking party the position of the enemy. The positions of the Austrians for that conflict were masterly. The calmness with which the battle was accepted but with a few troops, the perseverance with which unnecessary re-en-forcements were refused, the behavior of the troops themselves, the heroic defense of the brigade Strassaldo, the repulse of the attack upon Croce Bianca, all were admirable. An experienced theoretician pronounces that the defense of the Adige by the Austrians in the position of St. Lucia, most brilliantly mani-fested the truth of that theory, for which the science of war will be at all times most grateful to him, because here was exemplified the practical application of one of the most suc-cessful principles of the theory of self-defense.†

The victory of St. Lucia liberated the confined Austrian army for the remainder of the campaign from the advance of the enemy. It was a daring act on the part of the Piedmont-ese to advance so near to Verona, and which they probably never would have done but with the hope of the sympathy of the inhabitants. On this occasion, they experienced for the first time that it would not be quite so easy a task as they had contemplated, to proceed in an untroubled triumphal march to Vienna, and to prescribe (as Napoleon had done before) under the walls of that city the terms of peace to the old empire tot-tering under the agitations from within as well as the invasions from without. The old imperial battalions, inured to disci-pline, and distinguished for fidelity, relieved of their discordant

---

* The loss of the Piedmontese in this engagement is put down by an Italian author at fifteen hundred; that of the Austrians at about nine hundred.—Author of "Custoza."

† Williston's "Campaign of Lombardy."   ‡ Wiener Zeitung.

elements (seventeen battalions of Italian troops had deserted
their flag‡), were here for the first time, it might be said, opposed to the forces of the Italian insurrection.   Although it
was the desire of the veteran marshal, immediately after the
success, to assume the offensive, he was compelled by pruden-
tial motives to abstain from such a course.   Verona, with sixty
thousand inhabitants, had to be strictly guarded and strongly
occupied, and the army division under Count Nugent had not
yet arrived, and was not expected before the end of the month
of May.   The arrival of the first re-enforcement was necessary
to proceed successfully on the offensive, and even then it appeared doubtful, as, owing to the revolutionary state of the
country, it was improbable that considerable re-enforcements
could within a short time be sent into Italy.   These re-enforcements were, however, subsequently received, much to the credit
of Count Latour, the Minister of War, who conducted the military administration with great energy and success, amid all
the internal commotions of the empire.   The offensive was not
then seized immediately after the victory of St. Lucia, but determined on as soon as the junction of Nugent's forces with
Radetzky's should be effected.   The interval was occupied in
accomplishing particularly two things, still wanting to complete the strong system of defense around Verona, viz., the
strengthening of the positions before the city, by fortifying the
line before St. Lucia and St. Massimo, and the formation of a
small squadron on the Garda Lake.   The marshal's greatest
care was devoted to provisioning his army, rendered so difficult
by its position.   The only free communication which remained
to him was the great road through the Tyrol, and, as that region of country itself was incapable of furnishing any supplies
for an army, every thing had to be transported from a long
distance beyond it, and with great difficulty ; and to have provided the army for many weeks amid these difficulties reflected much credit on the administration.

MOVEMENTS OF GENERAL NUGENT.

After the evacuation of Venice by the Austrian troops, and
the insurrection of Udine, Osopo, Palma Nova, and Treviso,
General Victor de Pantis received orders to concentrate all the

troops who had been able to effect their retreat, and to prepare, in expectation of the main force under General Nugent, a sufficient van-guard on the Isonzo. Although all the Italian battalions (Wimpfen, Ferdinand d'Este, Albert, the marine troops at Venice) had deserted their standards, Major Geramb succeeded in collecting a force of Hungarian and German battalions of the garrisons of Udine and Treviso, and waited, in Görtz and the villages in the vicinity, the orders of General Victor. This general proceeded from Trieste, bringing with him the regiment, Kinski's, one battalion of Hungarian grenadiers, and one battalion of Croats, belonging to the late garrison of Venice, and one battalion of Furstenwerther, stationed in Trieste. Orders were transmitted to Fiume and Agram, and other parts of Croatia, to send forward their battalions of Croats, which were accordingly dispatched from Fiume to Trieste by steamer, and from Agram to Görtz by land.

On the 4th of April, General Victor had fourteen frontier battalions, four of infantry, two squadrons of cavalry, and four cannons under his orders, near the Isonzo.* The reserve corps was in Romano, and the outposts extended very near to Palma Nova. In this position he awaits the arrival of Nugent and his re-enforcements.†

General Nugent has his head-quarters at Görtz, fifteen thousand men, with four batteries of artillery, and four rocket batteries under his orders. No important engagement occurred.

On the 17th of April, General Nugent took the offensive, by attacking Visko, Talmico, and seven other villages, which, after a severe resistance, were burned. The inhabitants fled, leaving the country open to operations against Udine.

The head-quarters were then removed from Romano to Nogaredo. The 21st of April, Udine was bombarded during two hours, and, as the greatest confusion prevailed in the city, the white flag was hoisted, and *parliamentiares*, with propositions of capitulation, were sent to General Nugent's camp. On the 23d, General Nugent took possession of the city of Udine, where he found arms and munitions, but only three cannons. The garrison, which consisted of Piedmontese artillery, and the two

---

Italian batteries—Wimpfen's and d'Este's—retreated to Osopo, after having been repulsed at Ponteba by the Austrian troops. A great part of the insurgents, consisting mostly of volunteers, were dispersed in the mountains of Carinthia. Colonel Gorizutti had a strong force under his command at Gemona, to observe their movements, and to besiege Osopo. Prince Schwartzenberg had the command of the besieging forces at Palma Nova. Being so covered in his rear, General Nugent pushed his columns forward to the banks of the Tagliamento. A rowing flotilla, which had been armed in Trieste, entered the Tagliamento near Porto Buso and Lignano, and communicated with the Austrian troops, which covered the right shore of the Tagliamento as far as Portogruaro. On the 28th of April, the Tagliamento was crossed; and, on the 3d of May, the head-quarters of Nugent were at Conegliano. On the same day, General Nugent, in order to cover his left flank, ordered Major Geramb over Ceneda to Belluno. On the 4th of May, after very slight resistance, that place was occupied by the Austrian troops.

On the 8th of May, the Piave was passed at two points, Belluno and Capo di Ponte. Major General Culoz, with four thousand troops, was at this time in Feltre.

On the 8th, General Culoz forced a division of sixteen hundred Papal troops to retreat to Onigo. The attack was resumed on the 9th with equal success. Meantime, General Nugent had passed the Piave at Ponte della Priula, where a bridge had been built by the pioneers. On the 10th, Montebelluna was evacuated as soon as the Austrian troops approached. The van-guard of the Austrian corps had advanced to Spressiano and Visnadello. On the 11th, the Papal troops under Ferrari attacked the Austrians in their position, but were soon repulsed, and retreated to Treviso. On the 12th, Nugent's head-quarters were in Visnadello, one post-station from Treviso, and his *corps d'armée* posted *en échelons* on the roads leading to Treviso.

From that day the operations against Treviso were suspended, on account of the necessity of effecting the junction with Radetzky's main forces. General Nugent delivered his command at Treviso to General Sturmer, and he retired to Görtz

on account of ill health.   The command was, a few days afterward, given to Field-marshal General Welden.   It is said
that Nugent retarded all movements against Treviso, being
afraid that his daughter, who was a prisoner at that place,
would be sacrificed in the event of his advance, as the Provisional Government had threatened.

On the 18th of May, the main forces of the *corps d'armée*
of General Nugent, under the command of Prince Schwartzenberg, started from Visnadello, passing the Brenta, and directing their movements against Vicenza, where General
d'Aspre was to meet them.   Another column marched over
Bassano for the same purpose.   On the 23d the junction took
place, and the now united corps under D'Aspre, Thurn, and
Culoz, commanded in person by Radetzky, marched upon Vicenza.   On the 31st, General Welden received the command
of the besieging forces at Treviso.   From this day to the 14th,
when Treviso surrendered, nothing remarkable occurred.

The garrison of Treviso consisted of Piedmontese, Papal,
and Neapolitan troops, besides a number of Crociati—Crusaders, as they called themselves—the whole amounting to
eight thousand men.   In the latter part of the month of May,
the Neapolitan troops had received orders to return to their
country, in consequence of the late outbreak at Naples.   A
proclamation of Baron Welden to his troops, orders that no
quarter be given to any one of the Crociati, who had committed tremendous atrocities in a hospital at Villa Franca.   On
the 10th, General Sturmer made a movement toward Bassano and the mountain passes on the frontiers of the Tyrol,
which was attended with complete success.   The communication with the Tyrol was re-established, and the country
cleared of the ravaging bands of insurgents.   On the 14th of
June, Treviso surrendered, after a bombardment of twelve
hours.   On the 18th of June, Prince Lichtenstein entered
Mestre, which offered no resistance.   On the 17th of June,
Padua surrendered ; and on the 25th, the Fort Cavanella.
Thus the whole Venetian terra firma was again reduced to
subjection by Austria.

After the battle of St. Lucia, the Piedmontese army remained
motionless upon the Mincio, without even attempting to for-

tify its positions, which were liable to be attacked at any moment by an enemy concentrated at Verona, not more than two
leagues distant from the centre of his line. The besieging
batteries having at length arrived, the attack on Peschiera
was vigorously commenced. But even the capture of this
place was trifling in comparison with the advantage to the
Austrians arising from the junction of Nugent's army with
that of Radetzky, and which the Piedmontese made no effort
to prevent. Peschiera, situated at the southern extremity of
the Lake of Garda, at the point where the Mincio issues from
the lake, is a regular pentagon, well fortified, and traversed
and surrounded by the waters of the river. On each bank, a
fort covers the body of the town, and protects it from the
heights which, on either hand, command it. The garrison
was composed of two thousand Croats, commanded by the
aged General Rath, who had been governor of the place for
twenty-two years, and was much beloved by the inhabitants.

This fortress, being closely pressed, and unable to hold out
more than a few hours, Marshal Radetzky, re-enforced by the
arrival of Nugent's forces, under the command of Count Thurn,
left Verona on the evening of the 27th of May, and marched
all that night and the next day, on the flanks of the enemy,
toward Mantua (as by the direct road the Piedmontese positions were too strong), having, by a feint attack on the enemy, misled them, and thus concealed his march toward that
fortress. "By this maneuvering," says the field-marshal, "I
succeeded in throwing my forces rapidly on the extreme right
wing of the enemy; and thus I yesterday (the 29th) passed
the Mincio with my army, under cover of the guns of the fortress of Mantua." After this, on the same day, as Radetzky
further reports, "in order to attack the flanks of our enemy,
and to advance with my army into the plain, I was forced to
take the fortified position in the neighborhood of Mantua and
Cortatone. This difficult task was successfully executed; in
three hours all the lines were taken, and about two thousand
prisoners, among whom were one colonel, sixty-six officers,
one battalion of Neapolitan troops, five cannon, four powder-
casks, and one flag." The object of Radetzky was to follow
up the line of the Mincio, and to force the enemy, by that

movement, to leave the river, or to fight. A victory here would
have been of the greatest result. The enemy had, on the left
side of the Mincio, no other means of retreat but by the prolongation of his right flank, while he had in his rear the Garda Lake, the yet uncaptured fortress of Peschiera, and the high
Alps, while the Austrian army had a completely-secured line
of retreat toward Mantua. A more favorable, strategic plan
can scarcely be conceived. So secret and rapid had been the
movements of Radetzky, that it was not until the 29th, and
after he had passed Mantua, that Charles Albert became aware
that he had quitted Verona. He was, consequently, taken altogether by surprise, and his lines completely turned.

The Mincio, from Peschiera to Mantua, forms a larger lake
as it approaches the latter town. The Austrians had the
choice of issuing forth on either side of the lake and of the
Mincio. This rendered the investment of Mantua by the Piedmontese a difficult task. Accordingly, Charles Albert had
kept at a considerable distance, at Valeggio and Volta, leaving
merely light and irregular troops to watch Mantua.

Radetzky marched out of Mantua on the 29th, at the head
of about thirty thousand men. He issued southwest of the lake
and the Mincio, routed the irregular troops, and moved up the
Mincio on its Lombardian side, in order to divide, if possible,
the Piedmontese. The road from Verona to Cremona traverses
the Mincio at the bridge of Goito, and then strikes off, straight
as an arrow, to the village of Gazzoldo.* This road was the
line taken up by Charles Albert, his two first lines being in advance of Goito, and the reserve at Volta. In this position of
the parties, an attack was commenced, about one o'clock on the
30th, by Radetzky on the Piedmontese position. The result is
claimed as a great victory by the Piedmontese, but the engagement was but a slight one. The Piedmontese, about fifty thousand strong, were commanded by General Bava, assisted by
the King and the Duke of Savoy. Each party retained its
ground; but the Piedmontese had been turned, and Radetzky
found himself in the rear of the enemy. Had the Piedmontese been beaten in a pitched battle, they would have been cut

---

* Galignani's Messenger.

off from Cremona, Brescia, and Milan, and compelled to retreat to what was so lately their advance, viz., the left bank
of the Mincio, where they would have been exposed to an attack from Verona and Mantua, provided strong reserves had
been left in these fortresses.*   It was the intention of Marshal
Radetzky to have offered the decisive battle at this point, for
which reason he threw up barricades and intrenchments; but
two circumstances, altogether unforeseen, occurred, and caused
him to change his plans.   The first was the violent rain, which
fell without interruption from the 31st of May to the 3d of
June, and completely inundated the low and level country,
where his army was then located, rendering it utterly impracticable for him to operate, either with his cavalry or artillery.
The second was, the occurrences of the 26th of May, in Vienna, news of which had just reached him, that all the power
there had fallen into the hands of the students and populace;
and Radetzky, uncertain whether he would be sustained by
the government with such re-enforcements as might be necessary in case of his advance, concluded rather to forego the advantages of position than jeopardize his troops by risking a
battle.   Accordingly, on the night of the 3d of June, he abandoned his position, and returned, with all his forces, to Mantua.
While these operations were going on, on the right of the Piedmontese army, an Austrian column of Tyrolian chasseurs, advancing over Riva, attacked the left wing, in the vicinity of
Bardolino, on the Lake of Garda, and with a view of coming to
the relief of Peschiera.   The free corps of Pavia, which defended this point, were, after several hours' resistance, compelled to
give way, and Bardolino was taken.   Several regiments of
Savoy cavalry and infantry coming up to the assistance of the
Pavian volunteers, the Austrians were, in turn, forced to give
way before superior forces, and retreated to the neighborhood
of Caprino.

On the evening of the 30th of May, the fortress of Peschiera
surrendered to the Piedmontese under a capitulation highly
honorable to the brave garrison.   The first duty of the besiegers
was to distribute seventeen hundred rations to the famished

---

* Evening Mail.

inhabitants. The next day the garrison, sixteen hundred in number, under Baron Rath, marched out with flying banners and all the honors of war. They were to lay down their arms at a mile's distance from Peschiera, and then to march to Ancona, and there embark for Trieste. The capitulation stipulated that they should not take up arms against the Italians as long as the war of independence continued.* The defense of the fortress was the more meritorious, as the garrison had not been regularly provisioned since the 12th of May, having had no other nourishment since that time but mice and salt-petre, all the horses having been previously consumed. The artillery had been obliged to watch, for the last two months, day and night, without ceasing. The number of sick and wounded increased daily; they were without medicine, and but a single surgeon. Four thousand bombs had been discharged into the town, and a great portion of the buildings destroyed.† Though the little town suffered severely, the fortress itself was comparatively uninjured. As the works occupied a great extent, and were constructed with great solidity; and, as the waters of the Lake of Garda flowed around, through a deep ditch twenty feet wide, the Piedmontese would have found it a difficult matter to enter. In fact, it was very evident that Peschiera capitulated alone from the want of food, and not from any impression made by the besiegers. The opportune surrender, however, was an advantage to the King of Piedmont, not only from its being a good base for operations, and a desirable place for magazines, but from the extent of the force which he was thereby enabled to draw from before it to support his maneuvers in front of the enemy.

On the next day, after his return to Mantua, Marshal Radetzky started out on his return to Verona; and from his headquarters at Sanguinetto on the 5th, he writes, that his march over Mantua on the flanks of the enemy had not entirely fulfilled his expectations; and as the direct march back to Verona would be accompanied with much danger, he had concluded to cross the Adige at Legnano, and to attack Vicenza on his route; by which movement he would place himself in direct

---

* Risorgimento of Turin.   † Radetzky's Dispatch.

communication with the reserve corps under Baron Welden.
Accordingly, on the 9th, an imposing force of the imperial army
approached Vicenza from Comisano, and occupied the Basano
road. At the same time, the Austrians stationed at Montebello advanced toward Monteberico. On the 10th, at dawn,
the attack upon that position commenced. It was valiantly
defended until noon, when all the artillery of the besiegers
being directed against it, it became impossible to defend it
longer. The rest of the town was guarded and defended by
the whole garrison. Eighty bombs were discharged by the
Austrians into the city.

The fire was kept up until evening, when, all the fortifications being taken, the troops of the Pope, under General Durando, by whom the city was principally defended, surrendered.
The garrison was allowed to march out with the honors of war,
and to keep their arms, on condition of not fighting against
the Austrians for three months. The town was evacuated
before noon, and Radetzky returned the same day to Verona, reaching there on the night of the 13th of June. On
the 12th, D'Aspre, with the second army corps, took Padua,
without striking a blow. He had remained with two brigades
at Verona during the absence of Radetzky, and had only left
when the field-marshal was on the march back, in order to
maintain the communication with Vicenza, and thus secure
Radetzky's return. After the affair of Goito, and the sudden
retreat of Radetzky from that part of the field of operations,
Charles Albert extended his army north, to occupy the heights
of Rivoli. General Somnaz, at the head of three brigades, with
the necessary quantity of artillery, the first battalion of tirailleurs, and the volunteers of Pavia and Piacenza, moved, on the
9th, from Sega, Colmassino, Cavajon, and Costuman, to attack the formidable positions of the enemy on all sides. The
fourth division, commanded by the Duke of Genoa, occupied
the heights of Pessina, Boi, and Caprino. The king, who had
transferred his head-quarters to Garda, followed these movements with the columns of Piedmont and Pinerolo, and established himself at Gazzoli. The Piedmontese army thus extended from Goito to Rivoli; and the object seemed to be to
cut off Radetzky's communication with the Tyrol, cross the

Adige, take all the forts above Verona, and then capture that city. The favorable opportunities which the King of Piedmont possessed of executing this plan during the absence of Radetzky from Verona, were lost by unaccountable inaction. The consequence was, not only the sacrifice of a noble prize, almost within his grasp, but the troops, from this inaction, spent all their time in complaining of their officers; and the officers, equally idle, devoted themselves to condemning the plans of those whom accident, and not merit, had placed at their head. As these complaints were none of them unfounded, the train was laid for a rapid demoralization of the whole army.

A plan, it is understood, was made for the capture of Verona, while Radetzky was at Vicenza, and in which the Piedmontese were to have had the assistance of the people of Verona, but which failed through the indecision and inactivity of the king. The citizens of Verona, it is said, had positively agreed to give the Porta Nova to Charles Albert; and that, for the purpose of profiting by the offer, all the troops had been marched, on the 13th, within two miles of the city.* Had the movement taken place twelve hours sooner, complete success was assured; but the king delayed until Radetzky had time to return from Vicenza with ten thousand men; and at two o'clock on the morning of the 14th, when the attack was to begin (and the honor of first entering the town was allotted to the Duke of Savoy), a messenger came to head-quarters, at Alpo, to say that it was too late, and that the people, who were ready to act when the garrison was three thousand, declined to run the risk when it was augmented to thirteen thousand men. The propitious moment was lost, and the king and the army retired, equally dispirited and defeated, to Valeggio. A more striking example of the evil of delay than is exhibited at this time in the conduct of the King of Piedmont, and its consequences, has seldom occurred. The line of the Adige, upon which, according to the just opinion of Napoleon, the possession of Upper Italy depended, and the city of Verona, the acknowledged key to the whole Venetian territory, lay before him, both, at that time, feebly defended. By striking

---

* Evening Mail, June 28, 1848.

at that opportune moment, he would not only have secured those important points, but have cut off Radetzky from all communication with the heart of the empire—the receipt of provisions, as well as the arrival of re-enforcements—to say nothing of a safe and open retreat at any time, should defeat await him.   But, instead of turning his attention to this most important matter, his thoughts seemed to be occupied in securing, at least on paper, the enlargement of his kingdom, and the union of Lombardy and Piedmont.   It was on the afternoon of the 10th, when Radetzky, after a hard-fought battle, was signing the capitulation of Vicenza, that King Charles Albert was affixing his signature to the Act of Union of Lombardy to the kingdom of Sardinia, the document, ready to be signed, having been brought to him by M. Casati and two other members of the Provisional Government of Milan.   According to this compact, the Provisional Government of Milan was to cease its functions immediately, and to be replaced by a Commission of Regency, composed of Piedmontese and Milanese, under the presidentship of M. Casati.

The situation of Charles Albert was, however, not without its embarrassments.   About this time, the Piedmontese ministry gave in their resignations collectively, baffled and divided by the question whether the war should be carried on to the last extremity, or whether a temporizing policy should be adopted.   The ministry professed the latter opinion.   But a still greater source of annoyance to him was, the abrupt refusal of the Provisional Government of Milan to accept what was understood to be the proposition of the Austrian government for a settlement on the basis of the Adige or the Mincio. As long as the "holy war," for which so much idle boasting was heard, and so little in reality done, had even the semblance of being national, Charles Albert was willing to encounter all the risks which the prosecution of it demanded ; but, after having been deserted by Naples, by Rome, and but inefficiently supported by Tuscany ; when he perceived that the question was no longer Italian, but Piedmontese, his enthusiasm in the cause underwent some abatement.   The army, at the same time, became discouraged.   The Piedmontese had learned wisdom at the price of their blood, and, unable to disguise from

themselves that they were left alone to fight the national quarrel, they were beginning to calculate the extent of the sacrifices
that had been made, those which were still required, and such
as the effective prosecution of the war might yet demand.
They saw that all the coin of the realm had flowed to the seat
of war, that the strength of the people was exhausted in the
struggle, and that the fields at home absolutely remained un-
tilled, because the arms that should cultivate them were in
the camp. These sacrifices were willingly made so long as
success followed the operations of the king, and the other Italian troops joined in the national cause and contributed to its
maintenance; but now, when victory had become more doubtful, and the Piedmontese found that the whole burden had
fallen to their lot, they began to cool down in their ardor, and
to become clamorous for a settlement. Charles Albert was
willing to accept what the Austrians were desirous of giving,
and a nobleman in the confidence of the king, it was understood, was dispatched to Turin, with the intention of consulting
the ministry and the heads of the parties on the subject, and
that plain language had been used to the Provisional Government of Milan, for the purpose of securing its consent. But
the Milanese and the Venetians were more anxious that the
king should prosecute the war for the recovery of the Venetian
kingdom, which, with the exception of the capital, was every
foot of it in possession of the Austrians. To this proposal the
king declared, that he would only advance with the whole, and
not with a portion of his army; and he inquired if the Milanese had power to defend their own territory, and protect Brescia, Bergamo, and the capital itself. The Lombardians were
of opinion that an army corps of thirty thousand men were
quite sufficient to reconquer Venetia, and that the rest of the
force should be left to protect the line of the Mincio; but the
king wisely determined not to divide his army, or to compromise his own position by operating against an enemy who had
sixty-five thousand men in hand, without at least an equal
number.

For these reasons, the whole Piedmontese army, a force of
at least sixty-five thousand men, extending from the vicinity
of Mantua to Rivoli, a distance of nearly thirty miles, re

mained paralyzed, and without any movement or occurrence to disturb the inaction, except an occasional skirmish between the outposts.

About this time, the Emperor of Austria, deeming the moment when success attended the Austrian arms an appropriate one for advancing some proposals of reconciliation with the Lombardo-Venetian kingdom, orders Marshal Radetzky to suspend hostile operations for a brief period, and again dispatches Count Hartig on the errand of peace, and with his views as to the terms of settlement; but the opposition of Radetzky, and the whole Austrian army, to any suspension of hostilities at this moment was so great, that the emperor concluded to decline taking any such steps, and especially while the King of Piedmont remained an invader on the imperial territories.

There is no doubt that Charles Albert, and every person of reason and influence in the court and in the army, were at this time inclined to accept the terms lately offered by Austria, and to secure, by conceding the Tyrol and the Adige, the magnificent conquest of Lombardy, and the conversion of a monarchy, with only four millions of inhabitants, into a kingdom having nine millions at its disposal, and one of the richest and most productive soils of Italy. They both well knew that such a result of a first campaign has seldom been attained by the most successful conqueror, and that even his warm expectations, formed at the opening of the invasion, could scarcely have anticipated so important an acquisition at so small a cost. The king was fully aware that his dominions, as King of Piedmont, Savoy, and Lombardy, would be far more secure than if Venitia were added to them. In the one case, the Austrians would respect a frontier, which a wise policy shows is most beneficial to the empire; while, in the other, they knew that Austria would not freely relinquish the head of the Adriatic, and that the extreme frontier must ever be maintained in a state of war—defensive war. The union of Piedmont, Savoy, and Lombardy would not give offense to, or inspire alarm in the other powers of Italy; but, on the other hand, would not the Pope and the King of Naples be, in common prudence, compelled to preserve an armed neutrality, when they found the self-styled King of Italy in possession of the Alps, and the

two seas, and nine millions of inhabitants ?   And when France
should revive from the internal agony under which her best
energies for the moment were prostrated, would she behold on
the Italian frontier the creation of a powerful monarchy, without natural feelings of jealousy ?   It was a question, also, these
views would suggest, whether the annexation of Savoy to
France, on the same grounds of nationality and language that
formed the pretexts for this crusade, could not be with equal
justice demanded ; and Charles Albert, well aware of the influence of example, would scarcely hazard losing a province,
whence the best of his army was derived, for the doubtful acquisition of a territory whose fidelity could not be implicitly
relied on.   In short, every motive of reason and policy induced
the king to give a favorable ear to nogotiation ; but popular
clamor was so great, the vapid nonsense repeated about the
"holy war" and the national cause was so loud, that he doubtless felt himself forced in honor to persevere, when it was no
longer prudent, in his opinion, or consonant, perhaps, with the
plans with which he entered the contest.*

The two great political aims, of equal interest to the entire
community of Europe, and which seemed to engage the attention of the whole continent at this time, were involved in the
struggle then going on in the north of Italy.   The first was,
without doubt, the independence of that new state which had
been called into existence by the arms of the house of Savoy,
by the eventful circumstances of the times, and by the promise of a liberal Constitution under the tutelary genius of a
monarchy, to which several of the Italian states had already
spontaneously and unanimously adhered.   The second was the
re-establishment of peace upon terms consistent with the security of the Austrian empire, so that if the imperial court was
to be relieved from the government of a disaffected province,
and the danger of an exhausting war, Austria might have ample
security on her southern frontier against the possibility of foreign aggression, and, although she should lose a portion of her
Italian subjects, might still find in Italy a barrier and an ally
against the more formidable power of the French Republic.

---

* London Times.

In the state of Europe at this time, to settle the first of these questions was to contribute largely to the settlement of the second. By some it was thought not for the interest of Austria herself to attempt the reconquest of Lombardy, even if such an enterprise were possible in the face of the Piedmontese army and the decided hostility of the entire population. On the other hand, the establishment of a regular and monarchical government in the north of Italy was the best security against the extension of the revolutionary propaganda in that direction.* No power in Europe at this time, not even Austria herself perhaps, rent as she was by insurrection in all her provinces, and her very capital in the hands and under the control of revolutionists, supposed that it would ever be possible for her to regain the lost province; and the question then at issue, in its most practical form, seemed to be, which of the rivers that fall into the Adriatic should be the boundary of the Austrian empire — the Adige, the Piave, the Tagliamento, or the Isonzo? When Bonaparte had penetrated to Leoben, in 1796, after the annihilation of three Austrian armies, he extended the territory of the Cis-Alpine Republic to the last-mentioned stream, and his power touched in the Bay of Trieste, the most important maritime position of the Austrian empire and of Southern Germany.

But at this time, in the relative positions of both belligerents to each other, to Europe, and especially to France, such a concession was more than Austria could make or Charles Albert obtain. But the question was even more political than military. A serious reverse might depress the Italians, but what effect would it have upon the French? This was the point which most concerned the independence of Italy, the security of Austria, and the peace of Europe. A turbulent party in Paris might avail itself of this event, as it did in the Polish question, to raise the cry of war, and hurry its troops to the scene of action; while, on the other hand, it was currently believed that the German Confederation would actively espouse the cause of Austria in the quarrel, by sending the Federal troops of Bavaria and Wurtemberg to occupy the frontiers

---

* London Times.

of Tyrol as part of the territories of the German Confederation, in consequence of the blockade of Trieste by an Italian
squadron.   Thus would all Europe be once again involved in
war.*

While these speculations were indulged in throughout Europe, Marshal Radetzky, whose policy, it had long been evident, was to fight a decisive battle when and where he thought
fit, was slowly but gradualy collecting all his resources for the
great blow, which was certain sooner or later to come.   In the
mean time, as the period for final operations against the Piedmontese army had not yet arrived, Radetzky, having left sufficient forces in Verona and Mantua, proceeded with the balance
of his troops to reconquer the Venetian kingdom to the Austrian sceptre, as well as, by this diversion, to draw Charles Albert,
if possible, from his fortified position between the Adige and
the Mincio.   The King of Piedmont employed himself in executing the hydraulic operations against Mantua proposed by
Napoleon in his memoirs.   The waters of the lake were devi-
ated and lowered, so that the miasmatic effluvia produced fatal consequences to the garrison, and the water at Porta Moli-
na being drawn off; the mill stopped, and the inconvenience
and mortality in consequence were very great.

During these operations on the wings of the army, the two
main bodies, the one about Verona and the other along the
Mincio, with head-quarters at Villa-Franca, remained in a state
of inactivity, except in the preparations making for a more
vigorous prosecution of the war.

Slight engagements took place between the advanced posts,
and which were, by their respective parties, magnified by
high-sounding bulletins into great affairs, but which were
without the slightest result upon the general current of events.
One of these occurred on the 30th of June, on the plateau of
Rivoli, which resulted favorably to the Austrians, and in which
a large number of Piedmontese laid down their arms.

On the other hand, a " small affair," as termed by the disinterested, but characterized by the Italian bulletins as a brilliant victory, took place on the 18th of July, at Governolo, a

* London Times.

village on the Mincio, near the confluence .of that river with
the Po.   General Bava, with a few regiments of Piedmontese
troops, attacked three thousand Austrians, who were intrenched
in that position, carried the bridge by a brilliant charge of
cavalry and flying artillery, and took four hundred and fifty
prisoners, four pieces of artillery, two standards, and put the
Austrians to flight.

Meantime, heavy and vast preparations were making on
both sides for the decisive blow, which every one saw must
soon occur.   For some time great movements had been perceptible at Peschiera, in the arrival of Lombardian troops and
arms of all kinds.   The Piedmontese force at this time was
divided between Rivoli and the heights between the Lake of
Garda and the Upper Adige, and the ground occupied by Goito, Roverbella, and Villa-Franca, and these advantageous positions were strongly protected by several lines of fortifications.
Twenty thousand men were stationed on the left of the lines,
while at least forty thousand occupied the right, and protected
the Mincio.   About five thousand Tuscan troops had lately
arrived on the Mincio, and fifteen thousand Lombard levies on
the Oglio ; but upon these not much reliance was placed.

Works of circumvallation were being executed around Mantua, on the right side, while a large portion of the army were
so placed as to complete the blockade on the left bank, and
to oppose any aggression, either from Verona or Legnano.
Trenches were opened on the principal roads by which the
enemy might issue forth.   Strong works were at the same
time proceeding against Verona : many covert ways were ex-
cavated around the town, and movable barricades constructed to approach the walls, with loop-holes for heavy cannon, as
well as capable of being manned by sharp-shooters.   Heavy
intrenchments were also thrown up, from which they intended to bombard the road along the Adige, and to secure thereby the communication with the left side of the river.

On the other hand, Marshal Radetzky was gradually and effectually concentrating his forces around Verona ; nine regiments had reached there by the way of Vicenza, and the roads
for some days from Codroipo were crowded with men wending their way to head-quarters.   On the 21st, twelve thousand

Q

men entered Verona from Vicenza. Radetzky was busily engaged reconnoitering and feeling the lines of the enemy at various points, and resorting to every stratagem to draw him beyond his intrenchments, or entice him into the commission of some false step.

This opportunity soon occurred; for the King of Piedmont, interested in the blockade of Mantua, which he superintended in person, was guilty of the imprudence of stripping the valuable positions of Rivoli and the heights covering Peschiera, overlooking the plain of Verona; and, in violation of all the rules of war, by the occupation of a long straggling line, strong only in the point most distant from the centre of operations; and this in the face of a formidable enemy, who only awaited the first false move of his adversary to commence an overwhelming attack. The military eye of Radetzky in a moment detected this false step of his adversary, and every preparation was instantly made to take advantage of the imprudence of the enemy. On the 20th and 21st, all communication between Verona and Mantua were interrupted.

In anticipation of this movement on the part of the Piedmontese, the marshal, on the 21st, directed the third army corps, under Count Thurn, to march against the left wing of the enemy at Rivoli; and, on the afternoon of the 22d, informed by a report from Major-general Baron Simbschen, in Sanguinetto, that the enemy stood nine thousand strong at Governolo, four thousand at Castellano, and four thousand at Castelbelforte, his resolution for attack was immediately taken. The third army corps, which had been dispatched the day before, quietly passed the Upper Adige at the foot of the Montebaldo, or great mountain, which overlooks Rivoli, and is, as it were, the guardian giant of the river, and attacked the hostile position on La Corona, and carried it by storm. A re-enforcement of thirteen hundred infantry and half a battery of artillery retrieved for a time the disastrous state of affairs; but the Piedmontese stationed there were at length obliged to retreat before them to their position at Rivoli. On the next day the Austrians advanced from La Corona, and, after a vigorous resistance, carried the plateau and all the lines of Rivoli; the Piedmontese, in number about twenty-five thousand, who defended them, falling back in tolerable order to Sandra, a few miles beyond, abandoning two pieces of artillery, but securing their baggage. On the 24th, Count Thurn advanced to Pastrengo and Sandra to blockade Peschiera. While these operations were proceeding on the right, under the orders of Marshal Radetzky, the first and second reserve corps, on the night between the 22d and 23d, about one o'clock, started out from Verona during a frightful storm, and, to avoid any notice of their approach, having their horses' hoofs and the wheels of their carriages covered with cloth, and, two hours before day, appeared before Villa-Franca, Somma Campagna, and Sona. They were directed by · their veteran chief to storm those heights, and to advance, in case of success, to the Mincio at two different points. For that purpose, the first reserve corps marched over Gerastala and Oliosi, and the second reserve over San Giorgio. An infantry and cavalry brigade were ordered to occupy the enemy, between the road of Sona and Busolongo, by a sham fight, in order to deceive him as to the real point of attack.*

General Simbschen was directed to leave only a detachment at Legnano, and to march with his brigade over Villa Fontana and Isolalta to the heights of Custoza. All these orders, says the marshal, were executed promptly and bravely. At eight o'clock they reached the hostile intrenchments.; and while the force that had been so successful at Rivoli attacked the right flank of General Somnaz, these made a tremendous assault in front, and carried by storm, at ten o'clock, the heights of Sona, Somma Campagna, and Bosco, and all the elevations running from Busolongo on the Upper Adige to Valeggio, on the Mincio, and overlooking the vast plain in which the great fortress of Villa-Franca stands. The Italians occupying these points, consisting of the regiments of Pignorol, of a part of that of Savoy, of some Tuscan regular troops, Modenese volunteers, and Milanese levies (in all not exceeding five thousand), made a noble defense, and, it is said, put *hors de combat* no less than three thousand of the enemy ; but, before so formidable a force, and attacked in front and in flank, they were compelled to give

---

* Radetzky's Dispatch.

way, and, after a resistance of several hours, sought shelter in
Peschiera and on the other side of the Mincio.

On the evening of that day the victorious Austrians had their
head-quarters at San Giorgio; the first corps stood on the Mincio, the second in Castel Novo, and the van-guard against Peschiera.   They had thus covered the whole line of the left bank
of the Mincio, and regained the entire territory from the foot
of Monte Baldo, between the Upper Adige and the Lake of Garda, and all the heights between the Upper Adige and the Mincio, from Busolongo to Valeggio.   All this they accomplished
in one day, although it took the King of Piedmont two months
to establish himself in the same position.   " By this operation," says Marshal Radetzky, " I govern now all the hostile
passages over the Mincio at Peschiera, Salionze, and Monzanbano, and threaten that of Valeggio.   I have a strong position
against Villa-Franca and Roverbella, the communications with
the Tyrol are open, and that land free from further hostilities."
On Monday morning, the 24th, the Austrians attempted the
passage of the Mincio at two different points.   Under the fire
of the enemy, who had fallen back from Sondra, at Salionze,
three miles below Peschiera, the Austrians laid double pontoon
bridges across the river, and accomplished its passage with two
brigades of the reserve corps, and one of the first army corps;
and at Ponti, three miles on the right bank, captured three cannons and twenty-six wagons.   At the same time, another brigade of the latter corps advanced over Brentina to Monzanbano, took the bridge after a short engagement, and occupied the
latter town.   The brigade Strassaldo, of the division of Prince
Schwartzenberg of the first army corps, occupied it the same
day, and the brigade Wohlgemuth advancing the next morning
to Borghetto, opposite Valeggio, the bridge was immediately restored; three passages over the Mincio were thus secured to the
imperialists, and they were safe from an attack on either side
of the river.

On learning the disasters of Rivoli, the King of Piedmont
advanced at once with six thousand from Marmirol, in the
neighborhood of Mantua—the ill-chosen head-quarters whence
all his misfortunes date—giving orders to the Duke of Savoy
to follow with all his troops that could be collected.   In this

way, a body of about thirty thousand men were concentrated at Villa-Franca, and on that night (Tuesday) and the next morning the whole advanced in good order, and burning to avenge the defeat on the Mincio. On the evening previous, Marshal Radetzky was informed that the enemy had forced the brigade of Major-general Simbschen at Custoza, advanced to Monte Godio, and taken the heights of Custoza. Learning that they intended to attack his positions from Custoza to Valeggio, and to give a general battle, the marshal ordered the third army corps to march from Castel Novo against Peschiera, and to blockade that fortress from the right and from the left side of the Mincio; the second army corps, stationed at the same place, to occupy the position between Custoza and Somma Campagna; and the four brigades, stationed on the right side of the Mincio, to repair back that night across the river, over Salionze, Monzambano, and Borghetto, and to take place in the centre of the right wing of the army, as re-enforcement.* In that position, the Austrians, having every confidence in their superior skill and discipline over the enemy, calmly awaited the onset.

The principal attack was directed against Custoza, Somma Campagna, and Sona. The attack was impetuous, and the resistance obstinate; but the numbers and valor of the Piedmontese prevailed, and all the positions were, for a moment, in their possession; but the Austrians, re-enforced by the troops which Marshal Radetzky had prudently recrossed over the Mincio, the Piedmontese were driven back. Undaunted by this reverse, the gallant troops of Charles Albert re-formed at the foot of the heights, and again advanced, carrying every thing before them; but, as they ascended the heights, they were again met by increased forces, and the battle hung for some time in suspense. The Sardinian troops had now fought from five in the morning until five in the evening. As usual, they were left without refreshment, and no care had been taken to provide for a reverse. At this moment, by the orders of Radetzky, who seemed to have calculated every thing with the greatest precision, a large body of fresh troops issued from Verona, and fell upon

---

* Radetzky's Dispatch.

the flank of the exhausted Sardinians, while the other force renewed its attack in front.   Charles Albert was obliged to yield
victory and withdraw to Villa-Franca.   The troops on both
sides behaved with great gallantry.   The heat of the day was
so excessive, that several of the Austrian soldiers fell dead in
the ranks while marching.   During the thickest of the fight,
at Custoza, the king and his two sons, and the regiment of
carabineers, were completely surrounded, and must have fallen
into the hands of the Austrians, had not the brigade of Savoy
made a dash for them, and gallantly liberated their monarch
and the princes.

The conquered Piedmontese retired on Villa-Franca, a place
quite open to the plain, which the enemy might have carried,
had they not been prevented by exhaustion or other plans in
view; and the night closed, in that village, on the broken fortunes of the King of Piedmont, who was destined never again
to witness another prosperous day.   The imprudence and folly
of the king, which led to this, and consequently to all his disasters is by many, ascribed to the fact of his being the victim
of a stratagem practiced upon him.   It appears that, a few
days before, one of the most influential personages of the Austrian army (Prince Lichtenstein) was taken prisoner, and conducted to his majesty; and but little doubt was entertained
that he had put himself in the way of being captured, that he
might more fully concert the plot to which Charles Albert fell
a victim.   It was with great astonishment that the army saw
this personage liberated and allowed to re-enter Mantua; but
he was released, it was said, after having agreed with the king,
for the price of one million of francs, to deliver up the fortress.
The object of this stratagem was to get the King of Piedmont
to withdraw from the left of his lines a considerable proportion
of his forces, in which event Radetzky saw that he might strike
a severe blow.   To effect this, it was made one of the conditions of the transaction, that a great body of troops should be
drawn round Mantua, and an effective blockade established, in
order that it might be believed that the garrison surrendered
from necessity only, and from the fact that the gate nearest
the Piedmontese had been forced.

At the earliest dawn of day, the king abandoned Villa-Franca, and crossed the Mincio to Goito, which had been for some time his head-quarters, which was well fortified, and where he expected to have made an effectual stand.   On the same day, Radetzky marched, with his army in two columns, on Pozzalenga—not desiring to attack the strong position of Goito in front, or follow up the king in his retreat from Villa-Franca by Roverbella, across the Mincio to it—crossed a large body of troops over the Mincio at Salionze, a station higher up the river, and carried an overwhelming mass from Monzambano on Volta, and from that height attacked Goito in the rear, and quickly dislodged the Piedmontese.   Prodigies of valor were performed by the gallant Savoyards.   A regiment of Savoy troops actually retook and held Volta for several hours, by a charge of bayonets, against a strong battery of Croats, supported by double their number.   But the greatest courage, unaided by able and experienced officers, to direct the movements of the troops, could not prevail in opposition to highly disciplined soldiers, under the command of skillful and distinguished generals ; and the Piedmontese were forced to abandon, not only Volta, but their intrenched camp at Goito, beyond it, with all their cannon.   The defeat was so total, that the private coffers of the King of Piedmont, containing two millions of francs, as well as all the table service of silver, and his equipage, fell into the hands of the Austrians.   In consequence of this defeat, the king demanded a truce, which was granted by Marshal Radetzky, on the condition of his immediate retreat over the Oglio.   A longer truce, to extend until the 28th, prescribed the surrender of Venice, Peschiera, and Osopo to the Austrian troops, and an immediate retreat behind the Adda.

These terms, considered by Charles Albert too humiliating, were declined ; and the field-marshal, in consequence of the refusal, continued his pursuit of the enemy.   The king, in his retreat from Goito, passed the night of the 27th at Asola ; and the next day crossed the Oglio and proceeded to Bozzalo, a small town between the Oglio and the Po ; and the remains of " the grand army" were encamped in the same direction.   At three o'clock, on the morning of the 29th, the king, after leaving that place and making a short circuit to the different posts, proceeded to Cremona.

On the same day, the first army corps of the imperialists arrived at Casal Romana, the second corps at Cunetto. The vans of both corps stood on the Oglio. The reserves were at Aqua Negra. The fourth corps advanced from Mantua to Marcaria.

The king, on reaching Cremona, renewed his demand for a truce. But now Radetzky demands full reparation for all the expenses of the war. Of the grand Italian army, which lately numbered eighty thousand men, there were not twenty thousand in all available for service. The others were disposed of, on a rough calculation, in the following manner : in hospitals previous to the late affair, fifteen thousand; killed, wounded, and prisoners within the past week, ten thousand ; dispersed in regiments and half regiments, some at Brescia, some at Lonato, and others at Cremona, twenty thousand; deserters, principally Lombardians and Modanese, five thousand; stragglers that crossed the Po and returned toward Piedmont, ten thousand. The army was completely broken up, and could no longer be united ; though it was attempted to collect all those who retired on Brescia or Cremona, and again unite them with the divisions still under the orders of the king, consisting of the remains of the brigades of Aosta, of Guardo, of Savoy, and of Corny, and the major part of the artillery, and about twenty-two hundred lancers.

It was perfectly vain for the king to attempt with such a force to oppose a victorious army, high in spirits, supplied with every thing, and directed with consummate skill. What a striking instance of the uncertainty of all human affairs do not the events of these few days present! One week before, and the proud Piedmontese army, numbering from fifty to sixty thousand men, extended from the Upper Adige along the whole line of the Mincio to Mantua—every hill-top fortified and bristling, with an army exulting in the consciousness of strength, superior in numbers to the enemy, and now scattered to the winds, so that no *rappel* or trump of war can call together one third of their number.

For these disasters the king himself is, in a great measure, censurable. His own inexperience in battle, and his undue preference for generals who knew nothing of the art of war,

and who neither possessed or deserved the confidence of the
troops, were strong obstacles to his success.   One great error
of Charles Albert was his removal of the Duke of Genoa and
Colonel La Marmora from Rivoli, and intrusting that important point at the extreme of the left wing to a force not exceeding eight hundred men.   He was also wrong in depriving the
position commencing on the Adige and extending to Valeggio,
on the Mincio, of all but five thousand men ; and he was still
more unwise in collecting forty thousand men on the extreme
right, around Mantua, in such a manner that they were unable
to assist each other or re-enforce in time any part of the line.
Of all these blunders his veteran adversary knew how to take
full advantage.   He contrived, at the expense of a few men,
to occupy the king's attention at Governolo and at Ostiglia,
until his plans were ripe, his re-enforcements had arrived, and
he had prepared the torrent with which he overwhelmed his
adversary.   Marshal Radetzky, in like manner, evinced great
skill in not following the king to Villa-Franca and Goito, but
in crossing the Mincio in the centre of the line, winning the
race to the heights of Volta, and thus turning the position of
Goito, which had been strengthened with so much care against
an attack in front from Mantua ; by which the Piedmontese
were driven into the low grounds and kept there, while the
Austrian general commanded all the heights, and could extend
his lines without risk between the Mincio and the Oglio, so as
to force the enemy to the Po, while he could cross the Oglio
when and where he pleased.

But the King of Piedmont's disasters were ascribable not
only to his want of proficiency in the science of war, but to his
utter ignorance or neglect of the very details of service, especially in the organization of a good commissariat.   At a moderate calculation, one tenth of the Piedmontese, it was thought,
fell not from the fire of the enemy, but from want of food and
excessive fatigue.   For three days, and during the hardest
fighting, the troops were without proper supplies of food—men
dropping from hunger on the road, because fresh troops were
not detailed at the right moment, or necessary provisions sea-
sonably furnished.   Bread and wine, it is believed, were sent
at intervals to the men, but that the wagoners took to flight,

and, cutting their traces, escaped with their horses, leaving their loaded wagons in the road. The ammunition carts were said to have been deserted in like manner. These things were not accidents, but criminal oversights, because sufficient escorts were not sent to control the drivers or take their place in case of need.

Another great error was also committed, and which accounts for the rapidity of the defeat. All the new levies had been drafted into Sardinian second battalions, in the proportion of two and three to one, in the expectation that the good example of one third old soldiers would fortify the courage of the two thirds of younger. But the consequence was that the two thirds ran, and the one third who remained were slaughtered on the spot. A position thought to be defended by fifteen hundred was, in reality, defended only by five hundred; and thus points were given up which it was of the utmost importance to preserve.

At Cremona, the King of Piedmont published two orders of the day, to the effect that he, anxious to give the troops some repose after their late fatigues, had applied for an armistice; but the terms were not honorable to the army, and he had refused them. He therefore called on officers and men to remember that the enemy was still before them, and to join him in making due exertion to save the common cause and interest of all.

The deep thunder of the cannon heard at Cremona on the 30th of July gave notice that the Austrians were crossing the Oglio; and the king, quitting Cremona, began to make dispositions to receive the enemy; and, as the artillery was still in tolerable condition, and the cavalry not much cut up, sanguine hopes were entertained of being able to make an effective stand. The line of the Adda* was taken: the river immortalized by the affair of the bridge of Lodi, in Napoleon's campaign. The first line on the left bank, extending from Crema to Pizzighetone (a small fortress on that stream), and the second on the right bank, from Lodi to Codogno, a considerable

---

* On this stream occurred the victory of Aignadel, gained by the French on the 14th of May, 1509, which laid Lombardy prostrate.

town between Cremona and Lodi, and where the head-quarters of the king were established after abandoning Cremona.

To turn to the movements of the Austrians after the victory of Goito. By orders of Radetzky, Strassaldo advanced to Brescia. Every where the troops met with a most cordial reception from the peasantry.

The two cannons taken from the brigade Simbschen, on the heights of Custoza, were recaptured at Goito. Field-marshal Lichtenstein distributed among the army the two millions of francs belonging to Charles Albert, and taken in the battle of Goito.

Three army corps cross the Oglio, after a small engagement between the vans, on the 30th ; the fourth advanced from Marcaria over Bozzolo. The first and second army corps, with the reserves, take position at Godesco and St. Ambrogio, two miles from Cremona. The field-marshal took up his head-quarters that night in Cremona, which the same morning, in haste, Charles Albert had abandoned.

In that city Charles Albert could not procure provisions ; where, as soon as they heard of the king's approach, the Provisional Government dissolved, and the National Guard decamped. No preparations whatever were made for the troops : they were left without wine or provisions, and, to all appearance, were in an enemy's country. At the approach of the Austrians, how changed their conduct ! A deputation was sent out to announce the submission of the place, a flattering address delivered, bands playing, one hundred oxen presented, and provisions of all kinds, as well as a large sum in ready cash. The town was illuminated for three successive nights in honor of the emperor, and the Austrians every where hailed as their deliverers, with the cry, " *I nostri liberatori !*" The King of Piedmont, still at Codogno, had proposed to change his head-quarters to a small place called Casele, in the direction of Piacenza, but the unexpected arrival of Mr. Abercrombie, British minister at Turin (whose object was to tender his services toward procuring a truce between the parties), induced him to countermand that order.

Mr. Abercrombie, accompanied by the French minister to Turin, after two hours' interview with the king, started for

Cremona, in search of Marshal Radetzky. At the interview between the marshal and the ministers, Radetzky, so far from granting a six days' truce, refused to give a single hour ; and he stated firmly, but most courteously, to the ministers his intention of following up the Piedmontese army to the gates of Milan, and of entering it in triumph on the next or the succeeding day.*

The king, on hearing from Mr. Abercrombie, who returned immediately to Lodi (to which place his majesty's head-quarters had been changed), the result of the interview with Radetzky, instantly abandoned all idea of defending the line of the Adda, and resolved to concentrate all his troops before Milan, and there decline or accept a final battle with his enemy. The order of march was given, and the road to Milan was soon covered by the long train of artillery, cavalry, infantry, and luggage. The brigade of Savoy was left to cover the retreat, and to watch the ever-memorable, but now blazing bridge of Lodi, set fire to by orders of a captain of a Lombard company, much to the regret of all the high officers of the army.

The king and the royal dukes abandoned Lodi at ten o'clock. at night for Milan, and, whether in accordance with a declaration, made at the opening of the campaign, that he would not enter that city but as a conqueror, or for the purpose of encouraging the troops by sharing their quarters, the king did not, upon his arrival at the Lombardian capital, enter the gates, but took up his quarters in a small house a little removed from the Porta Romana.

The Piedmontese army occupied a line about two miles distant from Milan, the left resting on the villages in front of the Porta Romana, and the right on those in advance of the Porta Ticinese ; in fact, making face to the country through which the Austrians must advance from Lodi and the other points at which they crossed the Adda. To all appearance, it seemed at that time the intention of Charles Albert to decide the matter there, if the troops were resolved to do their duty.

---

* The old marshal, it would seem, was determined on restoring the status quo ante bellum, and of occupying Lombardy to the Po and the Ticino before the French troops, said to be on their way, could possibly arrive, and thus of converting them from an auxiliary into an invading force.

In the mean time, Radetzky, having left a brigade to garrison Cremona, continued his operations against the Adda with four army corps. On the 2d of August, he passed the Adda, with the first and second army corps, at Crotta d'Adda, and with the fourth army corps at Formigara. The enemy occupying the left of the river were driven back, and the marshal, surrounding the fortress of Pizzighettone, forced the enemy, by that operation, to abandon Formigara. The Austrians advanced incessantly toward Milan ; the wing passing through Crema encountered no opposition. After a short engagement between the Austrian van and Piedmontese rear, Lodi is taken. Radetzky then dispatches two cavalry divisions in the direction of Boffalara, to take Milan in the rear, while he would operate with the main forces in front.

The marshal, leaving Lodi on the morning of the 4th, advanced with the first and second army corps as far as San Donati, when they became engaged with the enemy in their positions before Milan. The first army corps occupied the enemy in front, while General Clamm succeeded in passing around, to take him on the right flank. The Piedmontese were soon overpowered, and driven back under the very walls of the city. A whole battery, four officers, and one hundred and twenty men, were captured. In consequence of this reverse, an order for all the troops to retire into the city was given. The king took up his head-quarters in the remains of the ruined citadel, and the enemy lined the bastions, which overlook and command the country.

At the same moment, it having been understood that the king meant to defend the city, a placard was posted up, ordering the tocsin to be sounded, and barricades to be erected in all the streets. The order was at once obeyed. While all the church bells were set in motion, the men, women, and children commenced the erection of barricades, and in the course of two hours the face of the city was quite changed ; barricades were constructed every twenty yards, and heaps of small paving stones carried up by the servants to the several floors, to be showered on the heads of the Croats, as was done during the five days. All this was great madness and folly ; for if the Austrians forced the city, every house would be sacked and plundered; and, with an army burning to revenge the treatment they received during the first outbreak, it might become a heap of ruins. The Provisional Government had been abolished, in order that the defense without the lines might not have the appearance of originating with the citizens, but undertaken simply by order of the king's governor, General Olivieri. But what excuse could now be rendered, when Radetzky would have the evidence of the barricades before his eyes, hear the tocsin sounded from every tower, and learn from his spies that the inhabitants were all compromised. About five o'clock, the French chargé d'affaires and the English consul proposed to visit the head-quarters of Radetzky, to claim a suspension of arms for a few hours, to enable them to provide for the safe exit of French and British subjects. The party set out; but by the time an escort was provided, it was ascertained that the Austrians had for the moment retired, and the mission did not then take place. With that facility of invention peculiar to the Italians, reports were immediately circulated that the enemy had been beaten off; that several pieces of cannon and several hundreds of prisoners had been taken; and the people, inspired by such favorable tidings, worked at the barricades more earnestly than ever, while every body capable of carrying a musket rushed to the bastions. Popular enthusiasm was now at its height; and if the people and army were really united, and the *morale* of the latter had not been lost, they might have offered a most formidable, if not effectual resistance. At eleven o'clock at night, two of the king's generals,* charged with a special message from his majesty, accompanied by the diplomatic authorities mentioned above, set out for the head-quarters of the Austrian commander. Owing to a mistake in the night-signals made by the Austrian outposts, the party were fired at several times, but at length reached the quarters of Radetzky. The missions being totally distinct, the diplomatic authorities declined being present at the interview of the Piedmontese officers with the Austrian commander. The generals were first admitted, and after a conference, which lasted two hours, withdrew. The consuls

---

* Generals Rossi and Lazzari.

were then admitted; and when they intimated their desire to
obtain a forty hours' truce, Radetzky exclaimed "For what
purpose, when they have capitulated?"   This was the first notice given of so important a fact; and on the diplomatists retiring, and questioning the generals on the subject, they admitted that the basis of a capitulation was drawn, with which
they were about returning to the king to obtain his sanction.
At seven o'clock in the morning the party returned to Milan.
The generals waited on the king; and they were followed, in
a short time, by the chargé and consul, for the purpose of ascertaining what his majesty's answer might be, as their ulterior proceedings depended on the capitulation being accepted
or declined.   During their stay at the citadel, a message was
dispatched to Radetzky, bearing the king's answer, acceding
to the terms of capitulation.   What were the terms was not
then known; but, whatever they might be, it was most shameful to have authorized and commanded the erection of barricades and the sounding of the tocsin, when, up to that time,
not a circumstance had occurred which could have given umbrage to the Austrians.   Why did not Charles Albert at once
retire beyond the Ticino, and allow Milan to follow the example of the other cities of Lombardy, and, after the persons most
compromised had fled, open its gates to its old masters.   Within a few minutes after the dispatch of the king's answer, accepting the terms laid down by Radetzky, the whole city was
in possession of the fact.   The excitement became intense;
and, as soon as the reports were confirmed by the departure
of some of the household troops, and many of the royal equipages, in the direction of Turin, it amounted almost to desperation.   Groups flew through all the streets exclaiming, "We
are sold!" "We are betrayed!"   The drums of the National
Guard beat to arms! and men, with muskets on their shoulders, ran like maniacs from place to place, willing to do mischief, but not knowing where to commence.

The populace were fortunately without leaders.   The most
violent of them collected in the square of the Scala theatre,
and in the Corsia del Giardino, before the Casa Greppi, in
which the king was now lodged, and there, finding several carriages prepared for the journey, they at once cut the harness,

withdrew the horses, and overturned the equipages. This was accompanied by the most insulting expressions against the king, but not against the Piedmontese ; and so great was the distinction made that the officers and dragoons who formed the escort of the carriages were compelled to dismount, and were embraced by the people with loud cries of " Long live the Piedmontese army, but death to the traitor Charles Albert!"

A body of National Guards at once took possession of the Casa Greppi, in effect constituting the king a prisoner, and several filled the rooms leading to the royal apartments, loudly declaring that, come what might, Charles Albert should not depart. At the same time, emissaries were dispatched to the several gates, and large bodies of National Guards, assisted by an unarmed mob, resolutely barred ingress or egress. The gates leading toward Turin were blocked up and barricaded, and, with the most violent denunciations, the people declared that the traitor should not be permitted to escape.

About this time, the only two persons belonging to the late Provisional Government, General Pompro Letta and the Abbé Annelli, who had not abandoned the people, drew up a paper to the following effect, which they first read to the crowd, and then sent into the king: " We, the only two members of the government who remain at our post, learning by public rumor that a capitulation, injurious to the honor of all Italy and of the city of Milan, has been made with the Austrian general, in the most urgent manner entreat your majesty to give us some explanation on this important matter." In a short time afterward, both these gentlemen appeared upon the square, and read a declaration of this nature : " The king has assured us on his word of honor, and he offers his life as a guarantee that he will fight with the force of the whole army to the last moment." This declaration calmed, in some degree, the violence of the crowd ; but it was no less generally believed that a capitulation had been made. Still, some color was given to the king's words by the march of the Piedmontese troops having been suspended, and the preparations for his majesty's departure abandoned. The same disorder prevailed during the day in every part of the city, and so far did it proceed that it is believed that the king was compelled to inform the field-marshal that it was not in his power to fulfill the terms of the capitulation.   Although in point of form the capitulation was broken off, in consequence of the violence of the people, Radetzky was not disposed to regard it in that light, and remained perfectly quiet, without a single shot being fired from his advanced posts.   The people did not partake of that opinion, and they were seen on every side strengthening their barricades, and apparently preparing for a resolute defense.   The day and afternoon passed in this manner; but at nightfall the tumult became so violent near the king's residence, that the Duke of Genoa came to the balcony and requested the people to abstain from such angry and violent demonstrations, as his majesty was much indisposed, and earnestly desired repose.   The amiable and gallant prince was received with a volley of hisses; the king was again called a traitor, and he a deceiver. The duke declared that he and his father were determined to fight to the last; but even this did not satisfy, and he withdrew amid cries of "Death to the traitor!" "Death to the impostor!"   Several houses in the suburbs were set on fire, and the horrors of the situation increased by the city being overhung for several hours of the night by a canopy of flame.

After this demonstration on the part of the people, the King of Piedmont, alarmed for his personal safety, resolved to leave Milan.   Taking advantage of the obscurity of the night, as well as of the great confusion which prevailed, surrounded by his household troops, who suddenly dispersed the crowd that blocked up the *contrada* by a charge of cavalry and blank discharges of artillery, the king escaped about three o'clock in the morning, amid the shots and curses of the populace.   Although some of his suite were wounded, the king and the Duke of Genoa fortunately escaped with their lives from the violent hands of the very population which, a few months before, hailed them as their deliverers.

During the night the Archbishop of Milan and the temporary podesta went out to the head-quarters of Field-marshal Radetzky, for the purpose of informing him of the true state of affairs within the city, and of deprecating his wrath.   This was a most judicious step; and it was quite evident, from the forbearance shown by the Austrian troops during the night and

R

next morning, that Radetzky felt aware that the king broke
off the agreement of capitulation merely to satisfy the clamor
of the moment, and that, after a few hours, when the temporary madness was over, its conditions would be fulfilled. At
five next morning the tumult had ceased, the tricolor flags
were withdrawn from many of the balconies, and the barricades were in a state of active demolition. It was evident
that the fever had passed away, and that the people were now
as much depressed as they were on the previous day excited.
Indeed, the best proof which can be given of their having returned to their senses is, that they allowed the free circulation
of the following printed notice :

"Agreeably to the basis of a convention, concluded by his
majesty Charles Albert and his excellency Field-marshal Radetzky, the latter will occupy militarily, at eight to-morrow
(this) morning, the Porta Romana, and at twelve will enter
the city. There is every reason to believe that the population
of Milan will not suffer. It is strongly recommended that the
barricades, tricolored flags, and cockades be removed as quickly as possible.

                              "BASSE, Podesta."
                              "TAVERNE, Assessor."

In fact, this advice was implicitly followed; all the barricades were removed with the same expedition with which they
were raised (save in the vicinity of the Porta Romana, where
the low mob still domineered); and even the pavement, ripped
up the day before in such haste, was rapidly re-laid.

The Austrian civil and military authorities took quiet possession of the city. The change was effected with the most
perfect order; not a rude expression was heard from the people during the passage of the troops; and as the Austrian army
ever maintains the strictest discipline, no offense was given on
their part. It being the Sabbath, nearly all the shops were
closed; and so many of the inhabitants being absent on account of the season, or had fled from fear, or accompanied the
retreat of the Piedmontese troops, that the city presented a dis-
mal appearance indeed. The windows of the Corso were not,

as usual, crowded, and the long array of artillery, dragoons, hussars, lancers, and infantry defiled through it in the most solemn silence. At an early hour, according to the capitulation, the principal gates were occupied; but it was not till late in the afternoon that the whole army made its triumphant entry. The troops were in fine condition; the uniforms varied and splendid, and their appearance, almost fit for parade, presented a striking contrast to the soiled dress and fatigued looks of the brave but defeated Piedmontese, who, during the night, and at an early hour, had taken their departure. The peace of the city was preserved, and the palaces of the nobility protected from further pillage by detachments of the National Guard, who, by order of the podesta, appeared in uniform for that purpose. The damage done by the mob was inconsiderable, save in the palaces of the Dukes of Litta and Visconti. In both, many of the finest pieces of furniture and glasses were broken; but most of the objects abstracted by the thieves were afterward recovered by the police. Before nightfall, all the measures of the Austrian civil and military authorities were taken, the few persons then in the city reposed in the most perfect security; and those who had taken refuge with their respective consuls returned to their own homes. No military precautions, however, were neglected by the commander-in-chief. The Austrian artillery were placed on the bastions as a hint to the ill disposed, and an order of the day issued, declaring the city in a state of siege, and stating that all offenses against good order would be punished according to martial law. By this hour the Piedmontese army had crossed the Ticino, and rested within its own frontiers.

The news now reached Marshal Radetzky that Pavia had surrendered to the fourth army corps; Brescia had opened its gates before the troops under D'Aspre on the 6th; on the following day, Prince Schwartzenberg had entered Bergamo under the acclamations of the people; the second army corps occupied the cities of Como, Lecco, and Sandria; the fortresses of Peschiera, Rocca d'Anfo, and Osopo were delivered up, agreeably to the terms of the truce* entered into with the

---

* For Armistice, see Appendix, note 6.

King of Piedmont, and the whole of Lombardy was evacuated by the enemy. Thus, in the short space of a fortnight from the time that Radetzky took the offensive, had the Piedmontese army—which, in the pride of their conquests, possessed themselves of the whole of Lombardy (with the exception alone of the little spot on which stands the fortress of Mantua), and a considerable portion of the Venetian kingdom—been defeated at Rivoli, Somma Campagna, Custoza, Volta, Cremona, Pizzighettone, and Milan, and driven completely beyond the frontiers of the imperial territories; in the language of Radetzky, in his address to his troops after entering Milan; "You have marched from victory to victory; and, in the short space of a fortnight, advanced victoriously from the Adige to the Ticino. The imperial flag waves again from the walls of Milan, and no enemy any longer treads the Lombardian territory."*

---

* Radetzky's Address.

CHAPTER III.

THE POLITICAL HISTORY OF VENICE, FROM ITS ORIGIN TO THE LATE REVO-
LUTION.—THE EXPULSION OF THE AUSTRIANS, AND PROCLAMATION OF THE
REPUBLIC OF ST. MARK.— ITS EXISTENCE FOR UPWARD OF A YEAR, AND
FINAL OVERTHROW.—BESIEGED BY LAND AND BLOCKADED BY SEA.

VENICE, the proud city of the lagoons, whether we contem-
plate her peculiar geographical position, her once boundless
power and commercial prosperity, or her political longevity,
without a parallel in the annals of human society, must be
regarded as one of the most interesting as well as remarkable
states that ever existed.

In the early part of the fifth century, a small band of fugitives, from Padua, Aquileia, and other adjacent Roman colonies, escaping from the all-wasting sword of Attila and the
devastations of the Goths, sought refuge amid the marshes
and shallows of the Adriatic, formed by the deposits of sand
carried down by the rivers which, descending from the Alps,
fall into that gulf; and there, amid the waters, founded a city
destined to preserve its independence for nearly fourteen hundred years, to resist successfully the combined arms of Europe,
become the conqueror of Constantinople and Athens, and "to
reign over the Archipelago, the Morea, Candia, Cyprus, and the
finest quarter of the Roman empire."

This remarkable state, emerging from the bosom of the
waves in the darkest ages of Italian misery, before the empire
of Rome was swept away, endured through the northern irruptions; and, having been finally extinguished within our own
times, its history forms a connecting chain—perhaps the only
one that can now be traced—between the Europe of the Romans, of the Middle Ages, and of modern times; or, as her
eloquent historian* has described her, enthroned upon the
gulf whence her palaces emerge, contemplating the successive

---

* Sismondi.

changes of dynasties and continual invasions, with the whole shifting scene of human revolutions, until, in her own time, as the last surviving witness of antiquity, and as the link between the two periods of civilization, she has herself bowed under the humbling hand of the destroyer.

Detestation of monarchy and love of independence, as her history discloses, were the leading principles by which Venice was guided from her birth as a nation—distinguished through all the changes of a long and eventful history—and which actuated, in a measure at least, the last movement, when, on the 17th of March, 1848, the double-headed eagle of Austria was torn from the standard before the cathedral, and its place supplied by the winged lion of St. Mark.

In submitting to the common necessity of obeying one leader in war, and having a supreme magistrate to guard their laws, maintain their religion, and preside over the ordinary tribunals, the Venetians never, for a moment, relinquished their right of conferring these powers by election, but continually asserted their power to degrade the possessor from the throne to which they had raised him (nor did they deem any means for the attainment of this end unlawful); and they gradually limited his authority, until at length they subjected him to the control of an aristocracy, which derived its constitutional claim to represent the people from the natural influence of wealth, and the respect derived from a long line of renowned ancestors.

To vest the substantial power in an oligarchy like this, arising from the very nature of civil society, it is only necessary that its members should act with some degree of concert; but the Venetian *few* matured this concert into an artful and organized conspiracy; and, by carefully preserving the republican forms, and cherishing the hatred of monarchy and love of independence, continued to augment their power without awakening suspicion; while, as a means of accommodating the primitive laws of the land to their exclusive interest, they seized on every opportunity of bringing into operation such arbitrary expedients as, in former ages, had only been resorted to in cases of extraordinary emergency. The authority and number of these unconstitutional precedents thus gradually increased, until they came to be regarded as practical parts of the Constitution, and, in fact, furnished the elements out of which the state inquisition was formed, and to which Venice must ascribe her gradual decay and ultimate downfall.

A brief reference to the history of Venice will not only illustrate these events, but exhibit a view of the stages by which democracy gradually dwindled into hereditary aristocracy, and that, in its turn, into a mysterious and unrelenting oligarchy.

The fugitives who first peopled the lagoons of the Adriatic were governed by magistrates sent from Padua, and the Constitution was consequently a consular one; but when the metropolis was, a short time after, devastated by the incursions of the barbarians (A.D. 450–60), the little colonies were emancipated from her guardianship, and left to maintain, as they could, their feeble independence. They established tribunes or judges, of which the number was twelve, and the election annual; and these officers were bound to govern the republic, with the concurrence of a popular Assembly.

This Constitution—which might be called a rude federative democracy—lasted for more than two centuries and a half.

Little inequality, and less ambition, could subsist so long as their manners remained simple and uncorrupted; but frugality and industry brought competence; this rapidly augmented into wealth; and then came the trial. Dissensions arose among those who aspired to govern, intrigues in the annual elections, licentiousness among the people, and all the symptoms of civil war existed, at the very time when their struggles with external enemies imperiously demanded union and co-operation. In this emergency, they elected, for the first time, a chief magistrate, called a doge, who was to hold his office for life (A.D. 697). This title, which is a corruption of Dux,* while it excluded the idea of sovereignty, more peculiarly indicated the office of leader of the national armies.

Having thus provided a conductor of their wars abroad, and combined vigor in the government with security to popular rights at home, their determination never to yield even the shadow of their political independence acquired new strength.

Their jealousy of the power of one man is also evidenced by

---

* Dux-leader.

the fates of their successive doges. Of the forty-three who
reigned in the course of three hundred years, scarcely one half
concluded their career in peace. Five were compelled to abdicate ; three were assassinated by conspirators ; one was condemned to death according to legal form; and nine sentenced to
be deposed and deprived of sight, or sent into exile ; and sometimes many of these punishments were united. Some only escaped them by dying on the field of battle. Yet few, if any,
of these victims had brought any great calamity on the republic, while many had extended her dominion and her fame, by
the acquisition of extensive provinces on the Adriatic, and by
planting some of those colonies in the Archipelago, which afterward facilitated her conquests in the East, and aided the
growth of her adventurous commerce.

Considering that these magistrates were restrained by no
specific forms, and punishable by no process but the blind fury
of the mob, it is wonderful how the state was preserved from
hereditary obedience to a ducal family.

The audacious attempt of a member of the family of Ur-
seolo to seat himself, without even the form of popular suffrage,
on the throne which several of his illustrious house had occupied with honor, awakened the jealousy of the Venetians, and
produced, in 1032, a fundamental law of state, that the reigning doge should never associate a son in the administration.

One hundred and forty years were suffered to elapse before
any further alteration was attempted in the Venetian Constitution; and it was at length, during the anarchy which followed the murder of a doge, that the Council of Justice, the
only permanent deliberative body of the state, persuaded the
people to adopt a political system, which at once offered security against the exercise of arbitrary power by the doge, and
obviated, at the same time, the inconvenience of the general
and tumultuous assemblies of the people. It is not known by
what skillful address the Council of Justice prevailed upon the
people to consent to an innovation which, in a great measure,
deprived the democracy of its influence ; but from this period
(1112) may certainly be dated the foundation of the oligarch-
ical government of Venice.

The persecutions and punishments which thus followed every attempt on the part of the doges to render the throne hereditary, and the judicial trials and executions by which the state repressed all schemes of personal ambition, afford the strongest proofs that the abhorrence of the Venetians for the government of one man continued unabated during the first seven centuries of their political existence.

Thus slowly and imperceptibly arose that aristocratical domination which prepared the way for the silent usurpations of the oligarchy, and was at length matured into the tremendous despotism of the State Inquisition. The doge was, in fact, no more than one of an oligarchy; their nominal chief was reduced to an expensive pageant; in authority he was scarcely a counselor; in the city he was a prisoner of state, and out of it only a private individual. The fit time for beginning to reduce an occasional example into a constant practice appeared to have arrived when the last of the forty-three doges abovementioned was assassinated, and his death succeeded by popular commotions. Eleven individuals, deputed by the council, then elected a doge, upon condition that he should ratify a new Constitution, the conditions of which were, that the people should have the right of confirming or annulling the elections of the doges, but not the power of electing them; that the doge should henceforth have no power to choose his own counselors, but that six individuals, to be called the *Signiors*, should be associated with him, subject, however, to his control, who should form an integral part of the supreme magistracy, and without whose concurrence none of his decrees should be valid; that whenever he might stand in need of a larger number of counselors, he should not, as formerly, request the assistance of those citizens whom he thought most capable of advising him, known as the *Pregadi*, but should consult the council.

The first doge elected in virtue of this Constitution (1172) refused the office; but it was not difficult to find another who accepted it. The second was carried in procession through the city, seated on a throne, and introduced the custom, ever after observed, of throwing gold and silver to the populace. So ready are men to sell their rights, and to admire as munificent liberality that despicable bribe, which they are always willing to receive as the price of their freedom. Meanwhile, the prosperity of the republic, the glory of her victories, and the extent of her conquests constantly increased.

At this time, too, Pope Alexander the Third, fleeing from the ravages of Frederick Barbarossa, sought a refuge in the threshold of St. Mark. Barbarossa pursued him, but received a severe defeat (A.D. 1177) by the Venetians; whereupon the Pope, as a mark of his gratitude, solemnly presented the victorious Doge Ziani with a ring in the cathedral, and accompanied his gift with these words: " Receive this as an earnest of the empire of the sea, and marry her to thee every year, in order that posterity may know that she is under thy jurisdiction by right of conquest, and that I consecrate the same to thee, placing her under thy dominion as I would subject a wife to that of her husband."* From that time the doges annually wedded the Adriatic, and a custom which appears ludicrous to us was looked upon as sacred, and was productive of important consequences in that and many succeeding ages.

The winged lion of St. Mark had now attained its maturity. The most important commercial power of the age, she monopolized the trade with India ; the great route from Western Europe and Augsburg (at that time the commercial metropolis) lay through Venice. The spices, precious stones, and Oriental luxuries, brought by caravans from the East through Candabar and Persia, or by the northern routes, and along the Caspian and Euxine Seas, or up the Euphrates and overland to some of the Syrian sea-ports, or by the way of the Red Sea and Egypt, were transported chiefly by Venetian vessels, and exchanged for European manufactures, rendered both continents tributary to the state, which held the power to supply their wants or relieve their necessities.

Their success in the India trade inspired them with the project of obtaining possession of Egypt, and opening the communication between the Red Sea and the Nile, or the Mediterranean — a project which, although duly appreciated by the great powers of Western Europe, is, perhaps, not nearer its

---

* The validity of this donation, though made by a Pope, was disputed at the time, and the controversy was continued through many centuries—a controversy not unlike that which is still agitated with regard to the same subject among more powerful nations, and which nothing but the right of the strongest is competent to decide.

accomplishment than it was six hundred years ago by the Venetians, although the route is now being surveyed by French and Austrian officers, and found altogether practicable.

The romantic age of the crusades was now at its height. A series of succeeding Popes through a century and a half, operating upon the superstitious weakness of the most powerful sovereigns of Europe, induced them to lead out expeditions from all the nations of the West to carry on religious wars against the East. This enthusiasm, so disastrous to the other nations, operated alone to the advancement and prosperity of Venice, as the transports for their immense armies could only be supplied by Venice, and were furnished by her at most exorbitant rates.

Still further to increase the power of the " Queen of the Adriatic," the kingdoms of Christendom regarded her as the power best able to resist Saladin, whose capture of Jerusalem, and triumphant march over Palestine and the coast of the Levant, had alarmed all Europe, and called forth to the scene of action such renowned warriors as Frederick Barbarossa, Richard Cœur de Lion, and Philip Augustus. Frederick Barbarossa met his death after bathing in the Salef (or, as some say, the Cydnus), and before he had reached the scene of action. Richard Cœur de Lion and Philip Augustus quarreled after the capture of Acre; the latter returned home, and the former was alone left to combat the victorious sultan.

About this time, the assistance of the republic was asked, and consent to co-operate obtained; but, through the influence of their most artful and far-sighted Doge Dandolo, quite a different direction was given to the expedition, as they were convinced by him that no surer means of regaining the Holy Sepulchre existed than by the establishment of legitimacy at Constantinople, and thus securing for themselves the necessary supplies and assistance for future proceedings. The capital of the Byzantine empire was captured, and all recollection of Jerusalem was obliterated in their division of " the quantity of gold, silver, precious stones, and other costly things found there" (which, as they wrote to his holiness the pope), " far exceeds all that could be collected in the city of Rome, and in all our Christendom."

Venice obtained the lion's share of all movable spoil, as well
as of all substantial authority and influence in the capital.
The former was valued at upward of a million of marks, equal
to ten millions of dollars. Her doge was invested with the
purple, as " Despot of Romania, and Lord of one fourth and a
half of the Roman Empire."

She purchased Candia for ten thousand, or, according to another account, for eighty thousand marks of silver; and retained feudal supremacy over Corfu, Cephalonia, Zante, Nax-
os, Paros, Melos, Andros, Mycone, Scyro, Cea, and Lemnos ; to
which Negropont and some of the most important fortresses in
the Morea were afterward added.

Victory seemed to wait upon her nod. The people, intoxicated with military glory, forgot their domestic interests, and
allowed their great men to effect one encroachment after another, until every vestige of liberty disappeared. Amid the
successes of an aggressive foreign policy, the fabric of aristocratic usurpation was strengthened, which afterward became
absolute sovereign of the nation, grasping the whole power of
the state, and perpetuating it in their privileged descendants.
This revolution, however, unlike most others, neither rushed
to its conclusion with precipitate speed, nor was brought about
by any sudden catastrophe ; but, proceeding by gradual and
silent encroachment, so ingrafted itself on the trunk of the
Constitution that, though its fruits were somewhat different
to the eye, the plant itself, in its nature, seemed to remain
unchanged.

One of the first steps in the progress of this revolution, and
which forms an era that gives a new aspect to the history of
the republic down to the hour of her dissolution, was a new
mode devised for electing the head of the government—a mode
which remained unchanged to the extinction of the republic.
It required that a number of electors, amounting sometimes
to forty, should be five times indicated by chance, after which
they were to be individually subjected, an equal number of
times, to a scrutiny by which most of them were excluded, in
order that their names might be replaced by others also drawn
by lot. The whole were then subjected to the most rigid examination, in order that those who were eventually retained

as electors might be such as were thoroughly acquainted with that precise combination of qualities which the circumstances of the times and the views of the ruling party required in a doge.* These complicated forms were admirably calculated at once to bewilder the people, and to lead them to imagine that individual interest and design were baffled by the impartial decrees of fate, while in their turn they exercised just that degree of control over fortune necessary to secure the republic against her blind and wayward caprices. With this step, the obvious tendency of which was to reduce the sovereignty of the people to a shadow, and at the same time to enlarge and consolidate the powers of the aristocracy, was mingled, for the sake of blinding the populace, a recurrence to early principles in certain enactments calculated to protect their cherished notion of political independence. First, that the doge should not marry any woman not a native of Venice. This remained ever after inviolate and unchanged. Secondly, that no Venetian should serve any foreign prince, either in war or peace. This, so far as patricians were concerned, was also rigorously observed, and the violation of it inexorably punished. The third, of the new laws, decreed that no Venetian should possess landed property on the continent of Italy. For a time this was enforced, since, with the exception of a few sterile stripes on the shore of the Adriatic, the government itself possessed none. The princely domains of the ancient families were accordingly all situated in the colonies; but in process of time, as they lost their colonies and extended their conquests in Italy, they admitted the most powerful families of the conquered cities into the body of the Venetian aristocracy, and this law was, in consequence, tacitly abolished.

These enactments, which were devised by the reigning party as a means of avoiding the opposite dangers of the revival of popular rights on the one hand, and the introduction of monarchy on the other, were no sooner introduced than they acquired stability and authority, and excited no suspicions in the nation, because they arose directly out of the two original and vital principles of every modification of Venetian government, and fell in with sentiments which appeared to be the indigen-

---

* Daru's History of Venice.

ous growth of every Venetian bosom, viz., complete national independence, and hatred of a domestic dictatorship.

A circumstance arising out of their foreign relations now tended to increase the power and influence of the oligarchy. The Church having taken upon itself to give the kingdom of Naples to Charles of Anjou, Martin the Fourth,* then occupant of the pontifical chair, proclaimed a crusade against the lawful heir; and, because the Venetian government would not suffer its subjects to take arms in the enterprise, and thus open Italy to French invasion, he launched an excommunication against them, and interdicted the celebration of religious rites within their territory. For three years, during which the republic submitted in silence, no priests officiated at her altars, nor were prayers or offerings presented in her churches. Martin's successor removed the interdict, but on condition that the Holy Inquisition, whose introduction the Venetians had hitherto resisted, should be admitted, and established in perpetuity (A.D. 1286).

Another advance of the oligarchy arose from the circumstance that the aristocratical faction, having the power, succeeded in placing at their head Pietro Grandenigo, who united the advantages of very ancient family and high military reputation, with an inflexible temper and the full vigor and fervor of youth. The right which the people still retained of confirming the election of the head of the republic was not formally abrogated, but was thenceforward, in substance, abolished. One of the electors advanced to a window of the palace, and proclaimed to the people, " *The doge is elected, if you approve him,*" and then, without waiting for an answer, retired.

Grandenigo ascended the throne with the resolute determination to found an hereditary aristocracy, or to perish in the effort. He obtained a succession of decrees from the Great Council, which may be esteemed the corner-stone upon which the future pure oligarchy was consolidated.† His encroachments began by effecting the object of a law which had been hitherto successfully resisted, excluding all from the Great Council, excepting such as had already held a seat there, or whose fathers, grandfathers, or great-grandfathers had been

---

* By some authors, Nicholas the Fourth.　　† Venetian History, Family Library.

members of that assembly. Assuming that, as the annual
elections had almost invariably fallen upon the same individuals, those individuals had therefore established a right; and
he did not so much support the claim of re-election to a body
of which he already held them to be constituent members, as
of determining whether they were still worthy of continuing
in it. The annual nomination was abolished as a useless ceremony. By this crowning statute of hereditary rights, every
Venetian noble whose paternal ancestors had been of the Great
Council became himself entitled to the same dignity on com-
pleting his twenty-fifth year. On proof of these qualifications
of descent and age, his name was inscribed in the *Golden
Book** of nobility, and he assumed his seat in the Great Council, whose numbers were no longer limited. This sovereign
body of nobility numbered in the sequel about twelve hundred
individuals. This law was afterward modified so as to restrict
the privilege to those who had already had a seat in the council for four years. It claimed the privilege of naming the
twelve electors by whom it was to be renewed, and consequently, in point of fact, re-elected itself; and, although they
appeared to be chosen from year to year, were in reality seated
for life. Shortly after, a law was introduced excluding from a
a seat in the Great Council all men who had recently risen
to opulence, and who were therein first described as *uomini
nuovi*, new men (A.D. 1300). Subsequently, a law was proposed and adopted, which Grandenigo, after placing the Great
Council exclusively in the hands of the ancient families, caused
to be received as a fundamental statute of the republic.

That no one should henceforward be elected nor eligible to
sit in the Great Council except those who were then members
of it, or their descendants. That this privilege should be hereditary in their families in perpetuity. That the Great
Council should be the sovereign power of the state, and that it
should elect all the magistrates from among its own body.
This decree, which bears in history the name of " *The closing
of the Council*,"† marks the point from which may be dated
the second period in the history of the republic, which ended
only with the fall of its power.

---

* Il Libro d'Oro.   † La Serrata del Mazor Conseio.

The period which followed was totally unlike the former, rather, however, in its substantial effects than in its external appearances. Contemplating, within the space of a few pages, the steps of this mighty change, the contrast between the earlier character of the government and that which it bore to its dissolution appears immense. But it must be recollected that this revolution was the result of changes so slow as to be almost imperceptible, changes tending to one conclusion, through a long course of ages, by the very nature of human society; it will be perceived that the nation was scarcely aware of them until it was too late to repair the evil, and that familiarity with slavery, and forgetfulness of absolute rights, gradually prepared it for deeper degradation.

This revolution, unexampled for the skillful combination of its causes and the permanence of its effects, was conducted in the arbitrary spirit of oligarchy, under the mask of republican equality, with premeditated iniquity, under the forms of justice, with a discretion which presented no front to its adversaries, but rather appeared to shrink from danger, and thus lulled suspicion, while it secretly extended and increased its powers. One conspiracy now followed another, in the vain attempts made by the people to regain their lost power; but these outbreaks of popular indignation were quenched in the blood of the citizens, while they served but to increase the strength, and to arm with new terrors this relentless oligarchy.

These conspiracies gave rise to the institution of the Council of Ten (I Dieci), one of the measures which assured the downfall of the republic. This body was at first nothing more than a committee of the Council of Forty, specially appointed to investigate and punish all persons implicated in the late insurrections. They were invested with a plenary, inquisitorial authority, with an entire sovereignty over every individual in the state, and with freedom from all responsibility and appeal.* The duration of their office was at first limited to ten days; but this was six times prolonged for a like period, then for a year, soon after for five, next for ten, and in the end the tribunal, with a great extension of power, with ample authori-

---

* Venetian History.

ty to make, alter, and repeal the regulations which were to
govern its proceedings, was declared permanent (A.D. 1325)
In their judicial administration, the members of this council
examined, sentenced, and punished according to what they
called " reasons of state." The public eye never penetrated
the mystery of their proceedings ; the accused was sometimes
not heard, never confronted with witnesses ; the condemnation
was as secret as the inquiry, the punishment undivulged, like
both.* Nor was this all : instituted solely for the cognizance
of state crimes, this tribunal attributed to itself the control of
every branch of government, and exercised despotic influence
over the questions of peace and war, over fiscal enactments,
military arrangements, and negotiations with foreign powers.
It annulled at pleasure the decrees of the Grand Council, degraded its members, and deposed, and even put to death, the
chief magistrate himself.

Henceforward, the body of nobles acted in strict unison,
without perceiving that their power was gradually arrogated
by a narrow oligarchy. Our wonder at the political problem
of its long-continued existence is not a little heightened when
it is remembered that the Great Council, upon which of all
classes it weighed with peculiar hardship, might, by refusing
its votes at any one of the four elections in each year, have
abolished its hateful yoke forever. That it did not do so, may
be attributed, in the outset, to a false view of the nature of the
magistracy, and to a belief that it was necessary for the preservation of the state. As its tyranny became more distinctly
manifest, it may have been protected by an ambitious but unworthy hope, which each noble cherished, of one day wielding
its immeasurable powers with his own hands. And, lastly,
after a lapse of years had so far interwoven it with the general
polity as to make it seem an almost inseparable part of the
whole, it might be saved by a mistaken but censurable reverence for antiquity, by that fond clinging to established institutions, which (perhaps not unwisely) is backward to remove
even an abuse, under the fear that its extirpation may endanger the entire fabric upon which it is ingrafted.

---

* Hallam's Middle Ages.

S

It is not difficult to conceive that such a tribunal would not be slow in swallowing up all power, and extinguishing all rights, whether high or low.   True to their early principles, a hatred of monarchy, their first attack was upon the doge, abridging his authority, and holding him up to the people as a fit object of jealousy, and responsible for every error of government; while, at the same time, they were not regardless of the other concomitant principle of their ancestors, love of independence. The law which forbade doges to take wives not natives of Venice was extended to their sons, who were also excluded from every place in the magistracy.   Every one employed about his person, of whatever rank he might be, was excluded from the lowest office connected directly or indirectly with the government. A fine was imposed on any one who should address him, either orally or in writing, in any other style than that of *Messer il Doge*.   While the naval and military force of the republic was no longer at the disposition of the doge, every war in which she engaged was ascribed to him as its author, and by this subtle policy the popular indignation was drawn down upon him whenever there occurred a doubtful or unsuccessful issue.   Another change went hand in hand with the degradation of the ducal authority.   The people were deprived, even in *appearance*, of that power of confirming the choice of a doge, of which they had been despoiled in *substance* a century before, at the election of Pietro Grandenigo.   On that occasion the nobility ventured, for the first time, to announce to the people, without waiting for the appropriate reply, " The doge is elected, if you approve him."   But, at this time, the nomination of Francesco Foscari was proclaimed to the people in the more concise and less respectful formula, " The doge is elected" (A.D. 1423).   But the encroachments of the oligarchy did not stop here.   The tribunal of Ten had now been in baneful operation a little more than a century ; when, during the reign of the last-named doge—as one usurpation unchecked is sure to be followed by another—it gave place to the still more portentous Tribunal of the *State Inquisition*.   On the 16th of June, 1454, a decree of the Grand Council was passed, by which the Ten, in consequence of the difficulty found in assembling their members with sufficient promptitude on every occasion on which their services might be requisite, were authorized to choose three persons under the above title: two (I Neri), the black, from their own council; and one (Il Rosso), the red, from that of the doge.

The powers granted by the Ten are briefly stated in a second decree of their own, passed three days afterward. By that ordinance the inquisitors were invested with all plenary authority possessed by their electors; over every person, of what degree soever in the republic, whether citizen, noble, magistrate, ecclesiastic, or even one of the Ten themselves; over all individuals, in short, who should in any way expose themselves to merited punishment. The penalties which they might inflict were left solely to their own discretion, and extended to death either by public or secret execution. The terrific dungeons, whether under the leaden roofs (I Piombi),* or beneath the water of the canals in the hollowed walls of the ducal palace (I Pozzi),† were placed at their disposal; they held the keys of the treasury of the Ten, without being accountable for the sums they might draw from it. All governors, commanders, and embassadors on foreign stations were enjoined implicit obedience to their mandates, and they were permitted to frame their own statutes, with the power of altering, rescinding, or adding to them from time to time. As the advantage with which the state could be served was considered to be strictly proportionate to the mystery in which this tribunal was enveloped, every process was forever kept secret. No inquisitor was known, and its citations, arrests, and other instruments, were issued in the name of the Ten; and its examinations conducted and its judgments pronounced by the mouths of secretaries, who were never present during their deliberations. Of a tribunal, whose chief elements were secrecy and terror, nothing like perfect authenticity as to all its proceedings can be expected; but, from the statutes of this most atrocious court which have recently come to light,‡ the declaration is warranted, that its decrees are the only ordinances reduced to writing in which a legislative body has ever dared to erect a code upon the avowed basis of perfidy and assassination.

---

* The leads.   † The wells.   ‡ Daru's History of Venice.

These regulations, contained originally in forty-eight articles, were extended, at different periods, to reach in the end
one hundred and three; were always written in the hand of
one of the three, and deposited in a chest, of which each member kept the key in rotation.   Erected for the pretended security of republican freedom, history has no parallel to its silent,
mysterious, and inexorable tyranny.   The inquisitors were empowered to use torture for the purpose of extracting evidence
and confessions of guilt.   No spot in Venice afforded protection to the individual who fell under the displeasure of the Inquisition.   As surely as he existed, he was certain to meet his
fate, either by poison, secret assassination, or being sunk at
midnight beneath the waters of the Orfano.*   At the corner
of every street, and even on the steps of the Ducal Palace,
where the stone image is still visible, lions' mouths yawned
to receive anonymous information which even private malice
might dictate, for the use of the inquisitors of state.   But so
jealous a tribunal was not contented with these voluntary and
detestable accusations.   Its universal and fiendish vigilance
was maintained by a multitude of spies in all the public places
of the city—under the piazzas of St. Mark, the favorite promenade of the nobles—on the Exchange, the quays, the markets,
and in every resort of the people.   There was not a church or
a religious meeting, a ball or a convivial party, even a den of
prostitution or an abode of infamy, into which some of its
emissaries did not penetrate.   Their informers infested all
ranks of society, from the highest to the lowest.   Nobles,
monks, prostitutes, gondoliers, and domestic servants enabled
them to watch the secret springs of action in fashion, religion,
passion, pleasure, and privacy.   Every thing was observed
with the eyes of an Argus and the ears of a cruel despotism,
more dreadful and sensitive than that of Dionysius, and which
found a channel of communication with the most confidential
intercourse.

Yet, under this dark and relentless administration, Venice
was the seat of pleasure—the chosen spot not only of Italian
but of European festivity.   Throned on her hundred isles, the

---

* One of the canals in Venice.

magnificence of her palladian elevations; her churches and palaces of every style and decoration, slumbering on their shadows in the "long-drawn aisles" of her canals; her docks and
her arsenals, stored with all the furniture of war; her quays,
so strangely crowded with the mingled costumes of the Eastern and Western World, glittering with the pageant or heaped
with costly merchandise; this proud city of the sea was but a
painted sepulchre, striking in its monumental grandeur, but
covering a political charnel-house. All this splendor, festivity,
and lively activity were consistent with scenes of secret but
excessive horror. Her palaces and her prisons were covered
by the same roof; and while the masque and the revel encircled the edifice of government, that ancient pile concealed
abodes of misery from which mercy and hope were alike excluded. During the gayest hours of Venetian pleasure, in the
throng of the Casino, or in the mazes of the Carnival, individuals disappeared from society and were heard of no more: to
breathe an inquiry after their fate, was a dangerous imprudence, to mourn their loss an actual guilt.

Under the influence of so searching a police, there was no
sweet privacy in domestic life—no confidence in familiar intercourse which was not chilled or violated by fears and suspicions, or a detestible treachery against which there was no assurance, which no caution could guard against and no sharp-
sightedness foresee.

"Never yet," says the historian, "did the principles of ill
establish so free a traffic for the interchange of crime, so un-
restricted a mart in which mankind might barter their iniquity; never was the committal of certain and irremediable evil so
fully authorized for the chance of questionable and ambiguous
good. Never was every generous emotion of moral instinct,
every accredited maxim of social duty so debased and subjugated to the baneful yoke of an assumed political expediency."*
The statutes of the Venetian Inquisition of State, now exposed
to the general eye, exceed every other product of human wick-
edness in premeditated, deliberate, systematic, unmixed, and
undissembled flagitiousness.

---

* Venetian History.

Ten centuries of Venetian history had past, but all her early virtue had departed, corruption and crime polluting every branch of her government, and every class of her people : from this hour her doom was sealed.

Extrinsic and remarkable events occurred at this time, viz., the Portuguese doubled the Cape of Good Hope, thus opening another route to India than that by Alexandria or the Persian Gulf; the Spaniards had discovered America, and thus giver another direction to enterprise and commerce ; and these would have produced her immediate downfall, had not that most execrable part of her government, the Inquisition, while it checked and stifled the internal prosperity of the republic, yet saved her for nearly four centuries from the causes of dissolution by which she was externally beset, skillfully concealed the progress of her decay, and covered her intrinsic weakness, down to the hour of her agony, with a specious and imposing appearance of strength.

For ages before the subversion of the republic her glories had utterly withered, her commerce and maritime enterprise had perished.   Even the energies which had marked the foreign policy of her rulers were extinct, and there remained, only to excite universal abhorrence, the iniquity of their domestic administration, and that corruption of private morals which they had encouraged in their subjects, to divert their attention from the affairs of state.   During the last seventy years of her career, the republic was reduced to a passive resistance.   Her name ceased to be heard in the discussions, the alliances, and the wars of other states of Europe.   Her commerce was annihilated ; her manufactures had dwindled, in one branch alone, in the annual manufacture of cloths, from 120,000 to 5,000 pieces ; and her revenue, during a long peace, fell far short of the expenses of her corrupt government.   Her claim to the sovereignty of the Adriatic was now contemptuously violated ; her naval force, which furnished three hundred sail to the cause of the Crusades, was reduced to eight or ten vessels of war ; and when the French entered her capital, they found vessels on the stocks which had remained unfinished, for want of materials, for above half a century.   In the higher classes all feelings of honor and patriotism had long been extinct.   Debauched, unprincipled, and needy, the aristocracy united only in desiring the removal of every restraint upon their peculations and their vices. In promoting dissoluteness of private life, the tyrants of Venice had trusted, perhaps, to their vigor to supply the place of morality and its attendant public spirit in the people; but their own vigor had fled, and the depravity of all classes continued to increase with frightful rapidity. Where patricians, in their robes of office, presided at the public gaming-tables; where mothers made a traffic of their daughters' honor, and the laws recognized their contracts; where miserable children of prostitution were employed as political agents in ruining men whose wealth might render them dangerous; and where, by the facility of divorce, the court of the patriarch was besieged, at the same moment, with nine hundred petitions for the privilege of legalized adultery! Where *virtue*, the foundation, as Montesquieu contends, of all republics, had so completely vanished, that not a trace was left behind, the epoch had arrived when it must have sunk under the weight of its own corruption; and our detestation of the treachery of its betrayers is mingled with the conviction that humanity has at least nothing to regret in the catastrophe.*

Such were the real causes of the catastrophe which extinguished the career of Venice in shame. The political earthquake, which had overturned despotism in France, could not fail to fill every minor despotism with alarm and dismay. The Venetian republic resolved to maintain, what it called, a perfect neutrality; but the weakness and profligacy under which she labored not only rendered her incompetent to the task, but made her an easy prey to French conspiracy. The admission of four thousand French troops was recommended to guard the city; the Great Council, at the exhortation of their president, resigned their offices; the ducal dignity, with its associations of eleven centuries, was forever abolished; and the tree of liberty was planted on the Piazza amid salvos of artillery, the shouts of thousands, and a solemn *Te Deum* from the cathedral of St. Mark.

The insignia of the ancient government were burned; a for-

---

* Venetian History.

eign army had entered that capital which had remained inviolate for one thousand three hundred and fifty years ; and, within four months, the treaty of Campo Formio transferred it, with
all its provinces, to Austria, as an indemnity for the Netherlands.   Thus this state, which began with Attila, ended with
Bonaparte; and to the desolating march of two formidable conquerors it owes alike its origin and its fall.

The Venetian provinces acquired by Austria in 1798, in
exchange for the Netherlands, were again lost to the empire in
1805, after the disastrous campaign of Austerlitz and the capture of Vienna, when, to purchase the peace of Pressburg,*
Napoleon compelled her to cede them to the kingdom of Italy,
to which they remained attached until the fall of the conqueror,
when they were restored to Austria by the treaty of Vienna.

After the peace of 1814, the Emperor Francis introduced a
new organization in the Venetian territories, as well as in the
province of Lombardy.   The details of the general and provincial administration were prescribed in a proclamation of the
24th of April, 1815, which is a quasi-charter for the Lombardo-
Venetian kingdom ; the scheme for the communes was subsequently arranged.   The plan of Francis was based upon the
system of his ancestress Maria Theresa, which went into operation in 1755, and reduced the duchies of Milan and Mantua
(after the peace of Utrecht, transferred to the German branch
of the house of Austria) to a position closely resembling that
of the hereditary Austrian states.   The proclamation of 1815
sets forth as its motive the emperor's desire to form colleges
of men from the different classes of the state, through whom
might be learned, in regular form, the wishes and desires of the
nation.†

Accordingly, the kingdom is divided into two general governments, the one of nine provinces (Territorio Milanese), having its seat at Milan, the other of eight provinces (Territorio
Veneto), having its seat at Venice, and both subject to the

---

* Austria resigned all she acquired from Venice (including, therefore, Dalmatia, formerly belonging to Venice, and bordering on the Turkish empire) to the
Italian kingdom, and recognized Napoleon as its king.—*Peace of Pressburg, Dec.*
26, 1805.

† Staats Lexikon.   Von Raumer's "Italy and the Italians."

resident viceroy. Based upon these divisions, the edict directs the formation of two sorts of representative assemblies. The higher are two central congregations, one for the government of Milan, the other for that of Venice. The inferior class comprises seventeen provincial congregations, being one for each of the provinces. The Constitution of the assemblies is as follows.

In each Provincial Congregation there are, in the first place, four, six, or eight land-holders, according to the population of the province, half being nobles and half commoners ; and, next, one representative for every city in the province which ranks as a royal borough. The special qualifications for eligibility are several: the party must be a citizen of the kingdom, and, if noble, must have a patent confirmed by the emperor ; he must be a resident of the city which he represents, thirty years of age, at least, and possess a capital of two thousand crowns, invested in land, trade, or manufactures.

The elections are conducted with great caution. For filling up the periodical vacancies (after the first election, over which, for both assemblies, the emperor reserved full right of control) each commune proposes two names, those of a nobleman and a commoner, and the lists so formed are submitted to the Provincial Congregation itself, which selects for each vacant place three qualified candidates, and transmits these purified lists to the Central Congregation ; which, again, may either object to any individual, or lay the lists, without remark, before the government at Milan or Venice respectively. The government, unless its members choose to exercise a special veto (the reasons of which they are bound to report to Vienna), appoint to the vacant places the persons first named in the lists. The delegate, or imperial governor of the province, is the president of the Provincial Congregation, and is responsible for the competency of any orders they issue to inferior boards. Its deputies have no salary, but possess honor and rank, and their duties are described by the proclamation, under four heads : the business of the taxation of the province, the superintendence of the affairs of the towns and communes (for which purpose the communal councils must annually submit their accounts to it), the superintendence of roads and of

operations regarding the canals and rivers (so far as these belong to the province, and not to the general government), and
the inspection of public charitable institutions.

Each Central Congregation contains two deputies, a nobleman and a commoner, for every province which the government contains, and one deputy for each of the royal cities.
The qualifications of a deputy are, the possession of real tax-
able property worth at least four thousand crowns; the age of
thirty years complete, the right of citizenship with (if the deputy is noble) a confirmed patent and residence in the kingdom,
or in Austria.

For the elections, the initiative is exercised in the same way
as in the other class of assemblies; but the lists from the towns
are transmitted directly to the Central Congregations, with a
recommendation of a particular name; and these bodies are
authorized to make a similar recommendation in submitting
the reduced lists of the other class to the government, the emperor reserving to himself the final right of nomination, and
the prerogative of expelling any members " who should show
themselves unworthy of the confidence reposed in them."

The deputies of the Central Congregations have honorary
rank, and salaries of two thousand florins. Their president is
the Governor of the Territorio Milanese, or the Territorio Veneto, respectively; and their functions are described under six
heads: the assessment and registration of any extraordinary
taxes that might be imposed by the sovereign; the completion
of the roll for the land-tax; the inspection of the communal
revenues, and the consideration of the apportionment of the
public burdens between the towns or communes, the provinces,
and the whole territory of the government; the allotment of
the military services; the superintendence of such bridges,
canals, and roads as the government does not choose to take
under its charge; the general inspection and supreme administration of charitable institutions: provided, that in all these
cases the Central Congregation shall have only the power of
superintendence, and only a consultative voice in regard to the
establishment and organization of expenditure not yet arranged; and that in the several branches of administration above
mentioned, all which relates to resolutions already sanctioned

or expenditure already arranged, shall be the business of the Provincial Congregations, *under the restrictions specified* in the part of the edict which relates to these assemblies : " We permit the Central Congregation," it is added, " to communicate to us the necessities, wishes, and petitions of the nation, and reserve to ourselves to ask them for advice when it shall seem good to us." The Central Congregation can neither issue ordinances nor impose contributions and taxes, nor exercise in its own name any power, legislative, judicial, or executive ; ' ut, in regard to all matters intrusted to it, as well as in the explanation of ordinances already subsisting, it must lay the result of its deliberations before the government, which will either ratify them, or, if it is not entitled to do so, will apply for *our* sovereign ratification. In cases where the government refuses ratification, the Central Congregation is entitled to make direct application to us.*

Such was the system of administration by which the Lombardo-Venetian kingdom was governed after the peace of 1815; and, although it was a mere mockery of a representative Constitution, their condition, quite equal to any, and far superior to some of the provinces of Austria, and all of the Italian states (except Tuscany perhaps),† was an improvement on their former situation ; and though there was little self-government intrusted to them, perhaps it was as much as their state of political advancement at that time would suffer them to bear, and as Solon, in reply to one who asked him if he had given the Athenians the best of laws—" The best," said he, " they are capable of receiving." And, although the members of these congregations, instead of being legislators, were but overseers of roads and canals, etc., yet, from the fact that their attention was not absorbed in matters of government, they were enabled to devote themselves more assiduously to the sphere of their duties, and by which their social condition was more strictly regarded and evidently improved. In its industry, its judicial and economical administration, but especially

---

* Von Raumer: Staats Lexikon.
† This fact is admitted by an Italian writer of great zeal in the cause of the regeneration of Italy, Marchese Massimo d'Azeglio.

in its system of instruction and in internal improvements, it has made a material advance on its former condition.

The Austrian empire is one of the countries of Europe in which popular education is most encouraged; and that system of universal instruction, in imitation of the Prussian states, is applied in full force to the Lombardo-Venetian kingdom.* There are two classes of elementary schools in Lombardy, minor and upper ones. The minor elementary schools are established in every commune or village; and, where the commune is too small or too poor, two are united for the purpose of supporting one school between them. The school is sustained at the expense of the commune, which however, if poor, is assisted by the treasury. The schoolmasters have a fixed salary of from two hundred and fifty to four hundred Austrian livres.† They must have attended the lessons on method or pedagogy in one of the normal schools, and have a certificate that they are qualified for teaching. All children from the age of six to twelve of each commune or parish are obliged to attend the schools, unless prevented by illness. The rector, and the inspector of the district, are answerable for the fulfillment of this regulation. The poor children have their books supplied from the scholastic fund. The upper elementary schools are established in the towns, and are supported by the public treasury. There are also schools for girls, consisting of three classes, and in which the instruction is adapted to the occupation and pursuits of the sex. Excellent moral and sanitary regulations are enforced in all these schools; all corporeal punishments strictly forbidden; cleanliness and health especially attended to; and habits of sincerity, cordiality, and propriety sedulously inculcated among the children.

In relation to internal improvements, it may be remarked that nowhere, perhaps, is the administration of roads and bridges so actively and usefully employed as in Lombardy. The roads are like the walks of a highly-cultivated garden. Even the patches of grass growing here and there are carefully picked out. The numerous rivers and canals which intersect the road are crossed by bridges of solid and handsome masonry. It is

---

* Botta's Account of Italy in 1807.   † A livre is about twenty-five cents.

computed that the preservation of the high-roads in Lombardy, for a length of one thousand five hunded and eighteen Italian miles, costs one million and a half of Austrian livres yearly. Besides the high-roads, which are maintained at the charge of the state, the communal roads (or roads throughout the different districts), which have been opened or repaired since the peace of 1814, amount to a total length of three thousand two hundred and ninety-four miles, for which the sum of twenty-four millions of livres has been spent by the various communes and municipalities. Forty years ago there were hardly any communal roads in Lombardy deserving the name. The communications between village and village, and between these and the nearest high-road, were wretched tracks, which served also as drains for the rain-water.

No one can be transported over the magnificent roads which now intersect the plains of Lombardy, observe the high state of cultivation, every foot of soil improved, behold the three crops maturing at the same moment, witness the unrivaled system of irrigation by which the limpid waters of the Lakes of Garda, Como, and Majora are conducted through it in canals of various size, without being struck with the evident marks of material prosperity.* The whole plain, as level as a floor, is planted (with the exception of that portion occupied by the road) with the trees of the mulberry, at a distance of about every forty feet. These are kept closely trimmed, and not suffered to grow to a greater height than from fifteen to twenty feet. By the side of each mulberry is planted the vine, which is entwined around it, and, after reaching to its height, is extended, and fastened to the vine, which has grown, in a similar manner, around the next mulberry; presenting, at a little distance, the appearance of one continued arbor; while in the intervening spaces, the ground, sufficiently open and exposed to the sun, is covered with a flourishing grain-crop. In the adjoining field, separated from it only by a bank of earth planted with willows—and which, as the only source of fuel for winter, are kept as closely trimmed as a friar's head—a rich and luxuriant crop of rice may be seen, so level, and so intersect-

---

* They could commence what business or calling they pleased, without leave of the government, necessary in the other province .

ed with canals and drains, that every spot of earth is equally moistened, and the water under such perfect command as to be introduced or excluded at any moment it may be desired. So far from the evidences of oppression and ruin, to the eye of the traveler no more thriving agricultural region can be met with throughout the length and breadth of the European Continent; certainly none in which every foot of land is so reduced to cultivation, or rendered subservient to the purposes of man.   In the neighborhood of Mantua, the birth-place of Virgil, which, with its formidable fortress, stands like a sentinel on the plain, the scholar may still behold the " sedgy banks of the Mincius," of which the poet sang; but a " grove," a " brook," or even a single " spreading beech" or " aerial elm," will be sought for in vain.*

If not from the period when the barbarian hordes first inundated the plains of Italy, at least from the time when Barbarossa and other German emperors razed their cities to the ground, the prejudice and hatred which the Italians entertain against the *Tedeschi* has never disappeared; and, notwithstanding the substantial and unmistakable indications of prosperity which their situation presents, the " barbarians," as they still call the Austrians, are regarded in the light of ruthless oppressors.

It is true, as they complain that the Lombardo-Venetian kingdom, while it contains in population but one seventh of the inhabitants of the empire, furnishes one fourth of the taxes for the support of the government, yet, as this is for the most part an *income*-tax laid upon the productions of the country, it should be no cause of complaint that, owing to its almost boundless resources, the amount derived from that source forms so great a proportion of the revenue of the state ; while a reference to the annexed table† shows that taxes demanded of the people of the Lombardo-Venetian kingdom amount per head to but a little more than one half the sum paid by the population of some other provinces of the empire.   Venice may have suffered some pecuniary loss, on account of the monopoly of navigation given to the Austrian Lloyd steamers; Milan,

---

* Personal observation.
† See Hübner's Table of Taxes, &c., Appendix, note No. 7.

because it was not allowed a bank of discount; Pavia, because it was deprived of its arsenal; Brescia, that it was obliged to stop her numerous armories; Bergamo, that it was forced to close its founderies. These were all matters of government favor, which, if from motives of imperious necessity she considered it her duty to withhold, such acts, instead of an infringement of private rights, or interference with personal liberty, ought rather to be considered as the legitimate effects of the arbitrary institutions under which they existed.

While there were many things in the administration of the government of which they had just cause of complaint, viz., that the officers placed over them were mostly German, who had no sympathy with the people or interest in the country; that the Central Congregations, composed of the minions of power, failed to convey their complaints to the ear of majesty; that the restrictions thrown around the press were too rigid; that they were infested by crowds of secret spies, and overrun by quantities of troops; yet these were all evils inseparable from the nature of the government under which they unfortunately lived, and which, perhaps, the peculiar attitude of the province to the general government seemed imperatively to demand.

In the political condition of Venice, its annexation to the Austrian empire, however galling the imperial yoke, any change must have been preferable to the awful terrors of the State Inquisition. While we can not but condemn the base treachery by which her independence was destroyed, as well as disapprove of that traffic, common among the monarchs of Europe, by which whole states, with their entire population, are transferred from one sovereign to another like chattels, without the slightest knowledge or assent on the part of the people, yet the fact can not be disguised that, so far at least as concerned the physical condition of the population and the prosperity of the city, the change to Venice could not but have been a desirable one.

In 1815, when Venice was again occupied by Austrian troops, it is said the suburbs were deserted and in ruins; life had gradually ebbed from the extremities, and seemed to flutter but faintly in its last retreat at the heart of the city, the Piazza of St. Mark. The ports, choked up with sand, were inacces-

sible to larger vessels.   The arsenal, which had furnished to
Dante that celebrated image of superhuman activity to which
he likens the never-ceasing labor of the " dark cherubim" of
his *Malebolge*, was now deserted and silent.   The stores were
moldering in the magazines ; the half-finished vessels were rot-
ting on the stocks.*

From this state of depression, a union with Austria offered
the only chance of escape.   To Austria alone the possession of
Venice was valuable, as affording a military position of great
strength, and as an emporium of commerce; while Austria
alone could give to Venice, in return, protection, wealth, and
importance.

• Under a stable government, commerce revived, property rose
in value, the city became again the resort of travelers, and the
wealthy proprietors of Germany seemed to delight in speculations which brought them to the beautiful shores of the Adriatic.

Such was the condition of Venice under Austrian rule.   But,
as Italians, the Venetians were not unconscious of that movement for the regeneration of Italy, which, commencing at Rome
with the reforms of Pius the Ninth, and followed up by other
liberal sovereigns of Italy, had spread itself throughout every
portion of Italian soil.

On the 21st of December, 1847, in imitation of a similar
movement adopted at Milan by Nazari, a deputy of the Central
Congregation for that kingdom, Daniel Manin, addressed to the
Central Congregation of the Venetian province the following
communication :

" That during thirty-two years there had existed in the Lombardo-Venetian kingdom a national representation (since the
Central Congregations had been in operation for that space of
time), and whose duty it was to inform the government of the
wants and desires of the country ; but that during this long
period none of those desires had ever been communicated by
the Central Congregation ; that the government would, consequently, be led to believe that the people had nothing of which
to complain, and were therefore perfectly contented and happy.

---

* Quarterly Review, 1850.

That the government was thus deceived by the silence of the Central Congregation, since it was evident that the people were neither contented nor happy, but were laboring under many wants and just desires. That the silence on the part of the Central Congregation was owing to the fear of doing something which might be displeasing to the government. But this fear was unjust and injurious to the government, in supposing that it could have conceded to the kingdom a national representation as a mere burlesque. That it had deceived, and was continuing to deceive, both this country and Europe, by making laws which they did not wish should be observed, and by prosecuting and punishing those who attempted to observe them. It was our duty to respect the government which rules over us ; and every one who does respect it should believe that the government desires to know the truth, and appreciates those who make them feel it, while it disapproves of those who conceal it. It was high time that the Central Congregation should break through its long silence, and make known by their acts that they are aware of the sacredness and importance of their calling. The Lombardian Congregation had already made the first step. One of its deputies, as a good citizen and subject, had presented the annexed document, wherein he suggests that a commission should be nominated to investigate the causes of discontent in the population, to search out the remedies, and to report them. If this proposition should be accepted, it might, as he believed, be attended with salutary results, and prevent, perhaps, sad collisions. The example of our sister state, Lombardy, was worthy of imitation ; and he trusted that the high Venetian Congregation would follow in her footsteps, and, by so doing, promote the honor, the national prosperity, and the public tranquillity."*

This address has been characterized as insolent in its language, and so extravagant in its demands, that the writer could only have intended to force upon the government prosecutions which would insure notoriety ; but, from the above most literal as well as faithful translation of the document, it is difficult to conceive how such a judgment in relation to it could

---

* Biography of Manin.

T

possibly have been formed. Such an opinion is doubtless founded in error, and no less palpable than the statement by which
it is accompanied, viz., that the address was signed both by
Daniel Manin and Niccolo Tomaseo.

On the 30th of December, nine days after, Niccolo Tomaseo
made a speech in the Athenæum of Venice, upon the subject
of the imperial decree of 1815, relative to the censorship of the
press, in which he introduced a petition to the emperor, praying that the people should be protected in the practical enjoyment of the rights granted in that decree. The petition was
altogether respectful, as well as his remarks, in which he sustained the application by reason and argument, as well as by
a reference to the laws of Austria and the adjoining states.

Niccolo Tomaseo, a Dalmatian by birth, has been known as
an author of some distinction ; he is a poet as well as a writer
of romances, and was at one time, on account of his liberal
opinions, excluded from the Austrian dominions.

Daniel Manin, although he bears the name of the last Doge
of Venice, is not connected with him by blood. He was the
son of Peter Manin, advocate, and Anna Bellotto, of Padua,
and was born at the capital, on the 20th of June, 1804. He
was educated at the college of St. Giustina, at Padua, and distinguished himself by his studious habits and rapid acquirements. He pursued the study of the law, and at the age of
twenty-eight years was admitted an advocate at the Venetian
bar.*

On the 18th of January, 1848, Daniel Manin and Niccolo
Tomaseo were arrested and thrown into prison. As the biographer of the former states, " the domicile of Manin was violated by Austrian police-officers, with their commissaries and
satellites, his privacy was invaded, his papers seized, and his
person placed under criminal arrest."†

During the month of January, as evidence of the growing
spirit of excitement among the people, an affair took place at
the theatre, which liked to have proved serious, and to have

---

* His intense application gave him a disease of the eyes. During his study
of law he translated Justinian's Pandects. Theresa Perrisinatti, daughter of a
Venetian advocate, read to him; this kindness ripened into love, and she afterward became his wife.   † Signor P. A. Monterossi.

brought on, at that time, a general outbreak. Cereto, the famous danseuse, appeared upon the stage, with her dress and decorations representing the white, red, and green colors, adopted every where, by universal consent, as the future symbols of independent Italy; and the enthusiasm which that slight circumstance awakened was so intense, that the police were obliged to enter the theatre, disperse the audience, and close the doors. Violence and bloodshed would probably have occurred on the occasion, had not the police taken the precaution to surround the theatre with so large a force as to render any attempt on the part of the people useless and absurd.

The news of the outbreaks occurring in various parts of Lombardy had not been without its effect upon the population of Venice, when, on the 16th of March, vague rumors of the Revolution in Vienna, and the fall of Metternich, produced an intense but deeply-smothered excitement. The joyful intelligence could be read most legibly in the dark countenances of the Italians; every one knew it; but, unable to contain themselves, they hurried from point to point, from group to group; and yet no one dared to communicate, and many not even to credit, the happy tidings.

On the following day, the 17th, the Austrian-Lloyd steamer from Trieste brought a full confirmation of the events which had transpired in Vienna; and, with the rapidity of electricity, it was immediately conveyed through the city. Soon after the arrival of the boat, a crowd was seen moving from the Piazza of St. Mark toward the harbor, animated by cries of mutual encouragement; the indolent loungers about the piazza, attracted by the noise, hurried in that direction; the guards who stood sentinels at the doge's palace seized their arms, when another band of about two hundred men, of the better class, both old and young, were observed coming from the sea-side, and moving toward the square of St. Mark, with rude banners flying, made by attaching white handkerchiefs to sticks; and this band reiterated every moment the cries of " Manin and Tomaseo !"*

---

* The piazza opening from St. Mark's to the sea in front, and lined on one side by the ducal, and on the other by the governor's palace, with its two superb pillars of granite, surmounted, one by the winged lion of St. Mark, and the other by

The united crowds now stopped in front of the governor's palace, which lies between the quai and the piazza; and immediately confused cries arose. Count Palfy, the civil governor, appeared on the open balcony; he commenced to speak of his attachment to Venice, but his voice was soon drowned by the loud interruptions of the crowd. Suddenly, a deputation was dispatched to the governor, to inform him of the desires of the people for the liberation of Manin and Tomaseo. The situation of Count Palfy was, perhaps, an embarrassing one. Some days before, his wife had been insulted in the open street, by persons of the better class, and followed home with cries of derision and contempt. Repeatedly, of late, he had received anonymous letters, threatening his life and that of his children. He stood in a land of strangers, without support; while the Vice-president Sabregandi enjoyed among his countrymen but slight consideration and esteem, and still less energetic assistance could be looked for from his other counselors. Unable or unwilling to resist the popular importunity, the governor accorded the boon. Appearing again upon the balcony, the trembling count commenced an address to the crowd with the remark, " Faccio quel che non dovrei,"* but the residue of the speech was delivered without an audience, as, with one simultaneous movement, they all hurried to the prisons. While these things were transpiring in front of the governor's palace, the people on the piazza were not idle; in a moment, the cafés, with which that grand square abounds, and which were respectively named in honor of the emperor or some other royal dignitary, had, as if by enchantment, changed their inscriptions, and were converted into Café of the "Union," Café Manin, Café Tomaseo, &c. Striking as was this change, it was less so than that of the countenances of the gathering crowd, transformed from their recent sadness, which pervaded all ranks, to glowing joy; but more remarkable than either change was the conduct of the Italians and Austrians, who had hitherto regarded each other with the most bitter jealousy and hatred, now embracing, and in raptures, exclaiming, " We are all brothers !" " we are all free !" And, indeed, the occasion

---

St. George and the Dragon, standing insulated in the centre, forms a grand, airy, and animated scene.   * I do what I ought not to do.

seemed to be regarded as a political millennium—the dawn of a brighter day upon the fortunes, both of Austria and Italy.

Manin and Tomaseo were released.   The latter retired immediately to his peaceful lodgings.   The former, with his neglected dress and disheveled hair, was conducted in triumph through the city.   "From this time," says the biographer, "these two heroes—these two friends of the people—commenced their reign in Venice; and at the same epoch the people themselves recovered all the pristine energy of the early days of their history."   Before the Cathedral of St. Mark, which forms one side of the grand piazza of that name, are three great standards, erected by the old republic, as symbols of its power over the three kingdoms of the Morea, Cyprus, and Candia; and on which, since the dominion of Austria, the white and red flag* was always hoisted on festive days.   Suddenly the Italian tricolor appeared on the top of one of these standards; and a few minutes after a man approaching with the imperial standard, with the view of hoisting it in the place of the other, it was immediately wrested from him, and torn into a thousand pieces.

The officers of government, recognizing in these revolutionary indications the commencement of an insurrection, immediately ordered alarm-guns to be fired from the military guardship in the harbor.   Although the meaning of those ominous six shots was well understood by the people, yet the tumult continued, despite the preparations.   Suddenly the tramp of military was heard from all directions; and in a moment the Piazza of St. Mark was crowded with troops and bristling with arms. The people, regarding each other with anxious and inquiring looks, demanded what was intended by these warlike preparations, as no enemy appeared, and the only thing observed in connection with this hostile display was the transportation of a long ladder to take down the Italian tricolor, which still waved from one of the standards.   The attempt was accordingly made, and failed; and, slight as the circumstance was, it spoke volumes, and was decisive of the fate of Austrian rule in Venice.   If the exhibition of the national symbol was so se-

---

* Flag of the Austrian Provinces.

rious an offense, why not have made use of the supple crews of
the navy, who were at hand, or felled the standard, and brought
the revolutionary flag to the ground ?   The government would
thus have shown that they were determined to act with energy, to be undaunted by opposition, and that they would not
surrender their power until desperate resistance had proved
unavailing; but by making a feeble attempt to displace the
Italian standard, they exhibited the importance they attached
to the revolutionary movement, while their hesitation to accomplish it taught the people to despise an authority which
they could thus brave with impunity.   By such weak and
vacillating conduct, the ardor of the troops was damped—the
activity of the police paralyzed; and the obstinate forbearance
of the governor tended rather to promote the collision it was
his object to prevent.   Later in the evening, the great alarm-
bell in the Cathedral of St. Mark was sounded.   The first impression which its startling tones produced was that a conflagration had occurred.   How could it have been otherwise,
as the garrison was posted next to the tower, and the ringing
of the alarm-bell was naturally thought to have originated with
the government?   It was, in truth, the storm-bell, and all the
mob and rabble were summoned from the piazza, to spread
disorder and tumult through the city.   A few bold and resolute Revolutionists had entered the tower, and sounded the
tocsin with all the violence in their power, until dislodged by
a division of grenadiers sent for that purpose.   But to neglect
the occupation of the tower, such a common measure of precaution when an insurrection was expected, and when so many
preparations were made to meet it, exhibited a want of proper foresight as difficult to explain as it would be impossible to
excuse.

The mob collected by the sound of the tocsin, increasing in
number from minute to minute, and becoming more and more
violent, rendered the danger of collision and bloodshed imminent; when the patriarch of the city, in his ecclesiastical robes,
presented himself upon the balcony of the governor's palace,
pronounced his benediction on the people, and enjoined on
them the preservation of order and tranquillity.   The masses,
supposing that the "holy father" was about to communicate

some message from the governor, rushed toward the palace. The military and its commanders, mistaking this movement for a general attack, advanced under the order of "Charge bayonet!" and the crowd, pressed in this manner, soon dispersed in wild flight. With the exception of some slight wounds, and a few broken panes in the glass doors of the *cafés*, this maneuver of the military was attended with no more serious result. The crowd dispersed, the military withdrew, and the night passed off quietly, while the Italian tricolor continued to wave from the standard of St. Mark. The governor that night, in consultation with the municipal authorities and Central Congregation, requested their views as to the best mode of calming the tumult, when Manin proposed the temporary establishment of a Civic Guard; but this proposition they immediately declined to entertain.

The next day, Saturday the 18th, every appearance indicated that some event of moment would ensue; for, at an early hour, all the shops were closed, the mob began to gather in the streets and on the piazza; the military approached. The mob that had collected on the piazza, and till then amused itself by ridiculing and insulting the troops, undisturbed in its petulancy, began now to tear up the large paving stones in the middle of the place, and to dash them down against the pavement with violence, in order to break them into smaller pieces capable of being thrown at the troops. As these things were transpiring under the eyes of the main guard, a division was dispatched to drive the actors away. The crowd immediately dispersed; but, as the troops turned to march back to their posts, a volley of stones was discharged at them by the mob. The troops immediately wheeled, and, facing the thoughtless rabble, fired in the air; but their adversaries, disregarding all the warnings they had received, still persisted in their insults and attacks, and the military next fired at their persons, when three fell dead, and seven were more or less dangerously wounded.

"The Germans have fired!" was soon heard and echoed throughout the whole city, and the excitement, already great, was vastly increased. "We must have our Civic Guard!" was the next cry; "we must protect ourselves against such

massacres." Although the governor had on. that day, for a
second time, refused the application of Manin for a Civic Guard,
yet, after the fire of the troops, his firmness gave way, and he
signed the order for the enrollment of that force ; and, as Signor Monterossi truly observes, with it signed the abdication of
Austrian authority in Venice. It was late in the afternoon
when placards announced this concession of the governor, but,
on the instant of their appearance, men of all classes and ages,
armed with any kind of weapon they could command, were
seen hurrying to the place of appointment. Tranquillity was
immediately restored throughout the city ; again every heart
was filled with joy, and a brilliant theatre formed the closing
scene of that eventful day. Later in the night, joyful shouts
again resounded in the Piazza of St. Mark, when the governor
communicated, as he had promised, the intelligence from Vienna (brought by the steamer which had just arrived) which
promised to the monarchy a new life, and, under the protection of Heaven, a more brilliant future.

Sunday, 19th of March. The Sabbath came. All rose
with light hearts ; the hour of threatening outbreak from the
wild fury of the mob seemed to have passed by. A few horrible specimens of the rabble flitted across the piazza, like dark
clouds across a clear sky ; but their day of triumph had rolled
by ; their power was gone, as the armed citizens, now formed
into a regular guard, it was thought would certainly keep them
in subjection. The Piazza of St. Mark, that grand saloon of
the fashionable world, was adorned as if for a festival. Rich
carpets were hung from all the windows. During the morning, white and red were the only colors visible ; but later in
the day a green was observed to have been added to the collection. White, by general acceptation in all the recent revolutions of Europe, signified *constitutional ;* white and red
were the provincial colors of Austria ; and white, red, and
green were the Italian tricolor. All classes of people, like the
gondolas on their own Grand Canal, seem to glide along with
buoyancy on a sea of enjoyment. The nobility, as well as the
wealthy and intelligent people who could appreciate the concessions of the government, were in transports at the thought
of the freedom which was in store for them ; while the lower

ranks and rabble had reason to be delighted, as their portion consisted in something more appreciable as well as substantial than imperial promises — since every salutation of "*Eviva l'Italia!*" addressed by them to the more decently attired, was sure to call forth a handful of livres.

But the most ominous feature in the occurrences of this day was the open fraternization which seemed to be every where going on between civilians and the Italian regular troops. Italian grenadiers arm in arm with persons in civil costume, might be seen lounging about the piazza, or wandering from one café or restaurant to another, with hands full of money, and Italian ribbons dangling from their button-holes. The same course was prosecuted, and with like success, with the navy and infantry. It was remarkable that no step should have been taken by the Austrian commanders, not the slightest effort made to prevent an association from which the most disastrous consequences could only have been looked for. A simple proclamation, explaining to the troops the concessions from the crown, and showing that it had created no change in their duties and relations to a flag which they had sworn to support, and under which they might still earn unfading laurels, could but have been attended with beneficial results; while a military festival in honor of the occasion would have been quite appropriate, have kept the troops together, occupied their attention, and preserved them from the seductions of idleness and intrigue.

The 20th and 21st of March passed over, without an outbreak or the commission of any overt act; but it was evident that something terrible was in contemplation. The people had suddenly acquired great boldness of speech, and discoursed without reserve of the matters of the day, instead of carefully looking to the right and to the left, to see that no listener was near, before they dared to whisper in the ear of a confidant. While the people had become emboldened, the government, on the other hand, had become intimidated. The yards and entrances of the governor's and viceroy's palaces were crowded with soldiers of the Grentzer regiment, the most loyal and reliable troops in Venice, who there, with arms in hand, seemed to await momentarily an attack. The authority of the gov-

ernment, in fact, was suspended, or, rather, transferred to the
Republican leaders; and their measures were marked with as
much shrewdness and audacity as those of Count Palfy with
weakness and vacillation.   A conspiracy was on foot, a scheme
in contemplation, for the success of which it became necessary
to put in circulation the most wild and exaggerated reports;
as, that the city was to be bombarded, or destroyed by mines
dug in various parts of it, or by rockets and other infernal devices designed to multiply death and destruction; and that all
these diabolical purposes were the invention of Marinovich,
the commandant of the arsenal.   It is an old proverb in Venice (dating, doubtless, from the days when the mighty thunder-
bolts prepared in that work-shop struck terror in every sea),
that "whoever is in possession of the arsenal is master of Venice;" this the insurgents knew, and to it tended all their measures.   Their plan was simple : first a Civic Guard, as numerous and well-informed as possible ; then its introduction, either
by stratagem or force, into the arsenal, and all was accomplished.   .The biographer of Manin states : " Already, on the
night preceding the 22d of March, Tomaseo, together with
many other generous patriots, had assembled at the house
of Manin, all anxious to co-operate in the liberation of their
country.   Various means were discussed, and it was at last
resolved to gain possession of the arsenal, and to cry out
' Viva San Marco.'   Our people would have paid no attention
to the promise of a constitutional government—few of their
number would have understood it.   It was necessary to arouse
that sleeping lion, which had remained on the belfry tower
during the universal monarchy of Napoleon, as well as under
the tyranny of Austria—in proof that neither should last forever.   This was the opinion of Manin, and his advice prevailed."*   For this purpose, Marinovich must die.   An assassination seemed the necessary precursor of all reforms, the indispensable prelude of all political changes of the year 1848.
At Rome, Vienna, Prague, Pesth, Frankfort, and Baden, this
method had been pursued under various circumstances of
treachery and cruelty.

* Monterossi.

Colonel Marinovich was a naval officer of much ability and talent; but with the marines and workmen under his command he was exceedingly unpopular, on account of the strict discipline which he exacted. He had been appointed expressly to reform the numerous abuses in that department, and by his indomitable energy this object was accomplished. The pilferings of wood from the arsenal by upward of one thousand workmen—and by means of which, in times past, whole houses had been built in Venice—were prevented by the insertion of iron gratings at all the outer windows, and a search of the men as they left the arsenal, and every offense committed was punished either by a deduction from their wages or immediate dismissal. These things had strongly embittered all the workmen against him, and that feeling was still increased by the circumstance, that he was rewarded by the government with honors and increased salary, while, upon his recommendation, their wages had been diminished.

As he was the source from whence every order issued in the arsenal, the odium of all the unpopular measures or severe restrictions necessarily fell on him; but of his fidelity to the Austrian government there can be no doubt; while, to his foresight and judgment, that power is indebted for the greatest part of the fleet which, in anticipation of such difficulties, he had dispatched to the more secure harbor of Pola.

Colonel Marinovich, on the afternoon of the 21st, with difficulty escaped a plot that had been laid for his destruction. The workmen of the arsenal had assembled in the squares and on the bridges leading to that building, after they were dismissed from labor, with the intention of waylaying and murdering the commandant, or, in the language of the official statement of the matter, " to watch the wild beast, as it issued from its lair, to assail it with stones and brickbats, and to knock it down and drown it." This plot was defeated by the presence of mind of Marinovich himself in the first instance; but some officers of the establishment having afterward obtained the help of a detachment of the Civic Guard, the leaders of that force, after much entreaty, procured the consent of the conspirators to the escape of their victim by the promise (for which he gave them no authority) that on the very same day he would send in his resignation. He was conducted on board the corvette that guarded the harbor, and there he passed the night.

March 22d. " Who would have thought," pursues the official document,* " that the following day (the 22d) he would have again returned to the arsenal ? It was by the special permission of Heaven that he should be blinded by his obstinacy, and should run upon his miserable fate ; for upon that life depended the destruction of Venice ; and on his death, its liberation from the yoke of the barbarians immediately ensued, with safety and regeneration—a real miracle of Providence."

On the morning of that day the friends of Marinovich attempted to dissuade him from the rashness of appearing at the arsenal among the enraged workmen. General De Martini endeavored even to detain the unfortunate man. But all their efforts proved unavailing. In accordance, however, with their suggestion, he resolved, instead of entering the great gate, and thus exciting observation, to obtain admission to the arsenal by a small side door. But this door being locked, he was obliged to send for the key. The messenger, being one of the plot, immediately notified all his companions of the approach of the commandant, whom they earnestly awaited, by the cry of " The key of the door for Colonel Marinovich." The commandant, immediately surrounded by a threatening crowd, directed his steps toward a round tower near the Porta Nuova, with the intention of securing himself there until the arrival of assistance. He found the door leading to the garret closed, and the entry door, which he had immediately locked behind him, was soon forced by the infuriated mob. The unfortunate man stood at the top of the stairs with two pistols and a drawn sword. Seeing that resistance was useless, he asked his pursuers if they " desired to take him alive or dead." " Alive," was the immediate reply ; and one seized his sword, a second struck him on his face, and a third, with a pointed weapon, ran him through the body. He fell to the floor, and was dragged down stairs, his head striking each step in his descent. Forming a circle around him in the yard, they seemed to enjoy the last agonies of this slowly-dying man. His body was pierced through with innumerable wounds, inflicted with in-

---

* " Authentic notices of the death of Colonel Marinovich."—*Raccolta.*

struments purposely selected, it was said, to mangle the flesh more hideously.* "Thus died," continues the document, "the bad man, visibly punished by the hand of God for having conceived the horrible design of ruining the country of which he was the unworthy and degenerate son."

As soon as the murder was committed, and the report of it had passed out of the arsenal, a division of the Civic Guard who were in the neighborhood, headed by Manin and Tomaseo, marched to the spot, where the slight resistance offered by the admiral, De Martini, was quickly overcome. Manin demanded the keys of the arsenal, and, on being refused, the doors were soon forced, and the arms seized and distributed among the crowd.

One division after another of the Civic Guard entered, until they amounted to about five or six hundred, when, with a full knowledge and consciousness that the hour for a decisive blow had arrived, they declared themselves in possession of the arsenal. Admiral Martini, treacherously called and caught, is pronounced a prisoner. The major of the battalion of naval troops, Budai, attempted to opppose with his force the Civic Guard, and commanded his men to fire; but they not only refused obedience to the order, but fell upon their commander, and wounded him most dangerously. The battalion of Grentzers stood by with loaded cannon, and, opposed by the civic artillery (whose cannons, it was afterward discovered, were not even charged), enter into a capitulation to lay down their arms. All opposition subdued, Manin, exercising the authority of a chief, bestowed the command of the arsenal on Colonel Graziani, promoted for the occasion. He and Tomaseo, from the steps of the building, then harangued the people. They announced the restoration of the old republic, and departed amid cries of "Viva San Marco." While these things were transpiring at the arsenal, the governor and military commandant, who had taken no pains either to avert the disaster, or to interrupt its progress, were closeted in the royal palace with the counselors.

---

* If this be true, their course was more brutal than that of the Spartans, after the battle of Platæa, when they proposed to inflict on the body of the fallen Mardonius the same indignities which the Persians had exhibited toward their own Leonidas.

The governor, Count Palfy, a Hungarian by birth, had re-
sided long in Venice, and been employed there even before its
government had been committed to his charge.   Frank and
open in his manners, easy of approach, and generally obliging,
he was personally liked and respected, and was never believed
capable of so much weakness and pusillanimity as he exhibited
in the last hours of his command.   General Count Zichy, the
military commandant, also a native of Hungary, had exhibited
in his youth all the courage and resolution that belong to his
country and profession ; but habits of indolence and self-indul-
gence had completely unmanned him, and shaken the firmness
of his nerves.   He possessed now none of that moral courage
and strength of purpose which the exigency of the times demanded.

The news of the capture of the arsenal and the murder of
Marinovich had carried the consternation of these officials to
its climax.   Shortly after appeared a deputation* from the
Municipal Assembly, with proposals for a general surrender.
Hereupon Count Palfy resigned his command to Count Zichy,
who entered into a capitulation with this self-constituted council, who found, to their infinite astonishment, that they had
actually succeeded in persuading an Austrian general, with
a garrison of five thousand men, to surrender without a defeat, nay, without even an effort to defend his trust.   Their
spokesman was a lawyer, Signor Avesani, and the argument
he adopted was the propriety of saving the city from the risk
of an attack, and the cruelty of exposing human life in a hopeless conflict.   Such, indeed, were the motives assigned by the
general himself, on trial before a court-martial at Olmütz ;
but the court failed to recognize their validity.   That the people possessed arms at all was owing to the folly and negligence
of the government ; but both Palfy and Zichy were well acquainted with the theatre of operations, and they should have
known that, even provided with arms, there was nothing to
fear from the people, who possessed neither the skill nor the
courage to use them.   The plea of humanity ostentatiously
advanced on this occasion, and so frequently pleaded in other

---

* Advocate Avesani, Leoni Pincherle, Fabbris (central deputy), and Mengaldo
were the deputation.

countries, is merely a paltry and hypocritical excuse for cowardice.   The heavy expense of maintaining armies and garri-
soning fortresses might indeed be retrenched, if, on the pretext
of *humanity*, their assistance is to be discarded when it is
most needed.   The first duty of every soldier is to maintain
the post committed to his charge; nor should it be considered
that the fine buildings of a town can be dearer to him than
his duty and his honor.*

On the present occasion, the plea of humanity admitted by
General Zichy could only hold good if he knew that no effort
would be made by his master to reconquer the rebellious city.
Had the contest begun at that moment, there can be little
question how it would have terminated; and, had the loss of
life and property risen to a higher amount than the largest
computation can carry it, it must have fallen very far short
of that which actually occurred during the prolonged siege and
final capture of Venice.   After a little undignified disputing,
which served only to enhance the triumph of the Venetians,
the capitulation was signed.†

It is reported of Zichy, and it is feared with too much truth,
that, as soon as he was apprised of the murder of Marinovich,
and the capture of the arsenal, he became so completely unnerved that he retired to bed, and there remained until the
arrival of the deputation with the capitulation.   On being informed that the document was all prepared, and that nothing
more would be necessary for him to do than simply to sign it;
quite relieved, he sprang up, without a moment's hesitation
affixed his signature to the instrument, and then, rubbing his
hands, with the most ineffable complacency exclaimed, "Now,
thank God, I shall eat my dinner in peace."

At the earnest entreaty of the governor, the last article of
the treaty, allowing the soldiers pay and subsistence for three
months, was agreed to, but all other requests were refused.
When any pretension was advanced that displeased the delegates, Signor Avesani overcame all opposition by threatening
war; and to the abject entreaties of Count Palfy not to be
detained as a hostage, appealing to his general good character

---

* London Quarterly, January, 1850.

† For the capitulation of the Austrians, see Appendix, note No. 8.

as a title of indulgence, he replied by giving a qualified approbation of his conduct till within the last three months, after
which period, " from pursuing the commands of Prince Metternich, he had committed the heaviest faults, faults shared
by the Nestor of diplomacy, which brought the Austrian monarchy to ruin."

The treaty was on the point of being interrupted a few
moments after its execution. In consequence of a misconstruction of the third article, an attempt was made to deprive
the Kinsky regiment of their arms. Officers and men alike
refused to submit to the indignity. Colonel Culoz closed the
doors of the barracks, and threatened an armed resistance.
The terrified victors began to doubt whether the refractory
regiment would retreat at all, and it was without much hesitation that the Venetians accorded them any terms to get rid
of them, the honors of war and whatever else it pleased them
to demand. Having witnessed with equal astonishment and
delight the departure of the Austrians, the whole crowd repaired to the Piazza St. Mark, where Manin, in a short and
animated speech, proclaimed victory, enjoined upon the people
order and moderation, and, under vivas for the Republic of St.
Mark, the crowd dispersed.*

With the capitulation of Venice, the Italian revolution in
Lombardy had arrived at its culminating point. As we have
seen in the preceding chapter Peschiera, had fallen into the
hands of the Piedmontese, and the Austrian forces were restricted to Verona and Mantua, and those intermediate posts by
which their communication was preserved with the Tyrol. A
period had now arrived when Italy had an opportunity of recovering her long-sought independence, and, could her counsels
but have been directed by prudence and moderation, success
would assuredly have crowned her efforts. At this time two
plans were presented by the imperial government, through its
agent, Count Hartig,† to the Lombards and Venetians, on ei-

---

* In half an hour after the republic was proclaimed, little boys were running,
tearing down the little tin signs marking the insured houses, because they contained the double-headed eagle, and throwing them into the water. The wonderful
Madonna of St. Mark, brought out for the worship of the crowd, and the death of
Marinovich proclaimed the first miracle.

† Count Hartig left Vienna on his errand of peace, 5th April, 1848.

ther of which, as a basis, Austria was willing to treat for
peace, and upon which the mediation of England was asked,
and by Lord Palmerston refused, on the ground that they
were not sufficiently liberal to suit the views of one of the
contending parties.

1st. The complete independence of the Lombardo-Venetian
kingdom (with the reservation of a supremacy, little more than
nominal, of the emperor), and possessing a viceroy, an administration, and an army of its own.   Or, 2d. The absolute cession of Lombardy, with the concentration of the Austrian forces
in Verona, and the continued occupation of the Venetian territory.*   But the course of the Austro-Italians furnished but another to the many examples with which history abounds, of
" vaulting ambition o'erleaping itself," or a refusal of just and
liberal terms in a vain struggle to obtain that which, in reason, they had no right to expect.

But their prosperity, produced by the temporary success
which attended their efforts; that the Milanese, without arms,
had driven off the well-disciplined and fully-equipped army of
Radetzky; that the King of Piedmont had, without opposition,
overrun the plains of Lombardy, inspired them with a blind
and fatal confidence.

The political state of Europe, too, tended still further to
delude them.   The Democratic cause was every where triumphant.   Austria, rent by civil war, was powerless, both in
the capital and in the provinces; foreign aid was not within
her call, for, in the state of anarchy to which Germany was
then reduced, she looked to that quarter in vain for support.
Nor could Russia venture to contract an alliance with the feeble ministry which the students of the Aula controlled, while
France, so far from operating against the rebellious provinces,
stood pledged, by the proclamation of Lamartine, to aid all
" oppressed nationalities."

What terms more liberal or advantageous than those actually offered could reasonably be expected from Austria, it is
difficult to conceive; but Italy, all Italy, all the sub-Alpine
regions, that never before were called Italy, all that was

* Blue Book of English Parliament.

U

necessary to give Italy security; Trient, the Italian Tyrol, the valley of the Isonzo, Istria, and Dalmatia, all were insufficient to gratify the expansive nationality of the patriotic leaders. The town and territory of Trieste even were claimed, without which the trade of Venice, it was said, would be injured, a demand not even made by the grasping ambition of Napoleon, after the victory of Austerlitz, the capture of the capital, and the subjugation of the entire surrounding country. But at this very moment, when the delirium of Italian self-confidence was at its highest, and they would have no arbiter but the sword, the tide of success was already turning, and the Austrian monarchy was thus saved from dismemberment, no less by the perverseness of Lord Palmerston in refusing his mediation, and the overweening self-confidence of the Italians in declining the proffered terms, than by the irresistible sword of Radetzky, which drove the invaders from the soil, and subdued all opposition within the territory.

In justification of his course, the governor, Count Palfy, now made the following explanation: "I must acknowledge the afflicting feeling of sorrow on the occasion of the loss of Venice, (feelings honorable to every faithful subject of Austria); the fact is, several too hasty reports are put in circulation, which tend to cast censure on my conduct in that city, and which are altogether without foundation. I am, therefore, compelled to publish the following facts. Immediately after the commencement of the revolution on the part of the people and the municipality, I perceived the necessity of placing the unlimited authority into the hands of the imperial and royal commander of the military forces, which, according to the existing laws, was done on the 22d of March at two o'clock P.M. Shortly after this act, I was imprisoned, and confined under a strong guard at my apartment. In the same manner, I was conducted to the steamer, without coming in contact with any one. Therefore it is evident that I have not had any influence upon the capitulation, of which I was quite ignorant, and which is not signed by me. I protest, therefore, that I have taken no part in the aforesaid capitulation. On the 26th of March I made a full and detailed report (accompanied by all the documents) to the highest authority; and as

I have requested the ministry to publish a statement of the last occurrences, as far as it concerns my sphere of action and my conduct, I await quietly the result of my request. Every one will then be convinced that I never neglected my duty, either before or after the unfortunate catastrophe, as a servant of the state and as a man of honor."

A Provisional Government was instantly proclaimed, of which Manin was the chief, with Tomaseo as his principal adviser.* The various offices of state were divided among the different actors of the drama, or the most enthusiastic friends of the revolutionary movement.

Pincherlè, a Jew, to whom was assigned the Bureau of Commerce, was a man of ability, and had been Secretary of the Insurance Company of Venice, a post of note and responsibility; but Toffoli, the tailor, who also had a place in the ministry, was distinguished for nothing but the violence of his enthusiasm, and his activity in exciting the ardor of the population.

Religion was invoked to act upon a population, devout after their own fashion, and much addicted to superstition. The wonder-working picture of the Madonna, kept in the Cathedral of St. Mark, having been exposed on the piazza that day, the people immediately exclaimed that the revolution was a miracle of the Madonna.† The cardinal patriarch was called forth to pronounce a benediction, and to call down the blessings of Heaven on the new-born republic, while, at the same time, a placard was addressed to the people containing the following propositions: "Jesus Christ was crucified for sustaining the cause for which we are fighting. The patience with which we support our martyrdom proves that we are his chosen servants. If one among us should be found endeavoring to shake our firmness, let us slay him."

Owing to the insular position of Venice, as soon as the Aus-

---

* The Provisional Government was composed as follows: Messrs. Daniel Manin, President; Nicholas Tomaseo, Minister of Foreign Affairs; Antonio Padulucci, Minister of Marine; Jacopo Castelli, of Justice; General Solera, of War; Pietro Palcocopa, of Public Works; Francesco Camerata, of Finance; Leon Pincherlè, of Interior; Toffoli, without port-folio.

† "E un miraculo della madonna."

trians had sailed, the city was free from immediate attack and
alarm, as if she had been independent for centuries.

Nothing occurred to disturb the peace except the storming
of the Imperial Pawning Establishment by the mob.   The
Provisional Government devoted itself to the promulgation of
decrees.   Among the first of these was one establishing a flag
for the new republic, as follows : The flag of the Venetian republic was composed of three colors — green, white and red ;
the green next the staff, the white in the middle, and the red
at the end.   At the top, the yellow lion, on a white ground,
bordered with the three colors.   The three colors, common to
all the Italian flags, signify the Italian Confederation.   The
lion the particular symbol of one of the Italian states.

Instructions were issued to the commanders of fortresses,
and to the captains of the ports, relative to the admission of
foreign vessels to the city.   Correspondence between Bishops
and Popes to be free ; importation of arms allowed ; duties on
Sardinian wines, and stamp duties on newspapers, abolished.
Public officers not to accept bank-notes.   The engineer department, being a branch of the Vienna institution, abolished.   Every accused person to be furnished with an advocate.   Instead
of a Senate, or supreme tribunal, a commission of revision appointed.   People to make known their wishes through the
press and petitions, and not to indulge in mobs and riots.
But the most important decree, perhaps, was, that each of the
provinces which had given in its adhesion to the new republic should elect and send to Venice three counselors, and that
the Provisional Government should also elect three.   The
council so formed to meet on the 10th of April, to appoint its
own president, and to regulate the order of its discussions.
All other provinces which might send in their adhesions to acquire an equal right to elect three counselors.   The council
to assemble in the Ducal Palace, and maintain a direct correspondence with the Provisional Government.

The next task which occupied the attention of the Provisional Government of Venice was the preparation of addresses,
which were immediately dispatched to all the foreign powers,
the contents of which were as follows : In the note to the
Pope, they promise never to disturb the cause of order in the

neighboring states, and notify his holiness of their intention to become a party to the Italian Zoll-Verein. The addresses to France* and England contained nothing but assurances of friendship. In the address to the United States of America, they bring to the recollection of the government the historical fact that a citizen of one Italian republic had been the discoverer of their country, while a citizen of another Italian republic had given name to the new continent; that the new republic confesses that it has still much to learn from the republic beyond the ocean; and further states that it is her intention to maintain free and peacefully the inheritance of their ancestors, and to contribute, to the extent of their power, to the development and progress of mankind. The address to Greece refers to the former relations of friendship which existed between the Ionian Isles and Venice. They trust that common remembrances and hopes, for the future, as well as common interests, may still connect these two states more closely. In the collective note to Sardinia, Naples, and Tuscany, the desire is expressed to remain on intimate relations without claiming any separate advantage. At last, the joint note to Russia, Prussia, Turkey, Holland, Belgium, Switzerland, Denmark, Sweden, Spain, Portugal, Brazil, Bavaria, Hanover, &c., is as follows: "A part of the old Venetian states has constituted itself a republic. In communicating to you this fact we do not feel ourselves called upon to justify or explain it. Upon history will devolve this task. We shall enhance the glory of our triumph by moderation in our language and in our actions. God has made our victory easy, and that facility must inspire us with a still deeper feeling of duty. We hope to find our strength in that sentiment of duty; we shall meet all apprehensions of danger by respect for existing rights, and stamp with sacredness our revolution. We expect that our new Constitution, which sooner or later will unite all the peoples of the earth, will strengthen our ties, enlarge our increasing commercial relations, and make the peace of the world more and more necessary and honorable."

---

* France, as most was expected from her, was honored with a special deputation to bear the address—Messrs. Angelo Zanardini, Giacomo Nani, and Alvise Caotorta.

To this collection was added a special one to Milan :

"We hailed with infinite joy the account of the emancipation of our generous sister of Lombardy.   On the very day
when you shook off the Austrian yoke, a Provisional Government of the Venetian republic was proclaimed here under the
glorious banner of St. Mark.   We are influenced by no local
prejudice ; we are, above all, Italians, and the insignia of St.
Mark figures on the tricolored banner.   We are united to you,
Lombards, not only by the tie of affection, but also by a community of misfortunes and hopes.   When the hallowed soil of
the country shall have ceased to be sullied by the feet of the
foreign oppressor, we shall join you in discussing the form of
government most conducive to our common glory.   We intended at first to send you a special deputation ; but the important and multifarious labors with which we are overwhelmed
do not admit of our dispensing with the services of any of our
distinguished citizens.   We impatiently await your direct communications.
   "Viva l'Italia, Viva Milano, Viva liberta, fratellanza !
   "Venice, 26th March, 1848."

Having fully secured themselves in the possession of Venice
and its surrounding ports ; having published the various ini-
tiatory decrees, the next object of the Provisional Government
was to send re-enforcements to the relief of such portions of the
Venetian kingdom on the main land as had given in their adhesion to the new republic, and which were now threatened by
the imperial forces.
   The following were the towns which had already declared
themselves for the republic, viz. : Donate, Piave, Padua, Treviso, Sacile, Monfelice, Bassano, Belluno, Agordo, Asola, Noale,
Fontanna, Tribano, Conegliano, Serivalle, Ceneda, Adria, Este
Rovigo, Poidmone, Feltre, Udine, Salvore, Vicenza, and Chioggia.
   A corps of "youthful volunteers"* were at first dispatched
in the direction of Palma Nova, at that time besieged by the

---

* Colonel David Amigo, appointed by the Provisional Government, commander.

Austrians.   Considerable ceremony preceded the departure of
this band of patriots.   They were first blessed by the patriarch
in the Basilica, and afterward harangued by Manin, who promised them that the republic would provide for the families of
those who might fall in battle.

Martial enthusiasm was at its height.   A Barnabite monk,
Pater Gavazzi, a second Peter the Hermit, had, like his great
prototype, been preaching the crusades throughout many of the
towns of Italy, not for the expulsion of the Saracen and recovery of the holy sepulchre, but for driving out those whom
they regarded as equally "barbarians," and for regaining their
own sacred soil.

The next issue from Venice was a battalion of Crociati, or
Crusaders, distinguished from other volunteers by wearing on
the breast a tricolored cross; composed of facchini (porters),
gondoliers, and all vagabonds who could find no employment
in the city.   The officers were composed of musicians, paint-
ers, and such other artists as the times had deprived of the
means of subsistence, or who, with the Moor of Venice, could
exclaim, " Othello's occupation's gone!"   Another portion of
this holy band, still more remarkable, was a regiment of wom-
en, consisting of opera-dancers, and females of the most dissolute character in Venice.   This band, dismissed with priestly
benedictions, proceeded toward Treviso and Udine, under no
control, and indulging in every kind of license.   They might, it
was thought, more appropriately have been called Corsairs than
Crusaders.   So far from affording protection, they soon became
a greater terror to the inhabitants than the Austrians whom
they had enlisted to oppose.

For a considerable time after the reconquest of the Venetian
provinces, the attention of the Austrians was so much occupied
with the advancing army of the King of Sardinia, that they had
no leisure to enforce the blockade of Venice; but this was finally accomplished on the 25th of June, when Baron Welden took
the Fort Cavanella, and by which operation Venice was, by
land, entirely inclosed.

But before that had been effected, Venice was filled with
defenders.   Each town, as it fell into the possession of the
Austrians, added to the numerical force of the garrison around

Venice, as all who could effect their escape retired to the capital. Besides these, volunteers had flocked in from every part of Italy; and the portion of the Neapolitan army that had deserted under General Pépé secured to it a garrison of regular soldiers, and the assistance of experienced officers. About this time, Baron Welden makes the following official report of the military forces in and around Venice: "At one of the last parades held by the Neapolitan General Pépé, seventeen thousand men were reviewed by him in the Campo Marzo; forming, with the garrison of the forts, a total of twenty-one thousand men. Malghera has a garrison of one thousand eight hundred men—Neapolitan, Piedmontese, and volunteers—with sixty cannons. Malghera defends the entrance into the lagoons, and can only be taken by a regular siege, as the buildings are bomb-proof. From that point to Brondolo there are fortifications. Brondolo is garrisoned by one thousand Neapolitans, with sixty cannons. From thence, along the sea-shore, comprising Alberoni, Palestrina, and the Lido, there are three thousand men. Treporti, Burano, Mazorbo, are but feebly garrisoned, and an attack upon Venice could only be possible on that side."

The vast concourse of strangers driven into the city by the conquest of their territories had the worst effect upon the Venetians. The volunteers from the provinces, the demoralized soldiery from Naples and Rome, and the adventurers from every part of the world, all living in the luxury of a large city, amply provided, by the fear or affection of the natives, with all that could minister to their desires, spread abroad an atmosphere of licentiousness not to be described. Vices, practiced at first with some attempt at concealment, arrived, at length, at such a pitch of barefaced extravagance that observation was rather courted than shunned. The scenes which polluted the hospitals of Rome were repeated at Venice. Fever and disease of all sorts were the result, and much of the subsequent mortality attributed to the cholera was the natural effect of intemperance and debauchery.

Other difficulties soon arose. Money was the chief desideratum. The usual revenues of the town were, of course, suspended. New imposts were not to be thought of; and a re-

course to great capitalists in any quarter was hopeless, as no
security could be given. Voluntary loans produced but a few
dollars. Sundry silver spoons and old watch-cases, believed
to be the contributions of the poor, the silver snuff-box of Manin, and several mites guaranteed to have come from the pock-
ets of the widow, figured in the list of the patriotic gifts.

Forced loans were much more successful. All men known
to be wealthy, and especially those believed to be disaffected
to the Republican cause, were compelled to contribute most
freely. Such resources, ruinous to many respectable citizens,
were, however, quite insufficient for the expenses of a government which had to pay twenty-one thousand mercenary soldiers, and to maintain the dissolute population of a large town
in plenty and in idleness. The *volunteers*, moreover, were a
vast drain on the exchequer ; and the rabble of St. Mark's
Square, who were employed to demand what the government
had previously determined to grant, or to cheer and propagate
the false news which it became necessary to circulate, exacted a florin (fifty cents) for every hour of service ; and so resolute were they in keeping up the price of enthusiasm, that
they were repeatedly known to interrupt a political song or a
popular oration, observing to each other that they had cried out
enough for their livres, and that they should now go to the
wine-shop and drink.

To meet all these expenses, a large issue was made of paper money, to which a forced currency was given, and which
maintained a certain credit, in the belief that the Austrian
government would pursue the same humane system of which
Prince Windischgrätz afterward gave the example in Hungary, to the injury of the imperial exchequer, and to the benefit
of the struggling province. This method of extorting the costs
from the winning party, and of making the legitimate government defray the expenses of the insurrection, is an invention
of modern times, which, combined with the new code of international law, adopted by Sardinia and the other Italian powers, offers great encouragement to rebellion, and secures perfect impunity to aggression.

In concert with the movements going on in Venice, as early
as the 25th of May, a combined fleet, composed of Neapolitan,

Sardinian, and Venetian vessels, appeared off the harbor of Trieste, and threatened to place that city in a state of blockade ; but, by the interposition of the foreign consuls and the commanders of one or two English vessels then in port, they were induced to desist. No obstruction was at any time offered to the commerce of neutral nations. Soon after, the Neapolitan vessels, owing to the troubles in Naples, were recalled home, the Sardinian vessels sailed away, and the Venetian ships returned to their city.

On the 6th of June, the Sardinian fleet again made its appearance in the harbor of Trieste, and, approaching rather too near the city, was fired upon by the batteries on shore ; and, after two of the vessels were disabled, they all withdrew. On the morning of the 10th they again returned, and on the 12th placed the city under formal blockade. A communication from the commander of the fleet, Admiral Albini, was made to the authorities of the city, in which he declared that he was compelled now to " regard Trieste, not as a place of commerce only, but also as one of war." The military governor of the fort fearing, from the large number of men on board the enemy's ships, that their intention might be to land and storm the city, sent to Vienna for troops, and two battalions, consisting of one thousand men, were immediately dispatched to their relief.

The Austrian government had resolved on commencing the blockade of the city of Venice on the 23d of May, but the arrival of the combined fleet at Trieste prevented their vessels, which were much inferior, from going out and carrying that determination into effect.

The Sardinian fleet continued in the Adriatic, cruising between Venice and Trieste, without making any attack, until after the defeat of Charles Albert, at Milan, when, in accordance with the terms of the armistice then entered into, the blockade was raised, and, shortly after, they disappeared altogether from the waters of the Adriatic.

During the month of June, several sorties were made by the Italians at Fort Malghera, upon the Austrian force that was besieging Venice, but without any important success. General Pépé issues a proclamation, on the 18th of that month, in which he declares that the Venetian government, with the con-

sent of Lombardy and the Pope, had placed him at the head
of all the troops there assembled from all parts of Italy, to wage
war against the Austrians.   By his orders, the rail-road bridge,
connecting Venice with the main land, a length of six miles,
was blown up.   On the 26th, he visited all the forts along the
coast, up to the mouth of the Adige, and ordered General Ul-
loa, the chief of his staff, to form an intrenched camp from
the fort of Brondolo to the sea-coast.   The Austrians awaiting re-enforcements, and contenting themselves with cutting
off the supplies destined for Venice, no batteries or fortifications, up to that date, had been raised near Malghera.

While these military operations, both by sea and land, were
occurring, a civil movement, of much greater importance, was
progressing, occasioned, doubtless, by the conquest of all the
Venetian provinces by the imperial army, which had by this
time taken place.   The towns of Padua, Vicenza, Rovigo, and
Treviso, just before they fell into the hands of the Austrians,
and in contemplation of the dangers which imminently threatened them, having sent an address to Venice desiring her to
give an immediate decision as to her union with Lombardy and
Piedmont, the Provisional Government of Venice published a
decree, bearing date the 3d of June, convoking a General Assembly to decide that question.

The decree determines that the representation is to be based
on the population, the electoral districts to be regulated by the
parishes.   In every parish where the population does not exceed two thousand souls, one deputy is to be returned ; where
the population fluctuates between two thousand and four thousand, two are to be elected ; and where the population varies
from four thousand to six thousand, three will be chosen ; and
so on, in the same ratio.   The only restriction on the exercise
of the suffrage, and the eligibility of the individuals to act as
deputies, being age ; the electors to be twenty-one at least,
and the elected twenty-seven years of age.

On the 20th and 29th of June, demonstrations took place in
favor of Charles Albert.   The people assembled on the Piazza
of St. Mark, and vociferated, "Long live Charles Albert!"
"Down with the republic!"   "Away with Manin!" In a short
time the minds of the people had undergone a great change.

A few days before, no one dared to advocate the claims of the
King of Piedmont; so great was their antipathy to him, that a
merchant, whose sign was the " City of Hizza" (a Sardinian
watering-place), was compelled to take it down; and now no
one thinks of a republic. On the morning of the 3d of July,
at nine o'clock, the National Assembly met, in the Cathedral
of St. Mark, where his excellency, the cardinal patriarch, officiated at the mass, after which he made a short address. The
religious ceremonies being concluded, the deputies all convened
in the ducal palace, where they proceeded to the election of the
officers of the Assembly.

Pianton, mitred Abbot of St. Maria della Misericordia, was
elected president; Dataico, Medin, and Vicenzo Scarpa, secretaries, ad interim. At one o'clock, the deputies assembled in
the Hall of the Grand Council. They numbered one hund-
dred and twenty-eight members. Two committees were appointed to examine the executive power of the Assembly. The
attorney, Avesani, proposed to hurry the discussions, upon
which Ferari Bravo remarked that, fifty years before, the republic of Venice was lost by too hasty resolutions. Tomaseo
recommended the " festina lente" as the proper mode of procedure. At two o'clock, the Senate adjourned, and the committee proceeded to the scrutiny. At four o'clock, the session
reopened, and the elections, as declared, resulted as follows:
Rubbi, Peter Canal, Vari Dataico, Medin, Dolfin, Boldu, secretaries. The Minister of Justice, Castelli, read the articles to
be taken into consideration.

The first and second regarded the projected annexation with
Piedmont. The third respected the confirmation or new election of the ministers and government; the fourth, the power
of the president for preserving order in the Assembly; the fifth,
the substitution of the president; and the sixth, the adjournment and closing of the session.

The next morning, the 4th of July, a discussion took place
in the Assembly upon the subject of annexation with Piedmont. Manin favors the measure, and says it will be time
enough to determine the form of government after the war
shall have been concluded. That they should not dispute
whether they would be Republicans or Royalists; that that

question would afterward be decided at Rome.   The annexation was determined by a vote of one hundred and twenty-seven in favor, and six against the project.

A change of policy ordinarily involves a change of administration; but as this measure was one of necessity, rather than of choice, and as neither the delegates who voted the decree, nor the citizens who accepted it, made any concealment of their aversion to the measure, or of their intention to reassert their independence when the fortune of war should turn in their favor, a change in the persons of the administration was not necessarily demanded.

Manin was urged to resume the executive power; but, as he had little faith in the durability of Sardinian power over Venice, especially after the loss of Vicenza, Padua, and Udine, in fact, all the Venetian terra firma, he shrewdly avowed his attachment to the republican cause, his determination not to hold office under royalty, and resigned his trust into the hands of a ministry (ad interim) named by the Assembly.*

On the 7th of July, the Provisional Government, presided over by Castelli, surrendered the administration to the Sardinian commissaries, Messrs. Calli and Cibrario.†   This ceremony took place with the greatest pomp in the hall of the former library, in presence of the cardinal patriarch and General Pépé, commander-in-chief of the Venetian forces.   The Cross of Savoy and the Lion of St. Mark figured on the national banners. For the first time in the history of Italy the cross of Savoy superseded the winged lion of St. Mark.   By this ceremony, the republic was buried, and Venice became for a short time a part of " the united Italian kingdom."

A month elapsed, and on the 9th of August reports of the fall of Milan and the capitulation entered into by the King of Piedmont reached Venice, and produced a great excitement throughout the city.   The people assembled in the Piazza of St. Mark, and demanded of the government to be informed of

---

* The ministry thus named consisted of Jacopo Castelli, Pietro Paleocapa, Francisco Cancirata, Antonio Paolucci, Leopoldo Martinengo, Giovanni Battista Cavedalis, and Giuseppe Reali.

† On the very day that Radetzky entered Milan, Venice passed under the authority of commissioners representing the monarchy of Charles Albert.

the real state of affairs. The government, afraid that a serious riot would be the consequence, endeavored to conceal the
disastrous news. They had been apprised by Baron Welden
of the armistice entered into by Charles Albert and the Milanese, who at the same time inquired if Venice was disposed to
be included in the armistice, which was declined, as an acceptance of the armistice would have been an acknowledgment of
the capitulation. As the excitement continued hourly to increase, the royal Sardinian commissaries thought it advisable
to communicate with Manin, and who, upon their application,
promised to appear before the people on the evening of the
11th of August, at eight o'clock. He appeared accordingly;
and, after the announcement by M. Calli, the royal commissary, from the windows of the Procurata Nuove, of the defeat
and capitulation of Charles Albert, Manin told the people that
the rule of the commissioners had ceased, that an Assembly
should be summoned within forty-eight hours, and " in the interval," he added, " I govern."

The citizens, absolved, as they thought, by these events
from all allegiance to the King of Piedmont, the Sardinian flag
was struck in the Place of St. Mark, at the end of one month
from the time it had been raised; and the city of the doges
once more returned to its self-government.

On the morning of the 13th of August, at ten o'clock, the
Assembly opens, one hundred and eleven deputies present.
Among the absent is Castelli, late royal Sardinian commissary. Manin rises, and states that he is authorized by Castelli
to inquire of the Assembly whether his late employment as
royal commissary would deprive him of his rights as deputy.
The Assembly being of the opinion that the employment was
not an obstacle to the enjoyment of his rights as a member of
their body, Castelli is sent for. Deputy Tralli, premising that
the prospects of Charles Albert were not altogether hopeless,
proposes a continuance of the royal commissaries until further
notice. Violent interruptions ensue, and he is not allowed to
proceed. Manin suggests the immediate formation of a government, to secure order and domestic tranquillity. Deputy
Bellinato proposes Manin as sole dictator. Manin declines the
proposal on the ground that he is not possessed of military

science, so necessary for the crisis. Bellinato then proposes
to give him two assistants for the war and navy departments.
The proposition is carried, and Manin is elected to the civil
department, Giovanni Battista Cavedalis for the war department, and Leone Graziani for the navy. On a further motion,
it was determined that dictatorial power should be vested in
these three individuals, so long as the country should continue
in danger, and the Assembly, for the same reason, to remain
en permanence.

Tomaseo and Toffoli having been dispatched on the 11th, by
the dictator, to Paris, to ask for their armed intervention, Mal-
fati, the deputy, proposes to send a member of the Assembly to
Paris, for the purpose of confirming that the will of the dictator is also that of the Assembly and the people. Mengaldo is
sent, and Bragadin is promoted to his place, as commander of
the National Guard.

The new government entered upon its duties with great energy. On the 16th of August, they published two decrees:
the first naming a Council of War for the defense of the city
and fortress of Venice; the second ordering, on pain of confiscation and arrest, all the gold and silver in Venice to be brought
to the Mint within forty-eight hours. The Mint was directed
to give receipts, to be afterward exchanged for loan certificates
bearing interest.

On the 24th of August, Marshal Radetzky dispatches, by a
special courier, an open letter from the Sardinian Minister of
War and Marine, to Admiral Albini, ordering him to raise the
blockade, to quit the Gulf of Venice with his fleet, and to send
home the Sardinian troops to their country. Several weeks
still elapsed before this order was carried into effect.

Tomaseo arrived in Paris, and, on the 2d of August, had an
interview with M. Bastide; and, in reply to an application for
assistance, was informed that negotiations were going on having for their principal base the evacuation of all Italy by the
Austrians.

Mengaldo, the deputy of the Assembly, who arrived the following day, had an interview with General Cavaignac, and
was informed, in like manner, that France had offered her
mediation to Austria, on the invariable basis of the enfran-

chisement of all the Italian states—that he hoped this mediation would not be rejected; but, in that case, there would be
war.   He said, " It would not be myself alone who would be
for war.   It would be declared by a decree of the National
Assembly.   Write to your countrymen to hold out as long as
possible, and give to my words the greatest publicity."*

The great powers, England and France, who had refused
their mediation in the affairs of Italy when Austria sought it,
.so long as there seemed the slightest hope that the Italians
could conquer their independence—now, when the imperial
government, by its own unaided strength, had reconquered,
with the exception of a single city, the entire territory of both
revolting provinces, they were more than anxious to force their
mediation upon her.

Austria, at this time, very properly hesitated to accept the
tendered mediation; in fact, the subject was by no means free
from difficulty.   If the mediation was solely interposed between Austria and Sardinia, the belligerent states, it was of
necessity superfluous and ineffective, inasmuch as the contest
had already ceased, and the two countries had concluded an
armistice, on the *status quo ante bellum.*   And, if the mediation aspired to regulate and determine the rights and territorial authority of the court of Austria within its own Italian
dominions, it was easy to anticipate that such an effort, at that
time, would be held wholly inadmissible.   The mediation was,
however, afterward accepted by Austria, at least in principle,
she reserving to herself the faculty of submitting the propositions which might be made the subject of consideration, as
well as the privilege of giving to France and England, and to
the other powers who signed the final treaty of the Congress
of Vienna, a written answer, with the motives upon which it
might be founded.   This answer, as delivered to Lord Palmerston and M. Bastide, establishes the following three principal
points: First, that the war by King Charles Albert against
Austria, not being justifiable upon any principle of international law, could not afford the crown of Sardinia the least
pretension to any portion whatever of the Lombardo-Venetian

---

* Patrie, September 1st, 1848.

kingdom. Secondly, that Austria, by maintaining intact her possession of the Lombardo-Venetian kingdom, far from attempting to gain any territorial aggrandizement, only demanded the fulfillment of the guarantees established in her favor by the seven powers who signed the final treaty—guarantees which find an additional strength in the right of conquest, since Marshal Radetzky, by driving back the Sardinian army beyond the Ticino, re-established *de facto* the strict *status quo* as it was before the war, and taken as the basis of the armistice agreed upon at Milan between the two belligerent parties, on the 9th of August. Thirdly, that the mediation offered by France and England could in no case have for its object an alteration in the political balance of power in Europe, without the co-operation of all the powers who established and guaranteed it. All these being laid down, Austria, renewing in the most formal manner her reservations as to the possession of the Lombardo-Venetian kingdom, proposes that a general Congress shall be convoked, at which, with a common accord, between the principal powers of Europe, there might be concerted the most opportune measures for insuring, on the one hand, a national and independent government for the Lombardo-Venetian kingdom, and, on the other hand, for consolidating, in the most durable manner, the tranquillity of the Apennine peninsula.*

While this negotiation was pending, a serious difference of opinion arose between the mediating powers and the government of Austria, on the subject of the city of Venice. The British and French representatives at Vienna are said to have declared to Baron Wessenberg, the Minister for Foreign Affairs, that, in consequence of the mediation accepted by the Imperial Cabinet, the latter was bound to abstain from any act of hostility against Venice, until the future fate of that city should be fixed by the mediating powers. The Cabinet of Vienna is said to have replied to this declaration that, in signing the armistice with King Charles Albert, the Austrian government reserved its full right to adopt such measures against Venice as might be necessary to recover possession of it, the more so

---

* La Presse.

X

as the armistice in question declared expressly that Venice should be surrendered to the imperial troops within three days after the ratification of the armistice by King Charles Albert. The Baron de Wessenberg added that, at the period the armistice was concluded at Milan, the city of Venice was dependant, in fact, on the Sardinian government, and that, consequently, the engagement contracted by King Charles Albert to surrender Venice to Austria could not be weakened by the refusal of the present Venetian government, a revolutionary government, not recognized by any foreign power, and much less by Austria. Neither did Baron Wessenberg conceal from Lord Ponsonby and M. de Lacour that, as soon as the Sardinian fleet should have quitted Venice, the Austrian government would attack it by land and by sea.

The course which Austria had now resolved to pursue, and which her late conquests enabled her publicly to declare, was that she would go great lengths, exceeding even the most sanguine expectations, in the concession of constitutional rights and the establishment of self-responsible government; but that she would not condescend to debate, for the tithe of a second, the question of the territorial surrender of those provinces which she had possessed for centuries, and which the prowess of her arms had enabled her again to reconquer. She could not do so, it was obvious, without a total disregard of her peninsular interests. She could not consent to attach such a slur to the fame of the gallant armies that had asserted her supremacy. She could not thus damp and discourage the loyalty of her faithful legions. She could not thus reward the services of her marshals; nor could she hope (were she on such a point to cede) to escape reaction at home, and discontent among the united and loyal legions who had rallied round the empire to restore it to undiminished, if not augmented authority.

While these diplomatic negotiations were proceeding, the government of Venice was sorely pressed for the pecuniary means necessary to support the extraordinary exigencies of the state. Manin, in a private letter of the 2d of September, writes that "money is the most urgent want of Venice; if she can raise it, Venice will hold out, but not otherwise."

Voluntary contributions had produced but little; forced loan

after forced loan was decreed.   Defended as she was by twenty-one thousand men, one thousand cannon, and a squadron of
seven ships, the expense of this force was estimated to exceed
three millions of livres a month, while the revenue of the town
did not exceed two hundred thousand livres.   To meet the deficiency, a new and special forced loan was decreed, in the
month of October, of two millions of livres, to be divided between the hundred and fifty houses who contributed the first
voluntary loan.   In the early part of November, another forced
loan of one million of livres, to operate generally, was decreed.
In the latter part of the same month a new contribution of
twelve millions of francs was demanded ; to meet which a
quantity of paper, called " Money of the Commune of Venice,"
was to be issued.   From the 22d of March to the 31st of December, 1848, the expenditure amounted to 35,601,110 francs,
and there remained in hand 1,428,682 francs, and all the means
within the state were exhausted, and the government had to
look abroad for assistance.   Had they followed the example of
the Romans when placed under similar circumstances, and the
first men of the state—particularly those who could afford to
contribute—had come forward and placed all their possessions
at the command of the government, the result, as in that instance, might have been widely different.   When the Cartha-
ginians were invading Italy, and Hannibal, with his unconquered army, was laying waste the Italian plains, the consuls
decreed a contribution ; but the people, seeing that no efforts
were being made on the part of the higher classes proportioned to their abilities and the exigencies of the occasion, complained aloud, and gathering in crowds in the forum, declared
that no power on earth could force from them that which they
did not possess.   The Consul Lævinius, convinced of the necessity of the tax, as well as of the impossibility of carrying
it through, summoned the Senate, and told them that, before
they could call on the people to make sacrifices, they must set
the example.   " Let each senator keep his ring, and that of his
wife and his children ; but all the rest of the gold which we
possess, let us offer to the public service.   Next, let all of us
who have borne curule offices reserve the silver used in the
harness of our war-horses ; let us all, besides, keep one pound

of silver for the plate needful in sacrifices, and let us each keep
five thousand asses of copper money.   With these exceptions,
let us devote all our silver and copper to our country's use, as
we have devoted all our gold.   And let us do this without any
vote of the Senate, but of our own free gift as individual senators, and carry our contributions at once to the three commissioners for the currency.   Be sure that first the equestrian
order, and then the mass of the people, will follow our example."* He spoke to hearers who so thoroughly shared his spirit, that they voted their thanks to the consul for his suggestion.   The Senate instantly broke up, the senators hastened
home; and thence came crowding to the forum their slaves,
bearing all their stores of copper, and silver, and gold, each
man being anxious to have his contribution recorded first; so
that, Livy says, neither were there commissioners enough to
receive all the gifts that were brought, nor clerks enough to
record them.   The example, as the consul knew, was irresistible, the equestrian order and the commons poured in their
contributions with equal zeal, and no tax could have supplied
the treasury so plentifully as this free-will offering of the whole
people.

The internal resources exhausted, or not available, the Venetians were compelled to look for assistance beyond the confines of the republic, especially since the Venetian paper currency would not be received by the ship-masters, who had
brought in their ships ladened with provisions for the suffering
city.   A large loan was contracted at Rome; and the King of
Sardinia, not having yet relinquished the hope of one day possessing himself of the Lombardo-Venetian kingdom, decreed
the advance of six hundred thousand livres monthly to the aid
of the struggling republic.

The first installment of six hundred thousand livres reached
Venice on the 29th of January.   With this advance, however,
whether from the aggravated embarrassments at home or a
decline of enthusiasm in the cause of Italian independence, all
pecuniary relief ended.

In the month of January, the Provisional Government issued

---

* Polybius.   Livy.   Arnold's Rome.

a decree establishing a permanent Assembly of the representatives of the State of Venice, with the power of deciding upon every thing relating to the interior or exterior condition of the state; the deputies to be elected by direct universal suffrage, in the proportion of the population, of one to fifteen thousand; the elections to commence on the 20th of January; the representatives to meet immediately after, and their mandate to last six months.   This Assembly was in existence but a couple of weeks, when, by a decree of the Provisional Government, of the 9th of February, this Assembly was dissolved, and a new Assembly convoked for the 15th of February.

The Assembly meets, and elects Tomaseo presiding officer of that body.   He declines; but, at his suggestion, Calucci is chosen.   The Assembly resolves that the election of dictator rests with the Assembly; but the executive power was again confided to Manin, Cavedalis, and Graziani, so far as concerned the defense of the country.   The Assembly shortly after, in March, elects Manin unlimited dictator, but bound to submit to the sanction of the Assembly all important legislative dispositions.   Should he adjourn the Assembly, he must call it together again in fifteen days.

The Austrian government had now determined to prosecute with the utmost energy the siege of Venice.   The bombardment was directed to be opened against all the fortifications around the city without delay, while the Austrian fleet was dispatched from Pola, to commence the blockade by sea.   After the desertion of Naples, the Austrian occupation of Tuscany, the French intervention at Rome, and especially after the total defeat of the Piedmontese at Novara, and by which they were deprived of the efficient aid of the Sardinian navy, the Venetian Assembly resolved, on the 2d of April (in answer to the demand of General Haynau to surrender), to resist " at any cost, and to the last."   While this answer would denote an act of heroism worthy of Venice in her palmiest days, yet the determination is not free from the charge of rashness, when it is considered that, with all this resolution to resist at all hazards, and to the last extremity, no stores of provisions, so indispensable, were made for the siege, while the communication by sea was kept open by the Sardinian fleet, and the

Venetian trading-boats communicated, with so little interruption, with the terra firma; leaving the inevitable result,
that, even should they survive the formidable batteries of the
enemy, they must assuredly, and at no distant day, perish by
starvation.

To save the effusion of blood, as well as preserve a city
which the Austrians were loth to injure, Marshal Radetzky,
leaving his head-quarters at Milan, arrived at the quarters of
the besieging army on the evening of the 4th of May, and immediately sent into the city the following proclamation:

"Venetians! it is not my intention to address you to-day as
a soldier, or as a fortunate general, but I speak to you as a father.   One year of confusion—of anarchical and revolutionary movements—has passed away, and what are the results?
Your public treasury is exhausted—your property destroyed
—your city in misery and want.   By the victories which my
gallant army has gained over your allies, you can not fail to
be convinced that, in a short time, attacked from all sides, your
fortifications must be taken—all your communications cut off.
No opportunity of departure left you, you will be placed only
at the mercy of the conqueror.   I come from my head-quarters at Milan for no other purpose than to give you my last
admonition, with an olive-branch in one hand, if you are not
yet deaf to the voice of reason—with the sword in the other,
ready to prosecute a war of extermination if you persist in rebellion, and thus deprive yourselves of all claims on the clemency of your rightful sovereign.

"I shall remain in your neighborhood, at the head-quarters
of the *corps d'armé*, and will await your answer during the
space of forty-eight hours; that is, until the 6th of May, at
eight o'clock A.M.   In the name of my sovereign, I require
of you the fulfillment of the following conditions:

"1st. Unlimited, full, and entire submission.

"2d. Immediate surrender of the city, the fortifications, and
the arsenals, which will be occupied by my troops.   All the
vessels of war, in whatever epoch they may have been built;
all public edifices; *materiel* of war, and all objects which are
the property of the state, must be consigned to the troops.

"3d. Delivery of all arms belonging to the state or to private persons.

"I concede you the following points:

"1st. It is permitted to every person who may choose to do so, to leave the city, either by land or by water, during the space of forty-eight hours after the capitulation.

"2d. A general amnesty will be granted to all common soldiers and subordinate officers of the army and navy. On my part, hostilities will be suspended during the whole day of tomorrow, until the above-mentioned hour.

"Radetzky.

"Head-quarters, Casa Papadopili, 4th May, 1849."*

In answer to Radetzky's proclamation, in which are most kindly expressed terms more liberal than, under the circumstances, they had reason to expect, Manin communicates the resolution of the Assembly to resist at all hazards, and adds, at the same time, that he is directed by the Assembly to inform his excellency that, in consideration of the present condition of Italy, Venice had requested the interposition of the governments of France and England, since the receipt of a similar proclamation by Baron Haynau; that, as a favorable answer to this request might be expected in a few days, he would ask of the marshal a suspension of hostilities until the result of the application made to the cabinets of France and England, for their joint mediation, should be known. Field-marshal Radetzky replied to the dictator, that, "As his majesty had determined never to accept any intermediation of foreign powers between himself and his rebellious subjects, all hope of relief from such an application was vain, and tended only to deceive the already-deluded inhabitants of Venice; and that, as all negotiations by writing had proved unavailing, he regretted most deeply to be obliged to resort to the horrors of war."

The application† to which Manin alluded was made in a communication dated April 4th, and by both governments was refused, with civil regrets on the part of M. Drouyn de Lhuys

---

* Wiener Zeitung.   † Gazetta de Venezia.

and on Lord Palmerston's, with the advice to make terms with
Austria while it was yet possible. A request had also been
made to M. de Lacour, the French diplomatic agent at Vienna,
for his mediation; but his application was refused by Prince
Schwartzenberg, and the Venetian deputies were referred to
Marshal Radetzky, who was now invested with the full powers
of his sovereign.

All attempts at accommodation between the parties having
failed, the siege was now prosecuted with vigor, and the attack
of Malghera commenced on that day (the 6th of May). This
fortress, situated to the west of Venice, on the canal of Mestre,
commands the access to the city, and was at that time the
only spot of the *terra firma* still in the possession of the Venetians. For some time previously, the Austrians had been engaged on their works of approach to this fortress, through the
marsh which intervenes between it and Mestre. During a few
days, they advanced successfully with the first parallel, and
even reached the second; but the murderous fire from the fort,
and especially the sea of water which the Venetian engineers
threw over the enemy's works, by closing up the canal of Mestre, forced them to suspend their operations. The Austrians
were obliged to carry on their works waist-deep in water; and
at some important posts, they stood for twelve hours up to their
breasts in this manner. The rain, which fell in torrents, added
to the annoyance of the Austrians, keeping their fosses brim-
ful of water, until the night of the 15th, when they succeeded
in boring an outlet into the rail-road dike. On the morning
of the 24th, at five o'clock, the Austrians opened a fire from
ninety-six pieces of artillery, and continued it for seventy successive hours, without a moment's interruption. It was a perfect rain of bombs, and all other warlike projectiles. But the
Venetians were not intimidated; never did fellows stand better
to their guns than the young artillerymen of Malghera; for
sixty-five hours they replied with impetuosity, which, for an
ordinary fort of the third order, and feebly manned, was an
achievement of no slight importance. "We alone," says an
Austrian officer, describing the attack, "made fifty thousand
shots, exclusive of thirty-one bombs from mortars, fifteen howitzer grenades, and nine Paixhans. We have received at least

as many." On the third day of the attack, the fort was in ruins, and the bomb-proof buildings afforded no protection. Some
of the troops were even killed while sleeping, as they thought,
in security. Apprised of their situation, the Venetian government dispatched an order to the commandant to evacuate the
fort. At nine o'clock, on the evening of the 26th, the evacuation of Malghera commenced, and by twelve o'clock not a
soul was left within its walls. The cannons of the fort (those
old ones which were not spiked) were loaded, and, with slow
matches applied to them, they kept up a continued fire for
three hours after the fortress had been entirely abandoned.
The Austrians, completely deceived, continued their awful fire
until five the next morning, against nothing but bewitched or
spectral cannons, which were firing of themselves, without
gunners.

Amid this rain of bombs, the garrison all arrived safely in
Venice, and the second line of defense began its fire upon the
enemy at five o'clock the next morning, from a battery constructed on the rail-road bridge. It was a most fortunate circumstance for the Venetians that the enemy were so slow in
discovering that the fort had been abandoned, otherwise their
retreat would have been cut off, and all have been lost. The
next morning, at eight o'clock, when all was as silent as the
grave within the fortress of Malghera, the Austrians entered,
and found it a heap of ruins. Not a step could be taken without encountering traces of the endless destruction which had
been caused. Funnels of burst shells, damaged guns without
number, palisades and mounds demolished, and the few buildings it contained a mass of cinders. When the Austrian officers beheld the total wreck before them, and the guns almost
all disfigured with blood, they could not but express their admiration of an enemy who had braved the death and destruction of those awful days, without seeking safety in retreat,
which had been at all times open to them.

From the intrenchments of Malghera, the little fort San
Giulano, but a short distance off, and, like Malghera, deserted
by the Venetians, presented a fearful spectacle, lying prostrate
in the waves of the lagoons. As no boat could be procured, a
small party of men and a few officers, who could swim, imme-

diately dashed into the waves and swam across. The fort was
quite empty, though the guns were yet warm, from the rapid
and recent firing; the cannons were all spiked, with the exception of a miserable one which lay there loaded, with the lighted match alongside, and, strange to tell, pointed at the flying
enemy. The temptation to the Austrians was too great to be
resisted, and one of them, seizing the lighted torch, applied it
to the gun. The shot went off well, but, a few moments later, an awful mine exploded, which was connected by a train
with that cannon. The concussion was tremendous; it shook
sensibly the shores of the *terra firma*. Twenty men and three
gallant officers were whirled into the air, and some few fragments of their bodies were all the traces that could ever be discovered of those brave men who, but a moment before, were
exulting in victory. When the smoke and dust had cleared
away, as no movement or signs of life appeared among those
who had so recently taken possession of San Giuliano, a second
party, with some surgeons, were dispatched to investigate the
sad affair. It was found that one of the magazines had been
exploded by a well-conducted train; a further examination
led to the discovery of another lighted train, which connected
with the second magazine, and which, had it not been instantly extinguished, would in a few moments have launched the
second party into eternity.

During the siege of Malghera, Baron Haynau, commander
of the besieging force, was, by the government, transferred to
the field of operations in Hungary, and his place supplied by
the general, Count Thurn. On the 1st of June, M. De Bruck,
Minister of Commerce in the imperial cabinet, reached Mestre,
and addressed Manin a note, to inquire what he desired, and
what he intended to do. The day after, two commissioners,
Messrs. Calucci and Foscolo, were dispatched by the Venetian
government, to have a personal interview with him. On the
same day, the Venetian Assembly, with unanimity, confirmed
the decree of the 2d of April, of resistance at all hazards.

De Bruck, after reading to the Venetian commissioners a
general project, concluded by proposing three plans for the future government of Venice, of which he left the choice with
them. To these proposals the delegates declined giving any

reply without consulting their constituents. The offers of the Austrian commissioners were declined, and the correspondence, on their part, terminated with a tender of terms (in case of capitulation) nearly the same as those previously proposed by Marshal Radeizky. The negotiation concluded with the reply of Manin, viz.: that the Chamber, after "having deliberated on these proposals, had negatived them, by passing to the order of the day." Their heroism and union form a noble contrast to the base extinction of the republic in 1797, when it fell, without a struggle, from decrepitude and corruption. Malghera and San Guiliano were captured; but with these successes the fall of Venice was by no means assured. Six miles of water yet intervened between them and the devoted city of the doges, and which their guns, as yet, were equally unable to reach. But the enemy had now got an opening on the lagoons, and beheld before them the placid bay, studded with little fortified islands, besides San Secundo, two batteries on the remains of the rail-road dam, the *téte du pont* at Venice, and eight or ten well-armed ships, from all of which a perpetual and well-directed fire was constantly poured out upon the enemy.

No time was lost by the Austrians in clearing away the rubbish at Malghera, raising again its fallen battlements, and preparing it for action, under the double-headed eagle that now floated from its standard. Four thirty-pound mortar pieces were placed at San Giuliano, and a battery constructed at the head of the rail-road bridge, supplied with two howitzers and four thirty-pound mortar pieces.

The Provisional Government, apprehending that the rail-road bridge might be used as a *point d'appui* for the Austrian guns, ordered that, besides the five arches nearest to the city, which had been already destroyed, eight more should be blown up. For the defense of the bridge, one hundred gun-boats, each with four guns, were posted at different points on the lagoons.

The Austrians attempted, on the 7th of June, to cross the Brenta, near Busola, for the purpose of attacking Brondolo. Meanwhile the brig Montecuculli and the steamer Vulcano bombarded the batteries of Calino, and the steamer Custoza threw a great number of shells into Sottomarina, near Chioggia; but all these were unavailing, as the troops found it impossible to

resist the destructive fire of the ninety guns on the fort of
Brondolo. In consequence of this failure, the Austrians resolved to make no further attempt on Brondolo, but to await
its fall until Venice should be taken, as it would then be impossible for it to survive the parent city.

On the morning of the 15th of June, Radetzky being present, the Austrians opened a terrible fire from their batteries
on the bridge and the island of San Giuliano, at the Venetian
batteries, and also sent a few bombs against the city, three of
which struck an old shed and an old church, situated at the *extreme* limit of the town. The main fire was, however, directed
against the Venetian battery on the bridge and the small fortified island of San Secundo near it. They kept up an awful
fire for three days and nights, but with no great success, as
the balls, for the most part, fell short. Of upward of two
thousand bombs, which the Austrians threw, only an average
of two per day fell into the fort, all the rest falling into the
water or bursting in the air. One dead, and six or seven
wounded, was all the loss which the Venetians sustained in the
three days and nights of terrific firing.

The spectacle presented by this bombardment was indeed a
magnificent one. From the house-tops, in the extremity of
the city, totally out of danger, one might behold the scene with
the utmost tranquillity. With an ordinary telescope he could
observe all that was transpiring at Malghera, the tops of the
casernes crowded with Austrian officers gazing at the extraordinary spectacle — the enemy load and fire their guns and
mortars—the progress of the balls and bombs as they course
through the air, and at length fall into the water, casting huge
volumes of spray into the air. While, nearer, the Venetian
batteries on the bridge ; the *tête du pont* in the city, and the
little fort of San Secundo in the lagoons, were vying with each
other in the rapidity with which they returned the enemy's
fire. At night the scene was incomparably more grand ; men,
women, and children line the shores ; the water is covered with
barks and gondolas by the delighted spectators to witness the
gorgeous scene ; the lagoon, all along the bridge, filled with
armed boats of every description ; while the perfect shower of
balls and bombs from the batteries, in every direction lighting

up the whole heavens, and, at the same time, being reflected
in the water, presented a scene of awful grandeur rarely, if
ever, before witnessed.

The Venetians seemed now more than ever bent upon "resistance at all hazards." Amid the shower of balls and bombs,
on the 17th of June, the Assembly met and confirmed again
the resolution to resist, and broke up with enthusiasm, after
appointing a Committee of Defense, of three persons, with *unlimited powers;* also another committee of five, to govern the
town *ad latus* with Manin. The people were not all pleased
at the idea of Manin's treating with De Bruck upon any condition, and it was for the purpose of having some supervision
of his movements, it is said, that this last committee was
formed. All that portion of the city (the outward limits) occupied by the fishermen, which *might* be damaged by bombs,
was abandoned enthusiastically by the people, who were transferred to the marble palaces on the Grand Canal. Instead of
repining at being obliged to abandon their humble dwellings,
it was a perfect *fete* to them; and in the utmost glee as they
moved along with their scanty effects, " Let the old houses
go," they said; " we would rather have bombs than Croats."
On the 20th of June, propositions of capitulation were made
by the Venetians. Field-marshal Thurn suspended the bombardment, and dispatched a courier to Milan. Field-marshal
Radetzky rejects the proposals known as the *ultimatum* of
Manin, and soon the great guns begin to labor again. As the
lagoons prevented the approach of artillery, the troops not being advanced a yard beyond the position which they took on
the fall of Malghera, an attempt was made, on the 24th of June,
to bombard Venice by balloons. Five balloons, each twenty-
five feet in diameter, were constructed at Treviso. In a favorable wind these balloons were to be launched, and directed
as near as possible to Venice, and, on their being brought in a
vertical position over the town, the fire was to begin by means
of electro-magnetism. Each of the five bombs fixed to the boat
was in communication with a large galvanic battery placed on
the shore by means of a long isolated copper wire. The fusee
was to be ignited by cutting the wire. The bomb then falls
perpendicularly, and explodes on reaching the ground.

By this means twenty-five bombs a day, it was thought, might be thrown, supposing the wind to be favorable. Experiments, previously made at Treviso, had succeeded completely; but on the 24th, when tried over the lagoons, owing to a change in the wind after the balloons were discharged, the three attempts which were made failed, and the balls, instead of reaching the city, fell into the sea.

On the 1st of July, the bombardment was again suspended, on account of *parliamentiares* sent from Venice; the same terms are proposed; and the Venetian Assembly decides that " the conditions offered by Austria are so humiliating, that they can not be accepted;" and again it is resolved to resist. They could not rely, it was urged, upon the promises of the Austrians; as much had been promised in 1815, and but little carried into effect. Resistance now, however, without object and without hope, seemed to be the result of a spirit bordering on desperation.

Protected by their insular position and the extent of the lagoons, they might resist for a time; but assuredly the day would come, and that before long, when, for want of the means of subsistence, all resistance must cease. Already had food of all kinds become exceedingly scarce, and particularly those articles upon which the poorer classes subsisted. For many days past the entire population had begun to eat *black* bread, and it was fully evident that, in a few weeks, they would be deprived even of that humble diet.

As long as they remained supplied with any means of subsistence, they might defy the Austrian artillery; but that they must fall by hunger, in a short time, was now apparent to all. In this respect the whole city had been woefully deceived. The government had assured the people that Venice was furnished with provisions for a year; but the truth was now for the first time disclosed, that the provisions then in the city could last but six weeks, while the blockade, both by sea and land, was so close as to exclude all hope of obtaining the slightest addition to the stock. Despite this heart-rending development, the town continued perfectly tranquil, nor was the determination to resist the enemy in the slightest degree impaired. In the mean time, the roar of the enemy's cannon was heard unceasingly night and day. They continued to send a few bombs toward Venice; but, as they fell short of the city, they occasioned no concern among the population.

On the night of the 7th of July, as a matter of further precaution, the Venetians blew up six more arches of the railroad bridge. So tremendous was the concussion, that the inhabitants of Padua, a town at the distance of fifteen miles, felt the ground sensibly shake beneath them; while at Treviso, no less than twenty miles off, the population were aroused from sleep.

On the night of the 9th, the Austrians made a bold attempt, which succeeded beyond all expectation, and, had it been properly followed up, might have caused the immediate downfall of the city. Some twenty or thirty men, well armed, approached in boats a Venetian battery of seven guns, on the rail-road bridge, and, without being discovered, took possession of it, and held it for the space of forty minutes; they spiked the guns, but, before they could get away, re-enforcements arrived, four of them were left on the spot, and the others, who escaped in the boats, must have suffered greatly, as the tide next morning brought down convincing proofs. It was a desperately bold undertaking, and executed most gallantly. The Venetians, however, soon unspiked their guns, and, in three or four hours after, continued their usual fire.

Toward the end of July, the incessant roar of cannon, which for thirty-two days and nights, without intermission, had continued to sound and resound upon the ear of the Venetians, began now, from some cause unknown to them, gradually to subside. By some, this cessation of hostilities on the part of the Austrians was ascribed to the preparation necessary for a new and more terrible mode of attack. And, what added force to this conjecture, was the intelligence which had reached them that Marshal Radetzky was then at Mestre, busily engaged in inspecting all the works, and superintending the construction of strong howitzer batteries at St. Giuliano and other important positions, which had hitherto remained unoccupied.

Others very naturally supposed that the enemy, finding it a useless expenditure of powder and shot, had abandoned the idea of taking the city by storm, and were resolved to await until starvation should accomplish what their army could not effect. And, as the city began now to experience the first effects of famine, this seemed for the moment the more probable conclusion.

The crowds around the bakers' shops were already so dense that several persons had been pressed to death. Meat and wine were almost completely exhausted, and bread of the worst quality exceedingly scarce. Notwithstanding these severe demands upon their patriotism and courage, public opinion in Venice on the subject of resistance was still unchanged—the people seemed still resolved " to hold out to the last ;" while the activity at the arsenals, and at all the posts, appeared to indicate that some great enterprise was to be undertaken before the final catastrophe arrived. For some time previously, a rumor had been circulated in Venice that, on the 1st of August, the Austrians intended to commence another and more awful assault upon the city than any that had hitherto been witnessed ; but there were few of its pleasure-loving inhabitants who listened with credulity to this whisper of fancy, and even they dreamed not of any thing more disastrous than that which they had already encountered. But, when the silence which reigned over the waters of the lagoons had been for many days unbroken by a single hostile gun, on Sunday, the 31st of July, at midnight, when the lower classes were quietly reposing in their beds, and the higher and gayer circles, as was their custom, promenading the illuminated Piazza of St. Mark, or seated under its extended balconies, carelessly sipping their coffee or puffing their cigars—no sooner had the bell in the tower of St. Mark tolled the hour of twelve, and announced the fact that the 1st of August had appeared, than they found themselves in the midst of a shower of red-hot shot, more terrible than the irruption of Vesuvius on Pompeii, and covering at once nearly three fourths of the city. In a moment, all Venice was alive. The streets were crowded with the residents of the invaded section—men, women, and children, all hurrying toward the Castillo and the public gardens, where the projectiles did not reach, and running, as it were, the gauntlet through those narrow ways, amid the shot and rubbish,

.broken chimneys, and severed cornices that were at every step rattling down about their heads. Yet not a complaint was uttered, not a tear shed. The people of the exposed districts quartered themselves upon the occupants of the other sections with as much composure as if they had been members of one family; and nothing was heard but imprecations upon an enemy who, avoiding the breasts of soldiers ready and willing to receive them, attempted to force a capitulation upon the town, by routing the women and children from their beds, in hopes, through their screams and tears, to accomplish that which their personal valor had been unable to effect.

The torrent of balls, which continued to fall incessantly, night and day, had no other result than to destroy property and demolish the most beautiful works of architecture and sculpture. On the Grand Canal, nearly every palace was perforated, and some, particularly those of Mocenigo (which Lord Byron occupied), had thirty-six balls; Balbi, Persico, etc., boast of having received as many as thirty or forty balls each. A number of the churches, viz., the Frari, the Scalzi, San Giovanni e Paolo, etc., with their splendid marble and statuary, suffered severely.*

The means by which the Austrians succeeded at length in throwing their projectiles into the city, a point which they had endeavored in vain for months to accomplish, was by mounting at San Giuliano pieces of eighty pounds and Paixhan guns of the heaviest calibre, and firing with muzzles raised to a considerable elevation; the balls then, in describing the parabolic curve, would descend and fall within the city; whereas, discharged on a level, or aimed directly at the object, as had previously been done, at a distance of five or six miles, the balls invariably fell short of their destination, and sank without effect beneath the waters.

On the 1st of August, the day upon which this awful bombardment commenced, two thousand Venetians made a sally from Brondolo, and, after capturing a few hundred oxen, retired. During the evening the tidings of that expedition reached Venice; and while the population of that gay capital were

---

* One shot struck the *Rialto*.

Y

quietly seated in the magnificent Fenice under the shower of red-hot shot (for the theatre was in the invaded district), enjoying, as composedly as though nothing had happened, the performance of "William Tell," the enthusiasm which the narration of this slight success created was so great, that the continuation of the drama was dispensed with, and the occasion converted into a national festival.

Day after day, unceasingly, the cannonading continues; at many points the bombs set fire to the buildings, but these are soon extinguished without much injury; and as the balls seldom, if ever, penetrated further than the roof and one story, the population are unconcerned. Provisions become hourly more scarce; the supply can last but two weeks longer, and yet the people very quietly say, "We will hold out until we have nothing more to eat, and then the Croats may come and do what they please."

To add to the horrors of their situation, the cholera broke out among the inhabitants in its most dreadful and malignant form, its ravages, doubtless, increased by the scanty and unwholesome food upon which they had been for some time compelled to subsist; and yet, amid all these disasters, the city remained tranquil, the Place of St. Mark was as much frequented as ever, and the countenances of the Venetians as bright as though enjoying the sunshine of the palmiest days of the republic.

On the 14th of August, Marshal Radetzky, aware of the state to which the city was reduced, renewed his efforts to induce it to capitulate, by offering nearly the same terms that had been previously rejected. Strange that now, when ammunition, food, medicine, drink, even water was failing—when to the general misery and squalor the cholera is added, carrying off from eighty to one hundred a day, in Venice and Chioggia, families without bread, without a roof, in search of shelter and victuals, old men, women, and children crammed into the public store-houses, or under the naked sky exposed to all the inclemencies of the weather and all the bombs and balls of the Austrians, these terms, quite as moderate as could possibly have been expected, were again rejected.

On the 17th, the president of the republic, warned by the

rapid progress of public danger that longer resistance was impossible, in consultation with the commandant of the French squadron and the French consul, it was decided, as the only and last means of safety, to send a Venetian deputation to the Austrian camp with an offer of capitulation. General Gergowski, commander of the Austrian troops before Venice, received the deputation on the 19th; and, in reply to their application, stated that he had no power to treat, but that he would immediately forward their note to Milan, and that during the time necessary to receive a reply from Marshal Radetzky he would consent to slacken his fire on the city; and further, that Venice might confide in the paternal intentions of the emperor, and in the enlightened and liberal spirit of his government. The deputation, comprehending the exact value to be attached to such phrases, returned dejected and disconsolate to Venice.

Time rolls on, the reply from Milan is hourly expected, the destiny of a nation hangs on the balance, and a day becomes an age. The fire of the enemy, somewhat slackened on the 20th and 21st, is renewed on the night of the latter with as great severity as ever. What will be the nature of the reply from Milan? What terms will an all-powerful and long-provoked enemy inflict upon an utterly weak and prostrate foe?

No one knows, but all fear they will be rigorous in the extreme. The republic approaches its end. Venice has but two days' provisions left, and those of the worst kind. The progress of the cholera is frightful. The absolute and unconditional surrender of the city within two days, inevitable. The 22d of August arrives, and with it the answer of the field-marshal. That octogenarian commander, as magnanimous as renowned, has affixed no additional stipulations on his fallen foe; the terms are accepted by the municipality of Venice, in whose favor the Provisional Government and the National Assembly have abdicated their powers; the firing has ceased on both sides, and the republic of Venice is no more.

Her defense stands alone—like her marble palaces and her renown—in the midst of seas and of the ages of the world. She falls as she has lived, free from excesses, free from violence; and, while enduring incredible privations, has never yielded to anarchy. Overpowered by superior forces, and yielding to the weight of events which it was impossible to withstand, ruined in every thing but spirit, Venice falls battling heroically for her ancient and long-cherished independence.*

General Gorzgowsky entered Venice on the 28th, and Marshal Radetzky, in great state, on the 30th. At nine o'clock on that morning, the thunder of the cannons of Malghera announced that the steamer on which he had embarked had commenced her passage through the lagoons. The batteries of San Secundo and Piazzale del Ponti saluted the hero as he passed. At the entrance of the Canasegio, where the marshal and his staff descended into the gondolas prepared for the occasion, his reception was solemn and imposing. As they sailed up the Grand Canal, the windows were decorated as in the happiest and most glorious days of Venice. From all the towers the bells sounded joyously ; and, on reaching the Piazetta, the large bells of St. Mark were heard amid the salvos of artillery from all the war-ships in port. After reviewing the troops in the Place of St. Mark, Radetzky attended mass in the cathedral, and later in the day sat down to a sumptuous banquet which had been prepared, surrounded by all the civil and military authorities. In the evening, the Piazza was brilliantly illuminated in his honor, while the air resounded

---

* The treaty was signed by General Gorzgowsky[1] on the part of the imperial government, and by the Podesta Correr on that of the Venetians. The Austrian troops, in a formal manner, occupied the city ; and, one after the other, all the forts surrounding it ; disarmed the Venetian soldiers, and took possession of the navy. Manin took his departure on the 27th, in the French steamer Pluto, for Corfu ; and the rest of the proscribed were conveyed away in eight merchant vessels to Corfu, Patras, Alexandria, and Constantinople. Not less than sixty thousand shot and shells were expended on Venice, besides the fifty-seven thousand thrown into Malghera. The costs of the siege to the Austrians, as estimated by General Hess, are ten thousand deaths ; number of invalids and sick, fifteen thousand ; and the cost of war material one million of florins. More than another million will be required for the repair of the fortifications and to make good the losses to the treasury. For the repair of the rail-road bridge (according to Negrelli), two hundred thousand florins, a moderate calculation, considering thirty-four arches are destroyed, and three ready to tumble in. The amount of Venetian paper out is forty-five millions of livres, or one million four hundred thousand pounds sterling, an enormous burden to be incurred by a city of one hundred and fifty thousand inhabitants.

---

[1] For the capitulation of the Venetians, see Appendix, note 9.

with *vivas* to his name.   The imperial eagle supplanted upon the standards the lion of St. Mark ; and joy, and plenty, and gladness now reigned where, a few days before, there was naught but misery, starvation, and suffering, a striking example of the vicissitudes of human existence.

CHAPTER IV.

HISTORICAL ACCOUNT OF THE EARLY POLITICAL INSTITUTIONS OF BOHEMIA.
—ITS CONVERSION BY THE HABSBURG DYNASTY FROM A CONSTITUTIONAL
AND ELECTIVE MONARCHY INTO AN UNLIMITED AND HEREDITARY KINGDOM.
—THE OUTBREAK AT PRAGUE IN 1848, AND ESTABLISHMENT OF A PROVISION-
AL GOVERNMENT.—CONFLICT BETWEEN THE TROOPS AND PEOPLE.—BOM-
BARDMENT AND SUBJUGATION OF THE CITY.

In the middle of the sixth century, Bohemia, then settled
by Germans, was overrun by a branch of the great Slavic nation known as the Czechi.* As her history from that day to
this consists chiefly of a struggle between the two races, a
short account of the former seems almost indispensable.

As to the origin of the Slavi, historical writers furnish us
with two prominent opinions. The first is, that the Slavi
were a foreign race, which, at the period of the great national
immigration, in the fourth and fifth centuries, appeared for
the first time on the historical stage, in connection with the
Huns and other Asiatic tribes.

The second theory is, that they were primitively a European
people who had long lived on that continent, among foreign
races which became subsequently extinct. The present number of the Slavi, the resemblance of many of their words to
those of the Greek and Roman, the absence of all proof as to
their immigration, the mixture with Gothic, old Scandinavian,
Scythian, Celtic, etc., words of now obsolete languages ; the
similarity of manners, customs, and legislation to those of the
most ancient nations in Europe ; and the identity of the names
of cities and rivers with Slavian terminations adopted by the
Greeks and Romans, are all facts that favor the conclusion
that the Slavi were not of Asiatic origin, but an aboriginal
European branch of the great Scythian race. Although con-

---

* In Bohemian, Czechowé, so called from Czech, their leader. The English
orthography, "Czecks," does not answer the Bohemian pronunciation, which
contains at the end the sound of the aspirate χ of the Greek, and which, pho-
netically, can not be devised in English.

founded by the ancients with the Scythians and Sarmatians,
their specific name among the Greeks was Ενετοι, of which
the Latin translation was Venetæ.   The Germans called them
Wenden, the Scandinavians Vanar, and the name by which
they called themselves was Serba or Sirbi.   The name Slavi,
or Slavonians, which has superseded them all, is derived by
Slavian philologists from the abstract word *Slava*, meaning
" glory ;" or *Slovo*, meaning " speech."*

The chief seat of the Slavi was the north of the Black Sea
and the Carpathian Mountains, and between the Baltic and
the Volga.   They are the most numerous of the European
races, and are estimated at this time at eighty millions.   This
race was at first agricultural, but chiefly pastoral and nomadic,
great horse-breeders and cattle-rearers, moving about along
the banks of the rivers that flow into the Black Sea, the Caspian, and the Baltic; but subsequently, toward the close of
the Roman period, when they exchanged the nomadic for the
settled and industrial mode of life, they embraced many thousand villages, scattered over the present limits of Russia and
Poland.   Toward the close of the fourth century, the Slavi,
overwhelmed by hordes of barbarians, much confusion arose
in the traditions concerning them; but soon they began to
emerge from the chaos around them.   They reappeared in history; and Christianity, which they received at one and the
same time from Byzantium and Rome, brought them once
more within the pale of civilization.   Their governments were
purely democratic, and conducted by popular assemblies, held,
like those of the early Greeks, in the open air, in which all
full-grown men, without distinction, had a right to participate.
Slavery was unknown among them, and even foreign captives
were, after a certain time, admitted to civil rights.

To no people was individual, despotic power more repugnant
to the national spirit than among the Slavi; a somewhat singular circumstance when contrasted with their present condition, subjected as those nations now are to the yoke of Russia,
Austria, and Turkey.   Spreading over so vast an extent of
country, and presenting such varieties of climate, soil, and

* North British Review.

neighborhood, it was but natural that the great Slavian mass
should gradually fall asunder into fragments, and be in time
distinguished from each other by peculiarities of feature, language, and customs. Indeed, three such spontaneous fragments appear very early to have exhibited themselves, in the
Northern Slavi, ancestors of the present Russians; the Central
Slavi, or the ancestors of the Poles ; and the Southern Slavi,
or ancestors of the present Bohemians, Moravians, and Slavonians of Hungary.   Had no foreign causes interfered, had the
three Slavian nationalities that were thus gradually forming
themselves been allowed to arrive at maturity, uninfluenced
by any thing from without, we should then have witnessed in
their history and their condition, at the present hour, the spectacle of a free development of the Slavic genius in all its force
and all its peculiarity. We should have seen in what form
of government, applicable to civilized states of large extent,
the peculiar democratic spirit of the original Slavi would in
course of time have resulted.   But the Slavic people were not
suffered uninterruptedly to work out their own destiny, or of
themselves to evolve a pure and peculiar civilization of their
own unaided energy ; but at the period of the great migrations
of nations, when Goths and Huns, Avars and Magyars, Franks
and Monguls, were rolling and dashing over the surface of Europe like the waves of a troubled ocean, they were assailed,
broken in upon, and disrupted into the four following fragments.   The Muscovites, or great Russians, extending from
the Baltic inland as far as the Dwina and the Volga, and ruled
over by a Scandinavian dynasty; the Lechs, or Poles, forming two independent nations of Lithuania and Poland Proper,
extending from the Oder to the Dnieper, and from the Baltic
to the Carpathian Mountains ; the Czechi, or Slavi, of the three
independent states of Bohemia, Moravia, and Hungary ; and
the medley of Græco-Slavic nations, Croats, Servians, Bulgarians, Slavonians, and Dalmatians, attached to the Greek empire.   Such, in the ninth century, were the four leading divisions of the Slavic family ; and these divisions, owing to the
stationary character of the Slavi, remained permanent for nine
centuries, creating isolated states, and producing, in course of
time, the difference of accent and terminations which at this

day characteristically mark the various Slavic languages. At the commencement of the eighteenth century, the same four divisions remained, though not quite identical with those of the ninth century, since, at this time, they had become divided and shared out between the powerful nations which they adjoined, and which had in the interim extended their respective sceptres over them. The Muscovite or Russian fragment of them, which was then but assuming shape under the sway of the Scandinavian chiefs, has since, by various additions, been swelled into the Slavic nucleus of an immense and complicated empire, and governed in the most absolute manner by the will of the Czar. Out of the principal mass of the Lechs, or Central Slavi, again originally divided into Poles and Lithuanians, there had arisen a united Polish nation, consisting of a caste of free nobles and serfs. Again, out of the north-western fringe of the Lechs, added to the whole body of the ancient Czechi, and to the northern portion of the Græco-Slavi, there had been formed an immense Slavian population, attached to the confederated German empire, part adhering to Prussia, and governed by the Prussian kings, and the remainder (including the Bohemians, Moravians, Slovacks of Hungary, Croats, and Slavonians) adhering to Austria, and governed by the Austrian sovereigns. Finally, the former Græco-Slavic states of Servia, Bulgaria, and Bosnia had, after many vicissitudes, been detached altogether from the Christian world, and annexed to the motley empire of the Turks, to be governed or misgoverned by Turkish *pashas*, depending on the sultan and the Ottoman Porte. Since the last-mentioned period no political change has taken place in regard to the Slavic race, except that the great Polish nation, occupying the lands to the south of Russia, from the Oder to the Dnieper, and stretching at one time from the Baltic to the Black Sea, has been conquered and divided between the three more powerful states of Russia, Austria, and Prussia, and her name effaced from the map of Europe. From the general view of the Slavic race, we pass for a moment to the consideration of those of the Slavi who are subject to and reside within the limits of Austria, and whose number far exceeds those of all the other races of the empire, as the following table demonstrates:

Of the	2,317,864	inhabitants of the Archduchy of Austria..	17,864	are Slavi.
"	997,200	" Styria...................	380,452	"
"	1,269,477	" Illyria	825,604	"
"	848,177	" Tyrol....................		"
*	4,318,732	" Bohemia................	3,065,232	"
"	2,242,167	" Moravia and Silesia	1,556,500	"
"	10,500,000	" Hungary, with Slavonia and		
		cir. Croatia	4,030,000	"
"	2,118,000	" Transylvania.............	400	"
"	1,235,466	" Military Frontier.........	895,966	"
"	405,854	" Dalmatia	251,340	"
"	4,876,549	" Lombardo-Venet. kingdom		
"	4,980,480	" Galicia.................	4,446,640	"
	36,110,272		15,769,998	

Of the 36,110,272 inhabitants of Austria, 7,817,711 are of the Roman race.

	7,071,825	"	German	"
	5,634,738	"	Asiatic	"
	15,469,998	"	Slavic	"

From the above estimatè, it might naturally be supposed that the Austrian was essentially a Slavic empire; but the intellectual condition of the people, as well as the geographical location of the Slavi, render their political preponderance impossible. The religion of this race in Austria is chiefly that of the Roman Catholic; for its greater part belongs to the Western Slavi, who received their religious forms from the West (A.D. 700–1000); while, on the other hand, the Græco-Slavi were converted by Greek missionaries (A.D. 640–1100), and consequently adopted the rites and doctrines of the Greek Church. From this fact it occurs that the Poles and the Czechi became members of the great confederacy of the Western nations, while the other fell back, as it were, into the arms of the East. This distinction was perpetuated by certain corresponding differences in the written characters used by the two groups of people. First, the Cyrilic alphabet (devised by the Greek monk Cyril 873) was used with the vernacular form of service, even in Bohemia and Moravia; where, indeed, Cyril preceded the Latin missionaries; ultimately, however, by the strenuous exertions of the Romish Church, the Latin character and the Latin form of service triumphed among all the Slavic Romanists, with the exception of some Romanist communities among the Græco-Slavi of the Adriatic, for whom an expressly new character was invented, called the Glagolitic, and who were allowed, besides, to retain their vernacular serv-

ice. The use of the Cyrilic character, therefore, became a
characteristic of the Slavi of the Greek Church. As was the
case formerly among the Germans, so among the Slavians,
the secession from the Catholic Church produced two parties
among the people, which operated injuriously upon the unity
of the nation. The Austrian Slavi may be said to be all Roman Catholics, with the exception of from one million nine
hundred thousand to two millions, in Croatia, Slavonia, and the
military frontier, who profess the Greek religion; and from sev-
en to eight hundred thousand in Hungary, who are Protestants. Among the Slavi of Austria there are eight distinct languages of the Græco-Slavic tongue, viz.: Bohemian, Slovackian, Polish, Ruthenian, Serbian, Croatian, Slovenian, and Illyrian.* The Latin character is employed in them all, except
with the Serbians, where the Cyril character has been adopted. Though all these dialects differ from one another, the
root being the same, men of education in either may make
themselves intelligible, while the illiterate of different provinces would find it difficult to be understood. Among them the
Polish, like the French in the Romanic race, is regarded as the
language of conversation; the Bohemian, like the English, the
language of science ; and those of the Southern Slavi like the
Italian and Spanish, the languages best adapted to poetry.
Civilization is further advanced among the Slavi than is in
general supposed. They have all passed already the first sta-
dium of literature, and their poetic effusions are marked by
all the glow of a more Eastern imagination; but, subdued
and oppressed as they have always been, the Slavic Muse still
preserves a gloomy, but martial character. The branches of
Slavian literature are six, viz.: Bohemian, Polish, Servian,
Croatian, Dalmatian, and Slovenian. Productions of no mean
merit have appeared in each; while excellent translations of
foreign works which they embrace exhibit the perfection to
which these languages have attained. To the two Western
races of Europe, the Slavic genius, no less than the Oriental,
is remarkable for its essential and striking originality. The
fact of this great difference may lead to important consequen-

---

* The inhabitants of Dalmatia and Istria.

ces, and at some future day transform the numerous, now isolated states, into three grand national confederations. That
antagonistic spirit of the Slavic race to the Germanic and Romanic people produced in our time the first step toward its
concentration.

When, in 1814, the Russians triumphed over the French;
and when, at a later period, in 1829, victory bore the Russian
eagles to the plains of Adrianople, the Slavi every where awoke
from their lethargy, and but a single thought occupied their
minds, and that was, that of their own approaching regeneration. Two prominent theories on this subject have been entertained; the one the so-called theory of Panslavism, the other
the theory of spontaneous separation into distinct nationalities.
Panslavism, in imitation of the Panhellenism among the Greeks,
implies the amalgamation of all Slavi, of every denomination,
either into one nation or confederation, or into a moral and intellectual community, based upon common origin and upon
similarity of language, though diversified by various idioms,
the general ground-work would form a literary language, to be
adopted by all, and thus create a firm bond of union between
them.   This theory, in its origin purely literary, was first
promulgated by John Kollar, a Slovack of Hungary. He demonstrated that, various as are the languages spoken by the
wide-spread Slavic race, these languages do not differ from
each other more than did the different dialects of the ancient
Greek, and, consequently, that, as the ancient Greek nations
had a common language and a common literature, so might
the modern Slavic nations, if they chose to decree it. To effect
this end, he proposed that there should be a literary reciprocity
among all the Slavic nations; that is, that all the Slavic literati,
Russian, Polish, Bohemian, and Servian, should make themselves acquainted with the different languages of their race, so
that the past as well as the future literary accumulation of
each Slavic people or tribe might be rendered accessible to all
Slavi, and a Panslavic literature be thereby instituted.   The
other theory—that of the spontaneous separation of the Slavic
mass into distinct nationalities—may be said to have originated
in the labors of an Illyrian, Dr. Ludovic Gay, who, in the year
1835, established at Agram the Croat Gazette (Lovine Hor-

vatzki), with a supplement, entitled the "Morning Star of Croatia, Slavonia, and Dalmatia." The leading idea of this journal was the consolidation of the several Slavic nations of the extreme South, both Austrian and Turkish, viz.: the Illyrians, Croats, Slavonians, Servians, Slovenians, Bosniaks, Montenegrins, and Bulgarians, into one body or state, to be called *Great Illyria*.

These nations, Gay argued, properly constituted but one mass; they all belonged to what historians had called the Græco-Slavic branch of the great nation, and, though dissevered by circumstances, should be united.*

The institutions of the old state and people of Bohemia, like those of the Slavi in general, were democratic in their nature, although not long after the acquisition of the country the seeds of aristocracy began to be developed, and later the monarchical principles. According to an old tradition, handed down by Cosmas (1125), the ducal authority had its origin in the assumption and exercise of *judicial* power.

A senate of twelve members, called *Kmety*, were assigned the duke, who, in the nature of a cabinet or council of ministers, aided him in the administration of the affairs of state; and, even as late as the fourteenth and fifteenth centuries, they continued to constitute the supreme tribunal of state. They were elected for life, and were not removable.

The higher population, or those possessed of property, com-

---

* That these tendencies were at first decidedly Panslavistic, can not be denied, as the following, one of the earliest articles in this newly-founded journal, will amply suffice to prove: "Europe," writes he in this article, "I would fain paint as a virgin, holding in her hand a triangular lyre. In past ages. the tones of this lyre yielded melody to every passing breeze; but suddenly, from north and east, and west and south, there came unchained storms and tempests, and the lyre was violently unstrung, and its music ceased. This lyre is Illyria, and the torn chords are the lands where once its tones were familiar—Corinthia, Carniola, Istria, Styria, Croatia, Slavonia, Dalmatia, Ragusa, Bosnia, Servia, Bulgaria, and Pannonia.

"What should we more ardently wish now, when unity seems to be the universal dream of nations, than that all these rent strings of Europe's lyre should once more unite in harmony? How can we attain this end, while each separate chord gives forth a different tone? Let us open the book of our country, and in it see how, in the antique Slavian, are noted down all the sweet sounds of our lyre—the treasured, priceless lyre of Illyria! Who that can understand this symbol," says Gay, at the end of his article, "can for one instant doubt the absolute necessity of unity in language and literature for all Illyria?"

prised three classes or ranks, viz., Kmety, Lechowé, and Vladiky, similar to the divisions which distinguished the judicial
tribunal of Libussa, the first princess of Bohemia.

The *Kmety* embraced the council of ministers alluded to
above. The Lechowé comprised the large territorial proprietors, to which also belonged the priests (the word *Knez* signifying both priest and prince) ; and these together constituted the
high nobility, and from which subsequently sprang the lords.*

The next class, or Vladiky, were the smaller proprietors,
deriving their name from *Vladika*, the chief of a family, as
when an inheritance was undivided, the most able of the family was always elected to manage the common interests, and
this personage was called Vladika. They represented the people in the Diet, and their descendants formed, in course of time,
the lower nobility. Persons without property were divided
into two classes : 1st. Those entitled to personal freedom ; and,
2d. Those enjoying no freedom. The latter cultivated the fields
of the Lechowé, and performed court service to them ; the
former were personally free, but liable to the payment of certain taxes, or to be called into service.

As early as the ninth century, the country was divided into
districts or circles called *Zupa*, each governed by a high functionary called *Zupan* (*comes, prefectus*), with several inferior
officers under them.

Every *zupa* or circle was provided with a fortified town or
fortress, demanded by the troubled state of the times, and used
as a place of refuge in cases of hostile invasion. As all such
castles or fortresses were considered the property of the duke,
it is probable that the zupans or officers were appointed by the
duke and his counselors, and were the peculiar privileges of the
Lechowé.

Private castles were also constructed and inhabited by the
Lechowé. These castles were usually built on the highest elevations which could be found ; and hence to this day every important summit in the kingdom is crowned with ruins, attract-
ing the eye of the traveler, and speaking to him of the early
troubles and trials of Bohemia.

---

* Palacky's History of Bohemia.

The Diet of Bohemia was composed of the *Kmety*, Lechowé, and Vladiky.   By that body were all important regulations made, all laws framed, and controversies affecting the internal peace of the state decided in the last resort.   Questions were determined by a majority, and not by unanimity, as was the case among the Luticians, and afterward among the Poles, where a single vote was sufficient to defeat a measure.   The Diet was the supreme tribunal for the whole country ; but beside this, each capital of a circle had their own courts, presided over by their own judges.

As her history shows, Bohemia always maintained her state sovereignty ; and although the emperors of Germany, since the year 1002, claimed her as a fief of the empire, and her princes as feudal vassals, they never attempted to interfere with her internal administration.   But the first blow affecting her independence was given when Boleslaus the Third was driven out of the kingdom, and Ladislaus of Poland elected in his stead.   He visited Regensburg (the seat of the empire) for the purpose of seeking the protection of the emperor, Henry the Second, and won his favor by promises of submission, and by declaring himself a vassal of the German empire—an example afterward invariably pursued by those princes who did not feel themselves quite secure upon their seats on the Bohemian throne.

And when, a little more than half a century later, the Emperors of Germany raised Bohemia into a kingdom, the real object of the measure was to connect to the empire, by the bond of vassalage, the large and influential principality of Bohemia. Notwithstanding these proceedings, however, the German emperors never exercised any right of jurisdiction, collected any revenue, or exercised any fiscal prerogatives in Bohemia.   Certain reciprocal obligations, it is true, were entered into between the monarchs ; as, for example : First, the Bohemian princes were obliged to obey the imperial summons, whenever the emperors thought proper to call them before them ; they reserving the right to announce their arrival with fire and flame (*in flamma et igne veniant*) ; and, in return, on their accession to the throne, upon the emperors devolved the duty of confirming them in their new dignity.   Second, the Bohemian princes engaged to furnish a contingent of three hundred armed men, to attend the emperor to Rome on the occasion of his coronation ; and, for this service, the princes obtained the right to vote at the election of the Roman emperors. The Bohemian princes, with their Diet, made all the laws, declared war, concluded treaties, and allotted lands and fiefs, without submitting their decrees for the sanction of the emperors.

Every circle possessed a superior and inferior court, which sat four times a year, and were open to the public. The competency of the tribunal had no reference, as is the case at present in Bohemia, to the condition of the parties, but was regulated, as is now done in all free countries, alone by the nature and importance of the cause. The judges, who presided, were assisted by the ministers of state, and, although the courts were regarded as prerogatives of the crown, the presiding officers never relinquished their independence.

In difficult cases, a trial by jury was arranged. The jurymen were selected by the parties, were sworn before the altar, gave their opinion only on the facts, and a bare majority of their number was sufficient to decide. This important attribute of freedom existed in Bohemia long before it was enjoyed in England, and disappeared only under Charles the Fourth, when, with the election of a German king, German customs gained ascendency.

In short, Bohemia, at this time, presented every where evidences of a Constitution more theoretically free than that of any other of the states of Europe. The peasant might appeal from the magistrate of his own town even to the King's Court, at Prague ; while the humblest citizen could, in this court, institute an action against the king himself.

Under the old Slavic institutions, which prevailed until the end of the thirteenth century, there was as little absolutism in Bohemia as in Poland or Hungary. Nay more, rights which in those countries were claimed and exercised alone by a powerful aristocracy, descended in Bohemia to the humblest citizen. It was the glory of this land that, when feudalism prevailed every where else in Europe, her peasants were not serfs, nor her citizens slaves. From Przemysl, the Bohemian peasant, whom Libussa taking from the plow, espoused and made the first Duke of Bohemia, in 805, to Wenzel the Third, there reigned twenty-three dukes and seven kings; but when Wenzel was killed, at Olmütz, in 1306, the line of Slavic kings became extinct.   In very early times, the Dukes of Bohemia were controlled in the exercise of their prerogatives only by the chiefs or representatives of certain powerful clans, which assisted their forefathers in winning the land, and were still ready and prompt to defend it.

But as time advanced this system changed.   The ancient distinctions of Kmety, Lechowé, and Vladiky disappeared, and three other divisions representing the same ranks, and in character closely resembling the former, were formed under the appellation of nobles, knights, and citizens.*   The high nobility consisted of barons, who went to war with their own men and fought under their own standards; the knights comprised the lower nobility and the burghers, on whom Ottocar conferred political rights, and called their deputies to the Diet, constituted the three classes of the people and the three orders of the Estates (Stände).

Whenever enactments were required which, in their operation, were calculated to affect the well-being of the entire community, the delegates from each of these three orders met to deliberate on them; and these, when passed, if sanctioned by the duke or king, became part of the law of the land.†   In the Constitution of Bohemia, consisting originally of oral and traditionary rights and customs, as it came to be settled as early as the close of the 10th century, and as it continued to work with more or less purity until after the 17th century, we accordingly find an executive, with three separate, and, as it were, independent but subordinate estates under it, each enjoying its own privileges and asserting its own rights, without giving the least umbrage or offering the slightest injury to the rest.

The executive was, of course, wielded by the crown, and the order of succession in two ways; that is to say, the hereditary line was generally adopted, and the custom of primogeniture prevailed; but, in the event of a failure, or in the case of abuse, or for other causes deemed sufficient, the people

---

* Gleig's Bohemia and Hungary.   † Ibid.

claimed, and frequently exercised, the right of electing whom they pleased for their sovereign. The right of the people to elect was never questioned by others or surrendered by themselves; and the accession even of a son, or the demise of his father, was always accompanied by the forms of an election; and to mark that such was not a mere empty ceremony, the utmost degree of religious solemnity characterized the performance.* The throne having been declared vacant by the estates or orders assembled, the regalia were brought with great pomp from the neighboring fortress of Stein, which was set apart for their safe-keeping. They were conveyed to the citadel of Prague, where they were arranged in the great hall within which the states assembled to act upon the emergency which had arisen, and, the burgrave or chief magistrate taking the chair, lots were cast to determine who should be king. The ballot over, the burgrave arose, and thus announced the vote: " In the name of the Most High, whose favor and protection we invoke for this realm, I, supreme burgrave of Prague, by virtue of my office, declare that the choice of the Estates has fallen upon the high and mighty prince (naming him), and I require that he be accepted as King of Bohemia." Immediately an officer proclaimed it from the window that a new king had been elected. The crowds which waited below raised a shout in testimony of satisfaction, and, the process of election concluded, it remained only to go forward with the more solemn parts of the ceremony. Accordingly, the regalia were borne back in procession to the strong depositary; the king elect proceeded in great state to the cathedral, where he received the holy sacrament, and was crowned and anointed by the archbishop, having first of all sworn upon the holy Evangelists that he would govern according to the law of the land, preserve the property of the nation, and defend the rights and privileges of all classes of his subjects from every aggressor.

After the extinction of the line of native Bohemian kings. the Diet elected John of Luxemburg, son of Henry the Seventh, in 1311, to the vacant throne.

Under the German kings of this dynasty, Bohemia reached

---

* Gleig's Bohemia and Hungary.

her greatest splendor, particularly under the reign of the Emperor Charles the Fourth, who encouraged commerce, mining, and agriculture; promoted science; founding at Prague the first German university, Bohemia became the central point of German education, and the foundation was laid of that high intellectual elevation which, breaking forth about a century after in religious frenzy, was to involve all Europe in the flames of war.*

Upon ascending the throne, John of Luxemburg gave to the orders "*a letter of assurance*," which is the First Document of the Bohemian Constitution. In that letter (1310) he gave the assurance that the property, the rights, and the privileges of the clergy and the nobility should undergo no alteration in their institutions. He declared that the nobility and people of Bohemia and Moravia should not be compelled to march in any war beyond the frontier, and that, in case they should go, they would be entitled to payment for their services; that universal taxes could only be levied on two occasions, at the coronation of the king, and at the nuptials of his daughters. He reaffirmed the old right that, in case of a failure of male and female heirs, relatives to the fourth degree might inherit, and that only in want of all these would the estate revert to the crown; that confiscation should only take place in the case of property belonging to criminals sentenced to death; that foreigners could not be admitted to court offices; and that all strangers who might acquire property in Bohemia, by inheritance, marriage, or gift, should be compelled, in the course of one year, to dispose of the same to some citizen of Bohemia.†

The next document, in chronological order, which appeared upon the subject of Bohemian rights, and forming, consequently, a portion of the Constitution, was that known as the "Golden Bull" (*Aurea Bulla*) of the Emperor Charles the Fourth, 1356. This document, in the rude Latin of the day, embraces twenty-one chapters, relating all to the affairs of the German empire, with the exception of the eighth, which treats of certain immunities of the princes and people of Bohemia. In this article it is declared, that "no prince, baron, noble, soldier, client, citizen,

---

* Menzel's Germany.   † Palacky's History of Bohemia.

inhabitant, or other person in Bohemia, of whatever rank, dignity, or condition, shall be called to answer to any charge before any other tribunal than that of the King of Bohemia himself, or before some of the courts of his kingdom, and that any such call shall be utterly void and of non-effect."

Charles the Fourth (or as he was also known as Charles the First, a prince of learning and character) was of Bohemian descent—his mother, having been a native of that country, exhibited a strong partiality toward a land with which he was so strongly identified. "In 1348, he bestowed a new code of laws upon Bohemia; in 1355, declared Moravia, Silesia, and the Lusatia inseparable from that country. He also granted the greatest privileges to the aristocracy and to the cities; encouraged mining and agriculture; rendered the Moldau navigable as far as the Elbe; brought German artificers into the country; and converted the whole of Bohemia into a garden."*

In the midst of the smiling country stood the noble city of Prague, whose fine public edifices, the regal Hradshin, as well as the celebrated bridges, are his works; while the university which he had established, called together, according to the most moderate accounts, no less than twenty thousand students from all parts of Germany.

But this state of unparalleled prosperity was but of short duration. In a few years the great Bohemian reformer, the pioneer of Protestantism, preceding Luther by a hundred years, arose. This bold reformer, with a view to restore to the corrupt Church the simplicity and purity of scriptural Christianity, ventured to censure publicly the immorality of the priests, to preach against the sale of indulgences in Bohemia; declared masses for the dead, image worship, monastic life, auricular confessions, fasts, etc., to be inventions of spiritual despotism and superstition, and the withholding the cup at the Lord's Supper unscriptural.

The promulgation of such heresies, as they were considered, amid the universal ascendency of Catholicism, could not fail to provoke against him all the thunders of the Vatican. Huss was burned at the stake (and his ashes thrown into the Rhine); but the flame which he had raised, and in which he was con-

---

* Coxe's House of Austria.

sumed, was not extinguished when his ashes were committed to the rapid waters of the Rhine, but led to the most bloody and terrible wars, in which whole villages were burned and the inhabitants put to the sword, convents and churches plundered and destroyed, and monks and priests murdered, even the emperor himself suffocated, and this most flourishing kingdom almost transformed into a desert. The wild Hussite wars, under their famous blind warrior, Ziska, continued for sixteen years; but at length, weakened by divisions among themselves, and the multitudes of sects into which they were separated, the Catholics succeeded at length in treading out every spark of that mighty conflagration which the Reformers had raised.*

As these wars were not merely religious contests, but also national struggles, the emperor and his priests being as hateful as *foreign* rulers, as on account of their *theological errors*, the defeat of the Bohemians was of course the triumph of the Germans; and, after the death of Louis the First, king of Bohemia and Hungary, in the battle of Mohacs, 1526, his brother-in-law, Ferdinand the First of Austria, brother of Charles the Fifth, was, by the Stände, elected king of Bohemia. The crowns of Austria, Bohemia, and Hungary were thus united.

Louis being the last male of his family, Ferdinand claimed both crowns under a double title, the one derived from family compacts, which secured the reversion to the house of Austria on failure of male issue to the reigning family, and the other in right of his wife Anne, the only sister of the deceased monarch. But the natives of Hungary and Bohemia were too much attached to their rights of election to respect these compacts, or even to acknowledge his claims as husband of the princess; and Ferdinand, prudently, therefore, waving his pretensions, offered himself as a candidate according to the usual mode of election, and being only opposed in Bohemia by Albert, duke of Bavaria, he was, on the 26th of October, 1526, elected by a committee of twenty persons, who were appointed by the Stände to choose a king.

On her connection with Austria, Bohemia was in the full enjoyment of all her liberty as a limited and elective monarchy.

---

* Menzel's Germany.

" On his accession to the throne, the king was always constrained to acknowledge the right of election, and all the privileges of his subjects, and promised to govern according to the
ancient constitution and statutes, particularly those of the emperor, Charles the Fourth.   The power of the crown was extremely limited, as well by the privileges of the different orders as by the authority of the Diet, without which he could
not impose taxes, raise troops, make war or peace, coin money,
or institute and abrogate laws ; and thus, in public affairs, he
was reduced to a mere cipher."*

When the emperor, Charles the Fifth, determined on subduing the Smalkaldic league of Protestant powers, his brother
Ferdinand endeavored to march an army to his assistance ;
but the Bohemians, being mostly Lutherans, claiming the benefit of that provision of their Constitution which did not allow
of their being forced beyond the frontiers of the kingdom, refused to furnish the proffered assistance.   They persisted for
some time in the course of manly opposition ; they entered into
confederation among the different states of the kingdom, and
raised an army to defend themselves against the foreign troops
that were now entering the kingdom, on their way to the Elector of Saxony ; and they disregarded the orders of the royal
commissaries, who, in the king's name, required them to dismiss their troops and dissolve the confederacy.

In the mean time, Ferdinand labored, by all the means in
his power, to check the progress of the Reformation, and exercised the utmost rigor against those who disseminated religious
opinions not tolerated by law.   As means of diminishing the
influence of the capital, he removed several magistrates, and
again separated the magistracy of the old and new towns ; he
re-established the Archiepiscopal See of Prague, and empowered the archbishop to consecrate the Calixtine as well as Catholic priests.   But, above all, in total disregard of that document signed and executed by him on his accession to the
throne, and by which he acknowledged and declared that "the
barons, nobles, citizens, and the whole community of Bohemia
had elected him king, not from any duty or obligation, but of

---

* Coxe's House of Austria.

their own free and good will, and according to the liberty of the kingdom"*—he formally revoked the document, and declared himself *hereditary* sovereign, in virtue of his marriage with Anne (sister of Louis the First), and the exploded compacts between the Austrian and Bohemian princes. This unpopular and glaring breach of faith could not fail to excite the highest indignation among a people so jealous of their privileges, and might have resulted in the total overthrow of the monarch and a restoration of their ancient liberty, had not the tidings of the disastrous battle of Mühlberg, and the total defeat and capture of their ally, the Elector of Saxony, inopportunely arrived at this moment to destroy their projects and crush their hopes.

Those very men who, with the hope of foreign assistance, had displayed such resolution to assert their liberties—the descendants of those who, under Ziska, had singly resisted or deposed their sovereigns, and spread terror throughout Germany, no sooner saw themselves deprived of foreign support, than they sunk into a servility and despondency as degrading as their former decision and boldness had been honorable and praiseworthy. The Stände congratulated the king on the victory, disbanded their forces, and, hurrying to the feet of the monarch, vied with each other in their eager and disgusting demonstrations of loyalty. Ferdinand made no other reply to these tardy offers of submission than threats and reproaches, and, without a moment's delay, prepared to avail himself of all the advantages which this timely victory had given him over his humiliated subjects.

After a memorial, presented to the king by the Stände, declaring that their only object in joining the confederacy was to promote the advantage of the country and protect the prerogatives of the crown, and promising that they would the next day erase their signatures and tear off their seals, and defend the sovereign against all his enemies with their lives and fortunes, Ferdinand condescended to forgive them, but reserved his severest vengeance for the contumacious citizens of Prague. Entering the capital at the head of a numerous army, the king summoned to the palace the mayor, burgomasters,

---

* For the original, see the Appendix, note No. 10.

magistrates, counselors, jurors, elders, and two hundred and forty of the most distinguished citizens of the three towns.   On the day appointed, these persons, amounting to more than six hundred, repaired to the palace, and had no sooner entered than the gates were closed and guarded.   The king being thus master of the principal members of the three towns, and those who by their talents or influence might have roused the people to a desperate resistance, was enabled to impose his own terms.

After subjecting them to the utmost humiliation, at the intercession of the archdukes, princes, and lords, and of *his own natural clemency*, he graciously pardoned their offenses on the following conditions.   They were to renounce their confederacy with the other states, and, at the next Diet, to break their seals and erase their signatures, and to deliver up all their letters and writings relating to their confederacy ; to surrender, without exception, all the acts relating to their privileges and immunities, and to be satisfied with whatever the king should ordain or graciously restore ; to bring all their artillery and ammunition to the palace, and the burghers their muskets, and all other arms except swords, to the town-house ; to resign all their vassals and property to the king, and to his heirs the sovereigns of Bohemia; to cede all the tolls of the three towns ; and to bind themselves to pay his majesty, and his successors forever, a certain tax on beer and malt.*

Having extorted from them an immediate ratification of these hard terms, they were dismissed, except forty of the most dangerous, whom he had reserved to chastise, for the sake of justice and the welfare of the kingdom.

In the mean time, Ferdinand had sent a similar summons to all the towns of the realm, except the loyal cities of Pilsen, Budweis, and Aussig.   The chief burgomasters, counselors, and elders of all the other cities were compelled, in like manner, to repair to the palace, and, like those of Prague, were imprisoned until they had surrendered all their estates, tolls, revenues, and privileges, and paid considerable penalties.

As an appropriate conclusion to these proceedings, a Diet was summoned by the king, to meet at the palace of Prague on the 22d of August, 1547, and, with a view to strike addi-

* Coxe's House of Austria.

tional terror, was opened with the execution of four of his principal prisoners, and from which circumstance that assembly has always been distinguished by the appellation of the *Bloody Diet*. After this eight were publicly whipped in each of the three towns; and before each flagellation, the executioner proclaimed, "These men are punished because they were traitors, and because they excited the people against their *hereditary master*."*

Having, by these rigorous measures, restored tranquillity and suppressed almost all seeds of future insurrections, Ferdinand introduced various measures calculated to secure and strengthen his authority. He appointed in each town a judicial officer, whose duty it should be to be present at all public meetings, and to take care that the public authority received no detriment. For the suppression of Lutheranism, to which he ascribed the principal opposition to his designs, he established in Bohemia, in 1556, the order of Jesuits, and intrusted to them the care of public education; he fettered the press, by the establishment of a board for the revision and censure of all publications, in less than a century from the time that the first work was published in Bohemia. Finally, he changed Bohemia from an elective to a hereditary monarchy,† crushed the spirit of a brave people, depressed that energy of mind and military ardor which are inseparable from a free government, and checked that active commercial spirit which flourishes in the consciousness of independence. From these causes, the towns, which had hitherto been remarkable for their commerce, wealth, and population, exhibited, under his reign, the first symptoms of decline, and the Bohemians began to lose that military fame which had rendered them at once the example and the terror of Europe.

Ferdinand was succeeded by his son Maximilian, who, notwithstanding his transformation of Bohemia from an elective to a hereditary monarchy, he took care should be elected by the Stände, and crowned during his life. Maximilian was an amiable prince; and being at heart a Lutheran, and granting to

---

* Coxe's House of Austria.

† And from that period, as was the case after the same change in Poland, commenced the decline of the kingdom.

his subjects great toleration, both in religion and literature, no difficulties occurred during his reign.

He was succeeded by his son, Rhodolph the Second. The Reformation rapidly approaching, and the power of the Protestants greatly augmenting, the latter were enabled to extort from Rhodolph (through fear of the rivalry of his brother Mathias) a document known as the *Majestic Letter*, considered as the paladium of Bohemia, and by which the ancient religious liberties were restored.

The following is the substance of the *Third Document* of the Bohemian Constitution :

" In answer to the petition of the Stände, in favor of the Utraquists,

" 1st. It grants that they may take the holy sacrament under both forms (the wine as well as the bread). That both sects, the *Sub Una* and *Sub Utraque*, shall exercise their religion according to the respective creeds which they had presented, to the full extent, as it had been confirmed by Maximilian ; that these parties should have full and free exercise of religion, and that no one should put any impediments in their way.* A perfect equality should be introduced in the erection of churches and founding of schools ; that no party should interfere with another in the exercise of any religious ceremony ; that no one from the higher classes, or the inhabitants of cities or country, could be *forced* by any authority, civil or spiritual, to change his religion ; that he and his successors to the throne should respect these privileges, and that any obstacle or change attempted, either by him or his successors, should be void and of non-effect ; that no efforts should be undertaken in opposition to the disposition expressed in the *Majestic Letter*, he orders his superior and inferior officers of the land-table to keep a copy of the document in their records, and that the original be deposited for safe-keeping in the Castle of Stein."†

Two years after the execution of this document, Rhodolph,

---

* And, as a security for their religious privileges, were to choose certain persons from their body, under the title of Defenders of the Faith, who were to be confirmed by the sovereign, and whose duty it was to watch over the affairs of religion, and prevent any infringement of this edict.

† Pelzel's Bohemia; *Goldasti's Commentarius de Bohemiæ Regno.*

whose converse was more with the stars of heaven than the affairs of earth, was deposed by his brother Mathias. Mathias was chosen king, with all the forms of an elective monarchy, in 1611, and, after confirming the rights and privileges of the nation, civil and religious, was crowned with great splendor and magnificence. He reigned but a few years, and having no heirs, prevailed upon the Diet to accept his cousin, Ferdinand the Second, son of the Archduke Charles, of the Styrian line. He was duly crowned in 1616, after confirming the privileges of the kingdom in the usual forms, and promising not to interfere in the government during the life of Mathias. Ferdinand the Second was the most intolerant of princes; and the Bohemians refused to receive a prince whose acts were in dreadful accordance with his words, that "Bohemia had better be a desert than a country full of heretics." On the 23d of May, 1618, a day from which dates the commencement of the "Thirty Years' War," they threw from the window of the Council-house, on the Hradshin, in Prague, a height of about eighty feet, the two regents of Ferdinand and their secretary; and in the following year the Diet of Stände elected to the throne Frederick the Fifth, elector of the Pfalz. Frederick's reign terminated in a season; and hence he has been distinguished by the *soubriquet* of the "Winter King." The fatal battle on the White Mountain, near Prague, in October, 1620, not only sealed his doom, but crushed forever the hopes and strength of the Protestants, and decided the fate of Bohemia for the two hundred and thirty years that have since elapsed.

The pictures presented to us by the Bohemian historians of the condition of the country, under the mild emperors and kings who reigned toward the close of the sixteenth century, are most gratifying to every friend of freedom and intelligence. The arts and sciences flourished. Prague, the modern Athens, was the seat of learning and refinement. There Tycho Brahé, Kepler, and other eminent minds of the age, studied, wrote, and taught; while, according to their exaggerated accounts, sixty thousand students were congregated from all parts of Europe to gather knowledge at this fount. Poets and orators sung and declaimed; and the works then written still serve as classical models of language.

Of the standard of intellectual advancement which the Bohemians had at this time reached, their language, that unfailing test of the enlightenment of a people, furnishes abundant
and striking testimony. While, in some of the provinces of
Austria, the language was too imperfect and meagre to bear
a translation of the new code adopted on the imperial decrees issued in 1848, the rich and musical Czeckish language
was not only amply full and refined for that purpose, but
also admitted of admirable translations both of the Greek
and Roman classics, as well as the standard works of German literature.*

In religion, too, great toleration prevailed, and the several
denominations of Catholics, Protestants, Utraquists, Hussites,
and Calixtines lived and worshiped together in peace and
friendship.

The Czeckish power had, under these benign influences, attained its maximum. In a Diet held in Prague, in 1615, the
question was gravely discussed whether it would not be better
to erect Bohemia into a republic like Switzerland or Holland
than to elect Frederick of the Palatinate to the throne ; no one
venturing the question whether the crown was elective or hereditary. In the same sitting, it was decided that all sermons
should be delivered in the Czeckish language ; that no one
should acquire the right of citizenship without a knowledge
of that tongue ; and that all the enemies of the Bohemian race
should be exiled.

But after their defeat on the White Mountain, where the
Duke of Bavaria, Ferdinand's general, prevailed over the Winter King, that power was cloven to the earth. The imperial
troops overrunning the land, held it like a victim bound to the
stake ; while Ferdinand, in obedience to the suggestions of his
Jesuits, subjected it to a series of tortures of the most elabo-

---

* No more highly-organized language, we are told, was ever spoken on earth,
than the Slavic ; vying, in grammatical devices, with the ancient Greek ; possessing, for example, numerous declensions, an ablative case, a dual number, a pat-
ronymic termination, diminutive and augmentative nouns, frequentative and in-
ceptive verbs, various preterit and future tenses, inflexions of verbs rendering
pronouns unnecessary, unlimited powers of compounding words, and a host of
serviceable particles ; besides all which, it includes every articulate human sound
known, except the English *th.—North Brit. Review.*

rate and refined cruelty. It was therein minutely determined who should be executed with the ax, and who with the sword; who should have his arm cut off, and who his tongue torn out; who was to be cut into four, and who into eight pieces; and on what gates these several pieces were to be exposed to the public gaze.* By execution, exile, and confiscation, Protestantism, to which three fourths of the population adhered, was completely abolished. Whoever refused to embrace the Catholic religion was declared incompetent to exercise any corporate trade, and was generally deprived of his property and exiled from the country. So far was the system of persecution carried, that the Protestant poor and sick were turned out of the hospitals, and orders given that none but Catholics should be admitted. Not even the dead were suffered to escape. Rokysana's remains were disinterred and burned; and Ziska's monument, and every visible memorial of the heroism of Bohemia, totally demolished. The Letter of Grace of Rhodolph the Second was annulled, and all traces of religious liberty annihilated. The emperor, disregarding his promise to the Elector of Saxony in regard to the Lutherans, declared himself bound in conscience to exterminate all heretics. Ferdinand abolished all the privileges of the Stände, and excluded the Bohemian language from the churches and the law tribunals. All the Bohemian works were collected and burned; and their national language, which they had proudly spoken at the court of the German emperors, now banished from all refined society, and confined alone to the peasantry of the land, disappeared for a long time from the list of written languages.

Perhaps there is not a parallel instance of such a complete change as Bohemia underwent during the reign of Ferdinand the Second. In fact, as the native† historian remarks, at the close of his reflections upon the consequences of the battle of the White Mountain, "Here the history of Bohemia closes, and the history of other nations in Bohemia commences."

---

* Menzel's Germany.

† Until the battle of the White Mountain, as Menzel states, the Stände enjoyed more exclusive privileges than the Parliament of England. They enacted laws, imposed taxes, contracted alliances, declared war and peace, and chose and con firmed their kings; but all these they have now lost.

After this persecution had been carried on for the space of
seven years, the emperor came to Prague, with his family; and,
having summoned a Diet, had his son Ferdinand crowned as
king.

On the 10th of May, 1627, he decreed a new set of statutes
upon the subject of police regulations and affairs of internal administration, reserving to himself the right to increase, amend,
and alter such regulations. He stated, at the same time, that
another decree, upon the subject of political rights, would be
issued in a short time.

On the 27th of the same month, the second decree made its
appearance, and in which, in affecting to display his clemency,
as well as with a view of preventing the immigration which
was daily taking place (nearly forty thousand families, either
through banishment or voluntary exile, having left the kingdom), he confirmed all the ancient rights and privileges, with
the exception of that of religious freedom, as guaranteed in
Rhodolph the Second's Majestic Letter, and the right of the
Stände to elect the king.

This *diploma* of Ferdinand the Second, as it is called, and
which constitutes the Fourth article in the Bohemian Constitution, is in substance as follows:

He renews and confirms all the Bohemian privileges, excepting those contained in the Majestic Letter of Rhodolph the
Second.* That there had been a great rebellion, which, by force
of arms and the help of God, he had put down; that for this
reason he had the right to abolish all privileges peculiar to this
kingdom, so far as they concerned the power and extent of the
authority of the Stände; but that, in consideration that there
were so many faithful subjects in his kingdom, who preferred
rather to emigrate than to oppose his will—in consideration
that so many faithful counselors and servants had moved into
the kingdom, he had resolved, of his own inborn mildness, to
preserve all privileges, liberties, and Majestic Letters, as far as
they were not contrary to the renewed statutes or regulations
of the country; but he declared as null and void the two Ma-

---

* Ferdinand the Second, in the presence of the Stände, with a pair of scissors,
cut to pieces and entirely destroyed the Majestic Letter of Rhodolph the Second.

jestic Letters of Rhodolph the Second, of which one concerned religion, and the other punishments and confiscation. He declared, also, that he would preserve all the rights of the Stände in the *hereditary* kingdom of Bohemia, not to impose constitutional taxes, except with the consent of the Stände, and that no other contribution whatever should be enforced ; that against no member of the Stände would he proceed summarily (de facto), but that every one should be examined and tried by the tribunals of justice ; and that, since differences of religious faith had been the cause of the late rebellion, he must and would preserve all the people of Bohemia in the unity of the holy Roman Church, and not permit other faith, religion, and exercise in the said kingdom ; and that all those who had not yet adopted the Catholic religion must be brought by convenient means to it, in order to form the unity of faith and feeling, to serve us better, and to advance the common welfare.   That he would establish a new order of coin, to favor the purposes of commerce."*

The historians of this period graphically describe the excess of misery which the reign of this tyrant had produced.   " Ferdinand the Second, on his accession to the throne, found Austria Lutheran, thickly populated, and prosperous; he left her Catholic, depopulated, and impoverished.   He found in Bohemia three millions of Hussites, dwelling in flourishing cities and villages ; he left merely seven hundred and eighty thousand Catholic beggars."

From this blow Bohemia has never recovered.

Ferdinand the Second was succeeded by his son Ferdinand the Third, 1637, who, though a more tolerant prince, for the honor, as he conceived, of his father, felt himself obliged to continue, in a measure, the contest which he had left him.   In 1640, however, he accorded an instrument known as the *Novella Declaratoria*, in confirmation of the rights of his subjects and of the Stände ; and the ninth article, regarded as the *Fifth Document* in the Bohemian Constitution, grants to the Stände

---

* " His imperial majesty reserves to himself, to his heirs and successors, the complete control of religion, according to the principle, ' cujus regio ejus religio.' He felt himself bound in conscience to exterminate all heretics."—*Menzel's Germany.*

the right to legislate on all matters which do not affect the sovereign rights of the king, and to adopt resolutions which must receive the sanction of the king.

With Ferdinand the Third ended the long series of wars growing out of the religious revolution accomplished by Luther and Calvin, followed by the peace of Westphalia, 1648. This great transaction marks an important era in the progress of European civilization. It established the equality of the three religious communities—of Catholics, Lutherans, and Calvinists—in Germany, and sought to oppose a perpetual barrier to further religious innovations and secularization of ecclesiastical property.

The peace of Westphalia continued to form the basis of the conventional law of Europe, and was constantly renewed and confirmed in every successive treaty of peace between its central states, until the French Revolution.

The reign of Leopold the First (1657 to 1705) was darkened by the insurrection of the peasants in many of the districts, who refused to pay the enormous socage demanded. Under him and his son Joseph the First (1705 to 1711), who reigned over his empire with intelligence and energy, Bohemia began slowly to recover, principally through the introduction of German colonies, and by a greater religious forbearance and a diminution of the labor of the peasantry. Charles the Sixth (1711 to 1740), who succeeded, involved in uninterrupted wars, was not able to effect much for the welfare of the country. And the same causes operated against Bohemia during the first years of the reign of his daughter, Maria Theresa, as this land became again the scene of the War of the Succession, as well as of the Seven Years' War with Frederick the Great. It was only in later years that she was enabled to effect any thing for the welfare of the country. She ameliorated the condition of the peasantry, removed several obstructions to agriculture, opposed the increase of convents, and abolished many old abuses.

During the reigns of Charles the Sixth and Maria Theresa, renewed attempts were made in Bohemia for the revival and emancipation of the Czeckic nationality ; but these efforts suddenly ceased when Joseph the Second ascended the throne. This imperial reformer was beset with the plan of destroying all the various nationalities, and blending the whole Austrian monarchy into one consolidated German empire. But this idea, which he labored so assiduously to accomplish, was unrealized when he died. In Bohemia, as elsewhere in the empire, his zeal in the cause of reform so completely outstripped his judgment and experience, that the Stände, after his death, handed to his successor, Leopold the Second, a bill of complaints against many of his decrees, some of which had been characterized by the very best intentions. Leopold the Second, who succeeded his brother Joseph, granted, at the request of the Stände, a Bohemian pulpit, and on the 12th of August, of the same year, 1791, published a decree which constitutes another article of the Bohemian Constitution, and by which it was determined that "no alteration could be made in the existing constitutional regulations without bringing the matter before the deliberation of the Stände."

In the reign of Francis, which followed, still further contributions to the Bohemian Constitution took place.

1st. In the guarantees contained in the 13th article of the Chart of the German Confederacy, which grants to all German provinces a Constitution.

2d. Articles 54 to 56 of the Treaty of Vienna.

These enactments already cited, together with the coronation oath, taken by all the sovereigns, even to Ferdinand, the last emperor of Austria—wherein he swears " to preserve and maintain to the lords, nobles, and knights of Prague and other places, as well as to the whole people of the kingdom of Bohemia, their regulations, rights, privileges, institutions, liberties, and justice to all ancient and laudable customs, and to alienate and change nothing of this Bohemian kingdom, but especially augment and increase it, and do every thing which should advance the honor and the welfare of this kingdom"— constitute and form the Constitution of Bohemia.

Since the commencement of the present century no change has taken place in the political condition of Bohemia. Her people much attached to their own institutions, and jealous of all innovation, have never been cordially reconciled to the house of Austria.* While, on the other hand, Austria, which at first

* To revive and strengthen their nationality, a few years since a Bohemian

A A

claimed only to govern by election and according to law, now acts as if Bohemia were her own by right of conquest.

The *form* of the Constitution has survived, but its spirit has departed, and all that was real in its privileges been gradually abolished. The Stände is still called together annually, some nominal vote of supply is passed, and they adjourn. Meanwhile, all the rights of the humbler orders are set aside, the nobles become feudal lords, holding their estates of the crown by tenure of service, and dealing with their vassals as feudal lords were wont to do. New laws were enacted, new usages established, and, worst of all, a new language introduced into the courts.

For years past Bohemia has been treated as an integral portion of Germany. German customs and language, instead of Bohemian, prevail, and every effort made to extinguish the very memory of former independence, and to induce the persuasion, both at home and abroad, that as Bohemia had always owed obedience to the Germanic Confederation, so, in subjecting its inhabitants to the common usages of Germany, no violence whatever had been offered to the principles of right and justice.

Although the Stände for a length of time never placed much value upon their privileges as a body, yet they never entirely lost sight of them ; and a few years ago, when an opportunity was imprudently presented by the conduct of the Hofkanzley, or Bureau of Administration at Vienna, they ventured once more upon an assertion of their long-dormant powers. At first they protested only against any interference with their own peculiar rights and privileges ; afterward, as they acquired more confidence, against those which concerned the rights of the whole kingdom.

The appointment of Count Salm to the office of High Burgrave, who had not filled the office of *Landes-Officier*, and who was not possessed of any real property in the kingdom, both of which, agreeably to the statutes, were requisite, induced the Stände to complain to the government of the con-

Walhalla was attempted to be established, to be filled with the statues and busts of Bohemian princes and heroes. Many of the unfinished pieces may yet be seen in the studio of the late sculptor Schwanthaller, at Munich.

tempt shown for their rights. The protest of the Stände proved effectual, and the disqualifications of Count Salm were removed. Subsequent differences occurred between the imperial government and the Stände upon the subject of funds over which that body claimed control; but it was not until the year 1845 that these bodies came to an open rupture. The cities of Bohemia finding the expenses of the criminal courts too heavy, the matter was represented to the government, and the government subsequently directed the Stände to pay annually the sum of fifty thousand florins (twenty-five thousand dollars) out of their funds for that object. The Stände declined on the ground that it was an expense which should be met by the government. The government paid the amount, but increased the taxes of Bohemia to that extent, in order to cover the sum so appropriated, and which taxes were really paid in the years 1845 and 1846. Although in the Diet of the year 1847 only the same amount of taxes was demanded as in the two previous years, yet the Stände thought it their right and duty to demand of the government the reason of the increase since 1845. No reason was assigned by the government for the increase of taxes, as such a step was not usual, and would, at the same time, have been a dangerous admission to the Stände of a right to control the employment of the public funds; but, in answer, the government referred to the course usual on such occasions, summoned the Stände to an immediate partition or assessment of the taxes, and at the same time reminded that body of the right of the king "to increase, amend, or alter" the statutes at pleasure.

Upon the receipt of this communication, the Stände appointed a committee to examine into and to report upon the subject. A very voluminous report was drawn up, under the direction of Palacky (the historian of Bohemia), in which their rights were historically reviewed, but which proved so considerable that it was concluded not to present the document in its totality, but to preserve it in their archives for future use, and to communicate the results only to the emperor. This report proceeded to establish, from historical facts, documents, and treaties, that the rights of the Stände were not founded on the statutes of the 10th of May, 1627, as alleged by the

administration, but upon the old Constitution of the country,
and the confirmation of King Ferdinand the Second, of the
27th of May, 1627 ;* that this confirmation had afterward been
always renewed by all the kings of Bohemia in their oaths of
coronation ; that this conclusion was drawn from documents
belonging to the archives, and from which it would be manifest that the political institutions were originally of a democratic nature ; that the people of Bohemia possessed great political liberties when the monarchical principle was only in its
infancy ; that from this principle was derived the right of free
election of their sovereign by the people ; that this people,
represented by a corporation of the free landed proprietors, had
always preserved their most important rights ; that the Stände
were, according to undoubted historical proofs, the descendants of the free landed proprietors, and their rights were essentially the same ; that if, in the course of time, some of
these rights, such as the election of the bishop, or the right of
electing the sovereign after the death of every king, had been
lost, the right of co-operation by acts of legislation, and especially upon the subject of taxes, had always been maintained ;
that these statutes were issued and became fundamental laws
as early as the middle of the fourteenth century, under Charles
the First; that the right of the lords and knighthood to make
their own laws and that of the citizens, and which could not
be altered without their consent, and that the same were confirmed in the year 1500, and again in 1564 ; that the statutes
of 1564 were to be considered as a treaty between the king
and the Stände of Bohemia, which, even after the suppression
of the Bohemian revolution, could not be altered, but gave
full power to the respective parties to enforce the reciprocal
fulfillment of the treaty ; that the Stände would not enter into
a particular discussion of these facts, as they had documents
of a much later date in their possession to prove sufficiently
these assertions ; that after the battle on the White Mountain, King Ferdinand decreed, on the 10th of May, 1627, a new
set of statutes, reserving to himself the right to increase,
amend, or alter those statutes ; but that those statutes em-

* Staats Lexikon.

braced only regulations of police administration, stating at the same time, most expressly, that upon the subject of political rights a new decree would be issued. This decree appeared on the 27th of May, 1627, confirming all the rights and liberties of the Stände, in so far as they were in accordance with the new regulations. (It excepts the two decrees of Rhodolph the Second, respecting religion, punishments, and confiscations.) That besides, King Ferdinand, in the same decree, gives the assurance that no taxes or contribution of taxes would be exacted without having been first debated in the Assembly of the Stände, and that only such sums as they voluntarily agreed to pay could be demanded; that the Emperor Leopold the Second, in one of his decrees, had decided that no alteration could be made in the existing constitutional regulations without its being first subjected to the deliberation of the Stände; that these rights were annually acknowledged in the demands from the throne upon which the taxes were granted, and were expressly acknowledged and confirmed by the coronation oath taken by each of the sovereigns, even including Ferdinand, the present king of Bohemia.

After recapitulating the various statutes which form the Bohemian Constitution, the report concludes that, in consideration of the very clear elucidation of their rights afforded by these documents, the committee invites the Stände to inform the king: First, that the Stände are fully conscious of the extent of their rights and liberties. Second, that they protest most solemnly against all alterations of their Constitution, or infringements of their rights and privileges. Third, that they are resolved to sustain their own and their country's rights by all the constitutional means in their power.*

The Stände declined to pay the fifty thousand florins, and requested to be informed of the necessity of such an expenditure. The government, in the usual bureaucratic language, declared "the conduct of the Stände most strange and reprehensible;" it stated further, that "explanation upon the subject of the employment of the funds would be given, but that an immediate compliance with the present request was expect-

* Staats Lexikon.

ed, as well as a closing of the sessions without delay." The
debates upon the question shortly afterward followed. On this
occasion, the bureaucratic president (the burgrave) of the Diet
said the Stände would have to bear the consequences, "if the
warning of the father should be changed into the punishment
of the master."* It was answered that, "even were an armed
force thundering at the doors, their resolution would be unchanged." On the 31st of August, the request was declined,
the vote being twenty-six against and ten in favor of the
measure.

After that decision, the government ordered the taxes to be
collected, and directed the Burgrave Count Salm, if necessary,
"to charge the imperial authorities with the execution of the
measure; and, in case of a refusal, to employ all the force at
his command."

Backed by a military power too gigantic to resist, the government prevailed; the taxes were paid in utter disregard of
the voice of the Stände, the only remaining feature of the
Constitution annihilated, and, by the hand of a Habsburg, by
which it had been first assailed, perished the last vestige of
Bohemian liberty.

When the first Habsburg ascended the throne of Bohemia,
as the partial eulogist of the "House of Austria" relates, the
people were all-powerful, and the monarch a cipher; but,
when the last of the same dynasty quitted the throne, the
monarch was all-powerful, and the people a cipher. When
Ferdinand the First was elected King of Bohemia, he could
not impose taxes, raise troops, make war or peace, coin money,
or institute or abrogate laws; he possessed none of these essential elements of sovereignty. And yet the apologists of the
imperial house will prate of the inherited sovereign power.
From whom was this sovereign power derived? The answer
is, from Ferdinand the First; for it had no existence before
his time. And where did he obtain it, when, in the language
of the historian, "he acknowledged, by public act, his election
to the monarchy, as the free choice of the barons, nobles, and
states of Bohemia, and disowned all other rights and preten-

---

* An imitation of the language of the Emperor of Russia to the Poles.

sions ?"   The question is left to the decision of those fawning
sycophants around the imperial throne who speak of it as a
matter of unparalleled insolence on the part of the Stände of
Bohemia to dare to remind the emperor of his oath of coronation, by which he had sworn to maintain their rights.   History records no more clear and palpable example of usurpation
than that afforded by the reign of the house of Habsburg over
the kingdom of Bohemia, where they found a people in the full
enjoyment of all the essential elements of freedom, especially
those of electing their own sovereign, and making their own
laws, etc. ; and this dynasty have left it so completely sunk in
slavery that the will of their Legislature is immediately annulled by military force, and when, as the only act of resistance to arbitrary power, that body presumes respectfully to
remind the emperor of those rights, such a step is regarded as
a matter of " unparalleled insolence."

Such was the political situation of Bohemia in 1847 ; and
it may readily be conceived that when, in the following year,
it was announced that the period had arrived for the resuscitation of all oppressed nationalities, that people was fully ripe
for the movement, and for the assertion of their long-lost
rights.

The state of disorder and confusion into which Europe was
thrown by the French Revolution of 1848, afforded to the
Czechi of Bohemia a favorable opportunity for the indulgence
of their national sentiments, as well as dreams of freedom and
independence, which two centuries of Austrian bondage had
failed to destroy.

Imitating the conduct of the rest of the empire, and jealous,
in particular, of the Frankfort Assembly, in whose schemes for
the Germanization of Eastern Europe it was feared that the
interests of the Slavi would be too much overlooked, the Czechi
of Bohemia protested against every measure tending to identify
them with the Germanic Confederation, and demanded a national existence equivalent in its relations with the empire to
that enjoyed by the Hungarians.

Refused their demands by the emperor, on the 1st of May
an address was published summoning all the Slavic provinces
of the empire to meet in a Slavic Congress, to be held at Prague

on the 31st of the same month, to take counsel. for the interest of their race, and especially to counteract the absorbing
influence of the Germanic body about to assemble at Frankfort.

"The populations of Europe," says Count Joseph Mathias
Thun, in his proclamation convoking the Assembly, "are beginning to comprehend each other, and to unite.   The Germans have, for their work of unity, called together a Parliament
in Frankfort, whereof one principal object is that Austria shall
give up to German sway so much of its possessions as are necessary to constitute German unity.   This would not only destroy the unity of Austria, but would annihilate also the union
of the Slavic races, whose national independence would be
threatened.   The time is come when we Slavians must understand one another and unite in our resolves."

This Congress, consisting, besides the Bohemian members,
of sixteen deputies, sent respectively from each of the southern
Slavic groups of nations (Russia, for obvious reasons, not being included), had met agreeably to appointment, and were
discussing the various theories of Slavic regeneration, when the
inhabitants of Prague, tired of inaction, rose in open revolt.

For some years previously, a secret association had existed
at Prague among the lower classes of citizens of Bohemian descent, and by whom only Bohemian was spoken.   On the occurrence of the revolution at Paris, this body at once avowed
its political character, and, on the 9th of March, a meeting was
called at the St. Wenzelsbad, where a petition to the emperor
was adopted.   The authorities had warned the citizens not to
attend this meeting, but no measures had been taken to prevent them.   A gathering of about thirteen hundred persons of
the lowest rank took place, who elected by acclamation a committee as the nucleus of the movement party, and this committee assumed a permanent authority.   As each succeeding
day increased the force of the revolution, a second petition was
shortly afterward prepared, chiefly by a party of students, demanding popular representation on the broadest basis, and a
responsible Bohemian ministry residing in Prague.   The committee, accompanied by two hundred armed students, forced
the governor general of the kingdom, Count Rhodolph Stadion,

not only to receive, but to sign the document, and a deputation was immediately dispatched with it to the emperor; Count Stadion, at the same time, advising Baron Pillersdorf, president of the ministry at Vienna, that "he could answer for nothing if all was not granted."

The previous petition had also been sent to Vienna, asking a number of concessions, some of which were granted and others refused. On their return to Prague, the deputation illuminated their windows in honor of the privileges granted; but the people, on hearing the result of their efforts, were so incensed because *all* their demands were not granted that they broke the windows of all the deputies; they then appointed a second deputation to repair to Vienna and renew the application to his majesty, making loud threats in case their second effort should be attended with no better success. The second application was successful. All was granted. A National Guard, with the Bohemian cockade, was formed. Committees were appointed to suggest the most extensive reforms for the approaching Diet; and these committees were by another popular demonstration converted into a species of national *Ausschuss*, or committee of administration, which was likewise recognized by the governor. After these acts of weakness, Count Stadion resigned, and Count Leo Thun, a young nobleman of great firmness and judgment, was raised to the post, which his predecessor had only quitted after he had abandoned every defensible point, and thus given an uncontrollable impulse to the Revolution.

A Slavic detachment of the National Guard, which was, in truth, an armed club (composed mostly of students), assumed the name of Swornost; another club, called the "Slovanska Lipa" (Slavic Linden), was formed on the 24th of May, and whose numbers amounted to six hundred. The objects of which were,

1st. To observe the further development of the constitutional principle.

2d. To watch over the confirmation and equal rights of the two nationalities in schools and offices.

3d. Strict union of Bohemia, Moravia, and Silesia, for the preservation of their independence, especially against the German Confederacy.

4th. To establish a reciprocity among all Slavic nations.

5th. Commercial intercourse with all Slavic countries, especially in the South.

This club, as its name imports—"the Oak of Bohemia"—was composed of the most radical spirits of the day, who considered any attempt to sustain order as reactionary. At their first meeting, a motion to abide by the concessions of the emperor made on the 15th of May, and to proceed to the election of members of the Diet, met with great opposition. They insisted upon the resignation of the mayor, and that the National Guard should join the students in a petition to the Minister of War for the removal of Prince Windischgrätz from his post as military commander of the city.

Ernst Alfred, Prince of Windischgrätz, one of the highest nobles of Austria, is, on his father's side, a descendant of the old counts, later Princes of Windischgrätz, whose ancestor, Weriand von Grätz, was a branch of the family of Weimar, that existed in the eleventh century. On his mother's side, he claims descent from the famous Waldstein (Wallenstein), *Duke of Friedland*—a title which the emperor, after the prince's successes at Prague and Vienna, in 1848, conferred on him,* together with that of marshal of the empire. There is, perhaps, in all Germany, no name more hateful to a portion of the population than that of Prince Windischgrätz; nor is it surprising that such should be the case, since, although a well-bred and highly-polished gentleman, he is cold, distant, and haughty. They ascribe to him the expression, "In my opinion, no man exists who is not at least a baron;" or, in other words, that all below barons were mere animals; and, whether guilty or not of the charge, this circumstance has doubtless tended to aggravate the animosity toward him during the Revolution, under the supposition that, with his utter indifference to all untitled human life, he would not hesitate to order wholesale slaughters, so long as no scions of nobility were included among the victims. But the falsity of such a supposition, the whole conduct of the prince at Prague, subsequently at Vienna, and

---

* He has been for many years endeavoring to obtain from the government of Austria some portion, if not the whole, of the immense estates of Waldstein, which had been subjected to confiscation.

still later in Hungary, most clearly establishes.   On these occasions, as his bitterest enemies are constrained to admit, he exhibited a forbearance rarely if ever surpassed.   The moment after his wife had been inhumanly murdered before his eyes, instead of threatening vengeance—instead of executing it—which the force at his command would have enabled him to effect, "Now," said he, in tones of heart-broken anguish, "the greatest moderation will be necessary. or I shall be supposed to act from feelings of revenge."

This seemed to be his ruling apprehension, to be thought capable of revenging himself.   With the most perfect control over himself, or a total absence of all feeling, which can alone account for the remarkable self-possession he displayed on the occasion just cited, during the siege of Vienna, this man of iron nerves was found to weep; and on being asked the cause, replied, " I feel that severity is absolutely required of me, and I am tortured by the thought that what I do may be imputed to vengeance."

As soon as the lawless proceedings of the 26th of May in Vienna, by which the whole power of the government became vested in the students, was known at Prague, whether from the force of example or* from the desire of being independent of the control of an administration of boys, on the 27th of May, the president of the government in Prague, in concert with the other officers of all its branches, decided upon the establishment of a Provisional Government; the ministry to be composed of eight members, and no longer to be under the control of the government at Vienna.   Two of the ministers immediately started for Innspruck, to obtain, if possible, the sanction of the emperor to their proceedings.   The ministry at Vienna, as soon as they had received official intelligence of the proceedings at Prague, hastened to inform the emperor of the illegal character of the measure, in order to anticipate all intervention on the part of the deputation applying for its confirmation.

---

* Count Thun gives as reasons for the movement, that the actual condition of matters required rapid and energetic measures, which exceed the limits of the existing authorities, and that official communication with the ministry at Vienna had been interrupted by the late events in that city.

At the same time, the Minister of the Interior addressed a
letter to the Governor of Bohemia, in which he declares the
measure illegal, and calls on him, on his responsibility, not to
permit it to progress, and, by proclamation, directed all the under officers not to obey the instructions of the Provisional Government of Prague until it shall first have received the sanction
of the emperor. To this protest of the Austrian ministry against
the formation of a Provisional Government for Bohemia, Count
Leo Thun boldly replied, and, after quoting the leading points
of the ministerial protest, states that he has sent a report of
his proceedings to his majesty the emperor, and that he was unwilling to retrace his steps or suspend his resolution, until the
emperor's decision should arrive. As to the responsibility with
which the Austrian ministry had threatened him, he protested
that he readily took it upon himself, and that he, and he alone,
was responsible for all the measures of the Provisional Government of Bohemia. The period for the meeting of the Slavic
Congress approached, and the picturesque streets of Prague
were thronged with the rich and varied costumes, and resounded with the many tongues of Poles, Moravians, Slovacks, Servians, Illyrians—all the Slavic nations of the empire. On the 2d
of June, the Congress opened its proceedings, thus giving fresh
stimulants to the prevailing excitement. " The old hymn of
St. Wenceslas was sung around the relics of the Bohemian martyrs, and in churches which had rung with the controversies
of John Huss and the Utraquists; a Serbian Pope said mass
before the statue of King Wenceslas, in the Rossmarkt; and
passions as fierce as the flames of Constance, or as fatal as the
rout of the White Mountain, started into life from that bridge,
from which St. John Nepomuck had been plunged into the Moldau."

Palacky, the historian of Bohemia, was named president *pro*
tempore of the Congress; and a president was also appointed
for each of the three sections formed according to the principal
Slavic tribes of Austria, the Czechi, the Eastern and the Southern Slavi.* The members present amounted to three hundred,

---

* The ministry consisted of eight members: Palacky, Rieger, Brauner, Barroslk,
Count Nastiz, and Strohback. Rieger and Nastiz proceeded to Innspruck, to receive, if possible, the sanction of the emperor to their proceedings.

and at the first sitting it was resolved that Austria should be a Slavic empire, as the Slavi, throughout its limits, greatly preponderated. The subject which principally occupied their attention was the Diet at Frankfort, and they resolved to have no connection with it.

In the mean time, the disorder of the city continued from day to day to increase, and Prince Windischgrätz, the military commander, and who had witnessed in Vienna, on the 14th of March, the consequences of a want of preparation against a popular insurrection, began to take the necessary military precautions. These, of course, were regarded as reactionary tendencies. On the 7th of June, a large meeting of the people resolved to petition the emperor for the removal of Windischgrätz, and the appointment of one of the archdukes.

On the 10th, a vast assemblage of citizens and students took place in the Carolinum, the building of the university founded by the Emperor Charles the Fourth, at which a Storm Petition was resolved upon, to demand of Prince Windischgrätz, military commander of the city, the withdrawal of the troops from certain strategical points which they had occupied on the Vissehrad, and a distribution of two thousand muskets and eighty thousand cartridges, and a battery of cannon for the use of the town, under the pretext of being obliged to defend themselves against reactionary movements. The common council proceeded to the Aula, and endeavored, but in vain, to quell the agitation. A deputation of students, headed by the mayor, and accompanied by several deputies, waited on Prince Windischgrätz. The latter personages were only interested in the third article of the petition, viz., the removal of the battery in the Joseph's Barracks, on the Vissehrad. The prince refused to grant the petition; but, in compliance with the wish of the citizens, as well as that of the Civil Governor, Count Thun, he caused the battery in the Joseph's Barracks to be removed to the Hradshin.

On the morning of the 11th, a public meeting was called for the evening of the same day, in the Wenzelsbad. At this meeting the greater part of the persons present were students, and members of the Swornost; several exciting speeches were delivered, and the people informed that Prince Windischgrätz had refused the delivery of arms; it was thereupon resolved to drive the garrison out of the city, as the moment had arrived when it devolved upon the people to make their own laws. The next day had been fixed upon for the celebration of a great mass in the Rossmarkt. Eight days previously, Prince Lobkowitz, commander of the National Guard, had been notified that a mass would be celebrated on the following Monday, and that the corps of the Swornost would be present to preserve the order and quiet of the city, pledging themselves that no riotous conduct should be allowed.

On the next day, between ten and eleven o'clock, the time fixed on for the mass, about two thousand workmen, a great number of the Swornost, students, and other people in Slavic costume, assembled on the Rossmarkt. During the mass, the soldiers at the guard-house and the officers on duty were insulted, although they had not been wanting in all the military ceremonies and honors appropriate to the occasion.

After the mass was concluded, it was resolved to proceed to the quarters of Prince Windischgrätz, and to inflict upon him a mock-serenade. The masses then put in motion, proceeded toward the quarters of the military commander, singing Slavic songs, in which they contemptuously mingled his name, screaming out " Okolo,* Windischgrätz !" endeavoring in every possible manner to provoke and insult him.

A company of the regular troops stationed before the commander's quarters ordered the crowd to preserve silence, and not being obeyed, they placed themselves before the singers, and prevented their further passage. Forced by this measure to withdraw, the populace retired in all directions to their houses in search of arms; and re-assembling again on the Graben, immediately commenced the construction of barricades. About this time, a deputation of citizens waited on Prince Windischgrätz, assured him of their loyalty, and requested his interference for the preservation of order and tranquillity. On their return, they met the noisy and riotous crowd, making warlike demonstrations, and crying out " Down with Windischgrätz !" " The rascal must hang from his own balcony !" A lieutenant

---

* *Okolo,* same as the Italian *eccolo ;* nearest approach in English is halloo.

of the regular troops, Tablouski, who came to the Graben to
release the soldiers on duty there, ordered his half company to
drive back the crowd, which was effected without injury to any
one. He was beaten on the head with a stick by one student,
while another attacked him with a sabre. The students were
arrested, and confined in the quarters of the general commandant. The people made another rush on the soldiers, stormed a
house in which they were stationed, and began to throw stones
and brick-bats. They were again driven back, and, only after
a second attempt, the above-named officer ordered his men to
load. The cry of treason and barricades now resounded from
all parts. Major Schütte sent his aid-de-camp to the barracks
to bring out the troops. He was attacked with stones thrown
from the houses. A student encountering him with a sabre, a
contest ensued, when a party of grenadiers came up to his relief. When the soldiers approached, the mob retired. toward
the Museum, which served as a *corps de garde* to the Swornost,
and there commenced tearing up the pavement, for the purpose
of erecting barricades. About this time the throng increased
to such an extent, that the soldiers on duty, on the *Alt Stadter-
ring*, were forced to retire with their cannons. Barricades were
now commenced in every street, a Swornost superintending and
giving instructions for their erection ; this, together with the
fact that the barricades were built upon the most approved
plan, induced the belief that the tumult was not sudden and
unexpected, but premeditated and well arranged.

Two companies of grenadiers were ordered to charge the
barricades at the Museum ; they were received with two discharges, but without effect ; upon which the second company
fired a volley against the Museum. That barricade was destroyed, and the soldiers retired. The troops now began with
energetic measures, and the conflict in several streets was
quite severe, particularly in the *Alt Stadt*, or Old Town, where
the narrow streets and high barricades obstructed the passage
of the troops, and exposed them to the fire from the windows,
as well as to injury from the heavy stones, tiles, &c., which
were thrown from the roofs of the houses on to them. Captain
Müller marched with two companies on to the fruit-market,
where he was ordered to take the *Clementinum.* One com-

pany was posted at the great entry in front; and the other, penetrating the building from behind, was received with shots and stones. The attack was vigorously repelled; several persons were killed or wounded, and fifty-six, principally Sworn-osts, students, and workmen, were taken prisoners, a great quantity of arms, and several thousand cartridges found in the building (another proof of premeditation), captured. A deputation of the people called on Prince Windischgrätz, and demanded the release of the prisoners ; to whom the prince replied, that the prisoners would be liberated as soon as the barricades should be removed. This was promised; and, to facilitate its fulfillment, some of the students in confinement were released ; these endeavored to effect the removal of the barricades, but the more violent defenders refused, and the students, unable to effect a reconciliation, returned to their prison.

A party of National Guards* preceded the troops, to show that only in case of extreme necessity would the soldiers be employed. This proved of no avail ; the defenders of the barricades declared to the troops that, if they were attacked, Count Thun (who, with several of the ministers, they had taken prisoner) should die.† After all this negotiation had failed, Colonel Mainan stated that he had orders to destroy the barricades with bomb-shells, but that he would give them still a respite of half an hour to remove the barricades and to disperse. During this interval, the barricades, so far from being removed, were more strongly fortified.

At this time the Archduke Ferdinand appeared in the streets, accompanied by the mayor and several members of the city council. All his endeavors to effect a pacification failed; Prince Lubkowitz, the mayor, who accompanied him, was shot at, and Lieutenant Gustaker, another of his attendants, had a horse killed under him. In the evening, Marie Eléonore, the Princess of Schwartzenberg, consort of the Prince Windischgrätz (sister of the present prime minister, and niece of the unfortunate Princess Schwartzenberg, who, in 1812, perished in

---

* These were the German citizens who sided with the troops against the Swornost, or Bohemian National Guard.

† Quarterly Review, 1850.

so tragic a manner at Paris, on the occasion of the *fêtes* in honor of the Archduchess Maria Louisa, just married to Napoleon), was killed in her own house by a shot discharged from one of the upper windows of the hotel, " The Golden Angel," which was immediately opposite to the quarters of the general commandant. A few moments after this event the prince descended into the street and addressed the crowd, who were making a demonstration before his quarters, with the most remarkable calmness and good temper. " Gentlemen," said he, " if the object of this vile serenade be to insult me as an individual, because I belong to the aristocracy, then you should go before my own hotel, where, unmolested, you may gratify your desire ; but if, in making the demonstration before *this* building, you design to cast contempt upon the military commander of the city, I warn you that I shall punish such an attempt by every means in my power. Notwithstanding my wife lies now behind me in her blood, I conjure you in all kindness to depart, and not compel me to use against you all the force and power at my command." As soon as Prince Windischgrätz had finished these words, several of the crowd rushing up, seized him, and were hurrying him to the nearest lamppost, where, with a cord which they had prepared, they intended to hang him, when he was rescued by the timely interference of some of his troops. These insults and injuries to the high officers of the government were the signal of battle, and the conflict was renewed at all points with increased vigor. General Schütte attacked the barricades with cannon and demolished them with bombs ; and, after a hard fight of several hours, succeeded in re-establishing the communication between the old city and the Klein Seite. The River Moldau, or, as it is afterward known as the Elbe, flowing through the city of Prague, divides it into two parts ; the greater portion, lying on the right bank, is called the Alt Stadt, or Old Town, with its narrow streets and antique buildings, one of the oldest, and, at one time, the most splendid city in Europe. The other, connected by a fine stone bridge adorned with time-worn statues, is called the Klein Seite, or small side, and contains the royal palace, the citadel, and other government buildings. On that side the land rises into a high bluff of several hundred feet, commanding completely the level positions of the old town opposite; and it was there, on the Vissehrad, that the first battery was erected which gave the citizens so much alarm, and which the military commander, at the request of Count Thun, consented to withdraw.

On the next morning, Tuesday, the 13th, the military commander, who had, the evening previous, withdrawn his forces to the Klein Seite, dispatched a messenger with a white flag into the old town, and summoned the Slavi to surrender, threatening, in the event of their refusal, to bombard the city. The Slavi disregarding the summons, the prince ordered twenty bombs to be discharged into the city. This was done, and, producing no effect, he directed that the firing should be continued until ten o'clock. In the afternoon, the insurgents sent a flag of truce to the military commander. Prince Windischgrätz insisted on the barricades being removed, but did not require the people to surrender their arms. This was refused. Thereupon the conflict was renewed. The fighting in detached parties continued during the day and throughout the night. The main streets and the principal squares of the city were in the hands of the troops. The insurgents were established in the Karolmenthal.

The number of killed on Tuesday night was computed at six hundred. One Austrian general was killed, and twenty officers either killed or wounded; among the latter, the son of Prince Windischgrätz. The bombardment of the city had continued, at intervals, during the 14th and 15th, and, so far from producing submission, the Slavic students had left the city in great numbers, to gather and bring to their relief all the Bohemian peasants from the surrounding country. Count Thun, who had been arrested by the people, was set at liberty on the 14th.

On the evening of the 15th, Prince Windischgrätz having been assured by the National Guard that his retirement from the command of the city would alone effect a pacification of the citizens, resigned his office into the hands of Count Mensdorf, sent from Vienna to supersede him. The cannonading ceased, and the re-establishment of tranquillity was confidently expected. But the Slavi were false to their engagement:

so far from removing the barricades, and returning to order, as was promised upon the resignation of Prince Windischgrätz, the interim was employed in gathering fresh forces, and making further preparations for action.

But a few hours elapsed before the treachery was discovered. Count Mensdorf himself comprehended the necessity of resistance, Prince Windischgrätz again resumed the command, and operations were once more successfully renewed. A heavy fire was opened from the heights on the left bank of the Moldau; the city was set fire to in many places; the loss of life and damage to property was considerable. The barricades were attacked with great vigor by the troops, and one after another carried by storm; and, after three days of severe fighting, the city surrendered.

On Saturday night, at eleven o'clock, after almost an entire week of fighting, the bombardment ceased. The fire in the city extinguished, the capitulation commenced; the streets were cleared of barricades and occupied by the military. The disarming of the students and people, with the exception of the National Guard, began, and fourteen of the leaders of the insurrection were retained as hostages for the tranquillity of the city.

With the entire submission of Prague, the Slavic Congress was broken up, and its members obliged to leave the city. The National Committee, many of whose members were implicated in the insurrection, was dissolved; and the projected Diet of Bohemia indefinitely postponed.

The city placed under martial law, or in a state of siege, the public order was not again disturbed; and this conflict proved not only the first, but the most successful effort of the restored military power of the empire.

The tranquillity of the Bohemian capital was not again disturbed, notwithstanding the subsequent outbreaks in Vienna, and in other portions of the empire, although the army was afterward, from necessity, withdrawn; and subsequently, the Bohemian party in the Diet at Vienna, and at Kremsier, constituted the chief supporters of the throne and government.*

* This was but the result of the strong Slavic feeling, and consequent hatred of the Germans. They would not follow the German Radicals, though they promised liberty, but awaited the general union and emancipation of the Slavi.

Without any direct agency in the liberal movements of the eventful year of 1848, but serving rather as the instruments of conservative, if not of reactionary principles, the Slavic nations of Austria seem to be the only portion of the population to whom the late irruptions have afforded any positively beneficial results.

Previous to that period, possessed of no proper individuality, their political nationality was unacknowledged, and for centuries, consequently, they exercised no influence in the political councils of Europe. The storms of 1848 and 1849 raised them to consideration, and even to power.

The course pursued by the Austrian Slavi was widely different from that adopted by the other races of the empire; and this doubtless, more than any other cause, contributed to the results we have stated. Confident of their eventual emancipation from a foreign yoke, the Slavi of Austria seemed carefully to avoid the premature and hasty examples of the revolutionary states of France, Germany, and Italy, but continued to labor silently and in patience for their own liberation; and, instead of desiring to accelerate that event, sought rather to render themselves prepared for its appreciation and enjoyment.

This tendency of the Austrian Slavi, as well as of the whole Slavic race, was nowhere more evidently displayed than in Vienna.

The geographical position of this capital, sufficiently central as regards all the Slavic nations, and, at the same time, the nearest point for the more free and enlightened governments of Western Europe, had made Vienna, for many years previously, the seat of the Slavic Amphictyons. The first step taken by the Slavi, after being rendered conscious of their existence as a great race, was to enlighten the people on the subject of their national unity. To this end all the powers of philology (for which the Slavi have a peculiar and native talent) were invoked, to show that the branches of their race possess a greater approximation and stronger affinity than exists in those of Romanic or Teutonic origin. The striking points of affinity developed by this critical comparison of languages, excited the vivid imaginations of the Panslavists, and very naturally suggested the ideas of a political union. Indi-

viduals of the various nations meeting together, became suddenly friends, through no other talisman than the mere affinity
of their idioms.   Small meetings began next to be held by the
different Slavi of the empire, in the metropolis, and under the
very eyes of imperial authority.   The mass of visitors regarded
these pleasant assemblies as insignificant ; but a few of the
most sanguine did not fail to consider them in the light of an
overture to a long and serious drama.

The police of the city, apprised of these regular festivals, became watchful ; and prudence on the part of the Slavi being
requisite, was strictly exercised.   The time and place of holding these so-called " Slavic Unions" were frequently changed,
and announced with great secrecy only a few hours before
they commenced.   The order and quiet with which they were
conducted causing no uneasiness in the minds of either the
police or of the government, permission was soon granted the
Slavi to hold public concerts and balls (the latter *en costume*),
even during the last years of the administration of Prince Metternich.

At a later period, these conclaves became more open, and
took place in a coffee-house called, *par excellence*, " The Slavic."   Every stranger, if a Slave, whether civilian or soldier,
was there introduced to the most prominent and erudite men
of the race.   There Slavic languages were exclusively spoken,
and Slavic newspapers read by Bohemians, Poles, Croatians,
and Carniolians, who clustered in groups around their several
tables, and discoursed in their various dialects.   Articles of
general interest, from the periodicals, were read aloud ; and
letters of importance from the different countries secretly circulated ; ethnographical maps disclosed the practicability of
Panslavism, and the interchange of views among the learned
rendered its objects more clear and defined.

Nationality in every respect, but particularly in intellectual
pursuits, was encouraged, in the hope that a common literature would, in time, produce political union ; and the *Xivio
Slava*, with which all their meetings in Vienna terminated,
became now the watch-word, resounding through the empire,
and deeply exciting every mind.

Such was the prudent course pursued by the Austrian Slavi

for the realization of this historic idea ; when the revolution of 1848, occurring too soon for their still undeveloped plans, embarrassed rather than facilitated their designs. Influenced by no sympathy with the Democratic movements of Germany, they remained passive and immovable throughout the shock which appeared to convulse all Europe ; and it was not until the whole list of liberal requisitions had received the sanction of the imperial government, that the Panslavist Congress commenced its sittings at Prague.

To that Congress came delegates from every branch of the Slavic race—Czechs, Lekhs, Slovacks, Rhuthenes, Serbs, and Slovenes ; and during its session, abruptly terminated by the outbreak of the populace, the great scheme for making the Austrian empire instrumental for the aggrandizement of the Slavic race, first took shape and form—a scheme unthought of at the date of the Polish insurrection of 1830, and having no existence when the republic of Cracow breathed its last, in 1846.

According to this plan, the Austrian empire was to form a centre around which all the members of the Slavic family were gradually to cluster, and under the shadow of which they were to acquire strength and consistency, such as would secure their existence, and entitle them to a place as an integral part of the European system.   To render this project completely successful required the annihilation of the Magyars ; and this, no doubt, was one of the principal motives which induced the late intervention of Russia in Hungary.

The Czar, holding imperial sway over sixty out of eighty millions of Slavi in Europe, very naturally considers himself at the head of that race ; and his defeat of the Magyars, the great enemy of the Slavi, furnishes him, as he doubtless thinks, with additional claims to the title of protector Both the protector and the protected seem, however, to be actuated by very different objects in the attainment of the same great end—the union of the Slavic race.   That of the former would seem to be to accomplish, through the lethargy of the Austrian and Turkish governments, the subjugation of the entire Slavic race to his sceptre, and to create thus an enslaved Panslavism ; while that of the latter, by the diffusion of literary and political knowledge, is to promote a distinct national existence, with the hope that, upon the downfall of Austria and Turkey, they may be enabled to erect upon the ruins of these empires one united, free, and great Slavic nation.

If Austria were truly wise, half-Slavic as she is (having more than sixteen millions of Slavic subjects*), she would leave Germany to its plans of federalization, and place herself at the head of a grand Slavic movement; and, if the Turkish empire is destined to crumble to pieces, its scattered fragments should be gathered together in a Slavic empire, rather than add to the colossal power of Russia, and enlarge the dominion of its semi-barbaric institutions. The incapable Greeks of the present day have sometimes dreamed of having Constantinople for their capital; but how much better could the Slavi establish and maintain themselves there, should the predictions of the fall of the Turkish empire be verified. A Christian successor to the Moslem would thus be secured, without the Turkish empire becoming a possession of the Czar. The attainment of such a result might reasonably be hoped for, if a common feeling in favor of liberty united the German and Slavic populations.

---

* The three united kingdoms (Croatia, Slavonia, and Dalmatia), though representing but the *thirty-fifth* portion of the empire of Austria, furnish the *third* portion of the Austrian infantry, and are capable of furnishing double the number, if required.

END OF VOL. I.

AUSTRIA IN 1848-49

AUSTRIA IN 1848-49:

BEING A HISTORY OF THE

LATE POLITICAL MOVEMENTS

IN

VIENNA, MILAN, VENICE, AND PRAGUE,

WITH

DETAILS OF THE CAMPAIGNS OF LOMBARDY AND NOVARA;
A FULL ACCOUNT OF THE

REVOLUTION IN HUNGARY;

AND HISTORICAL SKETCHES OF THE AUSTRIAN GOVERNMENT AND THE
PROVINCES OF THE EMPIRE.

BY WILLIAM H. STILES,

LATE CHARGÉ D'AFFAIRES OF THE UNITED STATES AT THE COURT OF VIENNA.

WITH

Portraits of the Emperor, Metternich, Radetzky, Jellacic, and Kossuth.

IN TWO VOLUMES.

VOL. II.

NEW YORK:

HARPER & BROTHERS, PUBLISHERS,

329 & 331 PEARL STREET,

FRANKLIN SQUARE.

1852.

CONTENTS OF VOL. II.

BOOK II.—(Continued.)

CHAPTER V.

CHAPTER VI.

CHAPTER VII.

CHAPTER VIII.

CHAPTER IX.

APPENDIX.

AUSTRIA IN 1848 AND 1849.

BOOK II.—(Continued.)

CHAPTER V.

For at least seven centuries after the appearance of the Magyars in Europe, by whom the kingdom was founded, Hungary maintained an entirely distinct and separate existence, until, in 1526, it became connected with the Austrian crown. To understand the origin and progress of the late contest between Austria and Hungary, as well as to appreciate the precise objects for which that gallant people have battled, single-handed, against the most fearful combination of power, it will be necessary briefly to consider, first, the political condition of Hungary previous to its connection with Austria, then the nature or terms of that connection; and, finally, the subsequent conduct of the parties; or, in other words, whether the terms of that engagement have been complied with or violated. What was the political condition of Hungary previous to its connection with Austria?

Toward the close of the ninth century (889), seven tribes of Magyar wanderers, under the conduct of Almus, and of his son Arpad, entered the country near the Theiss River, and gradually won settlements for themselves in the fertile plains of Dacia.† To concentrate their strength, they chose Arpad as their

---

* Sometimes written Jelachich; but the author has thought that the better guide as to the spelling of proper names was the manner adopted by the parties themselves. This rule he has also adhered to in writing *Habsburg*.

† The degenerate descendants of Trajan's Roman legions, who now call them-

duke or leader, and a solemn compact was entered into between him and the heads of the tribes, to the effect that the office of chief magistrate should be hereditary in his line, and that the right of the tribes to choose their governor should never be questioned. It was, in short, a federal aristocracy, or union of clans, owing a limited obedience to a superior chief—for there appeared to have been an express stipulation made by the heads of the tribes that the ducal title, on every new accession to the leadership, should be solemnly acknowledged by the state; and that a refusal to take certain oaths prescribed, to observe the popular liberties, should be followed by rejection. The conquered territory was at first distributed only among the chiefs of the tribes; but the duke soon acquired the right of rewarding the courage of the soldiers by the investiture of lands without regard to rank. These estates were held on condition of military service; the chiefs, or possessors of them, engaged to defend the country from internal turmoil and foreign invasion, and were bound to bring into the field, at the call of the duke or Diet, a number of soldiers proportioned to the extent of their lands, but these were never to be forced beyond the limits of the country.

Geysa, the third in descent from Arpad, embraced Christianity; and his son Stephen, who attained the dukedom in the year 1000, under the proselyting patronage of the Roman See, was rewarded for his services in " extirpating the heathen," by a crown from Pope Sylvester the Second, which, manufactured as was superstitiously supposed by the hands of angels, has by the Magyars been ever preserved and held in the utmost reverence, as inseparably connected with Hungarian independence.*

---

selves Roumani or Wallachs, and the ancient Slavic races, who were probably the aborigines of the country, offered but a feeble resistance to these fierce invaders.

   * THE CROWN OF HUNGARY.—One of the many subjects of speculation at the present moment is the fate of the Hungarian crown —not, by a figure of speech, the Hungarian monarchy, but the actual "round and top of sovereignty," the golden diadem itself. It is generally believed that Kossuth took it with him in his flight; if so, it has for a second time crossed the frontiers of Turkey. The past history of this crown is a curious one, and as full of vicissitudes as the lives of some of those who have worn it. The Magyars attach a superstitious value to the relic of their ancient monarchy; there is a legend that it was wrought by the

Thus Stephen founded the kingdom which, according to the notions of that period, he endeavored to strengthen by increas-

---

hands of angels for St. Stephen, who was crowned with it in 1001; history, with a more limited faith, records that it was sent as a present to Stephen by Pope Sylvester the Second. In 1072, Duke Geysa received from the Greek emperor a golden circlet or royal band for his brow; when he was afterward made King of Hungary, he joined this circlet to the diadem—so that the crown is really composed of two kingly emblems united. When the race of the Arpads became extinct, in 1301, there was a double election to the vacant throne; one party chose Robert of Anjou and Naples, the other Wenzel, the younger, of Bohemia. The cause of the latter did not prosper, and his affairs were taking an unfortunate turn. when his father, Wenzel, King of Bohemia, marched an army to Ofen, and carried off his son and the crown with him to Prague. The Hungarians then definitively elected Otto, of Bavaria, and old Wenzel, for reasons not stated, gave up the crown to him. Otto, to take possession of his kingdom, had to ride incognito through Austria, carrying the crown as a "property" with him. It was packed in a little cask, and hung at the saddle-bow of a German count, who discovered one morning that he had lost his precious charge during the night. The party had then arrived at Fischerment, below Vienna, where they were about to cross the Donau; they retraced their steps, and by great good luck found cask and crown again. In 1307. Otto went to Siebenburgen, on a visit to the Vayvode Ladislas, intending to win him over to his party; he must have failed in his attempt, for the vayvode seized the crown, and made the king a prisoner. After some time, he saw fit to let Otto go, but kept firm possession of the diadem for three years. In 1310, on threats of war and extermination, he gave it up. For more than a century after this its history is a blank; but in 1439, on the death of the Emperor Albert the Fourth, there was again a double election, the two rivals being Wladislaw, of Poland, and Ladislas, the infant son of Albert. The empress resolved to have the child crowned, and for that purpose the diadem was stolen from the Castle of Vissehrad, by one of her maids of honor, who undertook the task and succeeded. In 1441, the empress made a less dignified use of it: she pledged it to the Emperor Frederick the Fourth for two thousand five hundred guldens. It was redeemed by Mathias Corvinus, and taken back to Vissehrad; from hence, after the battle of Mohacs, it was again stolen, and again by a woman, in order to crown John Zapolya. Zapolya gave it in charge to Preny, who delivered it to Ferdinand the First; he was crowned with it in 1527, and then it fell into the hands of the Turks. As Solyman returned from the siege of Vienna, he publicly exhibited the crown to his army in Ofen, but told his soldiers it was that of the renowned Persian ruler Nushirvan; he' then sent it back to his *protégé* Zapolya, on whose death it was again given up by his widow to the Emperor Ferdinand. Rhodolph the Second sent the crown to Prague; Mathias the Second brought it back to Pressburg, where, in 1619, it was seized by Bethlem Gabor; on the conclusion of the peace of Nikolsburger, he gave it up to Ferdinand the Second. The Emperor Joseph had it brought to Vienna; afterward he sent it back again to Hungary, where it remained till the taking of Pesth by Windischgrätz, when it was removed by Kossuth, and has ever since been kept at the seat of the Hungarian government; that being broken up and dispersed, the crown has resumed its wanderings. As to what has become of it, there are many rumors; it is said to be buried in a secret place. According to others, Kossuth has it in his personal possession; but

ing the power of the hierarchy and the aristocracy. He established ten richly-endowed bishoprics, and divided the whole empire into seventy-two comitats or counties, with an officer at the
head of each, responsible only to the king, and invested with
full military and civil power. These officers and bishops formed
the House of Magnates, or Senate of the kingdom, and, with
their concurrence, King Stephen (in the year 1001) granted a
Constitution, the principal features of which are still preserved.
On his death, without issue, the country for a time lapsed into
a state of anarchy ; but order was restored by the election of
Wladislaw of Poland, the representative of a junior branch of
the house of Arpad, in 1077. It was during this reign that
Croatia and Slavonia were annexed to the Hungarian crown.*

Nothing of political interest then occurred until the first
quarter of the thirteenth century, which may be regarded as a
highly interesting era in Hungarian history—as marking the
establishment of the rudiments of a regularly defined constitutional and representative system.   Andrew the Second, the
reigning monarch at this time, participated in the first crusade,
in the thirteenth century, and was named, by the Pope, " King
of Jerusalem ;" which title has descended to all the kings of
Hungary.   But, while abroad acquiring titles and reputation,
his power and influence at home became seriously undermined
Upon his return, the rich nobility and clergy availed themselves of his weakness to extort from him a confirmation and
extension of their privileges, in a charter known as the *Aurea
Bulla†* (or Golden Bull), in 1222 (seven years after the Barons
of England had compelled John to grant the *Magna Charta*),
the thirty-first article of which authorized any Hungarian to
resist and oppose the monarch who might violate the Constitution.

This charter, which is to Hungary what Magna Charta is
to England, except that it secures to the nobility only their
rights, leaving the peasant and the subject nations precisely
where they were before its adoption—a prey to the oppression

---

where this gift of a pope to a saint now may be, is, as M. Pulzky told the author,
" the great secret."

* King Koloman in 1095 completed the subjugation of Croatia, and its incorporation with Hungary   † For original, see Appendix, note No. 11.

both of the barons and the crown.   It also guarantees to the nobles freedom from arrest, except by due course of law; perpetual immunity from all taxation whatever; the right, when their privileges are attacked, of legal resistance, without incurring the penalties of treason; and freedom from any obligation to obey the king until after his regular coronation.

After recognizing the ancient privileges of the nobility, this charter, in substance, provided that the magnates should sit as hereditary legislators in the National Diet or Assembly; and that the inferior nobility, or untitled gentry, with the body of the clergy, should be represented by members of their respective bodies; but all other classes of the community were beyond the pale of citizenship.   With the progress of social civilization, there gradually arose a middle class between the nobles and their serfs; and, about a century and a half after the Golden Bull was granted, this order received a quasi political recognition, and the representative branch of the Legislature was increased by a burgess class, the deputies from the free towns and royal cities.

The form of government in Hungary is a limited monarchy, at first elective, but since 1687 hereditary, in the dynasty of Habsburg.

The principal laws of the kingdom, which, as in Great Britain, form the bases of the Constitution, are,

1st. *The Golden Bull of Andreas the Second.*   Each king, upon his accession to the throne, is obliged to acknowledge and confirm it by a solemn oath, excepting the famous clause (the thirty-first) which accords to each Hungarian noble the right of a veto upon the unconstitutional acts of the king, and which, having often lighted the torch of discord in the country, was in 1687, under the reign of Leopold the First, abolished.

2d. *The four principal privileges of the Hungarian nobility,* but especially that which exempts the nobles from all taxes and from every public charge.   These were enacted into a fundamental law of the kingdom, by a decree of the Diet of 1741.*

3d. *The treaties of peace—of Vienna, in the year* 1606, *and*

---

* Demain, Tableau de la Hongrie.

that of Lintz in 1645.   Both acknowledge the free exercise
of religion for the Protestants.   These were made fundamental
laws by the Diets following, and reconfirmed in 1791.

4th. *The right of succession,* which assures the crown of
Hungary to the heirs male of the Archdukes of Austria, recog-
nized and confirmed by a fundamental law of the Diet of 1687,
and afterward accorded to females by the acceptance of the
Pragmatic Sanction of the Emperor Charles the Sixth by the
Diet of 1723.

5th. The diploma of inauguration and the oath which the
king takes at his coronation, and by which he engages to maintain and protect the privileges of the kingdom.   This oath is
each time inserted in the Hungarian Code (corpus juris) as a
constitutional law.

The King of Hungary is clothed with complete regal authority ; he alone exercises the *executive* power to its full extent ;
but as to the legislative power, this he exercises conjointly
with the Diet of the kingdom, legitimately convoked.

The person of the king is sacred.   By him are all civil appointments made ; he is the temporal head of the Church —
appoints to all ecclesiastical dignities, and receives the proceeds
of all vacant benefices ; he is the head of the army—the arbiter of peace ; and with him rests the power to summon and
dissolve the Diet.   The Constitution requires that, within six
months after his accession, the sovereign shall call together the
states of the realm, and take the oath of fealty to the Constitution, and that he shall be invested with all the insignia of
royalty.*

---

* CEREMONY OF CORONATION.—The king, in Hungarian costume, preceded by
the banners of the kingdom and the barons who carry the attributes of royalty,
enters the church, and, kneeling before the altar, swears to " preserve the churches, lordly prelates, barons, magnates, nobles, free cities, and all inhabitants, in their
immunities and liberties, rights, laws. privileges, and in all former good and approved customs, and to do justice to all ;" and, further, " to observe the decrees
of the most serene King Andreas" (with the exception of the thirty-first article).
After which, he is anointed with the holy oil—clothed in the garments of St. Stephen—the grand mass commences, and, at the end, the Primate of Hungary presents to the king the naked sword of St. Stephen, and the archbishop and palatine
place the crown upon his head, and he is proclaimed king, amid the eljens of the
people and the salvos of artillery.   The ceremony in the cathedral over, the king,
with the lords, magnates, and bishops, the cortège all on horseback, and with still

The next officer to the king in point of rank is the Palatine, or lord lieutenant of the kingdom, who discharges the functions of viceroy of Hungary Proper during the absence of the monarch. While the sovereign is in the country, the Palatine acts as a kind of mediator for the whole nation between king and people, with the view of preventing, on the one hand, an encroachment upon the popular liberties, and on the other an invasion of the royal prerogatives. The Palatine is elected for life, from a list of four persons presented by the king. Till the Reform Act of 1848, the administration of the kingdom was conducted through the Hungarian Court of Chancery, at Vienna.

The Diet of Hungary is divided into two Chambers, or Tables, as they are termed—the Lords and the Commons, or the Senate and Representatives of the kingdom. The first Table is that of the magnates, and may be said to be composed of three classes : first, the higher clergy ; second, the barons and counts of the kingdom (magnates by office, and named by the crown) ; and, thirdly, the magnates by birth and title.

This House is hereditary, and the members number from six to seven hundred. Only thirty or forty, in ordinary times, are usually present. The Palatine presides over this Assembly, as well as over the highest court of justice, the Septemviral Table. The second Table consists of the deputies from the comitats, that is, the representatives of the untitled gentry, and from the enfranchised cities and towns. There is a third, and very singular element, viz., the elected representatives of those nobles who do not personally attend in the Upper House, and are called *Ablegati Absentium.* The total number of deputies does not exceed two hundred and fifty. The representatives are paid by their constituents. The speaker (whose

---

more pomp, proceed to the *Königsberg* (or King's Mount), a circular mound which stands on the banks of the Danube, at Pressburg, and made expressly for this ceremony. Arrived at the base of the mound, with uplifted hand he again repeats the pledges exacted of him in the cathedral; and while his nobles, and knights, and clergy, with their picturesque costumes, their costly arms and housings, gather in a mass round its base, the king gallops to the top of the hill, and cutting the air with the sword of St. Stephen, toward the four cardinal points, thereby indicates that he will defend his crown and kingdom against all enemies who may dare to attack it, come from whatever quarter they may.

official title is *Personalis presentiæ Regiæ in judiciis locum tenens*) is presiding officer of this House.

Formerly the two Chambers sat together, and were not entirely separated until the Diet held in 1562, under Ferdinand the first, the first monarch of the line of Habsburg.

The legislative duties of these two bodies are, according to Fessler, "to maintain thè old Magyar Constitution; to support it by constitutional laws; and to assert and secure the rights, liberties, and ancient customs of the nation; to frame laws for particular cases; to grant the supplies, and to ordain the manner and form of their collection; to provide means for securing the independence of the kingdom, its safety from foreign influence, and deliverance from all enemies; to examine and encourage public undertakings and establishments of general utility; to superintend the Mint, and to confer on foreigners the privileges of nobility, the permission to colonize the country, and enjoy the rights of Hungarians."* But the election of a new sovereign, in the event of the extinction of a dynasty, or of the confirmation of a successor in the case of an ordinary demise, the election of Palatine of Hungary, the imposition of taxes, and the power of confirming or rejecting new laws proposed by the executive power, are certainly functions neither less important or less clearly within the scope of their duties and authority.

To return from this requisite digression to the narrative of the leading events in Hungarian history. On the death of Andreas the Third in 1301, the male line of Arpad became extinct; and from that period to the middle of the sixteenth century, the time of its connectĭon with Austria, Hungary, of her own free choice, elected and called to the throne five different dynasties.

1st. Charles Martel, of the Neapolitan branch of the house of Anjou—a family which, through the female line, claimed descent from Arpad.

2d. Wladislaw, King of Poland, was called to the throne through the influence of John Hunniades, surnamed Corvinus, a Wallachian by birth—a chivalrous soldier, who, from the essential service rendered the country in defense of the front-

---

* Padgette's Hungary.

iers against the Turks, had acquired high reputation and great influence in the nation.

3d. Upon the death of Wladislaw, in the fatal battle of Warnau (1444), Hunniades was elected captain general, and ruled the country for ten years successfully, when, upon his death, in 1456, the Diet made choice of his son Mathias Corvinus as their king.

4th. Upon the death of Mathias in 1490, after one of the most successful and brilliant reigns in Hungarian annals, Ladislas, King of Bohemia, was, by the votes of the Diet, elevated to the throne. Ladislas was succeeded by his son Louis, a youth who fell in the battle of Mohacs in 1526, when Solyman defeated, and drove the flower of Magyar chivalry into the fatal swamp of Czetze, and the throne of Hungary became for the fifth time unoccupied. Two rival candidates now presented themselves—Count Zapolya, a powerful magnate, and Ferdinand of Austria, brother of the Emperor Charles the Fifth, who had married Anna, daughter of Ladislas and sister of Louis, the deceased monarch. Both candidates were, by different Diets, elected to the throne. A civil war ensued, in which Ferdinand was victor; and, though he had been elected by the Diet at Pressburg as early as 1526, and had at Stuhlweisenburg gone through the ceremony of coronation, it was not until 1547 that he was fully acknowledged and confirmed in possession of the throne, which has ever since been occupied by his descendants, the emperors of Germany or Austria, and kings of Hungary.

Thus originated the connection between Hungary and Austria—a connection not arising from conquest or purchase, nor, at first, considered complete or permanent, but partial and temporary, simply arising from the fact of two independent kingdoms owing allegiance to the same sovereign. Hungary, being an elective monarchy, made choice of a sovereign from the house of Austria; and the great inducement, at that time, to such an arrangement was the continued and terrible invasions of the Turks. Hungary was then the bulwark of Christendom against the encroachments of the infidel hordes. The interest which Austria, from her proximity, felt in that struggle, and the support which Ferdinand might be expected to obtain from his brother, the emperor of Germany, were, in the minds of the Hungarian Diet, strong reasons for his promotion. The union of Hungary and Austria has erroneously been compared to that of Ireland and Great Britain; but a superficial examination is only necessary to expose the fallacy of such a parallel; the resemblance to the union of Great Britain and Hanover is the more striking, where one sovereign holds two kingdoms, both *de jure and de facto*, independent of each other; and where the crowns, after being united for four generations, were separated in the fifth, as one was settled on heirs male *or* female, the other on heirs *male alone*. In both instances the connection was one of association, and not of subjection.

What were the terms of that union? and was the independence of Hungary *de jure*, thereby impaired? The union being one only through the sovereign, the terms must be gathered from some act which may have occurred, or some document which may have been executed between the sovereign and nation on this subject. What are those acts or documents? The first act between the parties was the election of the sovereign by the Diet; second, the signing and publishing by the sovereign of the Diploma of Inauguration; third, the formal act of coronation by the nation; fourth, the solemn oath taken by the sovereign to maintain and protect the privileges of the nation.

These acts, constituting the compact between the parties, are worthy of a little more consideration.

The Act of Election by the Diet was a free and voluntary one. Ferdinand, indeed, did lay claim to the crown, under a double title—the one derived from family compacts, which secured the reversion, as was pretended, to the house of Austria; the other in right of his wife Anne, the only sister of the deceased monarch. But the Hungarians were too much attached to their rights of election to respect these compacts, or even to acknowledge his claims as husband of the princess; and Ferdinand, prudently waiving his claims, offered himself as a candidate, according to the usual mode of election.

The Diploma of Inauguration.—The day before the coronation, the king, seated upon the throne, presents, through the High Chancellor of Hungary, to the members of the Diet assembled in his presence, the Diploma of Inauguration, written upon parchment, and furnished with the royal seal. As the coronation could only take place at the conclusion of a Diet, this diploma is always inserted in the Book of Decrees of the Diet before its close. The new king then swears in the diploma to the following articles :*

1. To preserve and maintain scrupulously the liberties, privileges, rights, laws, and usages of the kingdom (except the clause of the decree of Andrew the Second).

2. Not to carry out of the kingdom the Hungarian crown, but to confide it to two secular guardians, taken indifferently from Catholics and Protestants.

3. To reunite to the crown of Hungary all the countries which they formerly possessed, after the same shall have been reconquered. Afterward the following two were added :

4. To render back to the Diet of the kingdom the right of election, after the extinction of the line of descendants of Charles the Sixth, of Joseph the First, and of Leopold the First.

5. Each one of his successors shall be bound, in virtue of the third article of the law of 1791, to sanction this conservative act of the Diet at his coronation, in the space of six months after his accession, and to confirm it by an oath.†

The *formal act of coronation* and the *solemn oath* of the monarch are but public ratifications of the covenant between the sovereign and people, as formed by the act of election and the signing of the Diploma of Inauguration.

Ferdinand the Fifth, the late monarch, took but the same oath‡ which had been administered to his predecessors, and the forms and ceremonies were the same as had been adopted on every previous occasion, when Martel of Naples, Wladislaw of Poland, Mathias Corvinus of Hungary, and Ladislas of Bohemia, were successively called to the throne. The covenant or contract was identical, and the union or connection with Austria was, therefore, the same as that formed with Naples, Poland, or with Bohemia, when Martel, Wladislaw, and La-

---

* Such was that of Maria Theresa, Leopold the Second, and Francis the Second.—*Demain's Tableau de la Hongrie.* † Demain, 257.

‡ For copy of Oath, see Appendix, note No. 12.

dislas were at different times elevated to the same dignity, and by which it will not be pretended that the independence of Hungary, *de facto* or *de jure*, was in any degree impaired.

From the accession of Ferdinand the First, until the Hungarian throne was made hereditary in the house of Habsburg, in 1687, seven princes had ruled over the country in the following succession : Ferdinand the First, 1526, virtually (or, by formal recognition, in 1547) to 1564 ; Maximilian, 1564 to 1572 ; Rhodolph, 1572 to 1607 ; all in succession of primogeniture. Mathias the Second, his brother, 1607 to 1618, when he relinquished the crown in favor of his cousin-German, Ferdinand the Second, 1618 to 1625 ; Ferdinand the Third, his son, 1625 to 1655 ; Leopold, from 1655 to 1687. During this period the situation of Hungary, in regard to its independence, underwent no change ; the throne, although practically confined to the house of Habsburg, was elective by the Diet of the kingdom, and the succession of that house had been secured by the practice of the emperor-kings, in the exertion of their influence and power in procuring the election and coronation of their heirs during their own terms of office.

The policy of Leopold was most despotic ; his aim was to subvert the national institutions of Hungary, and bring the country entirely under imperial sway. Mutual jealousies reigned between the sovereign and the nobles : they suspected Leopold of an intention to subvert their liberties, and he attributed to a party of the most violent kind a design to assassinate him. In the midst of these contentions, a secret conspiracy was actually formed by the intrigues of the Palatine Wesseleni, under the sanction of that clause in the Coronation Oath which authorized the nobles to associate in defense of their privileges.* The Ban of Croatia, the Governor of Styria, and many of the most powerful and talented magnates, were parties to the movement.

The conduct of the imperial court greatly increased the strength of this faction ; for Leopold not only declined assembling a Diet, and filling the office of Palatine, but connived at the excesses of his troops, and encouraged the Catholics to persecute the Protestants. Discontents spread rapidly through the

---

* Coxe's House of Austria.

kingdom. The chiefs of the confederacy formed connections with the Prince of Transylvania, by his intervention secretly appealed to the Porte, and in 1670 assembled a Diet at Kaschau, in virtue of the law which allowed the nation to elect a Palatine if the office remained vacant for three years. This meeting enabling them to consolidate their union, they made arrangements for raising a military force, and thirteen of the counties entered into a formal association.

Meanwhile, Leopold, apprised of the progress of the conspiracy, acted with a vigor and promptitude which confounded the insurgents. Troops were dispatched into Upper Hungary against Rakoczy, and into Croatia and Styria, against the other chiefs. The leaders were all secured, either by artifice or force, and, being found guilty of rebellion, were publicly executed; the sons of the Ban of Croatia were sentenced to perpetual imprisonment; and, as a means of rooting out their family's influence, the children of the delinquents were compelled to change their names.

The emperor, emboldened by his success, immediately commenced a movement having for its object to change the Constitution of Hungary, and to render the monarchy hereditary, like that of Bohemia. He published the acts of the process, declared that the whole nation, by participating in the conspiracy, had forfeited its freedom, and summoned a Diet at Pressburg. As the majority of the nobles, instead of obeying the summons, fled into Transylvania, he issued a proclamation on the 21st of March, in which, although owing his powers as a monarch to the *election of the people*, he undertakes " to enjoin all persons to submit, without excuse or delay, to that *power which he had received from above*, and was determined to maintain by force of arms." Afterward, when Sobieski, the King of Poland, with his brave troops, had saved his capital, from which he had ignominiously fled, and had driven the Turkish hordes under Kara Mustapha from the walls of Vienna; and when new victories followed the imperial arms under the direction of the Duke of Loraine, the Margrave of Baden, the Duke of Bavaria, and Prince Eugène, he availed himself of these successes to prosecute his long-meditated design of rendering the crown hereditary.

Taking advantage of the disaffection which still subsisted among those who had submitted to his authority, he established, for the trial of pretended conspirators, a horrible tribunal at Eperies, whose cruelties scarcely find a parallel in the proscriptions of Marius or Sylla, or the massacres of the cold-blooded Tiberius. In vain the accused persisted in their innocence—in vain those who had taken up arms appealed to the general amnesty; thirty executioners, with their assistants, found constant employment, and a scaffold erected in the midst of the town, as the place of execution, is commemorated in history by the expressive appellation of *the Bloody Court of Eperies.** As Joseph the Second, a century after, in regard to Belgium, so now thought Leopold, " it was necessary to quench the flames of insurrection with blood." When these long-continued and unexampled cruelties had completely broken the spirit of the nation, Leopold, in the full license of despotism, with a stroke of his pen repealed the electoral formalities of seven centuries, and abrogated a right which the Hungarians had ever regarded as the palladium of their liberties. Yet, notwithstanding the wretched condition to which Hungary was reduced—by these despotic cruelties, these foreign invasions and internal wars—the people adhered, with singular pertinacity, to the cherished privilege of electing their own monarch; and though every subterfuge employed, and every expedient offered, were unavailing to save the right, so far as regarded the male line, yet no threats, bribes, or concessions of the monarch could extort their consent to render the succession hereditary in the female line.

The Diet, thus forced, agreed to the coronation of Joseph as an hereditary sovereign, and confirmed the succession in the males, both of the German and Spanish branches; but still reserved to the nation the right of election on the extinction of the male line.

Although the Hungarians had thus temporarily parted with a most important right, viz., that of the election of their monarch during the existence of male heirs in the house of Habs-

---

* The executions which took place at Eperies are said to have been more few in number, and less atrocious, than those which occurred recently in Hungary, upon the instigation of Haynau.

burg, yet the independence of the kingdom, either in the estimation of the monarch or his subjects, was not thereby affected, as the subsequent history of the reign of Joseph will prove.

The popular struggle against the encroachments of the crown still continued, in the beginning of the next century, with the same zeal of purpose but uncertainty of success which had previously characterized the military efforts of the insurgents. Under the leadership of Rakoczy, they baffled all the efforts of the imperial court to subdue them. At length, the emperor-king, desirous of drawing his troops from Hungary, in order to employ them against France and Spain, opened a new negotiation with the insurgents. A mediation of Great Britain and the States-General of Holland, respectively represented by Lord Sutherland and the Honorable George Stepney, and Count Rechteren, ensued at Tyrnau.* The national independence of Hungary was admitted as the basis of that interference, and, in the terms of the treaty of peace, the insurgents are recognized as the " Federal States of the Hungarian Empire."

Thus in 1705, after the kingdom had been made hereditary .in the male line of the Habsburg dynasty, the national independence of Hungary was admitted by the very monarch in whose lifetime and for whose benefit that step had been taken.

But these negotiations were unavailing. The overtures of Joseph for peace were rejected, and, at a grand council of the patriot Hungarians, it was resolved that they should on no pretense lay down their arms until they had first obtained their demands. They likewise declared " that the Protestant religion should be maintained in the country ; that the proceedings of the Diet held at Pressburg in 1687 were illegal, and contrary to the written law of Hungary ; that they must be annulled, and the ancient liberty to choose their king, whenever a vacancy occurred, restored to the people ; that, without express permission of the Diet, no troops should garrison the country but those of Hungary ; and that all offices of trust should be filled by Hungarians, unless the Diet specially declared that signal service to the state entitled foreigners to reward."†

The war still continued, and the patriots increased in num-

---

* Coxe's House of Austria.   † The same concessions asked for in 1848.

bers, as well as in the earnestness of their demands. But by
the success of Prince Eugène over the Turks, at Zenta, in 1697,
and which was followed by the peace of Carlowitz in 1699,
the emperor was enabled to direct his entire forces against the
Hungarians, and which, by the end of 1710, accomplished their
entire overthrow. Joseph died in 1711, and, during the interregnum of six months, the dowager Empress Eleonora Mag-
dalen administered power in all the hereditary states. By the
treaty of Szathmar (1711), a general pacification took place in
Hungary.

Charles the Third (Charles the Sixth of Germany) succeeded his brother. According to the family compact formed by
Leopold, and confirmed by Joseph and Charles, the succession
was entailed on the daughters of Joseph, in preference to those
of Charles, should they both die without male issue. Charles,
however, had scarcely ascended the throne, though at that time
without children, than he revised this compact, and settled the
right of succession, in default of male issue, first on his own
daughters, then on the daughters of Joseph, and afterward on
the Queen of Portugal and other daughters of Leopold. Since
the promulgation of that decree, the empress had borne a son,
who died in his infancy, and three daughters, Maria Theresa,
Maria Anne, and Maria Amelia. With a view to insure the
succession of these daughters, and to exclude those of his
brother Joseph, he published the Pragmatic Sanction, and compelled his nieces to renounce their pretensions on their mar-
riages with the Electors of Saxony and Bavaria. Aware, however, that the strongest renunciations are disregarded, he obtained from the different states of his extensive dominions the
acknowledgment of the Pragmatic Sanction, and made it the
great object of his reign, to which he sacrificed every other
consideration, to procure the guarantee of the European powers.* By the powerful influence of the monarch, and the liberal distribution of court favors, the Diet of Hungary of 1723†
ratified the Pragmatic Sanction, and accepted the terms of succession therein stipulated. This further concession of their

---

* Coxe's House of Austria.
† From this period, the affairs of Hungary were conducted by a "Hungarian
Board of Chancery," established in Vienna.

rights on the part of the Diet, while it did not weaken the independence of the kingdom, brought to the throne the famous Maria Theresa in 1740. This princess, by her voluntary recognition of the ancient laws and liberties of Hungary, and by her personal qualities and misfortunes, won the hearts of the chivalrous Magyars. The fact that, in the hour of her need, with her infant in her arms, she entered the Hungarian Parliament and implored their aid, and that every sword leaped from its scabbard and every tongue exclaimed, *" Moriamur pro regio nostro Maria Theresia !"* constitutes indeed one of the noble incidents of history.

An attempt has been made, with reference to recent events, to found on the Pragmatic Sanction pretensions that might derogate from the absolute independence of Hungary; but a reference to the document will defeat any such undertaking. The Pragmatic Sanction* does not affect the ancient Constitution of Hungary; it created no new union between Austria and Hungary; it altered not the political relations of the two countries; but only provided that Hungary should accept the terms of succession therein stipulated. The first article guarantees to the Hungarians the preservation of all "documentary and other rights, liberties, privileges, immunities, customs, prerogatives, and laws already conceded and established, or to be established by the present and future Diets." The latter part of the same article contains only a single word of doubt; but upon this the apologists of the Habsburg house, availing themselves of the obscure and defective Latin of the day, attempt to found a surrender, on the part of Hungary, of her entire independence. In it the female succession of the house of Habsburg is established, " according to the form accepted in the other kingdoms and hereditary provinces of his sacred majesty, both in and out of Germany, as had been ordered, established, published, and accepted *inseparably.*" Upon the Latin word *inseparabiliter* the cavilers would build up a *national* union between Austria and Hungary; but by the most obvious construction, that term has reference only to the succession of the Habsburg house—is consequently but a *personal* union; and the conclusion of the article, in explanation of the

---

* For Pragmatic Sanction, see Appendix, note No. 13.

II.   B

phrase, fully confirms the construction, when it says, " so that (*ita ut*) the heirs of the kingdoms and provinces of the Austrian house, male or female, may be known, and crowned *also* as infallible King of Hungary," &c.

Great stress is also laid upon the last two words, *indivisibiliter* and *inseparabiliter*, in the second article, where the meaning is equally clear and free from doubt.

After defining how the succession to the throne is to be governed after failure of the heirs of Charles, and that it shall descend to the female heirs, first of his brother Joseph, and then those of his father Leopold, it asserts that " the kingdoms and hereditary provinces, in and out of Germany, are to be possessed indivisibly and inseparably, jointly, mutually, and at once, with the kingdom of Hungary." The incorporation of the two kingdoms was expressly guarded against by the words of the text, which distinctly state that they shall be ruled *in vicem, in simul et una ;* therefore, the internal independence and the constitutional rights of the Hungarians were fully recognized, even had there been no enactments to that effect.

That the connection " indivisible and inseparable," here alluded to, is limited to the subsistence of the entail of Charles the Sixth, is not only evident from what precedes, but is placed beyond the power of cavil or controversy by the conclusion, which asserts that, " upon the failure of the heirs of the said line, there shall revive and come into operation the ancient and approved custom and prerogative of the Diet in the election and coronation of a king."

Nothing can be more futile than an attempt to destroy the independence of Hungary by the production of a document which sets out with a full admission of all the rights, privileges, and immunities of the kingdom, and concludes with an acknowledgment that, upon the extinction of the present dynasty, the union with Austria is at an end, and Hungary must resort to the exercise of her ancient and cherished prerogative of electing and crowning her own monarch.

The son and successor of Maria Theresa made many attempts to amalgamate or incorporate Hungary with Austria, under that system of centralization or bureaucratic rule which has ever been the policy of the imperial court; but the nation boldly and successfully resisted them. Although Joseph had acknowledged the rights and privileges of the Hungarian states by his circular letter on the death of his mother, yet it is a historical truth that he declined the ceremony of coronation from an unwillingness to confirm those rights and privileges by a solemn oath.

That it was the opinion of Joseph that Hungary was a free and independent country, no better evidence could be desired than his efforts for its amalgamation with Austria, and his refusal to take the oath of coronation, which would pledge him to sustain that independence, and thus conflict with the most cherished object of his reign. Although the reign of Joseph the Second was short, it was sufficiently long to enable him to correct many of the errors into which imprudent zeal had betrayed him; but it was, unfortunately, only in his last days that he listened with complacency to the demands of the Hungarians—restored their Constitution, as it existed at his accession—promised speedily to solemnize the ceremony of his coronation, and, as an earnest of his intention, sent back the crown of St. Stephen, which by his wanton order had been forcibly removed from Pressburg to Vienna.

The efforts of Joseph to subvert the institutions of the country produced an excitement in Hungary, which even the death of that monarch was powerless to quell. Some of the public gazettes declared the hereditary rights of the Habsburg dynasty forfeited by their unconstitutional course. The comitats of Pesth, Zemplén, and Szabolcz called to arms, and the people every where raised the cry recently made, "We want no Austrian king!"

Joseph was followed by his brother, Leopold the Second, and the condition of affairs at the period when he came forward was such as obliged the Diet to exact of him securities against a renewal of the arbitrary proceedings to which Joseph had resorted.

For this purpose, certain articles were prepared by the Diet of 1790, in the nature of declaratory acts, implying no new concessions, but merely reasserting what the Hungarian Constitution had provided long before the first Habsburg ascended the throne, and which Leopold did not hesitate to recognize and confirm. Of these articles the following are the most important:

Article 10th. " That Hungary is a free and independent nation in her entire system of legislation and government; that she was not subject to any other people or any other state; but that she shall have her own separate existence and her own Constitution, and should, consequently, be governed by kings crowned according to her national laws and customs."

Article 12th. " That the power to enact, to interpret, and to abrogate the laws, was vested conjointly in the king, legitimately crowned, and the Diet, and that all the royal patents not issued in conjunction with the Diet are and shall be illegal, null, and void."

All these acts received the formal assent of Leopold the Second, and thus became statutes of the kingdom.

Language can not express more fully, or render more clear than it has done in Article 10th, the rights of Hungary and the nature of its connection with Austria. Comment upon it is superfluous, and misinterpretation impossible.

That clause may, indeed, be regarded as the palladium of her rights; so long as it remains a part of the Constitution of the land, the liberties of Hungary are safe; when it falls, her liberties are gone.

It seems, too, designed to meet the very crisis which has occurred.

In the first part of the clause the Hungarians designed to protect their independence from all encroachments of Austria, by forcing the monarch to acknowledge that "Hungary is a *free and independent* nation in her entire system of legislation and government ;" and, as if that language was not sufficiently strong to guard against the encroachments of the imperial government, the same idea is repeated in still more forcible terms, viz., that she was "*not subject to any other people or any other state.*" In other words, deeming the positive affirmation of her rights of independence insufficient to guard against the efforts of an usurping nation, they endeavor to add to her defense by a direct and palpable denial of all right of control over her on the part of others. The latter part of the clause carries out the same idea, and explains how it is to be accomplished, while it clearly defines the nature of the connection of the two countries, resting upon the identity of a common sovereign. " But that she shall have her own separate existence and her own Constitution, and should, consequently, be governed by kings crowned according to her national laws and customs ;" or, as may be more briefly expressed, in consequence of her separate existence, a coronation "according to the national laws and customs" was an indispensable prerequisite to government. A monarch might be king *de facto* by succession, but *de jure* he was not recognized as sovereign till he had fulfilled the conditions of the Constitution, and been crowned according to her national laws and customs.

But one sovereign before the present one has ever refused to enter into the coronation compact, and to be crowned according to the national laws and customs. This was Joseph the Second, and as he died without the observance of this ceremony, he has never been acknowledged by Hungary ; his name is not recorded on the list of her sovereigns, and all his acts considered illegal, null, and void.

Nor was there any thing unusual or unreasonable in such a requirement ; the only safeguard for the liberties and independence of Hungary rested upon her Constitution, and the only precaution which she could adopt for the safety of that Constitution rested upon the monarch's coronation oath to preserve it.

Had the union established by the Pragmatic Sanction been a *national* and permanent one, as contended for by the house of Habsburg, would Leopold the Second, eighty years after, have so fully acknowledged and proclaimed its independence ?

When Francis the Second, son of Leopold, succeeded him to the throne in 1792, there was no question as to the independence of Hungary, which had been so fully and so recently recognized by his father.

The prescribed oath was administered to him at his coronation, which was conducted in the usual manner ; and in his reply to the address of the Diet, he showed no disposition to invade the constitutional rights of the Hungarians, but declared, "I shall be the guardian of the Constitution. My will shall be no other than that of the law, and my efforts shall have no other guides than honor, good faith, and unalterable confidence in the magnanimous Hungarian nation."

For the first twenty years of his reign, involved in the wars of Napoleon, he assembled the Diet regularly; but one of its members at length had the boldness to proclaim that his only object in calling them together, was to ask for money and men, which, in their romantic generosity, they never failed to grant, although all the demands of the nation were, during that period, totally disregarded.*   At length, when, in 1815, peace was restored to Europe, and the Holy Alliance formed, the Austrian cabinet, which had always flattered the hopes of Hungary when it needed her assistance, now boldly resolved to govern the kingdom without the aid of a Diet.   In vain did the county Assemblies call for a convocation of the National Parliament, which the king was bound, by the laws which he had sworn to support, to summon every three years.   Their addresses were not even honored with an answer.

In 1822, an attempt was made to levy imposts and raise troops by royal edicts. The Comitats (county Assemblies) refused to enforce them.   In 1823, bodies of troops were sent to overawe, and then to coerce them.   The county officers concealed their archives and official seals, and dispersed.   Royal commissioners were appointed to perform their functions, and were almost every where resisted.   The whole administration of the country, civil and judicial, was in confusion; and after a severe contest, the cabinet found it necessary, in 1825, to yield, and to summon a Diet after an interval of twelve years. The attempt of Francis to subvert the Constitution of Hungary terminated, as the similar attempt of Joseph the Second thirty-five years before, in renewed acknowledgments of the independence of Hungary and the constitutional rights of the Hungarians.†

Ferdinand the Fifth, the last king of Hungary, succeeded

---

* The Diets were convoked to grant supplies, and to be dismissed as soon as they spoke of grievances.

† The well-known Article 3d, of 1827, was sanctioned by Francis.   In it the king reiterates his promise "*to uphold the Constitution in accordance with his coronation oath, especially in regard to Articles 10, &c., of* 1790."

his father Francis to the throne in 1835. He not only took the same oath, acknowledging the rights, liberties, and independence of Hungary, administered to all his predecessors, but he made a more decisive step than any of his long line of ancestry toward the establishment in Hungary of a national and independent government.

On the 15th of March, 1848, a few days after the outbreak of the first Revolution in Vienna, and when the monarch conceded to the people of his hereditary states the rights and privileges which they demanded, a deputation from the Diet of Hungary appeared before the throne, asking for their kingdom liberty of the press, a responsible ministry, an annual Diet, equality of rights and duties, &c.; and these were not only granted without hesitation, but on the 11th of April Ferdinand appeared in person before the Diet at Pressburg, and there solemnly confirmed all the statutes passed by that body for carrying their wishes into effect, and their separate and independent existence into immediate practical operation.

From this hasty sketch of the political history of Hungary, it will be observed that the throne was elective from its first establishment, under Stephen, in the year 1000, to the year 1687; when, through the coercion of the Diet by Leopold the First, it became hereditary, upon certain conditions, in the male line of the house of Austria. That it remained unchanged in the *male* line until 1723, when, upon failure of the heirs of Charles the Third, through his influence with the Diet he procured their assent to the Pragmatic Sanction, which transferred the succession to the *female* line.*

That this alteration in the disposition of the throne created no change in the character of the monarchy, the Constitution and laws remaining the same, and the coronation treaty between the monarch and people being identical under the hereditary as it had been under the elective monarchy.

It results, therefore, that Hungary is not a province of Austria, but a free and independent nation, possessed of its own

---

* These conditions, originally laid down, and repeatedly confirmed by solemn compacts by that family on the one part, and the Hungarian nation on the other have not been adhered to by the house of Habsburg, and the legitimate deduction is, that it has forfeited all claims to the throne of Hungary.

separate and distinct Constitution and laws, and exercising
alone, in case of vacancy, the power to dispose of the throne
of the kingdom ; that the only connection *de jure* between the
two governments consists in the temporary union of the two
crowns in the same person ; that the said connection would be
at an end to-morrow should the house of Habsburg become
extinct, and might at any time be dissolved by a violation of
the compact on which that connection is founded.

This historical view of the rights of the two governments,
although perhaps uninteresting to many, seemed indispensable
to a proper appreciation of the struggle which follows, and will
enable the reader to determine whether the parties confined
themselves within the strict lines of authority and duty, or
whether they have willfully transcended them ; whether Hungary, in the assertion of her independence, was engaged in the
commission of a revolutionary or of a conservative act ; and
whether Austria, in invoking foreign aid to crush her own
subjects, acted in self-defense, or with the most uncalled for
and unauthorized tyranny.

After a struggle of about three centuries, the cabinet of Vienna, of late years, seemed to have abandoned, by overt acts,
the projects of incorporating Hungary with Austria. Discouraged by the warm resistance of the Hungarians, she no longer
attempted to enforce illegal edicts, but depended on effecting
surreptitiously that which could not be done openly and by
force. Through the exercise of the royal prerogative in appointing lords and high officers of the realm, the cabinet could
command a majority in the House of Magnates ; while, by endeavoring to influence the elections, it hoped to secure an ascendency in the House of Deputies. For many years, also, the
affairs of Hungary, instead of being regulated in the kingdom
and by native Hungarians, were managed by a bureau or chancery in Vienna, under the direct supervision and control of the
Austrian cabinet.

These attempts on the part of the imperial government to
impose upon Hungary the patriarchal system of Austria, was
not long in producing two parties in the country ; of which
one, from supporting the views of the court, was considered
Austrian ; the other, from its desire to sustain the separate

nationality of Hungary, was considered Hungarian, and took the designation of the Liberal or Patriotic party.

The Diet had been summoned for November, 1847; and, in June of that year, the Liberal party put forth an exposition of its views preparatory to the elections, which in Hungary are renewed for every triennial meeting of the Diet. In that document they declare: "Our grievances, so often set forth through a long course of years, during which we have urged and endured, have to this day remained unredressed." After enumerating some of these grievances, they proceed to state their demands.

1st. The equal distribution of the public burdens among all the citizens; that the Diet should decide on the employment of the public revenue, and that it should be accounted for by responsible administrators.

2d. Participation by the citizens not noble in legislation and in municipal rights.

3d. Civil equality.

4th. The abolition, by a compulsory law, of the labor and dues exacted from the peasants, with indemnity to the proprietors.

5th. Security to property and to credit, by the abolition of the *aviticity* (the rights of heirs to recover lands alienated by sale).

They go on to declare that, in carrying out these views, they will never forget the relations which, in the terms of the Pragmatic Sanction, exist between Hungary and the hereditary states of Austria; that they hold firmly to Article 10th of 1790, by which the royal word, sanctified by an oath, guarantees the independence of Hungary; that they do not desire to place the interests of the country in contradiction with the unity or security of the monarchy, but they regard as contrary to the laws and to justice that the interests of Hungary should be made subordinate to those of any other country; that they are ready, in justice and sincerity, to accommodate all questions upon which the interests of Austria and Hungary may be opposed, but they will never consent to let the interests and Constitution of Hungary be sacrificed to *unity of the system of government*, which certain persons are fond of citing as the leading maxim, instead of the *unity of the monarchy*.

The Diet was opened at Pressburg on the 11th of November, by the king in person,* who had come from Vienna for that purpose. On the 12th, a joint meeting, or, as they term it, a " mixed sitting" of both Houses was held. The magnates and delegates then repaired to the primatial palace to receive the royal propositions. On their return to their own Chamber, they proceeded, in conformity with the first proposition, to elect a Palatine, when the Archduke Stephen, son of the late Palatine, was determined on by general acclamation, the royal rescript containing the names of four candidates (two Catholics and two Protestants, as prescribed by law) remaining unopened.

The Archduke Stephen, it is true, was not only the choice of all the imperial family, but of most of the Hungarians themselves ; but their election of him without venturing even to open the communication of the emperor, to see whether *his* name was really inscribed there, or that of the other individu-

---

* On the morning of the 12th of November, all the Diet, consisting of the *magnates*, or Upper House, and the *deputies*, or Lower House, in their gaudy uniforms, plumed caps, and embossed swords, assembled in the great hall of the Primate's palace, around the very throne on which the empress queen, Maria Theresa, sat when she appealed with such success to the hearts of her romantic and enthusiastic Hungarians. The galleries (the balusters of which were covered with Turkey carpets) were filled with ladies, except two small spaces, the one occupied by the diplomatic corps of Vienna, and the other by the empress and her ladies of honor, the archdukes and duchesses. The dresses of the members of the Diet were exceedingly rich and tasteful, and consisted invariably of a close frock of some brilliant-colored cloth, highly embroidered, and with buttons composed of diamonds or some other precious stones ; pantaloons tight, boots outside, and reaching to the knee ; while over the shoulders hung a mantle of velvet, bound around both collar and skirt with fur. The cap was also of fur, and decorated with a plume—sometimes that of the costly black heron, sometimes a single feather from the wing of an eagle or a pheasant, and not unfrequently it consisted of a lofty sprig of jewels. The general shape or cut of the dresses was the same ; but as to the material, its color and its ornaments, these were regulated solely by the taste or fancy of the wearer. Many of these dresses were pointed out to the author as having cost upward of one hundred thousand florins—equal, in our currency, to fifty thousand dollars. But these were tame in comparison with that of Prince Esterhazy, who is also one of the magnates, and the value of whose dress is estimated at half a million of florins, or two hundred and fifty thousand dollars. The dress, or rather the most valuable part of it, the jewels, have descended to him from an ancestor, who made, it is said, in his will, the singular provision that his other heirs, to whom he also left property, should contribute to sustain the splendor of this dress—a tax by no means insignificant, since every time it is worn the depreciation in value. arising from the loss of jewels, amounts, as is said, to many thousands of dollars.

als proposed, exhibited a degree of fawning subserviency to the throne scarcely to be looked for in a people possessed of a Constitution and characterized by the warmest aspirations for liberty.

And what rendered this craven spirit still more apparent was, that several comitats had expressly instructed their deputies to insist on the opening of the emperor's message, for fear that a failure to do so would constitute a precedent by which they might, in time, be deprived of all voice in the choice of their chief magistrate; but when the moment for action arrived—for carrying out the instructions of their constituents, and for asserting their own constitutional rights, there was not a man of them, instructed delegates and all, who had the moral firmness to open his lips in opposition to a motion made to elect the Archduke Stephen by acclamation, and without breaking the seal of the royal communication.

On the 15th, another "mixed sitting" was held, when the newly-elected Palatine was duly installed, and made a suitable speech on the occasion. On the 16th, the royal propositions, eleven in number,* were read at a dietal† sitting of the delegates.

ADDRESS TO THE THRONE.

On November 22d, the debate on the address, in answer to the royal propositions, commenced in the Chamber of Delegates (circular sitting).

The address was composed of eighteen paragraphs. From one to six, inclusive, conveyed the customary expression of

---

* For royal propositions, see Appendix, note No. 14.

† The delegates hold *circular* sittings and *dietal* sittings. The former are presided over by two delegates (taken in rotation), and correspond, in a great measure, to what, in parliamentary language, is called a Committee of the Whole House. The resolutions passed at these circular sittings are not valid unless confirmed at a dietal sitting, which is presided over by the Chief Justice of the King's Bench (*Tabula Regia*), or the Personal (*Personalis presentiæ Regiæ locum tenens*), as he is called. The *circular* sittings have, however, of late, become by far the most important, the resolutions passed at them being generally confirmed at a dietal sitting without much discussion, by the majority crying out "*Maradjon!*" Let it remain! *i. e.*, as it was decided at the circular sittings. It is only at the dietal sittings that the delegates wear their sabres and appear in the Hungarian costume.—*Blue Book*. Blackwell. Correspondence with the British government.

thanks to the throne, and were passed unanimously by both Houses.

In paragraphs sixteen and seventeen, his majesty is requested to summon a Diet annually at Pesth. These paragraphs would also have been unanimously adopted, but the word *annually* precluded the magnates of the government party from assenting to the proposal, although many of them were fully convinced that the summoning of an annual Diet was a measure imperatively required, and which could not be much longer delayed.

The fourteenth section expressed, in answer to the seventh royal proposition, the willingness of the Diet to pass measures " for adjusting the conflicting interests of Hungary and Austria." A somewhat vague expression, inserted probably to meet the views of all parties.

The contemplated removal of the intermediate customs' line between the two countries was a measure calculated to encounter the most violent opposition. The Liberal party in Hungary have always regarded this line as one of the safeguards of Hungarian nationality ; and though its removal might have been advantageous to Hungary in a commercial point of view, the Liberals, regarding it only in a political sense, declared that, if it were possible, they would convert it into a wall of brass.

Paragraphs seven to thirteen relate to the *gravamina*, or so-called grievances of the nation. It was these paragraphs, especially the eleventh, which furnished the principal topic of discussion in the two Houses.

The great question of the day at this time in Hungary was, in fact, the nomination of administrators, alluded to in the eleventh paragraph, an expedient resorted to by Count Apponyi (the late chancellor) to increase the influence of the imperial government, by rendering the office of lord lieutenant of a county merely nominal, and appointing in the same administrators, to exercise all the functions of lords lieutenant.

The Conservative, or so-called Government party, desired to limit the address to the usual expression of thanks; the Opposition, or so-called Liberal or National party, contended that an allusion ought to be made to the *gravamina*, and especially to the recent nominations of administrators of counties, which they held to be an unconstitutional measure of the most dangerous tendency.

Kossuth, delegate of the county of Pesth, regarded as the leader of the Opposition in the Lower House, made a lengthy speech on the occasion, and concluded by reading the draft of an address embodying the sentiments of his party. He was answered by Count Stephen Széchényi, who sat in the Lower House as delegate of the county of Moson (Wieselburg), and professing, at least, not to belong to any party. The address which he proposed, after the usual expression of thanks, alluded in general terms to the *gravamina*, with the remark that the Diet would subsequently send up a representation respecting them. He agreed, however, with Kossuth, that, both on account of these *gravamina* and the numerous measures that required to be taken into consideration, his majesty should be requested to summon a Diet to meet *annually* in the city of Pesth.

On the 27th, after a six-days' debate, Kossuth's motion was carried, but only by a single vote (twenty-eight to twenty-seven); and on the 1st December this resolution was confirmed at a dietal sitting, and the address thus voted sent up to the magnates.* On the 4th of December, the address thus voted by the delegates was read in the Chamber of Magnates, and gave rise to a six-days' debate—all the amendments proposed by the Conservatives having been carried by considerable majorities.

On the 13th, the address was sent back to the delegates with a *renuncium*,† in which the magnates stated that they would prefer laying before the throne the simple expression of their thanks, without alluding to the *gravamina*, especially as these *gravamina* would have to be considered and submitted to his majesty during the course of the Diet. If, however, the delegates insisted on alluding to them, they (the magnates)

---

* For copy of address, see Appendix, note No. 15.

† The magnates do not make what is known in parliamentary language as amendments to a bill, but state, in a so-called *renuncium*, on what points they differed from the delegates, suggest the propriety of omitting certain clauses, and of modifying others, &c.—*Blackwell.*

were of opinion that it ought to be in general terms; that the nomination of administrators was a question in which they would not enter, but were of opinion that until it could be proved that such nomination was an unconstitutional measure, it could not be called a grievance, and ought not to be alluded to. They therefore suggested the propriety of omitting altogether the eighth, ninth, and eleventh paragraphs. They further stated that, although they fully agreed with the delegates on the expediency of holding the Diet in the city of Pesth, the general wish of the nation in this respect had been already laid before the throne in several dietal representations; and (without entering into the question of annual Diets) they were of opinion that it would be more appropriate to send up a special representation on the subject than to mention it in the address, and for these reasons must also suggest the propriety of omitting the sixteenth and seventeenth paragraphs.

On the 15th, 16th, and 17th, a very stormy debate took place in the circular sitting of the Chamber of Delegates on this renuncium, in which some of the Liberal delegates undertook to compare the administrators with the district captains of Galicia, and to stigmatize them as the " salaried tools of an arbitrary government, ready, when called upon, to do the same dirty work as their Galician colleagues."

The debate was brought to a conclusion by Kossuth, who declared that, as the two Houses differed on constitutional principles, it would be a mere waste of time to continue the further discussion of the address, or to send it back to the magnates. He therefore moved that it should be deposited or dropped (*i. e.*, that no further notice should be taken of it), adding, that they would have an opportunity of expressing their thanks to his majesty for opening the Diet in one of the dietal representations.

Kossuth's motion was carried by a majority of four, twenty-five counties voting for, and twenty-one against it—two or three counties having furnished their delegates with fresh instructions, either to vote for it or to insist upon the paragraph respecting administrators being retained. The address to the throne being thus disposed of, the other proceedings of the Diet, as they progressed, may be classified as follows:

1st. *Measures recommended to be taken into Consideration in the Royal Propositions.*

a. The alimentation of the troops stationed in Hungary (second royal proposition).

b. Co-ordination of the royal free towns (third and fourth royal propositions).

c. The laws relating to the mortgages of manorial estates (fifth royal proposition).

d. Urbarial laws (sixth royal proposition).

2d. *Measures not mentioned in the Royal Propositions.*

a. The late Palatine.

b. Croatian affairs.

c. General taxation.

d. Liberty of the press.

e. Magyarism, or measures relating to the Hungarian language and nationality.

f. Comitatal administration question.

Of these questions, the most important, as well as those having a direct influence on the approaching struggle, were:

The Urbarial Laws.

The expediency of amending the existing laws that define the mutual relations of manorial lords and their tenant peasantry, was discussed in the Chamber of Delegates, December 3d and 6th, and all parties seemed to agree that the *roboth*** should be abolished.   The Hungarians were fully aware of the rock on which the Poles had always struck—that, in all the efforts made by the Polish nobility for freedom, it never had occurred to them to secure the co-operation of their peasantry by relieving them from the abject servitude to which they were subjected, and the consequence was that, in every struggle which they made for freedom, the peasantry would be found on the side of the government, slaughtering the nobles to secure their own liberty.

In the early periods of Hungarian history, the peasantry

---

* *Roboth,* the labor devolving on peasants.

were involved in the most abject servitude. A decree of Sigismond the Second in 1405, allowing them free migration, was confirmed, and its provisions extended by a dietal act passed in 1458. This act was, however, annulled, in consequence of the sanguinary insurrection which took place under George Dozsa ; but free migration was again allowed by the acts of Ferdinand the First in 1547, and Maximilian the First, 1566. The condition of the peasantry was further ameliorated by the *urbarial* regulations introduced under the reign of Maria Theresa, regulations which in 1791 obtained the force of law, and which were further extended by the acts of 1836 and 1840.

Notwithstanding these laws, the condition of the Hungarian peasantry up to this period was any thing but enviable. He might truly be said to have possessed no rights, either civil or political ; for, though allowed free migration, as was boasted, he never possessed the means of removing, and was consequently, in the same manner as with the serf of Russia, as often bought and sold with the land as any horse or ox on the estate.

On him, too, fell all the burdens of the state. It is on their property that county rates are exclusively levied, and that too in the most arbitrary manner imaginable. Nobles, in general, pay no taxes, and, even when they do, they are easily indemnified by the exactions which they make upon their peasantry. If roads or bridges are to be made or repaired, it is the peasantry who are to do it, and yet they are the only persons of whom toll is ever demanded.

They are obliged to furnish all the military of the country, and their sons, as soon as they become of age, instead of remaining at home to labor for the support of their parents in their declining years, are hurried off to be enlisted in the army, either to be slain in battle or to waste away formerly fourteen now eight years of the most valuable portion of their lives, at a compensation of about four cents a day, out of which they are obliged to furnish their own meat, and every other necessary or luxury—clothing, quarters, and bread, with which they are supplied, alone excepted.

A peasant's *holding* or *session*, as it is called, varies in extent, according to the nature of the soil and local usage, but is fixed by the *urbarial* laws at a certain number of acres in each county, the minimum being about twenty-five, the maximum sixty-five acres. A peasant may hold a whole session, a half session, or a quarter session. For a whole session, he is compelled to labor one hundred and four days in the year for the lord of the manor, besides contributing to the lord one ninth of the produce of the session *in natura*, and to the Church one tenth annually. There are various other services to which the peasantry are subjected. All the nobles or government officers have the right of impressing the horses of the serfs to take them upon their journeys—a privilege called *Vorspan*, and one which during seed-time, or harvest, or whenever particularly occupied, must be a matter of most serious inconvenience to the peasant, to abandon his crop in order to transport some idle noble or government officer wherever his fancies or his duties may direct.

But this is not all. Until the year 1835, when the Constitution of Hungary underwent a change, each nobleman possessed almost unlimited power of punishment over his peasants, and into the manner in which he might be disposed to exercise that power no one ever took the slightest trouble to inquire. In fact, by an old law of Hungary, a noble was only subjected to a fine of forty florins (that is, twenty dollars) for the killing of a *serf;* and, although this odious enactment is now abolished, a prison, with its bolts and chains, is still considered a necessary appendage to every estate, and the rod as freely used, perhaps, as in the more barbarous days of the Middle Ages.

In the discussions of the *urbarial* question, the House of Delegates was unanimously of opinion that, as the acts of the Diets of 1836 and 1840 had not been effective, a compulsory law ought to be passed by the present Diet. Several delegates contended that the law ought to be compulsory for both parties; that the peasantry should be compelled either to redeem their *roboth* for perpetuity, or to commute it into an annual money rent, in the manner specified in the above-mentioned acts of the Diets of 1836 and 1840; and that the landlords should likewise be compelled to accept this redemption or commutation. It was, however, decided that the law should only

II. C

be compulsory for the landlords, they being entitled to a full compensation for the loss which, by the change of system, they would have to sustain. A resolution was also passed to appoint a committee to draw up a bill on the subject.

These resolutions were confirmed at a dietal sitting (on the 21st of December), and a *nuncium* sent to the magnates requesting them to agree to the appointment of a dietal committee, on the conditions that the contemplated measures should be framed in conformity with the resolutions passed by the delegates.

This *nuncium* came up before the Upper House in February, and the majority of the leading magnates, Liberals as well as Conservatives, expressed their disapprobation of the principle that the measures should be coercive upon the landlords.

It was contended that if the law was coercive, it ought unquestionably to be coercive for both parties; but, under existing circumstances, the most appropriate course to be pursued would be to extend the provisions of the act of 1840; that is to say, to afford greater facilities for the commutation of the *roboth*, by the mutual agreement of the parties concerned, only rendering the law coercive for both parties in some particular cases, which the committee would have to point out in their report. It was therefore moved that, in their *renuncium*, they should express the willingness of the magnates to agree to the appointment of a dietal committee on the above-mentioned conditions, the attention of the committee to be chiefly directed to the removal of the existing obstacles in the way of commutation by mutual agreement, and, above all, to the most expedient manner of raising the capital required for the commutation or redemption of the *roboth* in a way that would afford full compensation to the landlords without ruining the peasantry. This motion, supported by the leading members of both parties, was carried without division, and a *renuncium* drawn up in conformity with the motion was read and authenticated.

The following are the acts finally passed upon the subject, and sanctioned by the emperor:

ACT 9TH.

Abolishes the *roboth*, the tithe of one ninth of the produce to the landlord, and all other *urbarial* services whatsoever, from the day cn which the act is published (April 11th). *Manorial* courts are also abolished. The landlords are to receive an indemnification, rather vaguely expressed by a high-flown Magyar phrase, viz. : " The Legislature places the indemnification of the landed proprietors under the protecting shield of the national public honor."*

Acts 10th, 11th, and 12th.

Acts passed as supplementary to the preceding act, respecting certain *urbarial* rights enjoyed by the peasantry, such as that of cutting wood in the manorial forests, &c.; also respecting *urbarial* lawsuits, and suits brought before the manorial courts.

Act 13th.

Abolishes tithes to the clergy without compensation, or, according to the words made use of, simply records the fact of the clergy having voluntarily renounced taking tithes, without claiming compensation. The poorer clergy, whose incomes were principally derived from tithes, to be duly provided for.

Lay persons, who have acquired possession of tithes by contract, &c., to receive a compensation.

Next question of importance before the Diet, and having a bearing on the approaching struggle, was,

The Comitatal Administration Question.

There are in Hungary fifty-five counties, forty-nine (including the three reincorporated Transylvanian counties) in Hungary Proper, and six in the *partes adnexæ*, i. e., in Slavonia and Croatia; and that all the magistrates and officers of a Hungarian county are elected triennially by the noblest (free-

---

* Correspondence on Hungary.--*Blue Book.*

† The word "noble" has a very different signification in Hungary from that attached to it in other countries, and is, strictly speaking, applied to designate a man enjoying certain rights and privileges; among which, that of being exempt from taxation has hitherto been the most highly prized. The Hungarian nobles may, however, be classed as follows: 1st. The titled nobles—princes, counts, barons, or the nobility, as they would be called in other countries. 2d. The untitled

holders) of the county, at a general congregation, with the exception of the *comes supremas*, or lord lieutenant. In three counties this dignity is held *ex officio*; the Palatine, the Primate, and the Archbishop of Erlau being respectively the lords lieutenant *ex officio* of the counties of Pesth, Gran, and Heves. In seven other counties the dignity is hereditary. In the remaining forty-five counties the lords lieutenant are appointed by the crown.

The office of lord lieutenant is that of mediator between the county and the crown, in the same manner as the Palatine is the mediator between the crown and the nation. He therefore, like the Palatine, holds his office for life, and, according to the strict letter of the law, is only removable for crimes and misdemeanors proved against him before a competent tribunal. He has no salary from the government, but receives a remuneration, for official expenses, of six hundred dollars per annum from the county *cassa*. The lords lieutenant are generally noblemen of rank and fortune; the office may, however, be held by a noble (in contradistinction to nobleman), who then becomes a magnate *ex officio*, and has a seat and vote in the Upper House.

For the counties in which the dignity is held *ex officio*, it has been a long-established custom to appoint administrators, or deputy lords lieutenant, as they might be termed in English. For a county in which the dignity is hereditary, it has also been the custom to appoint an administrator whenever the lord lieutenant happened to be a minor, the functions of that administrator ceasing with the minority of the lord lieutenant.

The word "county" is rather an inappropriate term to designate a *comitat*, or one of the fifty-five districts into which Hungary is divided, these districts having a much greater analogy to the Swiss Cantons, or the states of the American

---

nobles, viz.: *a.* Those who possess estates, or who have studied law; a class from which county magistrates and the delegates are elected, and which are in England called the "landed gentry." *b.* The half-spurred nobles, as they are termed, or those who possess only a small piece of ground, or, to use the Hungarian expression, "a house and four plum-trees." These form the mass of the electors. *c.* Landless nobles, who are consequently deprived of the elective franchise, and may be found gaining their livelihood in all capacities. The Hussars of the nobility frequently belong to this class.—*Blackwell.*

Union, than they have either to the counties of England or the departments of France. They may, in fact, almost be regarded as the independent states of a confederation under the rule of an hereditary monarch, whose constitutional authority is circumscribed within the narrowest possible limits. With such a system, it is obvious that the only direct legitimate influence which the government can exercise in a county is through its lord lieutenant.

According to a dietal act passed in the beginning of the last century, a lord lieutenant ought habitually to reside in his county, to preside over the county congregations, and perform several other duties therein specified; but this act, like too many other Hungarian laws, has remained a dead letter, a lord lieutenant being, generally speaking, a man of rank and fashion, unacquainted with business, and, until within the last ten or fifteen years, even unfamiliar with the vernacular idiom, in nine cases out of ten residing either in Pesth or Vienna, and paying occasional visits to his county, usually for the purpose of giving a splendid banquet at a restoration, as they term the election of the county magistrates.

When Count Apponyi took the seals of office and became the chancellor of the kingdom, he deemed it advisable to effect a radical change in this system of county administration. He accordingly persuaded, with two or three exceptions, the lords lieutenant who were magnates by birth to consent to the appointment of administrators, or, in other words, virtually to abandon their offices; for, although these gentlemen still retain the title of lords lieutenant, the duties of the office are *de facto* performed by administrators. It is the administrator who presides at the county congregations, corresponds with the government, and who is, in fact, the *bona fide* lord lieutenant of the county. An administrator has also a salary of three thousand dollars per annum, paid, not from a fund over which the Hungarians have any control, but from the royal treasury, being a part of the income derived from the salt monopoly, the royal mines, Hungarian customs' duties, and other sources.

This system of Count Apponyi's was a well-concerted plan, and having a tendency, if not for its object, to ingraft a kind of Austrian *bureaucracy* on the Hungarian institutions. A talented administrator would be rewarded for his services by being made a lord lieutenant. The candidates for comitatal offices, a very numerous class in Hungary, would make the office of administrator, with its three thousand dollars, and the prospect of a lord lieutenancy, the highest object of their ambition; to obtain which, they would only have to renounce their ideas of Hungarian nationality and independence, and thus would the ultimate result of the system be the conversion of Hungary into an Austrian province, and the Diet into a mere registrative board, or, at most, an administrative council, similar to the Land Stände of the hereditary provinces.

When the motion for the deposition of the address was carried in the Lower House, the delegates passed a resolution to the effect that the committee on Croatian affairs should be charged to inquire into and make a report on the system of comitatal administration introduced by the present chancellor; but before that committee had reported, a mixed sitting of the Diet was held, on the 1st of February, for the purpose of hearing read a document which the Palatine had brought with him from Vienna, entitled "Royal Rescript respecting the measures relating to comitatal administration taken since the last Diet."

In this rescript his majesty is pleased to say, "It is precisely because our paternal intentions are far removed from attempting to evade the laws of the land that, in strict adherence to the sense of the Royal Rescript of May 28th, 1827 (sub. No. 6888), we hereby declare that it is our firm resolution to reserve the nomination of administrators of lords lieutenant for exceptional cases, and at the same time to maintain in full vigor the ancient comitatal administrative system, as well as the legitimacy of the dignity of lord lieutenant, and, as soon as the above-mentioned obstacles shall be removed, every where to replace the lords lieutenant in the full exercise of their legitimate functions."

Neither party appeared satisfied with the rescript; the Conservatives, because they regarded it as too great a concession to public opinion; the Liberals, because they saw in it nothing but vague promises, never intended to be fulfilled. In this respect, however, a difference of opinion prevailed among the Liberals.

At a circular sitting on the 5th of February, Szentiványi,

first delegate of the county of Gömör, rose and said, that although the rescript was far from being as satisfactory as he could have wished, he would nevertheless regard it as a step toward restoring that confidence between the throne and the nation which had been almost utterly destroyed. He should therefore move that they should, in their representation, express their thanks to his majesty for having at heart the maintenance of the Constitution, and for his intention of replacing the lords lieutenant in the exercise of their legitimate functions, but at the same time should state that their anxiety was far from being groundless; and that, while his majesty's promise afforded them great satisfaction, they must humbly request that this promise be realized during the present Diet, by the total abolition of the system of comitatal administration recently introduced, intimating, at the same time, that on this condition they would abstain from entering into a special examination of the national grievances, and follow the path of moderation which they had hitherto pursued, &c.

Lónyay, first delegate of the county of Beregh (also a Liberal county), said that, as he differed in some respects from the honorable delegate from Gömör, he should move that they should state in their representation that, although the numerous nominations of administrators had caused a considerable degree of anxiety to prevail, they would not dwell any longer upon the subject, as his majesty had been graciously pleased to assure them that he regarded these nominations as exceptional cases, and that it was his firm intention to replace the lords lieutenant in the exercise of their legitimate functions. Relying with confidence on this assurance, they would proceed to the consideration of the questions of social reform, &c.

These different motions did not fail to produce debate, in which Kossuth participated, and, rising amid the most enthusiastic cheering, attempted to show that the new system of comitatal administration constituted a national grievance. That the system was *anti*-constitutional in its tendency, not only on account of thirty salaried administrators, but also because those lords lieutenant who had been suffered to remain at their posts, from motives which the House would know how to appreciate, were obliged to perform duties incompatible with their legitimate functions. A lord lieutenant was not intrusted with the administration of his county, but had merely the chief inspection over the magistrates, in whose hands this administration had been exclusively placed, both by law and long-established usage; that another anti-constitutional feature of the system was the practice, that became every day more prevalent, of transmitting the instructions, ordonnances, &c., of the government to the counties, through the Hungarian Chancery in Vienna; whereas, it was needless for him to observe that the Hungarian Vice-regal Council was the only supreme administrative authority which the counties were bound to recognize, &c. He concluded by lending his support to the motion of the delegates of Gömör.

After a few more speeches, the voting commenced; the votes in favor of the Gömör motion giving rise to loud cheers from the galleries, while those for the Beregh motion were received by groans and other signs of popular disapprobation. The final result of this stormy voting was, that each motion was supported by the votes of twenty-three counties; on which the delegate from Croatia (whose right of voting was contested by the Opposition) gave his vote in favor of the Beregh motion, which was consequently carried, to the great disappointment of the Liberals. An indescribable scene of confusion followed. Hot words passed between several delegates (in consequence of which two duels were fought the next morning), and the chairman tried in vain to restore something like order.

When the uproar had somewhat subsided, Kossuth rose and said, that it was a notorious fact that thirty counties had declared Count Apponyi's system of comitatal administration to be a national grievance; and how several honorable delegates could therefore reconcile it with their consciences to support the Beregh motion, he could not understand.

Simon, first delegate of the county of Soprony (Oedenburg), frankly avowed that he had voted contrary to his instructions, as those instructions were drawn up at a congregation in which the Liberals obtained a factitious majority by a party maneuver, and he was persuaded that his present vote would be approved at the next congregation, which would be held under more favorable auspices.

Szemere, in a speech which was listened to, as usual, with profound attention, commented on the Royal Rescript, phrase by phrase, in order to show that it contained no definite promise.

After a long altercation, the debate was adjourned until the following Monday (7th), without any resolution having been pronounced by the chairman. The debate was continued on the 7th and 8th, without leading to any result. On the 10th, Kossuth and the delegates of Gömör, Beregh, and Békés met in conference at the house of Szemere, when Szemere drew up a representation, which it was finally agreed should be supported by the whole Opposition. This representation was read the next day, in a circular sitting, and ordered to be printed. This representation to his majesty was a kind of combination of the Gömör and Beregh motions, or a sort of compromise between them, with the following addition: that, "relying on the sacredness of the royal word, shall await with sincere confidence the effective execution of your majesty's royal will; and we moreover declare, in a spirit of humble loyalty, that the above-mentioned measures being set aside, as incompatible with the fundamental articles 70 and 12 (1790), we trust and expect that the supreme comitatal administration will be exercised by the vice-regal council, in such a manner that the royal rescripts, decrees, etc., be addressed to the counties themselves; and the right which the counties possess of sending representations to the throne, as well as other comitatal rights and privileges guaranteed by the act 58 (1790), be fully maintained."

In the circular sitting of February 12th, the printed representation was read, and, after a short debate, in which the representation was supported by the delegates of Beregh on the one hand, and Kossuth on the other, was carried by a majority of thirteen; thirty-one counties voting for, and eighteen against its adoption. A dietal sitting was then held, when the *personal** endeavored to persuade the Liberals to strike out several phrases in the representation. He was, however, answered by a general cry of *Maradjon* (let it remain as it is)!

---

* Personalis presentiæ Regiæ in judiciis locum tenens (or the second judicial officer of the realm).

and was finally obliged to announce that the decision of the circular sitting had been confirmed.

Another bill* of engrossing interest before the Hungarian Diet, and one which exercised an important influence in the approaching contest, was that entitled

MAGYARISM; OR, MEASURES RELATING TO HUNGARIAN LANGUAGE AND NATIONALITY, NATURALIZATION, &c.

The Liberals had previously succeeded in their efforts respecting Magyarism, so far that the Magyar language had been by law established as the language of the Legislature, the courts of justice, and, with the exception of the post-office and the customs, of every department of the administration. These two last they had been obliged to strike out of the bill which was passed by the last Diet on the subject, in order that it might receive the royal sanction.

These exceptions it was now proposed to embrace in the present bill, by decreeing that the Magyar be the official language of every department of the state, civil and ecclesiastical, with

---

* The following is the bill:

1st. Is merely the insertion of a fact, stating that his majesty had been graciously pleased to assure the Diet that care had been taken to have the members of the imperial family duly instructed in the Hungarian (Magyar) language ; this assurance had been inserted in the act as a guarantee for the future.

The other clauses are imperative.

2d. Decreeing that the Hungarian (Magyar) be exclusively used as the official language of every department of the state, civil and ecclesiastical, with the exceptions mentioned in 5, 6, and 7. Official documents drawn up in any other language to be invalid.

3d. The Hungarian language to be also exclusively used for public instruction in all the schools, colleges, and universities in the kingdom.

4th. All Hungarian coins and seals of office to bear Hungarian devices and inscriptions in the Hungarian language. The vessels of the Hungarian littoral to bear exclusively the Hungarian flag (consequently not the Austrian).

5th. The three Slavic counties to be still allowed to make use of Latin, and the Hungarian littoral either of Latin or Italian for the space of six years, commencing with the close of the present Diet, but only for local (comitatal) affairs.

6th and 7th. The provisions of p. 2 to be only extended to the *partes adnexæ* (Croatia), in so far that the authorities of the *partes* (the Croatian authorities) will have to correspond with the Hungarian authorities in the Hungarian language, but are permitted still to make use of the Latin language for the administration of local affairs.

8th. The provisions of p. 3 not to extend to the *partes*, but the Hungarian language to be taught in all the public schools of the *partes*.

the exceptions therein mentioned; that official seals of every department of the administration bear Magyar inscriptions; that a coinage, bearing also Magyar devices, be struck for Hungary; and that vessels belonging to the Hungarian *littoral* bear the Hungarian, and not the Austrian flag.

This bill gave rise, in its progress through the House, to very warm debates, that is to say, to the usual conflict between the Magyar and Slavic races. Magyarism was said to be represented in the Lower House by the forty-six counties of Hungary Proper, and Slavism by the three Slavonian counties and Croatia, the three counties only having one vote.

Ossegovich, the Croatian delegate, defended with much zeal what he considered the rights of Croatia. He contended that under the denomination partes (*partes adnexæ*), which was consecrated by long usage, ought to be understood Croatia, Slavonia, and the Hungarian littoral, which formed one kingdom united with, but not dependent on Hungary, for this kingdom had its own Diet (the so-called Croatian Provincial General Congregation), and its own municipal laws and usages.

This was, of course, denied by the Hungarian delegates, who cited various documents to show that the three Slavonian counties had always formed an integral part of Hungary, and that the phrase *partes adnexæ* was only applicable to Croatia, in which sense it was to be understood in the bill then under discussion.

Ossegovich also protested against the right assumed by the Hungarian Diet to decree what language should be made use of by the local authorities of Croatia for the administration of local affairs. Such a right, he contended, belonged exclusively to the United Provincial Congregation (Diet of Croatia), and he would not suffer it to be called in question.

Both Ossegovich and the Slavonian delegates complained of the injustice of forcing the Croatian and Slavonian authorities to correspond with the Hungarian authorities in the Hungarian instead of the Latin language. The Hungarian delegates answered by accusing them of agitating for a repeal of the union, and attributing to them the secret design of forming an Illyrian kingdom, either dependent on or independent of Austria, as circumstances might dictate, which was, in fact, tantamount to accusing them of high treason. Notwithstanding the protest of the Croatian and Slavonian delegates, the bill was passed amid a general cry of " *Maradjon.*"

The debate took place in the Upper House, on February 4th and 5th.

When the bill had been read, Bishop Lonovics rose, and, after expressing in general terms his approbation of the bill, observed that some of its provisions might perhaps be deemed too stringent ; but on such a cherished and revered subject, this stringency could only be ascribed to a patriotic zeal in the sacred cause of Hungarian nationality, and in such a cause it was the bounden duty of the magnates not to suffer themselves to be surpassed in zeal by the delegates. The first clause, he said, was exceedingly gratifying, as it would serve as a perpetual testimony of the patriotic sentiments by which the imperial family was animated. Their present beloved monarch had done more for the propagation and cultivation of the Hungarian language than all the sovereigns who had ever worn the ancient diadem of St. Stephen.

Respecting the second clause, he would merely observe that the official language of the clergy should be understood to mean the language used in their correspondence with lay authorities and for public documents, and not to be applicable to their correspondence with ecclesiastical authorities, or for documents relating strictly to the affairs of the Church. It was in this sense he understood the provision, and he trusted that the delegates would give it that signification.

To the third clause the bishop proposed an amendment, with which the delegates were delighted. They had inserted an exceptional clause, purporting that the language of public instruction for elementary schools should be left to the decision of the local authorities ; whereas the bishop proposed to confine this to the two lowest classes in the schools, and to make it imperative that the upper classes should be taught in the Hungarian language, which he said would be the best to Magyarize the towns that are still, in the eyes of the Hungarian, too German. To the fourth clause, with its Hungarian coins, and seals, and tricolored flag, the bishop said that he had nothing to object.

In respect to the sixth and seventh clauses, he thought that they would do well to allay the agitation that prevailed in Croatia, by showing that, while they made use of all legitimate means in their power for the propagation of the Hungarian language, they would not adopt any measures that might be deemed hostile to the nationality of Croatia.

He should, therefore, suggest that, in respect to the administration of affairs strictly local by the Croatian local authorities, the use of the Latin language should not be made imperative, but potential; the clause to be worded not that "the Latin language *shall* be used," but that "Latin language *may* be used;" which would not exclude the use of the national idiom of Croatia, though no mention ought to be made of it in the act.

Bishop Lonovics had been often interrupted in his speech by loud cheering from the galleries. Haulik, bishop of Agram, who spoke after him in defense of Croatian nationality, was as often interrupted by hisses and other signs of public disapprobation.

Count Louis Batthiányi (the leader of the Opposition) then rose and said he trusted that the House and the galleries would listen to him patiently, and abstain from hissing; for he was aware that they would be too much inclined to receive unfavorably what he was about to propose.

"I fully concur," he continued, "in the opinions expressed by the enlightened Bishop of Csanad, and approve of every amendment suggested by his excellency, with the exception of that relating to the sixth clause. Here I must differ from our patriotic prelate, for, in my opinion, it is neither reconcilable with sound sense, nor with sound policy—least of all with the principles of equity and justice—to force the Croatians to make use of a dead language. Such a proceeding will be an act of tyranny still unrecorded in the pages of history, and expose us, and justly expose us, to the derision of the civilized world. Conquerors have frequently forced their own language on a subjugated people, but where shall we find an instance of a people having been compelled to make use of a dead language? I shall, therefore, propose that, for the administration of their local affairs, the Croatians be permitted to make use of the Croatian instead of the Latin language." (Marks of disapprobation from the galleries.) "I should, I must confess," continued the count, "have hesitated in suggesting such an amendment to the sixth and seventh clauses of the bill, if I entertained the slightest fear respecting the Hungarian language and nationality; but this is far from being the case. Our language has taken firm root in the country, and is no longer in danger. Our nationality is a *fait accompli*, a bright and glorious reality. It is to the development of our Constitution, and not to our nationality, that our future efforts ought to be directed. Our nationality was for centuries a dream, a mere illusion; our constitutionality is so still. Let us, therefore, conciliate our Croatian brethren, and they will unite their efforts with ours, to work out the regeneration of our common father-land. The amendment I have proposed is a step that will surpass their most sanguine expectations, and, if it be adopted, we shall no longer be reproached for our exclusive nationalism and liberalism."

Count Anthony Szécsén (the leader of the Conservatives) expressed his satisfaction at the speech they had just heard, and was overjoyed to find that he could give his cordial support to an amendment proposed by Count Louis Batthiányi. He must, however, remark that the word "nationality" was susceptible of a distinction being made in its signification. It might be applied to designate either the language or the material power and independence of a people. It was in the former acceptation of the term that he should make use of it. After a few more remarks, Count Szécsén concluded by saying that he should vote for Count Batthiányi's amendment to the sixth and seventh clauses, and for the Bishop of Csanad's amendments to the other clauses of the bill.

All the leading members of the Opposition followed; and, after eulogizing what they termed "the truly generous amendment proposed by their noble friend Count Batthiányi," regretted to say that they could not give it their support. They, the Hungarians or Liberals, had friends in Croatia (the so-called Magyar-Croatian party), whom they must not abandon. Hungarian nationality was, they feared, not so deeply rooted in the country as their noble friend supposed.

All declared that, although they should prefer leaving the

sixth and seventh clauses as they stood, yet, to show that they were also willing to follow a conciliatory policy, they would vote for the amendment of the Bishop of Csanad.

Busan, the delegate of Croatia, said that their nationality was as much cherished by the Croatians as Hungarian nationality was by the Hungarians. Hungarian nationality was now triumphant; the Hungarian was the official language of the country, and had been spoken from the throne; and still they refused to make a just concession to the Croatians. The Croatians were grieved at the bitterness displayed against them in both Houses; but what grieved them most was, that the authorities of the Hungarian *littoral* were allowed to make use of the Italian language, whereas the vernacular idiom of the *littoral* was the Illyrian. (Cries of " No, no !") " He was not," he declared, " the person to be put down by cries of No, no." He regarded these cries as the mere negation of a fact, and he should persist in maintaining, as his colleague had done in the Lower House, that the *littoral* was an integral part of Croatia ; and he presumed that, although Italian was spoken in the sea-ports, no one would pretend to deny that the bulk were of the Slavic race.

This assertion gave rise to the usual controversy respecting the true signification of the term *partes adnexæ* and Magyarism and Illyrianism were again in violent conflict.

On the second day of the debate, Bishop Lonovics said that there was no essential difference between his amendment and that of Count Batthiányi; the latter was, however, more explicit, and he should modify his own amendment by proposing that the words " the Croatian language may also be made use of " be inserted.

Count Emilius Dessewffy observed that three amendments had been proposed ; one by the Bishop of Csanad, that " Latin can be used ;" another, also by his excellency, that " Croatian may also be used ;" and a third by Batthiányi, "that the Croatian language be used instead of the Latin." He must, however, remind the House that, while they were deliberating whether Latin ought to continue, *de jure* at least, the official language of Croatia, the Croatians had *de facto* made their own national idiom the official language for the administration of local affairs. He thought, therefore, mention ought not to be made of any language, but that the clause should be worded "the language to be made use of for the administration of local affairs shall be left to the judgment of the local authorities."

When the Palatine had summed up the votes, he announced that the majority was in favor of the Bishop of Csanad's second amendment, with the modification of Count Dessewffy. Count Ladislaus Teleki observed that this was a contradiction; whereupon the *Judex Curiæ*, Count George Mailath, observed that there was no contradiction, the Bishop of Csanad's amendment having been modified or replaced by Count Dessewffy's amendment, and it was obviously this modification, or, in other words, Count Dessewffy's amendment, that had been carried. He was, therefore, of opinion that the majority had pronounced in favor of Count Dessewffy's amendment of the sixth and seventh clauses, and of the Bishop of Csanad's amendment to the other clauses of the bill.

This decision of the *Judex Curiæ* having met with the approbation of the House, a *renuncium* was ordered to be drawn up accordingly.

This *renuncium* was read and duly authenticated,* at a sitting of the 29th of February.

The Croatians were thus allowed, by the action of both Houses, to continue the use of their own language, a privilege in the enjoyment of which they had not previously been disturbed.

NEWS OF THE REVOLUTION IN PARIS.

Thus progressed the legislative proceedings of the Diet of Hungary, until the 2d day of March (1848) arrived, and with it the astounding news of the Revolution in Paris, which immediately put an end to the tedious routine of dietal proceedings, and threw the city of Pressburg into the utmost consternation.

The Hungarian legislators now felt that some decisive step must be taken, and frequent conferences were accordingly held during the day by both parties. Count Stephen Széchényi

---

* The authentication of a *renuncium* means that the document was read to the House, and found to be strictly conformable to the resolution on which it was founded

proposed that they should proceed in a body to the Palatine, and request him to make known their wishes to his majesty, but this proposal was not approved. It was finally decided that, on the following day, Kossuth should make a motion to the effect that, in a representation to his majesty, they should express their sentiments of loyalty and attachment to the imperial house, &c., but at the same time intimate that the system of policy hitherto pursued must be entirely changed, for which they should request his majesty to appoint, without delay a certain number of men in whom the nation could place confidence, as members of the *Vice-regal Council;* that these counselors should forthwith attend the Diet, in order that the questions under discussion might be terminated in a few weeks, without going through the tedious process of representation, royal rescript, &c.; and that the said counselors should afterward be intrusted with the execution of the laws and be responsible to the Legislature; which was, in other words, demanding a *responsible ministry*, to be composed of the *Liberal* party.*

The reason for adopting this mode of proceeding was, that *de jure*, though not *de facto*, the members of the Vice-regal Council, were responsible to the Diet for their official conduct. Should his majesty, therefore, name six members of the Liberal party as vice-regal counselors, and each of them be charged with the execution of laws relating to a special branch of the administration, Hungary would possess, under another name, a responsible ministry. At a conference held in the evening, the Conservative delegates agreed to give their tacit support to the motion; or, in other words, that the motion should be carried (without a single observation being made from either side of the House) by general acclamation.

A circular sitting was accordingly held the next morning at half past ten; Kossuth made a very animated though moderate speech. He began by alluding to a proposal previously made by the delegate of the county of Raab, respecting the

---

* The delegates foresaw that if they demanded, in plain language, a responsible ministry—a Minister of Finance, of War, &c.—their representation would not be adopted by the magnates, or, if adopted by them, would not be listened to in Vienna. Hence they merely request his majesty to send vice-regal counselors, &c.

solvency of the Austrian National Bank. This, he said, had now become an object of secondary consideration; what they wanted, and must have, was a responsible Hungarian Minister of Finance. This was the only way to save Hungary from being involved in the national bankruptcy with which Austria was threatened. But the time was already come when their demands must not be limited to the nomination of a responsible Finance Minister; they must tell his majesty in plain language that the only chance left of saving the empire from dissolution would be to place all the people under his sceptre in the enjoyment of constitutional freedom.

Kossuth then proceeded to show what Hungary especially required, his speech being, in fact, a mere amplification of the representation, which (he concluded by moving) should be laid before his majesty without a moment's delay. This motion, by the tacit consent of the Conservatives, as previously stated, was carried by acclamation.

This representation, thus duly sanctioned by the Lower House, was on the following day (4th) read at a sitting of the magnates, when the *Judex Curiæ*, Count George Mailath (President of the Chamber in the absence of the Palatine), requested them to await the return of the Palatine from Vienna before taking so important a document into consideration, especially as a satisfactory result was only to be anticipated through the mediation of his royal highness. After a few remarks from Count Louis Batthiányi, the House assented to the proposal of the *Judex Curiæ.* For several days following, the magnates held no sittings, owing to the absence of the Palatine and the *Judex Curiæ* at Vienna.

On the 9th, the delegates voted that a *nuncium* should be sent to the magnates, to urge them to take the representation into consideration, and at the same time to express the marked disapprobation of the delegates at their proceedings.

As the *personal* was at Vienna, Sarközy, the Vice-Palatine, presided at the dietal sitting at which this *nuncium* was adopted by acclamation.

The Vienna conferences having terminated, most of the officials and delegates, who assisted at them, returned to Pressburg on the 11th and 12th.

The magnates were to have held a sitting on the 13th; but it was decided, at a private conference, to await the result of a petition to the Austrian Land Stände in Vienna, which it was understood would on that day be presented.

A sitting was also announced for the following morning, but was postponed in consequence of the events which had taken place at Vienna. It was, however, finally concluded, at a private conference, that both Houses should meet at three o'clock on the same afternoon (14th), and pass the representation, with an additional paragraph, by acclamation.

Long before three o'clock the galleries were taken possession of by the jurists,* and when the sitting commenced the House was crowded to suffocation.

The representation was duly voted by acclamation, together with the additional paragraph demanding, in express terms, liberty of the press, trial by jury, and annual Diets at Pesth. A *renuncium* was immediately sent to the delegates, who also passed the representation, thus amended, by acclamation. The representation was then signed and sealed, at a mixed sitting, with the customary formalities; but, instead of being transmitted in the usual manner, through the Hungarian Chancery, it was, on the following day (15th), by a numerous deputation of magnates and delegates, at the head of which was the Palatine, presented in person to his majesty.

Arrived at Vienna at the opportune moment when the emperor was acceding to the demands of his subjects of the hereditary provinces, his majesty, without much hesitation, yielded, as was understood, to the imposing delegation from Hungary, all the concessions which they sought, and, in furtherance of their views, appointed Count Louis Batthiányi prime minister, with authority to form a ministry for Hungary.

With feelings of the highest exultation, the Hungarian deputation returned to Pressburg, and proceeded at once to pass the necessary laws for carrying the royal concessions into effect.

On the 23d of March the bill respecting the ministry passed the Chamber of Magnates, when Count Batthiányi announced

* The students of law, and those who had just been admitted to the bar, and were without practice.

that he had formed a ministry (the arrangements having been completed during the night), and would make known the names of his colleagues previous to their being submitted to his majesty. This novel and not very respectful proceeding toward the emperor was a matter of necessity, produced by the receipt, on the night previous, of an estafette from the Committee of Public Safety at Pesth, stating, in plain language, that if they (the committee) were not able to announce the definite formation of a ministry within twenty-four hours, the National Guards would storm the arsenal at Buda, and summon a National Convention to meet at Pesth without delay.

The ministry thus formed consisted of the most moderate men of the Liberal party, and was composed as follows:

Premier (without *portefeuille*), Count Louis Batthiányi, more distinguished for his patriotic sacrifices and the historical and spotless name of his family than by any superiority of mental endowment.

Interior (Home Department), Szemere, a man of decided talent, and one of the most efficient debaters in the House of Delegates.

Foreign (or International) *Affairs*, Prince Paul Esterhazy, of great wealth, and formerly Austrian embassador to Great Britain.

Finance, Louis Kossuth, the eloquent and distinguished agitator.

War, Meszaros, a colonel of hussars, then at Milan under Radetzky.

Public Works, the highly-esteemed and enterprising patriot, Count Stephen Széchényi.

Public Instruction and Religious Worship, the literary Baron Eötvös.

Trade, Agriculture, and Manufacturing Industry, Klauzal, one of the most celebrated delegates of the last Diet.

Justice, Deak, one of the profoundest jurists in the kingdom.

Immediately after the announcement of the ministry to the Hungarian Diet, Count Batthiányi hastened to Vienna to submit the bill, with the names of the ministry, for the royal sanction. He was followed by the Palatine and Deak, and joined in the capital by Prince Esterhazy.

Notwithstanding the high character of the names presented
for the ministry, it was with great difficulty that the emperor's
sanction* could be obtained.   A strange infatuation seemed to
have seized the emperor's advisers, viz., that because no blood
had been shed in Hungary, a revolution had not yet taken place
in that country, and that the Hungarian government must still
continue, in some manner at least, dependent on the imperial
cabinet.   Another circumstance, which doubtless operated
against obtaining the royal sanction to the ministry bill, was
the idea which the Austrian cabinet had conceived, viz., that
the students in Vienna had been instigated to the bold step
which they had taken, and that led to the resignation of
Prince Metternich, by Kossuth and other Hungarian Liberals;
whereas nothing could have been more erroneous, from the
best evidence which can be obtained.   The revolution in Vienna took every one in Pressburg by surprise.   Kossuth and
Szemere, particularly, were known to have been astonished at
the intelligence.   The famous programme of the Liberals, in
which, without the least disguise, they declared their determination to use all the efforts in their power to obtain a responsible ministry, liberty of the press, &c., at the same time recommended his majesty to grant Constitutions to the hereditary states of the empire.   This programme and the representation of March the 3d, together with Kossuth's speeches in
the Lower House, no doubt exercised a great influence on public opinion in Vienna; but this was the only kind of conspiracy of which the Hungarian Liberals were guilty.   They were
resolved to realize their views by constitutional means, and by
constitutional means only.

On the 29th, the Palatine returned from Vienna, with a royal
resolution respecting the ministerial bill, the principal feature
of which was the adoption of the " collegial system" of having
recourse to royal propositions; in other words, retaining the
Hungarian Chancery in Vienna, when it is obvious that, with
a responsible ministry, a chancery was superfluous.

This resolution, as might have been expected, caused the
greatest dissatisfaction, and all the printed copies of it which

---

* His principal objections were against a separate ministry of war and finance.

the jurists could get hold of were publicly burned on the promenade.

In the discussion of the subject which took place the same evening in the Chamber of Delegates, Kossuth uttered but little ; but what he did say evinced the determination of the Liberals not to give way. Count Stephen Széchényi, who of late years had been regarded as a Conservative, made a speech that reminded the auditors of the time when he was the fiery leader of the Opposition. He concluded by announcing his intention to repair to Vienna the next morning, and to use his utmost exertions to induce them to give way. The Palatine also made a solemn declaration in the Chamber of Magnates, that he should set out in the course of the night for Vienna, and, to-morrow, either bring back the ministerial bill with the royal sanction, or resign his office.

The emperor, unable longer to resist the appeals made to him on the subject, yielded his sanction to the ministerial bill, and thus terminated that unpleasant controversy.

The following resolutions were then adopted by the Diet, and formed the basis of the future administration of the government :

The executive power to be exercised exclusively through the ministry. The ministerial body to reside at Buda-Pesth, with the exception of one of the members, who resides near the court at Vienna. The Palatine to be invested with all royal power (in the absence of the king), with the exception of the appointments of the high clerical functionaries and military officers, the high barons of the kingdom, and the disposal of the army out of Hungary. Each member of the ministry responsible for his official acts. The ministers may be impeached by decree of the House of Representatives, and are to be tried by a committee of the Upper Chamber " for any acts or decrees prejudicial to the independence of the country, to her constitutional guarantees, to existing laws, to individual liberty, or to private property ; for dereliction of duty, fraud, or misapplication of money ; for neglect·in the execution of laws or in the maintenance of the public tranquillity and security." The right of pardon not to be exercised in case of condemned ministers but on an occasion of general amnesty.

The sessions of the Diet to be held in Pesth.   The laws passed to be sanctioned by the king during the session.   The President of the House of Magnates to be named by the king; the President of the House of Delegates elected by the House itself.

Perfect equality of civil rights and public burdens among all classes, denominations, and races in Hungary and its provinces, and complete toleration for every form of religious worship. The elective franchise extended to every man possessed of property to the value of three hundred florins,* or of an income of one hundred florins; to every one who has received a diploma from a university; and to every artisan who employs an apprentice.

All *corvées*, tithes, and money-payments in lieu of *corvées* abolished.

With the concurrence of both countries, Hungary and Transylvania, and their Diets, hitherto separate, were incorporated. The number of representatives which Croatia was to send to the Diet increased from three to eighteen, while the internal institutions of that province were to remain unchanged.

The whole of the acts thus passed in March received the royal assent which on the 11th of April, 1848, the emperor personally confirmed at Pressburg, in the midst of the Diet.†

The Diet was closed on the same day (11th April), and his majesty, having acceded to all the demands of the Hungarians, was received with the usual manifestations of popular satisfaction.

The last and probably most important concession—in order to obtain which the Palatine was again forced to appear before the imperial throne—was that respecting the "military frontiers."   The Diet required, as a matter of course, that the border troops should be placed under the authority of the Hungarian Minister of War.   They did not pass a bill to incorporate the frontiers with the adjacent counties, leaving that to be done by their next Diet; but in the bill respecting the elective franchise, the "military frontiers" are regarded as an integral part of the kingdom, and therefore empowered to send representatives to what is now termed the National Assembly.

---

* A florin, in ordinary times, is estimated at forty-eight cents.

† For acts passed by the Hungarian Diet, see Appendix, note No. 16.

The Austrian government wished, first, to retain the command of the border troops; and, second, that the decision respecting the extension of the franchise to the military frontiers should be left to the next Diet. They were, however, finally obliged to give way on both points. The military frontiers are now consequently under the authority of the Hungarian ministry, and will send representatives to the Hungarian Legislative Assembly.

The ameliorations which had been effected produced the utmost satisfaction throughout the kingdom; but this bright day in Hungarian history was of short duration.

In the first place, the change was too sudden, from the restraints of a rigid government to the enjoyment of constitutional liberty, and the people,* with no knowledge or experience of rational freedom, gave way to the utmost license; while the new government, scarcely organized, was too feeble to check their excesses, or afford protection to the persons and property of the more peaceful inhabitants.

Demonstrations, consequently, occurred in various portions of the kingdom, which would have disgraced the barbarism of the darker ages, and could not have been looked for in the nineteenth century in any portion of the civilized globe.

In the Eisenburger comitat an attack was made by the mob upon the Jews, plundering and maltreating this unfortunate race without cause, and only for the gratification of a national antipathy. In the Szatmar comitat, the poor landlords rose against the rich ones, and, equally without reason, slaughtered the nobles and destroyed their princely dwellings. In Middle Szolnok, so weak were the authorities, that a sworn jury fell victims to the popular rage. At Chemnitz, and in its neighborhood, the Slavic national fanaticism became daily more dangerous. At Neusatz, the mob took down the Hungarian flag and burned it, and then raised a red one in its place; at the same time, they seized the first fiscal officer of the town, brought him into the market-place, and there cut him literally in pieces. At Kikinda, and other points, outrages occurred too horrible to relate. These isolated atrocities of the mob could

---

* The masses, who previously enjoyed no privileges.

easily have been quelled by the presence of an efficient military force; but at that time the number of regular troops throughout the whole kingdom did not exceed eighteen thousand men. Repeatedly did the Hungarian ministry appeal to the Austrian government for assistance to suppress this anarchy; and it was only after these urgent and repeated applications had been attended with no success that the first threats of separation escaped the nation.

But about this period there arose for Hungary a far more alarming danger, and one which operated more seriously than any other cause in producing her ultimate downfall, and that was the opposition against her in several of the provinces of the kingdom.

Among the concessions exacted of the emperor, by the Magyars at the outbreak of the revolution, was the decreed connection of Transylvania with Hungary, and the subordination of that portion of the Croatian territory known as the "military frontier." It was the great error of the Hungarians, and the rock upon which their bark of state was wrecked, that while they were struggling with the imperial government for the establishment of their own nationality, they were reluctant altogether to respect the nationality of those provinces which lay within their borders. It must, however, be admitted that they subsequently, as will be seen, made every effort to retrieve this error. At six different epochs during the early stage of their differences did they invite the Croatian leader, Baron Jellacic, to an interview with the Hungarian authorities, urge him to lay before them the complaints of the Croatians, and assure him of their anxious desire to adjust the unhappy dissensions which separated them.

Instead of increasing by these measures the hostility of the neigboring provinces, had the Hungarian ministers taken the necessary steps to appease that feeling, and, by respecting their different nationalities, have secured their confidence and support, they would have united in their cause a force which would, in defense of their soil, and with the peculiar advantages of the country for their mode of warfare, have been perhaps invincible by any armies which Austria, either alone or when aided by Russia, could bring against them. The popu-

lation of Hungary and its provinces is estimated at about fourteen millions; of this number a little over five millions only
are Magyars, and the remainder (nearly nine millions), instead of battling with them, were, by the course of the Hungarian Diet and ministry, driven into the ranks of their opponents.

As soon as the tidings of the March Revolution in Vienna
had reached Agram, the Illyrian party (*i. e.*, the southern Slavi
of the Austrian empire), increasing in energy and violence,
dispatched a deputation to the emperor with a petition,* which
commenced by expressing " the desire of continuing as heretofore under the Hungarian crown ;" concluded by asking for
their own national independence, their own Diet, their own independent ministry, their national funds, National Guard, and
national troops to be under their own control ; in short, perfect independence of Hungarian rule.

At the same time, they demanded the appointment of Baron
Jellacic, colonel of the frontier troops, as Ban.   The emperor,
in reply to the application, promoted the Colonel Baron Jellacic to the rank of major general, and appointed him Ban, but
declared that, as to the other points, he could not act but in
accordance with his Hungarian ministry.

The Baron Jellacic was not the brilliant officer and extraordinary man that the sycophants around the imperial throne
have represented him.   He had distinguished himself neither
by strategy in the field, nor by ability in council; but, possessed of many qualities to endear him to his friends—a poet,
scholar, and wit ; a bold, chivalrous, and generous officer, he
was highly popular among his troops.   In mediæval times,
the Ban might have been a gallant and adventurous knight
for the troubadour's lay, or for a name in romance ; but he falls
immeasurably short of the position which his injudicious eu-
logists would claim for him, that of being " the only man that
the Revolutions of 1848–9 have produced."

The only thing remarkable about Jellacic was his sudden
and extensive reputation, produced not by any exalted merit
of his own, but arising simply from the promotions of royal

---

* For Croatian Petition, see Appendix, note No. 17.

favor, and the force of circumstances in which these promotions naturally involved him. The advancement of Macbeth, as foretold him by the witches, as "Thane of Glamis," "Thane of Cawdor," and "that shalt be king hereafter," were less sudden and inconsistent than those showered upon the colonel of a Grentzer regiment, who in a few months became Field-marshal Lieutenant, Ban of Croatia, and then civil and military Governor of Hungary. Descended from a family which had rendered considerable military service to the empire, Baron Joseph Jellacic was born on the 16th of October, 1801, at Peterwardine, and educated at the Therisanium, or charity school for young aristocrats in Vienna. He is of medium height and size; his bearing is upright and military; his gait quick, as, indeed, are all his movements. His face, which is of a somewhat brownish tinge, has in it something free, winning, and yet determined. The eyes are large, hazel-colored, and full of expression. His head is bald at the top, but encircled with a fringe of jet-black hair. He leaves the impression upon the observer of a man of a mild but determined character, fully confident of his own powers. He is adored by his Croat regiments; and it is said of him, that, whether "in battle, after the most fatiguing march, in *bivouac*, exposed to pouring rain, whenever and wherever the border soldier espies his Ban, he joyously shouts his *zivio*, and, for the moment, bullets, hunger, weariness, and bad weather are nothing at all to him."

Croatia, at a distance from the Hungarian centre, and directly subject to the influence of the court of Vienna, in consequence of its military organization and of its peculiar administration, became now the focus of the anti-Hungarian movement. How far these demonstrations were the result, on the part of the Croatians, of a sense of dreaded injury—in other words, in defense of their own nationality—or how far the actors were the servile instruments of the Austrian *Camarilla*, it is obviously impossible at this time to determine. That there was a party about the imperial court opposed to all concessions, and desirous still to resort to the patriarchal system, which had been overturned, there can be no doubt. Louis Gai was at Vienna at the time of the Revolution in March, and a few weeks after he is said to have declared, in an assembly at

Agram, that he was charged by high persons in Vienna to produce a counter-revolution among the Croatians. The Hungarians believe that, in the opinion of this reactionary party at
the capital, "the rights recognized to Hungary were regarded
in the light of forced concessions which it was necessary to destroy at any cost, even at that of their blood;" and that, at
their instigation, the imperial government commenced the
work by stirring up a civil war in Hungary, and exciting Croat
and Serb against Magyar, that it might with military force interfere and overwhelm the liberties of their nation.

The Wallachians, more properly Roumani or Romans, the
descendants of Trajan's scattered legions, for a long time refused to take up the cause of the Slavi, whom they considered
allied, by the tie of a common origin, to the Russians, those
oppressors of the Danubian principalities. They would have
preferred to be on good terms with the Hungarians, and to this
end they asked only the recognition of their nationality, and
the freedom that had been so fully promised in the resolutions
of the Hungarian Diet to all the races inhabiting the kingdom.
The moderate party among the Magyars were quite willing to
assent to the just demands of a people who were the natural
allies of their race. It was thus that Count Wesselenyi, a blind
old man, who sat in the Diet at Pesth, remarked in the session
of the 29th of May: "The horizon of my country is darker
than the night of my eyes; our only means of safety consist
in holding out a fraternal hand to the Roumani, and proposing
an intimate alliance with them; for, like them, we too are isolated in the vast ocean of nations; our interest, as well as
theirs, requires a close alliance between us; I ask you, therefore, to pass a law that the nationality of the Roumani shall be
respected." Kossuth opposed the motion, declaring that he
knew nothing of a Roumanic, or a Croatian people, and that
he recognized only Hungarian citizens.*

The Hungarians believe, with great apparent reason, that
the mission of Gai, but especially the appointment of Jellacic
as Ban of Croatia, without the knowledge of the Hungarian
ministry (whose assent and counter-signature they contended

---

* M. De Bourgong.

were necessary to give validity to the appointment), were but different means of attaining one end at which the Austrian government aimed, viz., a breach with Hungary.

On the other hand, it may be said, that the other nations, especially the Slavic, very soon began to fear that the object of the Hungarians was to obliterate and dissolve all other nationalities, and that the separation of Hungary from the Austrian central government was the first step toward it;* and it was quite natural that they should have been unwilling, as the Magyars themselves were, to surrender without a struggle their rights and liberties.   Jellacic and his Croatians may not have been at the onset the servile instruments of reaction, at least in an illiberal sense; they had rights to contend for, and with the Southern Slavi an equality of rights in a national point of view as regards the whole empire; but the means adopted by them to secure and maintain these rights can not be approved.   They made no effort to obtain redress in a legal or peaceful manner; they did not seek to prevail by the force of public opinion, and by enlightening the people; their members, in the Hungarian Diet even, did not protest against these innovations; but their course was to draw the sword, excite to its utmost extent the blind fury of fanaticism, invade a foreign state, and restore by revolution and civil war the cherished unity of the empire.

Jellacic became now the decided head of the Croatian movement; and notwithstanding the Hungarian ministers had a right to protest against his nomination as Ban, yet, to avoid causes of difference, they acquiesced in the appointment, and invited the Ban to put himself in communication with them Jellacic replied to the invitation of the Hungarian ministry by declaring, in a circular, the constitutional connection between Hungary and Croatia as changed, and forbidding the Croat

* About this time (14th of May) the Hungarian ministry did dispatch two envoys, Messrs. Pazmandy and Szalay, to represent the Hungarian government at the government and Parliament of Germany; and, what is equally strange, the commissions of these envoys were signed by the archduke and countersigned by the Austrian ministry at Vienna, and they were recognized by the Archduke John the regent, as well as by the government of Frankfort.   Later, Count Teleki was sent to Paris, M. Pulszky to London, and Splenyi to Turin, &c.—*Schlessinger's War in Hungary.*

magistrates from holding any communication* whatever with the Hungarian government; and declaring martial law against those of his countrymen who should make any reference to the legal connection between Hungary and Croatia. The Hungarian ministry called upon the Ban to retract these orders, but without effect.

The Archduke Palatine, in exercise of his right, hereupon addressed the Ban of Croatia, pronounced as unconstitutional his promulgation of martial law, and the trial of such offenses as were never before subjected to the decision of a court-martial, illegal. He ordered him to recall both without delay, and reminded him that he had not as yet taken his oath, and that, agreeably to the customs of the realm, he was not yet installed in the office of Ban.†

Jellacic having refused to appear personally in Ofen, as he had been summoned, and having committed various other illegalities, the Palatine charged the commanding general of Slavonia and Servia, Baron Hrabowsky, to declare all appointments made by Jellacic as illegitimate; to reinstate the former authorities, which had been removed by him; to oblige them by oath to execute the decrees of the Palatine viceroy, and ministers; to arrest all those who had participated in the dissolution of the crown and of the empire; to suspend Jellacic from his military dignity, and declare him under accusation for his treachery; and, finally, to conduct with all energy the military and civil power, and to delare publicly that, " in respect to language, right of moving, professions, trades, tithes, and feudal service, &c., the inhabitants of the military frontier stand on the same footing of equality with other Hungarians."

---

* The rescript from the Hungarian government, received at Vankavar, Essek, and other principal towns in Slavonia, required the authorities to attend solely to the directions which might be conveyed to them from the Hungarian Departments of State; and immediately afterward, the Ban laid his injunctions on the same functionaries, to yield obedience to no commands save those of " the Ban of Croatia, Slavonia, and Dalmatia," as he is styled in his patent.—*Consul-general Fonblanque*, c. ix., p. 71.

† When these orders of the Palatine reached Agram, on the 16th May, after much noise and confusion, the orders were about to be destroyed by fire, and were only saved at the earnest instance of the Ban. In this state of excitement, the portraits of the Palatine and his ministers were publicly burned in the open square before the council-house.

His majesty, the emperor-king, also, by a communication bearing date the 7th of May, at the instance of the Hungarian ministry, summons him to yield obedience to the crown of Hungary, and to desist from all efforts at separation. Jellacic, throwing off the mask, declared that he in no manner recognized the authority of the Hungarian ministry, which was but a usurpation of power, and convoked the General Assembly of Croatia for the 5th of June, by his own authority and contrary to the constitutional laws, which required the consent of the king.

The Illyrian party, as might have been anticipated, declared all charges imputing to the Ban violations of the Constitution as false, and pretended that the Ban had not as yet performed a single act of which his majesty and his brother, the Archduke Francis Charles, had not been immediately informed, and of which they had not entirely approved. Upon these delarations, promulgated on the authority of the Ban, the Hungarian ministry called upon the sovereign formally to contradict the reports, and to bring Jellacic to obedience. The king, acceding to his wish, in an autograph letter of the 29th of May, forbade Jellacic to convoke an Assembly, and ordered him to repair to Innspruck within twenty-four hours after the receipt of the summons. But Jellacic, far from obeying the commands of the emperor, opened the General Assembly in Croatia, composed of his own nominees, under the title of "Croato-Slavo-Dalmatian Diet." This outrage against the central authority of Hungary produced a strong remonstrance on the part of the Hungarian ministry at the imperial court, and the emperor was forced, on the 10th of June, to issue an ordinance which suspended Jellacic from all his functions, civil and military, declared him guilty of high treason, and ordered him before a tribunal.*

Jellacic at length proceeded, in company with a deputation from the Croatian Diet, for Innspruck, and in an audience of the 19th of June, he was informed, in the presence of Prince Esterhazy, the Hungarian minister residing near the court, that his majesty felt deeply offended by the disobedience of the

---

* For original, see Appendix, note No. 18.

Ban; that he declared the assembled Congregation at Agram illegal; that he could consider the deputies but as private individuals; that he would maintain the unity of the Hungarian crown, to which Croatia had ,belonged for seven hundred years; and that the Archduke John was charged with the mediation between the two countries.

The Ban of Croatia left Innspruck, and, on his journey home, received, for the first time, the imperial ordinance of the 10th of June, in which he was denounced, countersigned by no Hungarian minister, and which was issued before he reached Innspruck.

Upon this document the Hungarians laid great stress, and vainly supposed that such a blow, inflicted by the emperor upon the very " head and front" of that rebellious movement, must subdue all opposition, and that peace and order would soon be restored to the country.   But they were imposed upon by the treachery of the court; there was no sincerity in the act; and, as subsequent events fully established, the manifesto was a mere blind for their deception.

Had the imperial court considered him in the light in which it denounced him, Jellacic would have been in the presence of his God, instead of that of his emperor; or, even if regarded as less criminal than originally charged, he would at least have been condemned to the Castle of Olmütz or Spielberg, rather than called to the imperial palace; while, on his own part, the Ban would never have ventured to disobey with such audacity, had he not been sustained secretly by the approbation and connivance of the court.*   Jellacic, fully advised as to the force of the manifesto, quietly wends his way to Agram, and there, instead of returning in disgrace " deprived of his functions" and " placed before a tribunal," was carried about the streets in the arms of the people, and greeted by one of the most enthusiastic and brilliant receptions which was ever witnessed.

The Archduke John, to whom, with the consent of the parties, the emperor had submitted this controversy, now summoned this imperially-denounced traitor (whom he addressed

---

* That the imperial family encouraged the insurrections against Hungary was generally believed; and Jellacic himself wrote to this effect, in a letter dated the 4th of June, and addressed to the frontier regiments stationed in Italy.

as his dear Ban Baron Jellacic) to Vienna, to hold a conference
with the Hungarian ministry. Count Batthiányi, on the part
of Hungary, and the Ban Jellacic, on the part of Croatia, appeared, in obedience to the summons, before the Archduke John,
who simply introduced the parties to each other, entreated them
to arrange the matter amicably, and then left Vienna for Frankfort to enter upon the duties of Regent of the German empire, to which, by the voice of the Diet, he had just been called. In this interview the Ban demanded, agreeably to the
Croatian petition, a government quasi responsible, charged
with the internal management of the country, and leaving
the most important branches, viz., the departments of war, of
finance, and of commerce, in the hands of the central power at
Vienna. To this proposal the president of the Hungarian ministry would not accede, being unwilling to depart from the
legal ground upon which the concessions of March had placed
his country, the historical independence of Hungary and her
sovereignty over Croatia.

The proposal of Jellacic was mere insolence and ignorance.
The affairs of Hungary have at all times been managed, ostensibly at least, independently of any Viennese minister. They
were conducted by an Hungarian chancellor resident at Vienna; and by the new arrangement the Hungarian Minister of
Foreign Affairs was also to take up his abode at the capital,
and become the channel of communication.

The objection of Jellacic arose from ignorance; while his denial of the right of Hungary to have a finance minister, at a
time, too, when the same officer in Austria was under the control of the Viennese Assembly, was to subject the fiscal affairs
of Hungary to the influence of the Austrian deputies.

The pretensions of Jellacic, if sincere, were ludicrously absurd; but it is probable that the demand of terms to which
they knew the Hungarians would never accede, was but a
part of the plan devised to bring on a war, and thus to subjugate Hungary, an object upon which the Camarilla was now
intent, and which their instrument, Jellacic, had been deputed
to execute.

Upon the unsuccessful termination of the first interview,
Jellacic inquired of Count Batthiányi, " Shall we meet again?"

II.   E

" Upon the Drave, perhaps," replied the Hungarian minister ;
" I now join the army." " Not on the Drave," quickly rejoined
Jellacic, " but even on the Danube."

While these events were occurring, the partial revolt of Croatia was aided by a conspiracy against Hungary in the Banat
and in the counties of Bacs and Szerem, in concert with the
Serbs of Serbia.

" The population of these countries," says Count Teleki,
" of the Greek religion and of the Serb race, took refuge in
Hungary at different periods, to escape Turkish oppression.
At the time of their settling in the country, they obtained the
same rights as Hungarians ; but the imperial government, the
enemy of religious liberty, and which at that time persecuted
the Hungarian Protestants, did not allow them the free enjoyment of their form of worship.   The states of Hungary succeeded, by different efforts, in ameliorating the lot of the members of the Greek Church ; but it was the Diet of 1848, to which
it was granted to diffuse liberty universally, which assured
their legitimate rights, by pronouncing the perfect equality of
all creeds.   The Hungarian government, in order to become
acquainted with the further demands that the Greek Church
might put forward, convoked a meeting of the Greek clergy
for the 27th of May, which was to be charged with the investigation of the questions of instruction and religion.   The
Serbs, grateful for what the Diet had done for them, declared
themselves perfectly satisfied, and testified their attachment to
the Hungarian people.   But after a little, the influence which
had agitated and divided Croatia commenced to react upon
them also.   Stephen Suplikacz, a colonel, like Jellacic, of a
frontier regiment, put himself at the head of the Serb movement.   Under the pretext of holding a meeting preparatory to
that which was to take place on the 27th of May, the Serbs
convoked a National Assembly for the 13th, to which a great
number of the Ottoman Serbs were called.   The Assembly,
opened first at Ujvidek, was moved afterward to Carlowitz.
The Serbs named patriarch Joseph Rajacsis, archbishop of Carlowitz, and elected Stephen Suplikacz, colonel, like Jellacic, of
a border regiment, and then serving in Italy, as vayvode.   Putting forth the most illegitimate pretext, they formed the Vay-

vodat of the Banat and the military frontiers, with the counties of Bacs, Szerem, and Baranya, thus being the first to violate the rights of nationality, which they invoked, inasmuch as a considerable portion of this country is peopled by Hungarians, Wallachs, and Germans. They decreed that the Serb Vayvodat should form an alliance with Croatia, and nominated a permanent committee to govern it. Finally, a deputation was commissioned to make these determinations known to the king."*

The Serbian revolt was now carried forward with great vehemence, and distinguished by the utmost atrocity. Whole towns and villages, once flourishing, were laid waste, the inhabitants, even without resistance, massacred, and lovely districts converted into a wilderness. The Hungarian government had only at its disposal a few troops, hastily assembled, and for the most part foreign soldiers or National Guards, ill armed or not armed at all, while the enemy's forces were composed principally of soldiers of the frontier regiments, perfectly disciplined.

It was at this time that the Hungarian government, intrusted with the security and lives of the people, at length determined on active hostilities ; and the first efforts at civilized warfare were made on the 12th of June, 1848, when commenced the bombardment of Carlowitz, the metropolis or holy city of the Serbs. The object of this first expedition, commanded by the imperial general, Hrabowsky, and which issued from the neighboring fortress of Peterwardein, was to obtain possession of all the stores in the principal fortification, the bulwark of the Servian nation, and to disperse the crowds which had gathered in that city.

This expedition was not successful. Hrabowsky's troops penetrated, it is true, into the suburbs of the city, where they burned fourteen houses ; but, owing to the brave defense of

---

* The Emperor of Russia, about this time, through his consul at Belgrade, made proposals to protect the Servians, as co-religionists, provided they would make to him a petition to that effect. Rajacsis, the archbishop of Carlowitz, and leading man among the Servians, declined the proposals, but advised Mayerhofer, consul general of Austria at Belgrade, of the application. Mayerhofer immediately tendered them, on the part of Austria, every assistance and concession that they might desire, if they would but adhere faithfully to her.—*Pulszky.*

the city, under Stratimirowitch,* and the arrival of re-enforcements of volunteers from the independent principality of Servia, who hastened up to the assistance of their brethren in the Austrian province, the Magyars were driven back into the fortress of Peterwardein. From this time the whole Servian race in the Banat, and the provinces bordering on this part of the Danube, rose in rebellion, and this region became the scene of a furious contest. The Theiss was frequently crossed and recrossed by the two parties; the triangular peninsula situated at the confluence of that river and the Danube (the very spot that was, in 1697, the theatre that witnessed the splendid victories of Eugène of Savoy over the Turks, and which were followed by the peace of Carlowitz, that memorable era in the history of the house of Austria and of Europe), again, as a centre of operations, became the scene of most sanguinary conflicts.†

As the Servian insurgents continued to advance their cause in the name of the emperor-king, the Hungarian ministers requested his majesty to come in person to Pesth, on the occasion of the approaching convocation of the Diet, in order by his presence to give a positive contradiction to the enemies of Hungary. But the invitation was without effect.

On the 2d of July, the new National Assembly, returned for the first time by the suffrage of all classes of the nation, was opened at Pesth.

An immense crowd of people had early in the morning of this important day stationed themselves in all the streets, on the bridges, and places where their curiosity and interest were most likely to be gratified. The space from the royal palace to the Assembly-house was kept open by the National Guards of Pesth and Ofen, two battalions of infantry, and a troop of cuirassiers. The procession was opened by M. Perczel, the Commissioner of the Police for Hungary. He was followed by the two bürgermeisters of the cities of Pesth and Ofen, in their state carriages.

After them came the ministry, consisting of Messrs. Széché-

---

* Stratimirowitch had been educated at the Engineer Academy in Vienna, a young man of only twenty-five years, but of much military talent.

† One battle was fought behind the Roman intrenchments. repaired and employed by Eugène of Savoy, and still undemolished.

nyi, Mészaros, Szemere, Kossuth, Klausal, Dèak, and Eötvös, followed by a troop of mounted National Guards. The Archduke Palatine and the President of the Ministry, Batthiányi, came next, and troops of mounted National Guards brought up the rear.

Each part of the procession was received with cheers by the public. Deputations from the Upper and Lower Houses waited upon the Archduke Palatine at the foot of the great stairs of the Assembly-house, and conducted him and the ministry to the grand hall, where the Diet hold their sittings; he took his seat on the throne, and the ministers stood on his right and left.

After the tumultuous joy of the Assembly had subsided, his highness said:

" His majesty, our beloved king, intended himself to open the Diet; but the king is prevented by ill health from acting up to his own wishes, and he has therefore commissioned me to open the Diet. I herewith lay upon the table of the House the king's decree upon that subject, and another decree by which the king's sole power is provisionally placed in my hands."

The two royal decrees were then read by one of the ministers, and the names of the king and Palatine, whenever they occurred in the text, were enthusiastically cheered by the galleries. The speech from the throne was next read by the Archduke Palatine himself. It is to the following effect:

" In the name of our beloved king, Ferdinand the Fifth, I open this Diet; for the present condition of our country, especially the disturbances in Croatia, the Lower Danube, and Slavic frontiers, makes an immediate opening of the Diet necessary. His majesty wishes for a general restoration of peace and order.

" There is reason to hope that the financial questions will be definitely, beneficially settled, by a series of laws which the ministry propose to submit to the Assembly.

" His majesty has been grieved to learn that quiet and order have been disturbed in several of his countries, at the very time that his majesty with paternal care has fulfilled all wishes for the happiness of his people

"Malevolent individuals, by fomenting national and religious discords in Croatia, have caused an open resistance to the laws and orders of his majesty, and they have even dared to take his majesty and the members of the royal family as a pretext and authority for their lawless endeavors.

"His majesty scorns such insinuations; the king and his royal family will at all times respect the laws and protect the liberties granted to his people.

"His majesty has been happy to sanction the union with Transylvania, for his beloved Hungary will gain in strength by this union, and it will the more staunchly stand by the throne. The ministry have prepared some further laws respecting this union, which they will submit to the Diet. His majesty is grieved to inform you that his Italian subjects, with the assistance of foreign troops, have attacked his majesty's forces. The war resulting from this melancholy event has not yet been brought to a termination; but it is the king's wish that Italy, too, may soon enjoy the blessings of peace. His majesty stands in the most friendly relations with foreign powers, and hopes for a continuance of those relations. His majesty doubts not that the faithful Diet of Hungary will do all it can for the glory of the crown and the welfare of the country.

"I can assure you of the king's earnest and sincere love for you."*

This speech was followed by loud cheers and waving of swords and hats, in the midst of which the archduke and ministry left.

The Diet, rejoiced by these assurances, immediately dispatched a deputation to Vienna to entreat the king to repair to Pesth. The solicitude of the Hungarians on this subject was quite natural. The actual presence of the king in the country could alone convince the insurgent population that he spoke sincerely. All the decrees he issued, all the words he uttered, were represented to the insurgents as drawn from him by force; and

---

* This opening speech of the Palatine has been considered, by the friends of the Austrian dynasty, as a remarkable one, from the fact that it contains not one word of the union of the two crowns; of the rights established by the Pragmatic Sanction; of the bond between the two monarchies (*Monarchie-Verband*), which was the condition of the emperor's concessions.—*Baroness Blaze de Bury's " Germania."*

the flight of the emperor from his capital gave to these suppositions a semblance of reality. Jellacic had also thus explained the ordinance which stripped him of his offices. The Hungarians, therefore, tested the sincerity of the king when they asked his presence at Pesth. They were refused.

Meanwhile the Servian revolt gained ground. Troops were concentrated on the frontiers of Croatia, evidently for the purpose of invasion. At length the Austrian cabinet, in a communication to the Hungarian ministry dated the 29th of June, just three days previous to the speech of the Palatine, so full of amicable assurances, announced the intention of the Austrian ministry to put an end to the neutrality it had observed hitherto, and to support Croatia openly. This event confirmed the suspicions of the Hungarian government, which it had for some time entertained, that the disobedience of the foreign troops, to whom the defense of the country had been intrusted, had been ordered at Vienna; and brought home to them the conviction that the Constitution and independence of the country must be defended by force of arms.

After an eloquent and able speech from Kossuth* the Diet forthwith decreed a levy of troops, which raised the Hungarian army to 200,000 men, and opened the credit which this measure required. The two enactments passed to this effect were presented for the royal sanction by the prime minister and the Minister of Justice; but a long time elapsed before these ministers could obtain a reply. In the mean time, the situation of the country becoming daily more alarming, and the Diet being persuaded that this state of things would lead to the total ruin of the kingdom, sent a deputation to the king headed by the president of the Chamber of Deputies.† It demanded the sanction of those laws which were requisite to save the country; requested the recall of the Hungarian troops quartered out of the country;‡ and begged the king to order the foreign troops, appointed to defend the nation, to discharge their duty faith-

---

* For Kossuth's speech, see Appendix, note 19.

† For address of Hungarian deputation and reply of the emperor, see Appendix, note 20.

‡ Latour, Minister of War, told Batthiányi that he could send no troops into Hungary; and upon his reply that Hungary would be obliged to look to her own security, " Then," replied Latour, " I will send troops to Hungary."

fully; and, finally, the king was again entreated to come into his kingdom, to restore peace and order to the country. The deputation received an evasive reply. But at the same time, and while the two ministers, Batthiányi and Deak, were still at Vienna, the king, without acquainting them, dispatched on the 31st of August a letter to the Palatine,* directing him to send several members of the Hungarian ministry to Vienna, for the two-fold object of adopting measures in concert with the Austrian ministry; to consolidate and insure the unity of the government of the monarchy; and to open negotiations with the Croats, in order to reconcile their interests with those of Hungary. The king declared it as an indispensable condition to every attempt for this purpose, that the Baron Jellacic should take part in the conferences, that all preparations for war should cease on both sides, and that the districts of the military frontier (which had always formed part of Hungary) should be provisionally subject to the Austrian ministry. In the same document, a communication was made to the Hungarian ministry of a note of the Austrian cabinet on the relations to be established between Austria and Hungary. It was also stated that the provisions of the law of 1848, by which the Archduke Palatine had been appointed depository of the royal authority, and chief of the executive power in the absence of the king, and that by which a responsible ministry had been conceded to Hungary, detaching from the central government of Vienna the administration of war, of finance, and of commerce, were contrary to the Pragmatic Sanction, opposed to the legal relations between Austria and Hungary, and detrimental alike to the interests of both countries.

It is a favorite plea with the Austrian cabinet and its partisans, that the concessions of 1848 were not only extorted from the emperor, but were also at variance with the spirit of the Hungarian Constitution, and with the Pragmatic Sanction in particular.†

---

* For copy of letter, see Appendix, note 21.

† By a letter from the Archduke Palatine to the emperor, dated the 24th of March, 1848 (discovered among his papers after he had left Pesth), it would seem that the royal word was not intended by the imperial advisers to be a real security, and that the Viennese cabinet secretly reserved the liberty of retracting its

Is it reasonable to suppose that a hundred members of the Hungarian Diet could have had the magic power to extort concessions, by violence, of the sovereign in his own palace, surrounded as he was by eighteen thousand faithful troops, and have imposed on him in the Austrian capital laws hostile to Austria? Could the terror they inspired have been so great as to have induced him, nearly a month later (11th of April), to quit his capital and go to Pressburg, to confirm by his sanction the laws extracted of him by force? Could the spell thrown around his majesty by these hundred deputies have been such as to compel him nearly three months afterward, in his speech from the throne (on the 2d of July), formally and voluntarily to recognize them all?

If not extracted by force from the sovereign, were these confirmations of 1848 at variance with the spirit of the Hungarian Constitution or of the Pragmatic Sanction? The two concessions complained of are, first, that which conferred executive power on the Palatine in the absence of the king; and, second, that which constituted a responsible ministry for Hungary. Were these inallowable innovations? Both these questions may at once be answered by reference to the law of 1608. By the 18th Article of that law it is provided, " That when the king is kept out of the country by serious causes, and prolongs his absence, the Palatine is to be invested with full powers to govern and administer the kingdom of Hungary according to the laws and national customs."

By Article 5th of the same law, the king is obliged to name a High Treasurer of the kingdom, independent of the powers of Vienna, whose duty it is to discharge the functions of his ministry without reference to the Austrian Chamber of Finance. Besides, the demand for a separate ministry for Hungary was not a new idea, but was based on numerous statutes, that of Charles the Sixth (1715), of Maria Theresa (1741), of Leopold the Second (1790), and, more recently, of Francis in

---

concessions on the first opportunity; and, accordingly, the archduke proposes in that letter three methods of abrogating the Hungarian immunities—a peasant war to be excited against the nobles, a commissioner to be armed with martial law, or a temporary compromise with Count Batthiányi, the then head of the Hungarian ministry. For this remarkable letter, see Appendix, note 22.

1827. Hungary was always alive to this privilege, and did not cease to protest against its violations.

But the principal, and indeed the only plausible objection urged against the concession of a separate and independent ministry for Hungary has been that it violated that unity of the empire established by the Pragmatic Sanction. But this objection is based upon an assumption altogether untenable.

The Pragmatic Sanction, as has been already shown, created no union between the hereditary states of Austria and Hungary, but that which exists in the identity of a common sovereign. No treaty is in existence which decrees the dominion of one state over the other. Hungary is as independent of the ‘ hereditary states as the hereditary states are of Hungary. If the King of Hungary thinks proper, in concert with the Diet, to extend or modify the powers of the Diet and the Constitution, Austria and the emperor have no right to make an objection.

The independence of Hungary has been recognized, both by her relations with the hereditary states and in the recognized states of Europe. The hereditary states, for example, have been successively annexed to the Roman-German Empire and to the Germanic Confederation, but the kingdom of Hungary has never constituted a part of either the one or the other. All foreign powers have invariably given the emperor-king the double title of Emperor of Germany, afterward of Austria, and King of Hungary. In consequence of these considerations, the Austrian subjects of the emperor-king are alluded to in the Hungarian laws as *foreigners*. A mass of laws enact that *foreigners* can not take any part in the administration of Hungary, nor in her affairs; and that the king can not rule but with the assistance of Hungarian counselors. Neither the answers nor the ordinances of the king have ever borne the signature of any foreign minister. The affairs of Hungary have ostensibly never been managed but by Hungarians. By what right can it, then, be pretended to submit the decisions of the Hungarian legislative body, approved by the King of Hungary, to the approbation of an Austrian ministry? Compare these concessions, too, with the guarantees imposed upon Leopold the Second in 1790, and accepted by his successor in 1792, and

which, until recently, were the bases of the relations between
Austria and Hungary.

The twenty-five articles of the Diploma of Inauguration in
1790, after generally affirming the independence of the crown,
the laws and the privileges of Hungary, proceed to decree,
among other enactments, triennial convocation of the Diet, exclusion of *foreigners* (that is, of Austrians) from the government, and the residence of the emperor-king, during a portion
of every year, in his Hungarian dominions. They declare that
the king can neither make laws nor impose taxes without the
consent of the Diet, and that royal proclamations, unless countersigned by one, at least, of the boards of the Hungarian government, are null and void.

There are many other details, but these alone are sufficient
to show that the demands of the Hungarians in 1848 did not,
as regards Austria at least, introduce any sudden or violent
innovations into the federal relations between the two countries.

It remains only to be seen whether, in the interval of nearly
sixty years (1790 to 1848), Austria performed her portion of
this compact, and whether Hungary has protested unreasona-
bly and prematurely against her grievances.* This interval
of more than half a century may be divided into two periods :
the first comprising the wars which followed the first French
Revolution, and which ended in 1815 ; the second beginning
from that date, and terminating with the present civil convulsions.

In the former of these periods, the adage *silent leges inter
arma* was once more exemplified, and the Hungarian nation
was too much occupied with wars and rumors of wars to proceed regularly or zealously with constitutional or social reforms. Francis the First, when the victories of Napoleon were
shattering the unity of Austria, reminded the Diet of its response to Maria Theresa at a similar crisis, and on each appeal
was met with equal devotion, if not with equal enthusiasm.
The chivalrous nature of the people, and their loyalty to the
Kaiser's throne, led them not only to reject with disdain the
proposals for independence made them by Napoleon, but to

* Edinburgh Review.

submit to repeated and exorbitant demands for men and money, without exacting a corresponding redress of grievances.*

For twenty years this unequal contest was continued, as has been shown, between a generous people and an exacting prince, until it became a matter of general observation and notoriety that the Diets were convoked to grant supplies and to be dismissed whenever they spoke of grievances.

With the restoration of peace in 1815, a new era began for Hungary. In spite of wars, and levies, and bad government, the kingdom had advanced in material prosperity, and it was expected that peace would afford leisure for carrying out the social and constitutional reforms which the commission of 1790 had recommended. But it was an era of brief promise and protracted disappointment. Austria, as a member of the Holy Alliance, was now more than ever determined to place Hungary upon the same footing with the hereditary states. A court party was sedulously fostered in the country and in the Chambers; Austrian officers were put in command of Hungarian regiments; the bondage of the press was rigorously enforced; new shackles were imposed on trade; the currency was depreciated; for twelve years no Diet was summoned, and nearly every article of the Constitution of 1790 was assailed by violence or evaded by intrigue. At length the arbitrary measures by which, in 1822 and 1823, the Austrian cabinet attempted the express violations of the Diploma of Leopold, were arrested by the imposing attitude of the Diet in 1825. Francis the First retracted and apologized, and from that period the operations of the Austrian government became less daring and more insidious. Such, then, have been the relations of Hungary to Austria during one of the most momentous eras in the annals of the world. Twenty years of nearly incessant war were followed by an even longer interval of almost uninterrupted peace. During the former period, Hungary was Austria's foremost bulwark, furnished her best troops, her commissariat, and her magazines. During the latter period, Austria has requited Hungary for these services and sacrifices with successive and systematic endeavors to abridge or cancel her

---

* Edinburgh Review.

indisputable immunities ; to degrade into a subject province "an old and haughty people, brave in arms ;" and, finally, to clog and crush its spirit of enterprise with vexatious imposts and absurd fiscal regulations. The reforms of 1848 may have been imperative in their tone, but the results of sixty years endurance can scarcely be termed *sudden*, nor the assertion of rights, sanctioned for centuries and as often invaded, be justly designated as *unseasonable* or *unconstitutional.**

The opposition of the Austrian cabinet to the late concessions, and which displayed itself only months after the concessions were made, resulted, it is more probable, not from any constitutional scruples which should have been excited the moment the violation had been committed, but from the altered condition of the empire, consequent upon the late triumphs of the imperial arms in Italy.

When, during the months of April, May, and June, Radetzky, driven out of Milan, and pent up with his army in the fortress of Verona, the cabinet of Austria were daily expecting the tidings of his surrender to the King of Piedmont, who not only surrounded him, but with five times his force covered the entire plains of Lombardy, no dissatisfaction was manifested at the course of the Hungarians. It was only during the months of July and August, when the gallant veteran Radetzky, sufficiently re-enforced, issues from behind the walls of Verona, assumes the offensive, and by a succession of brilliant victories, drives the Piedmontese from the territory of Austria, and enters in triumph the gates of Milan ; it is then, but not till then, that we hear for the first time the cry of unseasonable and unconstitutional concessions !

The policy of Austria, for a long time as two-faced as that emblem the double-headed eagle which she bears on her standard, now unmasked itself, and the ministers boldly evinced their intention to subvert the Constitution of Hungary, subjugate the country, compel the Magyars to purchase peace at the price of their independence, and thus blend the various parts of the emperor's dominions into one undistinguished mass. On the 4th of September, the Hungarians determined

---

* Edinburgh Review.

by a vote of the Diet, to make one more effort with the emperor; and accordingly dispatched another deputation to Vienna, to urge his majesty to sanction the two proposed laws, and to come himself to Pesth to oppose to the rebels his royal name. The application was again refused.

On the same day, the 4th of September, the emperor, at the instigation of the Austrian ministry, signed a manifesto* recalling the decree which suspended Jellacic from all his dignities under a charge of treason, on the pretext that the accusations against the Ban were false, and that he had exhibited undeviating fidelity to the house of Austria.   Jellacic was, consequently, reinstated in all his offices, although he was at the time actually encamped with his army on the frontiers of Hungary, ready to invade the country, and awaiting, perhaps, this very decree to wipe off the stigma upon him, before he proceeded to carry his designs into effect, which he did in five or six days after, about the time that it would have taken the decree to reach him.

When the tidings of this retraction on the part of the monarch of the charges against Jellacic reached Pesth, and when, about the same period, the enraged deputation from the Diet, their caps adorned with red plumes, returned with a rejection of their application by the emperor, the Hungarian ministry, which had been appointed in March, tendered their resignations.

The Palatine then, by virtue of his powers, called on Count Louis Batthiányi, president of the ministry which had just resigned, to form a new ministry.

All hope of a peaceful adjustment seemed to be at an end ; but, as a last resource, a deputation of Hungarian deputies (sixteen in number, and headed by Deak) was sent to propose to the Diet of Austria, then sitting at Vienna, that the two countries should mutually guarantee their Constitutions and their independence.

Upon the presentation of their credentials, the President of the Assembly declared that the rules of the House did not permit the admission of such a deputation.   One of the members desired that an exception should be made in this instance ; a

---

* For this document, see Appendix, note No. 23.

long debate ensued upon the subject of their admission, when
the Diet finally concluded, that as Hungary, since the revolution in March last, had constituted itself into a nation separate
and independent from the Austrian empire, the deputation could
only be considered as one from a foreign country, which they
had no right or power to receive.

Commissioned to form a ministry, Louis Batthiányi took up
the direction of affairs, upon the condition that Jellacic, whose
troops had already invaded Hungary, should be ordered to retire beyond the frontiers.

He was answered by the king that this condition could not
be accepted before the other ministry was known.   Batthiányi
lost no time in presenting his list at Vienna ; but what affords
strong proof of the treachery of the movement, Jellacic had in
the interim passed the borders with his Croat and Austrian
regiments, and was at that moment an invader upon the soil
of Hungary.

On the 9th of September, Jellacic crossed the Drave (the
boundary between Croatia and Hungary), at Zegrad, at the
head of his Croat troops, and there, joined by the Austrian regiments, which had marched from various parts of Southern
Hungary to put themselves under his orders, he proceeded
without resistance to Kanisa.*

Jellacic, almost wholly unprovided with cavalry, issued to
all regiments stationed in Hungary a proclamation summoning them to join him, and loitered about the neighborhood of
Kanisa to await the results of his proclamations.   The colonel
of a regiment of *cuirassiers* (Hardig), who with his troops
was on his way to Austria, where his Bohemians were to be
exchanged for a Hungarian regiment of hussars, refused obedience to the Hungarian ministry, and submitted to the order
of Jellacic.

---

* About this time Hungarian shepherds surprised a courier from Jellacic with
letters directed to Latour, which plainly evinced the understanding which existed between the Viennese Minister of War and Jellacic.   The latter, in his dispatch, *acknowledged the receipt of military stores, requested more, and solicited his
public recognition by the emperor, with full authority to carry on his enterprise energetically.*   But a short time before, Latour had, on a question put to him in the
Diet, pledged his word of honor " that he had no official relations with Jellacic.'
—*Pulszky*, 171.

At this point General Teleki, a Hungarian commander, surrendered himself with his troops to the Ban. On the entrance of the Ban into Letenye, he was received by the population with the most joyful manifestations. Here he gained an accession to his force of fourteen thousand men, with sixty-two cannons, to which the troops of Kempen, sixteen thousand men, and twelve cannons, were afterward added. Another division, Hartbell, entered Czaknthurn, with eighteen thousand men and twenty-four cannons, without striking a blow. The National Guard every where dissolved at their approach, and the united army took up the line of march from Kanisa toward Pesth.*

The die was now cast—the Rubicon passed. The Diet appealed to the heroism of the nation. The people rose *en masse;* defenders of their country flocked from all quarters. The Hungarian regiments of the line, until then shaken by the intrigues of the reactionary party, were carried away by universal enthusiasm. But the forces thus collected to resist the invasion were still without a commander-in-chief or a staff, without sufficient arms or ammunition, and, for the most part, without military discipline or organization; and the small army of five thousand disciplined troops, with a few thousand raw levies, had to retire before the overwhelming force of the enemy.

Under these circumstances, the representatives of the nation offered the command of the Hungarian forces to the Palatine Viceroy, in his capacity of captain general of the country, in order that, by the authority attached to his position and his person, he should render all hesitation in the camp impossible, and give to the movements of the army that unity and energy necessary to success.

The Palatine, after the measure had been approved by the king, accepted the command, and proceeded to Vesprim, at the north point of the Platten Sea, where the regiments which had retreated before Jellacic from the borders, and the new recruits from Pesth were concentrated. Both parties, the invaders and the invaded, appeared at this time to be acting under the countenance and direction of the emperor-king.† After joining the

---

* When the news of Jellacic's invasion reached Pesth, the Diet decreed the issue of Hungarian money, and the immediate increase of the army.

† " Since Jellacic crossed the Drave, enlistments for Hungary had publicly taken

army and hastily organizing it, the Palatine opened communications with the Ban, encamped at the southern side of the lake, and made an effort for a meeting.

He proceeded down the lake in a steamer adorned with the Hungarian tricolor, and, on nearing the opposite point, dispatched his adjutant ashore and summoned the Ban to a conference in the steamer. Jellacic having his allotted task to fulfill, and knowing that an interview could be attended with no useful result, declined it, with the very unmilitary excuse that his officers would not suffer him to comply with the command of his imperial highness.* The Palatine then (summoned to Vienna as an archduke by the emperor) left the army, passed

place in Vienna, with the knowledge of the Minister of the Interior. Baron Dobblhof looked on the Croatian invasion of Hungary as a matter in which he was wholly neutral. He permitted the enlistment for the Hungarians, and simultaneously an enrollment for Jellacic. Lads, from eighteen to twenty-two years of age, were to be seen, some with the Hungarian, others with the Croatian 'tricolor,' drinking together at one and the same table in the tavern, and thus spending their enlistment-money together. These poor youths associated and joked good humoredly with one another; nevertheless, they knew that their next meeting was to be in opposite ranks, on the bloody field of battle."—*Pulszky.*

* Jellacic was invited by the Hungarians, on six different occasions, to a conference for the settlement of their differences:

1st. About the last of March, he was invited by the Palatine of Hungary, at Vienna, to an interview.

2d. About the same time, he was requested by Louis Batthiányi to come to Pressburg on the 11th of April, when the emperor was to be present for the purpose of approving of the laws passed by the Diet.

3d. On the 10th of May, he was summoned by the Palatine and ministry of Hungary to come to Pesth, for the adjustment of their difficulties.

4th. On the 4th of June, at Innspruck, he was invited by the Hungarian ministers, Batthiányi and Esterhazy, to a consultation.

5th. On the 4th of July, he was summoned to Vienna by the Archduke John, to meet the Hungarian ministry, and to lay their respective complaints before him.

6th. On the 27th of September, he was invited by the Palatine of Hungary to a conference on board the steamer in the Platten Sea.

The Vienna Gazette publishes the following report of what was said by Jellacic to a professor who conversed with him, in the course of a visit paid to a brother under the orders of the Ban:

"I am not an enemy of liberty. I spoke and acted for it at a time when no one in Vienna dared to open his mouth in its favor. I can not bear oppression. I have considered it a sacred duty to call the people to whom I belong to arms, because it was endeavored to oppress them. It is for liberty, and not for oppression, that I have drawn my sword. I will neither effect a reaction myself at Vienna, nor serve as an instrument in the hands of others to do so. I am not a servant of the Camarilla."

If these statements of Jellacic were sincere, why, it may be asked, did he de

II.   F

through Pesth, and, on his arrival in Vienna, sent in to the Hungarians his resignation of the office of Palatine, and retired to his private residence on the Rhine, despite his enthusiastic boast that "history would not find him among the traitors of the nation." If the contest in which he was engaged was illegal and unjust, why did he enter it? and if legal and just, why did he abandon it?

In the mean time, Count Louis Batthiányi received the official notification that the ministry he proposed was not accepted by the king; and another member of the Diet, the Baron Nicholas Vay, was commissioned by the king to form a ministry. Finally, a royal ordinance,* dated the 25th of September, which was not countersigned by any minister, placed all the troops stationed in Hungary under the command of Count Francis Lamberg, as "Commissioner Plenipotentiary," and instructing him to effect at once an armistice between the contending armies in the Hungarian territory, and to make every effort to bring about " a pacification of the internal quarrels, and to restore between his Hungarian and non-Hungarian subjects that harmony which had existed for centuries, and which was assured by the Pragmatic Sanction." On the same day, the emperor issued a proclamation† to his Hungarian army, declaring that, as he was determined not to suffer, under any circumstances, a conflict between his troops under the command of the Hungarian ministry and those under the Ban of Croatia, he had directed his imperial plenipotentiary, Count Lamberg, to repair at once to the head-quarters of the Hungarian army, and to put an end to all hostilities; that he had, at the same time, sent a similar order to Baron Jellacic, in command of the Croatian forces, and that he expected their obedience, and that they would terminate the unnatural contest between troops who had sworn allegiance to the same flag, and whose duty it was to fight only for the same objects and in defense of a common country.

This effort of the emperor-king at pacification may, on his

---

cline all these invitations for a conference except one, and at that one, as has been seen, exhibit no disposition toward the settlement of their controversy?

* For this document in full, see Appendix, note No. 24.

† For this proclamation, see Appendix, note No. 25.

part, have been sincere and honest; but the Hungarians construed it as full of the deepest treachery. Jellacic, they said, had invaded the country, relying on meeting with no opposition from troops trained under Austrian discipline; letters of his that were intercepted revealed this deception, and the fear that was felt of seeing a collision take place. It was, they thought, to guard against this collision, to take away from Hungary her only chance of success, and to deliver her up defenseless to the enemy, that the court, conspiring with Jellacic, gave the command of the national forces to Count Lamberg, who was ordered not to allow them to act.

Jellacic's unprovoked invasion of Hungary, his refusal to meet the Palatine, whose only object could have been pacification, and his continued advance toward the capital of the kingdom after the receipt of the emperor's communication enjoining a cessation of hostilities, are all strong facts in confirmation of the suspicions of the Hungarians.

Meanwhile Jellacic with his forces advances toward the capital, the feeble Hungarian army retreating before him. Without resistance he enters, with flaming torches, the city of Stuhlweissenburg, and, after establishing himself, appoints Count Eugen Zichy, with whom he had entered the city arm-in-arm, as administrator of the comitat, an appointment which afterward cost the recipient his life.*

---

* Zichy was seized by Görgey's orders, brought before a court-martial, presided over by the latter, accused of high treason against the nation, and of having secreted treasures wherewith to enable the Ban Jellacic to defray the expenses of his army, and was thereupon sentenced to death, and forthwith hung. Schütte, in speaking of this event, says, " From that moment the name of Görgey was popular, and the eyes of Kossuth were now directed toward him."

THE LAST MOMENTS OF COUNT ZICHY.—We read in the Hamburgh *Boersenhalle :*—" The following facts have been communicated respecting the murder of Zichy. He was traveling in company with his brother, the captain, in the direction of Weissenburg, when the carriage was stopped by our outposts. The various questions put were replied to by Captain Zichy. The outposts were on the point of letting the carriage drive on, when Count Zichy, who was of a very arrogant temper, seized his pistols. For this indiscretion the sentinels conducted him to the Loreke camp, where Major Görgey held an investigation, and then found the letters which proved a connection with Jellacic. A council of war was immediately summoned, and five hours after his seizure Count Zichy was hanging on the gallows. He retained his presence of mind to the last moment, and, as he was ascending the gallows, he said, ' I die quietly. I have always loved my country, and never was a traitor. God grant that I may be the last

The city of Pesth was now, by these occurrences, thrown into a state of the utmost excitement, and the cry of treason sounded from every lip. The treacherous behavior of Dreyhaun, the doubtful conduct of Blomberg, the surprising course of Teleki, the desertion of the Italian light horse, for fourteen years stationed in Hungary, the continual retreat of the Magyar force under Moga, the sudden resignation of the Palatine, the unpatriotic course of Zichy, and the approach of the enemy to Velencze, only twenty miles from the capital, caused an agitation in Pesth which it is not difficult to imagine, but would be impossible to describe.

On the night of the 27th of September, the Hungarian Diet, in a public session, discussed the appointment of Count Lamberg as royal commissioner, countersigned by no minister. The debate was concluded by the adoption of a decree declaring the appointment of Count Lamberg illegal and unconstitutional; the Constitution enacting "that the ordinances, decrees, and appointments of the king are not legal but when they bear the countersignature of one of the ministers sitting at Buda-Pesth."* They called upon the authority of the country, the citizens, the army, and Count Lamberg himself, to obey this decree under pain of high treason.

On the 28th, the rumor was circulated through the city that Lamberg was in Pesth; that, in the name of the king, he had forbidden the dispatch of troops, provisions, or arms to the camp at Velencze; that the gates of Buda were to be closed, at the order of the count; and that he was in conference with suspicious officers of high rank. The furious and excited populace rushed into the fortress of Ofen, and examined many houses in search of him; and only by the determination and promptitude of the police and National Guard were prevented from committing the utmost violence.

---

victim for my country, and may God bless it.' On the last step but one he remained standing, and replied to the executioner who desired him to come up, 'What, must I mount yet higher?' He then drew a small vial from his pocket, and drank off the poison which it contained, mounted the other step, and begged the executioner to bring a strong rope, upon which the latter replied, 'The one that is here is quite good enough for your excellency.' In a moment after the count was no more."

* See Appendix, Article 3d, sec. 3d, Constitution of 1848.

The unfortunate Count Lamberg, in obedience to the orders of his sovereign, left Vienna on the 27th; and on the 28th, at noon, had just arrived in Buda, attended only by his servant, in search of Count Batthiányi, to countersign his commission, and was proceeding in a carriage over the pontoon bridge across the Danube, which connects that city with Ofen, when he was recognized by a sergeant, who violently dragged him from his carriage; and by a German student and a young Hungarian from Transylvania, Kalossy by name, he was struck down.*

In vain did he exhibit to the ruthless mob his royal passport and commission—in vain did he demand to be carried before Kossuth. He was murdered on the spot, and his scarcely lifeless body dragged through the streets of the Hungarian capital. This horrible deed was the act of an infuriated mob, which the fearful excitement of the city might easily explain, but which no circumstances on earth can justify.

The Diet, it is true, expressed its sorrow at the bloody deed, and ordered criminal proceedings to be instituted against the murderers; but no criminals were taken, no investigation had, and no efficient means adopted by the representatives of the people to remove this awful stain from the national escutcheon.†

On the following day, the 29th of September, a decisive battle was fought against Jellacic, at Pacoszd, in the neighborhood of Velencze, within twenty miles of the Hungarian capital.

The Hungarians were determined to make that spot either their Marathon or Thermopylæ: there, like the Athenians, they must repel the invaders; or, like the Spartans, they "must die there, in obedience to their country's laws."

The eloquence and the energy of Kossuth had collected a considerable body of troops. "It is an eternal law of God," said he, in his proclamation, "that whosoever abandoneth himself will be forsaken by the Lord. It is an eternal law that, whosoever assisteth himself, him will the Lord assist. It is a

---

* Pulszky.

† One of the murderers. Kalossy, who first fled into Transylvania, afterward returned, and was caught and hung by Haynau, in November, 1849.

divine law that false swearing, by its results, chastiseth itself. It is a law of our Lord, that whosoever availeth himself of perjury and injustice, prepareth himself the triumph of justice. Standing on these eternal laws of the Universe, I swear that my prophesy will be fulfilled : it is that the freedom of Hungary will be effected by this invasion of Hungary by Jellacic. Between Veszprim and Weissenburg, the women shall dig a deep grave, in which we will bury the name, the honor, the nation of Hungary, or our enemies. And on this grave shall stand a monument inscribed with a record of our shame, 'So God punishes cowardice !' or we will plant on it the tree of freedom, eternally green, from out of whose foliage shall be heard the voice of God speaking as from the fiery bush to Moses, ' The spot on which thou standeth is holy ground—thus do I reward the brave. To the Magyars freedom, renown, well-being, and happiness !' "

This noble invocation was nobly answered. The patriot citizens hastened to the field. Jellacic was repulsed, and the capital saved. After his defeat, the Ban asked for and obtained of the Hungarians an armistice of forty-eight hours,* on the condition that, during that time, no change should take place in the position of the respective armies. But, faithless to his engagement, he fled, abandoning to their fate the detached corps of his army, and the Croat rear-guard, ten thousand strong, marching to his assistance under the command of Generals Roth and Philipovich, and which, at Ozora, on the 5th of October, fell into the hands of the Hungarians. Sixty officers were taken prisoners ; twelve cannons, seven standards, and eleven thousand muskets were the trophies of the day.

When the brutal murder of Count Lamberg reached Vienna, the emperor-king, by a new ordinance, nominated Count Adam Recsey President of the Hungarian Ministry. This ordinance had no other countersignature than Recsey's. Another ordinance,† bearing date the 3d of October, and also countersigned by Recsey, declared : 1st. The Hungarian Diet dis-

---

* According to Pulszky, " three days."
† For this document, see Appendix, note No. 26.

solved. 2d. Its decrees which had not yet been sanctioned, annulled. 3d. Jellacic appointed royal commissioner, with full executive power throughout the entire kingdom; the civil laws suspended, and the country placed in a state of siege.

This ordinance of his majesty produced, as might have been expected, the utmost dissatisfaction and excitement among the Hungarians.

Taking their stand upon the Constitution, which enacts that royal ordinances are not legal unless countersigned by one of the responsible Hungarian ministry, and which further enacts that the Diet can neither be closed nor dissolved before the vote of the budget; convinced that the king had not the right to leave the country at the mercy of an armed enemy; to abolish the Constitution, and take the legislative power from the Hungarian National Assembly, the representatives of the nation declared the self-styled royal ordinance null and void, and the measures which accompanied it illegal and unconstitutional, both in form and substance.

The Diet further decided that it would continue its sittings, and would persist in the fulfillment of its duties. It declared Joseph Jellacic, and all those who aided him, traitors to the country; and decreed that Adam Recsey, for having countersigned an illegal ordinance, should be brought to trial, in accordance with the Constitution.*

Finally, in the absence of a ministry, the country not being able to remain without a government, the executive power was intrusted to a Committee of Defense, which had been previously formed to assist the administration of Count Batthiányi, and which, from that time, was invested with the extraordinary power which the crisis demanded.†

---

* For Article 3d, 1848, act 3, section 32, see Appendix, note No. 27.

† At this stage of proceedings in Hungary, a number of the high aristocracy—such as Louis Batthiányi, Deak, Széchényi, Wesseleni, and others, called by some the *Girondists* of Hungary, and who had, up to this time, supported all the measures of the movement party—alarmed at the violence of the Diet, "indignant at the murder of Count Lamberg," and fearful that Kossuth was hurrying the country into revolution, withdrew altogether from the struggle. They were advocates of reform, they were not yet ready for rebellion. Kossuth, on the other hand, deprived of this conservative portion of his party, was compelled to seek support from, and consequently to fall under the influence of, the more anarchical faction.

Louis Kossuth, representative of the people, and until then Minister of Finance, was named president of this committee. Descended of a poor but noble family of Slavic origin, Louis Kossuth was born the 27th April, 1802, at Monok, a small town in the Zemplén comitat, in the north of Hungary. After a university education, he commenced the study of the law. In the year 1837, he was selected by two peeresses and a magnate as the representative of their *seigneuries* in the Hungarian Diet. In that capacity he transmitted periodical letters to his patronesses, with an account of the proceedings of the Assembly. The want of any communication by the press gave great importance to these documents. They were circulated from hand to hand; copies were at first multiplied in manuscript, and afterward in lithograph. The reputation of the young jurist's epistles had already excited the suspicion of the Austrian authorities, and this last step gave them the opportunity they were seeking. The lithographed sheets came under the denomination of a newspaper, and unlicensed newspapers were prohibited in Hungary. In May, 1837, under the reactionary ministry of Palfy, Kossuth was arrested for refusing to obey a ministerial order forbidding the appearance of his manuscript journal, and for having declared that order illegal. After awaiting in confinement for two years, his trial, which had excited great interest, came on. His personal defense was eloquent and masterly; but he was found guilty, and sentenced to imprisonment for three years. This increased the ferment of the country; and, after an earnest protestation by the Diet, Kossuth was released from his imprisonment, under the general amnesty of 1840, granted by Count Mailath, the successor of Palfy. On quitting his prison, he began to edit the *Pesthi Hirlap*, the first Liberal journal published in Hungary, which he continued until 1844; when, owing to some misunderstanding among the members of his party, he relinquished his connection with the press. In 1847, he was elected a deputy for the comitat of Pesth by a large majority; and in the Diet, by his fervid eloquence, skillful debating talent, and thorough knowledge of public affairs, he at once became the head of the party which had now attained the majority.

Such was his position when, a few months later, the revolutions of Europe broke forth, and his history since then is that of Hungary itself.*

After the defeat of Jellacic and his troops at Velencze, and during the existence of the armistice of forty-eight hours, which he had sought for and obtained, contrary to the stipulations of that convention, he, instead of remaining on the spot, withdrew his forces in the night from Weissenburg to Raab. Upon the expiration of the armistice he took possession of Raab, and then marched on Pressburg. After some negotiation, the latter city surrendered to him; but he had not time to collect a tribute laid upon the town, when the Hungarian army coming up, he retreated across the Leytha into Austria, and there, about the first days of October, dispatched a messenger to the Minister of War at Vienna for additional troops to carry on his operations against Pesth. The Minister of War, Count Latour, in obedience to that call, was dispatching troops on the 6th of October to the aid of Jellacic, when the revolution broke out in Vienna, in the effort there made to prevent the departure of the troops.

Upon receiving the tidings of the outbreak in Vienna, Jellacic with his army marched to Laxemburg, in the neighborhood of Vienna, where he subsequently united his forces with those of Prince Windischgrätz in the subjugation of the capital.

---

* The *character* of Kossuth will be considered after his acts shall have been detailed; or, in other words, his career in Hungary concluded.

CHAPTER VI.

THE Revolution in Vienna, of the 13th March, as has been
described, was followed by a complete prostration of civil authority and a suspension of military power. The emperor,
not accustomed to grant concessions, nor the people to receive
them, neither party knew when and where to stop. The people, intoxicated with the idea of liberty, gave themselves up
to the utmost license, which the government, in its weakness,
found itself unable to restrain; victories were, in consequence,
won, without a blow, by undisciplined mobs over veteran
troops; and the capital was abandoned to the caprices of a
band of students and National Guards; while the ministers
and their sovereign, who had previously exercised unlimited
power, stooped now to the most abject capitulation, or sought
safety in ignominious flight.

During the entire summer, the city had been abandoned to
the rule of the populace, to preserve order whenever it suited
them to do so, or to indulge in disorder and license whenever
such a course was more compatible with their inclinations.

The aristocracy had fled, their splendid equipages and rich
liveries had vanished, and even the ordinary civil dress of modern times had almost entirely disappeared from the streets.

Students, in their Calabrian hats and feathers, blue frocks,
with their shirt-collars à la Byron, German ribbons dangling
at their button-holes, and large cavalry swords swinging at
their sides and at every step striking the pavement, were alone
seen strutting through the streets, with airs as consequential
as if they had been the lords of the soil.

The university and the Democratic clubs, composed of Radicals, Socialists, and Terrorists combined, and presided over by foreign emissaries, usurped the entire control of the city, and the peaceful inhabitants were subjected to a terrorism as complete, though, from the absence of the guillotine, not so bloody, as that which reigned in France in 1789.

The students quartered themselves upon the inhabitants, who were not only forced to support, but also to supply them with funds and every luxury they might demand, even in some instances, among the lower classes, it is said, to the sacrifice of their daughters' virtue.

With one hundred thousand workmen at their command, whom, by the sound of the tocsin, they could gather in an hour, and who were ever ready to execute their order, regardless of consequences, the government, it will be perceived, had been changed from the palace to the university—from a government of order and respectability to a most cruel and unmitigated despotism.

One day, an order would be issued that the German flag should be suspended from the window of every house in the city; and at another, that an illumination should take place on a certain night, in honor of some Democratic triumph; and these orders were as readily and implicitly obeyed as if they had been the ukase of a czar; for if any one ventured on disobedience, his house would be attacked, the inmates treated with indignity and violence, every window smashed, and all articles of furniture demolished.

This anarchical spirit, which had kept the city for months on the brink of a convulsion, and which would sooner or later have destroyed itself by the excess of its own violence, was fostered by the divisions of hostile nationalities; and the Hungarian Radicals, it was said, availed themselves of the disaffected state of Vienna to produce an outbreak and create a diversion in their favor, when their danger became most imminent, and Jellacic and his invading army were within a day's march of Pesth.

Hostilities between the Croatians and Hungarians had been for some time progressing. The imperial commissioner, Count Lamberg, dispatched to Pesth, had been brutally murdered;

and, on the 3d of October, the Emperor of Austria issued a proclamation declaring that the Ban of Croatia should have command of all the forces in Hungary, and be constituted "Commissioner Plenipotentiary," with full powers and authority as the chief executive of Hungary. To sustain the purposes of this proclamation, and to reduce the revolting province to subjection, the emperor directed that the large military force then in Galicia should repair to the northern frontier of Hungary, and that several regiments from Vienna should be dispatched to the aid of the Ban of Croatia, now appointed military governor of Hungary, Croatia, Slavonia, and Dalmatia.

Several regiments of Italian infantry had left on the evening of the 5th of October, and on the next day, the 6th, in conformity to orders, the Richter battalion of grenadiers, for many years quartered in Vienna, and who had contracted numberless ties of intimacy with the population, were to take up the line of march for the same destination.

A body of students, and portions of the National Guard and citizens of the faubourg in which they had been quartered, determined to oppose their removal, whether bribed by Hungarian agents, as many believed, or as they themselves alleged, in order that the struggle for independence then going on in Hungary might not be effectually checked, and from an apprehension that the emperor intended, in the event of success in that country, to avail himself of the army which it would place at his command, to put down the constitutional system in Austria.

For some days this regiment had shown signs of insubordination, and, worked up to resistance by an excess of spirituous liquors, " which had been purposely administered in the well-known pot-houses,"* the order to march was, on the evening of the 5th, received by them with strong indications of mutiny.

The manufacturing population of the Gumpendorf suburb, in which the barracks of this regiment were situated, became excited ; and when it appeared that the grenadiers were on the verge of open revolt, a numerous deputation of the Democratic Association, composed of students, National Guards, women, and Magyars, with their national colors on their caps, march-

---

* Dunder's Revolution of the 6th of October in Vienna.

ed down to applaud and salute them. The grenadiers now refused to march, unless one of their comrades, who had been put
under arrest the preceding day, was restored to them. Count
Auersperg, then in military command of Vienna, underrating
the gravity of these circumstances, neither countermanded the
order, nor took the necessary precautions to enforce its fulfillment, but contented himself with replying to the committee that
reported them, " Do not be alarmed ; nothing will happen ; the
grenadiers will march off without their imprisoned comrade."

The National Guard and the disaffected began, meantime,
to muster in support of the refractory grenadiers. At four
o'clock, on the morning of the 6th, the peremptory order was
given to march ; and some other troops, less disposed to frater-
nize with the people, set the example ; but it was two hours
later before the Richter corps would move, and then, with every sign of insubordination, they broke to pieces all the implements and furniture in the *caserne.* At an early hour the
alarm-drum was beaten, without authority, in the Mariahülf
and Wieden, and the National Guards of those suburbs began
to assemble around the Gumpendorf *caserne,* although no orders to that effect had been given either by the commander-
in-chief or the district captain.

At half past five A.M., a regiment of cuirassiers arrived,
companies of grenadiers from other barracks also came up, and
the cavalry taking the disaffected grenadiers in the centre,
about six o'clock the march began. Repeated attempts were
made by the National Guard to stop the progress of the troops
on their way to the rail-road ; but these, by the promptness
and decision of the military escort, proving ineffectual, several
companies of Guards hurried off to the depot of the Northern
Rail-road, and there, while awaiting the arrival of the troops,
occupied themselves in tearing up the rails and destroying the
telegraph.

The march of the troops was the most irregular and confused—National Guards, women, and civilians walking in the
ranks of the military. As they passed along the *glacis,* the
grenadiers forcing the drummers to beat, in order to attract attention to them, drew together a mob of the most threatening
aspect.

The *rappel* was now beaten in the Leopold-Stadt and several other faubourgs, and National Guards without leaders, and workmen from all sides, rushed in, actuated apparently by the same motives, viz., to obstruct the departure of the troops, or, at least, to delay their advance until the Guards thought themselves strong enough to oppose effectually their passage.

When the troops reached the rail-road depôt, finding it occupied, and the rails torn up, the order was given to proceed to Gansersdorf; and they accordingly marched on through the Tabor line, with a view of crossing the bridges which span both arms of the Danube, and to enter the rail-road at Florisdorf, its first station.

Arrived at the Tabor Bridge, they found several arches of it torn up, and the lumber used to construct a barricade, which National Guards, students, and workmen had raised to prevent the passage of the troops. The battalion Richter arrived at the bridge, and the Hess division of it, headed by the major bearing the standard, passed the barricade and proceeded toward the second bridge; but the three other divisions of it refused, amid the cheers of the people.

Every instant the excitement increased. The university, now the centre of the revolutionary movement, was in commotion, and the Academic Legion marching to the rescue of the mutineers. Several students, mounting a wagon, harangued the populace, and declared that it was the will of the sovereign people to stand by the grenadiers, and that that will must be carried out, and the Camarilla and enemies of the people must be put down. While these things were transpiring, the imperial general, Breda, succeeded in collecting a small body of troops, with two cannons, and some sappers. He addressed the people, and tried to convince them that it was futile to attempt to restrain the military, who were bound implicitly to obey the orders of their commanders.

They endeavored to tear the general from his horse, and to treat him with other violence; and it was only upon his pledge to repair to the Minister of War, to receive new orders, that they suffered him to escape. During his absence, the troops were still more strongly pressed to stay; and by others the destruction of the Tabor Bridge was carried on. The pioneers attempted to repair it, but the National Guard, students, and workmen with spears prevented.

General Breda returned with the order from the Minister of War that the troops "must proceed." He crossed the river to announce the order to the division on that side, and on his return an attempt was made to throw him from the sleeper or beam of the bridge on which he was, into the Danube.

A short time after General Breda, a deputation of National Guards, students, and citizens called upon the Minister of War with the request that he would withdraw the order of march for the German grenadier battalions—which he most energetically refused, declaring to the deputation that, if they were possessed of any military knowledge, they might readily conceive that, while he might with propriety give counter orders to troops who obeyed, that to withdraw a given order to a mutinous corps because they refused to obey that order, could not be done without a destruction of all military discipline.

About ten o'clock, the National Guard and students occupied the rail-road dam ; below them, on the side of the road, stood the infantry regiment of Nassau, the pioneers, and cuirassiers, with three pieces of artillery. The battalion of German grenadiers stood upon the Great Tabor Bridge, surrounded by National Guards. The tocsin now rang in the city, the crowd became greater, and the excitement increased ; the detachments of troops which remained faithful to their duty were insulted. Still the hope of the government was to reduce the grenadiers to obedience without attacking the people. But they had yet to learn the disaffection of the great mass of the National Guard.

At eleven o'clock, while the pioneers were engaged in removing the barricade and repairing the bridge, an attempt was made by some workmen and others to capture a gun. The artillery officer retreated, and a powder wagon was all that they succeeded in carrying off. The workmen made a second attack with more success ; but at that moment, just as they had seized and were dragging off the gun, General Breda ordered the Nassau regiment of the line to fire, and the conflict began. The Academic Legion returned the discharge, and

Breda himself fell from his horse, pierced by two mortal wounds. Every one for a moment fled with loud cries, some over the bridges, others by the rail-road dam; while most of the Guards retreated to the cottages and trees in their rear, whence they began a murderous fire. An unarmed crowd that stood between the two fires fled in confusion, throwing the students standing on the rail-road down into the ditch; behind that ditch, and protected by it, the Academic Legion maintained a lively fire against the military. The action then became furious and general. The military attempted to take the dam by storm, but were beaten back, while it was at the same time attacked in the rear by the Guards and faithless grenadiers, who advanced over the bridge. About thirty were killed on the spot. Lieutenant-colonel Klein, of the Nassau regiment, fell at the head of his corps; but the Richter grenadiers, National Guard, and students so outnumbered the faithful military that the latter were driven back and forced to retreat, with the loss of two cannons.

To a want of decision on the part of General Breda, and his failure to make the proper dispositions for an energetic interference at the right moment, and suffering the crowd to approach so near as to obstruct the operations of the military, were ascribed, in a great measure, the repulse which the military sustained on that occasion. Their retreat was harassed by fire from the windows in the Augarten and in the Tabor Strasse. A second engagement took place between the Wrbna light horse and the mob on the Carmeliten Platz; but it was not till noon that any considerable detachment of troops entered the inner part of the city.

After routing the government troops, the insurgents marched from the suburbs into the town; the two captured cannons, the trophies of their victory, upon which were laid wounded students, were carried in triumph through the Leopold-Stadt by their comrades, National Guards, and faithless grenadiers, and deposited in the square of the university.

In consequence of the proceedings at the Tabor line, all the troops of the garrison of Vienna were dispatched by degrees to Schönbrunn; and but one battalion of Nassau infantry, and three companies of pioneers, remained in the city for its protection, and for the assistance of the loyal and well-disposed Guards.

At one o'clock a party of the insurgent guards were attacked on the Stephen's Platz by a party of loyal National Guards; but, after a short fight, the latter were forced to retire into the Cathedral of St. Stephen, the doors of which were then barricaded from within. But the insurgents battered down the doors, entered the church, and dislodged their antagonists, whose leader was killed on the very steps of the altar. The battle then raged in awful confusion round the walls of the cathedral. All ranks seemed mingled in one phrensy of civil war, National Guards, citizens, even soldiers fighting on both sides, without leaders, without order, and without result. At two o'clock the operations of the loyal force, consisting of three companies of pioneers, occupying one the *Hof*, another the *Graben*, and the third the *Stock am Eisen* (fronting the square of the cathedral), became more regular. The latter, insulted by the mob and Guards, gave the signal for the commencement of the fight. From the windows, roofs, and cellars a murderous fire was poured out upon the military; and they, in turn, discharged twenty rounds of grape-shot on the crowd. They were, however, too weak to maintain their position, and were again driven back with the loss of their guns. They retreated through the *Graben*, and up the Bogner Gasse to the Hof, on which the war office is situated, the fighting continuing the while, and the grape-shot producing havoc among the crowd, as well as defacing the fine buildings on either side, and penetrating the houses in every direction, notwithstanding the doors and window-shutters were cased with sheet-iron.

One of the city gates, the *Burg Thor*, still remained in possession of the government troops. Three companies of sappers and miners, with four guns, entered this gate at three o'clock in the afternoon. They were at once attacked and totally routed, in spite of the grape and canister which they uninterruptedly fired. Many of them were captured, disarmed, and confined in the university buildings. Formidable barricades were constructed while the fight was going on. The old fortifications of the city were occupied by the artillery of the National Guard.

II.   G

The Constituent Assembly, then sitting in Vienna, and which had long before assumed both legislative and executive powers, passed the day in idle communications with the ministers, and fierce international disputes among themselves. The ministers, partly from want of adequate military force, and partly from want of resolution to proceed to extremities against the people, took no decisive measures. They sent re-enforcements to the Stephen's Platz, when that spot was already in the hands of the insurgents ; and the cathedral itself, with its solemn grandeur and ancient monuments, had been already desecrated, and was then streaming with Austrian blood, shed by Austrian hands. The Minister of War dispatched orders that the firing should cease ; but it was too late, for the fury of an excited populace then knew no bounds, and blood alone could quench the flame which blood itself had kindled.

The cabinet remained in deliberation at the Ministry of War, situated at the corner of the square called the Hof. The tide of insurrection now rose to an unconquerable height. The nearest shots of the retiring cannons, the advancing shouts of the infuriated people, warned the ministers that all defense was rapidly becoming hopeless. The building itself still offered some means of resistance, and there were two cannons in the court ; but at that crisis was issued a written order, signed by Latour and Wessenberg, " to cease the fire at all points," and given to officers for distribution.*   It was in vain. The popular torrent rolled on toward the seat of government, which was destined ere long to be disgraced by atrocious crime. The Minister of War, Count Latour, prepared for defense. The military on guard in front of the War Office were withdrawn into the yard, with two pieces of artillery loaded with grape.

---

* The last order issued by the unfortunate Latour was intrusted to Colonel Gustave Schindler of the imperial engineers, an efficient officer, as well as a most amiable and accomplished gentleman, and one well and favorably known in the United States, from his kind attention to Americans who have visited the Austrian capital. The colonel was in the act of passing out of the great door of the War Office, which opens on to the Hof, when the mob reached that spot. Recognized by his imperial uniform, he was instantly surrounded and attacked. He received many blows over the head, inflicted by the crowd with clubs and iron bars ; was most severely wounded, and would probably have been killed but for the timely interference of one of the rabble, who, riding up on horseback between the colonel and the mob, shielded him from further blows, and finally effected his escape.

The gates were closed, the military distributed to the different threatened points, and the cannons directed toward the two gates. Soon the scene of battle had reached the Bogner Gasse, immediately under the windows of the War Department; the ministers in consultation heard the cry, "*The military retreat.*" The great square of the Hof was soon cleared, the soldiers retiring by the way of the Freyung. The Guards and Academic Legion pursuing, the military commander's quarters in the Freyung are soon captured. The retiring military, not being able to escape through the Schotten-Thor as they had expected—that gate being closed and barricaded—they cut their way through the *Herrn Gasse.*

So intent were the respective combatants, either in retreat or pursuit, that the whole tempest of war swept over the Hof, and left that square for a short time deserted and silent.

But that stillness was but of short duration; a few moments only had elapsed, when a number of straggling Guards, students, and people, came stealing silently from the Graben, through the Bogner, Nagler, and Glocken Gasse, on to the Hof, and removed the dead and the wounded into the neighboring dwellings, and into the deserted guard-house in the War Department. These were soon followed by a fierce and noisy mob, armed with axes, pikes, and iron bars, which halted before the War Office, and began to thunder at its massive doors.

The officer of ordnance in vain attempted to communicate to the crowd the order of the ministry, that all firing should cease. A member of the Academic Legion, from the window over the gateway, waved with a white handkerchief to the tumultuous masses, and, exhibiting the order signed by Latour and Wessenberg, read its contents to the crowd.

But a pacification was not to be thought of; the people were too excited, their fury could only be appeased by blood; that delayed measure was not sufficient; they made negative gesticulations, and summoned the student to come down and open the portals to their admission. The tumult increased from minute to minute; the closed doors at length gave way under the axes of the mob, and the people streamed in, led by a man "in a light gray coat."

The Secretary of War having by this time abandoned the

idea of defense, on the ground either that it was useless or impolitic, no shots were fired or active resistance offered ; but the
orderlies, with their horses, retired to the stables, and the grenadiers into an inner court.   At first only single individuals entered, and their course was not characterized by violence; then
groups, proceeding slowly, listening, and searching; and, at
last, the tumultuous masses thundered in the rear.

Ere long, the cry rung on the broad stair-case, " Where is
Latour ? he must die !"   At this moment, the ministers and
their followers in the building, with the exception of Latour
himself, found means to escape, or mingled with the throng.
The deputies, Smolka, Borrosch, Goldmark, and Sierakowski,
who had undertaken to guarantee protection to the threatened
ministers, arrived in the hope of restraining the mob.   The
numerous corridors and cabinets of the War Office (formerly a
monastery of the Jesuits) were filled with the crowd ; the tide
of insurrection now rose to an uncontrollable height ; and the
danger of Latour became every moment more imminent.   The
generals who were with him, perceiving the peril, entreated
him to throw himself upon the Nassau regiment, or the *Dutch
Meister* grenadiers, and retreat to their barracks.   He scorned
the proposal, denied the danger, and even refused, for some
time, to change his uniform for a civilian's dress, until the hazard becoming more evident, he put on plain clothes and went
up into a small room in the roof of the building, where he soon
after signed a paper declaring that, with his majesty's consent,
he was ready to resign the office of Minister of War.   A *Tec-
nicker*,* named Rauch, who, it was said, had come to relieve
the Secretary of War, was seized and hung in the court by his
own scarf, but fortunately cut down by a National Guard before life was extinct.   The mob rushed into the private apartments of the minister, but plundered it merely of the papers,
which were conveyed to the university.   They came with a
sterner purpose.   The act of resignation, exhibited to the crowd
by the Deputy Smolka, was scornfully received by the people,
while the freshness of the writing, the sand adhering still to
the ink, betrayed the proximity of the hand which had just

---

* A student of the Polytechnic School, for brevity, usually called *Tecnickers.*

traced it.   Meanwhile, the crowd had penetrated the corridors of the fourth story, and were not long in discovering the place of Latour's concealment.   Hearing their approach, and recognizing the voice of Smolka, vice-president of the Assembly, who was doubtless anxious to protect him, Latour came out of his retreat.   They descended together from the fourth story by a narrow stair-way, on the right-hand side of the building, and entered the yard by the pump.   At each successive landing-place, the tumult and the crowd increased; but the descent was slow, and rendered more and more difficult by the numbers which joined the crowd at every turn of the stairs.   At length they reached the court below, and Count Latour, although he had been severely pressed, was still unhurt; but here the populace, which awaited them, broke in upon the group that still clustered around Latour, and dispersed it.   In vain did the deputies, Smolka and Sierakowski, endeavor to protect the minister; in vain did Count Leopold Gondrecourt attempt to cover him by the exposure of his own body.   A workman struck the hat from his head; others pulled him by his gray locks—he defending himself with his hands, which were already bleeding.   At length a ruffian, disguised as a Magyar, gave him, from behind, a mortal blow with a hammer, the man in the gray coat cleft his face with a sabre, and another plunged a bayonet into his heart.   A hundred wounds followed, and, with the words "*I die innocent!*" he gave up his loyal and manly spirit.   A cry of exultation from the assembled crowd rent the air at this event.   Every indignity was offered to his body; before he had ceased to breathe even, they hung him by a cord to the grating of a window in the court of the War Office.   He had been suspended there but a few minutes when, from the outrages committed on it, the body fell.

They then dragged it to the Hof, and suspended it to one of the bronze candelabras that adorn that extensive and much-frequented square, and, there treated with every indignity, it remained for fourteen hours exposed to the gaze of a mocking populace.*

---

* Before the "Central Committee of Safety," which acted in concert with and by the authority of the Diet, appeared a man in a white jacket and apron, and

Yet all this time the soldiers stood to their post at the War Office, witnessing these atrocities, obedient to the last order of the minister himself, not to advance upon the people.

Lieutenant-general Count Theodore Latour was born at Vienna on the 15th of June, 1780, and was the only son of the imperial Master-general of Ordnance and President of the Council of War, Count Maximilian Baillet de Latour, who died in 1806, and was proprietor of the estate called the County of Latour, in the province of Luxembourg. This property was erected into a fief or entail in 1719; but the family mansion was destroyed during the French Revolution, and the property itself has passed into other hands. Educated at the Imperial Engineers' School, Theodore de Latour there received all that instruction and acquired that solid knowledge which was matured in after years, and which, at the commencement of his military career, caused him to be appointed on the quarter-master general's staff, in which duties he was enabled to render valuable service. During the period that the Austrian army was engaged in a constant succession of campaigns, Latour remained uninterruptedly on active service, and by his zeal and courage obtained rapid promotion; so that, at the commencement of what was called the War of Liberation, he had already obtained the rank of colonel. In January, 1814, he was appointed chief of the staff to the eighth army corps of the Confederation, then under the crown prince, now King of Wurtemburg. The able dispositions of Colonel Latour at the sanguinary engagements of Epinay, Brienne, Sens, Montereau, and La Ferre, were publicly acknowledged at the time, and obtained

---

with a long iron bar in his hand, who related, in a Viennese dialect, the following: "In the morning we were at the Wienerberg, and marched to the rail-road depôt from the Belvidere. Following the general alarm, we entered the faubourg, and erected barricades before the line. As we had finished with that, the cries for Latour became loud; we marched into the city to look for him. We first searched through the first story, and as we did not find him, then the *parterre*. Here we seized him, and I pierced him in the throat with my bar. Was not that right? The others struck him on the head with their tools; but I thought it better to hang him up. We hung him in the yard, but the rope broke. Then we dragged him out on the Hof, and hung him to the lamp-post. Was not that right?"—*Dunder's Revolution of the 6th of October.*

Notwithstanding this horrible confession made in their presence, no attempt whatever was made by the Committee of Safety for the arrest of the murderer.

for him the repeated thanks of the prince commanding and the allied sovereigns. The rank of general and many orders of knighthood were among his recompenses and honorable testimonies. During the long peace which succeeded the campaigns of 1813, 1814, and 1815, Count Latour filled various military offices with credit under the Austrian government.

Upon the abolition of the Aulic Council of War at Vienna, Latour, who had long attained the rank of lieutenant general, was by the Emperor Ferdinand appointed Minister of War and chief of the War Department. In this most difficult and perilous position he was enabled, by patience, firmness, and long experience, to temper the storm by which he was surrounded, and to accomplish what might have been considered impracticable. His combinations with Radetzky led to the successful issue of the late campaigns in Lombardy ; for he united to the talent of conception that of execution, and with these a wonderful faculty of economizing and producing resources. A man less gifted with courage and constancy under difficulties, and readiness for extracting great results from small means, would have yielded to the pressure of events and the embarrassments by which he was surrounded.

He could have retired from an office which, it is said, he did not covet ; but was withheld from so doing by his devotion to his emperor, by his disinterestedness, and by that generous, rational patriotism, which caused him to keep firmly at his post until death—a horrible, foul, and bloody death terminated his long and honorable career.

At five P.M., Smolka, with the deputation, returned. Leon Kowski re-entered the Diet with the words, " Latour is dead, and his corpse is hanging on the lamp-post on the Hof."

Howelka expressed his deep regret at the horrible deed, and at the disgraceful course which events had taken. He was answered by a deputy that if the Minister Bach, who had always ridiculed the sovereignty of the people, could be also hung up, he should witness the spectacle with pleasure.

The galleries of the House were now occupied by armed men, and one of the deputies calling the attention of the Assembly to the fact, summoned the individuals to leave the House ; but, instead of sustaining their own personal safety and freedom of action, the deputy Zimmer replied : " These arms have fought but a few months since in the streets for the liberty of the people ; they have, consequently, the right to appear here.   You betrayed that liberty—you may now suffer for it."

These demonstrations no longer left any doubt that the whole programme of frightful scenes announced at the barricades was about to be acted out.   Latour was already hung up, armed men had forced the galleries and were opposite to the right side of the House, and actually pointing their guns at the members seated on that side ; and these violations were approved by a representative of the people.

At this time, when the Assembly seemed to be completely in the hands of the mob, the minority controlling by terror the inclinations of the majority, the president, Strohbach, together with all the Bohemian deputies marked out for destruction, left the House, and saved themselves by flight.

At six o'clock, there was but one place of refuge left in the city for the troops and National Guards who took sides with the government, and that place was the arsenal—famous not only for the immense quantity of arms of all kinds which it contained, but for the valued trophies acquired in the crusades in the Holy Land, in the Turkish wars, and in the French campaigns.

All other places being in their possession, attempts were now made by the mob to carry this point by storm.   They first attempted to force the gates, but failing in this, operations were abandoned until after nightfall.   They next endeavored to gain entrance from the roofs of the adjoining houses, but this effort was attended with no better success, as the assailants were picked off by the sharpshooters in the arsenal as rapidly as they made their appearance.

At seven o'clock, and as soon as the shades of night afforded some concealment for their maneuvers, the attack was renewed with great vigor.   Two barricades were constructed not far distant from the arsenal, and in both the streets which met and formed right angles in front of the gate, and the fire was opened from all houses within reach, both in the Renn Gasse and Wiplingher Strasse ; while from the barricade on the Hohen Brücke the cannons poured forth their contents against the feeble gate, the concussion in the narrow streets and lofty houses shivering to atoms all the glass of the windows, and drowning all other sounds with its deafening thunder.

Captain Castell, commanding the only company of regulars left for the defense of the arsenal, prudently waited until the enemy's shot had made in the gate an aperture sufficiently large to enable him to point out the only but well-directed cannon which he had, and the effect of a few shots was indescribable—the streets were cleared, and the captain, venturing out with a few men, took the deserted cannons, which had been brought over the barricade for the purpose of attacking the arsenal from a nearer point.

The combat deepened, the garrison swept the Renn Gasse with grape and canister, and killed and disabled a great number of the populace, whose fury increased after each unsuccessful attempt to gain possession of the building. The assailants proceeded to the civic arsenal, and demanded cannon for the loudly expressed purpose of bombarding the military arsenal. With these they proceeded on the bastions, and attacked the building in the rear.

Parliamentaires were dispatched to the arsenal both by the Diet and the students, ordering the garrison to surrender, and the combat to cease; but these were shot as fast as they approached the building, not by the garrison, but, as was generally believed, by assassins posted in the opposite houses of the Renn Gasse.

At ten o'clock, the arsenal was bombarded from four different points. At eleven o'clock, from the discharge of Congreve rockets, the building took fire, and great apprehensions were entertained that the powder magazine would explode; yet the gallant little band intrusted with its defense held out undaunted. Some well-disposed citizens attempted to dispatch fire engines to the relief of the arsenal; but the enraged mob interfered, and prevented their departure. The fire fortunately communicated only with the wood and coal depôts, and, by the untiring exertions of the garrison, was kept under control. Every species of stratagem was resorted to to obtain possession of the arsenal, but all without effect.

One of these schemes was very near consummation, and had it been carried through, would have decided at once the fates both of the garrison and the arsenal. A little after midnight, a great sound of many voices was heard in the Wiplingher Strasse, and a band of mixed persons observed marching up to the arsenal, some bearing white flags, and others torches and candles. From afar they proclaimed words of peace, and requested a parley, and the garrison was inclined to listen to the most advanced speaker. Two loaded cannons were posted in the gateway and pointed down the street, and Captain Castell, with nearly his entire force of forty grenadiers, advanced toward the doubtful band ; and while there, listening to their communications, and preventing them from pressing too closely on the arsenal, the captain happening to cast a look behind, remarked a flash upon the tube of the double-loaded cannon. Amazed, he sprang toward the cannon, where he perceived a young *proletariat* searching with a burning match for the touch-hole of the gun, which in a second more would have discharged its murderous contents upon the backs of the grenadiers. An instantaneous cry directed the attention of the cannoniers to the youthful assassin, and the next moment one of them, with a rope hammer, struck him speechless to the earth. Incensed at the treachery which was attempted, Captain Castell immediately withdrew his grenadiers, and answered the faithless band by two discharges of grape, which produced great havoc in their ranks, and caused a death-like stillness through the street.

The attack and defense of the arsenal continued through the entire night. Never was more strikingly exhibited the advantage of skill and discipline over rude masses than occurred that night, when the handful of regular troops held out, with Spartan valor, against all the force which could be brought against them, and never yielded their post until next morning, when summoned to do so by their own commander, Count Auersperg, who had entered into stipulations with the Diet and common council for the surrender.

But the horrors of that awful night—the alarm-bells pealing from all the steeples in the city ; the arsenal at times wrapt in flames ; the uninterrupted musket-fire ; the thunder of the

heavy cannons, and the streets strewed with the dying and
the dead, will not soon be forgotten by the quiet and pleasure-
loving inhabitants of Vienna.

While these bloody deeds were occurring around them, the
transactions of the Austrian Diet, reduced, by the withdrawal
of the Bohemian deputies, to the "*rump*" of a faction, were
equally striking and significant, as the following short summary of the heads of their resolutions will not fail to exhibit.*

" Seven o'clock P.M.

"An executive committee, consisting of members of the left,
is appointed. M. Löhner moves an address to the emperor,
demanding the formation of a new and popular ministry, with
Messrs. Dobblhof and Hornbostel in it; the removal of Baron
Jellacic from his governorship of Hungary; the revocation of
the last proclamation against the Hungarians; and an amnesty for those implicated in the riots of that day. The House ac-
cepts the motion, and sends a deputation to the emperor."

While the disfigured body of Latour still hung to the lamp-
post on the Hof, and before the remains of Breda and all the
rest who had fallen on that day, had been committed to the
earth, while the streets were yet reeking with human gore, a
pardon was demanded by the Diet for all those who might be
connected with these atrocities.

" Half-past seven P.M.

" Resolved to appoint M. Scherzer Provisional Commander-
in-chief of the National Guard of Vienna and the suburbs.
Resolved to put a stop to the combat against the garrison of
the arsenal. Resolved to instruct the military commander,
Count Auersperg, to prevent the interference of the military.

" Eight o'clock.

" Resolved, with acclamation, to serve out fresh ammunition
to the Academical Legion.

" Nine o'clock.

" Resolved to instruct the directors of the Southern Rail-way
that they will not be suffered to convey troops to Vienna.

" Half-past eleven o'clock.

" The deputation returns. The emperor will consider about

---

* Wien und Buda-Pesth im Herbste, 1848, von Joh. Moshamer.

the address, and promises to appoint a popular ministry, with Dobblhof and Hornbostel in it.

"Twelve o'clock at night.

"The arsenal is reported to be on fire. Resolved to entreat the people to desist from the combat.

"Three o'clock A.M.

"Resolved to inform Count Auersperg that it is his duty not to obey any commands but those of the Diet."

As these extraordinary scenes were occurring in Vienna, the emperor, with the imperial family, clustered together in the summer palace at Schönbrunn, were receiving from time to time, with the utmost trepidation, intelligence of the treachery and defeat of his hitherto faithful and victorious troops— the shocking triumphs of the mob—the storming of the War Department, and brutal murder of the minister; while, from the upper windows of the palace, they beheld the arsenal in flames, and listened all night long to the uninterrupted musket-fire and incessant discharges of artillery.

The small garrison of the palace was re-enforced that night by the arrival of ten companies of infantry from St. Pölten and Stockerau; but these troops, from the forced march which they had undergone, were so fatigued, that had an attack then been made upon the palace, they would have been found unfit for duty. When, at early morn, a messenger arrived reporting that the arsenal was near its fall, and that the *proletaria* would soon all be armed, the emperor lost no time in resolving to flee a second time the palace of his fathers, and to abandon his capital again to the mercies of a triumphant rabble.

At seven o'clock the next morning, the imperial family, in light carriages with baggage, took their departure, escorted by six squadrons of cavalry, twenty companies of infantry, and eight pieces of artillery, and never ceased their flight until safely inclosed within the formidable fortress of Olmütz.

The flight of the emperor was imprudent in the extreme, as he thus cast loose the reins of government when madness ruled the hour, and subjected the empire to the danger of being again dissolved into its original elements. His retinue consisted of from twenty to thirty carriages; and his military escort, of six thousand troops and four cannons, accompanied him to his journey's end; but his reception in the towns through which he passed drew forth no display, either of approbation or disapprobation—it was grave and silent. The National Guard of the town of Krems, where he crossed the Danube, intended, it was said, to remove the bridge across the river, in order to induce the emperor not to leave the archduchy; but their intention was baffled. His departure from Vienna was regarded with so much indifference, and so completely failed in its effect, that the *Radical* journal of the day did not fail to tell its readers, " People, let the emperor go—let him abandon you a second time. Do not ask him to return; on the contrary, he must pray you to allow him to return."

At eight o'clock the brave little garrison, which, with a scarcity of ammunition, had all night long defended the arsenal amid fire and flame, surrendered it into the hands of its pledged protectors ;* and, marching unmolested through the tumultuous streets of the capital, reached in safety the encampment in the Schwartzenberg Garden, amid the enthusiastic cheers of their companions.

Scarcely had they left, when the populace, whose rage could no longer be restrained, rushed into the arsenal from every quarter, some even over the still burning ruins; and when the yard became full to overflowing with human beings, whose horrid faces and grotesque appearance beggared all description, the doors were burst open, and a general plunder commenced. So great was the rush to obtain arms, that, notwithstanding the fire had just again burst out with all its fury, and groups of thousands surrounded it on all sides, not a man could be obtained to assist in extinguishing it, and a number of boys, from twelve to fifteen years of age, could alone be gathered to work the engine ; and they really labored with great constancy until the flames were subdued.

The four long galleries, leading into each other and surrounding an immense hollow square, were filled with arms and trophies of every description; and so tasteful had been the arrangement of them, that that hall constituted one of the most attractive objects to the eye of the stranger that Vienna af-

---

* That the National Guard and Academical Legion would occupy and defend it.

forded. The two hundred thousand new muskets which it contained soon disappeared; and then followed the trophies, collected by the imperial government through many centuries, from the period of the crusades to the present day. Some strutted forth in complete suits of ancient armor; others were decorated only with helmets and gloves of mail; some brandished an ancient battle-ax, while others delighted only in a breast-plate and pike; some shouldered a Swedish blunderbuss, captured perhaps in the battle of Lutzen; and some waved a Turkish cimeter, taken probably at the siege of Vienna.

For hours the arsenal thus poured forth a rabble, in comparison with which Falstaff's regiment would have appeared a noble guard; all delighted with their spoils, and boasting of the havoc they would now make upon the military. The coat-of-mail of Libussa, the first princess of Bohemia; the buck-skin shirt, in which Gustavus Adolphus received his death-wound; the swords of Eugène of Savoy, of Wurmser, and of Schwartzenberg, and thousands of other invaluable relics, disappeared. Some were subsequently purchased for a Zwantzinger;* many have been lost forever.

On the night of the 6th, all the ministers, who felt that they did not enjoy the confidence of the people, escaped by flight. The Ministers of Finance and Commerce, who were popular with the people, alone remained. Baron Wessenberg, Minister of Foreign Affairs, and who was at the War Office when the mob broke in, and who walked out boldly through the crowd, owed his safety, doubtless, to the fact that he was not recognized.

On the succeeding morning, the following were the proceedings of the Diet:

"7th of October, ten o'clock A.M.

"Information received of the emperor's flight from his palace at Schönbrunn. The House appoints a committee to inquire into the truth of this statement.

"Half-past eleven o'clock A.M.

"The Minister of Finance, M. Kraus, informs the House of the emperor's departure."

---

* Twenty cents.

Ascending the tribune he said, "An hour since, one of the guards of the palace handed me a sealed letter, which contained a manifesto from the emperor, in nearly the following language: 'I have done every thing that a sovereign could do for the benefit of my people; I have renounced the absolute power left me by my ancestors. In the month of May, I was forced to quit the palace of my fathers, and afterward I came back without any other guarantee than my confidence in my people. A small faction—strong from its boldness—has urged things to the furthest extremity; pillage and crime reign in Vienna; and the Minister of War has been murdered. I have confidence in God and my right, and I quit the neighborhood of my capital to find means to afford assistance to my oppressed people. Let those who love Austria and her liberty, rally around the emperor.' "*

The minister added, that he had refused to countersign, as his majesty had directed him, this unconstitutional and threatening proclamation, proceeding upon the principle that, in a constitutional monarchy, the *whole* ministry should be held responsible for every thing, and that no opportunity had been afforded of consulting his colleagues on the subject; that, after an interview with Hornbostel, Minister of Commerce, he had concluded not to publish the manifesto, as such an act would be in violation of the oath of a constitutional minister; he therefore left the matter to the decision of the high and exalted Diet. A committee was accordingly appointed to decide on the manifesto, and they reported as follows:

1st. That the ministers, Hornbostel, Dobblhof, and Kraus, should discharge, temporarily, all the functions of the cabinet, and make propositions to his majesty to complete the ministry.

2d. That a proclamation should be addressed to the people, and a memorial sent to his majesty, on the events of the previous day.

3d. Resolved, that the House invest itself with both the deliberative and executive powers, and that this resolution be communicated to the provinces by special commissioners.†

The proclamation to the people was then issued by the Diet,

---

in which that assembly expresses its regret at the painful events that had occurred; its determination to remain *en permanence;* its intention to address itself, at the same time, to the monarch, and recommend to him to remove from his council all ministers not in the confidence of the people; and concluding by placing the safety of the city, its own inviolability, and that of the throne, under the protection of the National Guard of Vienna.

On the following day, they addressed a memorial to the emperor, in which, after making known the sentiments of unalterable affection which they feel for him, they express their surprise that he should have quitted the environs of his residence without a reassuring word, expressed in a constitutional manner, as to the object and the duration of that removal, which might tend to lessen the uneasiness of the people, inseparable from so afflicting an act. They supplicate the monarch to return to the seat of his government, in order to encourage the faithful sons of the country, and deprive the enemies of their liberty, of courage and hope; in order that every movement of anarchy and reaction may fail, and the work of the Constitution, in which the people of Austria seek their safety and the guarantee of their future welfare, may not be retarded; that his majesty might grant to all his people who await that return calmness and peace—put an end, according to the impulse of his noble heart, to a civil war, which, lighted up in one part of the empire, will promptly extend its devastating flame over a vast monarchy; that he would choose, for the accomplishment of this great duty, counselors possessing the confidence of his majesty, and that of a noble people loving liberty; and that the gratitude and the blessings of that people would be the noblest jewel in his majesty's crown.*

On the same day, the committee of students, acting by invitation in concert with the Central Committee of the Diet, made the following demands: "1st. That the emperor shall withdraw his manifesto. 2d. That all the ministers shall retire, and be replaced by a ministry composed by the deputy

---

* The Diet having assumed all the powers of government, both deliberative and executive, the following conclusions will show the folly and madness by which their movements were characterized.

Löhner of the extreme left of the National Assembly. 3d. That the army shall be subject to the civil authority. 4th. That all the regular troops shall quit the city. 5th. That the Archduke Louis, uncle of the emperor, and the Archduchess Sophia, his brother's wife, shall be banished from the Austrian states. 6th. That Marshal Radetzky shall be dismissed. 7th. That a civil government shall be established in Italy." The Diet adopted all these demands, with the exception of that relative to the banishment, which was reserved for special discussion. The manifesto of the emperor being generally understood to indicate that a concentration of troops would take place around Vienna, and the Diet, perhaps, anticipating that such a movement might interfere with the freedom of their deliberations, adopted, on the 8th, the following impotent and contradictory conclusions : " 1st. The Diet, which, in its quality of constituent Assembly, can not be dissolved before the completion of its mission, also declares that it will not dissolve under the most threatening circumstances, but will remain firmly faithful to its duty. 2d. The Diet is an indivisible body ; it represents all the different people of Austria, who have sent deputies to it. 3d. The Diet is, conformably to the imperial manifesto of the 6th of June, and to the free election of the people, the only legal and constitutional organ of the union between the constitutional monarch and the sovereign people, for the defense of the inviolable liberty of the people and of the hereditary throne. 4th. The Diet, being composed of the free representatives of a free people, will not impose a moral restraint on any deputy to compel him to remain. 5th. The Diet will remain with firmness on constitutional ground, to defend by legal and constitutional measures the country, the liberty of the people, and the hereditary throne. 6th. The Diet invites all its members who are absent, either with or without leave, to return to their post within a fortnight at the farthest."*

Count Auersperg, commander of the imperial forces in and about Vienna at the time of the outbreak, retired, upon the success of the insurgents, to the Schwartzenberg and Belvidere palaces (situated in the faubourg), with twelve thousand

---

* Moshamer.

II.   H

men; and there he seems to have been bewildered, and at a
loss to know what authority he should properly obey. The
ministers and Diet call upon him to come into the city, and
to aid in maintaining order within the walls; but really, it
was supposed, under that pretext to procure his surrender to
the insurrectionary force within the city. On his part, keeping up the pretense, at least, of official subordination, he professes to act under the responsible ministers, but pleads orders
from the Minister of War, the murdered Latour, and avers that
he only awaits the countermand of the minister's successor
duly appointed; he mistrusts the armed bodies in the capital,
and promises to enter if they are disarmed. Failing in the attempt to entice Auersperg into the city, and not satisfied that
he should continue to occupy his strong position at the Belvidere, and from which he might at any moment, with his batteries, lay Vienna in ruins, the Diet invited him to quit his
strong position. A day or two after, Auersperg receiving new
proofs of the increasing enmity of the ill-disposed people of
Vienna, determined on changing his position, and taking up
his head-quarters at Enzersdorf, a small village in the neighborhood, demanded of the Diet all the necessary objects for
his troops, as well as the privilege that his troops be allowed
to remove all their effects from the barracks. The committee
immediately caused the National Guard to occupy the position
abandoned by the troops.

When the outbreak first occurred, intelligence was sent by
a courier, who rode night and day, to Baron Jellacic, the Ban
of Croatia, and who was at that time with his army in the
neighborhood of Raab, in Hungary. Leaving orders for the
remainder to follow as rapidly as possible, Jellacic started with
that portion of his army about him for Vienna, and, by forced
marches, on the ninth he crossed the Austrian frontier and
took up a position at Ebersdorf, about two hours march from
the capital, with twelve thousand men.

The Hungarian army, which was in pursuit of Jellacic in
Hungary, as soon as they were apprised of his departure for
Vienna, as well as of the remarkable events of which that city
had been the theatre, followed rapidly in pursuit as far as the
Austrian frontier, and there took up a position for the time.

About the same period, two members of the Hungarian Diet
arrived in Vienna with an address to the Austrian Diet, to the
following effect : that the Hungarian nation was penetrated
with sentiments of the liveliest gratitude for the heroic devotedness with which the noble inhabitants of Vienna had risen to
prevent the arrival of re-enforcements to the army of the traitor Jellacic ; that it declares, before God and the universe, that
it will regard the liberty of Austria as its own, and consider it
its duty to contribute all in its power to maintain it; that the
Hungarian nation have given the Hungarian army the most
positive orders to pursue Jellacic wherever he may go ; that if
the Hungarian troops are obliged to pursue him on the Austrian territory, the Hungarian nation proclaims before God and
men that it has not the intention to violate the Austrian territory, but that it acts in conformity with sentiments of gratitude, which make it its duty not to leave the noble inhabitants
of Vienna without support against the common enemy ; that
the Hungarian government had given the severest orders that,
in case the army should advance, its maintenance on the soil
of Austria, sacred to them, should be at the expense of Hungary itself, and that it should not fall on the noble Austrian
people.*

Upon the arrival of Jellacic in the neighborhood of Vienna,
the Diet immediately dispatched a deputation to ascertain the
objects and intention which brought him to the capital.   Jellacic replied, by note, that the Diet might have confidence in
the sentiments which brought him before Vienna; that he himself was ready to protect the institutions of the country, and
that his intervention in Hungary was the proof of it.   He added, that it would be afflicting to see Vienna become the theatre of a bloody combat, and he desired a peace which should
establish order, liberty, and the happiness of the people.   To
this communication the Assembly replied: " The Constitutional Diet declares, that *there reigns in Vienna neither anarchy
nor brutal force.*   The Diet and the ministry are laboring to
maintain legal order, and the people are sustaining them.   The
people are in arms, as is natural when two armies of enemies

---

* Constitution Zeitung.

threaten them. The news of the arrival of the Hungarians has been received by the Diet with acclamation. We should also regret that Vienna should become the theatre of a bloody conflict, but the presence of your excellency would be the only cause. There is only one means to avoid it, viz., that your excellency retire. The address that we have sent to the emperor proves to your excellency that we strongly desire peace."*

It being understood that the Hungarian army were ready to come to Vienna on the call of the Diet, two days afterward the following communication from Jellacic and Auersperg, dated at the head-quarters at Enzersdorf, was presented to the High Diet: "We learn that the Diet has taken steps to establish peace by the intervention of the emperor. Above all, the Hungarians must not pass the frontier. The High Diet must prevent it, otherwise a battle will be inevitable, and the consequences incalculable. M. Pillersdorf has demanded of us to allow provisions to enter the capital; if this be granted, the soldiers must be allowed to enter it, to seek what they may require."

The following answer of the Diet to this communication was, after some discussion, adopted and ordered to be forwarded without delay: "A deputation has gone to his majesty to pray him to accept the propositions of peace that have been made. In the hope of success, the Diet has taken measures to prevent all hostility against the troops. Yesterday it learned that his majesty had declared to Lobkowitz that the generals should not attack; but various measures adopted by your excellency—such as disarming the National Guard, the refusal to allow provisions to be brought to Vienna, &c.—accord very little with the assurances of peace of the two generals, and the promise of the emperor. As to what concerns the Hungarians, the Diet did not call them, and can not send them away; besides, the Hungarian Diet has just informed us that it has given orders to its army to pursue your excellency in whatever direction you might take. The Diet then requires your excellency to restore their arms to the National Guard, disarmed by you, and immediately to retire to your own country. It is only

---

* Wiener Zeitung.

there that the Diet can charge itself with mediation, and invite the Hungarian army to conclude an armistice. Then only can the Diet, invoking the propositions of peace made to his majesty, order the Hungarian army to stop. The Diet thus fulfills its duty. If the conditions it lays down be not fulfilled, its pacific power will cease, and all will depend upon the battle with the Hungarians, for which those who have rendered it necessary will be responsible."*

Up to this period in the Revolution, so strange and contradictory had been the course of those possessed of power, and so complicated the internal conflict between them, that the position of the empire was rendered not only unprecedented, but almost unintelligible.

The Diet, on the one hand, while it palliates the murder of the emperor's minister, and seeks an amnesty for the perpetrators of this brutal act, professes to remain constitutional, and pursues the flying monarch with pressing invitations to return to the palace of his fathers. While, by its decrees, the same Assembly excites all the agitation and commotion which distracts the city, in the name of his majesty it calls upon Count Auersperg, commander of the imperial troops, to come in and aid in maintaining order within the walls. While professing sentiments of unalterable affection for his majesty, they call in the Hungarians, and thus invite his majesty's rebels to invade the metropolitan province, in order to clear it of his majesty's troops. The course of the emperor, on the other hand, is not less intricate. While a serious attack is made upon his authority and throne, instead of remaining at his post, and summoning all the force of his empire to protect him in their enjoyment, he runs off and surrenders them, without a struggle, into the hands of a revolutionary rabble that had assailed them. While professing undying attachment to his beloved subjects, he promises to send against them the means for their most effectual chastisement. While willing that the efforts of the Diet toward the " formation of a Constitution, which had been commenced, should be prosecuted without disturbance or interruption," he proclaims that he will not recognize any of

---

* Wiener Zeitung.

their decisions subsequent to the 6th of October, and that his generals will oppose their being carried into effect.

In tracing the causes which had brought the Austrian empire thus to the very brink of destruction, both parties must bear their share of censure. The policy of the Austrian cabinet, after the revolution of March, was characterized only by indecision and duplicity. It had been a policy of shifts, expedients, and of hesitating action, in which no party could discover the expression of its sentiments or the realization of its purposes. It contributed neither to consolidate the movement in which it originated, nor to counteract the evils to which that movement gave birth. It had been faithful to no principle it professed as its own. It had not protected the interest it promised to guard. It brought the imperial authority first into contempt, and then into danger. It had been weak, timid, vain. Nor were these errors its worst. It had been deceitful and false, intriguing and delusive. No small part of its dealings with Hungary was believed to have been of this character; raising hopes which it never meant to fulfill, making promises which it had no intention to perform, it thus greatly contributed to render formidable that insurrection which was now hurrying thousands of armed men to rescue from the menacing hands of loyalty the leagured capital of sedition and treason. Without question, it was the consciousness of the insincerity with which they had been treated that aggravated the hostile passions of the Hungarians, already too prone to recognize an insult and revenge an injury. To be satisfied of the duplicity which was practiced, it is necessary only to recall the proceedings toward the Hungarians and Croatians. On one day, the emperor grants to the Hungarians political government and control over the Croatians; on another, the Croatians are furnished with men, money, and arms, and encouraged to resist all encroachments of the Hungarians. At one time, the Ban of Croatia is proclaimed a traitor; at another, he is nominated to a high office. The extent of the emperor's complicity in those courses which condemn his administration to universal odium, it is obviously impossible to determine; but one thing is plain enough, that upon him has devolved chiefly the burden of enduring their consequences. He was compelled to abandon the palace of his ancestors—in an hour of the'utmost peril to surrender his capital to the mercies of an excited and triumphant rabble; and while his brave soldiery were seeking to restore the rigor of his authority in the remotest province of his empire, he was forced to show that he was unable to preserve it in his capital. Rumor, ever busy with men's names—ever claiming a right to determine men's motives, and to indicate their secret springs of action, has acquitted the emperor of any share in the errors to which unwilling reference is made; it ascribed to evil counselors, who betrayed his confidence and misled his judgment, the respon: ibility of the measures that had attracted to the imperial person the active hostility of his subjects. Whether this conjecture, which is not inconsistent with what is generally understood to have been the character of Ferdinand the First, be in truth well founded or not, one thing is certain that, by whoever committed, these errors brought the empire to the very verge of dissolution; a dissolution, to avoid which there was but a single course left, and that was one which the then administration seemed least likely to adopt—a sincere and vigorous policy. To save the throne of Habsburg, it was necessary that there should be no faltering now, no affected moderation that was not intended to be practiced, no apparent approval of measures to which it was determined to oppose an undeviating resistance.* The whole strength which the empire could command must be collected, and no fastidious repugnance must interfere with the employment of the only means available to the subjugation of a riotous mob, and the maintenance of legitimate authority.

The course of the Austrian Diet is still more censurable.

Besides a total ignorance of every parliamentary proceeding, and which was always involving them in the grossest absurdities, it was a body uncommonly deficient in talent. Called together as a Constituent Assembly, whose proper duty was only to prepare a Constitution for the empire, they began, in the very first days of their meeting, to assume *legislative* powers, and to make the laws necessary, in their views, to a constitutional government, which had not yet been formed.

---

* Galignani's Messenger.

The most patriotic and conservative portion of the Assembly were the deputies from the Slavic provinces ; and although a portion of them from Galicia, with their bundas and uncombed hair, had as little idea of politics as they had of the use of beds,* yet, not understanding a word that was spoken in the Assembly, they rested secure in the ancient faith.† But such was far from being the case with the German literati of the lower order, who constituted the extreme left of the Assembly, and who, by their idle interrogations of the ministry and absurd resolutions, were consuming the time of the House, and adding to the embarrassment of a cabinet in the prosecution of the new line of duties upon which they had just entered.

Among the first efforts of this patriotic clique was their attempt to dissolve the Austrian empire, and to add the German portions of it to the German Confederation, and let the Slavic, Mongul, and other provinces, take care of themselves. Thus the first effort of those who had met to unite and consolidate the empire under one common Constitution, was a project which, had it succeeded, would have shivered the empire to fragments. They were consistent but in one respect, viz., espousing every revolutionary excess which occurred either in Austria or other parts of Europe, down to the last, surpassing them all in savage brutality, committed under their very eyes in the Austrian capital, upon a member of their own body, and minister of the very government of which they professed to constitute a part.

If not privy to the occurrences which disgraced the 6th of October, they were certainly accessories after the fact, by the commendations which they paid to the perpetrators, and the efforts which they made to shield them from the punishment which they so richly merited.

---

* When they first reached Vienna, and bargaining for lodgings, they complained of the extravagance of the charges; and, upon the landlords explaining that they could not furnish beds for less, these Solons of Austria are said to have replied, "Beds! We want no beds. All we wish for is the floor, covered with straw, and twenty of us can occupy one room."

† The faith of the Slavic peasant of Austria exhibits the emperor in a constant struggle in favor of the serfs against the feudal aristocracy, and laboring with sincerity for their emancipation.

Instead of sustaining the authorities of the city, and displaying their activity in arresting the murderers of Latour, dissolving the Academic Legion and those companies of National
Guard who caused the struggle on the Tabor Bridge, they issued a proclamation declaring that the murder of the Minister
of War, and the violent overthrow of the ministry, was "nothing more than an act of popular self-preservation resulting from
regrettable circumstances;" and joined in a petition to the emperor praying "a general amnesty for all those who might be
in any manner implicated in the affair."

This vile insurrectionary mob they assumed to consider and
denominate as the *people*, and to allow it to take the law into
its own hands, to overthrow at its will a ministry that did not
please it, and to institute others according to its own liking,
when a Diet existed founded on the democratical basis of the
universal suffrage of the people.   It proceeded to pass decrees
without the number requisite for that purpose, and by the same
means to assume and appropriate to themselves full executive
power, until they finally placed themselves in a position of open
defiance to the emperor.

The complete tools of a metropolitan rabble, they exhibited
all the waywardness and inefficiency of a mob, without the
ability to profit by any advantages which the suddenness or
violence of their attack had opened to them in the temporary
prostration of their opponents.   Like children with their toys,
their only efficiency consisted in pulling down and destroying;
they had neither ability nor disposition to put together or re-
construct.

When by these acts of unparalleled barbarity, committed in
Vienna under their knowledge, they had frightened the emperor from his capital, and then possessed themselves of all his
power, they had not the moral courage to declare their independence, or take any steps to free themselves of a government
which they complained of as oppressive.

Later, when they took the resolution to arm the citizens of
Vienna from the rifled arsenal of the emperor, and to establish
corps, and to officer them in opposition to the imperial troops;
when, before the succor afforded by the forces of Windischgrätz and Jellacic had come to their assistance, and they could

with their immense force have annihilated Auersperg and his twelve thousand men, they refused the application of Messen-hauser, their own constituted commander, to be allowed to take the offensive.

And still later, when a Hungarian army of from twenty to thirty thousand men had come up to their rescue and remained on the frontiers of Austria, burning for an invitation to cross and come to their relief—when Windischgrätz, with his immense force, had not yet reached the scene of action, and a well-drilled army of thirty thousand men—with proper and efficient officers to direct the movements of the hundred thousand fighting men within the city, would have been invincible by any force which Austria could at that time have brought against them, they had not the boldness to assume the responsibility of extending the invitation. Strange conclusions, indeed, both of morality and policy, which could have dictated the murder of the em-peror's minister, the robbery of his arsenal, the seizing all his power, and then hesitate to take the steps most necessary for their defense, or best calculated to carry their purposes into ef-fect.

In the mean time, the course of the Diet and Common Coun-cil of Vienna, in open defiance of imperial authority, rendering it necessary for the emperor either quietly to submit to a total deprivation of his power or to recover the same by force of arms, makes a conflict inevitable, and all parties prepare themselves for the struggle.

Wessenberg, the Minister of Foreign Affairs, follows the em-peror to Olmütz, and there prepares and countersigns his proc-lamations. Dobblhof and Bach disappear, and, in communi-cations having no dates to betray the places of their conceal-ment, tender their resignations of office, which their precarious health, as they allege, will not suffer them longer to retain.

Hornbostel, as an intermediate, pendulates between the em-peror and the Diet; but, doubted by the former, and of no force with the latter, he can avail nothing. He lays his ministerial honors at the feet of his monarch; but his majesty will not suffer him to resign.

Kraus, the Minister of Finance, is the only one left; upon him has devolved the business of all the bureaus, the entire affairs of the empire; and, though a man of high integrity, is represented as feeble and careless, and but ill adapted to the gigantic task of steering the vessel of state amid the breakers which surround her.

The Bohemian members of the Diet have seceded *en masse*, and have protested energetically against the authority of a body which suffers itself to be made the instrument of a mere street mob; and subsequently sent deputations to the emperor, to request that he will either have peace restored in Vienna or remove the sittings of the Diet to some other portions of the empire, where its deliberations may be conducted without interruption. The "*Rump*" has returned the defiance; and declaring the Assembly at Vienna to be "the only legal constituent and lawgiving authority; that every attempt of deputies or individuals to assemble at another place, to pass resolutions, which alone appertains to the Diet, is illegal and of no effect; and the Diet hereby protests against resolutions so passed, and declares the authors thereof as solely responsible for the consequences."

The Diet demands the withdrawal of the imperial troops from the vicinity of the city. The commanders refuse to stir, and all hope of an arrangement has vanished. Every preparation is made to resist the anticipated attack from without; every inhabitant capable of bearing arms is summoned and provided with weapons; barricades are erected throughout the streets, and the entire fortifications surrounding the faubourgs are raised, mounted with cannons, and covered with men—students, National Guards, and workmen. During the day of the 10th of October, it being currently reported throughout the city that an attack might be hourly expected from the combined forces of Jellacic and Auersperg, the excitement became very great. National Guards from Brünn, Baden, Vöslauer, and the vicinity, were all day pouring into the city. The *Landsturm* of the neighborhood were every where rising and rushing to the rescue of the capital. In the evening, as soon as the army of the Ban was visible from the towers, the alarm was sounded, and the whole city was under arms. And when, a little later in the night, the watch-fires of Auersperg's army were found to have been extinguished, the attack was

considered as placed beyond all doubt, and might be momentarily expected.

By the older inhabitants, that night was considered the most
distracted one which Vienna had endured since its bombardment by Napoleon in 1809. In the streets, till early dawn,
only armed men were seen, who, either singly, in small irregular bodies, or in regulated companies, marched in solemn silence at a measured pace. At the corner of the streets, in the
open squares, and in front of the coffee-houses, stood sombre
groups in animated conversation or violent altercation.

Behind and upon the barricades, armed blousemen were
gathered around the watch-fires, and among them women and
girls of not very respectable exterior were scattered—some
sleeping upon heaps of stones, others laughing or singing.
The ramparts and bastions, in particular, presented a most
animated and picturesque appearance—watch-fire succeeded
watch-fire, each surrounded by a motley group—*legionnaires*
in their *kalabreses*, workmen in their sleeves, and National
Guards. Above the gates were mounted cannon, which commanded the entrance to the city; beside them were burning
torches, borne by the Burgher Artillery, scattered Academi-
cians, or workmen. Close by were ranged whole companies,
armed with every kind of weapon, whose patrols marched up
and down, keeping guard with a musket or rifle, carabine or
pike in hand, and almost every minute stopping some curious
spectator with the incessant cry, "*Halt wir da!*"

Fortunately for the undisciplined, ill-organized mass, the
night passed off without attack.

From that time they began to devote more attention to organization. The Diet issued a proclamation to quiet the agitation of the city, promising to watch with care and energy
over the interests of Vienna, and have ready all means of defense in case of attack.

In the course of the 13th, the command of the National
Guard was changed four times, and was at length provisionally confided to M. Messenhauser, a poet, and once an officer in
the Austrian army. To General Bem, a Pole, and a man of
remarkable military talent, as he afterward proved himself in
Hungary, was confided the command of the Mobile Guard.

The Diet decrees two millions of florins to afford relief to poor workmen, and two hundred thousand for the maintenance of those under arms. The civil authorities promise pensions to the relatives of those who might fall. The people are so full of warlike ardor, that the absolute order of the Diet was necessary to prevent them from attacking the Croats.

To add still further to the encouragement of the citizens in their attitude of resistance to imperial authority, a deputation from the extreme left of the National Assembly of Frankfort, headed by Messrs. Blum and Froebel, reached Vienna, to afford assistance and encouragement to the struggling Viennese. They waited on the Diet, and subsequently visited the committee of students, to whom the spokesman declared that the cause of the Viennese was that of Germany, and that Vienna must triumph, or all Germany would fly to its assistance. The deputation subsequently assumed the uniform of the Academic Legion, and issued an address to the inhabitants of Vienna, expressing " high esteem and profound gratitude for the services they had rendered to liberty."*

While these things are transpiring in and around Vienna, the emperor, quietly seated under the protection of the guns of the formidable fortress of Olmütz, after returning evasive answers to the unfortunate messengers from Vienna, and refusing to accept the resignations of the ministers in that city; when the military preparations were complete, he at last throws off all disguise, and comes forward in his proclamations of the 16th and 19th October, and assumes a decided and hostile position. " In virtue of my duties," he declares, " I have forced myself, but with a bleeding heart, to resist with arms the revolt which has audaciously reared its head in my capital and in other places, and contend against it until it is overcome, until order and tranquillity shall be restored, and the murderers of my faithful servants, the Counts De Lamberg and Latour, be brought to the avenging arms of justice. To attain this object, I send from different parts of the monarchy forces against Vienna, the seat of insurrection; and I confide to my marshal, the Prince de Windischgrätz, the control of all my

---

* Galignani's Messenger.

troops, with the exception of those commanded by Marshal
Count Radetzky. At the same time, I invest Prince Windischgrätz with full powers to accomplish as speedily as possible,
and according to his views, the work of peace in my empire."

Fortunately for the Emperor of Austria, the discipline of
this army, and the known fidelity of several of his other provinces, but above all, the feelings of national hostility which
many regarded as the weakness, but which in fact was always
the strength of the empire, enabled him to adopt this vigorous
course of policy, and to concentrate an overwhelming force
around the principal seat of rebellion.

The troops engaged in the reduction of the capital were almost altogether Slavic, who had no sympathies in common
with the Germans; in fact, independent of widely-distinctive
characteristics, the animosity between the two nations had been
kept up by the selfish policy of the government, which had
always sustained itself, and repressed all opposition by setting
one race to reduce the other. It had bombarded Prague with
German cannon, and was now about to subdue Vienna with
Bohemian bayonets.

The feelings by which the Slavi were actuated in the coming contest were shadowed forth in a written address made at
this time (22d of October) to the Slavic Association of Bohemia, called Slovanska-Lipa by Baron Jellacic, and in which,
among other things, he declares, "As I am animated with the
same love as you are for the Slavic nationality, and as you
are as well as I am convinced that Slavism is the strongest
support of Austria; as, on the other side, Austria is an indispensable condition for the existence of Slavism, to such an extent, that if Austria were not in existence, it must be created
for that end." "It was my duty, then, as a good Slavian, to
put down and destroy at Pesth the anti-Austrian party which
had risen against Slavism." "But when I marched against
Pesth, our common enemy made an insurrection at Vienna.
This is why I have turned with my whole army against Vienna, in order to chastise the adversaries of Slavism in the capital of the empire. I have experienced a lively joy on seeing
that our brothers of Bohemia, guided by the same conviction,
which has only been strengthened by the departure of the dep-

uties to the Diet, were hastening to range themselves under the victorious standards before Vienna, holding out the hand of fraternity to me, and this army of brothers which I command, to conquer like heroes or to die with glory. I have been led to present myself before Vienna only to combat with the enemies of Slavism ; and I flatter myself with the hope that you not only comprehend me, but will support me."* This letter was received by the Association in Prague with an enthusiasm (say the accounts) which it would be impossible to describe.

About the middle of October, Prince Windischgrätz, with a large body of troops from Bohemia, Moravia, and Galicia, takes up the line of march for Vienna ; and on the way from Lundenburg he issued, on the 20th, a proclamation to the people of Vienna, in which, after stating the commission with which he was vested, and the force with which he was armed for carrying its purposes into effect, pronounced the city of Vienna in a state of siege, and declared martial law.

Ten days had elapsed since the burghers of the beleagured city first looked down from the steeple of St. Stephen's on the motley host spreading itself over the spacious plain around them, and surveyed far and near, with a curiosity mingled with alarm, the uncouth garb and strange accoutrements, distinctive of the natives of those remote provinces which skirt the eastern frontier of the empire. The videttes of a Hungarian army had been in sight for nearly the same space of time ; and although no exact account of their numbers was received, there was every reason to believe that a very considerable body of Magyar troops were encamped upon the frontiers, just twenty-eight miles distant, anxiously awaiting the call of the Diet, and ready to march at a moment's warning to the relief of the besieged capital.

Journal of Operations during the Siege of Vienna.

Monday, October 23d. — Prince Windischgrätz, with his troops, reaches the neighborhood of Vienna on the north, crosses the Danube near Klosterneüberg by pontoon bridges, and, passing around the city, takes up his head-quarters at Hetzensdorf,

---

* Galignani's Messenger.

a small village about three miles from the capital on the south. The troops arriving with him increase the force around Vienna to about one hundred thousand men.

In the afternoon Prince Windischgrätz issues a proclamation summoning the city to surrender within forty-eight hours, and laying down the terms of submission. All communication with the city is cut off.

Tuesday, October 24th.—Before day a firing of artillery is heard, occasioned by an attack made on the outposts of the imperial troops by the forces from the city, but which is soon repulsed. The sentinels of both armies within gun-shot of each other ; those from the city extending to the vicinity of Hietzing.

The centre of the Imperialists, under the immediate command of Prince Windischgrätz, is at Hetzensdorf, immediately behind the Palace of Schönbrunn. The left wing extends by Breitensee and Lerchenfeld, lying on the west of the city ; while the right wing of the army, under Jellacic, rests on the Prater, situated on the east of the city.

Wednesday, October 25th.—This, as well as the previous day, is occupied by the imperial troops in preparations for an attack, while awaiting the answer of the city to the proclamation of the previous day, summoning the city to surrender. The troops are so drawn out and arranged as to surround the city completely. A battery is located on every eminence ; as far as the eye can reach, all is one entire camp ; their bright uniforms and glistening arms by day, and their extended watch-fires by night, present a martial scene of thrilling interest. On this day the prince addresses another proclamation to the citizens of Vienna, stating that pacific proposals had been made him for entering the city with his troops, and to execute the conditions prescribed ; he also appeals to the loyalty of a great portion of the citizens of Vienna, and inquires whether it be possible, after all that has passed—after his troops had been fired upon without a motive as soon as they appeared—he should enter the city, which is swarming with armed men filled with evil intentions, before this multitude has been disarmed, without bringing on a murderous combat in the streets. That during several days his troops had been continually attacked, although they had received orders not to return these attacks, except in case of extremity, which had occurred in several places. He once more asks if an arrangement is possible under the conditions proposed.

Thursday, October 26th.—The forty-eight hours given by Prince Windischgrätz having expired, and no arrangements entered into, in the morning early the firing begins. Before nine o'clock the videttes and outposts of the city forces are driven in. About ten o'clock a body of National Guards, making a *sortie* from the western part of the city, are repulsed and driven back. In the same quarter a fire is opened by the imperial artillery from the hill, back of Pensing, on to a battery constructed by the city forces in the cemetery of the Schmeltz, lying outside of the intrenchments of the city. After a short cannonade, the battery was carried by assault, and those who had manned it forced to retreat behind the fortifications of the city. The troops, discharging grenades from that battery, set fire to several houses in the opposite faubourg.* On the eastern side of the city, toward the Prater, a point against which Baron Jellacic was operating, the firing was more heavy all day ; the demonstrations on the western side being mere feints to distract the attention of the enemy while the more serious attack was progressing on the other side. After a combat of twelve hours, the exterior line of the faubourg Leopoldstadt—that is, the Prater, the Augarten, and Brigittenau—were occupied by the army ; but the faubourg itself, bristling with barricades, and courageously defended by National Guards and workmen, was not broken into. The firing continued until midnight. During this day a deputation from the city, headed by M. Pillersdorf, member of the Diet and late Minister of the Interior, waited on Prince Windischgrätz, demanding more humane propositions than those contained in the proclamation of the 23d, but Windischgrätz was inflexible.

" Well then," said Baron Pillersdorf, " may the responsibility of all the blood shed fall on your head." " I accept the responsibility," replied the general.

---

* The water and gas-pipes of the city were cut off. By a vigorous attack the city forces recover possession and command of the water-pipes, but they were not able to retain them.

II.   I

M. Kraus, Minister of Finance, also called, but met with no better success.

Friday, October 27th.—During this day all remains comparatively tranquil. No engagements are undertaken. Prince Windischgrätz has given orders to suspend firing at all points where it was not necessary. Not a shell was thrown into the city. It was hoped that some arrangement would be entered into which might render further hostilities unnecessary, but the day passes without any such result.

Saturday, October 28th. — The attack on the city commences on all sides with great vigor. All the batteries raised by the imperial troops, on every eminence around the city, open upon the intrenchments. At eight o'clock in the morning, the firing was particularly severe at four different points—the faubourg Leopoldstadt, Lerchenfeld, the Belvidere, and the barrier of St. Maxer. The reports of the cannonade and platoon firing succeed each other with frightful rapidity.

About nine o'clock, a large body of infantry, under the immediate command of Prince Windischgrätz, issuing from Schönbrunn, takes up the line of march, in different directions, for the city. Shortly after, a desperate engagement takes place between these troops and the forces of the city posted in the depôt of the Glognitz, or Southern Rail-road. During the fight, the depôt takes fire, and the buildings, with a number of cars and locomotives, are entirely consumed. To this attack the city forces responded with rare courage; but, being at length overpowered, are forced to retreat into the city. They are pursued by the imperial forces into the faubourg Wieden, and there the contest is continued. About the same time, a number of bombs are discharged by the batteries outside into this faubourg, eight or ten large houses are set fire to, and the conflagration spreads to an alarming extent. While these operations are progressing on the southern side of the city, the troops under Jellacic enter the faubourg of the Landstrasse, on the eastern side. They attack and take thirty barricades with the bayonets and side-arms. The Seressàners,* with their fiery-

---

* *Seressàners* are the wild border soldiers from Montenegro, and bearing a stronger resemblance to the Indians of the North American forests than to the ordinary troops of the European continent. The frame of such a borderer seems to

red cloaks and peculiarly grotesque costumes, inspired great terror in their opponents; and when the National Guards saw them carrying their cimeters in their mouths, and thus, with the use of both hands, mounting the barricades with all the activity of cats, they threw down their arms and betook themselves to flight. The workmen, however, stood their ground manfully; but at length the whole faubourg was compelled to lay down its arms. No students were seen; and hence it was believed that they had laid aside their peculiar costume, and put on workmen's blouses to escape detection.

The imperial troops next march into the adjoining faubourg of the Leopoldstadt, where they encounter a much more desperate resistance; but, before night, the greater part of that faubourg is also reduced to submission. Notwithstanding the desperate defense of the city forces at all points, the troops stood before night under the walls of the inner city, and along the Danube. The house of Invalids, the Mint, Custom-house, Hay-market Caserne, and the palace of Prince Schwartzen-

---

be nothing but sinew and muscle; and with ease, nay, without appearing to be at all affected by them, he endures hardships and fatigues to which the most seasoned soldiers are scarcely equal. A piece of oaten bread and a dram of *sklikowitz* (plum brandy) suffice him, on an emergency, a whole day, and with that refreshment alone will march on untired, alike in the most scorching heat and the most furious snow-storm; and when night comes, he desires no other couch than the bare ground, no other roof than the open sky. His costume is most peculiar, as well as picturesque. There is something half Albanian in some portions of the dress—in the leggings and full trowsers fastened at the knee, and in the heavily gold-embroidered crimson jacket. But that which gives decided character and striking originality to these sons of war is the cloak. Over these giant frames hangs a mantle of scarlet cloth, fastened tightly at the throat; below this, on the breast, depends the clasp of the jacket, a large silver egg, made so as to open and serve as a cup. In the loose girdle are to be seen the richly-mounted pistols and glittering kandjar—Turkish arms chiefly; for every *Seressäner* is held, by old tradition, to have won his first weapon from the Turk. The mantle has a cape, cut somewhat in the shape of a bat's wing, but which, joined together by hooks and eyes, forms a sharp-pointed hood, resembling those of the Venetian *marinari*, but higher and more peaked. Over the crimson cap, confined by a gold band upon the brow, falling with a gold tassel on the shoulder, rises this red hood, usually overshadowing such a countenance as a Murillo or a Vandyck would delight to portray. The brilliant rays of the long dark eye repose beneath a thick fringe of sable lashes; but you feel that, if awakened, they must flash forth in fire. The brow, the mouth, and the nose are all essentially noble features; and over all is spread a skin of such clear olive-brown, that you are inclined to think you have a Bedouin before you.

burg, were occupied by the imperial forces. The contest continues both in the Leopoldstadt and the Wieden faubourgs all night.

From the discharge of grenades, Congreve rockets, and shells, the city is set fire to in many points ; and so extensive was the conflagration that almost the whole of Vienna appeared enveloped in flames.

Although the brunt of the conflict during this day had been on the southern and eastern portions of the city, the batteries on the north and west kept up a slow but steady cannonade during the whole day.

Sunday, October 29th.—The firing, which had been kept up all night, ceased about eight o'clock this morning. Field-marshal Prince Windischgrätz hoped that the city, after the experience of the preceding day, would not fail to be convinced that a disorganized mass, however numerous, could not withstand a well-disciplined army, and that the city would accede to the terms of submission proposed ; and he, therefore, to afford time for sober reflection, remained during this day without making an attack. Toward evening, a deputation from the municipality of the city visited Prince Windischgrätz at the imperial palace at Schönbrunn (to which point his headquarters had now been transferred), bearing with them the written declaration that the city would submit itself unconditionally ; that they would accept the state of siege ; and that, in accordance with this declaration, the troops would occupy the next morning the city and its faubourgs. A commission was appointed to superintend the execution of the terms. The greater part of the citizens are anxious to surrender; but some of the more desperate, particularly the proscribed—who were fighting, as it were, with halters around their necks—being unwilling to comply with the terms, threw themselves into the faubourg of Mariahülf, and again renew the conflict ; but, after a struggle in which they are severely beaten, they agree to lay down their arms, and the contest ends for the night.

Monday, October 30th.—Early in the morning all is tranquil, and the report of the unconditional surrender of the city every where circulated. About eight o'clock, a heavy and brisk firing is heard in the direction of Hungary. General Messenhauser, commander of the city forces, perceiving from the tower of St. Stephen (where he uninterruptedly remained for the last two days) the approach of the Hungarian army, which had been for days hourly expected to come to their relief, immediately issues a summons calling the citizens again to arms, despite their engagements of surrender entered into the night before, and notwithstanding a deputation executing the terms of peace was at that moment at the head-quarters of Prince Windischgrätz.

As soon as the news of the advance of the Hungarians was spread through the city, where the people were in the act of disarming, the Guards and workmen refused to fulfill the terms of the capitulation, and fired on a body of troops unsuspiciously approaching to receive their weapons.

Arms are again resumed, and the contest continues during the remainder of the day. Prince Windischgrätz, to punish the violation of faith which had been committed, recommenced the bombardment of some of the faubourgs known as the most rebellious, and the firing was continued until nightfall.

The firing heard in the morning, in the direction of Hungary, proceeds from an engagement which took place at Schwechat, twelve miles from Vienna, between a Hungarian army of twenty-two thousand men, coming up to the aid of the city, and twenty-eight thousand imperial troops dispatched against them by Prince Windischgrätz, and intrusted to the command of Count Auersperg and Baron Jellacic.

The Hungarians had been awaiting on the frontiers, for many days, the call of the Austrian Diet. At last, on the 28th of October, Kossuth himself joined the army.* The twenty columns of fire that rose that night from amid the palaces of Vienna showed but too fearfully the need there was of a speedy aid for that devoted city; and, without waiting longer on the Austrian Diet, Kossuth gave the order to advance. It was too late, for on that very day had the fatal blow been struck, and Vienna was in the power of the Imperialists.

On the 30th of October, the Hungarians came up with the

---

* After Kossuth joined the army, two days were lost, one in reorganizing the army, leaving out those not disposed to cross the Austrian frontier, and the other in awaiting the return of a messenger sent to Prince Windischgrätz.

scattered detachments of the Imperialists, drove them out of Fischamend and Albern, carried Mannsworth by storm, and pushed on toward Vienna. In the mean time, the *corps d'armée*, under Jellacic, who had been directed against them, in most secure and advantageous positions awaited their approach.

The main part of the Hungarian army, under the lead of General Moga, was between the Danube and the so-called *Schwartzen Lachen*, a sluggish arm of that river, as broad and deep as the Danube itself. At the head of this body of water the Austrians, with a park of sixty guns, stood ready to receive them; while ten regiments, principally cavalry, had been sent out to gain their rear, and inclose them in the defile. So gross a blunder could not escape the military eye of Görgey, who was at that time invested with but an unimportant command, and he directed Kossuth's attention to the fact, and by an immediate retreat they narrowly escaped the trap and avoided a total defeat, in which an hour's advance would inevitably have involved them.

They were then pursued by the victorious Austrians, both that and the following day, and driven back across the frontiers into Hungary. This was the battle of Schwechat, in which Colonel Görgey, for the efficient service rendered in saving the Hungarian army from this *cul de sac*, was promoted on the ground to the rank of general.

Tuesday, October 31st.—In consequence of the bombardment of the previous day, the city on this morning declared, for a second time, its unconditional submission. A deputation from the municipality communicated to the field-marshal the fact that the greatest part of the citizens were willing to accept the proposed conditions without reservation, but that they were too feeble—in opposition to the increased power of the Radical club, the committee of students, and its instruments the armed mob—to carry their determination into effect; therefore, they request of the field-marshal his protection of their persons and their property, as the mob threatened to set the city on fire, and to bury themselves beneath its ruins.

White flags are seen suspended from the steeples of the churches in most of the faubourgs. It is understood that they

have all surrendered except the Mariahülf and the city proper.
In the Mariahülf the contest continues for a time in the morning ; but the city forces, finding themselves unable to continue
the struggle in the open streets, retreat behind the battlements
of the inner city. In the afternoon the imperial general ordered large bodies of troops into the faubourgs, the white flags
hanging from the bastions and the adjoining houses betokened their unconditional surrender ; but no sooner had the un-
suspecting troops made their appearance on the open glacis,
than their ranks were torn to pieces by the murderous fire of
grape and musketry poured upon them from the ramparts.

How far this crime was premeditated, or how far it arose
from the confusion and insubordination which reigned in the
city, is now left to conjecture ; but, whoever were the criminals, the city suffered the penalty of the crime, for Windischgrätz no longer hesitated to open his fire on the city, and especially the massy iron-bolted gates of the Burg Thor. The
gates were destroyed by cannon, and then stormed by two battalions, who soon effected an entrance, captured eight cannons
from the enemy, and soon overpowered all opposition. During
the attack on the Burg Thor, or palace-gate, the imperial residence, situated immediately in the rear of it (whether by accident or design accounts do not agree), takes fire in the roof of
that portion of the building which covers the Imperial Library,
cabinets of minerals and antiquities. The upper part of all that
portion of the palace is destroyed, but its contents escape uninjured. The Augustin church adjoining suffers still more severely ; the renowned piece of sculpture of Canova, as well as
the hearts of the .deceased members of the imperial house
which it contained, sustained no damage.

Wednesday, November 1st.—The conflict over, the imperial
troops enter the city, take up positions on the public square,
and occupy the gates and the public buildings, the barracks,
Imperial Arsenal, War Office, and Imperial Palace.

The combatants of the night before, students and workmen,
are nowhere to be seen. Prince Windischgrätz publishes a
proclamation, in which he declares the conditions previously
laid down to be null, owing to the rupture of the capitulation.
He establishes new ones, among which are the city and its

faubourgs placed in a state of siege ; the complete disbanding
of the Academic Legion; the dissolution of the National
Guard for an indefinite period ; the suspension of all journals
and associations; domiciliary visits for the discovery of concealed arms, &c. The Diet being in session, Prince Felix
Schwartzenberg, appointed Minister of Foreign Affairs, rides
up on horseback to the building, and, entering, disperses the
Assembly, causes the doors to be closed, and the tribunes to
be occupied by the military. Military cordons are drawn by
the imperial troops for miles around the city ; no one can pass
either in or out without the written permission of the commandant ; and the most diligent search is going on in every
house for arms and combatants.

The loss of property is immense, estimated at twelve millions of florins,* or six millions of dollars. Besides those portions of the city which have suffered by conflagration, in some
places whole streets have been demolished by the cannon. The
houses in the vicinity of those gates which were stormed, as
well as the faubourgs in which the severest fighting took place,
have been either completely destroyed or most seriously damaged. The loss of life, after so protracted and desperate a
struggle, is much less than might have been expected.

An official dispatch gives the following statement of the loss
of the imperial troops in the contests at Vienna and at Schwechat, from the 26th of October to the 31st inclusive, viz.: killed,
14 officers, 175 common soldiers, and 57 horses ; wounded, 42
officers, 774 men, and 11 horses.

The loss on the other side has not been, and probably never
will be ascertained. It is admitted to be ·much greater than
that on the part of the troops ; but on both sides the loss was
astonishingly small for six days' fighting ; but this was the result of the protected positions which the combatants on both
sides occupied.

Thus ends the last siege of Vienna—a siege not carried on
in the sixteenth, but in the nineteenth century ; not conducted
by barbarous Turks, but civilized Austrians; not waged against
a foreign and infidel city, but against their own beautiful and
justly admired capital.

---

* By some accounts, thirty millions.

After the entry of the imperial troops into the city, and their occupation of the different posts, nothing of special importance occurred except the continued search for the insurgents and their arms, which lasted for some weeks, and the trial and execution of such of the leaders as they succeeded in arresting.

The number of persons suffering capital punishment were very few (only nine) in comparison with the number implicated, or with the exaggerated reports that obtained circulation on the subject. The principal individuals were Messenhauser, commander of the National Guard, on the 10th of November; Drs. Becher and Jellinek, editors of the *Universal Gazette of Austria ;* and M. Sternau, a young writer of merit. Neither his duplicity, nor the fact that he had been appointed by the Diet, the highest authority then in the city, and charged with the defense of the capital, could save Messenhauser.

Among the persons seized and tried by court-martial were two members of the Diet at Frankfort, sent thence by the deputies of the extreme left, to aid by their counsels the insurrection in Vienna. The first, Robert Blum, member for Leipsic, somewhat distinguished as a popular orator, and who had been making revolutionary speeches in the university and at other points in the city, being taken *flagranti delicto,* was, despite his supposed inviolability as a deputy, tried by court-martial, and, "on his own confession of having delivered revolutionary speeches, and opposed armed resistance to the imperial troops,"* condemned and executed on the 9th of November.

---

* The Vienna Gazette publishes the following official notice of the execution of Blum :

" In virtue of a decree of court-martial of the 8th of this month, Robert Blum, bookseller, of Leipsic, convicted on his own confession of having delivered revolutionary speeches, and opposed armed resistance to the imperial troops, was, pursuant to the proclamations published the 20th and 23d by his excellency the Prince de Windischgrätz, condemned to death, and executed the 9th November, 1848, at half-past seven in the morning, on the Brigitteneau."

The Breslau Gazette gives the following details:

" On the 9th, at six o'clock in the morning, the decree of condemnation was read to Robert Blum in his prison. He heroically declared that he expected it, and only demanded time to write some words to his wife. ' Support with courage the intelligence of my lot,' he wrote, ' and bring up our children in such a way that they shall not fail in what is due to their name. I die for liberty !' At seven o'clock the *cortège* arrived at Brigitteneau. Blum, who was in a vehicle escorted by dragoons, did not lose his presence of mind for a moment. Uncov-

The second, Julius Froebel, member from Schwartzburg, Rudolstadt, president of the Democratic Society at Frankfort, a man
of much more depth and dignity than his colleague, was also
tried and condemned to death by hanging ; but, owing to some
extenuating circumstances, he was *pardoned* (not, like his
friend Blum, from hanging to be shot), but discharged from
all punishment, and sent away from the city.

The condemnation of these officials, it was supposed by many,
would produce a great sensation throughout Germany, and involve the imperial government in serious trouble ; but it was
not difficult to perceive that such consequences could not possibly follow.   Those deputies,* if they had not, in coming to
Vienna, transcended the limits of their inviolability, certainly
did identify themselves with a rebellion in which they could
not be properly and legitimately concerned.   So far from being sent *officially* by the Frankfort Assembly, they *voluntarily*
abandoned their duties as members of that body to engage in
a foreign insurrection, in which they were proven to have been
deeply implicated, and especially as, after the declaration of
martial law, of which they were duly advised, their *civil* rights,
even if they could operate as a protection in the commission
of such high offenses, became by the *supremacy* of *military*
power annulled.

General Bem, in the disguise of a coachman, escaped from
Vienna and passed into Hungary, where he subsequently highly distinguished himself.†

Of the sixteen hundred persons arrested, nine only were
punished with death, nine sentenced to imprisonment for a

---

ering his breast, he stated that he would look death in the face; but on being told
that that was not possible, he himself tied the handkerchief round his eyes and
knelt down.   The soldiers fired, and he fell dead, struck by two balls in the
breast and another in the head."

 * Neither the government at Frankfort or Dresden could have punished Blum
for abetting rebellion at Vienna ; and the whole matter, consequently, rested with
Austria.

 † The manner of Bem's escape was related at Vienna in a variety of fabulous
ways.   Some said he passed the strictly guarded gates in the dress of an Austrian
officer; others, as a sailor; again, others say he escaped in a coffin, as a corpse.
From Pressburg he took the steamer, and fell asleep in the cabin, not awaking till
it reached Komorn, when he heard that he was in the same boat with Kossuth,
to whom he introduced himself.—*Schlessinger.*

term of years, nine hundred and ninety-six discharged, and the remainder were tried by civil tribunal. Many of the most influential instigators and participators escaped by flight before the troops entered the city.

The insurrection, although abundantly supplied with men and means, never had the least chance of success, from the total absence of that talent, character, and experience indispensable to such an undertaking. In the first place, there was no head. Messenhauser, the commander-in-chief, was in all respects totally unsuited to the station which he was called upon to occupy. He prepared no plan of defense, made no proper disposition of his troops to resist the attack, established no organization or discipline among the people uninstructed in the use of arms; he did not even make use of the means of defense at his disposal—the number of cannon might have been doubled, the manufacture of powder was wholly neglected. He had no confidence in the strength of the force subjected to his command; he despaired of the success of his cause—the defense of Vienna against so serious an attack; he thought it too difficult, nay impossible, and his whole efforts seemed directed at securing the best conditions for the city. By many he was believed to be a traitor. On the 29th and 30th, his death was called for, and but for the opportune approach of the Hungarians, and consequent distraction of the public mind, his life could not have been saved. The character of the man, and the course which he labored to pursue, can not be better illustrated than by reference to the last proclamations which he issued. In the first, dated the 29th, he states that, having consulted all those who possessed the confidence of the companies as to the possibility of holding out, he had come to the conclusion that "it would only be leading the flower of the population to the slaughter-house." He adds that he has only been able to collect ammunition sufficient to hold out four hours longer; and that he therefore proposes a surrender, and engages to remind Prince Windischgrätz of the promises of his majesty. In the second, dated the 30th, at eight o'clock P.M., he announces that the Hungarian army had fought near Schwadorf, and had not gained the victory. He then, after praising his fellow-citizens for the disposition which they manifest of holding out if there is the least hope, announces that the field-marshal has declared that if by eight o'clock the town has not surrendered, he will attack the still remaining suburbs with the greatest energy, and reduce them to ashes, if necessary; and then asks the National Guard to give him a written answer to the question whether they will lay down their arms or not. In the third, dated the 31st, he solemnly protests against his having ordered the aggressive acts committed by some corps Mobiles against the imperial troops during the negotiation for a capitulation on the 30th; and that, on the contrary, he had been constantly engaged in disarming the National Guard since the morning, and had some cannons removed from the bastions.

In the next place, there was no body to the Revolution. The feeling of resistance was not a general or popular one; a large majority of the Viennese were inclined to peace and loyalty, but they were completely crushed by the terrorism of the Polish committee, the students, and the workmen. Martial law had been proclaimed in Vienna, and every able-bodied man who was found unarmed, or who refused to perform military service which the committee required of him, was immediately taken up as a traitor, and tried by court-martial. Nothing was more common than the name of traitor, for they had other tests besides the performance of military duties to try the wretched citizens' devotion to liberty. Students and workmen took up their quarters in any man's house that suited their fancy, and must be treated with every hospitality. People who declined the honor of receiving these distinguished guests, who winced under the summary disposal of their goods and chattels, or demurred against giving up their wives and daughters to the brutal lusts of the rulers of the hour, were treated as enemies of public liberty. They were accused and given up to the tender mercies of martial law.

And who were these rulers of the hour, these especial champions of the movement? Were they of the better class of citizens? Were they of the substantial burghers, the owners of property? No; they were the youth of the university, to whom the only government of which they had as yet any experience was that of a college; and the *ouvriers*, or workmen in the different fabrics of the faubourgs and the vicinity, who felt not a particle of interest either in the government or the country, who lived to-day on the earnings of yesterday, and whose only hope for the morrow rested on the earnings of to-day. To such a class, any change which might come must be for the better, as it could not possibly be for the worse. They are the bane of every government; to them the restraint of any regular authority, however free, is insupportable ; and their every effort is aimed at its destruction. Like certain animals, they are brought forth by, and can exist only in an atmosphere of dissolution. Their only conception of liberty is *licentiousness*—the liberty to do any thing and every thing which their inclinations or interests might dictate ; their only ideas of justice consist in an equal division of property—a doctrine which comports most admirably with their destitute condition, for, having nothing in the world to contribute, they can only be the gainers by the division. Such are the rank and file of the Communists of Germany and the Red Republicans of France.* The leaders (those who figure in their clubs and direct the movements of the animal mass) are atheists in religion as well as politics ; who look upon the creation as the work of chance, society as a state of slavery; who deny a Supreme Power in the guidance of things on earth, declare religion a scarecrow to frighten the vulgar. All these men worship one idol, that of their own will and of their own caprices.† Fortunately for the United States, such a class is unknown among them ; and although in the spring-tide of emigration, which has for a few years past been on the flood with us, but few of this class have been able to bear the expenses of transportation to our shores; and, even if they could, an almost inexhaustible West, where

---

* Chronicle.

† The various nations of Europe are attempting to solve the question in various ways. In France, since the Revolution of February, it has consisted in the planting of trees and the erection of barricades ; in the assertion of the right to labor and the practical cessation of demand. Berlin and Vienna, Hungary and Lombardy, and the German states, would return much the same answer to the question as at Paris. Every man is to do what he likes—is that it ? The definition would seem somewhat large. Some men are for cutting throats; others are for retaining throats uncut. A. desires B.'s horses, his side-board and plate, his realty, his chattels, his choses in action; B. desires, very naturally, to retain them for himself. The definition must at once be narrowed ; B. must be shorn of his goods or A. of his liberty, there is no escape from the dilemma.—*Galignani's M ssenger.*

they may settle down and acquire some substantial interest in the country and its institutions, will operate, for centuries to come, as a safety-valve to free us from the dangers of so fatal an element.

While such was the character and such the motives of the prime movers in this revolt, the considerations which incited the action of the imperial government can not, perhaps, be more correctly gathered than by reference to the following communication, bearing date at Olmütz on the 26th of October, and addressed by Baron de Wessenberg, president of the Austrian ministry, to the Austrian envoys at the German courts :

" The recent events at Vienna have been frequently erroneously interpreted in Germany. In order that the question may be correctly judged, the principal circumstances herein indicated should be borne in mind : the military operations which are at this moment taking place under the walls of Vienna have only one object—to combat anarchy and re-establish a legal state. The emperor and his government have no intention of retaking the liberties accorded, of realizing the scarecrow which the revolutionary party presents under the name of reaction, or of conquering for one of the Austrian nationalities a superiority over the other. It is not a struggle of nationalities, a transformation of the monarchy into a Slavic Austria, as the German press believes or causes to be believed ; it is a combat of order against anarchy, of legal power (without which there is no government) against terrorism, of conservation against revolution. It is a disregarding of facts, an erroneous judgment of things, to give to this combat another signification. The revolution has covered itself with a German mantle ; the German colors have become the ensign of the party of overthrow. It is not against liberty, the grandeur and the tie of Germany, which the Emperor of Austria thinks himself specially called on to protect ; it is against the party which makes an abusive use of those colors, and of different things, for the promotion of its criminal objects, that the efforts of the government and the army of his majesty are directed. I invite you to conserve this point of view, and to support it as much as possible in your circle of action. His majesty the emperor and the government are resolved to maintain this combat by all the means in their power. These means were set forth in imperial manifestoes of the 18th and 19th, which were communicated to you by a circular dispatch. Military measures have been already employed. An army of nearly sixty thousand men, conducted in person by Field-marshal Prince de Windischgrätz, who has taken up his headquarters at Hetzensdorf, closely surrounds the capital, and I have reason to hope that these operations will soon attain their object. His majesty, at the same time, finds himself constrained to remove the Diet from Vienna, and to convoke it, for the 15th of November, at Kremsier."

The battle over, and the exciting scenes which attended it having passed away, an opportunity is now afforded for a brief consideration of the peculiar character of the conflict, of which the Austrian capital has recently been the theatre. Such a contest is exceedingly apt to be misunderstood in our country. We are so much inclined to interpret all struggles between sovereigns and subjects according to analogies afforded by our own political history, that the notion of liberties denied and Constitutions violated appears inseparable from the idea of rebellion and civil war. Such was, however, far from being the case in the instance under consideration. That the war between the emperor and his Magyar subjects happened to come to a head, or to burst forth in the Austrian metropolis, and to have assumed something of a constitutional aspect, was really but little more than accidental. When the news arrived from Hungary of the butchery of Lamberg, the Radicals of the capital, professing to sympathize with their rebellious coadjutors at Pesth, were determined that Vienna should not be outstripped in patriotism, as it was profanely termed, and therefore got up an *émeute*, which ended with the murder of Latour and the flight of the emperor.* There was nothing either national, liberal, or general in the movement. Had it been a national struggle for liberty, in which the people on the one side were struggling with the monarch on the other, we should have watched the progress of the strife with a far different eye.

---

* F. Pulszky, in "Memoirs of an Hungarian Lady," defends himself and the Hungarians from the charge of instigating the Revolution of the 6th of October.

But the case was quite otherwise. We have seen the mob of the capital rise against the government, murder a responsible minister of the crown without a hand being raised to avenge him, and usurp the arbitrary power of swaying at will the general administration of the empire. In the scenes which followed, the people of the empire bore no part; of *its* will, the populace of Vienna was never constituted the exponent. The Diet itself, as a Constituent Assembly, was intrusted with no such office. Were it even, which it was not, a permanent legislative body, it would by no means have followed that the passive acquiescence or reluctant participation of a mere fraction of an Assembly could have the effect of implicating the nation in the quarrel, or of converting a local riot into a general rebellion. Had they been capable of governing, they would at this moment have been supreme in Vienna. They could not govern, they merely snatched at the reins, and afterward, when the horses were at full speed, were as powerless to guide as to check their mad career.* Before the rebellion broke out, they did but obstruct and embarrass the government, which they had neither the skill nor the moral weight to direct; and, throughout the deplorable scenes which ensued, they occupied themselves in issuing manifestoes to which nobody listened, and in passing resolutions which were soon expunged from their records. The great constitutional principle of which they were the champions, was the legalization of anarchy and crime; the patriots over whom they tried to extend the shield of their protection, were the perpetrators of a dastardly and atrocious murder.

Although it is impossible not to be penetrated with the deepest commiseration for the misguided victims of this great revolt, and although few events in modern history are more terrible than this attack by the forces of the empire on that ancient and splendid city, which has been for ages the seat of the imperial government and the sovereign of Central Europe, yet our sense of justice does no more recoil from the suppression and punishment of anarchical revolt than we should from the necessary infliction of the last rigor of the law on a convicted

---

* Chronicle.

offender. The firmness and ability of Prince Windischgrätz, and the gallantry of the imperial troops, might have been displayed with more unalloyed glory on a foreign field and against a foreign foe; yet few of the ordinary causes of war could so imperiously claim the devotion of an army as this conquest of a faction, by which the seat of government had been successfully invaded, and society itself menaced and assailed.

The cause of liberal institutions received a heavier blow and a greater disparagement from the incapacity and extravagance of the German Radicals and the Hungarian rabble than the cannons of Windischgrätz could inflict. The unfortunate effect of these horrors and follies will be to induce a timid people, which has only seen the effects of liberty in turbulence, ruin, and bloodshed, to cling to military power as the last defense of society.

The people of Vienna have had a taste of anarchy, and are not likely soon to forget its bitterness. The commercial classes will now prefer peace under the emperor, and without a Parliament, though bought with heavy taxes to support large armies, to the unchecked excesses of the mob, until these shall either be passed out of present memory or be balanced in estimate by some present evil traceable more or less truly to the absolute form of government.*

To us, who have the happiness to live in a country where the strong but simple forms of civil justice have ever averted or adequately punished all serious disturbances of public order, these terrible outbreaks of social madness, followed by the stern retributions of military power, are, by the blessings of Providence, unknown. But in observing the course of these events upon the continent of Europe, where the law is in reality weaker, and therefore more violent than it is among ourselves, we must not be led astray by misplaced sympathies with any cause which is not that of freedom or improvement. Had the people of Vienna been less servilely docile of old to the tutelary precautions of a government which has been often startled at shadows, they would not have fallen into the snares of a few itinerant demagogues, or sunk under the yoke of a

---

* Galignani's Messenger.

II.　　　　　　　K

sanguinary insurrection. The original blame, therefore, de-
servedly rests upon the policy of a government like that of
Metternich, which left the people emasculated, demoralized—
ignorant alike of their duties and their rights. Where so little had been done to make men good citizens and enlightened
subjects, the base and unmeaning cry of insurrection found a
ready response from ignorance and discontent.*

Upon this state of the population of Vienna the revolutionary societies confidently speculated, for none are better acquainted with the vices and weakness of a people than those
who trade upon its power. They hoped to strike a fatal blow
at peace and monarchical government in Europe by making
themselves masters of what was once their strong-hold. As far
as Vienna was concerned, they succeeded; but they had un-
derrated the power and loyalty of the Austrian army, and the
result was the severest check which the Revolution had yet
received.

Of old such a triumph would have rendered a usurper absolute. Yet now the counselors of these triumphant kings and
emperors instantly confess that military triumph is of slight
avail, and that in these days a monarchy can be no longer
based upon it. The first acts of the sovereigns are to crave
pardon of their people for such terrible coercion, excusing it as
salutary and necessary, but as temporary; while the most specious promises of constitutional and liberal government are
superadded, to allay the terrible master of popular discontent.

The emperor will return again to his capital, surrounded by
the faithful and gallant army who have encountered in his
cause a warfare a thousand times more awful than any struggle with a foreign foe could have been. But he returns to a
changed city and an altered people. It is not as it was. The
monarchs of the house of Austria had always lived in kind and
friendly intercourse with their people; if they were pressed
down with an iron hand, the surface, at least, was smooth—
they were treated indulgently and well. But the events of the
late siege have given a rude shock to the old ties of traditional
loyalty. The citizens can not look around them at their black-

* Galignani's Messenger.

ened homes and ruined churches, without being reminded that there has passed between them and their emperor that which both of them may forgive, but which neither can soon forget. Long years of internal prosperity and good government must elapse, fresh triumphs and fresh disasters must have linked together monarch and people, before the traces of the outbreak in 1848, and its terrible suppression, are erased from the hearts of the burghers of Vienna.

CHAPTER VII.

FIRST HUNGARIAN CAMPAIGN.—AUSTRIANS INVADE HUNGARY SIMULTANEOUSLY FROM NINE DIFFERENT POINTS. — THE CAPITAL ABANDONED, AND THE AUSTRIANS EVERY WHERE TRIUMPHANT.—AUSTRIANS REACH THE THEISS.—HUNGARIANS ASSUME THE OFFENSIVE, AND, BY A SUCCESSION OF BRILLIANT VICTORIES, DRIVE THE AUSTRIANS COMPLETELY FROM THEIR TERRITORY, WHILE THE DIET OF THE KINGDOM DECLARES THE INDEPENDENCE OF HUNGARY FROM THE SWAY OF THE HABSBURG DYNASTY.

ALTHOUGH the Hungarian Diet had, in the month of July, voted an enlistment of two hundred thousand men, their levy and equipment had proceeded but slowly. On the 3d of October, when the imperial manifesto, and the appointment of Jellacic as civil and military governor, produced the final rupture, the whole military force of Hungary consisted only of forty thousand men, and of these only twenty-four thousand took a decided part for the nation. Even the officers of many regiments that proved true subsequently either went over to the Imperialists or retired. By the 28th of October, fifteen thousand regular troops and eight thousand *Honvéds*,* or militia, were all that Kossuth could assemble to march to the relief of Vienna. After their repulse on the 30th at Schwechat, the Hungarian army retired within the frontiers of their own kingdom, and occupied a long line of posts from Oedenburg to Holics. A desperate conflict was now inevitable, and each party devoted itself to preparation for the struggle.

---

* Fifteen thousand troops of the line, ten *Honvéd* battalions, seventy squadrons of cavalry, and two regiments of Szecklers—in all, a force of thirty-six thousand men and seven thousand horses, were the foundation of the great Hungarian army. In the commencement of their difficulties, and during the insurrection in the south of Hungary, the greater part of the Hungarian troops were at this time fighting the Austrian battles in Italy. It was, therefore, necessary to raise new forces for the defense of the country; and ten battalions of volunteers were formed, of which the commanders were appointed by the king, the officers by the Palatine, Archduke Stephen. Their commissions were countersigned by the Hungarian War Office. These troops were called *Honvéds*, or " defenders of home," and, with the battalions of the line and the regiments of hussars, formed, at a later period, the nucleus of the Hungarian army.—*Klapka.*

In Hungary there was no lack of men, but in arms and ammunition they were sadly deficient.   Manufactories for these were there almost unknown, for, wishing to keep the country in this respect dependent on Austria, the imperial government had always discouraged their establishment.   They soon, however, arose like magic throughout the country.   In every town the anvils rang with the clang of the arms which the artisans forged by night and by day.   There was but little powder, and no sulphur to make it with; and this, at great cost, was extracted from copper ore.   Metal was also rare, but the bells of the churches were taken to supply the necessity.   Under the extraordinary energy of Kossuth, there sprang up with marvelous rapidity, at various points, founderies for cannon, armories for muskets, powder mills, and extensive saltpetre establishments, and manufactories for the production of fulminating silver and percussion caps.

Under the extraordinary expenses of the government money soon failed in the treasury; but, to supply this deficiency, paper was issued, which circulated like gold, so that in two months twenty-eight millions had already been issued.

Every where enlistment and equipment of the Honvéds proceeded, under the superintendence of the local committees of defense.

The nobles mortgaged their estates to aid with money the patriotic movement, and, heading their dependents, brought whole battalions and regiments into the field.   Even women, casting aside the vestments of their sex, took arms as soldiers.*   It was a great and generous movement.

It is true that many leading magnates adhered to the court at Vienna, in devotion to which they had spent their lives, and which, from a long residence, constituted their home; but there was hardly a great family of which some wealthy and influential members did not declare for their native land.†   A great

---

* Two women, entering the ranks, reached the post of captain before their sex was discovered.   Two regiments, altogether of females, were formed in the South, and tendered their services to Kossuth.   Kossuth was much annoyed; but, with his great tact, he accepted them both, and ordered one regiment to the hospitals to nurse the sick, and the other to the arsenal, to be engaged in making cartridges, clothes, &c.

† About one half the high aristocracy, particularly those of the Theiss and Tran-

majority of the resident aristocracy, the numerous class of resident country gentlemen, almost without exception, the body of inferior nobles or freeholders, the peasant proprietors, and the laboring population, espoused the cause of Hungary. The Protestant clergy in the Magyar country to a man, and the Roman Catholic clergy of Hungary in a body, urged their flocks to be patient and orderly, and to obey the government charged with the defense of the country, and to be faithful and valiant in defending it.

As soon as Prince Windischgrätz had completed the subordination of Vienna, and punished the leading insurrectionists, his whole attention was devoted to preparation for the invasion and subjugation of Hungary. The army of upward of one hundred thousand men, that had just assisted in the reduction of the capital, was in a state of readiness for marching immediately against Hungary ; but the preparations for so serious a campaign were necessarily much heavier than might, at the first glance, have been anticipated. The provision of the immense baggage-trains required for the transportation of all the ammunition, rations, and other necessaries, even to fuel, for so large an army, was found to be an extensive undertaking, and the scarcity of horses increased the difficulty. It was also thought advisable not to open the campaign until the severity of the winter had set in, and the roads, at other times almost impassable to heavy artillery, should become frozen, and thus rendered passable. These difficulties, with the usual Austrian tardiness, delayed for six weeks the departure of the army, which it was at first supposed would have marched in a very few days after the capture of Vienna.

On the 6th of November, the emperor issued from Olmütz a proclamation to the inhabitants of all the countries appertaining to the Hungarian crown, cautioning them against the stratagems of Louis Kossuth and his companions, and warning them that, unless they fulfilled their duties toward their king and country, they would be held as traitors to both, and the authorities be forced to treat them accordingly.

---

sylvania (those of the Danube country, from their connection with Vienna, were unfavorable), the untitled nobility, and clergy, sided almost unanimously with the country.

This proclamation of the emperor was followed by two others from Prince Windischgrätz, issued on the 12th and 13th of November, and directed to the people of Hungary and Transylvania, advising them of his intention, under the orders of the king, to invade the country, and proffering "protection to the faithful, pardon to the repentant, but death to the rebel." The other was addressed to the Field-marshal L. Moga, and to all imperial generals and officers in Hungary, calling upon them to return to their duty and their flag by the 26th of November, or, on failure to do so, they would be held traitors and rebels, and treated with the utmost rigors of martial law.

Wearied by contentions in which his character and feelings unfitted him to participate; distracted by diverse counsels; involved, by a series of intrigues, in conflicting engagements; dreading the new order of things, and diffident of his own ability to perform the duties it demanded of him, the Emperor Ferdinand, on the 2d of December, abdicated ; and, by a family arrangement, the crown of Austria was transferred, not to the next heir, but to the second in succession.

The Emperor Francis Joseph, son of the Archduke Francis Charles and of the Archduchess Sophia, is a youth of fine and manly appearance, tall and slender in stature, upright and military in his carriage, with an intelligent countenance, but, above all, distinguished for his remarkable self-possession. He is said to be endowed with an excellent mind, and to have acquired such a knowledge of the different languages of his empire as to enable him to address with fluency any portion of his subjects in their own tongue. His character, of course, remains yet to be developed ; and if the anecdote related of his conduct, when first apprised of his elevation to the throne, be not a fiction, favorable anticipations may be entertained as respects his future career. When informed that he was emperor, Francis Joseph, sinking back upon the sofa, and covering his face with his hands, exclaimed, *Meine Jugend ist hin!* My youth is over!* It was a noble exclamation for a boy of but nineteen years, for it told of duties accepted and of devotion to an arduous task. To be master in the fresh flush of

---

* Baroness Blaze de Bury.

youth of one of the greatest empires of the world, and to think
first of the sacrifices which duty imposes rather than of the
splendor which the position confers, exhibits an appreciation
of the task as rarely to be met with, as it is indispensable to
success in those that are born to rule.*

The crown of Hungary, as we have already seen, had been
settled, by statute, on the heirs of the house of Habsburg; but
no provision had been made for the case which had now arisen.
The Hungarians held that their king had no power to abdicate; that, so long as he lived, he must be their king; that,
if he became incapable of performing the regal functions, the

---

* On the 2d of December, 1848, the garrison of Olmütz was aroused at early
dawn, and bidden to the Place d'Armes, where some military ceremonies, for
purposes not specified, were to take place. Some said it was merely a review in
honor of Prince Windischgrätz and the Ban, who had arrived in the night; but
whatever it might be, some secret presentiment drove nearly the whole population to the spot where the troops were ordered to assemble. A regiment of infantry, a battalion of grenadiers, and several battalions of artillery, were ranged
in line of battle; the officers, in their full-dress uniforms, with their plumed hats,
and stars and crosses on their breasts, were assembled; carriages, full of ladies,
were hurrying by, no one knew why, unless it might be to see the Ban; the
crowd was unquiet, and it scarce knew wherefore; and the ignorance and vague
curiosity of all found vent in a thousand questions. It was half past eight, and the
rays of the morning sun began to illuminate the blue winter-sky; then began those
strange prophetic murmurs, for whose existence no one alive can assign a reasonable cause, but which so often divine the truth; but none would give a loud current to thoughts which seemed to every one almost an offense. Suddenly, the
Archduke Ferdinand d'Este dashed forward on his horse, and, calling around him
all the staff-officers present, announced to them the abdication of the Emperor
Ferdinand, and of his brother, the Archduke Franz Karl, in favor of the Archduke
Franz Josef, the emperor's nephew. The regeneration, the new youthful age of
Austria was complete; it was a great, an incalculably great measure; but the first
impression was one of sadness. The first spontaneous words of the whole crowd,
turn to which side one might, were words of sympathy, of affliction, of regret for
Ferdinand. It would seem that suddenly his people had been struck with re-
morse for all he had suffered; he, so good, so gentle; he, in whose simple heart
had never dwelt a thought that was not for their welfare, *der armer, guter Ferdinand!* Those were the first sounds that ran along the crowd. At the end of
half an hour, a general movement announced the arrival of the new monarch;
and, followed by his brothers and cousins, attended by the heroes of the late
events, Windischgrätz, and the Ban, and Schlick, attired in the simple colonel's
uniform, in which he was familiar to all around him, the young sovereign of Austria bounded forward, full twenty paces in advance of his suite, upon a splendid
charger, whose ardor seemed but to furnish proof of its rider's graceful skill.
Franz Josef der Erste! "the flower of Habsburg," as he has been called; the
successor to the throne of Rhodolph and Maximilian, emperor-Cæsar, and but of
nineteen years.—*Baroness Blaze de Bury.*

laws had reserved to the Diet the power to provide for their
due performance; that the crown of Hungary was settled by
statute on the *direct* heirs of the house of Habsburg, and the
Emperor Francis Joseph was not the *direct* heir; and that
conferring the crown on him changed the order of succession
to the throne—a change never effected, even in absolute countries, by virtue of the royal will alone.   Also, that the Hungarian crown was hereditary in the house of Habsburg under
certain conditions, which had been originally laid down and
repeatedly confirmed (particularly in 1687, 1722, 1790) by
solemn compacts between that family on the one part, and
the Hungarian nation on the other; that, if he claimed the
crown of Hungary as his legal right, he was bound to abide by
the laws or conditions upon which that right was founded;
that these laws or conditions required that the person claiming
the throne of Hungary should be crowned with the crown of
St. Stephen, according to the ancient forms and ceremonies,
within the realm of Hungary itself, and should, at his coronation, take a solemn oath to preserve inviolate the ancient liberties of the Hungarians, their Constitution, and laws.   These
requirements and conditions not having been complied with,
the Hungarian Diet held the decree of abdication null and void.
The abdication of the Emperor Ferdinand, and the accession
to the imperial throne of his youthful successor, presented another opportunity of which the Austrian government might
have gracefully availed itself, to terminate the differences with
Hungary.   The young emperor was totally uncommitted, was
fettered by no engagements, involved in none of the intrigues
that entangled his unwary predecessor, and which entailed so
great evils upon the country.   He was free to take a constitutional course in Hungary; to confirm the concessions which had
been voluntarily made, and which could not now be recalled;
to restore to the imperial government a character for good
faith, and thus to have won the hearts of the Hungarians.
The situation in which the young emperor was, by the force
of circumstances, thus placed, resembled very much that of his
ancestor Leopold the Second, on his accession to the throne,
when a Diet had not been held in Hungary for twenty-five
years—when the Hungarians, provoked by the persevering ef-

forts of his predecessor Joseph to Germanize the country, began to utter the cry, "We want no *Austrian* king."

Had he been possessed of the manly boldness, generous confidence, or great tact of his ancestor, to have gone, like him, immediately to the Hungarian capital, there to have unhesitatingly confirmed the concessions which had been granted, and which, without dishonor, could not have been recalled—with that romantic generosity so peculiar to the Hungarians, he would have been received by them with open arms; the unhappy difficulties would have been healed, and all the evils and bloodshed which have since occurred been prevented; while, supported by their loyal attachment to their king, he might have peacefully worked out such reforms in the government of his empire as the times and circumstances imperiously demanded.

Independent of its effect upon Hungary, the recent accession appeared destined to change completely the situation of things in Austria, to induce a perfect rupture with the past, and to form a new era for the monarchy.

In taking the sceptre from the hands of a prince whose deplorable infirmities of mind and body rendered his reign a most significant commentary upon the absurdity of the "divine right," he removed one great source of disaffection. But that alone was not sufficient: in the case of a simple abdication, the crown would have devolved on his brother, the Archduke Francis Charles, always known in Austria as a partisan of the system of Metternich. His ascension to the throne would not have appeared to offer to the moderate Liberal party the guarantees and hopes which it was desired to attach to the abdication of Ferdinand. It was necessary to indicate that it was not only a change of persons which was about to be effected, but that the crown was sincerely desirous of breaking with all the traditions of the past, contrary to the spirit of the times and of constitutional institutions. The Archduke Francis Joseph, too young to be bound in any respect by the past, or to be suspected of reserves or regrets for a system to which his age necessarily rendered him a stranger, was the proper person really to inaugurate the future of Austria. Even the sort of blank left in the transmission of the crown by the refusal of his father to ascend the throne, seemed to constitute a line of profound demarcation between the past and the future.

But evil counsels and despotic ambition prevailed, and this occasion for an amicable adjustment of the differences between the countries was suffered to pass unimproved. In fact, indications warranted the conclusion that it was deemed an advantage that the emperor, unfettered by personal engagements to Hungary, was free to prosecute its subjugation, to subvert its Constitution, and to force the Hungarians afterward to accept in its place the *Charte Octroyée* of Count Stadion; but this was a course which implied a determination rather to undertake the conquest of the kingdom than to claim the hereditary succession to a throne secured and guarded by statutes.

About the same time, another opportunity presented itself for the settlement of the unhappy difficulties which distracted the two countries, but which the imperial government, in the proud consciousness of its inexhaustible strength, thought proper to disregard. At the solicitation of Louis Kossuth, President of the Committee of Defense in Hungary, the Chargé d'Affaires of the United States at the court of Vienna, on the 3d of December, 1848, made application to the imperial government, with a view " to initiate the negotiations of an armistice for the winter between the two armies standing on the frontiers of Austria and Hungary, and to stop the calamities of a war so fatal to the interests of both countries."

" This application" (as Mr. Webster, Secretary of State of the United States government, advises M. Hülsemann, Chargé d'Affaires of Austria) " became the subject of a conference between Prince Schwartzenberg, the imperial Minister of Foreign Affairs, and Mr. Stiles. The prince commended the consideration and propriety with which Mr. Stiles had acted ; and, so far from disapproving his interference, advised him, in case he received a further communication from the revolutionary government in Hungary, to have an interview with Prince Windischgrätz, who was charged by the emperor with the proceedings determined on in relation to that kingdom."*

" A week after these occurrences, Mr. Stiles received, through

---

* Mr. Webster's reply to M. Hülsemann.

a secret channel, a communication signed by Louis Kossuth, President of the Committee of Defense, and countersigned by Francis Pulszky, Secretary of State.* On the receipt of the

---

* On the night of the 2d of December, 1848, when all communication between Hungary and Austria had ceased, large armies on either side guarding their respective frontiers, the author was seated in the office of the Legation of the United States at Vienna, when his servant introduced a young female, who desired, as she said, to see him at once upon urgent business. She was a most beautiful and graceful creature, and, though attired in the dress of a peasant, the grace and elegance of her manner, the fluency and correctness of her French, at once denoted that she was nearer a princess than a peasant. She sat and conversed for some time before she ventured to communicate the object of her visit. As soon as the author perceived that in the exercise of the utmost caution she desired only to convince herself that she was not in error as to the individual she sought, he told her that, upon the honor of a gentleman, she might rest assured that the individual she saw before her was the diplomatic agent of the United States at the court of Vienna. Upon that assurance, she immediately said, " Then, sir, I am the bearer of a communication to you." She then asked, " Have you a servant, sir, in whom you can rely, who can go with me into the street for a few moments ?" The author replied that he had no servant in whom he could rely, that he feared they were all in the pay of the police, but that he had a private secretary in whom he reposed confidence, and who could accompany her. The secretary was immediately called, they descended together into the street, and in a few moments returned, bearing with them the rack of a wagon. This rack, which is a fixture attached either to the fore or back part of a peasant's wagon, and intended to hold hay for the horses during a journey, was composed of small slats, about two inches wide and about the eighth of an inch thick, crossing each other at equal distances, constituted a semicircular net-work. As all these slats, wherever they crossed, were fastened together with either wooden or iron bolts, with our unskillful hands an hour nearly was consumed before we could get the rack in pieces. When this was accomplished, we saw nothing before us but a pile of slats; but the fair courier, taking them up one by one, and examining them very minutely, at length selected a piece, exclaiming, " This is it !" The slat selected resembled the others so completely, that the most rigid observer, unapprised of the fact, could not have detected the slightest difference between them; but, by the aid of a penknife, to separate its parts, this slat was found to be composed of two pieces, hollowed out in the middle, and affording space enough to hold a folded letter. In this space had been conveyed, with a secrecy which enabled it to pass the severe scrutiny of the Austrian sentinels, the communication addressed to the author by Louis Kossuth.

The mysterious personage, as intrepid as she was fair, who undertook the conveyance of this dispatch, at night, alone and unprotected, in an open peasant's wagon, in a dreadful snow-storm, through the midst of the Austrian army, when detection would have been certain death, was (as M. Pulszky has just informed the author) then a single lady, has since married, and is now the Countess M.

The statement, therefore, of a person assuming the title and name of Baroness Beck, and who, in a work upon the Hungarian war, published in England about two years ago, claiming for herself the credit of having been the bearer of the dispatch referred to, is altogether without foundation. This authoress, whose char-

communication, Mr. Stiles had an interview with Prince Windischgrätz, who received him with the utmost kindness, thanked
him for his efforts toward reconciling the existing difficulties,"
but replied in substance as follows : " I can do nothing in the
matter." " I must obey the orders of the emperor." " Hungary must submit." " I will occupy Pesth with my troops, and
then the emperor must decide what is to be done." " I can not
consent to treat with those who are in a state of rebellion."

The course of the imperial government was fixed, and, from
motives of pride as well as of policy, nothing short of the unconditional submission of Hungary, as Prince Windischgrätz
stated, would at that time for a moment be listened to.

Two recent victories over his own undisciplined and ill-arm-
ed subjects had given the young emperor a confidence in the
invincibility of his troops which nothing could shake. Prague,
battered by the cannon of Windischgrätz, had been but a short
time previously reduced to a state of the most fawning subserviency ; and Vienna, besieged, not by Turks, but by an overwhelming force of Austrian troops, had just surrendered, and
lay in all its agonies prostrate at his feet.

But as great an obstacle to the success of negotiations at this
time arose from the fact, that the constitutional privileges of
Hungary had ever been a thorn in the side of Austria ; and the
Schwartzenberg cabinet had arrived at the conclusion that the
present was a most favorable moment to rid themselves of these
troublesome encumbrances.

It was the boast of Wentworth, Earl of Strafford, when Viceroy of Ireland, that he had made King Charles, in that island,
" as absolute as any prince in the world could be," and the
ambition of the English statesman seems to have been the
leading motive which characterized the policy of Schwartzenberg's government of Hungary.

The *Vienna Gazette*, the acknowledged organ of the impe-

---

acter, as well as untimely and remarkable death, was involved in so much mystery, and excited for a time so much discussion in Europe, was (as M. Pulszky
represents) the servant of the Countess M., and thus became possessed of a knowledge of the incident above detailed.*

---

* For document containing the correspondence between M. Kossuth and W. H. Stiles, see Appendix, note No. 28.

rial cabinet, in its imprudent exultation over the triumphant commencement of the campaign, thus exposes the fixed policy of the ministry : " The Magyar tribe is now being thrown back upon its geographical territory, and the kingdom of Hungary, such as it has been, lies in its agonies, after existing for a thousand years. Its history is ended ; its future belongs to Austria."

COMMENCEMENT OF THE CAMPAIGN.

On the 15th of December, Prince Windischgrätz, intrusted with the command in chief, left Vienna with the last of his forces for Hungary ; and the subjugation of that country, so firmly resolved on, was then effectually and energetically commenced.

The plan of the campaign, so far as could be judged of from observation of their different movements, seems to have been arranged with great judgment, and to have been attended with thorough preparation. It consisted in invading the country, with formidable forces, from nine points at the same time, all simultaneously tending, with the utmost rapidity, to a common centre, viz., the capital of the kingdom ; subduing all opposition which they might encounter, and disarming the population as they proceeded in their victorious march. That these combinations were attended with the most rapid and complete success, the following details will make manifest.

OPERATIONS OF F. M. L.* SCHLICK.

On the north, F. M. L. Count Schlick, marching with a considerable force from Galicia, entered the town of Eperies, in Hungary, on the 10th of December, amid the acclamations of its inhabitants. He occupied that and the neighboring town of Soovar, while his advanced guard (a day's march before him) at the same time, after a severe conflict, carried by storm the fortified city of Kaschau.†

---

* F. M. L. meant to denote Field Marshal Lieutenant, less than Field Marshal, and about the rank of General. There are but two Field Marshals in Austria, Radetzky and Windischgrätz.

† Meszaros, the Minister of War in Hungary, was in command of the Hungarians in this action. He lost eleven cannons, and drew off but eight thousand of his sixteen thousand men. It is but right, however, to say that this corps was

Leaving brigades to garrison Eperies and Kaschau, Count Schlick dispatched one brigade against Hydasnemethi, followed by a second as a reserve, as far as Enyiezke. Two attempts to retake Eperies proceeding one from Leutschau on the west, and the other from Bartfeld on the east (portions of the country which had not been disarmed), were subsequently made, but the Hungarians in both instances were repulsed with loss.

On the 28th of December, the advancing brigades of Count Schlick having united, encountered the enemy, who had taken up a position at Szikszo; and, after an engagement of a few hours, the Hungarians were routed, and the imperial troops pursued their march toward Miskolcz.

The same force met, on the 4th of January, on the heights of Pareza, a formidable army of the enemy, consisting of fourteen battalions, with thirty-three pieces of cannon and eight hundred horsemen, commanded by Meszaros, and again completely defeated them.* The troops took, on the field of battle, two officers, ten cannons, two hundred muskets, and forty horses; and the light cavalry, pursuing the retreating enemy, captured six more cannons, a thousand muskets, and many horses.†

OPERATIONS OF THE AUSTRIAN ARMY UNDER F. M. L. SIMONIC.

Another wing of the imperial army, under F. M. L. Count Simonic, entered Hungary from Moravia, having forced the hostile position at Jablunka. His advanced guard, commanded by Lieutenant-colonel Frischeisen, on the 11th of December came up with the enemy, occupying a very favorable position

---

composed almost entirely of National Guards and recruits, of whom only one fifth were provided with fire-arms. The cannons even were served by novices. The eight thousand missing were neither killed nor taken prisoners (for Schlick did not leave his defensive position to pursue them), but dispersed to their homes.

* "The forces which the Hungarians had at this time," says Klapka, " were as nothing compared with the masses of our enemies. We had some garrisons in fortresses. Görgey and Perczel had thirty thousand men on the Upper Danube. In Upper Hungary, they had an ill-trained corps of eight thousand men; and in Transylvania they could not even dispose of six thousand troops. The most efficient force was still in the Bats country and in the Banat, where they fought against the Razen (or Servians). These troops, including the blockading corps round Arad, numbered twenty thousand men."—*Klapka's War in Hungary.*

† Austrian official bulletin.

in the vicinity of Budatin. The latter were defeated, and driv-
en back to Silein.

Proceeding on his march, F. M. L. Simonic, on the 14th of
December, encountered the enemy in the strong mountain pass
of Jablonitz; having dislodged, he pursued them in their retreat as far as Szered, when the Hungarians retired behind Tyrnau. At that place the enemy, availing himself of an advantageous position, and having received re-enforcements from
Pressburg, gave battle on the 16th of December, and were
again, after a fight of two hours, completely beaten, and seven
hundred and seventy-six prisoners, forty-three horses, five cannon, one flag, and a great number of small arms, fell into the
hands of the victorious troops.*

After the defeat at Tyrnau, the Hungarians retreated to Leopoldstadt, a strong fortress in the neighborhood, while F. M.
L. Count Simonic occupied Tyrnau, and awaited re-enforcements from Pressburg to attack it.

OPERATIONS OF THE AUSTRIAN ARMY UNDER FIELD-MARSHAL WINDISCHGRÄTZ.

Leaving Vienna on the 15th of December, Prince Windischgrätz commenced his march toward Hungary, and took up his
head-quarters that night at Petronell. On the morning of the
16th, he began operations by undertaking, with the main body
of the army, a general reconnoitre, from Bruck to Prellenkir-
chen, in hopes, in this manner, to bring the enemy to an engagement; but the Hungarians would not accept battle, and retreated at all points. On the same day, he dispatched Colonel
Baron Horvath, with three thousand men of the garrison of
Vienna, to penetrate the country lower down, pursuing the road
over Wiener-Neustadt to Oedenburg; while another portion
of the forces marched to the same point, over Hoflein, in order
to cover at the same time his left wing.

These forces met on the same day, at Volka-Brodersdorf, a
hostile division; and, in a short but spirited engagement, they
carried the town by assault, making two officers and twenty-
six men prisoners; thence continuing their route, they united

---

* Austrian official bulletin.

at Kingenbach, marched upon Oedenburg, and entered that place without resistance.* The enemy had withdrawn to Kapuvar.

In the mean time, Baron Jellacic, in command of the first army corps, who had been dispatched a day in advance of Prince Windischgrätz, marched from Vienna in the direction of Wieselburg (the Hungarians retiring before him at all points), and, on the night of the 16th of December, took up his head-quarters at Altenburg. The following day, the 17th, Prince Windischgrätz, with the second army corps, under the command of F. M. L. Count Wrbna, crossed the River March, occupied Stampfen, attacked Neudorf, and, advancing, entered Pressburg, the former capital of Hungary, without striking a blow, the Hungarians having evacuated the city on the previous night. The same day, the 18th, Baron Jellacic, after a fight of several hours, took possession of Wieselburg.

After the capture of Pressburg, Prince Windischgrätz, with the second army corps, recrossed to the right bank of the Danube, joining the first army corps under Jellacic. They marched together on Raab, a place strongly fortified, and where it was supposed that the decisive battle would take place. During the advance of these corps, the van-guard crossed the Rabnitz without encountering any resistance from the enemy.† While these operations were progressing on the part of the Imperialists, Görgey, in command of the Hungarian army on the frontiers of Austria, finding it quite impossible to resist such a force as that opposed to him, after several unimportant actions, already mentioned, ordered a general retreat to Raab.‡ Here intrenchments were thrown up, in which the noblest ladies toiled with their delicate hands. The weather, during the early part of the winter of 1848–9, was unusually mild, and from this cause Görgey hoped to be able to maintain his ground behind the three rivers and his strong intrenchments, and to check the further progress of the enemy. But the elements decided otherwise. On the 20th of December, the weather suddenly became intensely cold. By the 25th, the ice was so thick that a body of Austrian troops crossed the frozen waters

---

* Austrian official bulletin.   † Ibid.   ‡ Wiener Zeitung.

of the Little Danube, and took a position, with their artillery, below Raab. This circumstance rendered it necessary for Görgey to abandon the formidable fortifications at Raab, and to commence his retreat, which he conducted slowly, in order that he might form a junction with Perczel's army, which had been ordered up from the south, and thus give a decisive battle to the enemy before reaching Pesth.* The Austrian column under Colonel Horvath, which had occupied Oedenburg, by this time entered Kapuvar, in consequence of which the communication with the right wing of the army was established.

At the same time, another division of troops, from the garrison of Vienna, under Colonel Altham, marched over Güns to Steinamanger, where it united with the army corps under F. M. L. Count Nugent, which entered Hungary from the Styrian frontier, advancing over Lövo to Körmend.

Operations of the Austrian Army under F. M. L. Nugent.

On the 25th of December, Count Nugent, with his force of twelve thousand men, entering the country from Styria, took possession of Körmend, and pursued the flying enemy as far as Janoshaza, whence they took the route for Pápa. By this advance, the junction of his force with that under Colonel Altham was effected.† On the 27th, Prince Windischgrätz, with a view to cut off the retreat of the enemy, crossed one army corps below and the other above the city of Raab, while he himself, in command of the reserve, marched upon the city, and was met at the river (Rabnitz) by a deputation from the town, who delivered him the keys of the city, and informed him, at the same time, that the Hungarian army had evacuated the city and all the intrenchments around it, and had retired, as they understood, with the principal force to Komorn, and with some regiments to Pesth. The Hungarians had retired so effectually, that an officer and nine men were all the prisoners made.‡

Prince Windischgrätz then immediately dispatched Major-general Ottinger, with his cavalry brigade, in pursuit of the

---

* Pragay's Hungarian Struggle for Freedom.
† Austrian official bulletin.   ‡ Ibid.

enemy. After a forced march, Ottinger's brigade came up with
the rear-guard of Görgey's army, in the vicinity of Bobolna,
on the morning of the 28th of December, and attacked it without delay. Among the Hungarians, a battalion of the former
imperial regiment, "Prince of Prussia," about six hundred
strong, was attacked by two divisions of Walmoden cuirassiers, and the greater part of them either cut to pieces or taken
prisoners. Besides the cavalry above alluded to, there were
seven officers and seven hundred men (Honvéds) taken prisoners, an amunition wagon and flag captured.*

After this affair, the first army corps, under Baron Jellacic,
pursuing the road from Raab toward Stuhl-Weissenburg, when
he reached Kisbír, having learned that Perczel's corps had a
short time before left for Mör, immediately commenced a
forced march toward that point.

After proceeding the whole night along a high, narrow causeway leading through the frozen marshes, the icy north wind
which swept the plain was found so penetrating that the whole
of the hussars, unable to remain on horseback, dismounted,
and marched forward on foot, leading their horses by the bridle. At length, about ten o'clock the next morning, they fell
in with Perczel's corps, about an hour's march beyond Mör.†
The attack, on the part of the Imperialists, was executed with
great gallantry; in half an hour the Walmoden and Hardeg cuirassiers broke the enemy's centre. A part of the Hungarians,
particularly the regular cavalry, fought with great resolution;
the contest between these cavalry regiments, which had formerly belonged to the imperial army, composed of native Hungarians, the best horsemen in the world,‡ and the squadron of
heavy cuirassiers, with their cuirasses, helmets, and long *pal-
lashes*,§ making the very earth shake under them, was desperate indeed. But the number of the Hungarians was much
inferior to that of the enemy; their dispositions were bad;
there was a want of direction, of confidence in the officers;

---

* Austrian official bulletin.

† Scenes of the Civil War in Hungary.

‡ Hussar, a native Hungarian word, derived from Huss, signifying twenty.
Every twentieth man was formerly required to do military service, and hence
was called Hussar.

§ Long swords, more like Scottish claymores than any other weapon.

and the Honvéd battalions soon sought safety in flight, leaving on the field nine cannons, and several thousand dead, wounded, and prisoners.

The engagement at Mör is still involved in mystery. By some, all the evil consequences of this disastrous check have been ascribed solely to Perczel; he might, they assert, at a much earlier day have united with Görgey; but placing an overestimate upon his own merits after the defeat of Roth, he delayed as long as possible, placing himself under the command of a younger general:* that he was not obliged to accept battle, for he had arrived at Kisbír half a day earlier than Jellacic, and might have quietly pursued his march to Buda. Nevertheless, others acquit him of the fault, and throw it wholly upon Görgey, who is said to have had the ability, but not the inclination, to unite with him, even after ordering him to make a stand at Mör, and promising him succor in case of need. There is still a third view of the question entertained by many, and that is, that Perczel is stated to have received the order from Kossuth himself to arrest the enemy's march at any cost. "Every hour of delay is not too dearly purchased, even with a defeat."†

The result, to whomsoever belongs the blame, was, that the best troops, the heroes of Freidau, were entirely dispersed,‡ and Görgey's idea of a decisive battle before the enemy reached the capital rendered impossible.

Nothing now remained for Görgey but to retire slowly beyond the Danube, and which, after an engagement between his rear-guard and the enemy's cavalry at Zeth, he crossed at Pesth, on the 3d of January, 1849.

While these events were occurring on the right bank of the Danube, the fourth column proceeding on the left bank of the river from Pressburg to Komorn,§ F. M. L. Count Wrbna in

---

* Pragay.   † Schlessinger's War in Hungary.

‡ Perczel wrote that, immediately after the battle of Mör, his troops had so completely scattered that not two thousand could be seen; they had only concealed themselves from the enemy, which their superior knowledge of the country enabled them to do. Two days after, they gathered in their entire strength, with the exception of the few hundreds slain on the field of battle.

§ Ptolemy makes mention of the town of Chomara, and the name is by some historians derived from the Chomærians, a Scythian colony. The more general

command, on the 30th summoned that fortress (the strongest in Hungary, and which had successfully resisted all the invasions of the Turks) to surrender.* Mezthény, a former officer of the imperial government, charged with its defense by Kossuth, and preferring to support his cause to that of the Austrians, refused to yield.

---

opinion is, Oluptulma and his Kumanians, about A.D. 900, laid the foundation of this fortress, and named it Kumarum, whence is derived the name Komorn. It was taken and razed to the ground by the Czeck Ottokar, and was rebuilt in 1272. In 1340, it fell into the hands of the Bishopric of Gran; in 1527, it was defended by Zapolya against Ferdinand the First, and at length surrendered. In the following year it fell into the hands of the Turks; and in 1529 came again into the possession of Ferdinand, without ever having been taken by force of arms. In the sixteenth, seventeenth, and eighteenth centuries, both town and fortress were gradually extended, until they acquired their present size and importance.

* Komorn is the key of Hungary: this is a phrase continually repeated, but perhaps as often misunderstood. An army may be in possession of Komorn without being master of Hungary, but can never be master of Hungary without the possession of Komorn.

In point of strength, Peterwardein may be compared with Komorn; it likewise commands the Danube, but in the less important part of its course toward the southeast; whereas Komorn commands the river not far from its entrance into the country, and has the power of preventing the passage of any vessels from Monostor to the Black Sea, thus stopping the main artery of the country at its source. Hungary has not, as yet, any internal communication of roads and railways to supply its place. This power, together with its singular position, wonderfully fortified alike by nature and art, constitute the importance of Komorn.

The old fortress lies in the pointed angle formed by the confluence of the two branches of the Danube, at the extreme eastern point of the Isle of Schütt; and in a large semicircle before the town are situated the extensive works, which sufficiently cover the open side on the west. This is called the Palatinal line— an extent of ramparts which, at the instigation of the late Palatine, was completed to a length of three thousand fathoms, at a cost of some millions of florins, according to the rules of modern science. These ramparts protect both the old and new fortress, together with the town, on the land side, leaving large open spaces between these works and the town, serviceable for encampment, parades, reviews, and pasturage. More to the north, as far as Gutta, where the Traag joins the upper arm of the Danube, a strong crown-work prevents any hostile attempt to cross the river. Other works—bastions of three, four, and five lines—cover the old fortress on the river side. But a still stronger protection than these artificial works is afforded by the Danube, in connection with the Rivers Dudvoga, Penna, Waag, and Neutra, the embouchures of which form an intricate net of rivers, extending over a tract of inaccessible marshes.

In addition to all this defense, a fortified tête de pont on the right bank, opposite to the town, was converted by the Hungarians into a second fortress, by means of extensive ramparts; and an island, formed of alluvial deposit in the middle of the stream, between this tête de pont and the old fortress, was taken advantage of by the military engineer.—*Schlessinger.*

The Austrians surrounded the fortress, but suffered to pass unimproved the favorable opportunity for taking it, which occurs but seldom, when the Danube and the Waag, which form its principal intrenchments and the chief grounds of its invincibility, were so completely frozen as to be passed any where with the heaviest artillery.

After the victory at Mör, Baron Jellacic with the first army corps, pursued the enemy as far as Lovas Bereny, on his way to Buda-Pesth ; while Prince Windischgrätz, with the first army corps and reserve, advanced over Bieske and Bia also to the capital.

At Bieske, the prince was met by a deputation from the Hungarian Diet (still sitting in opposition to the orders of the emperor for its dissolution), composed of two of the former ministers of Hungary, Count Batthiányi,* and Deak, Bishop Lonovics, and Count Mailath.

The prince refused to receive a deputation from so illegal a body, but informed its members that no proposal for mediation coming from what source it might, could be entertained, and nothing short of unconditional surrender for a moment listened to.

On the 3d of January, the head-quarters of Prince Windischgrätz were at Bia, about three hours' march from Pesth ; those of Jellacic at Promontorium, about the same distance, and both entered the capital together, on the 5th of January, without striking a blow.   The prince immediately dispatched his son with the keys of both cities to his master the emperor at Olmütz.   The remnants of Perczel's army crossed the Danube at Pesth, on the 1st of January.

Kossuth and the government left that city on the 3d, for the fortress of Debreczin, in the southeastern part of the kingdom, taking with him all the public funds and the ancient and venerated crown of St. Stephen.

Operations in the South.

Such were the operations in the northern and middle parts

---

* They were all detained as prisoners by Prince Windischgrätz, but were soon released, except Count Batthiányi, who was kept in confinement until his execution, on the 6th of October, 1849.

of Hungary; and these were conducted agreeably to the rules
of civilized warfare, and with comparatively little loss of life;
but such was far from being the case in the more barbarous
districts of the south, which had been for many months the
scenes of frightful disorder and bloodshed. The many different
races inhabiting the southern districts, viz., Slavonians, Croatians, Servians, Wallachians, Saxons, and Szecklers, taking advantage of the insurrection of the Hungarians, and the consequent license which completely annulled all supreme authority, had risen and massacred each other; whole villages had
been demolished; every species of property pillaged; the rich
beggared, and the poor murdered; until the entire country
was reduced to one scene of devastation and horror. In Transylvania, occupied by Romans, Saxons, and Szecklers, the
scenes of murder and rapine were remarkably numerous and
frightful: in the conflict between these two races, the former,
for the most part, remained true to the imperial government,
while the latter espoused the cause of the Hungarians.*

At first the Szecklers, supported by some Hungarian regiments, invaded the Saxon and Roman districts with great success, destroying many villages, and, in some instances, the
richest towns, ravaging the country, and murdering men, wom-
en, and children. Later, F. M. L. Puchner, with an imperial
force at his command, having assumed the government of the
country, and organized the military force existing among the
Saxons and Romans, enlisting new regiments and raising companies of National Guards, at length acquired sufficient power
to meet and oppose successfully the combined Hungarians and
Szecklers; and, by his energy and courage, succeeded in subduing all opposition in Transylvania, and in establishing the
supremacy of the imperial government throughout that district.
After the important and rapidly acquired advantages in Transylvania, F. M. L. Puchner marched with a force of thirteen
hundred men, into the adjoining district of the Banat, where
the Hungarians and their allies were still in triumphant ascendency, and where the important fortress of Arad, manned
by imperial troops, was likely to fall before the besieging force

---

* Allgemeine Zeitung.

of fifteen thousand men. Calling to his aid a part of the garrison of Temesvar, in the same district, F. M. L. Puchner was joined, on the 14th of December, by two columns under Major-general Leiningen, at Engelsbrunn, and the united forces marched together to the relief of Arad. The attack upon the besieging enemy was executed with great success; after an engagement which lasted several hours, under the heaviest artillery fire, in the plain of St. Miklos, the Imperialists succeeded in turning the left wing of the enemy, and, by a judicious and opportune charge, put the Hungarians to flight; they retreated over the Maros, leaving in the hands of their adversaries two hundred prisoners, four howitzers, and a cannon.* But the greatest advantage derived by the Austrians from this battle was the relief of the fortress of Arad. Still further triumphs followed the imperial arms. At Panscova, also in the same district of the Banat, Colonel Mayerhofer, on the 2d of January, encountered the enemy, and, after a brilliant engagement, the Hungarians were completely routed, a great number of prisoners taken, and the commander of the hostile forces, Kiss, escaped with difficulty, attended by only six horsemen, to Allebunar.†

By these, as well as other less important successes which attended the Austrian arms throughout the southern districts, the supremacy of imperial authority was so completely re-established as to leave apparently but little probability that the Hungarians would ever be able again to resume the offensive, especially since the troops which had so successfully penetrated the country from the north and west to the centre, were now free to move in that direction, should subsequent events render such an advance necessary.

Thus, in less than three weeks from the entrance of Prince Windischgrätz into Hungary, and when the invasion of that kingdom might be considered as effectually commenced, almost the whole country had been reduced to subjection; the capital, as well as other principal cities, taken and occupied; the imperial functionaries reinstated in office, and order, to all appearance, completely restored.

---

* Austrian official bulletin.   † Ibid.

The conduct of the Hungarians in not giving battle, but almost invariably retreating before their adversaries, disappointed the general expectation, and shook the confidence long reposed in .their courage and chivalrous bearing. Some ascribed their course to the absence of practical talent in the administration of affairs, on account of which no properly organized system of defense had been prepared; but especially because they were possessed of no educated and skillful officers to command their forces, and the Honvéd, or militia and raw recruits of which their rank and file were chiefly composed, would not stand before the regularly organized and admirably disciplined troops of the imperial army.

But there were a few who recollected that John Zapolya and his descendants, in the sixteenth century, had held out for thirty years, invincible by any force which the Austrian monarchs could bring against them; that their course had always been to retreat to the great plains of Hungary, so well adapted for the operation of cavalry, the arm in which they were particularly efficient; and it was suggested that they now were but retiring in the same direction, and toward the banks of the marshy Theiss, where artillery, in which consisted the chief strength of their opponents, could not operate. In the eyes of such individuals, the retreat of the Hungarians seemed a matter not of compulsion but design, as clearly a settled plan of operations as the retirement of the Russians before Napoleon when he invaded their country; and that through another combination of the elements of nature with the power of man, the Austrians were destined to experience an overthrow alike unexpected and overwhelming.

Other considerations, divulged by Kossuth in his proclamation to the peasantry, besides those already mentioned, favor the opinion that the movement of the Hungarians ought not to be considered a flight, but as a strategical operation. It was disclosed that the object of the Hungarians in constructing heavy intrenchments at Raab, Wieselburg, and Pressburg, was not so much the defense of these points, as to force upon the Austrians the necessity of procuring additional cannon and additional horses ; in the hope that, during the time necessary for these operations, they might be able to make a general levy in

the Slavic comitats, to drill their army, and to receive the muskets ordered from Belgium. The subsequent retreat was also
a well-arranged plan, by which they expected to be able to
raise the *Landsturm* in the rear of the Austrian army, and
that would compel them to garrison all the towns which they
might capture, and thus weaken most effectually the main invading force of the enemy.

The first measures adopted by Prince Windischgrätz, after
establishing himself at Pesth, was to divide the subdued portion of the country into three military districts; placing the
first under the command of F. M. L. Kempen, with head-quarters at Pressburg; the second, under F. M. L. Wrbna, with
head-quarters at Pesth; and the third, under Major-general
Burics, with head-quarters at Oedenburg.

The next movement was an order, issued by the prince, to
place in a state of siege the provinces of Galicia, Cracow, and
Bukowina, to which the dispersed Hungarians were fleeing; to
disarm all individuals not belonging to the regular military
forces; to prohibit every where the publishing of journals, the
assembling of citizens, and to observe the strictest vigilance
along the entire frontiers of Hungary.

The first and second army corps were ordered to pursue the
military divisions, as well as the hordes of private individuals,
which fled from Pesth in every direction after the capture of
the city.

These dispositions were, perhaps, sufficiently proper and correct; but the course of Prince Windischgrätz is inexplicable in
delaying nearly two months at Pesth, engaged in the useless
task of attempting to reorganize the disordered administration
throughout the conquered comitats, instead of advancing, while
the spirit of his troops was elated, and that of the Hungarians
depressed, and subduing all opposition in the southern and
eastern portions of the kingdom, to which the Magyar forces
had retired; instead of suffering to pass unimproved the only
season of the year when their artillery could be made available, and granting to their opponents time to recover from their
consternation, and to gather recruits, as well as to organize
and discipline their forces.*

---

* Means altogether unworthy, it is asserted, were employed to induce Prince

Movements of the Austrians in Upper Hungary.

For a short time, at several points, unimportant successes still continued to follow the imperial arms.

In the Oedenburg and Eisenburg comitats, the corps under the command of Lieutenant-colonel Altham, having cleared that part of the country of all opposition, marched to Pápa, where he arrived on the 13th of January ; thence he proceeded to Vesprim and the Bakoneyer Wald, an immense forest, where some bands of Perczel's dispersed army were ravaging.*

On the same day, a brigade, under the command of Baron Neustadter, had an engagement with a hostile division at Aszod, on the left border of the Danube, in which they routed the enemy, but sustained the loss of Lieutenant-colonel Geramb. F. M. L. Czoric, who was ordered to pursue the retreating enemy under Görgey in the direction of Ipoly-Ságh, over Leva, and to press him to Schemnitz, advanced on the 13th, with eight battalions, six squadrons, and thirty-six cannons. At the same time, the column under the command of Major-general Götz advanced over Neusohl to Kremnitz.†

This officer, after the submission of the Turveyzer comitat, undertook, on the 16th, a reconnoiter of Neusohl and Kremnitz. The division sent out for this purpose met the enemy at Turezek, drove him from that position, and took Kremnitz ; but the approach of night stopped their triumphant march.

On the 17th, the Hungarians advanced with fresh forces to Kremnitz, to retake, if possible, the position lost on the previ-

Windischgrätz to remain inactive. High-born, influential members of the Magyar aristocracy surrounded the marshal, and assured him that it lay in his power to terminate the war almost without bloodshed. Conciliation was the hope deliberately given, while the most unquestionable treachery was abetted and planned. "You should have seen the countesses and baronesses at their Delilah work," said an old Austrian general who was present at all these scenes; "it was maddening to see how they took the marshal in, and how he confided in the asseverations and words of honor of the whole crew, just because he could not believe that people so well born could be so false. There were *soirées*, and there was music, and flirting, and *tea*," exclaimed he, with an accent of wrathful despair —for it seemed this last was an aggravation of all the too-credulous marshal's wrongs. "Tea," he added; "a pretty time for tea, forsooth, when Kossuth was at Debreczin, and they (the countesses and baronesses) were keeping him advised of all that was going on."—*Baroness Blaze de Bury.*

* After the defeat of Mör.   † Austrian official bulletin.

ous day; the imperial troops, however, made a strong and successful resistance, and the enemy, after a battle of four hours, in which they had one hundred killed, and one hundred and seventeen men and four officers taken prisoners, were discouraged, and fled.*   On the same day, F. M. L. Schlick, at Kaschau, knowing that a column of the imperial army was marching, under the command of F. M. L. Schulzig, from Pesth, over Gyöngyös, to Miskolz, and that another, under Major-general Götz, was moving over Kremnitz and Schemnitz to Zips, and aware that the operations were more favorable in Transylvania, from the last accounts, he, in order to prevent the escape of the leaders of the insurrection, commanded Major Kieswetter, with a suitable force, to occupy Leutshau, and that a flying column, issuing from Eperies, and passing over Hanusfalva, Varano, and Homano, should unite on the 17th with the second column, and operate afterward over Sarospatak against the Theiss.†

F. M. L. Schlick, having left at Kaschau the brigade Deym, marched with the main body to Tallya, where he expected to gather all his forces, and to advance from thence against Tokay, and afterward against Debreczin.   F. M. L. Simonic, who, after the capture of Tyrnau, was for some weeks occupied in besieging the fortress of Leopoldstadt, in the same vicinity, at length commenced, on the 2d of February, its bombardment with sixty and thirty-pound shells, and which produced so tremendous an effect, that in an hour that formidable fortress surrendered at discretion, although in possession of an abundant supply of ammunition and provision.

F. M. L. Simonic then marched, under the orders he had received, to Komorn, and commenced the siege of that fortress.

MOVEMENTS OF THE HUNGARIAN ARMY IN UPPER HUNGARY.

Upon the evacuation of Pesth, the Hungarian army, as well with a view to deceive the enemy as for the defense of the different portions of country, was then separated into two divisions.   While Perczel, with ten thousand men, marched toward the Theiss, Görgey, with the larger portion of the troops, took

---

* Austrian official bulletin.   † Ibid.

the direction of Waitzen, for the purpose of leading off the enemy from Debreczin, occupying the mountain cities, carrying off every where the government stores,* and disjoining, if possible, the Austrian generals Götz, Jablonovski, Deym, Ramberg, and Schlick.

As soon as Görgey reached Waitzen, he issued a proclamation, on the 5th of January, in which he declared that the Hungarian army fought for nothing else than for the laws of 1848, and for the legitimate king, Ferdinand the Fifth; and that it would defend the fatherland independently of any other authority.† This was, in fact, a repudiation of Kossuth and the Committee of Defense, and constituted the first overt act in his treasonable career.

Görgey now marched, in three columns, through Upper Hungary. Guyon commanded the rear, and, by his fortunate and heroic maneuver at Ipoly-Ságh, on the 10th of January, 1849, he covered the whole baggage train, and saved it thus from the pursuing enemy.‡

Near this place is a wooded height, on the summit of which are situated a chapel and a convent. At its foot extends a narrow ravine, separating the fenced convent garden from the hill on which the chapel stands; and in this garden Guyon had posted a strong division of Honvéds, with some cannon. He ordered loop-holes to be pierced in this boarded fence, for his fusileers and artillerymen, and then had these holes pasted over, so as to act as a screen.

The ravine was to serve as a trap for the Imperialists, and the stratagem succeeded. Their pioneers passed the ravine, and not a sound betrayed the vicinity of the enemy; but no sooner had the chief detachment reached the middle of the defile, than the guns opened a fire upon them from the whole line of fence, and several hundred Imperialists fell. Their vanguard was destroyed, and Görgey's rear-guard, under Benyicky, with their trophies of victory—a cannon and several hundred prisoners—followed the main body of the army, which was

---

* Not only was all the gold in this region, but the government stores, gunpowder, etc.

† For this document in full, see Appendix, note No. 29.

‡ Pulszky's Adventures of a Hungarian Lady.

advancing by forced marches in the direction of Kremnitz and Schemnitz.*

Görgey himself however, on the 21st of January, met with a decided check from F. M. L. Czoric, who, with a division of the second army corps, came up with him in the plateau before Schemnitz. The Austrians, commencing the attack, carried the village of Windschacht by storm, and drove the enemy from all points. The next morning, after a short fight with the hostile rear-guard, the Austrians entered Schemnitz. In this battle the Hungarians are reported to have sustained a loss of sixty killed, one hundred and twenty wounded, five hundred prisoners, twelve cannons, and ten mortars.† The loss of the Imperialists, by the official bulletin, was put down at two officers and six men killed, and thirteen wounded. Notwithstanding this repulse, the remarkable maneuvers of Görgey about this time deserve to rank beside the boldest and most splendid achievements of almost any period of history, not excepting the passage of the Little Bernard by Hannibal, the Great Bernard by Napoleon, or, that which perhaps exceeds them both, the crossing of the more lofty Splugen by M'Donald. In the depth of a severe winter, he led his troops and artillery over the Carpathians; one while appearing on the frontiers of Galicia; at another, escaping to the mountain towns and villages. His situation soon became extremely critical; pressed as he was on all sides, and making his winter marches and counter-marches over fields and mountains of ice and snow, he found himself, in his native country of Zips, suddenly shut in on three sides; while Hamerstein, in Galicia, was marshaling all the disposable troops to the frontier, to oppose his fourth and last exit.‡

Guyon, at the head of the northern column, was more successful, and carried off the gold and silver stores of the government from the mining districts, and, from Neusohl, the supplies of gunpowder. He reached the county of Zips without serious difficulty. At Neudorf, the Austrians took him by surprise in the night of the 2d of February; but, after a bloody struggle in the streets, the Hungarians were victorious, and

---

* Schlessinger's War in Hungary.   † Austrian official bulletin.
‡ Schlessinger.

dispersed the enemy.*   Guyon then advanced to the county of Sáros; here he found himself opposed by a division of Schlick, which occupied the defiles of the steep heights of the Branyiszko.   This rugged pass, which from its elevation was deemed impregnable, was the only road from Leutshau to Kaschau, and the sole outlet for Görgey and his troops, by which their connection with the army of the Theiss could be effected, and Guyon did not hesitate to storm it.   Attacking it from the valley below, and encountering a dreadful battery at every turn in this mountain road, he was obliged to sacrifice one fourth of his heroic troops before all the defiles were carried.

Guyon ordered four of his battalions to lay down their arms ; and for five whole hours they climbed up steep foot-paths, known only to the natives of the country, carrying the dismantled cannon piecemeal on their shoulders, or dragging them, together with the necessary ammunition, after them by ropes.

From eight o'clock in the evening till one o'clock in the morning this heroic band were winding up the steep mountain paths, making their way over rocks and snow-drifts, beset with incredible difficulties and hardships, in a cold winter's night ; while the rest of the troops, at the entrance of the pass, were continually making feigned attacks, to divert the attention of the Austrians, and prevent the silence of the night betraying the movement of the troops engaged in the ascent.

It was past midnight when the first cannon-shot came thundering from the heights down into the dark valley.   This was the signal for a general attack.   Ten successive times did the troops stationed below advance to the assault, braving death, while from above the shot thundered into the depths of the ravine.†   The Austrians witnessed with terror and dismay the destruction of their ranks : they abandoned one intrenchment after another, fighting as they retreated, and in the utmost confusion attempted to gain the opposite outlet of the pass. A great portion of their artillery and a third part of the troops were lost in this retreat ; the slaughter was unprecedented ; and, the next morning, Görgey's van-guard passed through the

---

* Pulszky.   † Schlessinger's War in Hungary.

defile which Guyon and his brave troops had unclosed to them. This obstruction removed, Görgey reached Eperies on the 6th of February, and re-established his communications (interrupted for four weeks) with the troops of the Theiss and the government at Debreczin.*

Operations on the Theiss.

While these occurrences were transpiring in the mountain districts, Prince Windischgrätz began to dispatch his forces toward the Theiss. The rail-road was reopened to Szolnok, and this important point was occupied by Ottinger's brigade. In this position, the Austrians were attacked on the 23d of January, and, owing to the negligence of their commander, suffered one of the most signal defeats that occurred during the whole war. The Hungarians, under Perczel and Damjanic, availing themselves of the frozen river, surrounded the vanguard of Ottinger, that held the bridge over the Theiss. The *Csikoses†* contributed greatly to the success of this surprise.

* When, through Guyon's messenger, Görgey was advised of the gallant achievement, and that the pass was now clear for the outlet of his troops, he is said to have remarked, with the utmost indifference, " Guyon was a great fool for his pains."—*Pulszky.*

† *Csikos.*—The Csikos is a man who, from his birth, some how or other finds himself seated upon a foal. Instinctively, the boy remains fixed upon the animal's back, and grows up in his seat as other children do in the cradle. The young Csikos soon feels himself at his ease on his cradle. The boy grows by degrees to a big horse herd. These herds range over a tract of many German square miles— for the most part level plains, with wood, marsh, heath, and moorland: they rove about where they please, multiply, and enjoy freedom of existence. Nevertheless, it is a common error to imagine that these horses, like a pack of wolves in the mountains, are left to themselves and nature, without any care or thought of man. Wild horses, in the proper sense of the term, are in Europe at the present day only met with in Bessarabia; whereas the so-called wild herds in Hungary may rather be compared to the animals ranging in large parks, which are attended to and watched.

The Csikos has the difficult task of keeping a watchful eye upon these herds. He knows their strength, their habits, the spots they frequent; he knows the birth day of every foal, and when the animal, fit for training, should be taken out of the herd. He has then a hard task upon his hands, compared with which a grand-ducal wild-boar hunt is child's play; for the horse has not only to be taken alive from the midst of the herd, but of course safe and sound in wind and limb. For this purpose the celebrated whip of the Csikos serves him.

This whip has a stout handle, from one and a half to two feet long, and a cord which measures not less than from eighteen to twenty-four feet in length. The cord is attached to a short iron chain, fixed to the top of the handle by an iron

They were close at hand before Szolnok when the trumpet of the Austrian cuirassiers sounded to horse, the generals barely saved themselves by flight, the officers rode off mostly without saddles, and the common soldiers were cut down in the stables before they could mount; eighteen hundred were made prisoners, and the remainder escaped to Czegléd.*

It was no battle, but the loss to the Austrians was greater than in a regular encounter, where the cannonade continues from morning to night. Subsequently, General Ottinger, re-

---

ring. A large leaden button is fastened to the end of the cord, and similar smaller buttons are distributed along it at distances, according to certain rules, derived from experience, of which we are ignorant. Armed with this weapon, which the Csikos carries in his belt, together with a short grappling-iron or hook, he sets out on his horse chase. Thus mounted and equipped, without saddle or stirrup, he flies like the storm-wind over the heath, with such velocity that the grass scarcely bends under the horse's hoofs; the step of his horse is not heard; and the whirling cloud of dust above his head alone marks his approach and disappearance. Although familiar with the use of a bridle, he despises such a troublesome article of luxury, and guides his horse with his voice, hands, and feet—nay, it almost seems as if he directed it by the mere exercise of the will, as we move our feet to the right or left, backward or forward, without its ever coming into our head to regulate our movements by a leather strap.

In this manner, for hours, he chases the flying herd, until at length he succeeds in approaching the animal which he is bent on catching. He then swings his whip round in immense circles, and throws the cord with such dexterity and precision that it twines around the neck of his victim. The leaden button at the end, and the knots along the cord, form a noose, which draws closer and tighter the faster the horse hastens on.

See how he flies along, with outstretched legs, his mane whistling in the wind, his eye darting fire, his mouth covered with foam, and the dust whirling aloft on all sides. But the noble animal breathes shorter, his eye grows wild and staring, his nostrils are reddened with blood, the veins of his neck are distended like cords, his legs refuse longer service—he sinks exhausted and powerless, a picture of death. But at the same instant the pursuing steed likewise stands still and fixed, as if turned to stone. An instant, and the Csikos has flung himself off his horse upon the ground, and inclining his body backward, to keep the noose tight, he seizes the cord alternately with the right and left hand, shorter and shorter, drawing himself by it nearer and nearer to the panting and prostrate animal, till at last, coming up to it, he flings his legs across its back. He now begins to slacken the noose gently, allowing the creature to recover breath; but hardly does the horse feel this relief than he leaps up, and darts off again in a wild course, as if still able to escape from his enemy. But the man is already bone of his bone and flesh of his flesh; he sits fixed upon his neck as if grown to it, and makes the horse feel his power at will, by tightening or slackening the cord. A second time the hunted animal sinks upon the ground; again he rises, and again breaks down, until at length, overpowered with exhaustion, he can no longer stir a limb.—*Schlessinger.*

* Schlessinger.

enforced by Prince Windischgrätz, advanced again upon Szolnok; but the Hungarians, so far from giving battle, as was expected, retreated across the Theiss.

F. M. L. Schlick, after his defeat of the Hungarians under Meszaros, on the heights of Pareza, on the 4th of January, was, as had been stated, marching upon Tokay, met the enemy at Szanto, and drove him back to Tokay.

The members of the Hungarian government, in their flight from Pesth to Debreczin, hearing this sad intelligence, immediately dispatched General Klapka to take command of the defeated army of Meszaros, now driven by Schlick to the neighborhood of Tokay. The defeated Hungarians, encouraged by the presence of Klapka, and under his directions, immediately took up a favorable position at Tokay, Tarczal, and Bodroy-Keresztur. Schlick attacked these positions separately, on the 22d, 23d, and 31st of January, and was by the Hungarians under Klapka, in three distinct battles, successively repulsed.* The advance of the Austrians on Debreczin was not only prevented, but they were driven back upon Kaschau and Eperies. Schlick, who had considered Görgey as buried alive, drew his sabre in a fury, when a major, on the 6th of February, brought him the news to Eperies of the defeat at Branyiszko. "Dogs that ye are—all of you dogs!" he exclaimed; "that pass I would have held against a hundred thousand men!"† He instantly decamped from Eperies, to escape Görgey's superior forces, and took the route to Kaschau. There he heard that Klapka was advancing, who, since the battle of the 31st of January, had lost sight of him, and he was now fixed in the same position as Görgey had been the very evening before. But Schlick was as familiar with the northern counties of Hungary as his enemy, and by masterly maneuvers he succeeded in escaping—by Jaszo, Rosenau, and Rima-Szombat—to Losoncz, and subsequently effected a junction with the main Austrian army. Of the army which he led from Galicia, not one fourth returned, and yet he might boldly claim the gratitude of the emperor. No other of the Austrian generals would have saved a single horse's shoe—probably not his own person—

---

* Klapka's War in Hungary.   † Schlessinger.

from the hands of the Hungarians amid the defiles of the Carpathians.*

During the operations on the Theiss, Perczel had so clearly displayed his inability to command, that he was compelled to retire, and his place supplied by General Dembinski, a Pole, who, about the 1st of February, arrived at Debreczin from Paris, and was, by Kossuth, shortly after invested with the command-in-chief of the Hungarian armies.

Dembinski, about sixty years of age, had received a military education at the Academy of Engineers in Vienna, had accompanied Napoleon in the Russian campaign, and, though quite young, been promoted to the rank of captain at Smolensk, by Napoleon himself. In the Polish Revolution of 1830, he had especially distinguished himself, and from commander of a battalion and chief of the Mobile Guard of Cracow was, by his brilliant services, advanced to the rank of general of division and governor of the capital.

The appointment of Dembinski to the chief command of the Hungarian armies, notwithstanding "he was called the first strategist of his age,"† was an unfortunate one for the Hungarians; for, whatever may have been his military merit, the Hungarian officers were jealous of the promotion of a foreigner over them, they censured and decried all his operations, and ascribed the failures which they experienced to "his absurd dispositions, extreme forgetfulness, and obstinacy," and to his "wretched selection of a general staff." His deportment, too, was calculated to increase rather than allay the prejudice of the Hungarians. To Klapka, who commanded a wing of the army under him, and who presumed upon suggestions relative to their military operations, Dembinski wrote, "You are to have views upon nothing; you have only to execute what is prescribed to you." Görgey was, at a later day, favored with a similar epistle. These, as was most natural, destroyed that confidence between officers so essential to success, brought down upon their author the enmity of the army, and to his "blunders and obstinacy" they did not hesitate to ascribe the

---

* Schlessinger's War in Hungary. † Ibid.

frequent escapes which Schlick made from the certain defeat which awaited him.*

This was doubtless, too, in part the cause that the necessary harmony was wanting in all the after operations, and that the battle of Kápolna, which soon followed, and which was the first general engagement that took place, did not fully answer previous expectations.

The escape of Schlick was doubtless owing to a want of concert on the part of the Hungarian commanders, as the following events most clearly exhibit. Several of the Austrian generals were dining, on the 14th of February, in Sagó Gömör. Suddenly cannons resounded from the north, in the direction of Aggtelek. The startled officers hastened to ascertain the cause; in half an hour the whole corps was in battle array. The third column of Görgey was fully expected. His outposts had, in fact, fired the shots which occasioned the alarm; but the Hungarians had retired again. The Austrians had scarcely encamped, when repeated shots were heard from the opposite side. General Dembinski, who had been at Miskolz, had in time been apprised of the movements of the Austrians, and now came, with eight thousand men, to take Schlick in the rear. The Austrians were panic-stricken. Eye-witnesses related that even officers ran about crying aloud, " We are surrounded—we are lost!" A violent cannonade ensued for several hours, but no close attack was made by Dembinski; he obviously awaited Görgey. The night silenced the cannonade. On the following morning the enemy had disappeared. Schlick had escaped with his corps to Rimaszomboth, thence to the mountain of Heves and to the plain of Kápolna, where at last, with his troops decimated by the Hungarians, as well as by the restless marches, he joined the main corps of Windischgrätz. Already then, in many quarters, the suspicion was entertained that Görgey, jealous of Dembinski, had intentionally failed to support him, and had, on this account, neglected to urge the pursuit of Schlick, who might easily have been destroyed by the co-operation of the Hungarian commanders.†

---

* Pragay's Hungarian Struggle for Freedom.   † Pulszky.

FURTHER OPERATIONS IN THE SOUTH.

Turning more to the southern districts, Major-general Count Nugent, intending to advance against Fünfkirchen on the 25th of January, ordered Major-general Baron Dietrich with his strong brigade to Kaposvar, to clear by this advance the comitats of Simegh and Barany of the roving bands of the enemy, while he marched against the Hungarians in the neighborhood of Fünfkirchen. The order was successfully executed by Baron Dietrich in taking possession of Kaposvar, and General Nugent himself, on the 29th, marched upon and took up his headquarters at Fünfkirchen without encountering any resistance, as the enemy, four thousand strong, with ten cannons, had abandoned the place on the 26th for Eszek.

Subsequently, Count Nugent pursued the enemy, retreating over Nemegyei to Eszek, and detached a division against Mohacs to occupy that place, and thus put himself in communication with the Serbians operating on the left bank of the Danube.

At the same time, F. M. L. Dahlen, organizing the frontier troops, and advancing on the right bank of the Danube against Eszek, after an engagement on the 18th with the enemy before Vershetz, takes possession of that town and Ziesidorf. Later, Major-general Frebersburg, who had for some time surrounded the city of Eszek, with the view of taking the formidable fortress which it contains, on the 30th of January attacked the faubourgs of the city, carried three of them by storm, and then summoned the fortress to surrender; but this summons the Hungarians would not obey until the arrival of Count Nugent, with his forces united to those of the besiegers, which rendered further resistance hopeless; and that strong fortress, with four thousand five hundred men, six hundred and fourteen cannons, seventy-four horses, four hundred oxen, and three thousand four hundred florins, surrendered to the Imperialists.*

In Transylvania, the Hungarians under General Bem (a Pole, who was commander of the Mobile Guard during the bombardment of Vienna), being driven from the Bukowina by

---

* Austrian official bulletin.

Colonel Urban, invaded the district of Transylvania, and, proceeding over Klausenburg to Hermanstadt, attacked that city on the 21st of January, held by F. M. L. Puchner in command of the imperial troops. The fore-posts of the Austrians opened upon the enemy, and were answered by six and twelve-pounders with such effect, that F. M. L. Puchner ordered an attack with the bayonet upon the hostile batteries. The storming column and squadron of cuirassiers, protected by cannon, advanced and threw the enemy out of his position, and subsequently the fight began along the whole line. After an engagement of seven hours, the Hungarians were forced to retreat, and were pursued by the Imperialists to Stolzenburg. Five cannons, four munition wagons, arms of all kinds, some provisions, and prisoners, were the result of this victory. From Stolzenburg Puchner withdrew his forces back to Hermanstadt; while Bem, with twelve thousand men and twenty-seven cannons, there took up a strong position under the cover of the castle.

On the 5th of February, Bem, with the view of making another attack on Hermanstadt, marched for this purpose to Salzburg, and planted his force on the heights near that town. F. M. L. Puchner, advised of the movements of the enemy, met him at Salzburg, and, advancing strongly upon him, Bem's forces were compelled to give way; at first they retired in order, but soon the retreat was turned into a flight. In this action the Hungarians lost seven hundred killed, and one hundred and forty taken prisoners; and lost, at the same time, thirteen cannons, ten powder wagons, and a great number of arms and baggage—among the latter that of the general himself.* The Austrians sustained a loss of seventy killed, and one hundred and sixty wounded. The imperial forces, subsequently pursuing Bem through Mühlenbach, Syasz-Varos, Deva, and Bürski, drove him over the confines of Transylvania, taking seven hundred more prisoners and four cannons, and clearing that district completely of the enemy.†

About the same time that the troops under Bem attacked Hermanstadt, another Hungarian force marched against the

---

* Austrian official bulletin.   † Ibid.

fortress of Arad in the adjoining district of the Banat, also in possession of the imperial troops. F. M. L. Glaser, in command of the fortress, ordered out two battalions of Peterwardein Grentzers to take the first houses of Alt-Arad, and afterward advanced the battalion of Leiningen and one of Illyrian Banat, to storm the positions of the Hungarians. After a desperate and bloody fight, the enemy were driven from all the intrenchments raised by them on the right bank of the Maros, and all the cannons therein (twenty-three pieces) taken.*

Campaign of the Theiss.

About the middle of February, the following dispositions were made by Dembinski for the maneuvers on the Theiss, and in Upper Hungary. The third corps, under Vécsey, and afterward under Damjanic, was to leave garrisons on the Maros, at Szegedin and Theresiopel, and to march up the Theiss to the road between Szolnok and Debreczin. The second corps, which had hitherto occupied that road, to occupy Füred, and the fords on the Theiss. The seventh and first corps, under Görgey and Klapka, were to advance on the Pesth road ; on the height of Poroszlo they were to be joined by the second corps, and to proceed to Gyöngyös. Damjanic was to cross the Theiss at Czibakhaza ; he was to take Szolnok, whence he was to advance, in forced marches, along the rail-road, in order to effect a junction with Dembinski, and to support that general's maneuvers against the *gros* of the Austrian army.

This was the plan of operations determined on, but the advance of the imperial army earlier than was expected prevented it from being carried fully into execution.†

While these things were occurring in the northern, middle, and southern portions of Hungary, the great body of the imperial army was gradually moving toward the scene of operations on the Theiss, and Prince Windischgrätz, having made all his dispositions relative to the conquered portions of the country, on the 24th of February left Buda for the seat of war.

On the 25th, he took up his head-quarters at Gyöngyös, and ordered Count Schlick, who had already reached Peter-

---

* Austrian official bulletin.   † Klapka.

vasaras, to march upon Verpeleth, and thus to effect the junction of the two army corps. On the 26th, the column of Count Wrbna marched from Gyöngyös to Kapolna; F. M. L. Schwartzenberg, with his column, from Arakszallas to Kaal.*

On the other side, Dembinski, apprised of the gradual approach of the Austrian army, resolved to hazard a decisive engagement. Klapka's corps was accordingly brought into line behind Tarna ; one division, under Klapka, was transferred to Verpeleth ; another, under Mariassy, to Kapolna. Schulz's brigade stood in reserve at Szolnok. Repassy's corps was ordered, on the 27th, to Kampolt ; one division of Görgey's army to Kapolna, two others to Felsö-Döbrö and Alsö-Döbrö, to take their place in the line of battle. Two other divisions were to form a reserve.†

The battle commenced on the 26th, about noon, by an attack made by Schwartzenberg's corps on Mariassy's division, in the neighborhood of Kapolna. When Wrbna, who was not far distant, heard the first cannon shot from Schwartzenberg's division, he immediately engaged the enemy also. Mariassy held his ground bravely, first attacking the left wing, and afterward attempting to break through the enemy's centre with his cavalry ; and the battle, with changing fortune, lasted till late in the night The Austrians, driving the enemy back to Kapolna, twice carried the village, and were as often expelled, and finally left it in the possession of the Hungarians.

F. M. L. Schlick, who intended to advance on the 26th as far as Verpeleth, in order to effect a junction with the main army, could not succeed on that day, as he found the defile of Sirok occupied by the enemy. After a severe fight, he succeeded in driving back the detachment sent by Dembinski to guard the pass ; but the approach of night prevented his further progress on that day. The next morning, resuming the offensive, he fell upon the right wing of the Hungarians, while Prince Windischgrätz, advised of Schlick's approach by the heavy cannonade on his left, renewed the attack by marching from Nánár and Vécs against the enemy's centre. Schlick pursued the Hungarians to Verpeleth, in which place they took position

---

* Austrian official bulletin.   † Pragay.

and offered a desperate resistance.   This village was taken by
storm, and the enemy retreated in great haste to the heights.
A division of the Hungarian army was thrown into the mountains of Erlau ; but the greatest part, following the centre, retired in order on the road to Miskolz.*   After several ineffectual attempts to retake the village of Kapolna, and when the
brigade Colloredo advanced over Döbrö, Prince Schwartzenberg took the village of Kaal by storm, and threatened thus
their right flank, the Hungarians retired and took up a position at Maklar, where the Austrians were too exhausted to
pursue them.

During the day and a half which this battle lasted, there
was hard fighting on both sides ; the Hungarians proved themselves worthy of that high reputation for gallantry which they
had enjoyed for centuries, and, had they been better directed,†
would have been victorious ; but the battle, notwithstanding
the loss on both sides, was without result.

The failure of success on the part of the Hungarians was
ascribed by some to Görgey, who led his troops merely to let
them figure as spectators : the entire right wing, which he
commanded, and upon whose attack the plan principally rested, remained inactive, and restricted itself to a defensive position.   The troops of Damjanic and Dembinski in vain stood
the fire of the Austrians, and were forced to abandon the field
to the enemy.‡

The Hungarians represent the Austrian loss in dead and
wounded at nearly four thousand—their own at two hundred
more ; while Prince Windischgrätz reports the Hungarian killed
as only three hundred.   Windischgrätz's force was estimated
at sixty thousand, that of the Hungarians at forty thousand.

At the close of the action, some divisions of the Hungarians
were posted on the heights behind Kericsend ; but the greater
body was ordered back the same night to Mezzökövesd, to be
followed by the remaining troops the next day.

On the 28th, Prince Windischgrätz advanced along the whole

---

* Austrian official bulletin.

† The line of battle extended fifteen miles, and, while the Austrians were acting with their entire strength, but a few of the Hungarian divisions could come
into action at the same time.—*Pragay.*   ‡ Schlessinger.

line, and removed his head-quarters to Maklar, just abandoned
by the retiring enemy.   No sooner were the Hungarians in
line, than an extensive and severe cavalry engagement took
place, in which they not only maintained their ground, but
compelled the Austrians to retreat with the loss of their guns.
The night passed without further interruption or change in the
position of the parties.   The Hungarians, elated by the last
success, awaited with anxiety, during the night, orders to advance, when, to their great astonishment, they received next
morning the command to fall back to Poroszlo, and thence behind the Theiss.

On the 2d of March, the Hungarians, pursued by the Austrians, crossed the Theiss at Tiza-Füred.   On the 3d, a council of war was held, under the presidency of Görgey, in which
the assembled officers expressed their want of confidence in
Dembinski, who, in consequence, resigned the same day ; and
upon General Vetter was conferred the principal command.*

The following were the positions of the Austrian army at
this time : Tokay was occupied by the brigade under General
Götz ; Miskolz, by Baron Jablonovsky ; F. M. L. Schlick's corps
was around Erlau, and extended thence to Szolnok ; while the
first army corps, under Jellacic, was at Czegléd, and the second, under Prince Windischgrätz, was between Buda and Hatvan.   On the part of the Hungarians, it was now determined to
resume the offensive, which had for a time, under Dembinski's
management, been changed to the defensive.

The plan was, that Görgey should cross the Theiss, move on
the enemy at Erlau, and drive him over Gyöngyös toward
Pesth ; that another wing of the army, under Vetter, with
Damjanic and Vécsey as their principal commanders, and
Klapka, as a reserve, should march on Szolnok, and subse-
quently pass over Nagy-Körös, and operate on Pesth.

On the 8th of March, Görgey recrossed the Theiss, Vetter
marched on Szolnok, and Aulick remained in Tiza-Füred.

Strange to say, the Austrians had taken no steps to secure
Szolnok, a place of great importance from its location on the
Theiss, and its connection with the left bank by a bridge.

---

* Pragay.   Some accounts state that Görgey had Dembinski placed under arrest.

Damjanic and Vécsey, advancing on the left bank unperceived, made upon the Austrian force, at this point, an attack so sudden and irresistible, that the troops, under Karger and Ottinger, were partly dispersed and partly driven into the stream Zagyva (which empties into the Theiss at that point), with a loss of five hundred prisoners, most of their cannon, military wagons, &c. This surprise was the commencement of that brilliant series of victories, by which, in battles and skirmishes following each other in rapid succession, the Austrians were forced to vacate the capital and many of the upper districts of the country. But the greatest benefit arising from this success was the confidence with which it inspired the Hungarian troops, that they were, through the vigor and impetuosity of their movements, a match for the better-drilled and more numerous forces of their enemy.

At the same time, Görgey, upon whom (owing to Vetter's illness) now devolved the chief command, coming up with the enemy at Erlau, after a short engagement, drove him back upon Gyöngyös. At Gyöngyös, the imperial rear-guard attempted to resist the march of the Hungarians, and thus protect the flight of the Austrians; but the first attack of the Magyar troops threw this guard upon the bulk of the army, and sixteen pieces of artillery, two standards, twenty-one wagons of ammunition, and fourteen hundred prisoners fell into the hands of the Hungarians.*

A division of Görgey's army, under General Gaspar, following up the Austrians from Gyöngyös on the road to Pesth, after a running fight of six hours, drove them behind Hatvan. On the same day, F. M. L. Schlick, in obedience to the orders of Prince Windischgrätz (who had heard, at his head-quarters in Pesth, that the enemy was concentrating in large numbers between Gyöngyös and Hatvan), undertook a reconnoitre from Hatvan in the direction of Hart; but he soon found that the enemy's strength was so superior, that he preferred to retire and occupy Gödöllö, the last tenable position between Hatvan and Pesth, and to await there the arrival of re-enforcements from Vienna. Accordingly, under a heavy artillery fire from

---

* Pragay.

the Hungarians, the Austrians succeeded in obstructing the further pursuit of the enemy, by destroying the bridge behind Hatvan, and placed themselves in a line of defense extending from Gödöllö to Hatvan and Czegléd. Their left wing, near Hatvan, was commanded by General Schlick ; their right, at Czegléd, was under Jellacic ; and the centre, at Gödöllö, commanded by Prince Windischgrätz in person, who arrived from Pesth, and took up his head-quarters, on the 3d, at Gödöllö, ordering up F. M. L. Czoric as a re-enforcement to the centre, and Jellacic to maintain communication with the corps under Schlick.* The Hungarian army opposed them in a line, which extended even beyond the wings of their enemies.

After the late successes of the Hungarians, Kossuth came to the head-quarters of the army, held a review, particularly of those battalions which had distinguished themselves, thanked them with glowing eloquence in the name of their country, and summoned them to further deeds of glory and renown.†

The strength of the Austrians at Körös rendering the advance in that direction impossible, and the illness of Vetter with the fever, causing a slight change in the plan of operations, it was then resolved, in a council of war, at which Kossuth was present, that the two Hungarian armies should operate together at a common centre, and, by so doing, flank Gödöllö, that position which was the very key of Pesth, and where a small force could hold whole armies in check.

In pursuance of this plan, Vetter's corps, now under the command of Klapka, having crossed the Theiss on the 27th of March, came on the 2d of April abreast of that division of Görgey's army, under General Gaspar, advancing on the direct road from Gyöngyös to Pesth.‡ Continuing their march, Klapka in advance, Damjanic in the centre, and Aulick (who had by this time come up) as a reserve, they met on the 4th, at Tapiobieske, with the right wing of the Austrians, being the first army corps, under Jellacic, and which, in obedience to the orders of the commander, had retired from Czegléd to Tapiobieske, in order to maintain his communications with the left wing. Their scouts having all agreed that Tapiobieske was defended ohly by two battalions and one battery, Klapka, in

---

* Austrian official bulletin.   † Pragay.   ‡ Ibid.

his ardor neglecting the necessary precautions, ordered his whole army across the only bridge over the Tapio, a muddy, unfordable stream, and, without proper examination, gave the orders to storm.   But what was their astonishment, when every house was found to be immediately changed into a redoubt, when numberless batteries opened upon them from the mountain behind the village, and Jellacic's entire corps was lying there in ambush awaiting them.*

This sudden appearance of the enemy on all sides had so injurious an effect upon the undisciplined Hungarians, that, after a short resistance, they began to retreat, and many battalions fled in confusion to the bridge.   The opportune arrival, however, of Damjanic's corps saved Klapka from a most disastrous defeat ; breaking their way through the fugitives, and amid the cross-fire of the enemy from the causeway, they carried the bridge at one charge, and restored the fight.   In less than half an hour, they not only recovered all advantages from the enemy, but forced them to retire from the village.†   By this victory was successfully executed the first step toward that grand strategical operation of flanking Gödöllö.   The next day, the Hungarians, pursuing the enemy and following up the advantages they had gained at Tapiobieske, came up with the entire first army corps, concentrated near Isaszeg.   Dispositions for a general engagement were made—especially as they learned that the entire Austrian army, under Windischgrätz, was collected at that place.   The main body, with a large number of cannon, occupied the heights behind Isaszeg, as also the village and forest in front.

Klapka approached by the road from Sass, Damjanic from Kapa, and Aulick formed a reserve between the two, toward the woods before Isaszeg.   About noon began a murderous fire, and the charge upon the forest.   The Hungarians carried the woods three times, but were as often expelled by the superior force of the Austrians.   At last, re-enforced by Aulick's corps and the cavalry of Gaspar, who had come up from Jura, they bore down all resistance—not only clearing the woods at one charge, but entering the village, now wrapped in flames.   When the Hungarians issued from the woods, they were exposed to

---

* Pragay.   † Ibid.

a severe fire of grape-shot from the heights; but, with great intrepidity, they stormed the enemy's strong-hold, and, before night, the Hungarian tricolor was planted on the hostile works, and waved gloriously in the last beams of the setting sun.* The loss on both sides, in dead and wounded, was several thousand.

Early the next morning, the Hungarians continued the pursuit, which excessive fatigue had prevented them from prosecuting on the previous night.   Both Hungarian armies directing their course to Gödöllö, the right wing, under Görgey, arrived first, and, on the morning of the 6th, had an engagement with the Austrians at Gödöllö, in which eight Austrian battalions, for the most part Croats, were routed, and twenty-six cannons, seven standards, thirty-eight wagons of ammunition, and thirty-two hundred prisoners, were captured.   Dembinski† reports the loss of the Austrians at five thousand, and that of the Hungarians two thousand.

As the loss of Isaszeg exposed the Austrian flank, they found it impossible to retain their position at Gödöllö, even against Görgey's division; and Klapka's corps reached the scene of action just in time to see the last columns of the retreating enemy as they left the field of battle, on the road to Pesth.

The battle at Gödöllö is mentioned in the Austrian bulletins as one of the "splendid successes" of Prince Windischgrätz, in which he had but two men killed; where "the Austrians compelled the Hungarians to retire, after taking from them six of their guns."

Nothing, indeed, can be more contradictory than the assertions of the two belligerent generals ; but the greater truth of Dembinski's statements is evident from the results.   If "the Austrians (who were at Gödöllö) compelled the Hungarians to retire," how happens it that the report of the action made by Dembinski, on the 7th of April, bears date at Gödöllö, while that of Prince Windischgrätz to his government is written on the same day at Pesth?   The result of Prince Windischgrätz's "reconnoitering expeditions" and "splendid successes" was

---

* Pragay.

† Dembinski, after relinquishing the chief command, continued in the army as a subordinate general.

the expeditious arrival of the imperial army on the plain of Rakos,* in front of Pesth ; its retreat over the Danube, and his recall by the emperor from the scene of his defeat. With his return to Pesth terminated his mission, and he was invited by an imperial note to Olmütz.

The Prince of Windischgrätz, although a man of high honor, personal courage, and iron firmness, yet needed the energy and enterprise, if not the military skill and experience necessary for the proper fulfillment of the responsible task which had been assigned him.

By unnecessary delay, after the capture of Pesth, devoting his attention to reorganizing the disordered administration throughout the conquered comitats, instead of pushing on and overcoming all opposition in the other districts of Hungary to which the Magyars had retired, he brought down a series of misfortunes upon a country for the prosperity and welfare of which the prince would doubtless have willingly laid down his life.

The material order was, indeed, re-established in those districts occupied by the imperial troops, but the moral pacification was not effected, and by these fruitless efforts much time was lost, of which the Hungarians availed themselves to organize and discipline their forces, as well as to gather recruits from every quarter.

In the month of January, when he had taken possession of their capital, the rivers were completely frozen, and the roads excellent.   The important fortress of Komorn might then have been attacked with every prospect of success, and the imperial forces have entered Debreczin, the last strong-hold of the Hungarians, comparatively without resistance ; for, at that time, the army was not only ill-prepared for such a contest, but a panic had taken possession of their troops ; whereas the Austrians were full of that confidence which insures success.

Instead of following up this advantage, the marshal delayed for nearly two months at Pesth, by which time the weather moderated, the thaws of spring came on, and these rendered it impossible for him to transport his heavy artillery, ammuni-

---

* The same plain on which the Estates formerly assembled in Parliament, and on horseback elected their kings, &c.

tion, and provision wagons across the low and marshy districts which intervened between him and the Hungarians. When, at length, the imperial forces marched out in pursuit of the enemy, and had with difficulty reached the River Theiss, they were then successfully met by the recruited and organized troops of the Hungarians, and after that time sustained a series of almost uninterrupted reverses.

SUCCESS OF THE HUNGARIANS IN THE SOUTH.

While these successes followed the Hungarian arms in the centre of the kingdom, a no less favorable turn of fortune occurred to their interests in the southern portions of the kingdom. When General Bem first took charge of the Magyar and Szekler troops in Transylvania, the army was so feeble, as well as demoralized, that he could not oppose, with any success, the well-disciplined imperial troops, fifteen thousand strong, under General Puchner, and he was defeated, as has been shown, in several engagements.

The Saxons and Wallachs, who form the bulk of the population in Transylvania, were from the commencement averse to Magyar domination, and steadily attached to the imperial crown; while the remaining inhabitants, the Szeklers, a wild, restless, and warlike race, espousing the side of the Hungarians, placed themselves under the command of Bem. This force Bem soon organized and disciplined; and, increased by recruits, and re-enforced by some troops which had evacuated the fortress of Arad, he was in a few weeks in a condition to resume the offensive. With this army, amounting to twenty thousand men, Bem first marched against General Gedeon, who stood with six thousand Austrians and Wallachs about Bistritz, and, after defeating him in several engagements, drove him out of Transylvania by the Burgo-pass into Bukowina, and cut him off entirely from the body of the army.*

Puchner, who was at this time in the Saxon district, and who had doubtless received authority in this regard, now called for aid upon the Russian general Lüders, who was stationed in Wallachia.

---

* Pragay.

General Lüders, who referred the matter to his emperor, received, by order of his majesty, the reply,* that in case the towns of Hermanstadt and Kronstadt should be seriously threatened by an invasion of Hungarian insurgents, at a time when the Austrian government did not possess the means of protecting them against such great disorder, he was authorized to send a sufficient force into these two towns; but that he ought only to do so in the event of inevitable necessity, and only at the express demand of the Austrian military authorities. When, after the granting of this authority, the danger of the towns became more imminent, in consequence of the successes of the Hungarians, General Lüders, at the call of the Austrian generals, caused the two towns to be occupied by detachments under General Skariatin, of the same effective force as when in possession of the Austrian generals, viz., six thousand to Hermanstadt, and four thousand to Kronstadt. Not discouraged, Bem pushed forward, and defeated the Austrian and Russian forces repeatedly.

At Deva, near the bridge of Pisci, the Austrians were repulsed with great loss. The battle was very serious, and lasted from eight o'clock in the morning until six in the evening. The regiment of infantry was almost totally cut to pieces. After his defeat, Puchner retreated to Hermanstadt. A few days later, a false report having reached General Puchner of an insurrection in Maros-Vasarhely, he proceeded to that spot, leaving Hermanstadt in charge of the Russians. Bem immediately marched against it. Near Modessy, he met an Austrian corps, which he defeated, and then marched down with his whole force on Hermanstadt.

As soon as advised of the approach of the Hungarians, General Skariatin, in command of the Russian forces, supposing that Bem was pursued by Puchner, sallied forth from Hermanstadt, with about four thousand men, in the direction of Stolzenburg, to meet him. The fire was actively kept up, chiefly of artillery, the infantry keeping at a distance until about half past eight, when the Russians precipitately retreated through Hermanstadt, and passed on to Talmacs.

---

* For text of Russian circular, see Appendix, note No. 30.

The Burgher Guard of Hermanstadt, on seeing this retreat, threw away their arms, and fled in all directions. The Hungarians closely pursued the Russians through the city, as far as the faubourg Schellenburg, where they established their outposts, and then took up their quarters in the different squares of the town and suburbs.

Not an act of pillage appears to have sullied their conduct —not a house was fired.* The men, wearied with nine hours' marching and five hours' fighting, demanded and took refreshments from such of the inhabitants as remained, and bivouacked, without committing any of the horrors which rumor had hitherto attributed to the Hungarian soldiery. It was only during the engagement that it became known that Bem commanded in person. He took up his head-quarters in the house of the burgomaster (mayor), whose name, three weeks previously, was appended to a proclamation offering a price for his head. The population was immediately disarmed, and order established the following day.

Puchner, hearing of Bem's rapid movement upon Hermanstadt, hastened after him, and arrived above the town in sufficient time to be made aware of the disaster which had happened to the Russians. A complete demoralizing panic seized the imperial forces; in a few hours their numbers dwindled down from about eight to two thousand; with which number Puchner, making a detour to the south of Hermanstadt, directed his course to the Wallachian frontier, and joined the Russians at Talmacs.

Leaving six thousand men to garrison Hermanstadt, General Bem proceeded with the remainder of his troops, about ten thousand men, on Kronstadt, where he learned that a considerable part of General Puchner's corps, to the amount of eight hundred infantry, nine hundred cavalry, and forty-three pieces of artillery, had gone after their separation from their commander.

As soon as the approach of Bem's forces was known at Kronstadt, the whole Austrian force evacuated the town, and hastened to the Wallachian frontier, whither they had been preced-

---

* English consul, Grant, official report.

ed the day before by the Russian troops, amounting to six thousand men. Bem's army entered Kronstadt without firing a shot. With the exception of the garrison of Klausenburg, and a few thousand Wallachs, who had retired to the mountains in small divisions under the lead of the partisan Junk; Bem, with an army of about twenty thousand men, was complete master of Transylvania.*

Pursuit of the Austrians by the Hungarian Army of the Theiss.

Kossuth, who, with some of his ministry and deputies, had followed the army of the Theiss in its victorious advance, and were with them at this time at the head-quarters at Gödöllö, after a council of war determining their future operations, now started for Debreczin, with the view of declaring the independence of the country, which the recent triumphs encouraged them to undertake.

In order to relieve the fortress of Komorn, which had been closely pressed for many months, and at the same time hold in check, as well as continually harass the hostile army in Pesth and Ofen, the Hungarian forces were disposed as follows : the corps of Klapka, Damjanic, and Gaspar, under the lead of Görgey, were to draw off toward Komorn ; Aulick, with his own corps and the division of Vienetz and Asboth, was to keep watch on Pesth.

Görgey departed for Komorn on the 8th of April, while Aulick remained behind, and, having defeated the Austrians in several different actions, obliged them to evacuate Pesth; but they left a garrison of between five and six thousand men, under General Henzi, in the fortress of Ofen.

On the 9th of April, Görgey reached and attacked Waitzen, with the full knowledge that the town was held by twelve thousand Austrians, under Generals Czoric and Götz. At the same time and in aid of this movement, Dembinski, who commanded the Hungarian forces before Pesth, leaving his vanguard on the field of Rakos, opposite to the imperial centre, occupied their left wing by an attack upon them at Szent

---

* English consul, General Colquhoun, official report.

Endre, by which the Austrians, under Czoric and Götz, at Waitzen, were completely cut off from the imperial left wing. The
Austrians at Waitzen, in expectation of the enemy, were drawn
up behind a row of sand hills in front of the town. Damjanic,
who was then leading the advance, attacked them as soon as
he came in sight, without waiting until the others had come
up, and pushed them so hotly, in spite of a violent rain, that,
when Klapka appeared on the right, they were already wavering, and soon after began their retreat. They were closely
followed into the town, which was carried by storm.

The Austrians again formed on the heights outside ; but F.
M. L. Czoric, finding it impossible to resist the superiority of
forces, as well as the impetuosity of the attack, retired on the
road to Gran. General Götz, and a number of officers of less
rank, lay dead upon the field. A number of cannons, military
wagons, and five hundred prisoners, fell into the hands of the
enemy. The Hungarian loss was comparatively small.*

Leaving a battalion of Honvéd troops to garrison Waitzen,
the Hungarian army the next day pursued their march toward
Komorn, and, to avoid the enemy, pursuing the mountain road,
saw nothing of the Austrians until reaching the Gran.

The imperial general, Wohlgemuth, commanding three brigades, fifteen thousand strong, was posted behind the Gran, as
a reserve, with head-quarters at Neühäusel.

On arriving at the Gran, a stream naturally rapid, and at
this time swollen, the Hungarians found the bridges destroyed,
and no materials for their reconstruction at hand. Nevertheless, with portions of house-roofs and timber, they commenced
the task, and, after three days, a bridge was constructed at
O'Bars and Levencz, without the slightest interruption from
the enemy.

The corps of Klapka and Damjanic consumed the whole of
the 18th in crossing the tottering bridge, which threatened
every moment to give way beneath them, and did not reach
Lök till late in the evening.

Meanwhile, F. M. L. Wohlgemuth, informed of this movement, left Kemend on the night of the 18th, to reconnoitre the

---

* Pragay.

positions of the enemy.   On the 19th, both armies met in the neighborhood of Nagy Sarlo.   The armies were nearly equal in number, commanded alike by able generals, and the battle was warmly contested from early morning until evening.   At first the result of the conflict was exceedingly doubtful; but soon the Hungarians succeeded in turning the right wing, by passing between the River Gran and the town, and while Damjanic thus surrounded the town, defended by four battalions, two rockets, and four field batteries, Kanzinczy carried it by a masterly assault.   The garrison defended themselves with great desperation.   Every room, every cellar, every door-way had to be stormed separately; but stormed they were, and the occupants either cut down or taken prisoners; but few made their escape.   When the Austrians had lost this support, they threw themselves violently, in strong columns, upon the Hungarian centre, which was almost without artillery, striving to break it through; but, about this time, a large flanking column of the enemy's cavalry breaking through their own left wing and flanking their centre, together with the opportune arrival for the Hungarians of two of their batteries, causing fearful destruction in their ranks, the Austrians were forced to retreat. When on the point of withdrawing, an oversight committed by the undrilled Hungarians was, in a moment, improved by the more disciplined troops of the imperial army, who hoped, by a rapid movement against flank and rear, to recover the ground which was lost; but the courage and impetuosity of the Hungarians was, on this occasion, an adequate substitute for skill and science, and they soon succeeded in recovering their right position without serious loss.   This effort thwarted, the retreat became general, and was kept up until ten at night, on the road to Gran.*   The Hungarians, on the next day, pursued their march uninterruptedly to Komorn.

The great and impregnable fortress of Komorn, situated at the confluence of the Waag and the Danube, probably the most formidable bulwark in the world, and one which, during the repeated invasions of the Turks, had never been subdued, for several months had been closely besieged, and, for weeks past,

---

* Pragay.

violently bombarded. Owing to the large force in this fortress, the provisions had become, it was understood, nearly exhausted, and its surrender, on that account, daily looked for. To hasten this result, the Austrians had detailed a very large force around it, to prevent the arrival of succor from any quarter; and to this operation, which diminished so materially the effective force of the Imperialists on the field, may be ascribed, in a great measure, the disasters which befell the Austrian arms on the borders of the Theiss and around Pesth.

Meanwhile, F. M. L. Welden, who had distinguished himself in the wars of Lombardy, and of late military governor of Vienna, a man of ability in his profession, and of popularity with the troops, was appointed, in place of Prince Windischgrätz, commander-in-chief of the armies in Hungary, left Vienna on the 15th of April for the scene of action, and was busily engaged in concentrating and organizing the imperial forces, with a view to prevent the further progress of the enemy.[*]

Under his direction, Pesth was evacuated; the first army corps, under Jellacic, dispatched to the south, over Stuhlweissenburg, to take part in the Servian war; while the second army corps, under Wrbna and Schlick, ascended the Danube, the one on the right and the other on the left bank, to Gran, where they were to join the fresh re-enforcements dispatched from Vienna, and aid in preventing the Hungarians from crossing the Gran, and, failing in this, to repair to Komorn, and thus prevent the relief of that long-besieged fortress, and, at all events, to sustain their communications with Vienna. After the evacuation of Pesth by the imperial troops, at the solicitation of the inhabitants, the Hungarian troops surrounding it declined to enter the city, for fear of subjecting it to bombardment from the garrison of Ofen, on the opposing heights across the Danube; but marched off to the northern part of the kingdom, to stop the advance of fresh Austrian troops which were entering, as was reported, from Jablunka.

---

[*] Welden seemed to think that the object of the Hungarians was the retaking of Pesth, and therefore first proceeded there, and prepared against it. But finding his mistake, and that the Hungarians had moved higher up the Danube, with a view of crossing the river between Pesth and Komorn, and thus cut the Austrians off from all communication with Vienna abandoned Pesth, and ascended the river toward Komorn.

On the next day (the 20th of April), Görgey reached Komorn, and by a *coup de main* soon raised the siege of the fortress.

That portion of the besiegers on the left of the Danube, attacked on one side by an army of nearly twenty thousand men, and charged, on the other, by a sally from the fortress, made by General Guyon* at the bridge over the Waag, were compelled to withdraw; and Görgey, by this communication, threw into the fortress two hundred oxen, exchanged some of his exhausted men for fresh troops from the garrison, and filled his munition wagons from the inexhaustible resources of the fortress.   Having thus achieved an entrance into Komorn, it only remained now to clear the right bank of the Danube, where was placed the main body of the Austrians, and whence the bombs were constantly discharged into the town and fortress.   To effect this object, the first step undertaken was that of restoring the bridge of boats over the Danube, that had formerly connected the fortress with the *tête de pont*, but had long since been shot away, and was now, in three days, despite an uninterrupted shower of bombs and balls, completed.   The great body of the Austrians had by this time ascended from Gran opposite to Komorn, and F. M. L. Welden had his headquarters at Acs, between Gönyo and Szöny, four German miles from Raab.

On the same evening, eight picked battalions, led by Colonel Knezic, were ordered over the bridge.   At two hours after midnight, they attacked the besieging force, under Simonic, stormed the hostile works opposite the fortress, which were already in the second parallel, captured all their defenders, and seized all their guns.   Before daylight, the same battalions stormed Old and New Szöny, took many additional prisoners and large supplies of war *materiel.*

At four in the morning, the Hungarian army corps, under Klapka and Damjanic, began to cross the bridge.

At eight o'clock the action commenced between the forces of Simonic and Schlick, under the chief command of Baron

---

* Guyon was now in command of Komorn; sent there by Kossuth, and disguised as a peddler, he succeeded in passing through the army of the besiegers, and entering the fortress.

Welden, on the one hand, and the troops of Klapka and Damjanic, under the chief command of Görgey, on the other. The fight began on the high grounds, near New Szöny, and was the most warmly-contested battle of the whole campaign. It was soon found that the imperial forces, with all the cool and unflinching courage for which they are so justly distinguished, could not withstand the impetuosity and desperation of the Magyars, who, rushing into action with the resistless force of a tornado, swept before them every obstacle, and bore down all opposition. The further back the Austrians were driven, the better and more elevated were the positions which they successively occupied and obstinately defended, until their left wing finally entered the wood before Acs, with their centre turning toward Puszta-Herkály, and their right wing to Nagy and Kis-Igmand. It was two o'clock in the afternoon, when General Nagy-Shandor,* commander of the Magyar cavalry, received orders to flank the enemy's right wing, and drive them over the Csonczo, which would have made a general retreat necessary. But this brave general, pushing forward with too much ardor, soon brought his cavalry into a formidable crossfire, while its flank was, at the same time, turned by Schlick's corps. A retreat in utter confusion was the result. When the Hungarian infantry at length recovered the advantages lost by the cavalry in this disaster, the fighting ceased on both sides, on account of the extreme heat, and each party encamped. During the night, the Imperialists withdrew toward the frontiers of Austria, partly in the direction of Raab and Hochstrass, and partly by the Island of Schütt. During the engagement, the Hungarians captured a number of cannon, took many prisoners, and gained possession of two camps, with more than three thousand tents and camp utensils.† The Hungarians compute the Austrian loss, in dead and wounded, at four thousand, and their own at one thousand. The Austrians report only that the result of the action was disastrous to the infantry, regiment Hesse cut to pieces, their intrenchments destroyed, and that forty thousand Hungarians contended against thirty thousand Austrians.‡ It was a matter of universal observation among the Hungarians, that the dispositions made

---

* The Murat of Hungary.　　† Pragay.　　‡ Austrian official bulletin.

by Görgey, in this action, were not characterized by that energy and military science which had previously distinguished
his operations.   They could not understand why it was that
his choice troops, those of his former corps, together with the
best artillery and cavalry, were not brought into action, but
were just crossing the river, at evening, when the general
staff were returning to the city after the victory.   Had they,
especially the cavalry, co-operated in the action, the enemy
might without doubt have been destroyed, and the city of
Vienna, between which and the Hungarians nothing but a
routed army remained, have easily been taken.   Had Görgey,
at that time, availed himself of the advantages which his
successful operations had secured him, or obeyed the urgent
recommendation which had been given him, " to follow up
the enemy with vigor," in two days they could have bivouacked in the Austrian capital, and Hungary perhaps have
been, at this time, ranked among the independent nations of
the world.

But Görgey contented himself with sending Gaspar's corps
to Raab, and a division under Kosztolányi to the Schütt; and,
after remaining eight days longer before Komorn, leisurely
proceeded to the siege of Buda.

" I will show the world that I too can reduce fortresses!"
said he to Damjanic and Aulick; and these words contained
the leading motives that induced him, in opposition to the orders of Kossuth, to encamp before Buda with thirty thousand
men, instead of pursuing Welden up to the gates of Vienna.
A single order of the day, subscribed " Arthur Görgey, from
head-quarters at Schönbrunn," would have been of infinitely
greater importance to the future prospects of Hungary and
Austria than the reduction of ten such strong-holds as Buda.*
Görgey was not insensible to this fact; but the plan to advance across the frontier had been formed by Dembinski and
approved by Kossuth, and this was a sufficient reason for Görgey to oppose its execution.   His military talent, however, was
so highly appreciated, and greatly needed in the situation in
which Hungary was then placed, that it was deemed advisable not to dismiss him from the service, but to remove him

---

* Schlessinger.

from his command in the army in a manner most honorable
and agreeable to his feelings, and appoint him Minister of War
—a post wherein his services would be of equal importance to
the government, while his opportunities for injury would be
vastly curtailed.   He accepted the appointment, but excused
himself from immediately entering upon its duties, on the
ground that there were no generals in the army to whom he
could safely intrust the chief command.

He desired, meantime, to send General Damjanic as his
substitute into the Ministry of War; and when this general,
from a personal injury sustained the day before that of his contemplated departure, was prevented from going, General Klapka, of whose popularity in the army he was jealous, was prevailed on to take his place, and he left Komorn for the seat of
government the same day that the three armies set out on
their march to Buda.

The day following the battle of Szöny, the Hungarians under Guyon, with Gaspar's corps, pursued and overtook the
Austrians at Raab; an action ensued, in which the Imperialists suffered greatly, and, with a loss of eighteen cannons, were
driven from the town.   About the same time, the Hungarians
took Tyrnau.   By this rapid succession of triumphs, the Hungarians drove the Imperialists to the frontiers of Austria in a
long line, extending from Oedenburg to Pressburg, and the
head-quarters removed to Laxemburg, within the Austrian
frontier, eight miles from Vienna.   While these things were
transpiring on the frontiers of Austria, Dembinski (who had
taken no part in the late actions), with the largest body of the
army, marches to the north, in order to prevent the arrival of
fresh re-enforcements on the part of the enemy; Vetter and
Casimir Batthyányi, with a corps of twenty thousand men,
march over Szolnok, south, in pursuit of Jellacic; while Bem,
having conquered Transylvania, crosses over into the adjoining
province, and attacks Temesvar; and with the fall of this fortress, the whole of the Banat (the granary of Hungary), and as
far as the Iron Gate, submitted to his authority.   In short,
Hungarian authority and power was in the ascendency every where, except in Buda alone, to which Görgey now hastened.

Görgey having reached the vicinity of Buda,* and fortified the neighboring heights, called the Blocksberg, Schwanenberg, and Adlersberg, which command it, on the 4th of May dispatched a note to General Henzi, the officer in command of the garrison, and demanded its surrender within three hours. The commander refused to surrender, and returned as further answer, that, should the Hungarians fire on him, he would immediately, from the heights of Buda, open a bombardment upon the exposed city of Pesth, lying opposite on the level banks of the Danube.

On the morning of the 5th of May, Görgey commenced the bombardment, and the garrison of Ofen, true to their threat, immediately answered the fire, and, at the same time, opened a bombardment on Pesth, which lasted until the evening of the 7th. On that day, the bombardment of Pesth was suspended, but the fire continued between the garrison of Ofen and the army of Görgey, on the surrounding heights. The bombardment of Pesth was resumed on the 14th, and a large portion of the inhabitants abandoned the city, and camped out, under tents, on the plain of Rakos, and at Stadtwaldchen, beyond the reach of the enemy's cannon, which had changed some of the finest streets, particularly the elegant rows on the river, into a heap of ruins.

After the firing against Ofen had continued uninterruptedly for a week, on the 17th, at one o'clock in the morning, the first assault was made. General Aulick was ordered to lead his troops through the Razenstadt suburb, to break through the castle gate into the park, and thence into the fortress. The breach, which was not quite practicable, was to be mounted by the first corps, under the command of General Nagy-Shandor. General Knezich and the third corps were directed against the Vienna gate and its bastions, and Colonel Kmetty had orders to take the strongly-fortified aqueduct. The Magyars reached the ramparts in several places, but, received with bombs, grenades, and red-hot balls, were repulsed with a loss of from four to five hundred, and at daybreak the fatigued troops were withdrawn.

---

* Buda and Ofen are but different names for the same place.

On the 19th, they made a second assault, at eleven at night. On that occasion they did not even reach the ramparts, and had several hundred killed.* But when at length the battering cannons and proper besieging materials from Komorn—which Görgey, with a negligence almost approaching guilt, had failed to bring with him, and was compelled subsequently to send for—arrived, a breach was soon effected.

When the Hungarian soldiers saw the breach which had been made, and when, on the other hand, they beheld the ruins of their much-loved capital, which the enemy's cannon had produced, and realized the disappointment which their repeated failures had occasioned, they burned with such impatience for the combat that it was with difficulty they could be restrained. They actually quarreled with each other for the privilege of joining the assaulting column, and the dispute was finally settled by lot.

At two o'clock, on the morning of the 21st of May, the assault commenced upon the breach, and, by means of ladders on all sides, the battlements upon a rock rising several hundred feet above the Danube were at length scaled. Two hundred and forty-seven cannons, and several thousand small arms vomited forth death and destruction upon the assailants ; but nothing could damp the ardor of their vengeance. They crept, and clung, and sprang like squirrels, from ladder to rock, and from crag to ladder. Here and there a ball would strike a ladder, with a man grasping every round, and hurl all together into the abyss.

At seven in the morning, the Hungarians were masters of the city, and the tricolor once again floated from the battlements. Major General Henzi, the commander of the garrison, with an intrepidity worthy of his profession, was found covered with wounds, and, though alive when the Hungarians entered, died soon after. Colonel Cecopieri was killed during the engagement, and, as was supposed, by the hands of his own regiment (of Italians), who laid down their arms as soon as the first Hungarians made their appearance on the breast-works.

---

* Nagy-Shandor, at this time, in a conversation with Klapka, complaining of the unpractical character of the dispositions, expressed his doubts of Görgey's *honesty.* —*Klapka.*

The entire garrison that survived, about thirty-five hundred, were made prisoners.

The Austrians fought nobly, but Ofen not being a fortress, the five or six thousand it contained could not hold out against a besieging force of thirty thousand men, especially when one of their own regiments, if not unfaithful, exhibited no zeal during the engagement.

To the Diet assembled at Debreczin, Görgey, in imitation of the comprehensive brevity of Cæsar, communicated his victory, like the Roman general, in three words, "*Hurra! Buda! Görgey!*"*

The reason why the Austrians, in their retreat, left a garrison at Buda, although unintelligible at first, upon reflection, can not fail to be evident. Their march was too precipitate to allow of their taking away the artillery and the stores of Buda and of Pesth, which cities for a time had served as their principal depôts; they had, moreover, reason to hope that the glaring bait thus carelessly thrown out would lure the Hungarians from the chief object of their operations, and that they would not venture upon invading Vienna so long as a hostile foot remained on the soil of Hungary. Events proved the just-

---

* The conquest by assault of the fortress of Buda in all but plain daylight, and with storming ladders only, General Klapka thinks the most brilliant feat of this war, and worthy to be quoted with the heroic deeds of all times and nations.

The magnificent bridge was about to be blown up by the Austrians; but, being clumsily executed, the discharge took place too soon, and, instead of injuring the bridge, destroyed Colonel Alnash, the officer charged with the enterprise.

The news of the conquest of Buda wrought a sudden change in the minds of the Diet on the subject of Görgey, whose popularity, owing to his repeated failures, was decidedly on the wane. In an extraordinary sitting, a resolution was passed that the thanks of the country be expressed to the victorious general and his army, and that the grand cross of the Hungarian order for military merit be awarded Görgey. A committee of members was appointed to convey this resolution to the army. Görgey declined the proffered reward, protesting that his principles would not allow him to accept a mark of distinction; that the mania for titles and orders was already rife among the officers of his army; and that, for the purpose of calling them back to the early purity of their purposes and tendencies, he felt it incumbent on himself to set them the example. Such were his words; but it was his hatred to Kossuth, it was supposed, by which he was actuated.—*Klapka.*

Klapka thinks Buda might and should have been taken by a *coup-de-main.* Had such a course failed, it might, without detriment, have been suffered to remain; and that, isolated as the garrison was in the heart of a hostile country, it was incapable of injury.

ness of their calculations.   Buda attracted, and for a time paralyzed their military forces; and turning aside, like the deluded Atalanta, to seize the golden apple, the Hungarians neglected to press on the heels of the flying enemy; they lost the race, and the Austrians saved their capital at the cost of a noble and most intrepid garrison.

During the period that these serious and extensive *military* operations were progressing between Austria and Hungary, two proceedings of a *civil* nature were carried on by their respective governments, no less important in their character, or influential in regard to the interests of the empire.

First, the granting by the monarch of a Constitution for the Austrian empire; second, the declaration by the Diet of Debreczin of the independence of Hungary.

CONSTITUTION OF AUSTRIA.

After summoning, in consequence of the March Revolution, a Constituent Assembly, for the purpose of forming a Constitution for the empire of Austria, and after that Assembly had been, with the interruption of a few weeks only, in session, from July, 1848, until March, 1849, the emperor discovers that "the task of framing the Constitution was beyond the limits of the Diet's vocation;" unceremoniously supersedes the dilatory Diet of Kremsier, and promulgates to his empire the Constitution of the 4th of March.

It is true that the proceedings of the Assembly were, beyond all question, tardy in the extreme; the tone of its discussions speculative and impracticable in the highest degree; and the whole affair an exemplification of the absurdity of expecting a practically free Constitution from the hands of those who had never enjoyed a day's freedom, and who were profoundly ignorant of political principles.   But to dismiss the Diet of Kremsier, on the ground of its incompetency to make a Constitution for those countries not represented in it, and then to present such an instrument for the empire, in which it is provided that the countries not represented at Kremsier shall be excluded from its operation, seems an absurdity still more glaring; or, in other words, a most bungling excuse for resuming the authority accorded to his subjects, and affording the amplest ev-

idence of how easy will be the task, when he desires it, to recall the privileges granted in the Constitution.*

This Constitution, or, more properly speaking, *Charte Octroyée*, vouchsafed by the Emperor of Austria to his subjects,
as it at present stands on the records of Europe, is but a project or plan to which the government has pledged itself, but
which it has not as yet exhibited either the disposition or ability to carry into effect.   It is only, in its present form, a general declaration of rights applicable to the people of Austria,
with a political organization for the empire, considered as an
imperial federation of states with a central government and
Parliament at Vienna.   Provincial Diets, with a local administration for local affairs in the respective communities, are also
proposed; but these, despite the repeated applications of the
different provinces, have not yet been promulgated.

So far as respects *form*, the newly-proposed Austrian system
seemed fair enough.   The mere *outlines*, except as respects
an hereditary monarchy, appear to have been an imitation of
the United States government.   The affairs of the several
provinces were to be managed by local Diets, while the general interests of the empire were confided to a Legislature composed (with the emperor himself) of two Chambers, answering
to the American Senate and House of Representatives.   The
members of the first are delegated by the local Diets, those
of the second chosen by a direct election on an uniform population basis.   The former sit for ten, the latter for five years.
The elective franchise is guarded by a tax-paying qualification
—the voting *viva voce*.   The emperor, who acts through a cabinet of responsible ministers, possesses all the usual prerogatives of a constitutional sovereign, including an absolute veto
on the decisions of the Chambers.   He is also clothed with the

---

* Which now (1st of January, 1852) he has done by the following decree:
" We. Francis Joseph, by the grace of God Emperor of Austria.
" In consequence of our ordinance of the 20th of August last, our council of ministers and our council of the empire have applied themselves to a thorough examination of the Constitution of March 4, 1849, and seeing that it results from
the deliberations which have taken place, that this Constitution is not adapted
to the position of the Austrian empire, and can not be executed in its entire arrangement, we consider it our duty, as the sovereign, after having well considered
all these reasons, to abrogate the said Constitution of March 4, 1849."

power of proroguing and dissolving the Chambers at pleasure ; but, in case of dissolution, a new Diet must be convened within three months.

The Constitution, too, professes to secure all the essential elements of freedom. It promises most freely all those sacred rights for which constitutional countries have struggled, viz., the right of religious freedom, of personal liberty, that of the press, of associations, and of instruction. But it does not require a very acute observer to perceive, that as with the system or plan of government which has been recommended, so with the possession of these sacred rights, the *form* alone has been preserved ; the *substance* is altogether wanting. The rights are granted by the Constitution ; but laws are subsequently to be made to restrain their efficient operation. The emperor's decree, preceding the Constitution, and in which all its essential elements are most boastfully paraded, affords an admirable index of the whole proceeding, and in this it will be discovered that there is not a single right granted which does not carry with it an accompanying reservation.

DECREE OF THE CONSTITUTION.

" We, Francis Joseph the First, by the grace of God Emperor of Austria, &c., &c., ordain for the provinces of the empire of Austria hereafter named ; that is to say, the Archduchy of Austria, Upper and Lower ; the Archduchy of Salzburg ; the Duchy of Styria ; the kingdom of Illyria, composed of the Duchies of Carinthia and Carniola, of the county and principality of Goritz and Gradiska ; the Margravate of Istria and the city of Trieste, with its territory ; the county and principality of the Tyrol and Vorarlberg ; the kingdom of Bohemia ; the Margravate of Moravia ; the Duchy of Upper and Lower Silesia ; the kingdom of Galicia and Lodomeria, with the Duchies of Aussihurtz and Zador ; the Grand Duchy of Cracow ; the Duchy of Bukowina ; and, finally, for the kingdom of Dalmatia, as follows, with the advice of our council of ministers, in acknowledgment and for the protection of the political rights guaranteed by the constitutional form which we have adopted. 1. Freedom of religious belief and the private exercise of forms of worship are guaranteed to all and every one. The enjoyment of civil and political right is independent of religious belief; *but* religious belief can not alter the duties of citizens. 2. Every church or religious society legally acknowledged has the right of exercising its worship publicly and in common ; it orders and directs its own affairs; it remains in the possession and enjoyment of its establishments, and the funds for carrying on its worship, for education, and for works of benevolence ; *but*, as well as every other society, it must be subject to the general laws of the state. 3. Science and instruction in it is free. Every citizen has a right to establish foundations for education, and therein give instruction, *provided* he has legally proved his qualifications. Domestic education is not subject to this restriction. 4. Instruction shall be given to the people in public establishments ; and in the provinces, where the population is mixed, the nationalities forming the minority shall receive necessary succor for the cultivation of their languages, and for instruction in them. Religious instruction in the schools shall be given by the respective churches and religious societies. The state has only the right of superintending the general instruction and education. 5. Every one shall have the right of freely publishing his opinions, in writing or by speech, in print or in any other manifestation, with his signature. The censorship can not be re-established. *A law shall be published for suppressing abuses of the press.* 6. Every one has the right of petitioning. Petitions under a collective name can *only* emanate from authorities or corporations legally recognized. 7. Austrian citizens have the right of assembling, and of forming associations, the object, the means, or the forms of which are not contrary to the laws, nor dangerous to public order. *The law regulates this right;* and the conditions on which may be acquired the rights of an association, and the exercise or loss of these rights, is also determined by the law. 8. Liberty of person is guaranteed. No arrest of person can be made, *except* in cases of *flagrante delicto, otherwise* than in virtue of the warrant of a judge or other judicial authority. Every warrant for arrest shall be shown to the person against whom it is issued at the time of his being arrested, or within twenty-four hours after. 9. The police is bound to set every one who has been

II.   O

arrested at liberty within forty-eight hours, or *to deliver him up to the competent tribunal.* 10. Every one's house and home is inviolable. No domiciliary visit or seizure of papers can be made, *except* in the cases and under the forms determined by the law. 11. Letters are inviolable. No seizure of letters can be made, *except* in time of war, or in virtue of an order issued by a judge. 12. In times of war or internal disturbances, the provisions of 5th and 11th sections may be temporarily suspended in certain places. This point shall be specified by a law. 13. Our council of ministers is charged with drawing up the ordinances, which are to be issued provisionally, for the execution of these provisions, until organic laws have been promulgated. Given in our capital this 4th day of March, 1849.   (Signed)   FRANCIS JOSEPH.

" Countersigned by the Ministers."

The more this charter is examined, the more apparent becomes the fact that the leading idea which influenced its production, and which prevails through all its branches and departments, is the consolidation of the empire. The primary object in view is not to give liberty to the people, but unity to the empire ; and, as the instrument itself declares, to consolidate and form " the constitutional, hereditary, free, independent, and indissoluble monarchy of Austria."

The only effort in the accomplishment of this great end seems to have been to fulfill, at least in *form*, the pledges previously given by the monarch to the people in the first revolutionary outbreak ; and this fact is therein pompously and boastfully alluded to. A great merit is attempted to be acquired from that circumstance, as though monarchs were either not in the habit of performing, or were not to be expected to execute the pledges which they might be pleased to accord.

To Count Stadion, Minister of the Interior, is ascribed the authorship of this Constitution. Between him and his colleague, the Minister of Foreign Affairs, a rivalry seems to have existed, having for its object to determine, not who could do most to advance the interest of his country or of his age, but who could do most to please their youthful, imperial master. And while Schwartzenberg, taking for his model the Earl of

Strafford, endeavored, like the English statesman, to "make his monarch as absolute as any sovereign in the world could be," Stadion, selecting his prototype from the opposite side of the Channel, labored, like the French minister, "to extend the powers of the crown by overthrowing the privileges of the great vassals," and to become for Austria what Richelieu was for France, "the founder of a united empire."

Richelieu's task, however gigantic, and with a colossal mind to perform it, was not to be compared, either in the state of the materials or that of the times, with the labor of Stadion. Richelieu's was an age of great violence on the part of authority, and of small resistance on the part of the subject class. Richelieu crushed the citizens with cannons, and sent their noble leaders to the scaffold. Stadion, by the arm of a Windischgrätz or a Haynau, might do the same. But the age had passed by when such a chastisement could be effectual; and, even if effectual in other countries, would be of no avail in such a country as Austria, where it could produce no brotherhood of feeling between the Slovack on the Carpathians and the Lombard in his rice-field.

It was a task which abler men in better times had tried and failed; where Kaunitz and Metternich had long labored in vain, and finally, abandoning in despair, had resorted to the opposite policy, "*divide et impera.*"

The capital difficulty, as will at once be perceived, of framing a general Constitution for the Austrian empire, lies in a proper combination of the element of federalism with that of national unity. The empire is a mass of conflicting nationalities, too distinct from each other to be compacted together by administrative centralization into a smooth uniformity of surface; on the other hand, so curiously intermingled that it would be difficult for any one race, without injury to the rest, to break off from the mass, and carve out for itself a separate national existence. The problem is, how to combine the greatest possible elasticity with the greatest possible strength; to bestow powers of local self-government sufficiently ample to protect all their provincial interests, without permitting the bond of union which confines the whole from being regarded as "a rope of sand;" in other words, to keep that whole so balanced about a common centre of gravity as to be adequate to the preservation of the general interests, without causing that bond to be considered as a galling yoke.

The most remarkable characteristic of the Austrian Constitution is that there is no hereditary chamber. The nobility are stripped of all right to hereditary legislative powers.

In comparison with her former system of government, the Constitution was a great advance toward liberal sentiments; but for it the government of Austria deserves "only the credit of submitting frankly and without reserve to what had become a political *necessity*."

In those portions of the empire where the people had never possessed or enjoyed political freedom, where their only safety lay in dependence on the unlimited power and unrestrained will of the monarch, this Constitution could not have been other than an acceptable gift. But far different was the case with those provinces (particularly Hungary) where the population had not only lived under a Constitution for centuries, but had enjoyed an independence of Austria in all but the union of the crowns in the person of the same monarch. It was unfortunate for the imperial government (as has been seen) that the young emperor, coming to the throne as he did wholly uncommitted on the subject, did not avail himself of so favorable an occasion to reconcile the difficulties existing between his government and the Hungarians; which noble duty, by a proper regard for the constitutional rights of the Magyars, might, doubtless, have been effected. But even had he failed in this, another opportunity now presented itself, by which he might still have avoided the evils and dangers that threatened his empire, by the addition of a *single* word to the Constitution then promulgated. That instrument contains a clause, that "a special statute (when the province shall be pacified) will fix the Constitution of Venetian Lombardy and the relation of those countries with the empire." The simple insertion of the word *Hungary* in that clause, and in that connection, and which, upon every principle of justice and policy, should have been done, would have spared, certainly at that time, and perhaps eventually, the vast amount of blood and treasure which its neglect did not fail to occasion.

But blindly adhering to an opposite course, and not only including Hungary (a kingdom then in the utmost revolt) under
the operation of the new charter, but by the terms of that instrument virtually annulling its Constitution, he drove the
Hungarian aristocracy at once from the support of the Austrian government, to which many of them were at that time
inclined, and forced them to the side of the Liberals; in short,
united the whole nation as one man, and inspired it with such
a spirit of determined resistance as enabled it, in a few weeks,
to overwhelm its adversaries, and to expel them almost completely from the soil of Hungary.

The following are the clauses of the new charter which conflict with the independence and constitutional rights of Hungary:

1st. " No custom duties can be established under any title
in the interior of the empire, and wherever they already exist
they are to be suppressed as immediately as possible."

By this clause, not only is Hungary prevented from levying
duties on foreign importations—an important attribute* of sovereignty, a strong mark of independence which she has always
enjoyed—but by it she is robbed of a large portion of her revenue, and deprived of all control over her financial interests.

2d. " All the countries subject to the crown are to be represented by Diets, in all affairs declared by the Constitution of
the empire to be the affairs of the country."

This clause virtually requires of Hungary a surrender of all
sovereignty and independence. The Constitution of the empire, which Hungary had no voice in forming, is to determine
what are and what are not the affairs of Hungary, and over
which their special Diet will have jurisdiction.

With such unlimited authority as that clause confers, can
it be difficult to determine what subjects the emperor will take
control of himself, what others he will confer on the Diet of
the empire, and, lastly, what he will suffer the stripped Hungarians to retain?

3d. " The Constitution of the kingdom of Hungary is maintained, but all the parts of it not in harmony with the Constitution of the empire are abrogated."

---

* Which even the sovereign states of *this* confederacy do not enjoy.

After, by the preceding clause, stripping Hungary of her most important and sacred rights, that act would be of no avail without a repealing clause to render null and void all the portions of the Hungarian Constitution by which those rights are sustained. This is, therefore, to the Austrian government a most important and indispensable provision.

4th. " Equality of rights of all nationalities, and the language of each country, are guaranteed by special institutions in the relations of public and civil life."

Not content with robbing Hungary of her rights and privileges, the object of this clause is to deprive her of those provinces which exist within her limits, and which are her just acquisitions. It is also designed to diminish the strength of Hungary, not only by depriving her of these essential parts of her kingdom, but by releasing them from her control to raise them in opposition to her. Instead of equal rights of all nationalities, this paragraph would be more properly translated, equal annihilation to all.*

5th. " The internal organization of the Constitution of Transylvania to be on the basis of complete independence of the kingdom of Hungary."

Not only has the *Charte Octroyée* deprived Hungary of her rights and privileges, and of all her nationality, but it takes away from her the province of Transylvania, the largest and most important of her dependencies, one which was acquired by conquest upward of five centuries before the connection of Austria and Hungary, and acknowledged by the emperor as late as the 11th of April, 1848. But this clause is still more significant, in showing that not one of the provinces or kingdoms of the empire shall be allowed a voice in their " internal organization" and Constitution. The coronation oath of the monarch, which fourteen kings in succession have taken, not only contains an express engagement, on the part of the sovereign, not to consent to any diminution of the Hungarian territory, but even makes it incumbent on him by every effort to reannex to that kingdom such portions as, in the progress of events and course of time, may have been torn from it.

---

* Westminster Review. Making a new vayvode of Servia, and giving it a separate administration.

Nor was this Austrian charter more acceptable to the other portions of the empire. The great merit claimed for it, of respecting the various nationalities, and which the deluded Croatians were induced to believe would render it so much more desirable to them than the Hungarian Constitution, was exactly the characteristic which it was found, on closer examination, especially to need. The great demand through all the Austrian provinces has long been for " national administrations." None, except Hungary, ever enjoyed this privilege. There was no one of their ancient liberties which the Hungarians, Croatians, and Transylvanians prized so much as that of being governed by natives of their own country; and that the foreigner, by which title they designated the German, should have no authority over them. When Metternich was driven from power, one universal demand for national government arose throughout the provinces. All asked for *employés* who should speak the language of the country, know the condition of the people, have a kind feeling for the province they were to officiate in, and a substantial interest in its prosperity. But the new Constitution guaranteed no *national* government ; on the contrary, that instrument declares, " *Throughout the Austrian empire there is but one citizenship, viz., Austrian.*" This sentence gives to the Austrian government the power of continuing the old system at their pleasure, of appointing to office strangers to the country where they are to have rule, unwelcome to its inhabitants, in opposition to their national feelings, in derogation of their national rights, and destructive of all prospects of harmony and peace. This single paragraph contains the lurking principle of the centralization of power, and the destruction of provincial individuality. Here, too, is the root of the almost universal opposition which the new Constitution experienced.

The *non*-German states of the Austrian empire had declared their hostility to the new Constitution by deeds as well as words. The *Bohemians*, whose deputies had hitherto voted in the Vienna Diet with the ministers, were foremost in the opposition. The charter has had the effect of uniting the hitherto irreconcilable parties of German, Bohemian, and Czecks. Scarcely any thing but the insult which that instrument offers to all their national feelings and traditions could have been attended with a similar result.

In Servia, the charter caused a burst of indignation, and a union with remonstrating and revolting Hungary. The Austrian ministry at Olmütz had so far yielded to the Servians as to ask them to send deputies to that city to confer upon the points of which they complained.

The Croats, who probably, in all their manifestations, include one third of the population of the Austrian empire, had most decidedly shown their opposition to the new Constitution by refusing to publish it; and they demanded in its place the confirmation of the resolutions which were passed by their own Diet in 1848. The Ban Jellacic himself, the pet of the emperor and the ministry, supported the Croatian protest with the whole weight of his personal influence. He was a personage not to be offended, for his services could not be dispensed with; and the ministry of Count Stadion has modified the charter according to the wishes which, in the name of his countrymen, the Ban had expressed.

DECLARATION OF INDEPENDENCE.

Although, as early as the 29th of June, 1848, the Austrian government, as we have seen, in a communication to the Hungarian ministry, announced that it was about to put an end to the neutrality it had previously observed in the contest between Hungary and Croatia, and to support Croatia openly;* and although, on the 9th of September, 1848, the Croatians, thus supported by Austria, crossed the River Drave, and invaded, in a most hostile and barbarous manner, the territories of Hungary; and although, on the 15th of December, Austria, with her own troops, entered Hungary at nine different points at the same time, taking both her capitals, subduing and disarming the population, and suppressing all Hungarian authority wherever they encountered it, it was not until after the promulgation of the *Charte Octroyée*, annulling, in the most essential

---

* It is not true, therefore, as has been stated, that "the Magyars declared the throne vacant only because Ferdinand had taken part with the *rebels*." If so, the declaration of independence would have taken place on the 29th of June, 1848, instead of the 14th of April, 1849.

points, the Constitution of Hungary, that the Magyars thought proper to *declare their independence* of the house of Habsburg.

Agreeably to the Hungarian Constitution, the king, upon his installation, was required to take an oath to sustain the Constitution and liberties of the Hungarian people ; when, instead of complying with this prerequisite, Francis Joseph declares his resolution not to accept the crown of Hungary, by issuing his royal charter, which virtually *destroys* the Hungarian Constitution, then, and not until then, did the Magyars express a determination to throw off all allegiance to the reigning dynasty.*

These acts would seem to evidence, if proof were necessary, the great reluctance which Hungary felt at a separation, and the sincerity of her assertion, when she declared, in her address to the throne, that it was " the firm wish and need of Hungary to remain indissolubly connected with the empire."

Owing to the existence of war, which prevailed at this time to the direst extent between the two countries, all communication having been cut off, a few weeks doubtless elapsed before intelligence of the new Constitution promulgated by the emperor penetrated Hungary. It was just one month and ten days after the new charter had made its appearance, and immediately upon the turn given to affairs by the victories of Szolnok, Tapiobieske, Isaszeg, and Gödöllö, that Kossuth and his associates, then at the head-quarters of the army, as has been

---

* It was for this reason, and not, as has been asserted, because the *Charte Octroyée* gave equality of rights to the Croatians, that Hungary declared her independence. Count Teleki, in his note to the Minister of Foreign Affairs of France, says that the fact of the Russian intervention, solicited in the name of the emperor-king of Hungary, is what, above all other things, led the National Assembly to declare its independence of the house of Habsburg.

Pulzsky, on the contrary, asserts that the Russian intervention was not known at Debreczin at that time. Schlessinger mentions, as an inducement to the step, that "Kossuth, while at the camp, received information of these secret cabals (going on at Debreczin during his absence with the army), which the zeal of his friends exaggerated and described as of the most formidable character. He resolved to put an end to them by burning the ships of his enemies behind their backs. His fear was greater than the danger, and this fear will explain the reason why the Declaration of Independence was proclaimed before the campaign had attained its object." Another reason assigned for bringing forward the declaration at this time was, that the officers of the army required the measure, to assure them that the Diet would not make its peace with Austria and sacrifice the army.

seen, left for Debreczin, to take the proper measures for declaring the independence of their country.

On the 14th of April, 1849, the representatives of the Hungarian nation met in the Protestant church in Debreczin.
Kossuth, in an eloquent address, reported the late victories,
presented the rights and claims of Hungary, the abuses and
perfidy of Austria, and called upon the Diet and the assembled
people, in the name of their country and their God, to shake
off the fetters that had bound them for three centuries, and to
take their place among the independent nations.   The following propositions were then unanimously adopted :

1st. Hungary with Transylvania, as legally united with it,
and the possessions and dependencies, are hereby declared to
constitute a free and independent sovereign state.   The territorial unity of this state is declared to be inviolable, and its
territory to be indivisible.

2d. The house of Habsburg-Lorraine having, by treachery,
perjury, and levying of war against the Hungarian nation, as
well as by its outrageous violation of all compacts in breaking up the integral territory of the kingdom, in the separation
of Transylvania, Croatia, Slavonia, Fiume, and its districts,
from Hungary ; further, by compassing the destruction of the
independence of the country by arms, and by calling in the
disciplined army of a foreign power for the purpose of annihilating its nationality ; by violation both of the Pragmatic Sanction, and of treaties concluded between Austria and Hungary,
on which the alliance between the two countries depended, is,
as treacherous and perjured, forever excluded from the throne
of the united states of Hungary and Transylvania, and all their
possessions and dependencies, and are hereby deprived of the
style and title, as well as of the armorial bearings belonging
to the crown of Hungary, and declared to be banished forever
from the united countries, their dependencies and possessions.
They are, therefore, declared to be deposed, degraded, and banished forever from the Hungarian territory.

3d. The Hungarian nation, in the exercise of its rights and
sovereign will, being determined to assume the position of a
free and independent state among the nations of Europe, declares it to be its intention to establish and maintain friendly

and neighborly relations with those states with which it was formerly united under the same sovereign, as well as to contract alliances with all other nations.

4th. The form of government to be adopted for the future will be fixed by the Diet of the nation.

But, until this point shall be decided on the basis of the foregoing fundamental principles, which have been recognized for ages, the government of the united countries, their possessions, and dependencies, shall be conducted, on the personal responsibility, and under the obligation to render an account of all acts, by Louis Kossuth, who has by acclamation, and with the unanimous approbation of the Diet, been named Governor (*Gubernator*), and the ministers whom he shall appoint.*

An eye-witness of this assembly states that the scene in that plain, unadorned house of prayer was the grandest one in the whole of the Hungarian Revolution. Never was Kossuth's eloquence more electrifying than when dictating the letter of renunciation of allegiance to the Habsburg dynasty; his glowing patriotism vied with his impassioned eloquence. The farewell curse thundered from his lips like a cataract; and, as the people beheld the history of their centuries of suffering, the deceptions practiced on them, and their unrequited and thankless sacrifices unrolled before them, and held up to their view like so many warning spirits, their hearts' blood stirred with feverish excitement; they trembled with irrepressible emotion. The thrill of present joy, the intoxicating presentiment of future freedom could alone adequately recompense the sufferings, the bootless struggles of ages, or efface the remembrance of past griefs. A shout of exultation broke from that immense assembly, and, swelling in its course like an avalanche, it was caught up by the multitude that thronged the streets without, and echoed far and wide throughout the country.†

"The declaration which the Hungarians issued," it has been urged, "was not so much a declaration of their own independence as a protest against the independence of Croatia and Slavonia; its object was not to justify their rebellion against Austria, but to accuse Croatia of rebelling against Hungary."

* For Declaration of Independence in full, see Appendix, note No. 31.
† Schlessinger's War in Hungary.

The truth is, as has been made evident, the Hungarians were contending for their ancient constitutional rights, altered and adapted to the demands of an advanced age ; and this fact is sufficiently obvious, when it is admitted by writers on both sides that "the Constitution (of Austria), treating them as rebels, with a dash of the pen erased all the ancient constitutional rights of Hungary, and, consolidating her with the empire of Austria, raised the Slavi to a political equality with their masters." And was not the promulgation of a Constitution which treated them as rebels, and which, with a dash of the pen, ignored all their ancient constitutional rights, sufficient to justify a declaration of independence ? What more could the most submissive desire by way of justification ? What right had this " *liberal*" Constitution, as it is sometimes characterized, to treat them as rebels ? They had not yet declared their independence; they had done nothing but defend their " *ancient constitutional rights.*"

What were the causes which impelled our American fathers to declare their independence of the mother country ? The colonies at that time were dependencies of Great Britain, and not constitutionally independent of her, as Hungary was of Austria ; and even *then* the most serious charge which we could bring against the British government, and which we conceived fully justified the bold experiment of our fathers, was "the taking away our charters, abolishing our most valuable laws, and altering fundamentally the forms of our governments." And what were these charters, of but few years' duration, granted by Great Britain herself, in comparison with those ancient constitutional rights, enjoyed by Hungary upward of five hundred years before her connection with Austria, and acknowledged by Austria for upward of three hundred years after that union ?

But the Hungarians did no more than declare their independence of the house of Habsburg ; they did not proclaim a republic, but simply left it to the Diet to establish the future form of government in all its details. This circumstance is by some cited against the cause of the Hungarians ; and the opinion is sought to be enforced that their struggle was not for national independence, nor for the establishment of liberal institutions, but only " to preserve the distinctions and immunities of the nobles."

To support this conclusion, a misinterpretation is given to the fourth resolution of their declaration. That resolution they interpret as follows : The form of government to be adopted for the future shall be fixed by the Diet of the nation ; but until this point shall be decided, *on the basis of the ancient and received principles which have been recognized for ages* (that is, as they construe it, acknowledging the absolute supremacy of the Magyar race in the country which they conquered, and where they have been lords of the soil and the dominant nation for eight or nine centuries), the government of the united countries, &c.

No unprejudiced mind, upon the perusal of the manifesto, can give to it this construction. There is not one word in the whole manifesto upon the subject of " acknowledging the absolute supremacy of the Magyars ;" but the burden of the complaint is, that " *the house of Austria has publicly used every effort to deprive the country of its legitimate independence and Constitution, designing to reduce it to a level with the other provinces, long since deprived of all freedom, and to unite all in a common sink of slavery.*"

A more correct translation of the resolution, however, would obviate the necessity of discovering the meaning of the passage, since no such phrase occurs in the original. The most approved translation of the fourth resolution is as follows : " The Diet of the nation shall establish the future form of government for the country, in all its details ; but, until this shall have been established, in conformity with the *above* or foregoing fundamental principles, Louis Kossuth, who has been, by acclamation and the unanimous approbation of the members of the Diet, named governing president, shall, together with the ministers, hereafter to be named by him, upon his own and their personal responsibility, and, under an obligation of accountability, govern the country in its whole extent."

The translator, by giving to *fönebi* (above or foregoing) the meaning of *former*, has perverted entirely the whole sense of the resolution. *Fönebi*, in the Hungarian language, signifies *above*, and refers to *space ;* while *elöbbi* signifies *former*, and

refers to *time*. Had the Hungarians intended to allude to their
former principles, would they have neglected the obvious use
of *elöbbi*, which would have conveyed their meaning, and have
adopted *fönebi*, which did not express their intention?

By the correct translation of the word *fönebi*, the whole
difficulty is obviated, and the sense of the fourth resolution
placed beyond all cavil, viz., "that, until this point shall be
decided on the foregoing principles (*i. e.*, as declared in the
first resolution, "that Hungary is a free, independent, sovereign state, its territorial unity inviolable, and its territory indivisible"), its government shall be conducted," &c.

What were these "distinctions and immunities of the nobles," which it is supposed the Hungarians made such efforts
to preserve? A species of the feudal system did prevail in
Hungary, until the year 1847, and the condition of the peasantry was indeed, as has already been described, deplorable;
but were these orders or distinctions regulated by and dependent upon the races? were the lords all of Magyar, and the
peasants altogether of Slavic origin?

The wealthy nobility of Slavic origin, scattered through all
the counties of Hungary, with their countless estates, surrounded by thousands of serfs, and in their princely mansions
rolling in luxury and Oriental magnificence, would be somewhat surprised to see themselves characterized as vassals, and
be certainly at a loss to divine in what style lords can live, if
their condition be regarded as one of abject slavery.

A reference to the statistics of Hungary is only necessary to
place this question beyond controversy. In the *Magyarors-
zág Leirása* of Fényes, the names of the largest proprietors
in each comitat are given; and by this it appears that in that
of Pesth, one of the most purely Magyar counties, as well as
that embracing the capital of the kingdom, out of five names
given as the largest proprietors, three are of Slavic origin.*

All of Slavic origin, then, were not serfs. Nor is there any
more correctness in the belief that all of Magyar descent were
lords.† The mass of the peasantry, in general, were of the

---

* Christian Examiner.

† The following facts will show that the Magyars are not exclusively the nobles. "In the Slovack county of Zólyom there are but two hundred Magyar in-

same race as their lords. In the Slovackian counties of the north, for example, they were Slovacks; in the Magyar counties of the centre, they were Magyars; and in the Slavic counties of the south, they were Slavi. This was but the natural result of the feudal system. In the early settlement of the country, the officers or petty chieftains, down to the lowest, received estates, the size of which was to be proportioned to their rank and to the number of men whom they had commanded. These men, the common soldiers, with their families, were to live on the estates of their officers, to labor for them, and support both themselves and their former commanders. The descendants of these officers form the present Hungarian nobility; the Magyar peasants are the offspring of the common soldiers or privates.*

The nine or ten millions of Slavi in the kingdom of Hungary were not then in the condition of abject slavery, as has been conceived, but were for the most part inhabitants of distinct provinces, having their own administrations and institutions; and though, as originally conquered provinces, they were somewhat under the control of the Hungarian government, yet their condition was almost the same as that of the Magyars. Possessed of their respective governors and Diets,† they made their own laws, and had a representation in the general Diet of Hungary.

Have they been, as has been supposed, enslaved for centuries, and was that the cause of their recent conflict with the Hungarians? The only manner in which oppression is complained of by the Croatians was as regards their language and their ancient rights.

---

habitants; there are in the county two thousand one hundred and fifty-two nobles. If we take it for granted that the two hundred Magyars are all nobles, there remain one thousand nine hundred and fifty-two Slovack nobles in this one county. In the Slovack county of Turócz, in which more than a tenth part of the population is noble, there are but two hundred Magyars; the number of nobles in this county is four thousand eight hundred. In the Slavic county of Pozsega, which has no Magyar population, there are six hundred and thirty-eight nobles. In the Slovack county of Trencsén, in which there are but one thousand five hundred Magyar inhabitants, the nobility number nine thousand eight hundred and thirteen."— *Christian Examiner.*

* F. A. Fessler's *Geschichten der Ungarn.*

† Transylvania had always a Diet of her own. Croatia and Slavonia united formed another.

In respect to the language, where has been the oppression? In 1805, in the Diet in which the Slavi were represented, all the native languages, even that of the Hungarians, were excluded, and the Latin adopted in their stead, for all public discussions.

It is not more than twenty years since the Hungarian language was applied to the public business of Hungary, and only in the year 1844 that an act was passed making it obligatory on the Deputies of Croatia to speak Hungarian in the Diet of Hungary after the expiration of six years from that time. How then, as regards language, can it be said that they have been oppressed for *centuries?* and where is the injustice of this last step? Some common medium of communication was found indispensable for those living under the same government; that being admitted, what more natural and reasonable determination on this point was there than the adoption of that language that was spoken by the greatest number of people, and this was the Magyar; for, although there were as many as nine or ten millions of Slavi, there were not more than about two millions speaking the same language, a number about half that speaking the Hungarian.

The use of the Croatian language in all the business of the country was guaranteed, and the Hungarians undertook even to address the Croats in their own tongue. In the Diet of 1847–8, in the month of February, before the Revolution of France, Count Louis Batthyányi, as we have seen,* in a speech received with acclamation by the Upper Chamber, and by the public universally, put forward the right of the Croats to use not only the Latin language, but their native tongue in all the internal affairs of their country, and this proposition was adopted by both Chambers of the Hungarian Diet. If the Hungarian government was then disposed to grant them what they asked before the events of March and April, how much more had the Croatians a right to expect justice after those events, since peace was the principal condition of the development of Hungarian improvement. Such was the tyranny exercised by the Hungarians over the Slavi for centuries in the way of language. What was the oppression as regarded

---

* Chapter V.

their ancient or political rights? Before the Revolution no complaint was heard, notwithstanding Croatia of all the provinces was most subject to Austrian influence, and where the Vienna cabinet had for a long time been intriguing to create sources of dissatisfaction against the liberal tendencies of the Hungarians.

With the results of the Revolution of 1848 the Croatians at first expressed their unqualified satisfaction. In fact, the conquest made by the Diet of Pressburg had been extended to Croatia, as well as throughout the length and breadth of the kingdom. Her ancient municipal rights, confirmed and secured by the Hungarian Diet of 1715, were in no manner assailed. They paid less taxes than the Hungarians, and at the same time were not liable, as were the Hungarians, to have the army quartered upon them. While the old feudal offices were abolished in Hungary, the dignity and power of the Ban of Croatia were preserved. The powers of the General Assembly of Croatia were increased in granting to it the right to regulate the number of deputies that should be sent to the Hungarian Diet, according to population. Until then Croatia was only represented in the Diet by three deputies, that number was now increased to eighteen* for the three counties, and their powers considerably enlarged. Croatians were called to fill the state employments, and particularly to hold the new offices which had just arisen from the creation of two Croat departments in the Hungarian ministry. The Croatian peasantry having received the same rights as the Hungarian, like them also received land, and Hungary agreed to indemnify the Croatian nobles, in the same manner as the Hungarian nobles, out of her own treasury.† Finally, the Hungarian government and Diet solemnly declared that if Croatia had any demands to make, they would undertake to investigate them carefully, and accede to them so far as was consistent with the national honor and the integrity of the crown.

In consequence of these concessions, the Croats enjoyed greater privileges than the Hungarians, inasmuch as all Croats are considered as Hungarians, while a considerable portion of the Hungarians are excluded from Croatia.

---

* A large representation for 1,400,000 inhabitants.   † Count Teleki's pamphlet.

This is the worse than Egyptian bondage which the Croatians* have suffered for the last eight centuries at the hands of the Magyars.

If the Slavi of Hungary were laboring under the intolerable servitude which some have endeavored so earnestly to show, how does it occur that that model of propriety and patriotism, "the gallant Ban of Croatia," should, as has been stated, "in July, 1848, have made overtures to Kossuth and his co-ministers, to make common cause with them against Austria, and offered to insure entire Hungarian independence on certain conditions," "which the Magyars indignantly rejected."

If their slavery was of the "abject character" sometimes affirmed, how can we explain the facts, that Kossuth the Slovack was the head of the Hungarian government; Vukovich, a Servian, Minister of Justice; and Duschek, a Slavonian, Minister of Finance?

It was not, therefore, for the maintenance of their "feudal institutions," and consequent supremacy over the Croatians, that the Magyars struggled for independence of Austria, since no such oppression of the Croatians existed; and because six months before the war began there existed no feudal institutions to maintain.†

Was it for the preservation of "the immunities of the nobles" that Hungary engaged in the contest?

The principal and most obnoxious immunity of the nobles of Hungary was their exemption from taxation of every kind, even to that of tolls over roads and bridges; but this had been swept away by an act passed eighteen years before.

The first blow at this immunity of the nobles, the first inroad upon this great privilege, was the work of Count Stephen Széchényi, one of the wealthiest and most influential magnates of the kingdom, as well as one of the purest patriots and best reformers of any age or country. The manner of its accomplishment was an act, passed by the Diet of 1836, for the

---

* The Croatians are the only ones here spoken of, because they were the only ones who preferred any complaints; the other Slavic provinces never uttered a murmur.

† The act emancipating the serfs was passed in the month of March; Jellacic's invasion of Hungary did not take place until September.

construction, at a cost of eight millions of florins, of a magnificent bridge across the Danube, connecting the two cities of
Ofen and Pesth; the object of this splendid structure being not
so much to facilitate the intercourse between the two cities as
to break in upon this exemption of the nobles from taxation,
as it was one of the stipulations of the charter, that all persons
who crossed on this bridge, of whatever rank, should be liable
to the payment of toll. Thus then, as early as 1836, through
the efforts of one of the principal nobles, did the Diet of Hungary, composed altogether of nobles or the representatives of
nobles, destroy in principle this their cherished immunity—
their entire exemption from all public contributions.

But the movement did not end here, the principle thus effectually invaded by the Diet of 1836 was still further encroached upon, at each successive meeting of that body, by efforts made toward obtaining a further relinquishment by the
nobles of their privilege of exemption from taxation. As illustrative of this fact, as well as in justice to Louis Kossuth, the
leader of the Revolution, who has been charged with the selfish advocacy of the privileges of a caste, the following extracts
from his speeches, in the Diets of 1841 and 1844, are inserted,
and can not fail to interest the reader, not only as part of the
history of the times, but as specimens of eloquence remarkable
for their force both of language and illustration.

On the 2d of January, 1841, Kossuth exhorted the magnates
of Hungary to renounce their cherished privilege of exemption
from taxation. "If they—the nobles," said he, "renounce nar-
row-heartedness, lovelessness, and unnationality; if they feel
that to do justice is not a sacrifice, but the best guaranty for
obtaining justice; if, then, on the peaceful path of national prosperity and constitutional development, they will carry forward
the white with the wreath-of-hope-adorned banner of steady
national progress; then the nation trustfully will hail them as
its leaders, and will, with two-fold spirit and excitement, follow on the paths of peace those old historic names whom on
the battle-field it has of yore so often followed, and will gladly
illumine the glory they thus acquire with the halo that encir-
cles the brows of their ancestors. But should there be among
them men who believe that the glorious name inherited from

their ancestors is an indestructible entail, which empowers them to indulge in inactive repose, or even entitles them to maintain their personal advantages against right and justice, and their private interests against the welfare of the nation; should men be found who, in their blind over-estimation of self, try to stay the wheel of the world, or to impede that steady progress which statesmanship guides, which the general want requires, and which national inspiration promotes, then, verily, the nation will do its duty. 'With you, through you, if you will; without you, ay, against you, if it must be!'"*

In 1844, addressing the same body, he said, "Like a second Sibyl, Fate stands before the nobles of Hungary, holding nine books in her hand. The first three books contain the secret how the national and constitutional independence of the country can be maintained, and by means of liberty be raised till it flourish; and that in such a way that a nobility, as the first-born of the nation, be intrusted with the office of leader on the constitutional path. In the second three books is recorded how well-being, mated with constitutional life, can be made general throughout the land, but without nobility. And finally, the last three books teach the secret how to create material well-being in the land, but without liberty or constitution. To purchase these nine books is to-day yet in the power of the nobility. The price exacted is renunciation of exemption from taxation. If the nobility delay to pay this price, the first three books fly into the fire, and with them the secret of the political future of the nobility. But the price of the remaining books is still the same. If the nobility further hesitate, the second three books vanish in smoke, and with them the secret of the constitutional future of the country; but the price of the last three books, which only offer brutish, material well-being, still remains the same. If the nobility again demur, the last three perish forever; and even then we must pay the price demanded for the nine; but in return we shall obtain only one vast grave, not even moistened by a tear of pity from free nations."†

---

* Mit euch, durch euch, wehn ihr willt; ohne euch, auch gegen euch, wenn es sein muss!   † Ludwig Kossuth, by J. E. Horn.

The first step taken in 1836 was followed, four years after, by a passage through the Diet of several other bills tending to a further abolition of the immunities of the nobles; and in 1844, at the like instigation of Count Széchényi (sustained by Kossuth), a law was passed, giving to the peasants a right of holding land and of filling office.   The reforms completed by the last Diet of Pressburg (1848), full six months before the commencement of hostilities, established civil equality and liberty throughout the kingdom of Hungary.   Political rights from that moment became the lot of every Hungarian, without distinction of race or creed.   The public direct taxes, of which until then the nobles bore no part, are now divided among all the inhabitants, in the proportion of their revenues; all seigniorial privileges, lay as well as ecclesiastical, completely abolished; and, " what never took place in any other country at any time, the nobility made to the peasants a free grant of the portions of land they held."*   " Thus, certainly," says Count Teleki, " there were many families ruined and fortunes shattered; but it was necessary to take advantage of the first day of liberty which shone upon their native land, and to assure to it a morrow."

There is another error relative to the causes of the war, which Austria, to blind the world as to her own arbitrary course, and to prevent its sympathies from being enlisted on the side of oppressed Hungary, has diligently circulated to entrap the unwary.   It is that of regarding the late struggle in the Austrian empire as a *war of races*, carried on between Magyar and Croat, instead of being, as it really was, a long-continued and systematic effort on the part of Austria to subdue Hungary, break down the constitutional privileges, and place her on a footing with the other provinces of the empire.

There was a conflict between races, it is true; no disturbance can arise in Austria without such a conflict; not only owing to the many nations of which the empire is composed, but because the policy to " divide and govern" has always been the mode by which Austria has been enabled to hold together

---

* Count Teleki's pamphlet.

her different parts, and maintain the supremacy of the little duchy over the whole.*   This conflict between the races was not the *end*, but only the *means*.   When did this war of races commence ?   Not until July, 1848, for at that time, as has been asserted by some who sustain this view of the question, "the gallant Ban of Croatia proposed to the Hungarians to join them against Austria."   And when did the struggle between Austria and Hungary begin ?   Upward of three hundred years ago, from the very first connection of the two countries.

The struggle could not, therefore, be characterized as a war of races ; its nature, if we have failed to show it in these pages, was most clearly stated in the British Parliament by Lord Palmerston, in 1849, as follows : "It is most undeniable, that Austria, by the course of policy she has pursued, has identified herself with obstruction to progress.   It is equally undeniable, that Hungary has been for centuries a state which, though united with Austria by the link of the crown, has nevertheless been separate and distinct from Austria by its own complete Constitution.   It is no less true, that the question (*i. e.*, the immediate question irrespective of results) now to be fought for on the plains of Hungary is this, whether Hungary shall continue to maintain a separate nationality as a distinct kingdom, and with a constitution of its own ; or whether it is to be incorporated, more or less, in the aggregate Constitution that is to be given to the Austrian empire."

It was not, then, a war of races ; and it is equally wide of the truth to believe, that the Croatians, Slavi, &c., were contending for liberty.   Such an idea was never asserted by them, and doubtless never for a moment seriously crossed their imaginations.   They have never at any time desired any government more free than that of Austria ; in fact, the ground always taken to his countrymen by their leader Jellacic was that the Hungarians aimed at their deliverance from the Austrian yoke, and that the duty of the Croatians was to prevent them from escaping its galling servitude.

---

* The strength of absolutism consists in the want of union of its opponents. To prevent or to impair such union is, therefore, the policy of the school of which Metternich, during his continuance in power, was always the head.

In all the negotiations held by the ministry or Diet of Hungary with Jellacic for a satisfactory settlement of the whole question between Croatia and Hungary, the Ban, waving all merely Croatian questions, plainly and invariably intimated that he would treat on no other basis than the submission of the Hungarians to the Austrian government.* But the unavoidable answers to two questions will prove conclusive on this point.   Are the Croatians at this moment dissatisfied with their present political condition?   No; for not a murmur has escaped their lips, while their leader Jellacic delights to revel at Vienna in all the luxury and splendor of the imperial court. Has their condition become ameliorated by the struggle?   No; for the recall by the emperor of the Constitution which he had given, so far from enhancing their freedom, has only deprived them of the little which they possessed.   If, then, the Croatians were struggling for liberty—if they have not only failed to obtain it, but lost even the little which they possessed, whence comes their present satisfaction and content?   Circumstances, then, would seem to warrant the conclusion that Jellacic and his Croatians, so far from contending for liberty, were the servile instruments of the Austrian government, to prevent the Hungarians from carrying into effect their purposes of maintaining their chartered independence.

The very circumstance, if true, which has been adduced, viz., the proposal of Jellacic to espouse the Hungarian cause, and engaging, on certain conditions, to effect her entire independence,† furnishes abundant and incontrovertible evidence of the hireling nature of his services ; and proves that, failing to sell himself to one of the parties, he immediately turned about, and bound himself body and soul to the other, and, in consideration of a slight modicum of court favor, sold the liberties of his country.

The Hungarians, it is true, did not establish a republic ;‡

---

* The absurdity of the intervention of the United States for the independence of Hungary can not be more forcibly illustrated than by the consideration that, of the fourteen millions of inhabitants in Hungary, nine millions desire no more free or better government than that under which they now live.

† The authenticity of this statement, however, the author is inclined to doubt.

‡ The weight of testimony would seem to have disclosed opposition to the adoption of a republican form of government. All the high nobility, it is natural to

they may never have intended to adopt such a form of government; that question was very properly as well as wisely deferred until after their independence had been achieved; but are they, on this account, less entitled to the sympathy of the American people? Is our sympathy with a people struggling to escape the yoke of arbitrary power to be dependent upon the form of government they may chose to establish when they have effected their freedom?

The Hungarians were contending for free institutions and popular government, and this not only their acts exhibited, but they did not hesitate to avow. Szemere, one of the Hungarian government, in the last session of the Diet, in July, 1849, states:

"There are three fundamental principles on which our Revolution rests, as upon so many pillars. The first principle, the reformation of our form of government. Hitherto the country, in regard to its government, was under tutelage. It was necessary then to introduce the parliamentary form of government, that the people might govern themselves, that the nation might direct its own fate.

"The second principle—the security of individual rights. It was necessary to abolish distinctions, to proclaim an equality of rights and obligations; that this principle being established, merit might be regarded, and not name and arms; that capacity might be rewarded, and not a long line of ancestry; that the prince, the count, the noble, might resign their dignities, and all who dwell in the country enjoy that equal dignity which is implied in the names *freeman, free citizen.*

suppose, would have been loth to part with their titles and other evidence of exalted birth. A large party in the country, embracing at one time both Kossuth and Görgey, were in favor of elevating the Duke of Leuchtenburg to the throne. Kossuth, after the battle of Kápolna, lost through the disaffection of the Hungarian commanders, said to Görgey, privately, " Brother, confess to me what thou desirest and wouldst have. Let me into the secret of thy wishes, and I will labor to satisfy them. Wouldst thou be dictator of Hungary? Thou shalt be it through me. Wouldst thou possess the crown of power? Thou shalt have it; only save our country!" But perhaps the greatest truth is expressed by the author of "Revelations of Russia," in his letter to M. Pulszky, when he says, "I need not tell you that Batthyányi and Kiss were the only decided aristocrats, as Szemere was the only republican, mixed up on the Hungarian side in this struggle, the remainder, whatever their tendency of opinion, occupying themselves as little with such questions as with geological theories."

" The third principle—the free development of nationalities. The free development of its nationality should be allowed to every race. Nationality is not an end, but a means for the perfecting of the man and the citizen. This development of nationalities should be limited only by a regard to the unity of the state, and to a prompt and exact administration of the government."

Popular government, security to individual rights, and a free development of nationalities, are all essential elements of freedom, and without which a republic could not exist. These are the *substance ;* the republic is but the *form.*

Is there no freedom without a republic, and does it always exist under such a form of government? Who can dispute the assertion, that vastly more liberty is to be found, at this day, under the monarchy of England than under the republic of France. The one diffuses her liberal and enlightened institutions throughout her extended empire, on which the sun never sets ; the other, while she stifles at home all freedom, both of opinion and of action, can find no more worthy object for the exercise of her military power abroad, than to crush, by force of arms, a young and feeble republic.

CHAPTER VIII.

SECOND WAR OF RADETZKY AND CHARLES ALBERT.—THE KING DENOUNCES THE ARMISTICE. — RADETZKY INVADES PIEDMONT.—THE BATTLES OF MORTARA AND NOVARA.—THE KING, DEFEATED IN BOTH BATTLES, ABDICATES, AND HIS SON, VICTOR EMANUEL, THE DUKE OF SAVOY, ELEVATED TO THE THRONE, CONCLUDES A TREATY OF PEACE WITH MARSHAL RADETZKY.

AFTER the Lombardian campaign in the summer of 1848, when, as we have seen, Marshal Radetzky defeated Charles Albert in seven battles, and drove him and his invading army across the Ticino into Piedmont, at the request of the king, an armistice was entered into between the belligerents on the 9th of August, and hostilities immediately ceased. The terms of this arrangement, granted by Marshal Radetzky at the intercession of the mediating powers, were as liberal as could have been expected, at a moment when there was no obstacle to the advance of the imperial forces to Turin, and their dictation, within the walls of that capital, of such a treaty of peace as would have severely punished their recent assailant, and thrown upon Sardinia the expenses of the war. And if the embassadors of France and England did not, by inducing the Austrian commander to abstain from taking advantage of a conquered foe, incur certain moral obligations with regard to its future course, the government of Austria certainly acquired thereby the confident expectation that the truce thus demanded would be employed for a different purpose than to refit a broken army, and prepare for the horrors of a fresh campaign. But such was the infatuation of the Italian party, that this very convention of General Salasco, which saved the north of Italy from instant occupation, was received with indignation by the people, who, after the signal defeat of their troops, looked for, and would have been satisfied with, such terms only as Charles Albert could have dictated on the ruins of Verona, with a French army at his back.

Encouraged, perhaps, by the injudicious pledges of foreign governments, the defeat of the King of Piedmont in the field had not been interpreted as it should have been, chiefly against the influence of those whose moderate support occasioned such a result. The moderate politicians had lost influence by the failure of the champion of monarchy, and the field was more open than before for the entrance of the Republicans. The ministry of Gioberti becoming too conservative, he himself "Austrianized," as was said; their services were dispensed with, and their places supplied by a ministry of a more genuine republican stamp, and whose first address was in every word an exhortation to hostilities.

The continual pressure on the people of a war expenditure, without any of the advantages of war ; the dangers arising from the prolonged excitement of the people ; the evident hopelessness of reconciling, by any mediation, claims so directly opposed as those of Sardinia and Austria ; and, finally, the chance of accelerating the effects of mediation by arms, were all advanced as reasons for action, and doubtless were all substantial ; but, as usual, prudence, on this occasion, only furnished arguments for the previous tendencies of feeling.

In a dispatch to his government, written by Mr. Abercrombie, the English minister at Turin, only four days before the denunciation of the armistice, he thus notices the failure of his efforts : " The deplorable infatuation which prevails upon the question of the realization of the kingdom of Upper Italy, of fighting the Austrians and driving them from Italy, has completely warped judgment and good sense.

" The yoke, it was argued by the people of Piedmont, which we strove so hard to break last year, is heavier than ever on the necks of our brethren in Lombardy. We went to war either to free them or without excuse, and there is now no hope of obtaining any thing for them except by force ; nor are we at peace with Austria now, but have eighty thousand men ready to assail her." It is not in human nature that such thoughts as these can have failed to produce their effect ; the war party naturally gained strength, and with it the political party most eager for the renewal of the contest, and the conclusion was readily arrived at, that it was treason to talk of peace with the foreigner ; there was one condition of peace and one only, that no " Tedesco"* should govern south of the Alps.

Another great obstacle to a pacific course arose from the position of Charles Albert himself, which, though created by his own acts, was not the less one of inextricable embarrassment. The choice of 1848 had become all but the necessity of 1849. If it had been ever right to assist the Lombardians to drive out the Austrians, was it less right to assist them now, when their own vote had given them the additional claim of subjects on his protection ? How could " the Sword of Italy,"† as he styled himself, the king of North Italy, the champion of Italian independence, with an army of eighty thousand brave men, ready to move at his command, deliberately and uncompelled renounce, without having gained a single advantage, a cause to which he was so deeply pledged ? Charles Albert was possessed of all that taste for arms and thirst for military glory, which has ever distinguished the princes of Savoy from Amadeus the First, the brave defender of the pass of Mont Cenis in the eleventh century, to Prince Eugène, the hero of Zante and the champion of Christendom against the Turks, in the eighteenth century. The Prince of Carignan, the late king of Piedmont, had served in the Spanish invasion as a volunteer, under the Duc d'Angoulême, and was present at the storming of Trocadero. With the blood of such heroic ancestry in his veins, and the remembrance of his former military exploits in his mind, the present king could, therefore, ill brook defeat, much less submit without a struggle to the signal chastisement he had received.

But a resort to war was not alone a matter of feeling with the unhappy monarch—it was one of judgment. It was to prevent the certain overthrow of his government at home that he risked the chances, desperate as they were, of subduing a government abroad. The Republicans had attained power in Piedmont, and nothing short of the liberation of Lombardy could now prevent the declaration of a republic. His embarrassing situation is graphically pictured by the king himself

---

* Tedesco, the ancient name given to the Germans by the Italians in the days of bitter hostility between the races.

† Spada d'Italia.

in an audience given the embassadors of France and England, when they sought in vain to dissuade him from his purpose. " Gentlemen," said he, " war is the desire of the nation; I must yield to this desire, if I would not expose my crown to greater dangers. I begin the war to escape the republic. If you, gentlemen, can not guarantee to me my crown, I dare not delay to employ the last measure remaining to me—the war."

These were the true reasons which induced the denunciation of the armistice; but not being of a nature to allow publicity, they differ materially from the causes advanced in a public manifesto issued on the 14th of March by the Sardinian ministry, and by them distributed to the different cabinets of Europe.

The following arguments comprise the substance of that lengthy and plausible document: That the vow of the Italian Revolution was for the restoration of national independence. The Italian governments could not oppose the desire of the people merely in obedience to the presumed rights of Austria. The Italian governments could not recognize Austria's right of possession to the Lombardo-Venetian kingdom, and further believed that her pretensions founded on treaties were not less groundless.

The Sardinian government did not shrink from the responsibility of having commenced the war of Italian independence.

Having first entered upon this war, consulting only the right and will of the nation, Sardinia had contracted more particularly the obligation of continuing it, since the fusion of the Lombardo-Venetian provinces, and of the duchies, with the Sardinian states, so unanimously willed by the people of those states.

But the days of misfortune came; Sardinia, betrayed by fortune, was obliged to bend to the necessities of the moment, and an armistice was concluded between the two armies.

The strong and unanimous protests which arose on all sides against the armistice and its consequences, convinced the Sardinian government that the thirst for national independence could not be allayed in the Italian people, either by the misfortunes they had suffered or those they were threatened with, till the last effort had been made. Some hoped that an honorable solution of the Italian question might be obtained by the observance of that military convention; but the Sardinian government soon became aware that such hope was vain, with the pretensions of Austria and her manner of interpreting and executing the said stipulation.

Austria had in several ways violated the express stipulations of the armistice, as well as the international condition of those countries which she was only to occupy in a military way, both according to the articles of the armistice and the obvious intention of the mediation.

She violated them by retaining one half of the park of siege-artillery of Peschiera, under the pretext that the Piedmontese troops had not evacuated Venice, but in reality to place Sardinia in the impossibility of recommencing the war.

She violated them by hostilities against Venice by sea and land, although the cessation of hostilities was sanctioned also for that wonderful city.

She violated them by the political restoration of the Duke of Modena, by all the government acts, and by prescribing government measures, which she published in the Lombardo-Venetian provinces and in the duchies.

She violated them by the excessive war taxes imposed upon various classes of emigrants, according to lists compiled in hatred and rage, and by the intimation to all emigrants to return within a very short time to their former abode, on pain of having all their property put under sequestration, a measure equivalent to confiscation.

She violated them by the edict of the 5th of January of this year, in which an imperial commissioner directed that deputies of the Lombardo-Venetian provinces should be elected and sent to Vienna to consult about the political reorganization of those provinces. She violated them by all those arbitrary laws, by all those fraudulent intrigues, calculated to give color to the assertion that the Revolution was completely stifled in the provinces occupied by her, and that the desire and love for the old state of things had been reawakened.

She violated them, at the same time infringing the eternal principles of right which regulate every civil compact, and treating with contempt the sacred feeling of humanity, by allowing her marshal and his lieutenants to have recourse in the territories occupied by them to the most atrocious exercise of violence, to the most outrageous rapine and most provoking insolence.

We, therefore, come to this necessary conclusion, that Austria has only seen in the benevolent interposition of the mediating powers an expedient to aggravate Sardinia with excessive charges, to ruin the occupied provinces, to drive the generous populations to desperate attempts, and to sow seeds of discord through the whole peninsula.

In such a state of things, the Sardinian government has felt it its duty seriously to consider its own condition of right and fact, its relation with the mediating powers, and the general condition of Italy, for the purpose of taking a course consistent with its honor and its most legitimate rights.

After all these considerations, the Sardinian government saw that there was but one course open to it; it had no choice but war, and it decided accordingly.*

Such were the proclaimed views of the Sardinian government, and the motives which impelled it to the recommencement of hostilities; but, to a proper appreciation of the controversy, it will be necessary, *audire alteram partem*, to refer to the views of the Austrian government, and the light in which they regarded the conduct of Sardinia, in the denunciation of the armistice.

The following are, in substance, the opinions of the imperial government, as soon as advised of the renunciation of the armistice, as published on the 18th of March, 1849.

" The armistice concluded on the 9th of August last with Sardinia has been renounced by that power, and consequently Austria must a second time draw the sword in defense of her just rights.

" In this war, now unhappily inevitable, she has the world for witness, that she had already done every thing to avoid it that her honor and her duty permitted.

" When, in the month of August last, the glorious imperial

* Piedmontese Gazette, March 14, 1849; Galignani's Messenger, March 19, 1849.

arms had obtained several decisive victories over the Piedmontese army, it was King Charles Albert who proposed the establishment of a permanent peace. It depended on the will of the imperial government to pursue the enemy to the utmost, and to dictate peace to him on his own territory. But Austria, animated by a sincere love of peace, gave to the world a new and irrefragable proof of her moderation, by checking the march of the victorious armies to the frontiers of Piedmont, in order to show that she had only taken up arms for the legitimate defense of the integrity of her territory. The armistice was, therefore, granted to the King of Sardinia, and a plenipotentiary named to open negotiations for peace.

"After a sanguinary conflict of six months, attended with the greatest sacrifices, the valiant armies of Austria defeated the enemy, and the conqueror restrained himself to demanding, independently of a just war indemnity, only what belonged to him through God and his right. No one will deny that such conduct bore the impress of the highest moderation, and the formal love of peace. The conduct of Sardinia, since the conclusion of the armistice, has been in opposition to this mode of proceeding.

"The Sardinian fleet, which, according to article fourth of the armistice, was to have quitted Venice immediately to return to the Sardinian States, did not withdraw until a late period, and not definitely. It has never quitted the Adriatic Sea, and is there at this moment. The manifest violation of the armistice on the part of Sardinia has alone placed Venice in a state to resist the imperial arms.

"Not content with this, Sardinia went further, by granting openly, and with the armistice in force, to this rebel city considerable sums in monthly payments. In the capital of Piedmont, there was formed a Lombardian *consulta*, composed, in a great measure, of the members of the government expelled from Milan. The court of Turin regarded it as a legal authority, and furnished it with the means of keeping up under its protection and its eye discord and hatred on the neighboring Austro-Italian provinces, and raising all imaginable obstacles to the efforts made by the imperial government to re-establish tranquillity and calm the public mind. Magyar emissaries and Polish refugees were also well received and protected at the court of Turin. Their object evidently was to establish a close fraternity between the Italian Revolution and the criminal party which had lighted up civil war in our country ; to bring about the dissolution of the Austrian monarchy. The official language of the Sardinian government was always in accordance with this manner of acting, which denoted the most hostile intentions.

When, at the commencement of the last month, the Legislative Assembly commenced its labors at Turin, Austria heard with indignation that the king had announced, in a solemn speech, a kingdom of Upper Italy, and had, without disguise, excited the Austro-Italian provinces to rise again and revolt against their legitimate government.

" Whatever may be the results, Austria can testify that she did not provoke the war, which the pride of her enemies force her to sustain. Austria has not been guided by ambitious views, has never coveted a foreign crown, has wished only to preserve that which belongs to her, and to defend against unjust pretensions the integrity of the monarchy acknowledged by solemn treaties,"* &c.

Hostilities were thus resolved on by the government of Sardinia, but never was a people so ill prepared, both morally and physically, to engage in such a conflict with one of the great military powers of Europe.

At the moment of the commencement of the war, the army might be said to have been without a general ; the government without a Minister of War ; and the troops in a state of the utmost moral and material inferiority.

The infantry regiments were totally devoid of men accustomed to war ; special permits had been given a large number of the old soldiers† to return to their homes, and new recruits, not inured to service, were enrolled in their places. The reorganization of a fourth battalion for every regiment was ordered ; and the recruits, instead of making up these new battalions, were divided among the old companies. In conse-

---

* Galignani's Messenger, March 23, 1849. Wiener Zeitung, March 18, 1849.

† Those who had survived the last campaign had been so much discredited and abused by the prints, that it was not possible to get them to serve.

quence of this, a general *dislocation* of the corps of officers took place ; soldiers were then separated from their officers, and officers from their men, to the total destruction of that mutual confidence so essential to the *morale* of an army. This change, which so completely disorganized the whole infantry, took place between the 11th and 14th of March. On the 15th, and after notice of the renunciation of the armistice had been given, and when the movements of concentration had commenced, the commanding general, who had been made answerable by the Chambers for the success of the campaign, ordered the re-establishment of the old corps. This measure, which was executed in great haste, served but to create still greater confusion. Owing to the sudden increase of the army by the accession of recruits, it became necessary to double the number of officers, and it proved difficult to fill the post of sergeants from the list of orderlies. These newly-promoted sergeants were totally deficient in military instruction, and were consequently inefficient in the administration and discipline of their companies. The greater part of the officers recently promoted were in the same condition.* A great number of Lombards, Tuscans, Neapolitans, and other foreigners, had been enlisted into the corps of officers ; and while the majority of these young men were totally ignorant of all that concerned the service, their promotion, through favor, over the heads of experienced and native officers had created the greatest jealousy and dissatisfaction.

In the introduction of that crowd of officers from all parts of Italy and other countries, the Piedmontese military character had been lost, without being replaced by any equally martial and efficient.

Nearly all the generals and staff officers were unacquainted with their brigades, regiments, and battalions. General Perron, who was killed on the field of Novara, received the command of his division just three days before the battle, and was a perfect stranger to the regiments under his orders. The new laws of promotion, therefore, had only created discontent, without procuring able officers. The chief command, after having

---

* Le Spectateur Militaire.

been tendered to and declined by many distinguished French generals, was conferred on a Polish officer, Chrzanowsky, to whom the war of 1831 against the Russians had given, as it had to many others, a certain reputation, which was due less to their talents than to the general sympathy then felt for unhappy Poland.   Chrzanowsky possessed a knowledge of the art and theory of war, and a familiarity with the details ; and this was the only superiority he enjoyed over the Piedmontese generals, like Bava and Sonnaz, who had held commands in the last campaign.   But he had not the real knowledge and qualities necessary for the head of an army ; he was not sufficiently imbued with the great principles of war, while he wanted decision and vigor in resolution, and activity and vigilance in execution.   To command an army or to govern a state, it is equally indispensable to have a profound knowledge of the character of those whom the leader is thus called upon to direct ; but Chrzanowsky was a stranger to the manners, and even to the language of the country ; he did not seek to know his army, or to be known by it ; and how could his men have confidence in one whose name they could scarce pronounce, and of whose great deeds and capacity they had never heard ?   Of a character cold, and an exterior neither imposing or military, there was nothing in him which could possibly excite the least enthusiasm in the minds of his soldiers ; he never showed himself, but passed his time in his cabinet, engaged in the details of organization, which completely absorbed him, and in which consisted his principal merit as a commander-in-chief.

The commissary's department was confided to inexperienced hands, sufficient means of transportation were needed to convey the military stores, so that provisions were wanting in the very first days of the campaign.

The reorganization of the medical department was greatly neglected, and only the day before the recommencement of hostilities the medical officers received orders concerning their further destination, and many did not join their divisions until after the battle of Novara.

The service of the trains was insufficient for the wants of the army.   A corps of militia had been organized for the purpose of increasing the means of transportation, but its bad organization rendered it almost useless.

The artillery had always justified its reputation, and for the reason that it had been subjected to less changes than the other corps ; but they, like the cavalry, were entirely too few in number, and thus created great disproportion in the army. The corps of engineers consisted almost entirely of new soldiers, and their *parc*, as well as that of the pioneers, was defective. On the day of the recommencement of hostilities, orders were given to employ the horses of the artillery in the *parc* of the pioneers, and the *parc* of the artillery was served by the horses of the militia trains.

Besides these defects, a strong germ of demoralization was already going on in the ranks of the army. The political complexion of affairs had greatly changed ; the enthusiasm of the "holy war," which had urged them throughout the last campaign, was extinguished ; the sad recollections of Milan, which had produced such painful impressions on the troops, were not yet effaced ; the holy father now disavowed the standards which he had blessed during the preceding year, and who could say, thought the superstitious soldier, that the Almighty himself had not withdrawn his favor and support.

Although the Piedmontese army labored under these defects in composition and organization, a still greater obstacle to success arose from the disposition and direction of the troops. Of the hundred and thirty-five thousand men forming, as was said, the total effective force, one hundred thousand only (and this was already a large calculation) were fit for active service; and this force was, at the moment of entering upon the campaign, reduced by sickness and other causes to about eighty thousand men.

But the greatest difficulty of all consisted in the fact that this force, instead of being concentrated on the most important points, was spread over a wide extent of country, stretching from Arone to Sarzane,* and separated by formidable rivers and mountains.

Opposed to this ill-composed army and incompetent officers

---

* The same error was committed the preceding year on the Mincio.

was the Austrian, one of the most efficient and best-disciplined armies in Europe.

As to their infantry, it presented an incontestible superiority to that of the Piedmontese ; recruited with great care, it was composed of large and able-bodied men, who had served in the ranks five or six years, were accustomed to discipline, familiar with all the details of the service, and, for the most part, inured to war.

The artillery and cavalry, though not physically superior to those of the Piedmontese, possessed in a high degree that in which their enemy was deficient — discipline, and without which their service was comparatively unavailing. The officers of the different arms, particularly those of the staff, were vastly better instructed than those of the Piedmontese ; and the soldiers, if inferior in martial spirit to their more impetuous foes, were actuated by a courage firm and indomitable, and which, under their chiefs, was of more consequence than the wildest bravery.

Nothing can exhibit in a more striking degree the force of good military institutions, than the comparison between Austrian and Italian troops.

Austria, with men of a nature less energetic, of a character cold, of a spirit heavy, knew how to make better soldiers, more formidable armies, and to become a more powerful empire ; while Italy, whose inhabitants were individually quite equal, if not superior to the Germans and the people of the north, possessed always the worst armies of Europe, and formed, in general, the most weak, inefficient, and ill-governed of the continental nations.

The same care and attention was bestowed by the Austrians to the minutest details of the service ; their trains, horses, weapons, and, in short, all accoutrements, were ample, and in the finest order.   The commissary's department was most admirably served, so that each Austrian soldier carried in his sack from two to three days' bread ; while the Piedmontese, on their own soil, were left to perish of hunger, or to subsist by plunder, as they did not fail to do after the battle was over.

The one hundred thousand men which composed the Austrian army, when reduced by a deduction of invalids, amount-

ed to about eighty thousand, formed six *corps d'armée*, each
of sixteen to eighteen thousand men. Each of these corps,
complete in troops of all arms, was composed of two divisions;
this organization in corps and divisions, of an effective not too
extensive, was preferable to that of the Piedmontese, in rendering the Austrian army more manageable, and easier of command.*

These fine corps were commanded by Generals Wratislaw,
D'Aspre, Appel, Thurn, and Wocher, all officers of experience
in war, and having, at the same time, able generals of division under them.

By far the greatest advantage possessed by the Imperialists
in the contest was that of being under the command in chief
of one who (if Wellington be excepted) may, without injustice
to any other, be called the most distinguished captain of the
age. Joseph, Count Radetzky, was born at Trebnitz, in Bohemia, in 1766, and began his military career as private cadet
in the regiment of Francis's cuirassiers in 1784. Gradually
rising through the grades of regular promotion, in 1799 he obtained the rank of lieutenant colonel of the general staff, a
post in which he was enabled to render the allied armies important services in their struggles with Napoleon, especially
on the battle-fields of Leipsic, of Culm, and of Brienne. In
1805, he commanded, as major general, a cavalry brigade in
the army in Italy. Having distinguished himself on the famous battle-field of Aspern,† under that distinguished general, the Archduke Charles, he was raised to the rank of field-
marshal lieutenant. In 1813, he acted as chief of the general
staff in the grand army of invasion under Prince Schwartzenberg, a position which required not only the qualities of a
soldier, but the intelligence of the diplomatist and minister.
General of cavalry in 1829, he was appointed to the command
in the Lombardo-Venetian kingdom in 1832, and in the year
1836 was promoted to the dignity of field-marshal, the highest rank in the service.‡

Although he had previously held high commands, and dis-

---

* *Compagne de Novare*, by the author of Custoza.
† The only battle in which Napoleon, on an open plain, and with a superior
force, was ever compelled to retreat.   ‡ Blackwood's Magazine, 1851.

charged important functions in the wars against Napoleon, yet
never, before the campaign of 1847, had he been intrusted
with the full command before an enemy.   Then it was, at an
age when the great proportion of mankind have passed from
this transitory stage, or, if they still linger on the shores of
time, are imbecile or unfit for active life, and especially for a
career in arms, that he really commenced to make for himself
a name, and to wreathe his brow with undying laurels.

One of the brightest pages of Austrian history will record
the deeds and triumphs of the old hero of '83, the idol of his
army, the determined soldier of an empire which seemed crum-
bling into atoms, the one prop of Austria in Italy, doing his
duty, whoever might fail in theirs, unmoved by the political
storms which surrounded him ; master of the ground he stood
on, and determined to preserve that, at least, though all the
rest be lost in the vortex of revolution, and though at the end
there should remain no crowned master to reward him for the
effort.

Radetzky's proclamations and addresses are models both of
sentiment and style.   Nowhere is more complete justice rendered to the merits of the Sardinian officers, to the bravery of
the Savoyard troops, to the courage of the princes who led
them on, than in the official reports of Radetzky.   While most
of the Piedmontese generals and officers found fault with each
other, in the marshal's reports alone was ample justice done
to his antagonists.   " The Piedmontese and Savoyards," said
he, in his official report, " fought like lions ; and the unfortunate Charles Albert threw himself madly into the thickest of
the danger upon every possible opportunity.   His two sons
also fought with brilliant courage."

The enthusiasm of the army for Radetzky knows no bounds ;
a kind of tender familiarity, tempered by veneration, renders
the manifestation of their sentiments for him inexpressibly
touching.   Upon one occasion, the anecdote is related, as the
marshal passed down the ranks, he perceived a soldier bare-
headed.   Riding up to him, "Where's your *chako*,* friend?"
asked he.   The man looked confused, and avowed he had no

---

* Cap.

*Feldziechen,** and therefore was ashamed to cover his head.
"Is that all?" rejoined Radetzky, smiling; and, taking off his
own hat, he divided the little verdant branch it bore, and,
"There, my friend," said he, tendering one half to the soldier,
"take that." The man pressed it to his lips, and, with tears
in his eyes, "Herr Marshal," answered he, with deep emotion, "not even to go to my children, should I ever have any,
shall it ever leave me. In my grave, upon my heart, there is
its place," and an irrepressible burst of applause from all
around approved the feeling. Many of the soldiers who died
of their wounds after the battle of Novara seemed almost paid
for the sacrifice of life by a shake of the hand from Radetzky,
and, by a proud glance of the eye, seemed to say, " I die content."

The marshal's great readiness to recognize the merit of others particularly distinguishes him. Of his quartermaster-gen-
eral, Hess, who served him through the Italian campaign, he
wrote to his wife, "If *I* have all the glory, *he* has all the
merit."

He was a boy of sixteen when Maria Therese died, and followed the whole of the two first campaigns against the Turks,
serving under Laudohn at the siege of Belgrade, and acting
as aide-de-camp to Field-marshal de Lacey. What Hess was
to him he was to De Lacey first, and afterward to Schwartzenberg.

Radetzky has served five sovereigns of the house of Austria
(Joseph the Second, Leopold the Second, Francis the First,
Ferdinand the First, and Francis Joseph), and two emperors of
the name of Joseph, between whom lie three generations, has
he seen in the thick of the *mêlée ;* Joseph the Second on the
Turkish frontiers, and Francis Joseph in Italy. Few can
boast of such a well-filled life; and, whatever danger threatens, Austria may feel secure, so long as she can, with the poet,
say to her octogenarian champion,†

"In deinem Lager ist Oesterreich"‡—*In thy camp is Austria.*

Agreeably to the stipulations entered into between the bel-

---

* A small sprig of green (usually oak), with which Austrian soldiers are required, on all gala occasions, to decorate their caps.

† Baroness Blaze de Bury.   ‡ Grillparzer.

ligerents upon the close of the late campaign, notice was to be given of the denunciation of the armistice eight days before the recommencement of hostilities; and, as the King of Piedmont seemed to have a peculiar fancy for opening the war on the 20th of March, a major of engineers (De Cordona) was hurried off on the 12th in all haste, to serve the notice on Radetzky, even before their own commander, at his head-quarters at Alexandria, had received the slightest intimation on the subject.

The Piedmontese ministry, in their remarkable prudence, had failed to advise their own general sooner, for fear that their intentions might possibly be communicated to Radetzky, and their army taken by surprise, but at the same time did not hesitate to commence a war, and declare a levy *en masse* of the Lombards and Venetians, notwithstanding their treasury was entirely empty, and no means of replenishing it either provided or even suggested.

The news of the denunciation of the armistice, although generally expected, struck with profound astonishment the country people throughout Piedmont, but failed to produce the slightest change in the disposition of the army. At Rome, in Tuscany, and other parts of Italy, it produced the utmost excitement, and a great exaltation in words; they elevated to the skies the names of Charles Albert and Piedmont, but no one proposed to offer any more substantial proofs of their approbation. The war-message, as soon as delivered to the old marshal at Milan, spread with telegraphic rapidity through the city, to the infinite delight of the garrison and the great consternation of the inhabitants.

Eight bands of music played in the evening the national anthem before the Villa Realle (the quarters of Radetzky), which was responded to with loud vivats in honor of the emperor and the venerable general by the assembled crowd. The same sentiment of joy again manifested itself in the theatre Della Scala, when the national hymn was again loudly called for and sung, amid the most enthusiastic applause of the audience.*

---

* When the armistice was denounced by Sardinia on the 12th of March, one would have supposed that to the garrison of Milan had been promised some over-

Marshal Radetzky, on the same day, issued a stirring order
to his troops, advising them that their " fondest desire had
been fulfilled, the armistice had ceased," summoning them
" to follow their old leader from victory to victory," and concluding with the inspiring injunction, " forward, then, soldiers! Turin is the watch-word; there alone shall we find
peace."*

Radetzky, without expecting so sudden a resumption of hos-

whelming joy. Through all ranks the news flew like wild-fire, and on all faces
only an enthusiastic anticipation of glory was to be read. " Toward evening,"
says an eye-witness, " the court of the Villa Realle (the residence of Radetzky)
was crowded with soldiers and their officers. Torches lighted up with their red
glare the house itself and the surrounding trees, and cast their flickering rays upon
the gold embroidery of the uniforms and upon the glittering arms. Eight bands
of music, followed by crowds of soldiers, marched into the court from different
sides, and, animated by spontaneous and simultaneous enthusiasm, gave a serenade to the marshal, to thank him for promising the troops that they should go to
Turin. ' Turin must be taken! Father Radetzky has said it; and what he has
said is as good as done!' These were the words upon every lip, accompanied by
thundering vivats. At last, when the field-marshal came forth upon the balcony
and looked around with his good-natured intelligent eyes, and spoke words of
heartfelt kindness to his children, the air was positively rent by acclamations, and
the phrensy of delight would not cease. Over many a bronzed cheek did I watch
the tears of emotion roll, and though I have often witnessed such scenes, often
heard the outbreak of popular feeling, never again shall I probably behold such
enthusiasm as this. With such an army, victory is sure. Of all those thousands
of hearts, there is not one that does not beat in unison with the heart of the leader; and, confident and trusting, they have but one will, to conquer with him, or
with him suffer defeat, but in good or evil fortune to bear together all."

    * The following order of the day was published at Milan, on the 12th:
"Soldiers! your most ardent wishes are fulfilled. The enemy has denounced
the armistice. A second time he stretches out his hand to grasp the crown of
Italy. But let him be taught that six months have not in any degree lessened
your fidelity to your emperor and king, or your bravery in supporting him. Having come forth from the gates of Verona, flying from victory to victory, and driven
the enemy back within his frontiers, you generously granted him an armistice.
While declaring that he was preparing to make pacific propositions, he was arming himself for renewing the war. We are all armed, and that peace which we
generously offered him we will gain by force in his own capital. Soldiers! the
conflict will not be long. It is the same enemy whom we have beaten at Saint
Lucia, Somma Campagna, Custoza, Volta, and before the gates of Milan. God
is with us, for our cause is just! Up once more, soldiers! follow your chief, who
has grown gray in arms, to war and victory. I shall be a witness of your exploits. It will be the last inspiring act of my long life, as a soldier, if in the capital of a disloyal enemy I can decorate the breasts of my brave comrades with the
insignia of their valor, gained by blood and glory. Let our war-cry then be,
' Forward, soldiers, to Turin!' It is there that we shall find the peace for which
we fight. Long live the emperor! Our country forever!   RADETZKY."

tilities, was nevertheless not taken by surprise, as the cabinet of Turin had been led to believe. Had he even supposed that the armistice was the end of the war, the accession of a democratic ministry would have undeceived him; while the language of the Piedmontese press, the recent Lombard emigration, and their partiality for the new cabinet, all indicated that a declaration of war would not long be postponed. Besides, Piedmont abounded in spies in the pay of Austria, many of them figuring in the highest circles, and from whom the projects of the government, however secretly concocted, were not concealed.

Nevertheless, the position of Radetzky, at the moment of the denunciation of the armistice, seemed difficult, and was, in truth, embarrassing; but he took his course boldly, and his able dispositions completely confounded the unfortunate Chrzanowsky.

The former was surrounded by many dangers, but he occupied himself with one alone, the most important, and which, if successfully overcome, would relieve him from all difficulty. If he evacuated Lombardy and the duchies, concentrating all his forces on the Ticino, crossing into Piedmont, giving battle immediately to the Sardinian army, he could destroy it—all would be finished—for, Piedmont vanquished, all the other insurrections would end with it.*

This plan, marked by the ability and boldness of its conception, was not less distinguished by the success and brilliancy of its execution. The Austrian army in Lombardy was composed of six corps: one rested upon the Mincio, the Adige, and in the Venetian kingdom; the five others, leaving garrisons only in the citadel of Milan, and in Brescia, Bergamo, Modena, at the *tête de pont* at Brescello, and in the citadel of Placentia (ten thousand men in all), were directed to repair forthwith to the confluence of the Ticino and the Po.

All orders had been given with so much promptitude and secrecy, and all the precautions so well taken, that, in the night of the 19th to the 20th, the army was all concentrated around Pavia, ready to take the offensive the very moment the armis-

---

* Campagne de Novara.

tice should expire, without the enemy's having any idea of the great concentrating movements that were progressing throughout all the roads of Lombardy. Radetzky, it is true, had said, like Scipio of old, that he would carry the war into the enemy's country; but every one refused to credit the assertion. The best method, at times, to distract or divert the attention from the true object, is to divulge one's projects; and principally from the fact that the marshal had announced his intention to take the offensive, by the most public and repeated declarations, persons in general, and the Piedmontese staff in particular, chose to remain perfectly incredulous.

The marshal had left Milan on the 17th, by the route of Melegnano and Lodi, to take up his head-quarters at St. Angelo, in the midst of his troops, arriving from all quarters; and the Milanese, seeing him issue with his troops from the Roman gate, readily conceived that he was retreating on the Adda, and this circumstance confirmed the Piedmontese in their error."*

The city of Milan had been left without troops, but the citadel in the suburbs placed in a state of defense, and provided with three thousand men and one hundred and sixty cannons pointing against the devoted city.

Marshal Radetzky was advised with sufficient exactness of the position of the Piedmontese forces, and knew that in debouching from Pavia he would cut their line in two, isolate all that portion of the troops on the right bank of the Po, and that, in bearing down rapidly against the principal mass, he could, in a single battle, terminate the campaign. Expedition was necessary for the execution of this plan, and it was not neglected.

On the morning of the 20th, two bridges were constructed by the pioneers over the Ticino, below the permanent bridge at Pavia. At eleven o'clock the corps of D'Aspre entered the isle opposite Pavia by the three bridges, and at twelve the armistice expired.

The troops then advanced in three columns on the road to Garlasco, crossing the Gravillone at three different points;

---

* Campagne de Novara.

that of the right waded the stream, the centre passed over the
bridge of boats on the route between Pavia and Piedmont, and
the left over a bridge of their own construction below.

All this was accomplished without encountering the slightest obstruction from the enemy. The division of Ramorino,
which ought to have occupied La Cava, and overlooked the
Gravillone, had remained on the right of the Po, in the vicinity of Casteggio, and had sent four battalions only on the left
bank ; one toward Zerboló, another to La Cava, and two at
Mezzana-Corte, to guard the bridge. The battalion of Zerboló,
cut off from Mezzana-Corte, retired in disorder toward Mortara ;
that which was at La Cava, and which approached the Gravillone, after exchanging a few shots with the Austrian corps, retreated in great haste toward Mezzana-Corte.

D'Aspre advanced in the direction of Garlasco, followed by
D'Appel, who was succeeded by Wratislaw, marching to the
right toward Zerboló ; while Thurn, who crossed the fourth,
proceeded to the left, toward La Cava. The reserve passed
also on the same day ; and at night the whole army encamped
within the territory of the enemy, the right at Zerboló, the
centre at Gropello, the left at Dorno, and the reserve a little
beyond the Gravillone.

One brigade of reserve rested at Pavia, to cover the rear of
the army ; two others, which did not pass that day, one belonging to the corps of Wratislaw, was stationed near Magenta, to deceive the enemy with the idea that a complete *corps
d'armée*, or some considerable mass of troops, remained at that
point, and which descended toward Bereguardo, to cross the
Ticino during the day of the 21st, and rejoin its corps. The
other, which made part of the reserve, was not to have reached
Pavia until the 22d. The total force of Austrians now in Piedmont, entering and about to enter, was sixty-nine or seventy
thousand, with two hundred and ten cannons ; and Chrzanowsky was not able to bring in opposition a greater number.

While the Austrian army entered so tranquilly into Piedmont from Pavia, the Piedmontese army awaited it near Buffalora, or believed it to be in retreat on the Adda.

On the morning of the expiration of the armistice, the five
divisions destined by Chrzanowsky either to cross or to defend

the Ticino, were at their posts.* The division of the Duke of Genoa in advance of Trecate, with one advanced guard near to the bridge of Buffalora; the division Perrone to the left, at Romentino and Galliate; the division Bes to the right, at Cerano and Castel Novo; the division Durando to the right also, but more in the rear around Vespolate; the division of reserve near Novara, on the road to Mortara. The brigade Solaroli was stationed on the extreme left, between Oleggio and Bellinzago, connected to the division Perrone by four battalions. At last the Lombard division, under the orders of Ramorino, which ought to have been at La Cava, with an advanced guard on the Gravellone, to keep clear the route to Bereguardo, where they would meet a part of the cavalry of the division of Bes, and four battalions placed under Vigevano to relieve these two divisions.

Ramorino had been ordered to suffer nothing to prevent his ascertaining the amount of the enemy's force by which he might be opposed, and, if not too considerable, to endeavor to get possession of Pavia on the morning of the 21st, and, if successful, to take the route immediately for Lodi. If, on the contrary, the Austrians debouched in too great force from Pavia, he should retard their march as much as possible, without endangering his command, and retire upon Mortara or upon Nazzaro; from either place he could easily reunite himself with the army, which, apprised by the cannonade, could advance immediately between Trumello and Mortara by the two par-

---

* General Chrzanowski, the commander-in-chief of the Piedmontese army, addressed to it the following proclamation, dated Alexandria the 14th:

"Soldiers! the days of the truce have passed away, and our wishes are granted. Charles Albert again comes to place himself at the head of your brave ranks. The armistice is renounced, and the days of glory for the arms of Italy are about to recommence. Soldiers! this is the supreme moment! Soldiers! march to the battle, which must be to certain victory. Following the example of your princes who fight in your ranks, and the voice of your king who leads you on, march, and prove to Europe that you are not only the bulwark of Italy, but the avengers of her rights. At the approach of your arms the oppressed populations will change their complainings into cries of joy, and our brothers, once more saved, will fly into your arms, participating in the intoxication of the triumph gained. Soldiers! the greater your alacrity may be, the more prompt will be your victory. The braver the battle, the sooner you will return into the bosoms of your families, crowned with laurels, and proud of having a free, independent, and happy country!"

allel routes extending in this direction. It has been seen that Ramorino entirely neglected these orders of the general commander, and remained beyond the Po, while the general supposed him to be at La Cava.

At mid-day the division of the Duke of Genoa was in mass opposite the bridge of Buffalora; no troops were to be seen thence to the river; nothing was heard from the direction of Pavia, and they remained in ignorance of the Austrians on the Lower Ticino.

About one o'clock it was determined to make a recognizance as far as Magenta. The king wished to cross first with a company of riflemen, and to have the honor of being the first to tread upon the soil of the enemy. They arrived at Magenta without encountering an enemy, or, in fact, seeing any, except at a distance a few pickets of cavalry. The enemy, it was evident, was not in this quarter, and the irresistible conclusion was, that he could only be either on the Adda or toward Pavia, and that Milan was just as free as the Upper Ticino.

In either case there was but one course to take, and that was to cross with the whole army at once between Milan and Pavia, and to advance immediately in the direction of Lodi.* This was precisely the maneuver which the Austrians were at that moment executing; but the commander of the Piedmontese had neither the intelligence nor the decision of Radetzky, and the absence of the enemy, instead of increasing his confidence, only augmented his irresolution.

He left the Duke of Genoa at Magenta, recrossed the Ticino with the king and his staff, ordered back the division Perrone, which he had advanced to the bridge to assist in the recognizance, and returned himself to Trecate to search or to await news.

---

* On the 17th of March, five days after the armistice had been denounced, Prince Eugène of Savoy issued a proclamation throughout the Lombardo-Venetian provinces, not only calling on the subjects of Austria to take up arms against their sovereign, but trying to force them into doing so by the following passage: "Each man who, within the space of five days after the promulgation of this decree, does not enroll himself upon the lists opened for that purpose, will be looked upon as a deserter, and punished as such according to the laws established against deserters in the part of the country to which he belongs. No plea for exemption from service will be admitted, except bodily infirmities positively preventing from bearing arms."

The inhabitants of Magenta having received the Piedmontese very coldly, refusing them quarters and provisions, and affording them no intelligence as to the movements of the enemy, the king dreading a similar reception at Milan, his ardor
to engage the enemy upon the soil of Lombardy diminished,
while his anxiety to know that they had not penetrated into
Piedmont increased.   On returning to Trecate, nothing could
be ascertained ; all were in utter ignorance of the movements
of the enemy.   One general, who felt the gravity of their situation and the value of time, kept all in readiness for action
around him, while he himself rode as rapidly as possible toward
Vigevano, to know as quickly as he could any thing of interest which may have transpired.   The Polish commander of the
Piedmontese in the mean time does nothing ; with the coolest
resignation he awaits intelligence, and sleeps tranquilly until
eight o'clock.   At nine an officer of the staff of Bes hastens
to announce the passage of the Austrians, and the absence of
Ramorino; and a little after, he receives, through his spies,
confirmation of the intelligence of the concentration of the
whole army of the enemy in the direction of Pavia.

The tardy announcement of the approach of the Austrians,
and the absence of the Lombard division from the post assigned, were without doubt both disastrous circumstances for the
Piedmontese ; but they were not entitled to the importance
which it was desired to be attributed to them.   With a little
activity, or with some modification of the projected manœuvers,
and by casting themselves before the enemy, it was easy to
repair one of these disadvantages ; and as for the other, the
absence of the Lombard division, not much confidence was
placed on those troops, and it is not probable that their co-operation would have changed much the course of events.

Ramorino, delivered over to a council of war, has been condemned to death and executed, but his blood can not wash
away from the skirts of the commander-in-chief the gross negligence with which he was justly chargeable.   Why did he not
order the occupation of La Cava before the 20th ?   Why confide a post of any importance to an officer in whom he could
place no confidence ?   Why remain many days without communicating with him, and assuring himself that his orders

would be obeyed? Why not have kept up a constant and efficient guard along the whole line of the Ticino to the Po, on the 19th, and even on the 20th, in the morning? Why did he not establish a telegraphic communication by signals or by relays of cavalry, to report promptly, instead of awaiting to be apprised of the enemy's presence by the report of his cannon?

Despite of all that had occurred, the project of Chrzanowsky of throwing himself before the enemy between Trumello and Mortara, remained still practicable, provided it was executed with great promptness and decision—for such were the traits of the enemy with whom he had to contend.

The country in which war was about to decide the fate of Italy, at least for a season, was a narrow strip of land comprised between the Ticino and the Sesia, inclosed on the south by the Po, and bounded on the north by the Alps, near the Lake Majora—its length about sixty-eight English miles, its breadth about twenty-five. It cuts perpendicularly the route from Milan to Turin. The Sesia runs an equal distance from both capitals, both situated on the left bank of the Po, about ninety miles apart—washing the walls of Verciel, which it leaves on the right, empties itself into the Po between Casale and Valence. The Ticino, whose course has been already indicated, runs, for a great distance, nearly parallel with the Sesia. Novara occupies the centre of this strip of land; below Novara is Vigevano, Mortara, and La Cava, which command the passage of the Ticino in the vicinity of Pavia, and that of the Po at Mezzana-Corte; above is situated Momo, Borgomanero, and Avona. It is a country but slightly broken, but covered and cut up by small rivers and canals, of which the general direction is parallel to those of the Ticino and the Sesia.

One of these lines of water, a canal called Roggia Biraga, passes about two or three miles below Mortara, and divides the two routes from that city to Pavia and to Vigevano. It was behind this canal, toward the road to Pavia, between Trumello and Mortara, that Chrzanowsky proposed to concentrate all his forces, and await the enemy; and he could have accomplished it without difficulty by marching without delay; but he lost time, and the combinations which he made of his troops were most unfortunate. Durando and Bes were the only corps

II.   R

placed under orders to move during the night; the former to advance before Mortara, the latter before Vigevano. The Duke of Savoy, Perrone, and the Duke of Genoa, were not to take up the line of march until the next morning; nor Solaroli, who had to descend from the bridge of Buffalora. These dispositions, slowly and irresolutely made, indicated that Chrzanowsky, at the moment when he took them, doubted whether the Austrians would ever abandon the Ticino and advance toward the Sesia; and that, if they should, he believed they would be checked by the heads of columns during the day of the 21st, and that concentration could take place during the morning of the 22d. Durando arrived late in the morning at Mortara, where he was joined, in the afternoon, by the Duke of Savoy. Bes, on his part, was at Vigevano at daybreak, and took up a good position in advance at La Sforzesca, and pushed an advanced guard as far as Borgo St. Siro, to observe the passage of the Ticino at Bereguardo.

On the morning of the 21st, the Austrian army advanced, as they had done on the previous day, in three columns, the left flank from Dona to Mortara, the centre from Gropello to Gamboló, and the right column from Zerboló to Vigevano. This last, consisting of the second corps and the van-guard division under Wohlgemuth, arrived about one o'clock at Borgo St. Siro, where it discovered the Piedmontese van-guard (which, as has been seen, was sent forward by General Bes) sustained by the brigade Strassaldo, which formed the head of the column of Wratislaw, which reached the spot about the same time, and attacked the enemy.

The Piedmontese, too feeble to confront such superior forces, gradually gave way, but slowly, and continually fighting. At St. Vittore they found two battalions, placed intermediately there to afford them support; and both together retired in good order to La Sforzesca. Bes, advised of the arrival of Durando at Mortara, recalled the brigade from Casale, but this brigade lost the way, and did not arrive in time. Nevertheless, Bes, with another brigade, two squadrons of cavalry, a battery, and some riflemen, resisted the enemy successfully, although more numerous, and checked all his attacks against La Sforzesca, which he endeavored to turn.

Repelled several times by the bayonets of the seventeenth
and twenty-third infantry, and charged then by the cavalry,
which threw them into disorder, the Austrians gave way, leaving a number of prisoners in the hands of the enemy; but,
opportunely re-enforced at this time by a part of the brigade
Gorger, which had been left the day before in Lombardy, and
which, agreeably to orders, were to cross at this time the Ticino at Bereguardo, they were enabled to maintain their positions.

During this time, Wratislaw, having arrived with the great
bulk of his corps at Gamboló, sent over a column in the evening to attack the Piedmontese detachment placed on the route
of Vigevano; but this attack was without success, and that
column soon retired.   The partial success had raised the spirits of the troops, and dispelled the disheartening impression
produced by the unexpected entrance of the Austrians and the
treachery of Ramorino.

Up to this point in the engagement the tide of war had been
favorable to the Piedmontese—they had met the enemy, and
had been able to sustain themselves before them; but, in order to have completed their triumph, they should have attacked
the enemy at Gamboló, as they would have had time the same
evening, after the arrival of their troops; or, what was still
better, they should have placed themselves immediately behind
La Biraga, in order to facilitate the movement of concentration on the following day; but Chrzanowsky, not holding in
sufficient estimation the value of time, and content with the
advantages obtained, postponed until the next day what should
have been done the same evening, and retired to rest, only to
be awakened at midnight and hear of the dreadful tidings
from Mortara.

While this engagement was proceeding in the vicinity of
Vigevano, the Austrian centre column, consisting of the division under the Archduke Albert, and the second army corps
under General D'Aspre, marched directly upon Mortara; and
at five o'clock in the afternoon, the engagement commenced
between them and the Piedmontese sent up for the defense of
that town.

Chrzanowsky, in directing Durando and the Duke of Savoy

to Mortara, had not given them any precise instructions; he had simply ordered Durando there to reconnoitre, and in case of attack to take a position defensive in advance of the city; and the duke, to cover the right of Durando's division and the city which might be turned on that side. Later, he sent them other instructions, which were no more explicit than the former, and which only tended to confusion; but a greater difficulty resulted from a want of knowledge of the country on the part of the troops, and particularly the staff. About three o'clock the division of Durando began to advance, and to take up a position about fifteen hundred yards only from the city, about a mile and a half short of the position which he should have taken, but which the rapid approach of the enemy at this time rendered it impossible for him to occupy. About half past four o'clock the corps of D'Aspre appeared in sight, advancing on the road from Garlasco, preceded by a party of cavalry and a cloud of riflemen, amounting in all to about fifteen thousand men, with forty-eight cannons.

D'Aspre, having been ordered to occupy and then to pass by Mortara, on seeing the town covered by the Piedmontese, did not desire, notwithstanding the lateness of the hour, to postpone operations until the next day; and therefore made as rapidly as possible his dispositions for battle.

The division of the Archduke Albert, which marched in advance, was formed into columns of attack on both sides of the road; the other rested in reserve, except a few detachments sent toward the cemetery and the convent (where Durando's division was stationed), to observe and retain the enemy upon those points.

The combat commenced by the discharge of four-and-twenty pieces, placed in front of the columns of attack; this fire was directed against the centre of Durando's division, and against an elevated spot of ground, where Durando, the Duke of Genoa, and La Marmora, to give an example of firmness to the troops, remained for a long time at this dangerous post, although their presence would have been useful at other points. The Piedmontese artillery, feeble at this point, could not sustain themselves against such great disadvantages; and a portion of the Queen's brigade (composed mostly of youths of eighteen, who

had seen but two months' service), overcome by the violence
of the attack, were thrown into disorder.

These difficulties, however, they were enabled to repair, and
the whole Piedmontese army maintained a sufficiently bold
front, when, just at the approach of night, D'Aspre gave orders for a vigorous charge at all points.

This severe attack could not be resisted.   The Piedmontese
immediately gave way, and retreated precipitately into the
city, where every thing was soon involved in the utmost confusion.   It was night, the inhabitants were fleeing for safety
in every direction, the artillery and baggage encumbered the
streets, and the enemy continued to advance, and to combat
pell-mell to the very entrance of the city.

The Austrians hesitated a little to penetrate into Mortara.
A single battalion, with two pieces, under the orders of Colonel Benedeck, was all that entered at first; but they were
afterward joined by a second battalion.   The great bulk of
the Austrian army remained without the city, and a part of it
combated for a time against the extreme right of the Piedmontese, on the side of St. Albin's, and which still continued
to resist.

Benedeck stripped the city, took the horses and equipage of
the Duke of Genoa, a great quantity of baggage, and established his two battalions upon the principal place and in the
grand street, which leads from the gate of Pavia to that of
Verciel.

The Austrians were then masters of Mortara, having put
to flight an enemy vastly superior in numbers, without sustaining much damage; but their triumph did not end here.
A singular circumstance, which occurred subsequently, tended
to render it vastly more important.   At the moment of the
attack, which broke the Piedmontese centre, the battalion
which was at St. Albin's, vigorously attacked also, had lost the
convent; then, with the assistance of another battalion, they
retook it, but both having subsequently lost it again, took position in the rear, and continued to hold front against the enemy, who were endeavoring to surround them.   La Marmora,
beholding the danger which threatened these troops, hurried
to them, and met at the Round Point of St. George the two

battalions of Cuneo, which the Duke of Savoy had sent. He made them rest there in reserve ; and, placing himself at the head of four or five hundred fugitives whom he rallied, advanced toward St. Albin's. But the enemy's sharp-shooters, in ambuscade behind the trees in that neighborhood, kept up so constant and deadly a fire, that it was impossible to make head against them. Deceived by this fusilade, as well as by the obscurity of the night, the battalions of Round Point fired upon this detachment of their own troops of St. Albin's, which was then forced to beat a retreat before the Austrians. The error was, however, soon discovered, the combat re-established and continued for some time, and the enemy, making no further advance, at length ceased altogether.

For some time the conflict appeared over in Mortara, and nothing being heard thence, or on the road to Garlasco, La Marmora, who had sent to ascertain what was passing in those quarters, was informed that the city was in the possession of the Austrians. It was now eight o'clock. La Marmora, thus outflanked, hesitated, knowing nothing of the spot in which he now found himself, ignorant of the road which led to Castel d'Agogna, and judging that a retreat across the fields would be impracticable, resolutely determined to pass through the city, conquer it, and take the road to Novara, along which many of the scattered forces had already fled.

He forms his troops in column, places the artillery in the midst, the battalion which had defended St. Albin's following in the rear, and marches boldly upon Mortara, leaving his soldiers ignorant of the presence of the enemy in the city. The column enters the city by the gate of St. George, situated to the left of that of Garlasco, through which the enemy had entered. He finds the streets encumbered with vehicles, the dead bodies of men and horses every where strewed around ; all the houses closed and lights extinguished ; the darkness was profound ; the Austrians whom they met, and who had believed the hostilities long since terminated, could not conceive whence had sprung this apparition of a hostile corps now charging upon them. La Marmora, to encourage his troops, sounded a charge, the Austrians beat the *rappel*, and a column, as if rising from the earth, debouches upon the public square and into the grand street, and there in close combat, breast to breast, the firing commences, amid a confusion frightful in the extreme. The Piedmontese were ignorant what route across the city to take which was not bristling with hostile bayonets, and the Austrians, on their part, unable to conjecture the extent of the enemy's force, were exceedingly disturbed.*

But these demonstrations, however dreadful, could not shake the courage or disturb the coolness of Benedeck ; with the rapidity of lightning, he concludes that the foe by which he is so unexpectedly opposed is but the troops of St. Albin's retarded and cut off, he promptly rallies his entire force, bars the issues of the public square and grand street, summons the Piedmontese to surrender, assuring them that they were completely surrounded, and that all resistance was vain. The Piedmontese made a vigorous effort to disengage themselves, and although there was but a small force opposed to them, still less on the right or on the left (for the great body of the Austrians remained without the city) ; but the ignorance of these facts, the obscurity, the confusion, the defeat of the day, all induced the belief that they were surrounded by forces innumerable. In such case, a true soldier would not have hesitated to attempt to open a passage for himself, let it cost what it might ; in such a conclusion there was one chance of escape, one glimmer of hope, while military pride prompts its possessor to confront any danger, and to meet death rather than dishonor. But these troops were too young, too little inured to the trials and dangers of war, not to be overpowered by the perilous situation in which they were involved, and, totally unnerved, they lay down their arms to the number of eight hundred.

La Marmora, however, who marched at their head, escaped with only fifty men, and was enabled to gain in safety the Castel d'Agogna, where he found the division of the Duke of Savoy, with which was also Durando, who, at the moment of the overthrow, became separated from his own corps, and was never able to rejoin them.† The loss of the Piedmontese in this engagement, in which the regular fighting did not last

---

* Author of Custoza.   † Ibid.

more than three hours, was five hundred killed or wounded, twenty-five prisoners, six staff, sixty sub-officers, and five cannons ; that of the Austrians was not more than three hundred men *hors de combat.**

This affair, partial though it was, produced such an effect, that it may be said to have decided the fate of the campaign. It was a proof of what intrepidity and energy in war can effect, and what terrible disasters, on the contrary, follow in the train of negligence and feebleness.

All the chances were in favor of the Piedmontese : more numerous, less fatigued, and with the choice of position. But on one side there was the boldness and promptitude of execution of D'Aspre, and the coolness and energy of Benedeck ; on the other hand, there was the indefinite order of Chrzanowsky, his want of energy, and improper dispositions, the timidity of his lieutenants, and the want of firmness in the troops. These circumstances rendered his condition most disastrous, and deprived the Italians of that victory which was almost within their grasp.

On the evening of this day (21st), while the Piedmontese had three divisions near Vigevano, two others in retreat from Mortara to Novara, and one brigade on the bridge of Buffalora, the Austrian army occupied the route from Pavia to Mortara, extending on the right as far as Gamboló, on the left to St. George. D'Aspre was at Mortara, Appel at Trumello, the reserve at Gropello, Wratislaw at Gamboló, Thurn at St. George.

The generals beaten at Mortara had not apprised Chrzanowsky of what occurred with the promptitude which circumstances required ; and it was only known through the accidental arrival of two of La Marmora's staff, who, not being able to find their way back, escaped to Vigevano, which they reached about one at night, and announced the total defeat they had sustained. This disaster, and the advanced position of the Austrians, not only rendered the projects of Chrzanowsky impossible, but placed the Piedmontese army in a most perilous situation.

The retreat upon Verciel being cut off, the only course left

* Austrian official bulletin.

them appeared to be to concentrate their forces as rapidly as possible, and then give battle.

Novara was the spot where this concentration of the Piedmontese forces could be most expeditiously executed, and it was there that Chrzanowsky resolved to test the fate of his army. To accomplish this it was necessary to hasten, as the enemy at Mortara and at Gamboló were not farther distant from Novara than the Piedmontese at Vigevano. Chrzanowsky, therefore, placed his troops in motion before day, and arrived at Trecate about noon, where he left in position until the next morning the division of the Duke of Genoa; the other division reached Novara in the evening. Arrived there, they found the division of Durando, and that of the Duke of Savoy, which, after making a considerable detour, had arrived at Novara in the night; at length the brigade Solaroli had come from Romentino, and the concentration was then effected.

To the south of Novara, between the rapid streams of Agogna and Terdoppio, there rises a kind of undulating plateau, on which is situated the village of La Bicocca, about a mile from the city, and occupying its highest point. At the foot of the hills of La Bicocca, that is to say, on the left when turning the back on Novara, the ground falls rapidly toward the Terdoppio, and is cut up by two small canals. To the right, from thence to the rivulet Arbogna, which runs a little distance from La Bicocca, it is a little broken, and presents only some small elevations toward the centre, but is covered with vines and trees disposed in long lines, scattered houses, and separated also by a canal running parallel to the Agogna.*

It was in this position that Chrzanowsky awaited the Austrians. The front of the battle line extended between Cortenova and La Bicocca, on a space of three thousand yards, and followed the cord of the *sector* of which Novara is the summit. Three divisions, placed in two lines, occupied this space; two other divisions were in *échellon*, in reserve, behind the wings of the line of battle. A part of the first division occupied the right wing, which was covered by a canal running parallel to the Agogna, of which the extreme right inclines toward Tor-

---

* Spectateur Militaire.

rione Quartara, and forms a kind of bastion, which had been used for defense. The remainder of the division, placed a little in the rear, covered the farm of Citadella, supporting its left by the farm of Rasario and the road to Torrione.

The second division occupied the centre, and was placed between the road to Torrione and the hamlet of La Bicocca, situated on the great road from Novara to Mortara.

The third division formed the left, and occupied the important point *à cheval* on the great road. The division of reserve was placed behind the right wing, between Novara and the road to Verciel.

The fourth division, placed behind the left wing, occupied the cemetery of San Nazzario.*

On the 22d, the Austrian army, at different points, took up the line of march toward Novara. The second army corps, under the command of D'Aspre, marched directly from Mortara on Novara, followed by the third and the reserve corps ; the fourth and first army corps moved in a parallel direction against the line of retreat of the enemy.

On the morning of the 23d, about eleven o'clock, the Austrians commenced the battle by an attack, executed by the second army corps, on the left wing of the Piedmontese at Biccocca. At first, the Piedmontese, making but a small display of forces, the Austrians were under the impression that it was but a rear-guard to protect the retreat of the army; and the Archduke Albert, in command of the van-guard, hurried rapidly forward with his division, followed at some distance by the division under F. M. L. Count Schaffgoth. But speedily the error was detected, when the fire became general along the whole line, and it was evident that the whole Piedmontese army of fifty thousand men was before them. A bloody engagement here took place ; the Piedmontese regiment Savona, posted in the first line, was obliged to give way ; but the brigade of Savoy coming to its assistance, was enabled to cover the lost ground. In the mean time, the division of the archduke being obliged to bear for some hours the entire brunt of the battle, the attack of the whole Piedmontese army, al-

---

* Le Spectateur Militaire.

though performing prodigies of valor (the archduke himself mingling in the thickest of the fight, and showing himself worthy of his heroic sire*), suffered greatly until the arrival of support. Shortly, the division of Schaffgoth entered the line of battle ; but the number of the enemy was still so great, that this incomparably small force would have been able to offer but a short resistance. The field-marshal, informed of the situation of these forces, immediately ordered up the third army corps and the reserve to advance in all haste to the support of D'Aspre. But before the third army corps and reserve, then some miles in the rear, could reach the scene of action, the situation of the Austrian army was perilous indeed. Pressed upon by such overpowering numbers, their ammunition became exhausted ; to replenish which they were obliged temporarily to retire (about a hundred steps).

The first and fourth corps had been dispatched by Marshal Radetzky to the other side of Agogna, to attack the right hostile flank. Both armies fought with determined courage, and the prospect of victory on either side for some time hung in the balance ; the Piedmontese believe that they must have triumphed, had the Austrian right flank been attacked before its reserve arrived. For a time the Austrian fire slackened on the left, and the whole weight of their forces was directed on a hamlet called La Citadella, which was taken and retaken several times. Here some of the hardest fighting of the day took place ; and on the Sardinian side, the brigades Casale, Acqui, and Parma particularly distinguished themselves.

About four o'clock, the third army corps, under F. M. L. D'Aspre, consisting of fourteen battalions, arrived on the field. Seven battalions immediately entered the line of battle, while the other seven followed the centre as a reserve.

At this period of the action, a fresh attack was directed by the Austrians with redoubled fury against Bicocca, which they succeeded in wresting from the Piedmontese. The loss of this position decided the fate of the day ; and although the Duke of Genoa, with the division which he led, made the most gallant efforts to re-establish the fortunes of the fight, they were unavailing.† The Sardinian position being thus turned, the

---

* Son of the Archduke Charles.   † Austrian official bulletin.

weight of the Austrian line was directed against the enemy's
right and centre; and when at this time (six o'clock), the
fourth army corps, under Count Thurn, arrived and took up its
position on the road to Verciel, and a concentrated attack was
then made upon the enemy at all points, they could resist no
longer, but retreated in the utmost confusion—some troops to
Memmo, others to the mountains, and the great bulk of them
into the city of Novara, which during the night was plundered
and set fire to by their own troops.

The loss sustained by the Piedmontese was four thousand
men killed or wounded, two generals killed, and sixteen killed
or wounded staff officers, from two to three thousand prisoners,
and twelve cannons.

The loss of the Austrians, which fell almost entirely upon
D'Aspre's corps, was about three thousand killed or wounded,
and each regiment of the first line of battle from ten to twenty
high officers killed and wounded.*

The numbers lost on either side vary but little; but that
is by no means the criterion by which the importance of the
battle is to be measured. The Piedmontese army was not only
defeated and demoralized, but it was beyond all possibility of
restoration. Piedmont was vanquished, and the fortunes of
Austria a second time triumphant. Piedmont disarmed, the
possession of Lombardy assured, and peace become certain—
such were the results to Austria of this short campaign.

If personal gallantry could redeem the errors of an insincere
and tortuous policy, Charles Albert might be held to have ex-
piated his misdeeds that day on the field of battle. He exposed himself to the enemy's fire on every point where the
danger was greatest.† He remained during the day within
musket range of the enemy on the point of the Bicocca, three
times taken and retaken. During the night, he continued to
direct the defense, now reduced to the town of Novara; and
to General Durando, who in vain tried to take him by the
arm and lead him away, he replied, " General, it is my last

---

* Le Spectateur Militaire.

† The Duke of Savoy, after exposing himself to all the dangers which his division encountered, twice repaired to the principal point of action when his troops
were not engaged. The Duke of Genoa, after having three horses shot under him,
led his troops on foot.

day; let me die." He had sent to demand an armistice of Marshal Radetzky, who had consented to accord it only upon the condition that his troops should occupy the country between the Ticino and the Sesia, and to hold the citadel of Alexandria, and leaving it to be understood, at the same time, that he could not confide in the engagements of the king to these terms, but would require the Duke of Savoy as a hostage.

When the king discovered that the army could hold out no longer, and that the terms of peace laid down by Radetzky were such as could not be submitted to, he, at nine o'clock, sent for the Dukes of Savoy and Genoa, the commander-in-chief, minister Cadorna, and the lieutenant generals and commanders of divisions at that time in Novara ; and when they had all assembled at the Bellini Palace, sad but calm, the king advanced with dignity, and said, "Gentlemen, fortune has betrayed your courage and my hopes ; our army is dissolved ; it would be impossible to prolong the struggle. My task is accomplished, and I think I shall render an important service by giving a last proof of devotedness, in abdicating in favor of my son, Victor Emmanuel, duke of Savoy. He will obtain from Austria conditions of peace, which she would refuse if treating with me."

The persons present burst into tears, but no emotion was visible in the face of Charles Albert; and all the efforts of the Duke of Savoy to shake his resolve were vain. The king embraced him and the Duke of Genoa, and all the persons present. He thanked them for the services they had rendered him, and said, "Gentlemen, I am no longer your king. Be faithful and devoted to my son, as you have been to me." He then withdrew to write to the queen, and charged the Duke of Savoy to deliver the letter of adieu with his own hand.

At half past one o'clock, an individual wrapped in a traveling cloak, and preceded by a valet out of livery, left the palace. He entered a carriage in waiting for him in a neighboring street, the postilion received orders to take the road for Porta Stura, and in a few hours Charles Albert had bid adieu not only to his crown, but his kingdom forever.*

---

* The spirit of the age and the lessons of experience were not altogether lost upon this prince, whose real character seems but recently to have been apprecia-

The next morning, just as the necessary measures had been taken by Marshal Radetzky for the pursuit of the enemy, *parliamentaires* arrived at the camp from the new king, applying for a truce, and requesting an interview.

The interview took place in a cottage near Vignale, between Radetzky and the young king, and an armistice entered into upon the terms previously laid down by Radetzky, viz., occupation by Austrians, with twenty thousand men, of the country between the Ticino and Sesia; joint occupation, with Piedmontese, of the fortress of Alexandria; disbanding by Piedmont of Lombard and other troops in her service. Negotiations for a permanent peace between the two countries to be entered on without delay, and upon the following bases: The *statu quo* territorial divisions of Italy, as established by the treaties of 1815, and by consequence the renunciations by Piedmont of all pretensions to the Lombardo-Venetian kingdom or the duchies; the reimbursement to Austria of all the expenses of the war; stipulations, or a treaty of commerce, removing all the causes which had at various times threatened the peace of the two powers. The armistice was signed on the evening of the 24th of March, 1849.*

On the succeeding day, Marshal Radetzky issued to his troops the following proclamation:

" Soldiers! you have well redeemed your word. You have

---

ted. We can desire no better evidence of his sincere love of country and benign projects than the fact that, many years since, when comparative tranquillity prevailed in Europe, he was accustomed to hold long and confidential interviews with our representative at his court, for the purpose of eliciting information as to the means and method of gradually ameliorating the institutions, not only of Sardinia, but of Italy. He long cherished the hope of giving her national unity, of combining from all her states an efficient army, and thus expelling the Austrians from the soil. This he believed to be the first step toward a constitutional government. Popular education and military training he more or less encouraged in his own dominions, with this great ultimate object in view; and he certainly possessed the most efficient native troops, and the best-founded popularity, among the Italian princes. Since his death, impartial observers concur in deeming him far more unfortunate than treacherous; a reaction has justly taken place in the public estimation of his motives and career; and no candid inquirer can fail to recognize in him a brave ruler, who gave a decided impulse to liberal ideas, advanced the Italian cause, and became one of its voluntary martyrs.—*Christian Examiner.*

* For a copy of the armistice, see Appendix, note No. 32.

undertaken a campaign against an enemy in numbers your superior, and you have ended it victoriously in five days. History will not gainsay, that never was a braver, truer army than that over which my lord and sovereign, the emperor, appointed me to command. Soldiers! in the name of your emperor and of your country, I thank you for your valorous deeds, for your devotion, for your truth. With sadness my looks repose upon the graves of our brethren, the glorious fallen, and I can not declare the expression of my gratitude to the living without giving a deeply-felt remembrance to the dead. Soldiers! our most persevering enemy, Charles Albert, has descended from the throne. With his successor, the young king, I have concluded an armistice, which guarantees to us the speedy conclusion of peace. Soldiers! with joy you were witnesses to it—with joy have the inhabitants of the country every where received us;* beholding in us, far from oppressors, saviors against anarchy. This expectation you must fulfill, and, by your severe observance of discipline, show to the world that the warriors of Austria's army are as terrible in war as they are honest and gentle in peace, and that we have come to protect, and not to destroy."

On receiving the intelligence of Charles Albert's abdication, Prince Eugène of Savoy-Carignani, lieutenant general of the kingdom, issued the following proclamation:

"I have to communicate to you a painful intelligence. The king, Charles Albert, after having with intrepidity confronted the enemy's balls, seeing the reverse sustained by our armies, has been unwilling to bend to ill fortune, preferring to crown his life with a new sacrifice. On the 23d he abdicated in favor of the Duke of Savoy. The gratitude of the people and our respectful attachment to him will be eternal. Let us ral-

---

* Through every Piedmontese village the passage of the Austrians was hailed with the cry, "*Evviva Radetzky!*" and "*Evvivani i nostri liberatori!*"

The campaign concluded, the victorious army (with the exception of one corps) leaves the Piedmontese territory. The first *corps d'armée* returns to Milan; second marches to Modena and Parma; third to Como, Brescia, and Bergamo; fifth corps takes position in Piedmont under the armistice. The first *corps de réserve* to Pavia.

ly round the new king, worthy emulator of his paternal valor
in battle, and upright guardian of the constitutional franchises
granted by his august father.   Long live King Victor Emmanuel!   Eugene de Savoie.

"Turin, 26th March."

This document was speedily followed by another proclamation from the new King of Sardinia, which is as follows:

"Citizens,—Fatal events and the will of my august father
have called me prematurely to the throne of my ancestors.
The circumstances in which I assume the reins of government
are such that, without the most efficacious support from all, I
could with difficulty accomplish my only vow, the welfare of
our common country.   The destiny of nations is matured in
the designs of God; man owes all his efforts to second them;
we have not failed in this duty.   Our present task must now
consist in maintaining our honor safe, in healing the wounds
of the public fortune, in consolidating our constitutional institutions.   It is to this task I conjure all my people to apply;
I prepare myself to swear to it solemnly, and I expect from
the nation, in return, assistance, love, and confidence.
                                   "Victor Emmanuel.*

"Turin, March 27."

While these successes attended the Austrian cause in Pied-

---

* The loss of the battle of Novara and the abdication of Charles Albert, though
apparently great misfortunes, have resulted in signal benefits.   After securing
peace from their adversaries, chiefly by a pecuniary sacrifice, the king and citizens of Piedmont turned their energies toward internal reform with a wisdom
and good faith which are rapidly yielding legitimate fruit.   Public schools were
instituted, the press made free, the Waldenses allowed to quit their valleys, build
churches, and elect representatives; the privileges of the clergy abolished, and
the two bishops, who ventured to oppose the authority of her state, tried, condemned, and banished; the Pope's interference repudiated; the right of suffrage
instituted; rail-roads from Turin to Genoa, and from Alexandria to Lago Maggiore constructed; the electric telegraph introduced, liberal commercial treaties
formed, docks built, and cheap postal laws enacted.   In a word, the great evils
that have so long weighed down the people of the Italian peninsula—unlimited
monarchical power, aristocratic and clerical immunities derived from the Middle
Ages, the censorship of the press, the espionage of the police, and intolerance of
all but the Catholic religion—no longer exist in Sardinia.—*Christian Examiner.*

mont, events of a different character were occurring in some of the Lombardian cities which they had just left. Brescia, the second city of Lombardy, with forty thousand inhabitants, was completely evacuated when an Austrian army had been raised for the invasion of Piedmont, and but five hundred men guarded the citadel.

The city had been already most strongly agitated, on account of her partiality for the Piedmontese, when (the 23d) the day of the battle of Novara, the arrival of a number of refugees determined them to improve the occasion of the withdrawal of the Austrian garrison to rise and strike for independence. The commandant of the citadel, surprised in the city, was made prisoner; the couriers from Milan and Verona were stopped, and the baggage of a regiment plundered. They endeavored to take the citadel, but the garrison easily repulsed all attacks, and cannonaded the city.

The insurgents, extending themselves beyond the town, advanced to the Castle of St. Euphemia, which they occupied; but the few troops established in the neighborhood were enabled to put them to flight, and forced the insurgents to shut themselves up in the place.

General Haynau, in command of the troops at that time blockading Venice, informed of the disturbances in Brescia, soon arrived with between three and four thousand troops, and on the 30th of March, Brescia was attacked by the garrison of the citadel, by the troops which were under the walls of the city, and by those of Haynau just arrived at the scene of action.

This unfortunate city, abandoned to its own forces, could not long resist, and would have submitted; but, deceived by certain insensate agitators, who dealt only in delusions, issuing forged proclamations of Chrzanowsky of the successes of the Piedmontese over the Austrians, calling all the people to arms, and assuring them that their friends and allies, the Piedmontese, would soon be seen on the Isonzo, they resolved to resist to the last extremity.

Conscious of their deficiency in military science and resources, the Brescians barricaded their streets and intrenched themselves in their houses, and, despising the summons to sur-

II. S

render, awaited the enemy's attack. The gates of the city were captured without the discharge of a gun; but then the contest commenced. A part of the town being in flames, the people endeavored in vain to escape over the walls, and were driven into a corner between the Porta St. Giovanni and Porta Piler. In this corner, fired at all points (for every house from which a gun was discharged was, agreeably to the orders of the Austrian general, to be set on fire at once), it is believed that a considerable body of the insurgents must have been burned to death. But the massacre did not end with the combat, though, when all resistance was over (says the official bulletin, which itself leaves no doubt as to the sanguinary character of this deplorable engagement), "the bodies of the insurgents lay in heaps in the streets and houses."

The most hideous incident of this terrible slaughter is reserved for the closing paragraph of the bulletin: "*All prisoners taken with arms in their hands were shot publicly!*"

The province of Brescia, now a heap of ruins, was mulcted to the amount of two millions of florins, and one million compensation money for the widows and orphans of the slain, for the wounded, and for the troops engaged.*

The imperial general who was guilty of these atrocities, so disgraceful to the age, and who publicly avows them in his report to the government, so far from being dismissed and dishonored, was in a few months promoted to a higher station, and intrusted with the command of all the Austrian troops engaged at that time in the subjugation of Hungary, where he was enabled to perpetrate deeds of enormity in comparison with which the treatment of the Brescians dwindles into comparative insignificance, and which has justly covered him with the unmitigated execration of the civilized world.

---

* Austrian official bulletin.

CHAPTER IX.

SECOND HUNGARIAN CAMPAIGN.—INTERVENTION OF RUSSIA.—JOINT INVASION OF HUNGARY.—THE DEFEAT OF BEM IN TRANSYLVANIA, AND OF DEMBINSKI AT SZOREG AND TEMESVAR.—THE DISSOLUTION OF THE GOVERNMENT.—THE DICTATORSHIP OF GÖRGEY.—THE SURRENDER OF VILAGOS.—THE FLIGHT OF KOSSUTH, AND THE DOWNFALL OF HUNGARY.—CHARACTER OF KOSSUTH.

AFTER the brilliant succession of victories that attended the conclusion of the first Austrian invasion, and by which the Imperialists were driven from the soil of Hungary, nothing but the scattered remnants of a defeated army intervening between them and the capital of the empire, the Magyars did not, as we should have supposed, bring about a cessation of hostilities, by advancing upon Vienna and dictating their own terms from the emperor's palace. A march of forty miles was all that was necessary to accomplish the grand object at which they aimed. As was said of the United States on a similar occasion, they had "pushed on until independence was within their grasp;" they had "only to reach forward to it, and it was theirs."[*]

But a division of counsel, treachery in the camp, a want of that boldness in action which characterizes those born and bred under the light of freedom, or perhaps all these causes combined, so operated that Hungary, instead of being at this day a free and independent nation of Europe, is deprived of her Constitution, robbed of her quasi independence, and reduced to a level with the hereditary provinces of the Austrian empire.

Nor did the Austrian government, on the other hand, attempt to meet the Hungarians with any terms of reconciliation, when a mere recognition of the constitutional rights of the kingdom as established for ages, and which Austria might

---

[*] Applied to John Adams by Webster, in his eulogy on the lives of Adams and Jefferson.

have acknowledged without dishonor, would have been quite sufficient to secure a lasting peace between them.

It might have been supposed that a legal acknowledgment of the positive obligations of their Constitution was no extravagant price to pay for the services and loyalty of twelve millions of subjects; and that, even if so regarded, the boon would not have been too great for a nation that had refused with disdain the independence proffered it by Napoleon,* and which had so often, by its bravery, saved the Austrian throne from annihilation; and we should have imagined that the Habsburg dynasty would not hesitate, as in days of former embarrassment and distress, to have thrown itself into the arms of its own magnanimous Hungary, or, as they styled her, that "all-beloved, most valiant, most loyal, and most illustrious nation."

The real policy of Austria would have been to foster the ancient Constitution of Hungary, developed by changes adapted to the exigencies of the time; to have imparted to all her provinces institutions in conformity with the spirit of the age, and not less liberal than those enjoyed by Hungary; and to have rallied around her the heterogeneous people which compose her empire by the watch-words of self-government, civilization, and free trade, in opposition to Russian despotism, barbarism, and restriction. But, unhappily, the Austrian statesmen then at the head of the government were incapable of embracing such an enlightened course of action.

They feared Russia much, but they feared liberal opinions more; as the least of the two evils, conquest was preferred to conciliation, and the intervention of Russia was asked. It will be unnecessary to record the acceptance on the part of Russia of such a task; the Czar would surely not have declined, when openly sought to perform, with the assent of the monarch and in the eyes of the world, that which for years he had been laboring to effect clandestinely and by intrigue.

---

* In 1809, after Napoleon had subdued the armies, and possessed himself of the capital of the Austrian empire, he issued a proclamation summoning the Hungarians to secede from the house of Habsburg, and to elect a king on the Rakos Field, as their fathers had done before them. But the loyal Hungarians indignantly rejected the invitation.

On the 1st of May, 1849, the Austrian journals published the following official proclamation :

" The insurrection in Hungary has, within the last month, grown to such an extent, and its present aspect exhibits so unmistakably the character of a union of all the forces of the revolutionary party in Europe, that all states are equally interested in assisting the imperial (*i. e*, Austrian) government in its contest against this spreading dissolution of all social order. Acting on these important reasons, his majesty the emperor's government has been induced to appeal to the assistance of his majesty the Czar of all the Russias, who generously and readily granted it to a most satisfactory extent. The measures which have been agreed on by the two sovereigns are now being executed."

The demand for assistance made by the Emperor of Austria on the Czar was neither rejected or delayed ; no inquiries were propounded, no preliminaries entered into ; and though it was only in the last days of April that the Austrians were driven out of Hungary,* it was as early as the 8th of May that a proclamation was published at St. Petersburg, concluding as follows : " In the midst of these disastrous events, the Emperor of Austria has addressed himself to us, demanding assistance against the common enemy. We shall not refuse the aid demanded. After having invoked the great leader of battles and the lord of armies to protect our just cause, we have issued orders to our army to commence its march, to put down the insurrection, and annihilate the reckless men who also threaten to disturb the quiet of our province. If God be with us, none can resist us. Of this let us be persuaded : let every man in our kingdom, which is under God's protection, every Russian and faithful subject, feel, hope, and speak thus, and Russia will fulfill its sacred calling." Some German journals, discussing the direct interest of Russia in this contest, spoke of a cession of part of Galicia as the price of her succor against the Hungarians ; others mentioned a compensation more definite and tangible, a port on the Adriatic, Catarro, which, sep-

---

* The Russian intervention was officially announced on the 29th of April. Resolution by Austria to make war on Hungary was supposed to have been determined in concert with Russia.—*Blackwood.*

arated from the rest of Dalmatia by an intervening portion of
Turkish territory, is therefore of little consequence to Austria;
but the indirect interest which Russia has in the preservation,
in the states around her, of those absolutist principles upon
which her existence depends, and the destruction (by the corruption of Austria and extinction of Hungary) of the only real
barrier to her encroachments on Western Europe or on Constantinople (the great aim of Russian ambition since the days
of Catharine), are motives which so forcibly appeal to her self-
interest as to render the hypothesis of a definite remuneration
quite gratuitous, and easily accounted for the ready sacrifice
of Russian gold and Russian soldiers. That such was the
opinion even of the Czar himself, a subsequent proclamation
issued by him clearly evinces : " I have placed at the disposal
of the Emperor of Austria eighty thousand men, besides the
corps which have already entered Transylvania. All the troops
are paid and kept up at *my* expense, and I claim no indemnification."

On the 12th of May, a proclamation of the Emperor of Austria appeared, and which concluded as follows :

" It is in conformity with our desire, and in accordance with
our wish, that the Russian armies have appeared in Hungary,
in order to terminate promptly, and by all the means in our
power, a war which devastates our fields. Do not regard them
as enemies of our country, but as friends of your king, who
second him in his firm project of delivering Hungary from the
heavy yoke of bad men, domestic and foreign. The Russian
troops will observe the same discipline as my troops, they will
protect persons and property, and with the same vigor labor
to put down the revolt, until the blessing of God shall bring
about the triumph of the good cause."*

COMMENCEMENT OF THE SECOND CAMPAIGN.

After a short time occupied in preparation, the second campaign for the subjugation of Hungary at length vigorously
commenced. The combined armies opposed to the Hungarians amounted to nearly four hundred thousand men—two

---

* Wiener Zeitung.

hundred and thirty thousand Austrians and one hundred and sixty thousand Russians—and were distributed as follows:

The first army corps, composed of Austrians and Russians, under the command of General Haynau, entering Hungary at Pressburg, advanced into the country over the island of Schütte, with the intention of taking the capital of Buda-Pesth.

The second army corps, entirely Russian, under Prince Paskievitch, coming in from the Galician frontier on the north, at Dukla, passed through Bartfeldt, Eperies, Kashau, and Miskolcz, with a view to capture the capital of Debreczin.

The third army corps, consisting of Russians and Austrians, under Field-marshal Puchner, penetrating Transylvania from the north, carried Bistricz by storm, and moved upon Klausenburg.

The fourth army corps, entirely Russian, under General Lüders, entering Transylvania from the south, through the Pass of Tömös, took Kronstadt, and marched upon Hermanstadt.

The fifth army corps, composed also exclusively of Russians, making their entrance into the country at Orsova, marched with a view of joining the Austro-Croatian army under Jellacic, operating in the territory formed by the confluence of the Danube and the Theiss.

Before the commencement of the second campaign, Baron Welden tendered to the emperor his resignation of the command of the imperial forces in Hungary, on the ground of ill health; and on the first of June there appeared in print the emperor's "hand-billet" to the general, in which his majesty, deeply deploring the necessity of the step, is induced to comply with the desire of the general, who had repeatedly expressed a wish to resign his post on the ground of ill health. For the present, his majesty offered to restore him to his command at Vienna, the post he had vacated. The imperial note concluded by nominating F. M. L. Haynau to be commander-in-chief of the army of Hungary and Transylvania. General Welden, although regarded as an able commander, lost immensely in public opinion after the fall of Buda, a disaster he might have avoided by sending timely succors of troops, of which he had abundance at his disposal. The fault was in trusting too much to the neutral and inoffensive attitude observed by the inhabitants of Pesth, and in neglecting to fortify the surrounding eminences which overhang and command it. The post there, if worth preserving, an adequate force for that purpose should have been provided.

Of his successor, besides the violence of his temper, which was quite notorious, little was known, except that he had long served with success under Radetzky, and that he was the general who had lately quelled the revolt in Brescia with a resolute but cruel hand. Beyond these, and the fact of his having put things in train at Mestre for the reduction of Venice, nothing was known of the military career of the man called suddenly to a task in which two predecessors, of vastly higher reputation for ability, had most signally failed.

HUNGARIAN PLAN OF DEFENSE.

When the Hungarian government became advised of a Russian invasion, at a cabinet council held on the 12th of May, the outlines of a plan for the defense of the country were agreed upon.

The leading idea of this plan was to divide the forces of the nation in such a manner as to make them equally efficient for a two-fold purpose—either, by a decisive blow, to hurry the war to a speedy close, or to extend its duration by avoiding a collision with the enemy's troops. Pursuant to this leading idea, it was resolved to make the fortress of Komorn the *point d'appui* of an intrenched camp for a garrison of thirty thousand men, and for the purpose of definitely impeding the advance of the main body of the Austrian army. The second and third corps (twenty thousand men), under General Aulick, were to take a position on the River Neutra, and communicate from thence, to the right with General Dembinski, and to the left with the garrison of Komorn. General Aulick was instructed to reconnoitre the hostile forces on the left bank of the Danube, to cover the mountain cities and districts, and, after ascertaining the enemy's intentions, to effect, by forced marches, a junction either with the garrison of Komorn, or the corps under the command of Dembinski, and thus to enable one of the two armies to leave the defensive, and to make an offensive retreat in the sight of the enemy.* General Dembinski was ordered to keep the mountain defiles in Upper Hungary, with the assistance of General Aulick, to throw the bulk of his army against the Russian corps which advanced from Arva, and, after annihilating it in the narrow valleys of the mountains, to concentrate his forces against the other Russian army, which invaded Hungary by way of Dukla. Numerous detachments in the north eastern counties were, for this purpose, placed at the disposal of General Dembinski.

But if the Russians, instead of advancing by Arva, were to push the bulk of their army forward on the road of Eperies and Pesth, the forces of the Generals Dembinski and Aulick were to be concentrated at Miskolcz, and their line of retreat was in that case marked out toward the Theiss, in the direction of Füred.

The blockade of the fortresses of Arad and Temesvar, and the protection of the Banat and the Batsk country, were committed to General Perczel, who for these purposes was placed in command of one half of his own corps and of the whole of General Vécsey's corps ; while General Bem was instructed to lead his troops and the second half of Perczel's corps against, and carry Tittel, and to complete the relief of the garrison of Peterwardein by dislocating the rest of the besieging army on the right bank of the Danube. This done, General Bem was to return, to advance along the banks of the Danube up the stream, to cross at a convenient place, to hoist the Hungarian colors on the right bank, to effect a junction with Colonel Kmetty, and to communicate with the garrison of Komorn. His line of retreat lay via Buda, in which direction he was to fall back on the great body of the Hungarian army, of which he was, in that case, to take the chief command. After the conquest of Buda, the division of Colonel Kmetty was to advance to the Platten Lake, to organize the insurrection in that part of the country, and to join the forces of General Bem.

The reserve corps were to assemble on the banks of the Theiss, where they were to wait for the orders of the War Office. The command of Transylvania was given to Colonel

---

* Klapka's War in Hungary.

Czecz, with instructions completely to suppress the Wallachi-an insurrection, to carry the fortified city of Karlsburg, and to prepare the defense of the defiles of the borders and of the mountains.

The Council of Ministers, as well as General Görgey, ex-pressed their concurrence with the views laid down in this plan ; and the necessary dispositions for its execution were immediately dispatched to the various commanders.*

The following were the forces which the Hungarians then held for carrying out this project :

First army corps (then around Buda), commander General Nagy-Shandor, ten battalions, ten squadrons of cavalry, and forty guns.

Second corps, commander General Aulick, ten battalions, fifteen squadrons, and forty guns.

Third corps, commander General Knezick, nine battalions, fourteen squadrons, and forty guns.

Colonel Kmetty's division, five battalions, six squadrons, and sixteen guns.

The following troops were in and around the city of Raab, in the island of Schütte, and in and around the fortress of Ko-morn :

Fourth corps, commanded by Colonel Pöltenberg ; and the fifth corps, commanded by General Lenkey. The former con-sisted of eleven battalions, seventeen squadrons, and forty-five guns ; and the latter of twelve battalions, four squadrons, and eighteen guns. Colonel Horvath's detachment of two battal-ions, three squadrons, and four guns was on the banks of the Neutra ; and a flying corps of two battalions, one squadron, and six guns, commanded by Major Armin Görgey, garrisoned the cities in the Carpathians.

The army on the Upper Danube was under the immediate command of Görgey, and amounted to a total of sixty-one bat-talions, seventy-two squadrons, two hundred and nine pieces of artillery, fifty thousand men, and seven thousand two hund-red horses. The rest of the Hungarians may be quoted as fol-lows :

1st. The army of the Banat, under the Generals Perczel

---

* Klapka.

and Vécsey, and afterward under Lieutenant-general Vetter. It numbered thirty thousand men.

2d. Bem's army in Transylvania, thirty-two thousand men.

3d. Lieutenant-general Dembinski's corps at Eperies, twelve thousand men.

4th. Colonel Kazintsky's division, in the Marmorosh, six thousand men.

5th. The garrison of Peterwardein, five thousand men.

The joint number of all these corps amounted to a total of one hundred and thirty-five thousand men, with four hundred pieces of artillery.*

Movements of F. M. L. Haynau.

General Haynau, in command of the first army corps, then resting around Pressburg, made no alterations in the positions of the Austrian army, but only applied himself to reorganize and newly divide it.

The re-enforcements which arrived from Austria Proper, Moravia, and Bohemia increased this army to fifty thousand men. A Russian division of sixteen thousand men entered Pressburg at this time, for the purpose of acting as a reserve force to the main army of the Austrians on the Upper Danube. The first corps of this army was under General Schlick, and the second, third, and fourth corps were commanded by Generals Czoric, Bamberg, and Wohlgemuth. At a later period, the fourth corps was commanded by Prince Lichtenstein. The cavalry division was under General Becthold, and the Russian reserve troops under General Paniutine.

Besides these forces, which were placed under General Haynau, as commander-in-chief and plenipotentiary of the emperor,

---

* Klapka.

According to Kossuth's statement, the number and distribution of the Magyar forces at this time were as follows:

Görgey's corps (after all losses) 45,000	men.
In the Banat.. 30,000	"
In Transylvania 40,000	"
On the Upper Theiss (county of Saros)............... 12,000	"
In the Marmorosh 6,000	"
In Peterwardein.................................... 8,000	"
Total....................................... 141,000	"

and which held an advantageous central position in and around
Pressburg, another reserve corps was concentrating at Pettau,
in Styria, under the auspices of General Nugent, who conducted this corps, at the end of June, to the county of Zala,
and thence against a powerful and well-organized rising of the
population around the Platten Sea.

A Russian corps, under General Grabbe, had meanwhile entered Hungary from Western Galicia, and advanced, though
slowly and cautiously, from the Arva, through the county of
Liptau, in the direction of the mountain districts.

The first engagement between the hostile forces took place
on the 13th of June, on the Rabnitz, near Csorna, where a
brigade of the Imperialists, under General Wyss, moving toward Raab to join the first division under F. M. L. Schlick,
was surprised by the Hungarians, and, after a severe conflict,
completely defeated. The accounts favorable to the Magyars
represent this battle as one of great importance, lasting for a
very long time, and ending in the slaughter of many thousands of Austrians and Russians ; while the Austrian papers
and bulletins make no mention whatever of the engagement.
The truth, so far as could be ascertained from impartial
sources, was, that the loss of the Imperialists, besides all their
cannon, amounted to several hundreds in killed, wounded, and
prisoners. Among the former was the commander, General
Wyss. On the following days, viz., the 14th and 16th, several engagements took place on the island of Schütte (lying immediately below Pressburg, and formed by the junction of the
Waag and Schwartzwasser Rivers with the Danube), at Kapo-
var, Szered, and Shintau, between the advanced posts of the two
armies, which were attended with alternating success. The
result, however, of these skirmishes was, that the Hungarians
abandoned to the Imperialists the island of Schütte, and, crossing the Waag at Guta, slowly retired before the pursuing enemy.

By this time Görgey had reached the scene of action, and,
after receiving intelligence of the defeat of the Hungarians on
the 16th, he resolved to take the command in person, and to
avenge the discomfiture of the Hungarian troops by a great
and brilliant feat of arms. On the 20th of June, four days

later, when, after reconnoitering extensively, the Imperialists
concluded to concentrate all their forces between the Waag
and the Neuhäusel Danube, Görgey, with thirty thousand
men and one hundred and eighty cannon, crossed these streams.
The second and third corps of the Hungarians attacked the
enemy between Szelly and Kiralyrev; while Klapka, with a
part of the eighth corps, endeavored to take Nyarasd, so as to
obtain command, if possible, of the passage over the Little Danube at Vásárut, and thus cut off the retreat of the Austrians.
But the Imperialists were in such numbers at Nyarasd and
its neighborhood, and several vigorous charges having been
made by the Uhlans and cuirassiers, who proved themselves
an overmatch for the hussars of Karolyi, Lehel, and Hunyadi
(who saw fire for the first time that day), they retreated, leaving their cannons behind.   Better success, however, attended
the Hungarians in another part of the field.   The second corps,
which was to cross the "Neuhäusel arm" early on the morning of the 20th, and to attack the enemy at Zsigard, under
cover of a dense fog, reached that point wholly unperceived
by the enemy.   This was the favorable moment for an attack
upon Zsigard, when the enemy was unprepared and open to a
surprise.   But no attack was made, as Görgey had ordered
them to wait for his arrival.   In a short time the sun arose,
the fog cleared away, and the Austrians beheld, to their great
astonishment, the Hungarian forces drawn up in battle array
at the distance of but one thousand yards.   They hastened to
regain the positions which they had occupied on the 16th.
Their movements were precipitate, and evidently confused, and
at that moment the roar of cannon sounded from the banks of
the Waag.   Major Rakovsky advanced with his troops against
Zsigard and the adjoining forest.   The Austrians, threatened
in their rear, and believing that an overpowering force was
marching against them, covered their retreat by a fight of thirty minutes' duration, abandoned their advantageous position
at Zsigard, and came to a stand between Pered and Szelly.

At ten o'clock in the morning, Colonel Ashboth ordered the
second corps to the charge without waiting for the arrival of
the commander-in-chief, and by this force, together with that
of Major Rakovsky, which had, in the mean while, joined the

main column, the enemy were driven from all the plantations
on the Waag into Pered. The preparations of the enemy
showed Pered to be the key of their position, and that the fortunes of the day were bound up in its occupation. Colonel
Ashboth, therefore, arranged a front attack of five battalions
and two batteries, while Rakovsky and his column advanced
on the left side* with a firm and steady pace, in the midst of
a furious fire of grape and grenades. The forty-eighth battalion had reached the church, when the Austrians uncovered a
masked battery, and opened a raking fire of ball and cartridge
upon them. The Hungarians were thrown back, but Colonel
Ashboth, deeply sensible of the importance of the moment,
rallied the retreating masses, and, placing himself at the head
of three battalions, he again led them to the charge. The brave
troops followed their intrepid leader. The main street was carried, every house, every garden, every court-yard was the scene
of a desperate combat. Austrians, Bohemians, Poles, stood front
to front, and breast to breast, with Magyars. The Imperialists
wavered at length. They moved backward, slowly and in good
order at first, but another charge dispersed them; and at two
o'clock at night, the Hungarians were in sole possession of Pered, with its dead, wounded, and captives. At this moment,
the third corps (nine battalions, fourteen squadrons, and forty
guns), under the command of General Knezick, arrived. Görgey, who had come up at the same time, had no sooner made
his appearance on the battle-field, than he took at once command of both corps, and ordered the troops to lie in bivouac at
Pered.†

He sent no troops in pursuit of the enemy in their flight to
Galantha and Deaki, which precaution might have been attended with important results; but Colonel Ashboth, notwithstanding the ability and gallantry he had that day exhibited,
was displaced for having proceeded to the attack before the
arrival of the commander-in-chief, and General Knezick met
with a similar fate on account of his slowness and indecision,
which had caused his late arrival on the scene of battle. General Knezick's place was given to Colonel Leiningen, and Ashboth's command was transferred to Colonel Kazony, the lead-

---

* Klapka.   † Ibid.

er of the cavalry of the third corps.*   This change of commanders was imprudent ; for it was difficult to replace the intimate knowledge of the peculiarities of their troops ; and on
the eve of a battle, against a vastly superior force, it was certainly altogether injudicious.

The following day (the 21st) the fight was renewed with
increased violence at Pered.   Görgey took his position in front
of Pered.   The Imperialists, strengthened by the arrival of
their reserved force, which had marched up in the night, the
Austrian brigade Polt and the Russian division Paniutine,
under the immediate command of F. M. L. Wohlgemuth, advanced and commenced the attack.   Although the Austrians
had been joined in the course of the night by an important re-
enforcement of Russian troops, they were at first repulsed ;
but, by their superiority in numbers,† they at length succeeded in turning the flank of the Hungarians, assailing their rear,
and forcing them to retire.   The action lasted from early
morning till eight o'clock at night.   The retreat of the Hungarians was conducted in the greatest order, although cut off
from the bridge, and the enemy had occupied Zsigard and Kiralyrev, through which their course lay, and which they were
forced to carry by storm.   The united loss of these two days,
on both sides, was estimated at nearly five thousand, in killed
and wounded.‡   The Hungarians retired to Komorn.

Immediately after this battle, the combined Austrian and
Russian armies transferred all their disposable force to the
right bank of the Danube, in order to begin their offensive
operations there.   On the 27th of the month, Raab§ was attacked by the allied forces, forty thousand strong.   The Hungarian garrison there, only nine thousand, under Pöltenberg,
Görgey failing to re-enforce him, held their position gallantly
from eight in the morning until three in the afternoon, when,

---

* Klapka.

† Pragay estimated the Hungarians at twenty-two thousand, and the Austrians
and Russians at ninety-five thousand.

‡ Klapka asserts the Hungarian loss on the 20th and 21st to have been two
thousand five hundred.

§ Haynau commenced his brutality here, by ordering Bö-Sarkany, all except
the church, to be burned to the ground, simply because the inhabitants sympathized with the Hungarians.

without any considerable loss of men and but two cannons, they retreated to Komorn.

This attack upon Raab occurred under the eyes of the Emperor of Austria, who was a witness of the whole engagement, and who entered the town in triumph as soon as it was abandoned by the enemy. After abandoning Raab, the Hungarians retired to the vicinity of Komorn, where, within the intrenched camp surrounding the head of the bridge, which led over to the fortress of Komorn, their army, consisting of the two corps under Görgey and Klapka and the garrison of Komorn, amounting to forty thousand strong, had concentrated. Hither the entire force of the Austrians and Russians, under the command of Haynau and the emperor, surrounded the enemy, with a view to throw them behind their intrenchments, and force them at length to submission.

Early on the morning of the 2d of July, the Hungarians were attacked on all sides. The Austrians, however, turned their main strength against the heights of Monosta, a position which commanded the entire Palatinal line, and from which the garrison itself could be annoyed by heavy ordnance. They carried the first four lines at the first charge. They then took the village of Szoney, into which the Hungarians had neglected to throw troops. The outer works being taken, the Austrian colors are hoisted on the walls, and the Hungarian battalions retreat to the inner line of fortifications. Again the Imperialists form, and prepare to attack the intrenchments, while a column, destined to operate against the rear, is pushed forward along the Danube, and protected by the high banks of that river. It was at this moment, when danger was most imminent, that the Hungarian staff appeared upon the field.

Görgey, contrary to his usual custom, appeared on this day in the splendid red and gold embroidered uniform of a general, and his tall white heron feathers were afterward seen at every point where any thing was to be disposed, ordered, or executed.* He took command of the right wing, committed the

---

* Görgey, having perhaps more to struggle against within himself than from the enemy, obviously sought death. With his conspicuous dress, he threw himself into the midst of the combat. He was wounded in the head by a cut from a sabre, but the balls seemed to avoid the general while they decimated those around

centre to Klapka, and the left to Leiningen. Encouraged
by his presence, the retreating troops rallied, and the combat
grew more violent as soon as these officers reached their respective posts.

Leiningen too soon prepared an unsuccessful cavalry charge,
which cost the Hungarians their bravest horse battery. This
battery accompanied the cavalry to the attack, and ventured
beyond their protected position; and when the latter were, by
the enemy's light horse, regiment Lichtenstein, suddenly repulsed, the battery also retreated at full speed, but, unhappily, in the direction of a ditch, which was not seen until it was
too late to rein in, and one cannon after another pitched into
it. The Imperialists, by superior force, took the guns, but it
was not until after they had slain every gallant soldier who attended them.

The battle, with various success, had lasted until past noon,
when one of Görgey's adjutants came to the centre with orders to Klapka to send help, if possible, to Leiningen, and to
take Szoney at any price, for he, Görgey, had already forced
the enemy from the lines on the heights, and driven their right
wing back to the wood of Acs. Klapka faithfully obeyed the
order, and in less than an hour, after two repulses, held Szoney in possession. The flying enemy were pursued in the direction of Todis. Görgey now, about six o'clock in the evening, came to the centre, took all the cavalry (twenty-nine
squadrons) and six batteries, and charged upon the hostile
centre, which he pursued till nightfall.

Haynau saw the danger. He advanced the Russian reserve,
and sent to his right wing for his cavalry. The Austrian horse
are beaten back, and the Hungarian squadrons sweep down
upon the Russian columns at Csém, where the career of the
bold horsemen is stopped by fifty guns from a covered position,
hurling death and destruction into their ranks. The Hungarian horse-batteries advance at the top of their speed; they
draw up, unlimber, and return the enemy's fire; but these batteries are soon silenced and forced to fall back.

---

him. The words he is said to have addressed to the Honvéds on this occasion
would seem to imply that he expected that day to be his last. "Forward, my
children; the ball to-day hits me alone!"

II.   T

The last great attack was equally unsuccessful, for the Austrians displayed large masses of cavalry against the Hungarian flank; and Görgey, while fighting in the *mêlée*, having been wounded in the head, was compelled to desist from his attempt to force the enemy's lines. Night came on, and at nine o'clock the last shots were fired on either side. The Austrians retired to their former positions, while the Hungarians again establish-ed themselves at the camp at Szoney, behind the intrench-ments.

The victory remained undecided; but the Austrians suffered far greater losses than their enemy. Haynau had become convinced that Görgey's positions were unassailable, while the latter perceived that Haynau's masses of troops were too compact to be broken. In each party claiming the victory as they did, they were both right, and both wrong. Each had failed in the attack; each had made a brilliant defense.

The Hungarian loss in dead and wounded is estimated at fifteen hundred; that of the Austrians, whose force was much larger, at three thousand.*

This brilliant repulse of a greatly superior force, although reflecting the highest credit upon the Hungarian arms, was afterward considered by them as more disastrous to the Hungarian cause than the most total defeat could possibly have been; for it unhappily confirmed their confidence in Görgey, which he subsequently so basely betrayed.

When returning to the city at a late hour in the evening, after setting the necessary guard, Klapka was met by a staff officer, who handed him an important dispatch from the government.† Its purport was to the effect that Görgey, who had refused, at the frequent and pressing request of the government, to retire with his troops to Pesth, but persisted in uselessly remaining about Komorn, while the capital of the country, the seat of government and the Diét, was abandoned to the enemy, should be removed from the chief command, and his place supplied by Meszaros.‡ Official letters of the same

---

* Klapka. Pragay puts down the Austro-Russian force in this action at ninety-five thousand; Klapka estimates them at thirty thousand.

† Pragay. Klapka.

‡ Görgey had but a few days before very coolly sent word to the government

tenor were sent with this document for the commanders of the several corps,'which Klapka was desired to deliver. The commanders of all the corps were assembled in the evening at Klapka's quarters. It was then concluded to say nothing to General Görgey, but to call a grand council of war the next day, at which this serious question should be discussed. The council met. At first there reigned a deep silence ; all seemed penetrated with the solemnity and importance of the occasion. The fate of the country hung upon their decision. That suspense lasted but for a moment. Feeling prevailed over judgment. With the romantic enthusiasm and generous confidence so peculiar to the Hungarians, and which had so often proved fatal to the best interests of their country, the silence was broken by the passionate cry, " No ! no ! Görgey must remain. We can not now serve under Meszaros.

A most unfortunate conjunction of circumstances then existed, which they felt it impossible to resist, and which afterward brought about the ruin of Hungary.

First. Görgey had but the day before made a noble stand against twice his own numbers, commanded by the emperor himself.

Secondly. This success was to be ascribed almost entirely to his bravery, for he had conducted in person the charge upon the lines that the enemy had already taken. He led in person the great column of cavalry that charged the enemy's centre.

Thirdly. The hero had been wounded on the day of his triumph.

Fourthly. General Meszaros, though a most honest patriot and brave man, was an unfortunate soldier, and consequently did not enjoy the confidence of the troops.

To have discarded Görgey just at that time and under those circumstances, would have required more than Roman firmness. It was resolved that Klapka and Nagy-Shandor should go to Pesth, and convey to the government the wishes of the army with respect to retaining Görgey. This was done, and the authority of the government preserved by following the

---

at Pesth that he was unable to protect them, and that if they had any regard for their safety they should fly.

suggestion of Kossuth; the appointment of Meszaros as commander-in-chief was unrevoked, but, upon Görgey's consent to
resign the ministry of war, he was to be made commander of
the army of the Upper Danube, to which he assented, and the
matter was thus arranged.

Thus was taken, through a misdirected confidence, the first
step toward the overthrow of Hungarian independence. Had
Kossuth come himself, had some other than Meszaros been appointed to the chief command, had the unlucky order arrived
but one day sooner, Görgey's fall, perhaps, would have been
accomplished, and Hungary saved.

From this time onward, Görgey paid but little attention to
the government, which still called him several times to the
protection of Pesth. He no longer considered himself appointed by the government, but chosen by the officers. For the future, all concert of action, so indispensable to success, was gone,
and the downfall of the country assured.

After their repulse at Acs, the Austrians withdrew to a short
distance, but still continued with the great body of the troops
surrounding the Hungarians, who remained about their intrenched camps, in the vicinity of Komorn.

Before Görgey had recovered from his wound, he devised a
plan for breaking through the Austrian army; then to move
toward Croatia, make requisitions of arms there, raise the siege
of Peterwardein, and either unite with the army of the south,
or with the main army of Dembinski, if that had been forced
so far down. The first part of this plan devolved upon Klapka
to execute. At eight in the morning of the 11th of July, the
troops were drawn up in the intrenched camp. At nine, the
eighth corps began their march upon the wood of Acs; the
seventh upon Puszta-Herkály; the third upon Csém; and the
first upon Mocsa. The fighting also soon commenced at all
points, and raged without intermission until three in the afternoon, without apparent advantage on either side.*

Klapka, in command of the third Hungarian corps, advanced
on the Igmand road, until they met the enemy at noon, in front
of Csém. This village, with its fenced farms, and the heights

---

* Klapka.

in its rear, was the key to the enemy's centre, who, when the
Hungarians attacked, occupied it with a brigade. After a short
fight, in which they silenced the enemy's artillery, the Hungarians carried the place at the point of the bayonet, and drove
the enemy before them; but, before the Hungarian reserve
columns could press to the charge and follow up their advantage, the gap in the enemy's battle-line was filled up by the
whole of the Austrian reserve, and by the Russian division
Paniutine, who received the fugitive brigade, rallied it, and
sent it, with a strong support, back to the charge, while eighty
field-pieces opened upon them from the neighboring heights.
For an hour the earth trembled with the roar of the cannons,
which, assembled on one point, were to decide the fate of the
day.   The effect on the Hungarian side was ruinous.   The
field was strewed with corpses.   Batteries were dismounted;
powder-carts exploded.   The Hungarians kept their position.
So did the Imperialists.   Some of the divisions retreated for a
time without the range of the fire; but they either returned
or were replaced by fresh troops.   If, according to the dispositions, Nagy-Shandor and Pigetti had advanced and joined the
attack of the third corps, they might have secured the victory;
for the enemy, wavering as they were, could not have resisted the impetus of their charge.   But Nagy-Shandor advanced
slowly, and Pigetti did not move at all.   The favorable moment
passed, and the Austrians, who were strongest in the centre,
seemed to prevail.   The Hungarians, thus finding it impossible either to drive the Austrians from their positions or to
break through their ranks, ceased fighting, and withdrew behind their intrenchments.

Movements of the Russians under Prince Paskievitch.

The Russian generals commenced the campaign against
Hungary with great precaution.   Before entering the country,
they sent to Vienna, and, through the Russian embassador,
obtained from the imperial archives copies of the dispatches
relating to the military operations in Hungary in former times,
under Charles of Lorraine, Eugène of Savoy, and Montecuculli, against Rakoczy, Tököly, and the Turks.

From these documents it appeared that all the invading gencrals of former days avoided, as much as possible, the plains of the Theiss. The city of Kashau was at that time the *point d'appui* of the imperial army, whence they crossed the Theiss, and drove the Hungarians under Rakoczy into the Szatmar comitat, and there dictated conditions of peace. Eugène of Savoy alone was obliged to select Szegedin as his place of operation, on account of the position of the Turkish army, and hence encountered great difficulties.

After the Emperor of Russia, with his son the Grand Duke Constantine, had accompanied the army under Prince Paskievitch as far as Dukla, in Galicia, near the frontiers of Hungary, he there reviewed the troops, and, urging them to deeds of glory, bade them adieu. He returned to Warsaw, and the army of eighty-seven thousand men crossed the frontiers into Hungary on the 18th of June. The Russians entered in three divisions; the one under General Rüdiger from Neumarkt, over Ajal to Lublyo; another from Dukla, over Komarieck to Bartfeldt; and the third directly on Eperies, to which point the movements of the three corps were directed, and where they were to concentrate.

With but slight opposition from the Hungarians, the divisions of the Russian army met at Eperies about the 20th of June, and thence pursued their march without serious interruption — General Wisocki's corps in the Carpathians being unable to oppose them—and with the loss of a few Cossacks in their advanced guard, reached Kashau about the 25th; and, after leaving a garrison there, marched on, and arrived at Miskolcz about the 30th. That army then separated into two divisions; one to march upon Debreczin, and the other upon Pesth; and both were entirely successful. The division marching upon Debreczin took possession of that capital without resistance on the 7th of July (the Hungarian Diet having, after the late victories, removed its sittings to Pesth, and upon the second Austrian invasion to Szegedin); while the other division under General Ramberg, proceeding on Pesth, captured that city on the 11th, without encountering opposition.* On the 17th, the first army corps under F. M. L. Haynau, which

* When Kossuth and his ministers, who were at that time at Pesth, heard of the approach of the Russians to the capital, they took their departure for Szegedin.

since the battle of Acs had established their head-quarters at
Nagy-Igmand, leaving the second army corps under F. M. L.
Czoric to besiege Komorn, broke up from that point, proceeded down the right bank of the Danube to Buda-Pesth, and entered the Hungarian capital on the 19th.*

Dembinski, toward the end of the last campaign, after the
brilliant succession of triumphs which distinguished its close,
proceeded, with a body of troops newly raised during the months
of April and May, to the northern frontier, for the purpose of
guarding it against a new invasion from Galicia.

Of this force, numbering in the beginning about twelve thousand, Dembinski, toward the end of May, resigned the command, because, as was said, the government would not approve
his plan of an irruption into Galicia.

His successor, General Wisocki, was not long able to hold
out against the overwhelming force of Russians that entered
under Paskievitch, and by the end of June was obliged to give
up his position ; and, constantly harassed by the daily advancing Cossacks, he gradually withdrew before them, and moved
down toward Pesth, in order, if possible, to protect the capital.

On reaching Szolnok, he was joined by Perczel's reserve of
fourteen thousand men, and to which, after the evacuation of
Pesth in the middle of July, were added the troops who had
been in that city, to the number of four thousand.   Notwithstanding the want of confidence generally expressed by the
corps of officers during the campaign of the previous winter,
Kossuth still rested his boldest hopes on Dembinski, and conferred upon him the chief command of this army, now thirty
thousand strong.

This appointment was made, not as some Austrian journals
state, on account of the fear which Kossuth had of seeing Görgey aspire to a military dictatorship, but principally for the
purpose of putting an end to the divisions and jealousies of the
native chiefs ; it was resolved to place the army under the
supreme command of a foreigner, whose position was less likely
to induce him to find fault with the measures of the Diet and
the government, and who could confine his authority to the

---

* In the march of the Russians to the centre of the kingdom, General Grabbe,
with a division of the army, occupied Cremnitz and Shemnitz, without resistance.

conduct of the war. But it was necessary also not to hurt the feelings of the Hungarian officers; for this purpose a great historical name was sought and found. Dembinski, the old Polish general, was placed at the head of all the Hungarian armies, and Görgey and all other Magyar officers were subjected to him.*

OPERATIONS IN THE SOUTH UNDER JELLACIC.

At the end of April, when the army of the Ban separated itself from the rest of the imperial forces in the centre of Hungary, he received instructions to form it into an army of the south by a junction with the divisions of Nugent and Puchner, and afterward with that of the Servian general, Knicanin. Events, however, only enabled the Ban to effect this junction with a few of the Servians and a portion of Nugent's corps. After a long march from Pesth to Eszek, and a halt of several days at the latter place, which delay was turned to account by the organization of new field batteries, clothing the troops, &c., he arrived, toward the end of May, in the vicinity of Peterwardein. Here the Ban determined to assume the offensive, and to cross the Danube, which was effected by the aid of steamers, from Szlankament to Tittel. He moved forward on the 5th, and found the Csaikisten circle, recently occupied by Perczel's army, abandoned, and the whole of that flourishing country laid waste. They had retired to Neusatz. On the 7th, Perczel's corps broke out unexpectedly from its intrenched camp near Neusatz, passed the Roman levies, and attacked the imperial army near Katsch. The Hungarians repulsed, returned to Neusatz. On the 10th, the Ban moved against Neusatz, and attacked the intrenched camp on the night of the 11th. Perczel abandoned his position at Neusatz; but owing to the heavy and continued fire from the fortress of Peterwardein, Jellacic could not take possession of the town.†

In relation to the operations in the southern part of Hungary but little information is obtainable, except through the dispatches of Baron Jellacic, and they are of so obviously partial

---

* Klapka.

† The cholera also raged terribly; all the wells filled with dead bodies, and the heat excessive.

a character that entire confidence can not be reposed in them. He reports a great victory over the enemy under Perczel, between Tittel and Römershanze, on the 7th of June, in which the Hungarians had " five hundred killed, and two hundred and twenty wounded ;" " whole battalions cut to pieces ;" " the field covered with the dead ;" while he again lost his favorite number of two men killed and twelve wounded.   In another bulletin, he says he has obtained a victory over the garrison of Peterwardein, when making a sortie, but lost several pieces of ordnance.

Those two triumphs (in consequence of which the funds of the Vienna Exchange rose) are reduced to the fact that the first was but an insignificant skirmish, in which Ottinger's Walmoden cuirassier's had made one successful charge ; and the second a perfect defeat of Jellacic ; for the garrison of Peterwardein made a sally against Kamenitz, took two intrenchments by storm, entirely destroyed them, spiked all the heavy guns, and carried the light ones into the fortress.   According to his own account, he had effected the conquest of Neusatz, the rescue of Temesvar, and the defeat of Perczel ; but as the formidable fortress of Peterwardein, in the immediate neighborhood, remained still in the hands of the Hungarians, and as advices from that quarter, arriving about the same time, reported the contemplated junction of the forces under Bem and Perczel, for the purpose of operating against him, it might with more propriety be concluded that, at the very date of these great victories, the Croatian general had not only accomplished but little, but that his own situation had become critical in the extreme.

After the slight engagement at Tittel, Perczel retired toward Theresiopel, and Jellacic to the neighborhood of Neusatz, whence he commenced to bombard the fortress of Peterwardein, while Colonel Mamula continued to fire into it from the opposite side at Kamenitz.

A little later, owing to the frequent collisions between Perczel and his officers, he was removed, and his place supplied by the appointment of General Vetter, who, gathering up the scattered fragments of Perczel's army, immediately confronted the enemy.   On the 14th of July, General Guyon, commanding

a wing of this army, attacked the Croats, and the very day that
Jellacic had designed for an attack on him. Informed by spies
of the position of the Magyars, he set out on the 14th of July,
with the intention of surprising them in the darkness of the
night; but the arrow recoiled upon the marksman. "Guyon,
having received timely information that the Ban, whom he
usually called 'The perjured Jack-Pudding,' contemplated hon-
oring him with a visit, made his arrangements quietly, though
hastily, to receive the uninvited guest in a becoming manner."*

At midnight, Jellacic set out from Verbasz, and advanced
at daybreak, with full expectation of success, into the defile of
Hegyes, without having even dispatched a side-detachment
toward Fékétehegy or Szeghegy. He was already entrapped
when the first cannon-shot thundered on the flanks of his troops.
The shades of night were still struggling with the morning
mists, when it became clear to the Austrians that every step
in advance was one nearer to destruction. Now began the
disastrous retreat through the cross-fire of the Hungarian batteries. The flight lasted without intermission to the Francis
canal, to Verbasz, to Ruma ; and even here, the Ban, not feeling secure, removed his head-quarters to Mitrovicz.

He there mustered his troops, not a third remaining of those
whom he had led over the canal on that night of horror ; the
rest had fallen, been taken prisoners, or were scattered to the
winds. To the undaunted valor of the Ottinger cavalry, which
protected his retreat, as well as they were able, at the sacrifice of their own lives, the Ban of Croatia alone owed the remains of his boasted army of the south.

He attributed the failure of his enterprise to the "knavery
of a traitor," and a captain whom he suspected of communicating intelligence of his movements to the enemy was arrested and executed.

This battle was one of the bloodiest during the whole contest, and the consequences of the victory to the Hungarians
were most important. The Bacska was freed from the enemy,
the Francis canal, Jellacic's most important line of operations,
was lost ; the army of the south decimated, its remains driven

---

* Schlessinger.

into a corner, scattered and demoralized; the fortress of Peterwardein, on the other side, was relieved, and supplied anew
with provisions, ammunition, and men.*

Guyon, an Irishman by birth, enlisted as a volunteer in the
expedition against Don Miguel; he afterward traveled on the
Continent, and, by chance, met at Trieste with some officers
of the second hussar regiment. He was pleased with the smart
uniform, and the social, brotherly life of the Austrian officers,
which, indeed, might serve as a model to all the armies in the
world. In consequence, he applied for a commission in the
imperial army, and entered the Archduke Joseph's hussar regiment as a cadet. In a very short time he was advanced to
the rank of first lieutenant, and was much esteemed in his
regiment as a true-hearted comrade, a brave officer, and a man
of education. He afterward obtained the post of aid-de-camp
to Baron Ignaz Splenyi, who was at that time commander of
the regiment and captain of the Hungarian noble guard.†

Guyon subsequently married a Hungarian lady of the Splenyi family,‡ left the regiment after the death of the old baron,
sold a portion of his property, and bought a small estate in
Hungary. Here, engaged in agricultural pursuits, he passed
a healthy and cheerful life in intercourse with the neighboring
landed proprietors, among whom he soon became famed far
and wide as the boldest of horsemen. Such was his mode of
life at the outbreak of the great Revolution. Kossuth offered
him a major's commission, and Guyon, who had become attached to the country with the whole energy of his character,
did not hesitate to draw the sword in defense of her rights.§

---

* Austrian journals related falsely that the battle of Hegyes was planned by
Bem. This erroneous statement was copied into most of the foreign journals.

† Schlessinger.

‡ Madame Guyon appears to possess much of the resolution of her husband.
In the course of the war, she exhibited her courage in various ways. When
Windischgrätz entered Pesth, every one who lived in Buda had to enter his or
her name in a book, in order that the prince might know whom he had about him
in the fortress. Among the rest, came the turn of Madame Guyon, who had remained behind with the old Baroness Splenyi, and her name is to be seen entered
in the above-mentioned book, written in her own hand, with the description affixed —" Wife of a rebel chief."

§ Guyon is thirty-four years of age, of middle stature, bold and resolute features,
elegant and winning manners. The chivalry of the Magyar and the nobility of
the high-born Englishman are worthily represented in his person.—*Schlessinger.*

After his defeat, Jellacic finding his situation critical, marched up the Theiss, with a view of joining the army of Haynau, then advancing south, as well as with a view to reach Szegedin, and eventually complete the occupation of the whole line of that river before Kossuth and Görgey could cross it between the northern and southern armies.

OPERATIONS IN TRANSYLVANIA BETWEEN THE RUSSIANS AND BEM.

About the middle of June, and at the same period that Prince Paskievitch and Rüdiger, with their immense armies, were entering Hungary on the north, three Russian corps, under Lüders, Grotjenhelm, and Hasford, were penetrating the country on the south. After the mountain passes had once been opened, the united forces of the enemy poured in like a flood, and threatened to overwhelm the defenders of the country from all sides. Bem, although he had completely subdued Transylvania,* and declared martial law throughout the province, was unable to resist successfully the overwhelming force, consisting, as was said, of forty thousand Russians and fourteen thousand Austrians, who approached on three different sides, as well as an insurrection of about thirty thousand Wallachians in their midst.

On the 15th, General Clam Gallas, at the head of the Austrian corps lately commanded by General Puchner, entered Transylvania from Wallachia, and marched upon Kronstadt. On the 20th, the main body of the Russians, under General Lüders, stormed, and carried at the point of the bayonet, the Tömös Pass. General Bem had committed the defense of that pass to the Hungarian colonel, Kisz. The fighting must have been severe, as a colonel of Cossacks was killed and General Dyk mortally wounded, but the Russians, by their numbers, prevailed. Colonel Kisz was taken prisoner, the Hungarians fled, and General Lüders, passing the quarantine station, bivouacked near the custom-house, and at the entrance of a long, narrow defile, which was to be stormed on the following day. On the next day the defile was carried, and

---

* Bem was laying siege to Temesvar, in the Banat, when he heard of the entrance of the Russians, but he immediately raised the siege, and returned into Transylvania to oppose them.

General Lüders advanced, and occupied Kronstadt the same day. He then, leaving Clam Gallas, with his force, in charge of Kronstadt, marched upon Hermanstadt, which, defended only by two thousand five hundred men, could not resist the Russian force of thirteen thousand five hundred, and, after a short resistance, surrendered. At the same time, General Engelhardt had penetrated the country through the Törzburg Pass, while the third Russian column, under General Freitag, at a great sacrifice of life, was endeavoring to hold the Ojtos Pass.

While these successes were attending the Russians under Lüders, the corps under General Hasford, entering Transylvania on the north, took possession of Bistricz, the chief town of the Saxonland, and drove back the Szeklers to Reismark. The Szeklers, however, returned and carried the city; but General Grotjenhelm coming up with a superior force, they abandoned it and fled.

General Bem had in the mean time passed over into Moldavia by the Ojtos Pass, hoping by his presence to put in motion all the revolutionary elements which had been accumulating for years past in the Principalities. In this, however, he failed. His rapid advance to Romau, as well as his proclamations, were equally without effect, and he consequently had no alternative left him but to return as hastily as possible to Transylvania.

Thus had the Austrians for a second time, entering Hungary at the four cardinal points, marched without serious opposition (the battles of Acs and Komorn alone excepted) into the very heart of the country, subduing all opposition as they advanced, and finally planting their victorious standards in the very capital of the kingdom, as they had done in the months of December and January preceding. The general plan of the campaign seemed to be to form a complete circle of the whole kingdom, and rapidly converge, so as to compress the Revolution in a ring of armies.

And so far it appeared to have been successfully executed. Haynau and Wohlgemuth, as has been seen, with the Austrian and Russian force, occupying the immediate frontier of Lower Austria and Moravia; Nugent and Jellacic operating on the

Danube and along the southern frontier, and the Russians, under Lüders and Paskievitch, embracing the semicircle to the north and east from the Rothenthurm Pass to the highest peak of the Carpathians.

On the other hand, what was the plan of the Hungarians? The months of April and May were to them a career of almost uninterrupted victory. They crossed the Theiss; they passed the Danube; they relieved Komorn; they stormed Buda, and their van-guard reached to the very frontiers of Austria on the north, while the army of the south, under Bem, had driven every hostile foot from the soil of Transylvania.

Yet here they paused. They failed to follow up these remarkable successes with vigor; no attempt was made to force the Austrians to treat, though Vienna itself lay unprotected before them. In short, under circumstances the most favorable to their cause, the Magyars turned their success and the evident weakness of their antagonists to little profit. This delay was precisely what the Russians most required. The Emperor Nicholas refused to be hurried to the field, or to operate otherwise than on the largest scale, and with a very extensive plan of campaign.

These very circumstances could have been made to operate most powerfully in their favor. Their situation did not require delay; they not only had an army raised and organized, but with all the experience furnished by a campaign through which they had just passed, flushed with victory, and confident of their invincibility. The mode of attack even, especially in its inception, afforded advantages to the Hungarians—for the superiority of forces was lost by their extreme dissemination, while the weaker party had the advantage of concentration. A general of great activity, and perfectly acquainted with the country, might bring a larger force to bear against some divisions of the allied army, defeat it in successive portions, and break the ring which had been formed around Hungary.

With such external defenses as Hungary is naturally girded, the mighty Carpathians bounding the country on three sides, and penetrable only at certain passes, which could have been so easily fortified and defended by a few troops against formidable armies, it is difficult to conceive why these passes

or entrances to the enemy should have been left open or abandoned without a blow, except on the obvious ground of policy,
and in connection with some settled plan of defense. It seemed
idle to suppose that this coincident falling back, north, east,
and west, of two hundred thousand men, elated with the indisputable successes that enabled them to clear their territory, at
the outset, without any attempt at serious resistance, could be
any thing but a strategic combination.

This mystery could only be explained on the ground of some
well-digested plan of defense that had been adopted by the
leaders, and the benefit of which would shortly be developed ;
or, on the more probable supposition that, owing to the jealousy and hatred which existed among the several commanders,
no suitable system of defense could be agreed upon, and each
was left to pursue such course as he might deem best, either
for the welfare of his country or for the advancement of his
own views.

Had the Hungarians not succeeded in so defending the passes
of the Carpathians as to prevent the admission of the enemy,
had they failed in so concentrating their forces on particular
points as not to have destroyed him in detail, a better plan, it
would seem, could not have been devised than to have retreated together to the Theiss.   The pestilential marshes of that
stream at that season would have been most disastrous to the
enemy, while to them, from habit, the malaria would have prov-
en innoxious.   On its low and miry banks, the heavy artillery
of the enemy, their principal arm of defense, would have been
rendered useless, while the great surrounding plains were peculiarly adapted to the operation of cavalry, in which their own
superiority consisted.   The most warlike portion of the Magyars inhabited principally the banks of the Theiss, and the
productive lands within this circle were still ladened with the
superabundant harvest of two years, which, in consequence of
political troubles, had not found in Austria their accustomed
mart.   And finally, within this narrowed sphere, the Magyars
could more fully enjoy the benefit of their concentric position,
and each army would not only be nearer to the other, but better able to yield assistance at any point more seriously threatened by the external ring of its assailants.

OPERATIONS UNDER GENERAL GÖRGEY.

The repeated directions of Kossuth to Görgey, to leave Komorn and proceed south, not only for the protection of the government, but to prevent being cut off from all connection with the Hungarian armies of the south by the advance of the Russians, he treated, as he had recently all the orders of the government, with utter contempt. In explanation of his remarkable course, Prince Wittgenstein, a Russian diplomatist,* in a circular dispatch from Frankfort, bearing date the 21st of July, affords some light when he states, " It is but fair to presume that Görgey, with the bulk of the Hungarian army, remained in and around Komorn for the special purpose of not being compelled to co-operate with Kossuth and the Poles, and *with the intention of treating with the Imperialist generals as soon as his retreat is cut off, by the occupation of Pesth and the country on the banks of the Theiss.* At Vienna they have reason to believe that *Görgey will treat and surrender within the next fortnight.*"† Görgey's negotiations with Paskievitch are supposed to have commenced some weeks previously, and, as corroborative of the suspicion, Klapka, in his memoirs, mentions, that as early as the 7th of July, at Komorn, several of Görgey's officers, when conversing on the divisions in the Hungarian army, said that " they were resolved to prefer the result of honorable *negotiations* to dissensions among themselves, and to the dissolution of the army."‡

When Görgey, after the battle of the 11th of July at Komorn, became sufficiently convinced that the project (which he had entertained merely with a view to avoid a union with the other Hungarian troops) of breaking through the Austrian armies on the right bank of the Danube could not be executed, leaving a sufficient force to garrison the fortress, which under Klapka made a feigned attack, to attract the attention of the enemy during his departure, he marched from Komorn down

---

* The Russians are regarded as the shrewdest diplomatists in Europe. They are the first to know every event of importance which occurs any where on the continent. The Russian minister at Vienna could always apprise the English and French embassadors of what was transpiring at London or Paris, and of which they had not the slightest conception.

† Pulszky. Appendix.   ‡ Klapka.

the left bank, on the 13th of July, toward Waitzen, then held
by a Russian division of Paskievitch's army under General
Sass, which had come up from Pesth.

Görgey's army amounted to forty-five thousand men, divided into three *corps d'armée*, under Generals Nagy-Shandor,
Count Leiningen, and Pöltenberg. They were the choicest
troops of Hungary (some of them the heroes of thirty battles),
provided with seven regiments of cavalry, mostly veteran, and
one hundred and forty-nine cannons excellently served.

On the afternoon of the 13th, Görgey's van-guard reached
Waitzen, and there engaged the Russian troops under Sass and
Rüdiger. The fight was prolonged until evening, and the result was in so far favorable to the Hungarians, that they maintained their position throughout the day and during the night,
while the Russians left the town and marched out to the
heights lying toward Pesth.

On the following morning, Görgey's two other corps came
up, and supported the van-guard in a general attack upon the
Russian troops. " But I became convinced," as Görgey himself writes, " that the enemy too had, in the course of the night,
received considerable re-enforcements from Gödöllö and Pesth,
and that their artillery force especially was by far superior to
the forces I could dispose of. This conviction, and a careful
review of our strength, caused me (in the interest of my country) to resign all thoughts of breaking the Russian lines at
Waitzen, and to proceed on a safe road to Losoncz, Putnok,
and Miskolcz.

In pursuance of this design, Görgey, at evening, issued orders
to begin the march, during the night, on the mountain road,
in order to reach the line of the Theiss. In obedience to this
order, the troops moved, at midnight, in perfect silence ; but
the great number of baggage-wagons impeded the march so
seriously, that at four in the morning the rear-guard, with
many wagons, was still in Waitzen. The Russians, about
dawn, observing the retreat, attacked the rear-guard, dispersed
several divisions, and seized all the baggage of the two corps,
together with some dismounted cannon. When the tidings of
this attack reached the commander-in-chief, he dispatched several divisions to the assistance of the rear, who, at six o'clock,

recaptured the baggage and expelled the Russians from the town.

But closely pursued by the corps under Rüdiger and Sass, and opposed in front by the Russian reserve under General Grabbe, that had just entered from Galicia into the passes of the Carpathians, Görgey, it was supposed, must be surrounded and cut off.

At Recsag, on the small lake formerly known by the name of "Ocellum Maris," an insignificant Russian corps made a stand against him; he was content to avoid it. At Vadkert he again fell in with the Russian troops; but here also, like a lion, he despised inferior prey, continued his march toward Balassa Gyarmath, and took up his head-quarters, on the 19th, in Ludany. He now stood on the River Ipoly, which rising a few miles to the north, in the Osztrosky Mountains, rushes, with impetuous force, through the valley; here, on the Rasos Pass, extending between the river and the wooded mountains, he had thought to gain a firm footing, but it was too late. Grabbe, who had preceded, drove him still further northward to Losoncz. Sass followed in his footsteps, and came up with his rear-guard at Losoncz, after the main corps had already marched out on the road to Gyöngyös. Nagy-Shandor, who commanded the rear-guard since the battle of Waitzen, withstood the shock bravely; and after a hot engagement, which spread into the streets of the town, was able to follow the main corps, united with which he, on the 25th, occupied the strong positions before Gömör.*

But the further Görgey proceeded eastward, and nearer he approached the Theiss, the more narrowed became the circle of the Russians, who were pursuing and awaiting him. Sass, who hung upon his heels, daily concentrating the scattered columns, was now in direct communication with Grabbe, and the two generals combined their maneuvers for a general chase in the mountains, while Tscheodajeff, in Miskolcz,† was waiting, like a sportsman at his post, until the noble prey was driven within shot.

---

* Schlessinger.
† It will be remembered that this general had gone back from Debreczin to Miskolcz.

Why Görgey, on his march, never once attempted to annihilate the inferior forces of Sass, and relieve himself of this dis-
agreeable escort, is irreconcilable with honesty of purpose, and
only consistent with the charge that he was keeping up negotiations, during the march, with the Prince of Warsaw.

The first visible negotiator between himself and the Russians appeared at Rima-Szombath, in the person of a nephew
of General Rüdiger, who brought him a present of Russian
arms ; and, at the same time, desired to conclude an armistice
of twenty-four hours. Görgey accepted the gift, and returned
the courtesy with a present of arms, but declined the proposed
armistice.*

His treasonable purposes became now daily more evident.
At the very next station he removed the chief of his general
staff, and substituted his own brother, Lieutenant-colonel
Armin Görgey, that he might be able to operate with more
secrecy. He intentionally and rapidly so weakened the physical and moral vigor of his forces, that he, a few days after,
at Putnok, ventured to speak openly and with impunity of a
surrender to the Russians. And still a few days later, at
Szikszo, where the first army corps then was, an aunt of
Görgey's was apprehended, and upon her person were discovered letters which she was conveying from him to Field-marshal Paskievitch, of a tenor that left no doubt as to his purposes of surrender. General Nagy-Shandor sent these letters
by special carriers in all haste to the government, and Kossuth
thereupon appointed a meeting for a conference with Görgey
at Czibakháza, which the latter declined to accept.† When
Nagy-Shandor, who was left by Görgey to protect his rear,
and, as that brave officer declared to Kossuth, out of mere hatred, purposely exposed by Görgey to danger, had fought with
his Honvéds, at Gömör and before Rosenau, against an enemy
three times his superior in numbers, at length, with his battalions, hunted down, starved, and decimated, reached the
main army at Miskolcz, he found Görgey engaged with Tscheodajeff.‡ Already, from afar, the thunder of the heavy artil-

* Pragay.
† Kossuth has assured the author of the correctness of the above statement.
‡ Schlessinger.

lery fell on his ear, and, with a last effort of his exhausted
troops, he pressed forward to the field of battle. The Russians soon retired, and Görgey was enabled to take very favorable positions from Onod to Zsolcza, to destroy the Sajo
bridge, and, protected by the stream, wood, and marsh, to
undertake the defense of this line. Nagy-Shandor and Pöltenberg performed here prodigies of valor on the 25th, while
Görgey conducted the engagement with the whole power of
his genius. The battle lasted from morning until night.
Görgey's superior tactics, and his keen perception in taking
advantage of the natural features of the ground, saved his
army from utter annihilation; and neither his officers nor the
Russian generals that evening doubted that he would at once
force the passage of the Theiss at Tisza-Füred. But Görgey,
contrary to all expectations, both of friend and foe, crossed the
Sajo and Hernad, and gave his troops a day's rest at Gesztely. In this position, Grabbe attacked him, and was driven
back to Onod (on the 28th). Another Russian column, ordered at the same time to advance toward Tokay, was likewise
arrested in its march at the Hernad. The head-quarters of
the Russians were removed to Tisza-Füred, and Görgey at
length crossed the Theiss.

About the 20th of July, when Görgey was at Putnok, the
Russian army, under Paskievitch, occupied the great road
from Miskolcz to Pesth, while Dembinski, with the new army
of thirty thousand men intrusted to his command, was on the
shores of the Theiss, near Szolnok.

A glimpse at the map of Hungary will show that Paskievitch at Miskolcz was just half way between Görgey at Putnok and Dembinski at Szolnok.

The situation of Paskievitch at this time between these two
hostile fires was perilous indeed, and had there been any understanding or concert of action between Görgey and Dembinski, he must have been annihilated.

Nothing could have been better timed, or apparently more
admirably conducted, than both these movements on the part
of the Hungarian generals. Paskievitch's force, although immense, was stretched out along an extensive line from Miskolcz to Pesth, with thousands of his men dead or dying daily

of cholera and Theiss fever, were incapable of moving, not-withstanding the repeated orders of his emperor to hasten op-erations.*

Dembinski, from various sources, had raised up as by mag-ic a large army on his front, while Görgey, by incredible forced marches, through a mountainous region and the brist-ling ranks of the enemy, had carved out for himself with the sword a way to his rear.† Could these generals but have un-derstood each other, and have advanced upon Paskievitch, and then united upon the field of victory over the routed Russians, their combined army could easily afterward have demolished the Austrians under Haynau.

But, alas! for their unhappy country, the discussions and jealousies of these two leaders prevented either from asking or rendering assistance to the other, or in any manner co-op-erating, although the object to be advanced was the welfare of a common country.

After two unimportant engagements with the Russians,‡ Dembinski, having his mind more occupied with defeat than victory, and fearful of an attack upon his position at Szolnok by Haynau, who was at that period with his army at Pesth, or that Haynau's advance south would place him between two fires, left ten thousand of his men at Czegled, under Perczel and Wisocki, who still awaited Görgey, and started with his main forces for Kecskemet, in order to await there the further operations of the Austrian army. When Haynau, leaving Pesth, directed his course south in pursuit of the Hungarian armies, Perczel and Wisocki, following Dembinski, retired south by way of Kecskemet to Szegedin.§

---

* Paskievitch, in one of his dispatches, states that he was compelled at one moment to halt, by the circumstance that five thousand men of the Russian army had been attacked by cholera in three days.

† One of the most energetic and successful moves of the war, for it defeated the first strategical combination of the imperial armies, broke their line, and placed a formidable enemy in the rear of the Russians. To fight was imperative. To have maneuvered in co-operation with Görgey, and to have fought Paskievitch to effect the junction, was what was universally expected.

‡ The Cologne Gazette reports a brilliant victory gained by Dembinski over Paskievitch, at Hatvan, on the night of the 24th of July, in which sixteen thou-sand Russians were killed; but this report is unsupported by other evidence than the supposed official bulletin of Dembinski.   § Pragay.

MOVEMENTS OF F. M. L. HAYNAU.

In the mean time Haynau arrived, as we have seen, in Pesth with his army on the 19th of July, and immediately commenced the same brutality which had marked his course in Pressburg. While at Pressburg, to the deep disgrace of the Austrian government, he ordered ladies of great respectability and high rank to be "publicly flogged for having held communication with the insurgents;"* and brave officers executed for no other offense than that of vindicating their country.

At Pesth his brutality found a new means of indulgence,

---

* The Hungarian commander of the fortress of Leopoldstadt (who surrendered unconditionally in the beginning of February to the Austrians), as well as the commander of the artillery at that place, were tried by court-martial and hung. The first of these gallant men, Baron Ladislaus Medniansky, belonged to a branch of one of the noblest families in Hungary. He had previously served in the Hungarian Noble Guards; but having retired from service, held no rank in the Austrian army. His father was privy counselor, president of the exchequer, and well known as an author and statesman. His imputed crime was that, in the council of war in which the surrender of the fortress was resolved, he voted for holding out to the last man. The second victim, Major Grube, who commanded the artillery of the fortress, was hanged for remaining with his regiment in the Hungarian army, having been an officer in the Austrian army. Haynau ordered him to be tried as a deserter. The commandant of the fortress, Lieutenant-colonel Ordody, in consideration of his having surrendered the place after the first bombardment, was sentenced to only eight years of close confinement in a fortress. Nor was Haynau satisfied with the execution of brave officers. He afterward ordered to be hanged the Protestant clergyman Razga, of Pressburg, a man of superior education, and one of the most celebrated preachers in Hungary. With true evangelical courage and devotion, at the foot of the gallows the noble victim harangued the crowd, telling them he forgave his enemies, and adjuring every one to love his country.

Madame von Udvarnoky, a "much respected, rich, and handsome Hungarian lady," was flogged at Pressburg. At Raab, Haynau had the daughter of a professor in the university (Geyer) flogged in the yard of the town hall; her offense was that she turned her back upon the emperor as he entered the city.—*Pulszky.*

At Ruskby, Madame'Madersbach received the same treatment under most aggravating circumstances, and it was attended with most disastrous consequences, as the following extract from her letter shows: "I am not aware that any of us committed any fault. I was suddenly, without a previous trial or examination, taken from my husband and children. I was dragged into a square formed by the troops, and, in the presence of the population which had been accustomed to honor me, not because I was the lady of the manor, but because the whole tenor of my life deserved it, I *was flogged with rods.* You see I can write the words without dying of shame; but my husband took his own life. Deprived of all other weapons, he shot himself with a small cannon. A general cry of horror was raised. I myself was taken to Karansebes."—*Klapka.*

which was to inflict upon the Jews of Buda-Pesth contributions in money so exorbitant as to be utterly destructive of
their fortunes. To this they were condemned nominally as
Jews, but really as Hungarian patriots. The public and private feeling of every inhabitant of the capital was known, and
Jews entertained no other political sentiments than their Christian brethren; but it seemed to be the opinion of this brutal
commander that Jews had less right than Christians to be liberal and patriotic.

He no sooner arrived in Pesth than (on the 19th) he addressed a proclamation to the inhabitants of the city, declaring, "Any individual who shall, either by word or action, or
by wearing any revolutionary signs or emblems, dare to support the cause of the rebels—any individual who shall insult
one of my soldiers or those of our brave allies, either by words
or blows, or any individual who shall enter into any criminal
relations with the enemies of the crown, or who shall seek to
kindle the flame of rebellion by reports spread for a sinister
purpose, or who shall be rash enough to conceal arms or not
deliver them up within the time fixed by my proclamation,
shall be put to death with the shortest possible delay, and
on the spot where the crime was committed, without distinction of age or sex."   This was addressed to the inhabitants of
Pesth; a few weeks later, he addressed another proclamation
to the people of the countries of the Theiss, still surpassing it
in fiendish brutality, and of which the following is an extract:
"Take care not to incur my vengeance by revolutionary movements.   Not being able in such case to find out the guilty
party, I shall be compelled to punish the whole district.   If
on the territory occupied by my army, or in its rear, any attempt shall be committed against my soldiers, or if any of the
convoys should be stopped, or a courier, or the transport of provisions prevented, an immediate punishment shall be inflicted
on the guilty commune—*it shall become the prey to flames,
and be leveled to the ground,* to serve as a frightful example
to other communes."

As soon as Haynau was advised of the appearance of Dembinski at Kecskemet, he immediately made every preparation
to overtake him.

The Russian division under Paniutine was dispatched on the 23d of July from Pesth, on the road to Kecskemet; on the 24th, the great body of the Austrian army; and on the 25th, after issuing a proclamation, and threatening the inhabitants of Buda-Pesth with the same chastisement he had inflicted on Brescia,* if they should attempt any thing in his absence, he left himself, attended by his staff.

F. M. L. Haynau, with his army, reached Kecskemet on the 26th, and, after a short struggle, Dembinski, finding that it would be impossible for him to oppose successfully so superior a force, abandoned the town to the Imperialists, and retreated toward Szegedin.

On the 27th, Haynau took possession of Kecskemet, and the next day continued the pursuit of Dembinski toward Szegedin. Field-marshal Paskievitch on the same day (27th) crossed the Theiss at Tisza-Füred, and marched on Debreczin, took possession of that capital, and thus placed himself between the army of Görgey and that of Dembinski.

MOVEMENTS OF GÖRGEY.

On the 29th, after his engagement with Grabbe, Görgey crossed the Theiss at Tokay, and proceeded south in two columns, with the first corps under the command of General Nagy-Shandor toward Debreczin, and with the 3d and 7th himself to Vamasperez and Grosswardein.

Görgey's motive at this time for dividing his army, when surrounded on all sides by the overwhelming forces of the Imperialists, has never been explained, and is difficult to be reconciled consistently with intelligence and honesty of purpose.

The first corps, eight thousand strong, with forty cannons, under General Nagy-Shandor, was attacked at noon, on the 2d of August, near Debreczin, by the main body of the Russians, consisting of eighty thousand men, under Paskievitch, and defeated.† The action lasted till evening. Meanwhile Görgey

---

* For his massacre at Brescia, see chapter viii.

† Görgey was well aware that Nagy-Shandor would be attacked that day. He said to his staff the preceding evening, "To-morrow Nagy-Shandor will get a dressing." And yet he took no measures to protect him from this "dressing." This was afterward told by his inferior tools, when they found that they also

was at Vamaspercz with the other two corps, at farthest a distance of not more than two hours' march from the field of battle, but did not come to the assistance of the first corps, who
owed only to the darkness an escape from total destruction.*

Not remaining at Grosswardein, where he added some new
troops to his army, Görgey hurried on with all possible haste
to Arad, pursued by the Russians under Paskievitch and Rüdiger.

Final Operations in Transylvania.

Upward of a month expired, after the entrance of the Russians into Transylvania, before they ventured to take the offensive vigorously.

They had possessed themselves of the principal towns, being
undefended, without difficulty; but they had in the former
campaign suffered so severely from the skill and indomitable
energy of Bem, that the Russian commanders seemed reluctant, notwithstanding their overpowering numbers, to enter the
field against him.

An opportunity occurred however, on the 31st of July, when
Bem, in order to prevent the junction of Lüders with Grotjen-
helm (who was at Maros-Vasarhely), attacked the former at
Shässburg. An important action took place between part of
the fifth Russian *corps d'armée* and the Hungarians under
Bem. The first shot on the part of the Hungarians killed the
Russian general, and chief of general quarter-master's staff,
Skariatin.

The engagement was on the point of terminating favorably
for the Hungarians, when, at that moment, two divisions of
lancers advanced against the infantry stationed before Weis-
kirchen, and attacked them, killing part on the spot and the rest
as they fled. The lancers took sanguinary vengeance for the
death of their general, and killed more than a thousand of the

---

were betrayed. " *Wicks*," the expression used by Görgey, and here translated
dressing, is a low word used by the vulgar instead of *Schläge*, blows.—*Pragay.*

* Nagy-Shandor sent repeated couriers to Görgey, imploring him to advance as
rapidly as possible; but Görgey, refusing to stir, with laconic brevity and cold-
ness merely reminded the brave Nagy-Shandor of the orders he had received to
evacuate Debreczin after an attempt at resistance.

enemy. Terror then seized the Hungarians, who proceeded in disorder to Kerefsten pursued by the Cossacks. Seven pieces of cannon, two flags, a great quantity of ammunition and baggage, the traveling carriage of General Bem, with important papers,* and the sword of honor presented to him by the inhabitants of Klausenburg, fell into the hands of the Russians, with five hundred prisoners. Bem escaped with difficulty to Mediastz, and, it was said, was wounded with a lance. The Russians had forty-four killed, and one hundred and six wounded, and among them six officers. On the same day in which the battle of Shässburg was fought, the Hungarians met with equally bad success in the neighborhood of Karlsburg, where General Hasford and Colonel Glebof put to flight the besieging force, and relieved the fortress. Seventeen hundred and seventy-five men laid down their arms, and seventeen officers and two cannons were taken.†

A few days only elapsed after these reverses, which were not sufficient to discourage him, when Bem, gathering the remnant of his forces, and with re-enforcements from Klausenburg, in all twelve thousand men, and seventeen pieces of cannon, attacked Hermanstadt on the 5th of August, then occupied by the divisions under Hasford, and, after a desperate struggle, Hasford, unable to sustain himself, was driven from the city as far as Talmacs.

Bem's triumph, like that of his enemy's, was short; for the following day (the 6th), Lüders, apprised of Bem's movements, appeared before the town, and another action ensued.

The Russians were posted on the heights of Gross-Scheurn. Bem had a portion of his troops before the city, and the remainder in reserve in the town; but he was greatly inferior in force, having dispatched a portion of his troops in pursuit of General Hasford. The engagement commenced about eight in the morning of the 6th, and lasted about four hours. General Hasford hearing the cannonade, advanced from Talmacs, and took Bem in the rear. Bem, forced to maintain a front against this second enemy, and Lüder's cavalry rendering it impossible for him to outflank their left wing, while the right was

* His correspondence with Kossuth and others.
† Austrian official bulletin.

sufficiently protected by the hilly nature of the ground, he was defeated at all points, and the result of the day's conflict was that he lost a thousand killed and wounded, and one thousand were taken prisoners, and fourteen out of seventeen pieces of cannon were captured. Even the general himself narrowly escaped being taken prisoner ; he was seized by a Russian soldier, but rescued by a Hungarian, who cut the Russian down.

Bem having lost four successive battles and all his war *materiel*, and unable to sustain himself longer against such superior forces, fled, with a few horsemen, across the Maros ; and, hurrying to the scene of war in Hungary, arrived on the field during the battle of Temesvar.

The last Meetings of the Hungarian Diet.

The Diet, driven from Pesth by the advance of the Imperialists, opened at Szegedin, on the 21st of July, the old and enthusiastic Paloczy presiding. At this sitting of the Diet, Szemere, with his usual ability, described the position of affairs, and the line of policy which the government had determined to pursue. He spoke of schemes of pacification with the hostile races, of past sufferings, and of sacrifices still to be made in the cause of liberty ; but, although expressly interrogated by Hernfalvi, he skillfully avoided unvailing, or explaining in any manner, that which the Parliament desired most to know, viz., the open breach which appeared to exist between the government and their first general.

The last efforts of the Diet, instead of being directed to preparation for the impending dangers, by the necessary military dispositions, dismissing unfaithful or disobedient officers, marshaling all the forces of the kingdom to meet the final struggle which imminently threatened, were devoted to a task which should have been accomplished before the conflict had commenced, viz., conciliation of the several nationalities. After repeated secret conferences, held to discuss the great question how the hostility of the Slavic and Wallachian races might be appeased, the Diet in its last sitting, on the 28th of July, adopted the following resolutions :

1st. That an amnesty should be accorded to all the people of different races, who had taken part in the war against the

Magyars; that the liberty of language should be guarantied to them, but that the Magyar should be the diplomatic language.

2d. That a credit of sixty millions of florins should be opened to the government.

3d. That the seat of government should be removed to Gross-wardein.

The exact object of the first resolution seems very naturally to be involved in doubt, and consequently to have been variously interpreted. Schlessinger, regarding it as a recognition of equal rights to all nationalities, declared it as not adapted to the times or circumstances. " The Magyar haughtiness, and the thirst for supremacy in the Hungarian nobility," he says, " never suffered a deeper humiliation than from the resolution passed at this sitting of the Diet—it was the last—the last great expiatory sin-offering of the representatives of the Hungarian nation for long years of injustice to the other races." Pulszky, on the contrary, pronounces this idea of Schlessinger as " incorrect," since " all the inhabitants of Hungary had, since March, 1848, possessed equal rights. The Diet only gave an amnesty to the Wallachs, Saxons, and Serbs, who were at this time all subdued by the Hungarians."

In the absence of further light upon the motives and objects which prompted the adoption of the resolution, the terms of the resolution would seem to sustain Pulszky's construction. The resolution certainly contains no " recognition of equal rights," but it does embrace an " amnesty to all the people of different races who had taken part in the war against the Magyars." It does declare that " the liberty of language should be guarantied to them," and that " the Magyar should be the diplomatic language ;" but this is precisely the act of March, 1848, and not a new concession. This clause, which is the only one capable of misconstruction, was, as Pulszky explains, a mere declaratory act, passed in conformity with a treaty just entered into between the government and Janku, the Wallachian leader, then at Szegedin, and by which a full amnesty was granted to the Wallachians.

On the 1st of August, three days after the passage of the above resolutions, when Dembinski had determined to abandon Szegedin, and when, from the towers of the city, the Austrian

outposts were distinctly visible, the members of the Diet and
the government left the town. The Diet was never again convened. The ministry met at Arad.

Last Battle between the Hungarians and Austrians.

Dembinski, retreating before Haynau from Kecskemet, reached Szegedin on the 1st of August. His forces were here increased by the addition of ten thousand troops hastily raised,
and the entire army of the south, numbering about twenty-five
thousand, which was there incorporated with it. In a week
the city itself was transformed, by the labors of one hundred
thousand hands, into a strong tenable position, while the government, which, with the Diet, had for a few weeks past made
their head-quarters at this place, had collected large supplies
of provisions, as well as munitions of war, before they were
compelled to leave for Arad.

Haynau, with the Russian division Paniutine, followed, and,
after a dreadful march through the deep sand, in excessively
hot weather and great suffering for water, as all the wells being filled with dead bodies, they were forced to exist on the
scanty but almost putrid supply brought with them, they reached Szegedin on the day following (2d) that of the arrival of
Dembinski.

Dembinski, for greater security, abandoned Szegedin, and,
crossing the Theiss, took up a position at Szoreg, a few leagues
to the south, and lying between the two rivers, near the confluence of the Maros with the Theiss. But notwithstanding
the fortifications,* and although his front was covered by the
Theiss, his right by the Maros, his left flank guarded by Peterwardein, and his rear by the army, which he might have
supposed in good condition, in Transylvania, as well as by the
blockading forces of Temesvar, and although he had between
sixty and seventy thousand men at his disposal, Dembinski declared himself unable to hold his ground as Haynau approached. The Imperialists, as soon as they reached Szegedin, about
four o'clock on the 3d, attempted to lay pontoon bridges over
the Theiss, but were resisted by the Hungarians on the oppo-

---

* They had intrenched the whole dike leading from the Maros to Szoreg.

site side of the river. A terrible cannonading ensued. The
bridges were destroyed, with all the brave men who had ventured upon them to gain the opposite shore. The yellow, muddy water of the Theiss, scarcely ever fit for drink, was dyed
red with the blood of the slain, and for a great distance, even
beyond Szenta, no dog would quench his thirst in those waters.* After an obstinate resistance the Hungarians were repulsed, and that night several pontoon bridges were extended
across the river.

After crossing on the 4th and 5th, the Imperialists, on the
afternoon of the latter day, attacked the Hungarian lines with
three corps, and a battle ensued, in which the Imperialist cavalry attempted to turn the left wing of the enemy, while the
whole of the artillery opened upon the Hungarian batteries,
which were posted in the intrenchments on the dike, and the
Imperialist foot advanced along the Maros to Szoreg. The
battle lasted several hours, and, by sunset, the Hungarians
were driven from all their positions, with a loss of five cannons
and four hundred prisoners. The approach of night prevented
the Imperialists from pursuing the enemy.

While this battle was going on at Szoreg, General Ramberg,
with the third division, and whom General Haynau had sent
around from Szegedin, forced the passage of the Theiss at Kanisa. On the following day, Jellacic, whose situation for some
time past had been exceedingly critical, pressed as he was,
and hedged in between the Danube and the Theiss, relieved
by the march of Haynau, advanced toward the scene of action,
and united his forces with those of Haynau, on the 6th, at
Mokrin. On the same day the line of the Maros was forced,
and Mako fell into the hands of the Imperialists.

By each of these successes, the imperial army, increased
and strengthened, continued to follow up their advantages
against the enemy, who retreated in the direction of Temesvar.† The imperial army continued its pursuit of the Hungarians during the 7th, 8th, and 9th of August; and it was

---

* Schlessinger.

† Dembinski was ordered by Kossuth, in case of defeat, to retreat to the fortress of Arad, which had he done, a junction with Görgey might have been effected, even against the will of the latter.

not until the latter day, not far from the fortress of Temesvar, that a decisive battle took place.

Haynau advanced on the enemy with the third army corps and the Walmoden cavalry division from Czatad to Kis-Becs-kerek, and with the Russian division Paniutine from Lovrin by Sillet, also to Kis-Becskerek, while he ordered the reserve corps to proceed from Peszak by Knez to Hodony and Karany, to attack the enemy's right flank. In the action on the 8th, Dembinski was unfortunately wounded in the shoulder by a shot; he fell from his horse, and was carried into a peasant's cottage, and for twenty-four hours the Hungarian army was without a commander.

At this stage of the conflict, defeated in Transylvania, and summoned by Kossuth to the army of Lower Hungary, Bem appeared on the field of battle, and immediately assumed the command. On the morning of the 9th, the battle of Temesvar commenced. Until half past four in the afternoon, Bem, who pressed forward personally with his left wing and chief force of artillery, drove the enemy from position to position, almost to Kis-Becskerek. The last reserves of Austrian and Russian cavalry charged to retrieve the day. They were beaten back by the hussars. At this time the battle was thought to have been won, and Haynau, it is stated, was seven miles from the field, when suddenly Bem's cannons ceased. His ammunition was exhausted. At this critical moment in the battle, Prince Lichtenstein, who had come from Hodos, appeared with his corps on the Hungarian left flank; and about the same time, Schlick, advancing from Mezöhegyes, made his appearance at Vinga. These re-enforcements to the repulsed wing of the Austrians caused them to rally, and return to the attack. The charge of the artillery commenced, and no fire being returned from the Hungarian side (when Bem broke a collar-bone by a fall from his horse, over which he had for some time lost sufficient control, covered as he was with wounds), the fate of the battle was now decided. In vain Guyon, with his hussars, charged the enemy's artillery : men and horses, having been for twenty-four hours without food or forage, were unequal to the attempt. The confusion into which the Hungarians were thrown led to a dispersion and flight such as Hungary had never before witnessed. Of the whole army, not one corps, with the exception of the Vécsey and Kmetty battalions (which, engaged in the siege of Temesvar, had taken no part in the battle), remained together. Instead of attempting to rally as they came up with the besieging corps at Temesvar, they fled by to the right and left, and the besieging force was quite too small to risk a battle with the Austrian army that was approaching to the relief of the garrison. The battalions dispersed in all directions, the smaller portions fleeing toward Orsova, and afterward reached Turkey; the larger number proceeded to Lugos.

Here they soon learned the resignation of Kossuth, the dissolution of the Diet and ministry, and the surrender of Görgey. Taking no further care of the bank-note press, the supplies of clothing, munitions of war, and the whole artillery, they dispersed entirely, each individual choosing what seemed to him the safest course. A few small bodies only remained united under Guyon and Kmetty. In the flight-like retreat from Temesvar to Lugos, the Hungarians left a large quantity of muskets, cannons, carriages, and munitions, and some thousands of the rear, in the hands of the pursuers. The Austrians estimate the loss of the Hungarians, after the battle of Szoreg, on the 5th of August, at eighteen thousand; a like number laid down their arms and returned home, so that the hostile infantry were completely dissolved.

The immediate result of the loss of this battle was the relief of the fortress of Temesvar. The uninterrupted bombardment of this fortress, during seventeen days and nights, had so demolished the city of Temesvar, that it presented an aspect of ruins which the most experienced soldiers had never before witnessed. As the numberless projectiles had been directed particularly against the arsenal, the neighboring houses were literally converted into piles of rubbish. Whether from accident or design, the black flag raised in such emergencies to excite the commiseration of the enemy, here fluttered in vain over the hospital crowded with sufferers. Every house bore marks of destruction, and threatened the lives of the exposed occupants. The bombs, which penetrated the roof and ceiling, were arrested only by the vaults of casemates; while the scur-

vy, typhus, hospital fever, and cholera, arising from the damp-
ness, want of wholesome air and food, decimated the citizens
and garrison.   Of six thousand soldiers intrusted with the defense of the fortress during one hundred and seven days (the
period of the siege), twenty-seven hundred died of different diseases, and three hundred only were killed by the balls of the
enemy.   Two thousand were found confined by sickness at the
moment of liberation.   Infantry and cavalry attended to the
cannons, for want of gunners.   Horse-flesh, upon which they
had lived for eighteen days, had become scarce, and supplies
of flour and wine sufficient for but a few days longer.   The
brave old commander, F. M. L. Rukowina, would in a short
time have been compelled to yield from famine, although he
remarked that the time for surrender would not arrive until
they had gnawed the last bone of their horses, or when the
handkerchief in his pocket should be set on fire.   The sensation produced by the entrance of the imperial troops, and
the consequent liberation of the garrison, exceeded all bounds.
Young and old, soldiers and citizens, women and children
laughed, wept, embraced each other, and kissed the hands and
clothes of the liberator.   But the most remarkable sight of all,
as well as the most convincing proof of the touching nature of
the scene, tears were absolutely seen to trickle down the long
gray mustache* of the iron-hearted Haynau.

SURRENDER OF GÖRGEY.

The Hungarian cause, from the defeats of Bem and of Dembinski, which so rapidly succeeded each other, was almost
hopeless, when the third and final blow soon followed in the
surrender of Görgey.

Görgey, who, as we have seen, had left Grosswardein for
Arad, was closely followed by General Rüdiger, who shortly
after occupied Grosswardein without resistance, and, after being re-enforced by nine regiments of cavalry, had advanced toward Arad; while Paskievitch, at Debreczin, was hourly expected to make his appearance on the scene of action.   Görgey reached Arad on the 8th of August, before Dembinski was

---

* F. M. L. Haynau wears a mustache of about eight or ten inches in length,
and it is perfectly white.

II.   X

defeated, and within half a day's march of the spot where his army was routed. Arriving, with his thirty thousand or forty thousand troops, at that opportune moment, when the combatants had been marching and fighting for several days previously, he might have turned the scale of victory, and rolled back the tide of war against the oppressors of his country. But that important day, when the destiny of the nation was suspended in the balance, as well as the following, were consumed in endeavoring to effect the dissolution of the government, and procuring for himself the appointment of dictator.

Surrounded by the enemy, and divided among themselves, the prospects of the Hungarians now rapidly declined. Reports having obtained circulation that the Russians were disposed to guarantee the Constitution of 1848, and to raise the Grand Duke Constantine to the throne of Hungary,* Kossuth dispatched two of the ministry, Szemere and Batthyányi, to the Russian camp ; but they soon returned, and reported the fallacy of these rumors.† The Diet had now separated, and was never reassembled. The ministry, upon the approach of Haynau to Szegedin, had scaped with the bank-note press to Arad. In the last full cabinet council, whether from a consideration of the hopeless condition of the country, the terrorism he exerted, òr the power he possessed, Görgey, whom each of the ministers knew or believed to be a traitor, "*received the commission to treat with Russia ;*" "on the condition," however, as Casimir Batthyányi states, "that the legal autonomy of Hungary be maintained, and a general amnesty granted."‡

Whether Görgey, under the authority thus intrusted to him, made any effort toward carrying out the wishes of the ministry ; or whether, as was more likely, aiming as he was at the position of *principal*, he wholly disregarded the office of *agent*, is a question it is yet impossible to decide.

To add to the embarrassments of the ministry, the tidings of the total defeat at Temesvar now reached Arad. Görgey, who, with his officers, for the last two days had been busily

---

* Wisocki, in his memoirs, states that Kossuth actually instructed the Minister of Foreign Affairs, Count Casimir Batthyányi, to prepare a memorandum offering the crown to a Russian prince.   † Pulszky.

‡ For letters of Hungarian ministers, Szemere, C. Batthyányi, Esterhazy, &c., on the abdication, see Appendix, note No. 33.

engaged in intriguing with some and exercising a terror over others, "now called upon Kossuth to abdicate, as a general alone could save the country in such a crisis."*

"Görgey," as Szemere states, "caused Kossuth to be requested to abdicate," and a proposal to that effect was presented to the governor by three of his ministers, viz., Vukovitch, Horvath, and Czanyi.† Without consulting his other ministers, three of whom (viz., Szemere, Batthyányi, and Dushek) were present in Arad, without even the call of a cabinet council, he took the important step of dissolving the government, and conferring upon General Arthur Görgey the supreme civil and military power. The following proclamation was then issued:

"KOSSUTH TO THE NATION.

"After the unfortunate battles wherewith God, in these latter days, has visited our people, we have no hope of our successful continuance of the defense against the allied forces of Russia and Austria. Under such circumstances, the salvation of the national existence, and the protection of its fortune, lies in the hands of the leaders of the army. It is my firm conviction that the continuance of the present government would not only prove useless, but also injurious to the nation. Acting upon this conviction, I proclaim, that, moved by those patriotic feelings which, throughout the course of my life, have impelled me to devote all my thoughts to the country, I, and with me the whole of the cabinet, resign the guidance of the public affairs; and that the supreme civil and military power is herewith conferred on General Arthur Görgey, until the nation, making use of its right, shall have disposed that power according to its will. I expect of the said General Görgey—and I

---

* Görgey now asked the governor whether he thought it possible alone to save the country. When Kossuth replied, "that he now could not do it unsupported by Görgey." The general then declared, "that he could and would save Hungary, but only if Kossuth immediately resigned and had him appointed dictator."—*Pulszky.*

† Szemere, in his letter to the Cologne Gazette, states, "I do not think that those three ministers, said to have agreed to it (out of the seven comprising the ministry), were guilty of having originated the proposal, but that the governor of the country (Kossuth) was to blame—one who, without asking the concurrence of the other three, though they were present, gave the decision."

make him responsible to God, the nation, and to history—that, according to the best of his ability, he will use this supreme power for the salvation of the national and political independence of our poor country and its future. May he love his country with that disinterested love which I bear it! May his endeavors to reconquer the independence and happiness of the nation be crowned with greater success than mine were!

" I have it no longer in my power to assist the country by actions. If my death can benefit it, I will gladly sacrifice my life. May the God of justice and of mercy watch over my poor people! " LOUIS KOSSUTH.

" S. VUCOVICS.

" L. CZANYI.

" M. HORVATH."

That so important an act as the dissolution of the government, even if, as is stated in the proclamation, its " continuance was not only useless, but injurious to the nation," should have taken place without a full cabinet, is indeed an event requiring explanation. But what is still more extraordinary, is, that Kossuth should have considered the supreme power intrusted to him by a vote of the Diet as transferable. This power, so confided to him, was not only a personal trust, and not transferable, but it was to be exercised by him conjointly with the ministry, who, by the vote of the Diet, received the power cotemporaneously with himself. Even then, had he chosen to resign the power which he held, and which he had a clear right to do, he could not resign that held by his ministry, and for the faithful exercise of which they were held strictly responsible. But what is by far the most inexplicable, as well as the most important aspect of the whole matter, was, that he should have thought proper to confide the power into the hands of one whom he had long had reason to regard as a traitor to his country.

Görgey, it is true, was at the head of the only army still unsubdued in Hungary; he was the only one possessed of power to serve the country; but this excuse will not avail, since, if the agent is unfaithful, the greater the power he possesses, the greater are his capacities for injury. But the military power then at the command of Görgey could not have been regarded as an important consideration, from the fact that, in the very proclamation of transfer, it is averred, "we have no hope of a successful continuance of the defense against the allied forces of Russia and Austria." It is exceedingly unfortunate for the reputation of Kossuth that, having thought a resignation of his power necessary, he had not concluded to surrender it to the Diet, whence he received it, or, in the event of their dissolution, to the ministry who, with himself, were conjointly and cotemporaneously empowered. Görgey accepted the supreme power, and issued the succeeding proclamation:

"Görgey to the Nation.

" Citizens !—The Provisional Government exists no longer. The governor and the ministers have voluntarily resigned their offices. Under these circumstances a military dictatorship is necessary, and it is I who take it, together with the civil power of the state.

" Citizens! whatever, in our precarious position, can be done for the country I intend to do, be it by means of arms or by negotiations. I intend to do all in my power to lessen the painful sacrifice of life and treasure, and to put a stop to persecution, cruelty, and murder.

" Citizens! the events of our time are astounding, and the blows of fate overwhelming. Such a state of things defies all calculation. My only advice and desire is that you should quietly return to your homes, and that you eschew assisting in the resistance and the combats, even in case your towns are occupied by the enemy. The safety of your persons and properties you can only obtain by quietly staying at the domestic hearth, and by peacefully following the course of your usual occupations.

" Citizens! it is ours to bear whatever it may please God, in his inscrutable wisdom, to send us. Let our strength be the strength of men, and let us find comfort in the conviction that right and justice must weather the storms of all times.

" Citizens! may God be with us!

"Arthur Görgey.

"Arad, August 11, 1849."

It was on the evening of the 10th, or the morning of the 11th, that Görgey received the full civil and military power; and what seems a strong corroboration of his guilt, or, at least, of a previous understanding with the enemy, is, that without the slightest attempt at resistance, or the least effort at negotiation, notwithstanding his assurance to Kossuth that he could, if possessed of dictatorial power, save the country, he immediately issued the foregoing proclamation, suppressing all opposition to the enemy, and advising the citizens to return to their homes, and to avoid assisting in any resistance or combats, even in defense of their own towns. That he had the surrender in view before he received the supreme power, and that it constituted the great object at which he aimed, is not only evident from the circumstances just mentioned, but is expressly admitted in his letters to Klapka and to Rüdiger.

On the same day (the 11th), at Alt-Arad he addressed a communication* to General Rüdiger, who had in the mean time advanced from Grosswardein to the neighborhood of Vilagos, announcing that, in consequence of the dissolution of the Provisional Government of Hungary, he felt called on to arrive at a solution, and he accordingly decided to submit without condition; and that he and all the officers of his *corps d'armée* were ready to lay down their arms before the army of his majesty the Emperor of Russia. He, at the same time, expressed the conviction that the other chiefs of the *corps d'armée* would follow his example, and offer their submission. By means of his subservient tools, he busily spread abroad the idea that he could not possibly hold out any longer, and that the Duke of Leuchtenberg, who had fully guaranteed the Constitution of 1848, would be placed, by the help of the Russians, on the Hungarian throne. He dispatched orders to all the armies and garrisons to yield to the Russians on the same conditions as those which he accepted for himself. He then left Arad, and maneuvered in the neighborhood until the 13th, when he surrendered to the Russians, whom he had daily apprised of his movements, that they might inclose his army, of which, in spite of its corrupted condition, he still stood in fear.

---

* For Görgey's letter in full, see Appendix, note No. 34.

Prince Paskievitch accepted the absolute submission of Gör-gey and his troops, in order, as he states, "to put an end to the effusion of blood, and to preserve a part of the states of the empire of Austria from the ravages of war." General Rüdiger received orders to disarm it.

As the bulletin of Prince Paskievitch declares, "Görgey, having left Arad with a *corps d'armée*, in conformity with the convention which he had formed with General Rüdiger, proceeded to Szöllös.   On the 13th, at midnight, Görgey advanced toward our army at the head of his staff.   He repeat-ed to General Rüdiger that he submitted without conditions, and only solicited, as a grace, the intercession of Prince Pas-kievitch.   At four o'clock in the afternoon the troops made their submission in the following manner : The Hungarian army was drawn up in two lines, in close columns, in the plains of the village of Szöllös.   The infantry and cavalry on the two wings occupied the first line, the artillery the second.*   The infantry, after presenting arms, laid them down, and the cavalry alighted from their horses, and attached their arms to the saddles.   The men then left the ranks and proceeded to-ward the town of Zarand, under the escort of three regiments of the second division of light cavalry.   The artillery and bag-gage were taken by a regiment.   The regiment Jellecki was charged to convey all the arms to Grosswardein.   Eleven gen-erals, twenty thousand infantry, and two thousand cavalry, laid down their arms, and one hundred and thirty pieces of ar-tillery were also given up.   Görgey, in approaching our troops, cried ' What can not be undertaken with such troops !'   Gör-gey then declared that he was disposed to cause the other di-visions of the army to yield.   Shortly after, two messengers from the fortress of Arad, presented themselves to General Rü-diger, and said they were authorized by the commandant, Dam-janic, and by the officers, to propose the surrender of the for-tress to the Russians.   On the 14th, the troops of General Rü-

---

* As an eye-witness of the surrender states : "Görgey's proposition to yield, with his thirty-five thousand men, at first excited distrust, and some trick of war or treason was feared.   He was required, accordingly, to blow up all that re-mained of his ammunition.   This he did, and the giving up of arms took place afterward."

diger took up their previous positions; the advanced guard at Simand, and the principal *corps d'armée* at Kis-Jenö, where he will remain until new orders from Field-marshal Paskievitch; the corps of Görgey is proceeding under escort to Grosswardein."

The act of laying down their arms by the Hungarians took place on the fields between Kis-Jenö and Szöllös; but in the little village of Vilagos the final terms were arranged, and hence this act will be designated in history as *the surrender of Vilagos.**

---

* On the 13th of August, the sun shone bright and hot; Görgey's army stood in regimental array, twenty-four thousand men strong, with one hundred and forty-four cannons. In the foremost ranks were the infantry, in the rear the artillery, on either side the regiments of cavalry. A death-like stillness pervaded the army, their looks were bent upon the ground. The soil was sacred—it was the grave of their honor.

From time to time the report of a shot broke the quiet of the scene. Some hussar fired the last charge of his carbine into the head of his faithful horse, determined that the brave animal, at least, should not survive the disgrace of its master and the fall of Hungary. Others of his comrades had unstrapped their saddles in the forest, and laid them aside with csiko and dolmany, as things which they could no longer call their own; they had then dashed off on their wild steeds over the plains, to resume their former course of life—the wild, free csikos of the heath. The hussars, too, in rank and file, took the saddles from their horses in silence, piled them in large heaps, together with their arms and standards, and stepped back to their horses. Here stood the Ferdinand regiment, with its brave colonel at its head, a picture of grief and despair: his sword was gone—he had flung it with a curse at Görgey's feet, when the latter succeeded in carrying his proposals of surrender in the last council of war. Beside them stood the Hanover hussars, Count Batthyányi, their commanding officer, at their head,[1] on foot: with his own hand he had killed his charger, the finest in the whole army, that it might never bear a Cossack on its back. Further on, the Nicolaus and Alexander regiments, Görgey's guardian angels in the Carpathians, Hungary's avenging angels in the victories of April—shadows of former greatness, remains of the old regiments, in which but a few still survived to serve as the frame-work of newly-organized battalions. Close at hand stood the Coburg and Würtemberg imperial hussars. The younger regiments of cavalry were distributed on the flanks; Lehel hussars, which had not yet had an opportunity of emulating the older regiments; the Hunyady corps, which had already won the respect of the veteran troops.

The generals stood gathered in a group, or rode slowly up and down between the battalions. Földvary approached the ninth battalion with tears in his eyes; under his command, in conjunction with the third, it had been the first to storm the ramparts of Buda. The men loved him as a father, and had rescued him from many a danger; for Földvary, one of the bravest of the brave, was short-sighted, and frequently rode into the very midst of the enemy, whence he had again and

---

[1] Now a private in the ranks.

Arthur Görgey was born in the year 1817, of noble and tolerably wealthy parents, at Busocz, in the county of Zips.

After finishing his studies at the Gymnasium of Késmark, he entered the Pioneer school at Tuln as a cadet, and from there an Austrian regiment, whence he was soon after transferred to a lieutenancy in the noble Hungarian body-guard.*

He was of an eccentric character, but greatly distinguished for his talents as well as his diligence as a scholar, and excelled especially in the mathematical sciences and chemistry.

In order to marry, he quitted the army, and occupied him-

again been extricated by his brave soldiers. At this moment, when they saw their former colonel up to bid a last farewell, as if electrified with one thought, they formed themselves unbidden into a large square; the standard-bearer hands the flag to his neighbor, and thus it passes from one to another up to the colonel. Every man kisses it: they then lay it upon a pile of fagots in the midst of the square, and look on in silence while the flag burns to ashes.

Nagy-Shandor—a Murat likewise in taste for costume—stands in conversation with Pöltenberg, dressed in a splendid uniform. The latter, undistinguished in outward appearance, with indolent features, concealing a spirit of true bravery, had always followed Görgey with blind devotion. The tranquillity of his countenance contrasted strongly with the visible excitement of Nagy-Shandor. Count Leiningen, Görgey's warmest friend, was pacing up and down near them; he was idolized by his comrades, but never made any pretensions to merit, content to assist in adding one stone to the temple of his friend's fame. Generals Löhner, Knezick, Kiss, Colonel Görgey, and others were on horseback, conversing on different subjects. Damjanic, the colossus in stature and courage, had remained as commander in Arad.

The new dictator appeared in the simple dress which he was accustomed to wear when on march. He endeavored to put on a cheerful face; but his features were more solemn, dark, and iron-bound than usual. He rode up and down before the hussars, murmuring here and there a word of encouragement, and slowly inspecting the Honvéd battalions, the scarred warriors of the former regiments, Schwartzenberg, Franz Karl, Prinz von Preussen, Don Miguel, Alexander, and Wasa. He then rode in front of the ranks, and declared himself ready to transfer the command to any one who believed himself capable of saving the army: this he was no longer able to do. A gray-headed hussar officer rode out of the ranks up to the staff, and declared that it was his and his comrades' determination to cut their way through the enemy. But Görgey warned him dryly against any "insubordination, which must be put down by musket-balls;" and so saying, he turned his back carelessly upon the officer.

From four o'clock in the afternoon until late that evening, continued the surrender of arms, the divisioning of the escorts, and departure of the troops. They were conducted to Sarkad, and from thence to Gyula, where they were transferred to the power of Austria.

At ten o'clock the fields before Vilagos were deserted.—*Schlessinger.*

* Other accounts state that he entered the regiment of Palatine hussars. He was a short time adjutant to Windischgrätz.—*Examiner.*

self in his favorite study of chemistry, which he was pursuing in Galicia, when the war broke out, and he immediatly return-ed home. On arriving in Hungary, he was appointed a captain of Honvéds, soon after a major in the National Guard, and on the field of Schwechat, as has been seen, he was promoted to the post of general, and appointed commander of the army of the Upper Danube.

As to the character of Görgey, opinions are as opposite as they are on the merits of the struggle between Austria and Hungary, and if truth can scarcely be discovered in relation to the events which transpired, when the accounts purely Aus-trian and those purely Hungarian are found totally irreconcil-able, some idea of the difficulties of the task may be conceived when it is attempted to approach the more delicate questions of demeanor, character, and motive. Whether Görgey was in fact a patriot or a traitor, is a question upon which the public mind is still divided, and in the consideration of which it would better accord both with justice and prudence, to review the leading circumstances which have induced such contradictory conclusions, than, by giving full credence to one set of state-ments and entirely rejecting another, to pronounce a definite opinion on the subject.

The following facts are apparently inconsistent with his treachery :

1st. His successful sally from Komorn, and desperate charge at Acs.

2d. His escape in the mountain districts from the toils with which Paskievitch endeavored to encompass him.

3d. His march from Waitzen to Arad, from the 17th of July to the 11th of August, a distance of nearly four hundred miles in twenty-five days, and fighting six battles and encountering no serious loss.

4th. His leaving that portion of Hungary above the Theiss, which was almost entirely free from the enemy, and penetra-ting south amid all the Austrian and Russian armies, amount-ing to five times his number.

5th. When at Arad, on the 11th of August, he learned that the corps of Bem in Transylvania, and Dembinski at Temesvar were completely routed ; that, while he could look for assistance from no quarter, he was himself completely surrounded, by Paskievitch at Debreczin, Rüdiger at Vilagos, Schlick at Mako, Lichtenstein at Lippa, Haynau at Temesvar, and Lüders advancing from Transylvania.

On the other hand, the following circumstances are adduced to found against him the charge of treason :

1st. His proclamation from Waitzen on the 5th of January, that the Hungarian army were fighting for nothing else than the laws of 1848, and for their legitimate king, Ferdinand V., and that they would defend the fatherland independently of any other authority. In fact, repudiating Kossuth and the Committee of Defense.

2d. That, after leaving Waitzen, Görgey, during his retreat, made several attempts to enter into negotiations with the Russian generals, Rüdiger* and Tscheodajeff, and with Marshal Paskievitch.†

3d. He intentionally and rapidly weakened the physical and moral soundness of his forces by extraordinary marches and great privations, by frequent parleys with the enemy, and open discussion of the propriety of a surrender.

4th. The arrest of Görgey's aunt at Szikszo, where the first army corps then was, carrying letters from him to Field-marshal Paskievitch, of a tenor that left no further doubt as to his purpose of surrender.‡

5th. Dividing his forces, after crossing the Theiss, and getting into the midst of the enemy.   Sending Nagy-Shandor by Debreczin, where he told his staff, on the evening previous, that Nagy-Shandor would get a "dressing" the next day, which was literally true, while he was at Vamasperoz, a distance of less than two hours' march from the scene.

6th. After reaching Arad, he makes no effort to assist Dembinski, struggling for existence within a few hours' march,

---

* Pragay.

† But as his letters only spoke of a desire of mediation, and not of submission without reserve, they were sent back unanswered.—*Vienna Gazette*, 24*th August*, 1849.

‡ The first visible negotiation between them appears at Rima-Szombath, in the person of a nephew of Rüdiger, who brought him a present of Russian arms. Görgey accepted the gift, and returned the courtesy with some of his own arms. —*Pragay.*

but remained at Arad with the government and Diet, endeavoring to procure for himself the office of dictator.

7th. He surrendered to the enemy, without making or attempting to make any reservations for his country or terms for his army, while, in his own language, he "had, it is true, one line of retreat from Arad, over Radna, to Transylvania."

8th. He "induced them (the government) to resign. They gave all the powers of the state into my hands. Time pressed, and I took the resolution (rash though it seems, it was *maturely* considered) to make an unconditional surrender to the troops of his majesty the Czar of Russia."*

9th. The charge of treason has been openly made against him. Görgey, if innocent, has it in his power to prove himself so ; yet upward of two years have elapsed, and he has not attempted a defense, or given to a deeply interested world the slightest explanation of his conduct.

Such are some of the considerations which may influence our determination as to the patriotism or treachery of Görgey ; but, before arriving at any conclusion, there is still another view of the subject, differing from both, and which, perhaps, may more nearly approach the truth than either. It is, that Görgey was neither patriot nor traitor, but a mere professional soldier ; that he was possessed, in a remarkable degree, both of skill and courage, but not one spark of nationality glowed within his bosom. His own illustration as a soldier, his own success, was evidently his first thought, and his country's safety or freedom a secondary consideration. Not to be beaten, or, when beaten, to take a speedy revenge; to keep his army together, not as constituting the defense and security of the country, but as illustrating the importance of the general, such were Görgey's aims. He cared not where he retreated or what he abandoned, provided he yielded not a flag and lost not a gun. And his last celebrated march (if not accomplished through the connivance of the enemy), a bold and martial achievement, seemed directed with infinite skill to the one great aim of surrendering *en masse*, with all his guns, troops, and arms, so as even if he thereby lost his country, he would gain credit with his enemies for the importance of his submis-

---

* Görgey's letter to Klapka.   See Appendix.

sion, and retain in the face of the world the reputation of a still unconquered general.

However divided may be the opinion as to his guilt or innocence as a traitor, his last act of unconditional surrender at Vilagos stands forth without palliation on the pages of history. To use his own words, he had " still one line of retreat open to him." He could not have lost more had he fought out the war for thirty years, like John Zapolya, amid the Carpathians, and disputed before the enemy the last inch of ground and the last blade of grass on the Hungarian pusztos. All his faithful comrades, who had stood by his side in many a hard-fought field, and had messed at his table, were left to the gallows or the prison. The brave soldiers who had followed him through his long and weary retreat with unshaken confidence and love, believing that their Görgey would come out right at last, were abandoned to Austrian dungeons, or drafted into the imperial regiments.*

And what has he gained by it? He has saved nothing but his own miserable existence. Instead of rendering up his life to save his country, he has basely rendered up his country to save his life, a life to be passed under the surveillance of Austrian spies, followed by the curses of all those widows and orphans that his surrender had occasioned, the wrath of the whole Hungarian nation, and the universal execration of mankind. Better, far better, a thousand honorable deaths to one such execrable life.

Upon the surrender of Görgey, the fortress of Arad in the neighborhood immediately tendered its submission ; and deputations of Russian and Austrian officers were immediately dispatched to all the armies and garrisons still holding out, with orders or solicitations from Görgey to yield to the Russians on the same conditions as those which he had accepted for himself.

To his friend Klapka, commanding the impregnable fortress of Komorn, something more than a mere verbal solicitation being necessary, he addressed a letter, not very flattering either to his head or heart, and remarkable only for involving in still greater doubt his own integrity of purpose.

---

* Brace.

"My dear Friend Klapka,—Events which, though by no means unexpected, are still decisive, have happened since I saw you last. The jealousy and the selfishness of some members of the government have brought affairs to the crisis which I prophesied to you they would bring them to.

"When, after many an honest battle with the Russians, I had crossed the Theiss at Tokay, I found that the Parliament declared that they desired me to take the chief command.

"Kossuth appointed Bem. He did it secretly.

"The country believed that I was commander-in-chief, for Kossuth returned a jesuitical reply to the motion of the Parliament.

"This piece of knavery was the source of all the later events. Dembinski was beaten at Szoreg. Bem's troops were routed at Maros-Vásárhely.

"Dembinski retreated to the walls of Temesvar. Bem hastened to the same place. He arrived on the field of battle at Temesvar, and succeeded in restoring the fight for a few hours; but afterward he was so fearfully beaten, that of fifty thousand men (according to Kossuth's calculations) only six thousand remained in the ranks. Vécsey informed me that all the rest were dispersed.

"The Austrians advanced meanwhile between Temesvar and Arad. The War Office had instructed Dembinski to retreat, as of course he ought to have done, upon our own fortress of Arad, and not upon Temesvar, which was held by our enemies.

"Dembinski—Heaven knows why—acted in opposition to this order. There are a great many facts which make me believe that he acted from motives of jealousy. He was jealous of me.

"The consequence was that I stood alone with the forces which I took from Komorn (minus the serious losses I had at Waitzen, Recsag, Görömböly, Zsolna, Gesztely, and Debreczin). From the south I was threatened by the Austrians, and from the north by the *gros* of the Russian army. I might, indeed, have retreated from Arad by way of Radna into Transylvania; but my affection for my country, and my desire to restore it to peace at any price, induced me to surrender.

" But, before taking that step, I convinced the Provisional Government of their inability to save the country, and of the certainty of a still greater ruin if they continued to remain in office. I induced them to resign.

" They gave all the powers of the state into my hands. Time pressed ; and I took the resolution (rash though it seems, it was maturely considered) to make an unconditional surrender to the troops of his majesty the Czar of Russia.

" My brave and gallant troops gave their assent. All the detachments in the vicinity of Arad volunteered to surrender with me. Damjanic commanded in Arad ; he declared that he would follow my example.

" Up to the present, the treatment we have met with was such as a brave soldier has a right to expect from a fellow-soldier.

" Consider what you can do, and what you ought to do.

" ARTHUR GÖRGEY.

" Great Warasdin, 16th August."

After the surrender of his power to Görgey, Kossuth left Arad, and directed his course to the Turkish frontier, by way of Radna and Lugos ; and when, as he thought, no hope remained of serving the cause of expiring Hungary, he escaped into Turkey, and delivered himself up to the Ottoman garrison at Widdin.

When Bem, after the defeat at Temesvar, reached Lugos, he found but a few feeble divisions in order, and these, as their commanders informed him, were so thoroughly demoralized that but little dependence could be placed in them ; yet the hero of Iganie and Ostralenka, whose spirit no reverses could subdue, was actively engaged in rallying the scattered forces, with a view of breaking through into Transylvania, and sustaining himself there. Under the hope still of success, he wrote to Kossuth, begging him to return. Bem and Guyon directed their march toward Transylvania ; but the Austrian main army pressed them on all sides, and when arrived at Dobra, where the news of Görgey's surrender reached them, their corps dispersed in all directions. The generals, left alone, fled together into Turkey, and bade farewell to a country endeared to them by many recollections, and whose cause, although not natives, they were the last to abandon.

The remnants of Stein's corps (he himself made his escape into Turkey), and the corps of General Count Vécsey and of Colonel Kazintsky, which, from having taken no part in the battle of Temesvar, were still a fine body of troops—following Görgey's example, or obeying his injunction to "unite with the Russians," marched along the Maros to meet the enemy, and lay down their arms; which was done on the 19th of August, without once inquiring into the nature of the pretended conditions. Kazintsky was shot; but Vécsey was hanged like a felon, notwithstanding his aged and highly respected father had saved the life, as it is said, of the Emperor Francis, in the French campaign, and was, for his gallantry on the field of Aspern, promoted by the Archduke Charles to the post of general, and is at this time Austrian general of cavalry, captain of the Hungarian noble guard, and one of the firmest props of the throne of Habsburg.*

HUNGARIAN SUCCESSES IN THE NORTH.

While these events, so disastrous to the Hungarian arms, were occurring in the southern part of the kingdom, quite a different fortune attended the efforts of the brave garrison left behind them in the fortress of Komorn. Komorn was, at this time, besieged by the second Austrian *corps d'armée*, under F. M. L. Czoric, who had his head-quarters in Acs ; Major General Polt, who was posted on the left bank of the Danube ; Major General Prince Collorado on the right bank ; and Major General Fiedler on the Schütte.

Such was the condition of things about the fortress, when it was observed that, owing to the long stay of the main army at Komorn, some of the provisions of the garrison began to fail. A sally was executed by Colonel Kosztolanyi, on the 24th of July, with entire success. They brought back the desired sup-

---

* Not content with this wound upon so worthy a family, the house of Habsburg, or its instruments, to palliate their brutal murder, have attempted to blacken the memory of their departed victim, true to the Jesuitical character which has ever distinguished it—"*calumniare audaciter semper aliquid hæret.*"

For the number of victims that suffered in Hungary under the rigor of Austrian court-martials, see Appendix, note No. 35.

plies, several loaded baggage-wagons, an Austrian diligence with money, together with eleven officers and the entire detachment of infantry at Todis as prisoners.

Encouraged by this and a second sally, which took place a few days after, on the left of the Danube, to rescue some of Görgey's dispersed rear-guard, General Klapka now determined to attack the besieging Austrian army with his entire force.

Accordingly, breaking up from their intrenched camp at midnight, on the 3d of August, Klapka dispatched two columns of about six battalions each, and the requisite quantity of cavalry. One, under Asserman, about four in the morning, stormed Almas. The garrison was partly cut down, partly put to flight. Having left a small force at Almas and Neszmély, he marched against Dotis, and, finding it unoccupied, next upon Kömlöd.

At eight o'clock, the other column, under Kosztolanyi, advanced directly against Mocsa, and appeared before this place just as the flanking column became visible on the heights of Kömlöd, immediately behind Mocsa. The garrison of Mocsa, which had heard nothing of the action against Almas, fell into great confusion on seeing itself thus suddenly surrounded. They retreated from the village, after a short resistance, and endeavored to escape into the open country to the left, but, being already flanked by Asserman's hussars, laid down their arms.

Both columns now pursued the course marked out for them.* One moving on Nagy-Igmand, the other advanced against the great redoubt of the Austrians between Csém and Herkaly. The latter, and by far the most formidable point, Shultz was ordered to attack *en face*. His execution of the order was truly heroic. He and his handful of men secured the Hungarians the honor of the day. Forming in a battle-line, with artillery and horse on either wing, preceded by only a weak line of tirailleurs, and cheering *Eljen á Magyar !* he led his troops through a fearful fire of grape and musketry to the very parapet of the enemy's works. His boldness startled the Austrians, who, fearing, from the side attack of the other troops, that their position was about to be surrounded, turned and fled in disorder upon Acs. Rapidly pursued to this point, and

---

* Pragay.

flanked on the right and left, the retreat of the enemy became universal, and all who could not conceal themselves in the fields and vineyards hastened to the bridge over the Danube, and nothing but the approach of night saved them from total annihilation. The Hungarian loss was trifling, that of the Austrians severe. Besides the dead which strewed the plain, the Hungarians took three thousand prisoners, captured twenty-seven cannons, and an enormous supply of provisions intended for the Austro-Russian army.*

On the next morning, Klapka sent forward more troops to Gönyö, where they made more prisoners and captured more ammunition; in fact, so great became the panic among the Imperialists, that, deserting their strong intrenchments, they fled in every direction, and the Hungarians took Raab on the following day without firing a shot, and with it, supplies and ammunition to the value of several millions of dollars.

At Pressburg, the consternation produced by the report of these movements was so great, that the population commenced immediately to throw up barricades, to arrest the expected march of the victorious troops. At Vienna, the few remaining available battalions were hastily collected, and dispatched by rail-road to Pressburg. But the heart of the soldiers (they were raw recruits, and apparently mere children) fairly gave way under the terrors of waging war in a land from which no Austrian army had ever returned to give an account of their dreadful Parthian foe.

The whole country being now freed from the Imperialists, Klapka, after taking the necessary precautions for securing Komorn, marched on the 5th of August, with the greater part of his garrison, on Raab.

The Hungarian troops entered that city, says Klapka, amid the touching, though silent and saddened sympathies of the inhabitants. They had seen the enormous masses of Austrians and Russians marching through their town, and that sight seemed to have stifled all hopes for the future.

Despite the successes of the moment, they could not believe that the small army within their walls would suffice to save

---

* Two thousand seven hundred oxen, forty loaded baggage-wagons, and the cargo of thirty-five large vessels on the right shore of the Danube.

their ill-starred country. Wreaths of flowers were, indeed, showered upon the heads of hussars and Honvéds, not in a spirit of exultation, but of sadness ; it was a mark of affection to a doomed favorite—it was but adorning the devoted lamb for the sacrifice which awaited it.

But far different from the gloomy feelings of the townspeople was the temper of the population of the country districts. Proud of the successes of their brethren, glorying in the spectacle of an Austrian rout, they cared little for the enemy's numbers or artillery. All they asked was, whether now the time had come for the people to rise *en masse.* Gray-bearded peasants shook the hands of the soldiers, and said, with that tranquillity which characterizes the Hungarian peasant, " Don't you care, we will get the better of the Russians too. Hitherto we sent our sons only, but now we, the old ones, will take horse !" They meant well, and would have acted up to their word. There is a dogged sturdiness in the peasant's nature, which eminently fits him for the duties and the hardships of a campaign.

Six days had passed since the entry of the Hungarian troops into Raab; the greater part of the stores had been conveyed to Komorn, the levy *en masse* was favorably proceeding on the right bank of the Danube, thousands of recruits had been raised, and the strong intrenchments which the enemy had thrown up at Acs, Aranyos, and Lel, were totally destroyed. Klapka now resolved to abandon his passive and protective position, and to concentrate his whole force for an offensive operation. There were three ways open for such an expedition : the first, to make a diversion into Styria ; the second, to attack and disperse the corps under Nugent ; the third, to advance into Austria and seize Vienna. The latter was by far the most brilliant, as well as hazardous undertaking, and, could it have been accomplished, would have produced by far the most important results; but Klapka, considering " the limited nature of the powers at his disposal," regarded it as a Quixotic plan, and, after mature reflection, determined on an expedition through the Eisenburg county into Styria. Every arrangement was now made for carrying this determination into effect, the troops in the Schütte were ordered up by forced marches to Raab, the enemy at Wieselberg, for the purpose of greater deception, to be attacked ; and while this was proceeding, the other divisions were, by forced marches, to enter Styria before the enemy could possibly be advised of their movements. Ten o'clock that night (the 11th) was fixed upon for the departure of the expedition. During the day, Klapka reviewed his troops which were to accompany him. They were tried soldiers, full of hope and courage. After divine service had been held, Klapka addressed the troops, and distributed medals among those who had most distinguished themselves in the late battles. When the troops were informed that they were on the eve of another expedition, and of fresh battles and victories, their exultation vented itself in thundering *Eljens !**

This happened on the very day on which Görgey, as Dictator of Hungary, announced to the people *that the wise and inscrutable decrees of Providence had sentenced them to ruin!"*

After the review, the staff-officers dined at the head-quarters of their commander. It was a merry feast. They drank health and prosperity to Kossuth and Görgey, the liberation of the country, the downfall of Austria, and the future greatness of Hungary. They were still at table, when it was announced that a peasant insisted on seeing the commander on urgent business. He was introduced. The man came forward, and his peasant dress, worn and soiled, covered a face and figure not unfamiliar to the company. It was Almasi, late speaker of the Lower House. He soon told, in accents of grief, that he was a fugitive, and that all was lost ; that Nagy-Shandor's troops were routed at Debreczin, Dembinski was defeated at Szoreg, Bem's troops were dispersed at Shässburg, the Diet routed, and the government in despair.

This news, and the reports of their own scouts, which reached them the same day that the corps of Nugent and the Russian division of Grabbe were returning from the pursuit of Görgey, that his late successes had enabled Haynau to send a large mass of disposable troops against Komorn, forced Klapka to renounce his intended enterprise, and, instead of advancing into Styria, to retire to Komorn.

Alas for the cause of the struggling Magyars ! the brilliant

---

* Klapka.

successes which followed the sallies from Komorn were fruitless.   They were the last glimmerings of the expiring flame,
which shoots forth with more than wonted brightness the moment before it sinks forever in eternal gloom.

The operations in the south having been closed, the entire
Austrian force was now centered around Komorn, and nothing
remained for the brave garrison, alone and without hope, but
either to bury themselves heroically under the ruins of the fortress, or to preserve themselves by an honorable military capitulation.   After many debates, the council of war accordingly resolved upon the latter course, for the following reasons :

1st. To alleviate the fate of their captured brethren, and to
put a stop to the frequent executions ; for they were encouraged to believe that all military persecutions and trials would
cease upon the surrender of Komorn.

2d. In order not to expose to utter ruin the city of Komorn
with its twenty thousand inhabitants, which had already severely suffered by fire, and by the bombardment of the previous
winter, that continued for five weeks.

3d. To save a numerous body of men, charged with political
offenses, who had taken refuge in Komorn.

4th. To relieve the inhabitants of the surrounding country,
already sufficiently impoverished, from the hardship of quartering Russian, and, still worse, Austrian soldiers.

5th, and lastly. To preserve twenty-seven thousand brave and
zealous soldiers for their country at a more auspicious future.

With the surrender of Komorn terminated the military operations in Hungary.*

Character of the Military Operations.

The military operations of the late Hungarian campaign will
receive, as they clearly merit, a closer and more complete examination than could be expected from one with no pretensions
to a knowledge of military science, or than could be given to
them during the rapid progress of the war, and with the imperfect and contradictory information which could alone be derived from that distant and unfrequented part of Europe.   The

---

* Komorn surrendered on the 29th of September.   Peterwardein had previously, on the 7th of the same month, opened her gates to the Austrians.

different plans of operations of attack on the one side, and of defense on the other, seem, to an uninstructed eye at least, to have been digested with great care and skill by both parties; but that there were failures in the execution of those plans, there can be no doubt; and the causes of those failures may be looked for in the deep jealousy of their respective leaders.

The plan of General Haynau for directing the movements of the army in Hungary was founded on that devised by Marshal Radetzky for overthrowing the Piedmontese on the plains of Novara.

The reason, it was thought, why the Hungarians had succeeded in the previous campaign, was the skill with which they had managed to baffle all the movements of Windischgrätz, until they succeeded in exhausting his strength and resources. The imperial commanders immediately saw that, in order to conquer the Hungarians, it was necessary to bring the scene of contest within a narrower circle, and to force them to come to a decisive battle by hemming them in on all sides.

In the prosecution of this plan, Haynau, with the bulk of the Austrian army, appeared to remain inactive on the banks of the Danube, until he learned that other Austrian and Russian corps, marching from opposite points toward the centre of Hungary, had effected a junction, and were ready to operate together. It was then that Haynau commenced his vigorous movements in accordance with this plan. But here the first error was committed in the prosecution of that plan, and which the Russian bulletin at that moment exposes, when it declares that here " the end assigned to the first part of the campaign was completely attained, and the whole of the upper course of the Danube became free." The Upper Danube was still commanded by the garrison of Komorn, and the *coup-de-main* of Klapka against Raab proved that even there the war was not terminated.

Neglecting Komorn, uncovering even Vienna, abandoning these lines of communication, with a hardihood seldom practiced in war, the Russians and Austrians hurried beyond the Theiss, determined to tread out at once, by their numbers, the brave and wary defenders of the soil, not so much in accordance with any skillful plan of co-operation, as an evident de-

sire of the different parties to outstrip each other and decide
the war alone. So evident was this haste, that Görgey is not
to be pardoned for neglecting to turn it to advantage.

Haynau was aware that Görgey was endeavoring to effect
a junction with Dembinski, and he pressed forward to defeat
the latter before their forces could be united, and which he
effected on the 9th of August. At the same time, the other
principal corps of the Austrian and Russian armies continued
to advance, and to hem in the Hungarians into a square of
which Arad was to be the centre. Görgey, outmarching the
Russians, reached Arad first, and there, on the 11th of August, he found Dembinski and Bem both defeated, and his
army surrounded. Encompassed on all sides by troops amounting to several times the number at his command, there was
no alternative left him but a hopeless contest or a surrender,*
and he adopted the latter.

On the other hand, the plan of defense adopted by the Hungarians was based upon the instructions of Kossuth to Bem.†
His orders were never to hazard an action, but to limit efforts
to harassing the enemy, cutting off his communication, and
prolonging the war.

This was strictly obeyed. The campaign may be said to
have lasted sixty days, from the entrance of the Russians to
the capitulation of Görgey. During the whole of that time, it
does not appear that one of those pitched battles in the open
field, which have in modern times decided the fate of empires,
was fought, unless Haynau's last action in the neighborhood
of Temesvar deserves that name.

The Hungarians, whether from instruction or voluntary inclination, were obviously reluctant to stake the success of their
cause on such an event. They probably dreaded the superiority of the disciplined infantry of the imperial armies, and they
relied principally on their own artillery and light cavalry,
which were their most effective arms.

This plan of defense was well adapted to, and succeeded ad-

---

* If we except the single line of retreat he mentions in his letter through Radna
to Transylvania.

† Found in his baggage. See Klapka, about the disputes between commanders, disobedience of War Department, &c.

mirably in the first campaign against the hundred thousand men that Windischgrätz led into Hungary, but against an overwhelming force of four hundred thousand men, supplied with all the resources of the two great empires, a mere guerilla system was hopeless. The only parallel to the invasion of Hungary, by the combined forces of Austria and Russia, is to be met with in the Seven Years' War, when Frederick the Great was assailed on different sides by the armies of Russia, of Austria, of France, and of Sweden. Eight hundred thousand men menaced old Fritz, who had scarcely one hundred thousand to oppose to them. Had he adopted the purely defensive and dilatory system, the Prussian monarchy would have died in 1757 the death of Hungarian independence in 1849. But Frederick attacked his enemies in detail, and with the fierce determination of the soldier, eager to repel invasion or to perish in the attempt, he finally triumphed over all his foes. It was evidently a part of the Hungarian plan, that Görgey should remain about Komorn only long enough to strike the Austrians a severe blow as they entered, and then to retreat suddenly beyond the Theiss, and connect his forces with those of Dembinski and Bem.* But why he should have remained at Komorn for several weeks, until the Russians, entering on the north, had reached the centre of the kingdom, taken possession of both capitals, and cut him off completely from the Hungarian armies of the south, has never yet been satisfactorily explained.

Although Hungary could scarcely have been expected to hold out for any great length of time against the fearful odds

---

* Joseph Bem was born at Tarnow, in Galicia, in 1795. He pursued his studies at Cracow, and, at a later period, in the military school at Warsaw. On their completion, he entered the Polish artillery-service, in which he made the campaign of 1812, against Russia, in Davoust's corps, and then in Macdonald's. On the breaking out of the Polish insurrection, he hastened to Warsaw, where the government appointed him major and commander of a battery of flying artillery. After the action of Iganie, in which he distinguished himself, he was made lieutenant colonel; after the battle of Ostrolenka, a colonel; and soon following this, was promoted to the command-in-chief of the Polish artillery. In October, 1848, Bem repaired to Vienna, and undertook the organization of the Garde Mobile, and the management of the military arrangements. After Bem fled into Turkey, he received a command in the Turkish army, where he died, in the year 1850, of the wounds received in the Hungarian war.

by which she was opposed ; taken by surprise, forced into a contest for which she was not prepared ; without an army, without generals, without arms, and, worse than all, her seaports in the hands of the enemy ; yet what she accomplished under these disadvantages—what a determined and energetic resistance she opposed to the united forces of the two empires, affords ample evidence of the internal resources, moral and material, which she possesses, and shows how firm a barrier Hungary, if independent, would have constituted against northern aggression, and how apt a guardian she would have proved of western civilization.

But no cause could hope for success when so little unanimity existed among its prominent supporters. So true as is the adage, that a house divided against itself can not stand, so true it is that Hungary has fallen under the weight of its own divisions.

Görgey, from the period of the first brilliant victory at Acs, when an attempt was made to displace him, gave but little heed to any order sent him by the government. The repeated directions given him by Kossuth to come south, and defend the Hungarian capitals, were treated with contempt ; the injunctions to unite with Dembinski totally disregarded.

Nor does the whole blame of their failure attach to Görgey. When he at length quitted Komorn, and, after an engagement at Waitzen, he, by a most dextrous movement, threw himself upon the rear of Paskievitch at Miskolcz, and was rapidly marching upon him from Kaschau. Dembinski, as has been shown, was at Szolnok on his front, and nothing could have been more natural or feasible than, by a mutual advance, to have crushed the Russian general. But Dembinski, as we have seen, instead of advancing, retreated, thus diminishing his own chances of safety, as well as those of Görgey, whom he abandoned to his fate. And when he resolved upon retreat, had he, instead of proceeding south to Szegedin, marched an equal distance east to Grosswardein, a junction with Görgey, who was wending his way to the latter place, could have been effected, at least three days sooner than by the route which he took, and quite a sufficient time, as it proved, to have united their forces before Haynau could have overtaken them.

When again, after his defeat at Szoreg, Dembinski, instead of retreating on Temesvar, still in possession of the Austrians, had proceeded to Arad (then in possession of the Hungarians), as he was expressly ordered to do, a junction would then have taken place, even in spite of Görgey's intention, and Hungary perhaps have yet been saved.

CHARACTER OF LOUIS KOSSUTH.

The time has not yet arrived for a full, impartial, and satisfactory estimate of the character and abilities of Louis Kossuth; but any sketch of the Hungarian contest would be quite imperfect that omitted an attempt to do justice to the genius of this eminent man.

Many causes unite to render the task difficult besides those that usually interfere with contemporary judgments. The European movement of 1848 was singularly barren of great men. Individuals of talent, of courage, and of enthusiasm it undoubtedly produced ; but no great social convulsion has ever before failed to evoke one or more master spirits, who to talent, courage, and enthusiasm have added the keen perception of character and resolute purpose which are indispensable to the character of a great leader. This absence of the highest order of ability has given increased prominence to him who, among the first to arouse the nations of Europe, was the last to surrender his post; who organized his country to resistance against one of the oldest governments of Europe, brought the ancient empire of Austria to the verge of destruction, and was at last overcome only by the inadequacy of his coadjutors and the colossal resources of Russia.

On the other hand, these achievements, their temporary success, and the consequences threatened by their ultimate triumph to the interests not only of Austria but of Europe, have tended to render his name more hated, because more feared, than that of any other leader in the movements of 1848, and therefore to raise up against him the greatest number of malignant detractors.

The situation of the country, also, to which Kossuth belonged, as well as its history and language, render it the more difficult justly to estimate his powers. Until the last revolution brought

Hungary into so conspicuous an attitude before the civilized world, she occupied scarcely any position on the theatre of European operations.   Her language being that of no other continental people, and having no commercial relations with any other nation, less was known of her history and institutions than of almost any other civilized land.

In this conflict of passions, and absence of the means of reliable information, it might be expedient to pause ; and, after faithfully recording those public acts of the Hungarian struggle which are of undoubted authenticity, to leave to later times the task of deciding upon the character and motives of the Hungarian leaders.   But the impatience of the human mind rejects this dictate of wisdom, and will not permit the curtain to fall upon the exciting scenes explored without a brief glance at the career of the late executive of this afflicted nation.   The epithet of great can in no proper sense be denied him, even by those who are least attached to his principles or course ; he has been too steadfast in devotion to his cause, too conspicuous in his functions, too prominent in his woes to be refused an epithet that has been often lavished on inferior men.

The early parliamentary labors of Kossuth entitle him to an eminent place among the legislators of Europe.   His temper, habits, and education seem, indeed, to have fitted him for parliamentary life, and, under a more free and enlightened government, he would doubtless have acquired the distinction of a great orator and politician.   He seems, indeed, during all the early part of his career, to have been actuated by no other ideas than those of a parliamentary and constitutional opposition to the Austrian government, and only to have been driven into revolution by the faithlessness and treachery of the imperial cabinet.   His incessant labors, his earnest struggles, and his noted sufferings between 1835 and 1848, entitle him to the esteem and sympathy of every admirer of genius and every lover of liberty.   It is in 1848, however, that began the more complicated phase of his career, and here the obstacles to an impartial judgment commence.

It had become a struggle for existence when the Austrian government, in its effort to revoke the concessions of March, aroused and armed the Croats on one side and the Serbs on the other, and there seemed no alternative left the Hungarians but unconditional surrender or desperate resistance. And if there be any good ground to question the sagacity of the policy of Kossuth during the year 1848, it was the tardiness with which resistance was commenced and the Declaration of Independence issued.

Had the declaration of Hungarian independence been made in the summer of 1848, when Austria evinced so openly her determination to revoke the concessions which she had granted in April, and when, to effect this object, instead of assuming, as was her duty, the province of *mediator* between Hungary and Croatia, she publicly announced her determination to become a *partisan*, and to enter the lists against the former and in favor of the latter, the result of the conflict might have been totally different.

The imperial aggressions at this time were amply sufficient to justify Hungary in throwing off her allegiance. The government of Austria had "become destructive of those ends for which it had been instituted," viz., "their safety and happiness," and "it was the right of the people" of Hungary "to alter or to abolish it." Besides, "when a long train of abuses and usurpations, pursuing invariably the same object, evinces a design to reduce them under absolute despotism, it was their duty to throw off such government, and to provide new guards for their future security."*

Had the Hungarians declared their independence in the summer or fall of 1848, they would not, a few weeks later, when on the frontiers of Austria, have been deterred by any scruples of duty, or fears of the traitor's doom, from obeying the call of the Viennese, and marching upon the capital to their relief.

Had the Hungarian army of twenty-two thousand men, as soon as they appeared on the frontiers of Austria, instead of delaying there, marched immediately on Vienna, Prince Windischgrätz, with his immense army, not having yet appeared, there was no force to obstruct their passage. The hundred and forty thousand fighting men in Vienna, properly organized and officered by Hungarians, with the Magyar army as a nu-

* American Declaration of Independence.

cleus, would have been invincible before any force which Windischgrätz and Jellacic combined could have brought against them, and the emperor would gladly have relieved his capital at so slight a cost as the acknowledgment of Hungarian independence.

But, even had the Hungarians not chosen to have embraced that occasion of marching upon the capital, and dictating their own terms from the emperor's palace, a still more favorable opportunity yet awaited them upon the conclusion of the first campaign, when the Austrian army was driven by the triumphant Hungarians from the centre of the kingdom over the borders, completely defeated and routed, and no efficient force remained between them and the defenseless capital.

Had she but declared her independence *previously*, the noble manner in which she *subsequently* achieved it with the sword was all that would have been requisite for the full accomplishment of her wishes. The moral force which such a course would inevitably have brought to her cause would have been more effectual than all the bayonets which could be enlisted in her behalf. In that event, the Austrians would never have ventured to seek or Russia to yield the assistance of her myrmidons against a nation which had so gallantly, both by word and deed, established her claims to freedom. There is not a civilized government that would not have cheerfully volunteered to recognize her independence, and even Ferdinand of Austria might have imitated the magnanimity of George the Third of England, and been, as the latter was in the case of the United States, the first to acknowledge an independence which he had found himself unable to prevent.

Kossuth has often said that in 1848 he held the house of Habsburg in his hand. If so, why did he spare a dynasty whose cruelty and perjury, as he states, were of centuries' duration? Was it humanity, was it fear of consequences, or was it want of nerve that impeded the exercise of his power? In the spring of 1848 he might have thought the public mind unprepared for extreme measures; but if so, why did he lend his sanction to the use of Hungarian troops in Italy, and why, above all, did he, in the fall of that eventful year, permit Windischgrätz, unopposed, to subdue Vienna, and at a blow to place the house of Habsburg in a position of impregnable authority ?

If these acts of his public life do not indicate a want of that resolute and unflinching purpose so indispensable to revolutionary leaders, they at least seem strongly to evince that revolution was then far from his mind, and a parliamentary and constitutional opposition the only one in which he was at that time ready to engage.

But the die was cast, and the struggle—more pregnant in consequences to Europe than any that has taken place since the fall of the Roman empire—commenced. Had Hungary established her independence, Austria must inevitably have sunk into a third or fourth rate power. Had she been able to establish a free Constitution, and, absorbing Croatia, opened to herself the ports of the Mediterranean, the future consequences to the freedom of Europe can not be overrated. The struggle, when once commenced, was one worthy of the utmost effort; and this was not wanting. The labors of Kossuth were Herculean; and, assisted by the most gallant people of Europe, no contest more worthy of the poet and the historian has ever been waged between the opposing spirits of freedom and tyranny, of good and evil, that have immemorially divided the world.

The labors of Kossuth during this period were doubtless of the highest order of merit. His voice, his pen, his indefatigable industry, his mastership of detail, his vivid imagination, his lofty aspirations, all were employed. A highly sensitive and poetic temperament, a peculiarly active and laborious mind, exhibited themselves in his efforts in rare and striking union; he aroused and armed the people, and, thus aroused and armed, his spirit led them into conflict. It is absurd to deny, as it is impossible to underrate, his efforts during this period; and those who criticise and decry him, would find it difficult to show higher instances of genius, enthusiasm, and devotion to the cause of liberty.

Nor does there seem, in this portion of his public life, any ground for the attempt of inimical writers to identify his character with that of the demagogue, or fix upon him the motives of an unscrupulous ambition.

He had used every effort to conciliate the cabinet of Vienna; he had forborne to use the power of injury he possessed; he had permitted the Hungarian arms to be employed for the subjugation of Italy; he had looked on while the watch-fires of Windischgrätz and Jellacic encircled Vienna with the girdle of destruction; he had reached the utmost limit of forbearance, and perhaps, indeed, hesitated too long, before he threw down the gauntlet and defied the imperial power. But after that decisive act, all the others became a necessary consequence. It was the dictate of the clearest policy and of inevitable necessity to abolish the distinctions of rank and race, and to give to the movement a direction absolutely popular. It was natural that the supreme power should be vested in the hands of the most able and active of the revolutionary leaders; and, if he looked forward to the chief magistracy of the state by the universal suffrage of free and independent Hungary, it was the dream of an honorable and laudable ambition—and, alas! it was but a dream.

These efforts were vain: the struggles of the leader and his brave followers were fruitless; and, after proving what heroism, constancy, and skill could effect, after defeating the power of Austria, they were destined to fall before the overwhelming legions of Russia.

We approach the final catastrophe. The Hungarians slowly retreat to the extreme limits of their country. But they still numbered one hundred and fifty thousand men in arms; their two strongest fortresses, Komorn and Peterwardein, yet held out; and, on the banks of the Danube, at least, the gallant nation stood at bay.

In this position of affairs, it is true, every thing appeared hopeless; indeed, the cause of Hungary was desperate; but in such a position some men are capable of great and immortal deeds. Kossuth, without a convention of his cabinet, confided the supreme power to a general whom he had repeatedly declared unworthy of confidence, and fled precipitately over the frontier. This act was succeeded by the immediate surrender of the army, and thus ended the brief life of independent Hungary. It is deeply to be regretted that no detailed account of the closing transactions has been given us by Kossuth himself, and that we are consequently obliged to grope our way amid conflicting statements of men all eager to shift both the responsibility and the disgrace on others. It appears certain that the trust of negotiating with the Russian commander was confided to Görgey by a full cabinet, and that the act of abdication was consented to only by three out of seven of the ministers, and without a formal council meeting. But the grant of power to treat shows the sense entertained by the whole ministry, not only of the hopelessness of their position, but of their dependence on Görgey. Why was the power to negotiate confided to an untrustworthy agent? Why, indeed, was not the faithless and insubordinate agent tried by court-martial months before?

The grant of authority to negotiate, given to a military leader, was in fact a practical surrender of the government; and, after this was acceded to by a united and unanimous cabinet, there is no reason to believe that the act of abdication would have been seriously opposed; and the endeavor, on the part of those members of the cabinet who were not concerned, to throw the blame on Kossuth and the remainder of the ministers, seems to be scarcely justifiable, and may, perhaps, be wholly attributed to that spirit of recrimination in which the partisans of a lost cause are too apt to indulge.

But if it is correct to ascribe to the entire government the responsibility of this transaction, what is to be said of Kossuth himself, who for years had been the soul of the resistance in Hungary, the martyr of the first struggles of the press in 1835, the leader of the parliamentary opposition for fifteen years, the prime mover of the revolution in 1848, and, finally, the first, the last, the only governor of Hungary? What explanation can be given of the act by which, at this essential climax of his country's fortunes, he abandoned his post, and, without any guarantee whatever, intrusted a power, which was not his to bestow, to a soldier whom he had repeatedly declared unworthy of confidence, and then sought his personal safety among the hereditary enemies of his country? Is there any new light to be thrown on this wretched termination; or is it to be inferred that the orator, the statesman, the man of genius, was unequal to the fierce conflict of arms, and that, overawed, subdued, and stunned by the storm he had himself aroused, he shrunk from the blast, and was as unable to protect his own fame as to defend the fortunes of his country ?

It is, after all, a personal question, affecting solely the character of the man, for there can be but little doubt that, when Kossuth fled into Turkey, the cause of Hungary was desperate, and that no object of public importance could be gained by his pursuing an opposite course.

Thus, for a time, Kossuth disappeared from the scene of Europe. If the testimony, that history has thus far furnished, leads to the conclusion that his highly nervous, sensitive, and poetical temperament has led him into conduct that a firmer heart and more deliberate judgment would have avoided, that his extraordinary powers of expression were not combined with a corresponding executive ability, and that his vivid imagination is better calculated to arouse the passions and kindle the aspirations of others, than to obtain for himself a dispassionate and practical view of events around him; still there remains more than enough of superiority in his character to justify the warm admiration of every lover of human freedom. His consummate oratory, his poetical fancy, his capacity for labor, his struggles and his sufferings in the great cause of civil liberty, will forever keep his name in the first rank of those who have magnanimously devoted their lives to extend the blessings of progress and equal rights, which are only the legitimate results of a free government.*

---

* The author has abstained from any observations on Kossuth's public efforts in England and the United States, since his release from exile. His conduct in his new position admits of varied interpretation; it is, however, quite independent of those events in the history of his native land to which this work is especially devoted.

II.   Z

APPENDIX.

Note No. 1.

ACT OF THE DIET OF THE CONFEDERATION OF FRANKFORT, PASSED JUNE 28, 1832.

1st. Whereas, according to the fifty-seventh article of the final act of the Congress of Vienna, 1820, the powers of the state ought to remain in the hands of its chief, and the sovereign ought not to be bound by the local Constitution to require the co-operation of the Chambers, except as to the exercise of certain specified rights, the sovereigns of Germany, as members of the confederation, have not only the right of rejecting the petitions of the Chambers contrary to this principle, but the object of the confederation makes it their duty to reject such petitions.

2d. Since, according to the spirit of the said fifty-seventh article of the final act and its inductions, as expressed in article fifty-eight, the Chambers can not refuse to any German sovereign the necessary means of fulfilling his federal obligations, and those imposed by the local Constitution ; the cases in which the Chambers endeavor to make their consent to the taxes necessary for these purposes depend upon the assent of the sovereign to their propositions upon any subject, are to be classed among those cases to which are applied the twenty-fifth and twenty-sixth articles of the final act, relating to resistance of the subjects against the government.

3d. The internal legislation of the states belonging to the Germanic Confederation can not prejudice the object as expressed in the second article of the original Act of Confederation, and in the first article of the final act; nor can this legislation obstruct in any manner the accomplishment of the federal obligations of the state, and especially the payment of the taxes necessary to fulfill them.

4th. In order to maintain the rights and dignity of the confederation, and of the Assembly representing it, against usurpations of every kind, and at the same time to facilitate to the states which are members of the confederation the maintenance of the constitutional relations between the local governments and the Legislative Chambers, there shall be appointed by the Diet, in the first instance for the term of six years, a commission charged with the supervision of the deliberations of the Chambers, and with directing their attention to the propositions and resolutions which may be found in opposition to the federal obligations as to the rights of sovereignty guaranteed by the compacts of the confederation. The commission is to report to the Diet, which, if it finds the matter proper for further consideration, will put itself in relation with the local government concerned. After the lapse of six years, a new arrangement is to be made for the prolongation of the commission.

5th. Since, according to the fifty-ninth article of the final act, in those states where the publication of the Chambers is secured by the Constitution, the free expression of opinion, either in the deliberations themselves or in their publication through the medium of the press, can not be so extended as to endanger the tranquillity of the state itself, or of the confederation in general, all governments belonging to it mutually bind themselves, as they are already bound by their federal relations, to adopt and maintain such measures as may be necessary to prevent and punish every attack against the confederation in the local Chambers.

6th. Since the Diet is already authorized, by the seventeenth article of the final act for the maintenance of the true meaning of the original act of the confederation, to give its provisions such an interpretation as may be consistent with its object, in case doubts should arise in this respect, it is understood that the confederation has the exclusive right of interpreting, so as to produce their legal effect, the original act of confederation and the final act, which right it exercises by its constitutional organ the Diet.

Note No. 2.

TABLE OF THE MONASTIC INSTITUTIONS IN THE VARIOUS PROVINCES OF THE EMPIRE.

Among which are included that of the Somaskers, the 14 Basilian Monasteries of the Greek Church, and the 3 of the Mechitarists, with their Dependencies. Hungary has 175 Monasteries, and 11 Nunneries of the Romish Church. Among the Nunneries are, 1 of Armenian Nuns, and 2 of the Basilian Order.

	Monasteries.			Nunneries.		
	No.	Priests.	Clerks and Laymen.	No.	Nuns.	Novices.
Province of Lower Austria	49	562	336	7	186	119
Province of Upper Austria	19	174	69	8	137	79
Styria	22	145	140	3	67	19
Carynthia and Carniola	11	88	34	4	95	28
Coast Land	18	87	77	4	65	19
Tyrol	57	488	341	19	237	215
Bohemia	75	541	312	6	125	26
Moravia and Silesia	34	502	147	4	48	18
Galicia	73	307	289	15	143	49
Dalmatia	54	231	118	8	38	6
Lombardy	10	63	97	19	420	236
Venice	27	284	324	15	286	164
Military Frontiers	11	63	35			
Transylvania	40	155	53	1	20	
Total	500	3390	2372	113	1867	978

The Monasteries may be divided among the following orders:

	No. of Monasteries.		No. of Monasteries.
Augustines	13	Crusaders	1
Charitable Brethren	20	Mechitarists	4
Barnabites	7	Minoritists	36
Basilians	15	Piarists	36
Benedictines	19	Philippinists	7
Regular Canons	14	Præmonstratenists	7
Dominicans	7	Redemptorists	6
Regular Hermits	30	Reformatists	11
Franciscans	3	Servitists	18
Jesuits	6	Terzianists	6
Capucins	86	Cistercians	11
Carmelites	8	Maltese	1

TABLE SHOWING THE ARCHBISHOPS AND BISHOPS IN THE AUSTRIAN EMPIRE.

Archbishops.   Bishops.

Vienna ......St. Pölten, Linz.

Salzburg ....Seckau, Leoben, Gurk, Lavant, Brixen, Trient.

Prague .....Budweis, Königgrätz, Leitmeritz.

Olmütz .....Brünn.

Lemberg....Przemisl, Tarnow.

Görz ....Laiback, Trieste and Capo d'Istria, Parenzo and Pola, Veglia.

Milan ......Bergamo, Brescia, Como, Crema, Cremona, Lodi, Mantua, Pavia.

Venice......Adria, Belluno and Feltre, Ceneda, Chioggia, Concordia, Padua,
            Treviso, Udine, Verona, Vicenza.

Zara........Spalato and Macarsca, Ragusa, Sebenico, Lesina, Brazza and Lissa,
            Cattaro.

Gran ....Fünfkirchen, Wesprim, Waizen, Raab, Neutra, Neusohl, Stein and
            Anger, Stuhlweissenburg, Siebenbürgen.

Colusca .....Grosswardein, Csanad, Agram, Diakowar, Zengg and Modrusz.

Erlau.......Kaschau, Rosenau, Zathmar, Zips.

The vicar-generalships are those for Vorarlberg at Feldkirch, and for the Breslau diocese in East Silesia.

Note No 3.

THE EIGHT UNIVERSITIES IN THE AUSTRIAN DOMINIONS ARE THOSE AT

	Professors.	Students.	Pensioners.	Pension Money in Florins.	Total Cost in Florins.
Vienna	84	4,991	233	21,706	186,479
Prague	63	3,479	36	1,988	72,355
Olmütz...............................	26	526	104	6,811	28,171
Leopol	42	1,375	50	3,839	59,210
Innspruck (No Faculty of Theology) ..	23	314	70	3,993	27,853
Gratz.................................	28	864	.46	2,067	26,866
Pavia	60	1,362	17	2,975	75,331
Padua.................................	36	1,433			99,131
Total....................	362	14,344	556	43,379	575,396

Cost in English Money, £57,539.

	Number.	Professors.	Students.	Pensioners.	Pension Money in Florins.	Total Cost in Florins.
Polytechnic Institution at Vienna	1	30	1104	4	150	59,628
" " at Prague	1	21	599			15,934
Mathematical School at Linz	1	1	50			300
School of Forestry at Marienbrunn	1	4	50			21,052
Schools of Utility at Trieste, Leopol, Brody, Rakonitz, and Reichenberg	5	44	235	2	253	30,419
Schools of Agriculture and Rural Economy at Olmütz, Brünn, and Kraumau	3	10	218			5,390
School of Practical Chemistry at Milan	1	3	19			2,260
Schools of Languages at Linz and Salzburg	3	3	54			1,058
Schools of Mathematics on Military Frontiers	8	34	386			2,200
Mining School at Schmnitz	1	7	178	55		11,500
Total	25	157	2893	61	403	149,741

The general establishments enumerated in the first table include the Theresarium and the noble school at Innspruck, the Academy of Oriental Languages, the Institute for Church Singing at Salzburg, the College for Rabbins at Padua, and for Unitarians at Klausenburg.

The female establishments include the schools of the Ursulines, and Sisters of Charity, those of different convents, and those for the education of the daughters of officers and *employés*.

The mixed schools for both sexes embrace the Deaf and Dumb Institutions, Orphan Houses, and the School of Music, at Milan, &c.

Among the special institutions in the second table are the Josephenian Academy for military surgeons, the Schools of Midwifery and Veterinary Surgery, and the Institution of Pious Ladies, at Chioggia.

Note No. 4.

PAY AND ALLOWANCE OF A REGIMENT IN GERMANY, HUNGARY, AND TRANSYLVANIA.

	PEACE								WAR							
	Germany		Hungary and Flat Country		Transylvania and Galicia				Monthly			Daily				
	Monthly	Daily	Monthly	Daily	Monthly	Daily	Bread	Horse	Pay	Field allowance	Total	Pay	Field allowance	Total	Bread	Horse
Inhaber	316 32	0	289 52	0	289 52	0	0	0	316 32	10 8	326 40	0	0	0	9	9
Colonel Commandant	149 33	0	138 24	0	145 12	0	0	0	149 33	4 46	154 19	0	0	0	9	10
Lieutenant Colonel	110 9	0	102 23	0	107 14	0	0	0	110 9	3 31	113 40	0	0	0	6	8
Major	79 49	0	73 2	0	77 10	0	3	0	88 49	2 50	91 39	0	0	0	6	8
Chaplain	23 25	0	22 11	0	23 2	0	0	0	23 25	0 44	24 9	0	0	0	2	3
Auditor and Secretary	34 43	0	32 33	0	33 53	0	0	0	34 43	0 6	35 49	0	0	0	3	3
Paymaster	25 31	0	24 4	0	25 31	0	0	0	25 31	0 49	26 20	0	0	0	2	3
Adjutant	19 42	0	18 14	0	19 13	0	1	0	19 42	0 38	20 20	0	0	0	2	2
Surgeon	25 31	0	24 4	0	25 2	0	0	0	25 31	0 49	26 20	0	0	0	2	3
Surgeon, Upper Assistant	14 0	0	19 0	0	19 0	0	1	0	14 0	1 0	15 0	0	1	1	1	1
Surgeon, Under Assistant	7 0	0	14 0	0	14 0	0	1	0	7 0	0 0	7 0	0	0	0	1	0
Cadets	14 0	0	13 45	0	13 0	0	1	0	14 0	1 0	15 5	0	1	1	1	0
Fourier	5 5	0	3 33	0	3 33	0	1	0	5 5	0 31	5 36	5	0	1	1	0
Regimental Drummer	0	5	0 0	0	0 0	0	1	0	0 0	0 0	0 0	10	1	1	3	0
Oboist	0	10	0	0	0	0	1	0	0 0	0 0	0 36	0	0	0	3	0
Master of Band	25 31	0	24 18	0	25 17	0	1	0	25 31	0	0	0	0	0	2	3
Provost	25 31	0	24 18	0	25 17	0	1	0	25 31	2 36	26 20	0	0	0	2	2
Captain	71 42	0	65 33	0	69 31	0	1	0	71 42	2 36	74 18	9	0	0	3	2
Captain Lieutenant	39 23	0	36 14	0	38 11	0	0	0	39 23	1 16	40 39	0	0	0	3	2
First Lieutenant	26 48	0	25 9	0	26 22	0	0	0	26 48	0 52	27 40	0	0	0	2	2
Second Lieutenant	22 37	0	21 9	0	22 7	0	0	0	22 37	0 43	23 20	0	0	0	2	2
Ensign	19 42	0	18 14	0	19 13	0	1	0	10 42	0 38	20 20	0	0	0	2	2
Sergeant	0	0 17	0	0 17	0	0 12	1	0	0	0	0	0 17	0 1	0 18	1	0
Corporal	0	0 10	0	0 7	0	0 7	1	0	0	0	0	0 10	0 1	0 11	1	0
Fourier, Grenadiers	0	0 6	0	0 4	0	0 4	1	0	0	0	0	0 6	0 1	0 7	1	0
Fourier, Fusileers	0	0 5	0	0 4	0	0 4	1	0	0	0	0	0 5	0 1	0 6	1	0
Drummer, Grenadiers	0	0 6	0	0 4	0	0 4	1	0	0	0	0	0 6	0 1	0 7	1	0
Drummer, Fusileers	0	0 5	0	0 4	0	0 4	1	0	0	0	0	0 5	0 1	0 6	1	0
Exempt	0	0 7	0	0 5	0	0 5	1	0	0	0	0	0 7	0 1	0 8	1	0
Barrackman, Grenadiers	0	0 6	0	0 4	0	0 4	1	0	0	0	0	0 6	0 1	0 7	1	0
Barrackman, Fusileers	0	0 5	0	0 4	0	0 4	1	0	0	0	0	0 5	0 1	0 6	1	0
Private, Grenadiers	0	0 6	0	0 4	0	0 4	1	0	0	0	0	0 6	0 1	0 7	1	0
Private, Fusileers	0	0 5	0	0 4	0	0 4	1	0	0	0	0	0 5	0 1	0 6	1	0

In garrison service the pay also varies in peace and war.

Note No. 5.

In Vienna, in March, 1848, previous to the Revolution.

Prince Metternich, Chancellor of State, Minister of Foreign Affairs, and President of the Council.

Count Kollowrat, Minister of Home Affairs.

Count Sedlnitzki, Minister of Police.

Baron Kübeck, President of the Treasury.

Count Taaffe, President of the Board of Justice.

Count Hardegg, President of the Board of War.

After the Revolution in March.

Count Fiquelmont, Foreign Affairs.

Count Kollowrat, Home Affairs.

Baron Kübeck, Finances.

Count Taaffe, Justice.

General Zannini, War.

Baron Pillersdorf, Public Instruction.

In May.

Baron Wessenberg, Foreign Affairs.

Baron Pillersdorf, Home Affairs.

Baron Kraus, Finances.

Baron Sommaruga, Justice.

Count Latour, War.

Baron Dobblhof, Trade.

M. Baumgarten, Public Works.

In June.

Baron Wessenberg, Foreign Affairs.

Baron Dobblhof, Home Affairs.

Baron Kraus, Finances.

Dr. Bach, Justice.

Count Latour, War.

Mr. Hornbostel, Trade.

Mr. Schwartzer, Public Works.

In November.

Prince Schwartzenberg, Foreign Affairs.

Count Stadion, Home Affairs.

Baron Kraus, Finances.

Dr. Bach, Justice.

General Cordon, War.

Mr. Bruck, Trade.

Mr. Thienfeldt, Public Works.

Baron Kulmer, Croatian Minister without Portefeuille.

In May, 1849.

Prince Schwartzenberg, Foreign Affairs.
Dr. Bach, Home Affairs.
Baron Kraus, Finances.
Mr. Schmerling, Justice.
Count Gylay, War.
Mr. Bruck, Trade.
Mr. Thienfeldt, Public Works.
Count Leo Thun, Public Instruction.
Baron Kulmer, Croatian Minister without Portefeuille.

In Hungary during the same Period, from March till September, 1848.

Count Louis Batthyányi, Prime Minister.
Bertalan Szemere, Home Affairs.
Louis Kossuth, Finances.
Francis Deak, Justice.
General Lazar Meszaros, War.
Gabor Klauzal, Trade.
Count Stephen Széchényi, Public Works.
Baron Josef Eötvös, Public Instruction.
Prince Paul Esterhazy, Minister around the person of the King, and intrusted
 with the regulation of international concerns between Hungary and the Aus-
 trian provinces, and therefore called Minister of Foreign Affairs.

In September.

Count Louis Batthyányi, alone.

From October to April, 1849. *The Committee of Public Defense.*

Kossuth, President.
Szemere.
Meszaros.
Baron Sigmund Perenyi.
Paul Nyary.
Count Michael Esterhazy.
Baron Nicholas Iosika.
John Palfy.
Francis Duschek.
Ladislas Madarasz.
Pazmandy, Pulszky, Zsembery, and Patay, were only from October to January
 Members of this Committee.

In April Kossuth was elected Governor-President, and formed the following
Cabinet:

Szemere, President of the Council, and Minister of Home Affairs.
Count Casimir Batthyányi, Foreign Affairs.
Sabbas Vucovics, Justice.
Francis Duschek, Finances.
Ladislas Csanyi, Public Works.
Bishop Michel Horvath, Public Instruction.
General Görgey, later General Aulick, War.

Note No. 6.

Head-quarters, Milan, August 9th, 1848.

1st. The demarcation between both armies shall be the frontiers of the respective states.

2d. The fortresses of Peschiera, Rocca D'Anfo, and Osopo, are to be evacuated by the Sardinian and allied troops, and surrendered to the Austrian troops. The surrender will take place three days after the publication of the present convention. The materiel of war belonging to the Austrians is to be restored to them. The withdrawing garrison shall take with it all the materiel of war, arms, ammunition, and regimentals, which it has brought thither, and shall return to the Sardinian states by the shortest route.

3d. The states of Parma, Modena, and the city of Placenza, are to be cleared of the troops of his majesty, the King of Sardinia, in three days after the publication of this convention.

4th. This convention extends even to the city and to the whole province of Venice; therefore the Sardinian forces by water and land will leave Venice the forts and ports, and return to the Sardinian states.

5th. Persons and property in the above-mentioned cities shall be put under the protection of the imperial government.

6th. This truce will continue for six weeks, to enable arrangements of a peace to be completed. After the expiration of this time, the truce will be lengthened by a mutual agreement, or otherwise to be revoked at least eight days before the commencement of hostilities.

7th. Commissioners are to be nominated by both parties, to effect the execution of the above-mentioned articles in the best and most friendly manner.

Note No. 7.

SCHEDULE OF TAXES PAID IN THE DIFFERENT PROVINCES OF AUSTRIA.

	Austrian sq. Miles.	Inhabitants.	Income in Guldens Conv. Money.	Per Head.	Per M le.
				Fl. Kr.	Florins.*
Austria below the Enns	344	1,456,925	18,056,024	12 24	52,490
Austria above the Enns	333	866,836	11,280,503	13	33,875
Styria	391	1,001,401	6,323,075	6 19	16,172
Carinthia and Carniola	354	780,329	4,498,973	5 45	12,709
Littorale	139	498,357	4,222,763	8 29	30,379
Tyrol	500	851,924	3,751,061	4 24	7,502
Bohemia	902	4,341,152	18,498,288	4 15	20,508
Moravia and Silesia	476	2,254,658	9,311,398	4 8	19,562
Galicia	1,545	5,192,445	14,086,416	2 43	9,117
Dalmatia	222	407,792	1,134,267	2 47	5,109
Lombardy and Venetia	789	4,901,369	37,376,946	7 37	17,373
Hungary, Trans., Milit. front.	5,600	13,885,328	22,320,683	1 36	3,986
Total	11,596	36,438,516	150,860,397	4 8	13,010

* The Florin or Gulden is about equal to forty-eight cents American currency.

Note No. 8.

CAPITULATION OF THE AUSTRIAN GOVERNMENT IN VENICE.

The municipality of Venice invited, in its official paper of the 22d of March, 1848, some of the most influential citizens to assist it in this critical moment.

The Assembly, consisting of the podestá and six municipal assessors, the secretary and Messrs. Giuseppe Reali, Luigi Revedin, the lawyer Gio. Francesco Avesani, Leone Pincherle, Giacomo Castelli, and Costi, were discussing upon the state of matters and the measures to be taken, when a communication was received, that the abhorred Colonel Marinovich had been killed by the working-men in the arsenal, and that Fr. Olivieri, the valorous chief of the Civic Guard belonging to the district of the Castel, had entered the arsenal with his troop, and caused another troop to take possession of the guard-ship.

Soon afterward, the Av. Angelo Mengaldo, commander of the National Guard, who, having been instructed previously by the municipality to demand from the civil and military governors, Counts Zichy and Palfy, the evacuation of the arsenal by the Croats, presented himself, reporting the result of his interviews. It was remarked to him by these two gentlemen, in presence of the Council of the government and the Vice-admiral Martini, that the number of demands were increasing rapidly, and that, even if that last should be admitted and granted, like the precedents, quietness and order would not yet be restored. Therefore, they desired to know the real intentions of the city. He answered, that order would not be restored until all means of offense and defense were put into the hands of the citizens. This was refused, as being almost the same as an abdication; and he stated further, that he was instructed to invite the municipality to present itself before the government and to explain the wishes of the people. The Assembly proceeded to elect a deputation of some of its members, who were authorized to repeat the demand to the two governors, for the purpose of saving the city from bloodshed. The deputation consisted of the Podestá Correr, the two assessors, Luigi Michiel and Dattacio Medin, Avocate Avesani, Leone Pincherle, and Fabris. Mengaldo arrived during the negotiations. They were introduced into the apartments of Count Palfy, governor of the Venetian provinces, who was surrounded by his government Council. He took the floor, beginning with a long complaint, and severely reproaching the false imputations against the government, which were tending only to produce dissatisfaction and excitement among the population. Avesani interrupted him, saying, "Are we called here to be reproached, according to old custom, or to negotiate?" upon which his excellency grew still more angry, asserting that his words were not directed to the Advocate Avesani, but to the podestá and the other gentlemen. He terminated his speech, complaining that order was promised after having obtained the granting of the people's wishes, but that, on the contrary, the excitement and the demands were still increasing; his Council was assembled to hear the demands, and to decide if they were such as to be admitted to a conference.

The podestá replied, stating that the municipality had selected a deputation, consisting of the present individuals, for the purpose of communicating to his excellency what was believed necessary to prevent bloodshed, and invited M. Avesani to take the floor.

The Advocate Avesani said that the governor must be aware that no demand belonging to the attributions of the Council of the government would be made to him, that all dissimulation was useless, that there was no time to be lost, and for this reason the deputation would not enter into any discussion about the inconvenient speech of his excellency, nor would any discussion be admitted upon the rights or the motives of the discontent of the people, and the tardy concessions of the government. A conclusion was urgent, and this conclusion is, "The Austrian government has to renounce its power." "If that is your demand," replied the governor, with great indignation, "I give up all my power as governor, to put it into the hands of the military governor, and thus the city will have to negotiate only with him." The Advocate Avesani then said that, a few moments ago, by the accidental opening of a door, he had seen his excellency the Count Zichy, and requested the Count Palfy to have him called immediately to hear the demands, and to give a final answer. The Count Palfy went himself, and, addressing him in a few words, explained the intentions and demands of the deputation, and gave all his powers as governor into the hands of the commander of the city and forts of Venice, ceasing from this moment to be governor. He recommended him to save, as much as possible, during the execution of his rigorous duties, this beautiful and monumental city from destruction, for which he professed a great affection. His excellency said he could not grant such demands; that he, too, loved Venice, but that his duty was dearer to him than his affection. Signor Avesani replied, that he took this answer for a refusal, and that his excellency would be responsible for all consequences when this should be announced to the people. Count Zichy requested him to act with moderation. Avesani replied, that moderation was impossible, and proposed the following conditions:

1st. The German troops will evacuate the city, and the Italian troops will— "Impossible," said the field-marshal lieutenant, "we will fight." "Well," replied Avesani, going to the door, "we shall fight." He was recalled by Count Zichy, who represented to him that it would cost him his head if he should consent to such a measure; to which Avesani replied, that on similar occasions the lives of all were equally in danger, and that already too much time had been lost. At last the first point was agreed upon, in the manner as already stated. Avesani further demanded,

2d. The troops will start immediately for Trieste. His excellency refused, for the reason, that he could not prevent the troops from rejoining their respective corps, and that they must depart protected by the forts. To which Avesani replied, that the forts must also be evacuated, and that the Venetians would not make a present to their Italian brothers of the troops driven out from Venice. He asked most peremptorily to be only answered Yes or No. The answer was, Agreed.

3d. The materiel of war remains in Venice.

4th. The chests remain in Venice.

The same refusal and the same final settlement.

Agreeable to the observation, that the salaries and the passage of the troops must be paid, it was stipulated that the necessary sum for that purpose should be provided for. Finally, the speaker of the deputation, Avesani, proposed that the two governors should remain as hostages for the faithful execution of the convention. Palfy complained of that measure, for the reason that, having already resigned before the conclusion of the treaty, and not having taken any part in it, he did not deserve such treatment, and called upon the whole deputation to testify, that he had always acted as a man of honor. "Yes, it is true," observed Avesani, "you have always been a man of honor, and affectionate toward the country; only the last three months you have committed many faults, beyond those ordered to you by that great man, who boasted of being the Nestor of diplomacy, and who has ruined the Austrian monarchy. Count Zichy complained, in the same manner, and, upon his promise to leave the city only after the departure of the troops, it was stipulated that a steamer should be kept at the disposal of his excellency and his suite. It was also stipulated that the necessary means should be provided for the departure of the troops, civil officers, and their families. The deputation then went away, proclaiming to the people the capitulation, and the end of the Austrian government in Venice. Signed,

CORRER, Podestá.
MEDIN, Assessor.
FABRIS.
LUIGI MICHIEL.
MENGALDO.
FRANCESCO AVESANI.

His excellency Count Palfy, desirous to prevent bloodshed, and having been informed by Count Correr, podestá, and other citizens, that this could not be done without fulfilling the conditions proposed by them, has recommended to Count Zichy all possible regard for that beautiful and monumental city, to which he is deeply attached. In consequence of his recommendation, and in consideration of the urgent circumstances, and to save the city from the horrors of bloodshed, he and the undersigned have agreed upon the following treaty:

1st. From this day the Austrian military and civil government has ceased, both on land and sea, and is surrendered to the Provisional Government, consisting of the undersigned citizens.

2d. The regiment Kinsky, the Croats, the artillery, and the corps of engineers, will evacuate the city and the forts; the Italian troops and Italian officers will remain.

3d. All materiel of war will remain in Venice.

4th. The evacuation by the troops will take place immediately, and they will direct themselves to Trieste.

5th. The families of all the officers will be protected by the Provisional Government, and they will be provided with the necessary means.

6th. All the civil officers, their families, and property, will be protected by the Provisional Government.

7th. His excellency Count Zichy gives his word of honor to remain in Venice till after the execution of the above conditions. A steamer will be kept at the disposal of his excellency, his suite, and the last soldiers.

8th. All the chests remain in Venice, and the necessary sum for the transport and the salaries of the troops will be paid. The salaries will be paid for three months.

COUNT ZICHY,
Commander of the City and Forts.
GIOVANNI CORRER.
LUIGI MICHIEL.
DATARIO MEDIN.
PIETRO FABRIS.
FRANCESCO AVESANI.
ANGELO MENGALDO.
LEONE PINCHERLE.

FRANCESCO D. BETRANE,
ANTONIO MUZZANI,   } Witnesses.
COSTANTINO ALBERTI,

Note No. 9.

TERMS OF THE SURRENDER OF VENICE.

"Minutes of the conference held at the Villa Pappadopoli, near Mestre, the head-quarters of the second *corps d'armée* of reserve, on the 22d of August. Present: his excellency the cavalry general Chevalier Gorzkowski, commanding the second *corps d'armée* of reserve; his excellency the artillery general Baron de Hess, quarter-master of the imperial army; Count Marzani, attached to his excellency the cavalry general for civil affairs. There appeared Messrs. Nicolo Priuli, Count Datario Medin, and Advocate Calucci, all three representing the municipality; Engineer Cavedalis, representing the army; and Signor Antonini, representing the merchants, who, having explained the determination of their constituents and of the population of Venice to make their submission to his imperial and royal apostolic majesty, and to come to an understanding concerning the surrender of the city and its dependencies, the following has been mutually agreed upon : 1st. The submission shall take place according to the precise terms of the proclamation of his excellency Field-marshal Count Radetzky, dated the 14th of August instant. 2d. The surrender of all that is mentioned in the said proclamation of the 14th instant shall be effected in the course of four days, from the day after to-morrow, in the manner to be agreed upon by a military commission, composed of their excellencies the cavalry general Chevalier Gorzkowski and the artillery general Baron de Hess, Colonels Schlitter, adjutant-general of his excellency Field-marshal Count Radetzky, and Chevalier Schiller, chief of the staff of the second *corps d'armée* of reserve, on one side, and Engineer Cavedalis on the other, assisted by a superior officer of marine. And whereas the gentlemen deputed by Venice have pointed to the necessity of some explanations concerning the measures contemplated by articles four and five of the above-mentioned proclamation, it is declared that the persons who are to leave Venice are, in the first place, all imperial and royal officers who have borne arms against their legitimate sovereign; in the second place, all foreign military of whatever grade ; and, in the third place, the civil persons named in the list, which will be given to the Venetian deputies. With respect to the circumstance that there is at present exclusively in circulation at Venice a large quantity of paper-money, of which the poorer class of the numerous population could not be deprived without serious consequences for their subsistence, and owing to the necessity of regulating this point before the entrance of the imperial and royal troops, it is agreed that the paper-money in circulation under the name of 'communal paper,' shall be reduced to half its nominal value, and shall have a forced currency only in Venice, Chioggia, and the other places of the estuary for the said diminished amount, till it shall have been withdrawn and another substituted in its stead, in consequence of measures to be agreed upon with the Venetian municipality, which operation shall take place in a short time. The city of Venice and the estuary shall bear the whole charge of redeeming the said new paper-money by the annual tax of twenty-five centimes for every livre, and with other subsidiary measures, which may be calculated to hasten the operation. In consideration of this charge, no war-contribution shall be imposed, and those already inflicted upon the continental possessions of some inhabitants of Venice shall be reconsidered. As to the paper called patriotic, which is to be entirely withdrawn from circulation, and other certificates of the public debt, they shall be taken under consideration at a future period. Done in duplicate, and signed *manu propria*, on the day and in the place hereinbefore mentioned.

GORZKOWSKI, M. P., Cavalry General;

HEP, M. P., Artillery General and Quarter-master;

MARZANI, M. P.;

NICOLO PRIULI, M. P.;

DATARIO MEDIN, M. P.;

GIUSEPPE CALUCCI, M. P.;

ANDREA ANTONINI, M. P.;

E. CAVEDALIS, M. P."

The minutes of conference farther add: " On the 24th and following days, the surrender of the place and estuary will take place as follows: 1. Departure from Venice of the Venetian and Lombard battalions, commanded by Meneghetti by land, *vià* Fusina. 2. Occupation of the forts on the 25th, namely, S. Secondo, Piazzale, S. Giorgio, S. Angelo, and the one on the rail-road station. 3. Departure of the corps of the Euganei and the Sile on the 26th, *vià* Fusina. 4. Occupation of the city, surrender of the arsenal and fleet on the 27th; assembly of the officers at the fort of the Lido. 5. Departure of the corps of the Friuli, Brenta, and Galateo, on the 28th; dissolution of the two regiments. 6. Occupation of Chioggia, Burano, and respective districts on the 29th. 7. Departure on the 30th of the Neapolitans by sea; occupation of S. Niccolo and the coast. 8. Departure on the 31st of the officers, and surrender of the fort of the Lido.

Note No. 10.

DOCUMENT CONTAINING THE RECOGNITION OF FERDINAND I., 1526, OF HIS FREE ELECTION TO THE BOHEMIAN CROWN.

RECOGNITIO FERDINANDI I. IMPERATORIS DE LIBERA ELECTIONE BOHEMICA, DE ANNO 1526.

Nos Ferdinandus Dei gratia Bohemiæ Rex, Infans Hispaniarum, Archidux Austriæ, Marchio Moraviæ Dux Lucemburgiæ, Silesiæ, et Marchio Lusatiæ, etc. Notum facimus tenore præsentium universis: Quemadmodum Barones, Nobiles, et etiam Civitates, al sota communitas Regni Bohemiæ ex sua libera et Cona voluntate juxta libertates Regni elegerunt nos in Regem Bohemiæ, quapropter recognoscimus quod hoc ipsum ab Oratoribus ipsorum abunde intelleximus, et re-ipsa cognovimus et comperimus, quod præfati status et communitas illius Regni; non ex aliquo debito, sed ita prout supra scriptum est, eam *electionem eligentes nos in Regem Bohemiæ ex libera et bona voluntate hoc fecerunt.* Harum testimonio literarum sigilli nostri quo hactenus tanquam Archidux Austriæ usi sumus, appensione roboratarum. Datum in civitate nostra Vienna, die tertia decima mensis Decembris, Anno Domini Millesimo, Quingentesimo, Vicesimo Sexto, Regni vero nostri Anno Primo.

Note No. 11.

GOLDEN BULL OF ANDREW II.

The *Bulla Aurea* of King Andreas the Second was given in the year 1222. The preamble to this bull sets forth "that the liberties of the nobility, and of certain other natives of these realms, as founded by King Stephen the Saint, having suffered great detriment and curtailment by the violence of sundry kings, who were impelled by their own evil propensities, and by the advice of certain malicious persons, and partly by the cravings of their own insatiable cupidity, the nobles of the country had preferred frequent petitions for the confirmation of the Constitution of these realms, to such an extent that, in utter contempt of his (the king's) royal authority, violent discussions and accusations had arisen." The king declares further that "he is now willing to confirm and maintain, for all times to come, the nobility and the freemen of the country in all their rights, privileges, and immunities, as provided by the statutes of St. Stephen." In specification of these rights, privileges, and immunities, it is enacted,

1. That the nobility and their possessions shall not for the future be subject to taxes and impositions.

2. That no man shall be either accused or arrested, sentenced, or punished for a crime unless he have received a legal summons, and until a judicial inquiry into his case shall have taken place.

3. The nobles and franklins shall be bound to do military service at their own expense, but it shall not be legal to force them to cross the frontier of the country. In a foreign war, the king is bound to pay the knights and the troops of the counties.

4. The king has no right to entail whole counties and the high offices of the kingdom.

5. The king is not allowed to farm to Jews and Ismaelites his domains, the taxes, the coinage, or the salt-mines.

In conclusion, the king declares " that if he or any of his successors should ever be found to transgress the provisions of this bill, that the bishops, the high dignitaries, and the whole of the nobility for all times to come, shall, by virtue of this bill, be entitled and empowered, jointly or severally, to oppose and contradict the king and his successors after him, as the case may be, without for so doing incurring the penalties of high treason."

These provisions, and those which we have quoted above, were embodied into thirty-one chapters, and in the form of a *Bulla Aurea;* seven copies were made and delivered " in the keep and trust of the Papal archives, of the Knights of the Hospital of St. John, of the Knight Templars in Hungary and Slavonia, of the king, of the Archbishops of Gran and Kalotsa, and of the palatine and his successors, with strict injunctions to the latter "to be very mindful of the said Golden Bull, even so that neither he in his own person shall transgress its articles, nor shall he allow either the king, or the nobility, or others to transgress the same. But he ought to watch that every man was left in the full enjoyment of his legal liberties, and that, in return, due respect and loyalty were paid to the king and his successors after him."

Note No. 12.

OATH OF CORONATION TAKEN BY FERDINAND THE FIRST, KING OF HUNGARY.

We, Ferdinand, by the grace of God, of Hungary, Bohemia, Dalmatia, Croatia, Slavonia, etc., apostolic king, Archduke of Austria, etc. We swear, as king of the first said kingdom of Hungary, and other kingdoms and parts annexed to it, by the living God, by his holiest mother the Virgin Mary, and by all saints, to conserve the churches (ecclesias Dei dominos), prelates, barons, magnates, nobles, free cities, and all inhabitants in their immunities and liberties, rights, laws, privileges, and in all former good and approved customs, and so do justice to all; we shall observe the decrees of the most serene King Andreas, with the exclusion, however, and withdrawment (semota) of the thirty-first article of that decree, commencing from Quod si vero nos, etc., to the words, in perpetuam facultatem. We shall never abalienate neither diminish the frontiers of our kingdom, Hungary, and those parts which belong to it by whatever right or title, but in as much as we shall, can, increase and extend them, and do all that what we can justly do for the public welfare, honor, and increment of all states, and of the whole Hungarian kingdom; so God help us and all saints.

Note No. 13.

SANCTIO PRAGMATICA.

CAROLUS VI., IMPERATORIS ET REGIS HUNGARIÆ III.

DECRETUM II. ANNI 1723.

ARTICULUS I.

Status et Ordines Regni, Partiumque eidem annexarum, Sacræ Cæsareæ, et Regiæ Majestati, pro Libertatum et Prærogativarum Eorundem Paterna et Clementissima Confirmatione; et Suæ in medium Statuum Sacratissimæ Personæ adventu; gratias quam maximas referunt.

Paternam sane, et Clementissimam Sacratissimæ Cæsareæ, et Regiæ Majestatis erga Status et Ordines Regni in præsenti Diæta, felicissime, et in frequentissimo, vix aliquando viso numero congregatos propensionem; et ad permansionem Eorundem, ac incrementum publici Status Regni Hungariæ, Partiumque eidem annexarum, proque stabilienda in omnem casum, etiam contra Vim externam, cum vicinis Regnis, et Provinciis Hæreditariis Unione, et conservanda domestica tranquillitate directam curam et sollicitudinem, ex benignis Ejusdem Sacratissimæ Cæsareæ et Regiæ Majestatis, ad Status et Ordines Regni, Partiumque eidem annexarum Clementissime emanatis Literis Regalibus ac novissime factis Propositionibus; devoto sane homagialis Fidelitatis Eorundem zelo, et constanti fervore humillime intelligentes; pro hoc erga Eosdem Clementissime exhibito Paterni affectus Gratiarum singulari voto, quodve non obstantibus in adversum quibusvis gravissimis, Sacrum Romanum Imperium, et Europæam quietem tangentibus curis et laboribus, in medium fidelium Suorum Statuum semet conferre; et Eosdem in Altissima, iisdem summe Veneranda Persona sua, paterne consolari; et primum ac ante omnia, nullaque prævia fidelium Statuum et Ordinum eatenus præmissa humillima Supplicatione, ex puro erga Eosdem paterno affectu, universos Status et Ordines Regni sui Hæreditarii Hungariæ, Partiumque, Regnorum, et Provinciarum eidem annexarum, *in omnibus tam Diplomaticis, quam aliis quibusvis Juribus, Libertatibus, Privilegiis, Immunitatibus, Consuetudinibus, Prærogativis, et Legibus,* hactenus concessis, et conditis, ac in præsenti Diæta, et in futurum etiam Diætaliter condendis, conservaturam offerre; et eosdem, ac earundem singulas, clementissime confirmare dignata fuisset; humillimas, et quam possunt, maximas Sacratissimæ Cæsareæ ac Regiæ Majestati ideo etiam gratias referunt;

§ 1. Quod Fœmineum quoque Sexum Augustissimæ Domus Suæ Austriacæ usque ad Ejusdem, et ab Eodem Descendentium defectum, ad Regiam Hungariæ Coronam, Partesque, Regna, et Provincias, ad eandem Sacram Coronam pertinentes, unanimi Universorum Statuum et Ordinum Regni, Partiumque eidem annexarum libero voto proclamatum; et per solennem Eorundem Statuum et Ordinum ad Sacratissimam Cæsaream et Regiam Majestatem, Viennam expeditam Deputationem vocatum;

II.   A A

§ 2. Et ejusmodi oblationem, tam pie, et clementer gratoque animo acceptare ; et fidelium Statuum et Ordinum suorum piis, ac salutaribus Votis, non tantum annuere dignata asset ;

§ 3. Sed ejusmodi in Sacra Regni Hungariæ Corona, et Partibus, Regnis, et Provinciis eidem annexis Successionem, eodem quo Masculorum Primogenituræ Ordine, secundum normam in reliquis Suæ Majestatis Sacratissimæ Regnis, et Provinciis Hæreditariis, in, et extra Germaniam sitis, jam per Eandem ordinatam, stabilitam, publicatam, et acceptatam, inseparabiliter, habitaque in graduum æqualitate ejusdem Lineæ, Prærogativæ Masculorum ratione, dirigi, servari, et custodiri vellet ;

§ 4. Ita, ut illa, vel Masculus Ejusdem Hæres, qui, vel quæ, præmissorum Augustæ Domus Austriacæ Regnorum et Provinciarum Hæres, juxta memoratam normam Primogenituræ in Augusta Domo Austriaca receptam, existet ; eodem Successionis, pro his et futuris quibuscunque casibus, Hæreditario Jure, etiam pro infallibili Rege Hungariæ, Partiumque, Regnorum, et Provinciarum eidem annexarum, æque *indivisibiliter intelligendarum*, habeatur et coronetur.

ARTICULUS II.

De Regia Hæreditaria Sacratissimæ Cæsareæ et Regiæ Majestatis Sexus Fœminei Augustæ Domus Austriacæ in Sacra Regni Hungariæ Corona, et Partibus eidem ab antiquo annexis, continua Successione.

Tametsi Suæ Sacratissimæ Cæsaræ et Regiæ Majestatis Fideles Status et Ordines Regni Hungariæ, Partiumque eidem annexarum, vividam et florentem, optimeque constitutam Ætatem, Vires, et Valitudinem conspicientes Divinæque Benedictioni quam optime confisi, Eandem Magnis, et gloriosis Sexus Masculini Successoribus, ad præces quoque fidelium suorum Statuum eo fine ad DEUM Ter Optimum fusas, et incessanter fundendas, largissime benedicendam, et indefinenti Masculorum Hæredum suorum ordine fideles Status Regni consolandos fore, vel maxime confiderent ;

§ 1. Quia vero apprime etiam perspectum haberent ; Reges pariter, et Principes, æquali aliorum hominum mortalitatis sorti subjectos esse ; mature proinde, et consulto perpendentes, tot et tanta, cum Prædecessorum Suæ Sacratissima Cæsareæ et Regiæ Majestatis, Divorum olim Leopoldi Genitoris, et Josephi fratris, Gloriosissimorum Hungariæ Regum ; tum vel maxime propria Clementissime Regnantis Suæ Sacratissimæ Cæsareæ et Regiæ Majestatis, pro incremento Boni Patrii publici, prove fidelium Civium suorum perenni salute, Bello æque ac Pace, exantlata Gloriosissima Acta, et Facta ; dum non modo Hæreditarium Regnum hoc suum Hungariæ, Partesque, Regna, et Provincias eidem annexas, in statu per præattactos gloriosos Prædecessores suos positum, conservavit ; sed occasione etiam novissimi Ottomanici Belli, contra ferventissimos ejusdem impetus, idem animose tutata ; victricibus, felicibusque Armis, in annexa eidem Regna, et Provincias, cum immortali sui Nominis Gloria, Statuumque et Ordinum, ac privatorum Regni Civium perenni securitate protenderit : ut successivis quibusvis temporibus, ab omnibus externis, et etiam domesticis confusionibus et periculis proservari ; imo in alma, et continua tranquillitate, ac sincere animorum unione, *adversus omnem Vim etiam externam* felicissime perennare possit ;

§ 2. Quosvis præterea etiam *internos Motus*, et facile solita, ipsis Statibus et Ordinibus Regni ab antiquo optime cognita *Interregni mala*, sollicite præcavere cupientes ;

§ 3. Majorum suorum laudabilibus Exemplis incitati ;

§ 4. Volentesque erga Sacratissimam Cæsaream, et Regiam Majestatem, Dominum Dominum Eorum Clementissimum, gratos, et fideles semet exhibere ;

§ 5. In defectu Sexus Masculini Sacratissimæ Cæsareæ et Regiæ Majestatis (quem defectum DEUS clementissime avertere dignetur), Ius hæreditarium succcedendi in Hungariæ Regnum, et Coronam, ad eandemque Partes pertinentes, Provincias, et Regna, jam Divino auxilio recuperata, et recuperanda; etiam in Sexum Augustæ Suæ Domus Austriacæ Fœmineum, primo loco quidem ab altefata modo Regnante Sacratissima Cæsarea et Regia Majestate;

§ 6. Dein in hujus defectu; a Divo olim Josepho;

§ 7. His quoque deficientibus; ex Lumbis Divi olim Leopoldi, Imperatorum, et Regum Hungariæ Descendentes, Eorundemque legitimos Romano-Catholicos Successores utriusque Sexus Austriæ Archiduces, juxta stabilitum per Sacratissimam Cæsaream et Regiam Regnantem Majestatem in aliis quoque suis Regnis et Provinciis Hæreditariis, in et extra Germaniam sitis, Primogenituræ Ordinem, Jure et Ordine præmisso, *indivisibiliter*, ac *inseparabiliter, invicem*, et *insimil*, ac una cum Regno Hungariæ, et Provinciis, Partibus et Regnis eidem annexis, *hæreditarie possidendis*, regendum et gubernandam transferunt;

§ 8. Et memoratum Successionem acceptant;

§ 9. Taliterque eandem *Successionem Fœmineam*, in Augusto Domo Austriaca introductam, et agnitam (extensis ad eam nunc pro tunc Articulis 2 et 3, 1687, et pariter 2 et 3, Anni 1715) juxta ordinem supradictum *stabiliunt;*

§ 10. Per præattactum Fœmineum Sexum Augustæ Domus ejusdem, prævio modo declaratos Hæredes, et Successores utriusque Sexus Archiduces Austriæ, *acceptandam ratihabendam*, et una cum prœmissis, æque modo prævio per Sacratissimam Cæsaream et Regiam Majestatem clementissime confirmatis *Diplomaticis*, aliisque prædeclaratis Statuum et Ordinum Regni, Partiumque, Regnorum, et Provinciarum eidem annexarum *Libertatibus*, et *Prærogativis*, ad tenorem præcitatorum Articulorum, futuris semper temporibus, occasione Coronationis *observandam determinant;*

§ 11. Et nonnisi post omnimodum prædicti Sexus defectum *avitam et veterem, approbatamque, et receptam Consuetudinem* Prærogativamque Statuum et Ordinum, *in Electione, et Coronatione Regum*, locum habituram: reservant intelligendam.

Articulus III.

Jura, Prærogativæ, et Libertates Statuum et Ordinum Regni, Partiumque eidem annexarum confirmantur.

Sacratissima Cæsarea et Regia Majestas, universorum fidelium Statuum et Ordinum Regni, Partiumque eidem annexarum, omnia tam *Diplomatica*, quam alia quævis *Jura, Libertates, et Privilegia, Immunitates, Prærogativas, Legesque conditas, et approbatas Consuetudines* (in conformitate Articulorum 1 et 2 modernæ Dietæ, in sensu Articulorum 1, 2, et 3, Anni 1715. Formulæque Juramenti ibidem contentæ, intelligendorum) clementer *confirmat, et observabit:*

§ 1. Pariterque *Successores*, legitime *coronandi* Hungariæ et Partium eidem annexarum Rêges; in iisdem Prærogativis, et præmissis Immunitatibus et Legibus, Status et Ordines Regni Partiumque eidem annexarum *inviolabiliter conservabunt;*

§ 2. Quas et quæ, præterea sua Majestas Sacratissima, per suos *cnjuscunque Status* gradus et conditionis subditos, *observari faciet.*

LEOPOLDI II. IMPER. ET REGIS HUNGARIÆ.
DECRETUM I. ANNI 1790-91.
Articulus X.

De Independentia Regni Hungariæ, Partiumque eidem annexarum.

ERGA demissam Statuum et Ordinum Regni Propositionem, Sua quoque Majes-

tas Sacratissima benigne agnoscere dignata est, quod licet Successio Sexus fœminei Augustæ Domus Austriacæ per Articulos 1 et 2, 1723, in Regno Hungariæ,
Partibusque eidem adnexis stabilita, eundem, quem in reliquis Regnis et Ditioni-
bus hæreditariis, in et extra Germaniam sitis, juxta stabilitum successionis Ordinem inseparabiliter ac indivisibiliter possidendis, Principem concernat, Hungaria
nihilominus cum Partibus adnexis, *sit Regnum liberum*, et relate ad totam legalem
Regiminis formam (huc intellectis quibusvis Dicasteriis suis) *independens*, id est
nulli alteri Regno aut populo obnoxium, sed *propriam habens Consistentiam, et
Constitutionem*, proinde a legitime coronato hæreditario Rege suo ; adeoque etiam
a Sua Majestate Sacratissima, Successoribusque ejus Hungariæ Regibus, *propriis
legibus, et Consuetudinibus, non vero ad normam aliarum Provinciarum*, dictanti-
bus id Articulis 3, 1715, item 8 et 11, 1791, *regendum et gubernandum*.

Note No. 14.

ROYAL PROPOSITIONS PRESENTED TO THE DIET OF HUNGARY IN 1847–8.

1st. To elect a Palatine in conformity with the Dietal Act 3, 1608 ; and to take
into consideration various important measures specified in the following propositions, viz. :

2d. The manner of provisioning and quartering the troops stationed in Hungary ; the royal rescript of November 10, 1844 ; and the bill annexed to these
propositions, to serve as the basis of their deliberations.

3d. The claim of the royal free towns to exercise the right of voting at the Diet,
and the expediency of extending this constitutional right to the ecclesiastical corporations (chapters of cathedrals) and the free districts.

4th. The co-ordination (*i. e.*, the reform of the corporations) of the royal free
towns ; a bill for which object is annexed to the propositions, and submitted to
the Diet.

5th. The laws and usages relating to mortgages of manorial estates ; for the
amendment of which a bill is annexed to the propositions, its chief feature being
the introduction of a system of registration (hypothecary registers).

6th. The urbarial laws (*i. e.*, the laws relating to the lords of manors and their
peasant tenantry), with a view of abolishing the roboth (covée) ; the Dietal Acts
8, 1836, and 7, 1840, which permit this roboth to be commuted into a money rent,
or to be redeemed for perpetuity, by mutual agreement of the parties concerned,
not having been found effective.

7th. The regulation of the commercial relations of Hungary and Austria in a
manner conformable to the interests of both countries ; his majesty being, moreover, of opinion that nothing would be more conducive to these interests than the
removal of the intermediate customs' line. Such a measure, he states, will require the most mature deliberation, on account of the peculiar circumstances connected with it and the questions it involves, as well as in respect to its bearing on
the Austrian states and the royal revenue. His majesty, therefore, wishes the
Diet to inquire into the means by which so desirable a result may be obtained,
and to submit their views to him as soon as possible ; for which purpose his majesty has been graciously pleased to order that the official data respecting the
trade of Hungary be laid before them.

8th. In this proposition his majesty states that all the efforts for extending the
trade of Hungary have hitherto been unavailing, on account of the want of roads
and other facilities for the conveyance of merchandise ; he has deemed it expedient

to form a special section, or board of public works, in the vice-regal council; and has, moreover, assisted, by loans and money, several private undertakings, as, for instance, the Central Hungarian Rail-way Company, and the company for the regulation of the Theiss. His majesty, therefore, wishes the Diet to take the important question of public works into their serious consideration; and, among other matters, to direct their attention to the representation (bill) presented by the last Diet, respecting a rail-way to Fiume, in which neither a satisfactory estimate of the cost, nor the sources from which is to be derived the sum that would probably be required to cover the guarantee of interest to a company, are sufficiently specified.

9th. His majesty recommends the states (3) to take into their consideration the documents which will be laid before them respecting the reincorporated Transylvanian counties (4).

10th. His majesty expresses a hope that the states will resume their labors on the criminal code, the code presented by the last Diet, and for which that drawn up by a Dietal commission appointed for the purpose in the year 1844 served as bases, not being sufficiently complete to receive his majesty's sanction.

11th. His majesty requests the payment of £53,828, advanced by the royal treasure for national purposes.

Note No. 15.

ADDRESS OF THE HUNGARIAN DIET TO THE EMPEROR, 1847–8.

1. Your majesty's faithful states summoned to the present Diet enter with pleasure on the laborious task of legislation, incited by the hope of their efforts leading to a favorable result.

2. With pleasure, because this has been the first time for centuries that the Hungarian nation has had the happiness of hearing from the lips of its crowned sovereign the cherished tones of its native tongue.

3. With the hope of their efforts leading to a favorable result, from the consideration of your majesty having presented the Archduke Stephen to the nation, and by this pledge of mutual affection strengthened that tie by which we are indissolubly attached—by law, by interest, and by predilection—to the imperial dynasty, and through this dynasty to the entire monarchy.

4. May your majesty therefore be graciously pleased to accept the ardent thanks of the nation.

5. We also can not refrain from mentioning that, by the royal propositions read to us on the 11th of November, several questions have been submitted to our consideration, the decision of which has long formed one of our most ardent desires. We trust that this may be regarded as a proof that between the nation and its ruler no misunderstanding subsists.

6. Having succeeded in responding to the first of the royal propositions in a manner strictly conformable to the interests both of the government and the nation, there is nothing we more ardently desire than to acquire the conviction that in treating the other questions contained in the propositions, as well as the ulterior measures which the necessities of the country imperatively demand, this fortunate coincidence may not be wanting: that the views of the monarch and the wishes of the nation may have the same tendency.

7. While we, therefore, joyfully embrace this opportunity of conveying to your majesty the expression of our sincere thanks and our unshaken loyalty, we also

regard it as our duty frankly to make mention of those obstacles without the removal of which we can perceive no guarantee for the future.

8. The chief obstacle to our social progress consists, in our opinion, in the Dietal Act 10, 1790, not having hitherto been fully realized; for the government of our country does not yet possess that independence which, according to law, it ought to possess.

9. This obstacle is the more serious on account of the very essential difference that exists in the fundamental principles of our legislative and administrative systems. It is owing to this circumstance that, in considering the questions submitted to us at our Diets and called for by the wants of the age, we can not calculate with any degree of certainty how far the views of the government and those of the nation may coincide.

10. Our preliminary and other grievances (*gravamina*) which we have repeatedly laid before the throne from Diet to Diet, still remain unredressed, which increases the doubt that we must necessarily entertain of the operation even of the most wholesome laws that may be enacted, a doubt which is justified by the fact that the execution and promulgation of our laws is not fully guaranteed. It is thus that the Dietal Act 20, 1836, has not yet been put in execution; and that the acts on religious affairs and on bills of exchange have not even been promulgated in the districts constituting the military frontiers.

11. To this must be added that, along with a tendency to set aside the influence of the Legislature, a tendency to increase the power of the administration is also clearly apparent. As a proof of what we here advance, we may cite those recent measures for reducing into a system the hitherto exceptional employ of county administrators, as well as those respecting the county congregations; measures which are at variance with our comitatal administration, as established by the Dietal Acts 56, 1723, and 36, 1536.

12. The special cases herein mentioned will serve to give your majesty a general idea of our present position. We shall hereafter venture to submit our views also respecting the details, with the remark that we regard the removal of these obstacles as an essential condition of the organic reform of our social institutions.

13. We are convinced that the expediency of removing these obstacles, and equitably adjusting the conflicting interests they give rise to, will not escape your majesty's paternal solicitude, solely directed to the welfare of your people. With this hope we enter willingly into the consideration of the questions contained in the royal propositions, and which have been called for by the exigencies of the nation. We shall also not neglect to lay our grievances before your majesty, in conformity with the Dietal Act 13, 1790.

14. We have no hesitation in stating that we are willing to pass such measures as may lead to an equitable adjustment of the conflicting interests of Hungary and the hereditary states; the more so as we are convinced that the difficulties in the way of this adjustment do not proceed from the nature of the relations themselves.

15. Great and arduous is the task of the coming times! It is ours to develop to the utmost extent our social institutions, grounded on constitutional rights, as well as our material resources. It is that of your majesty to make these coincide with the intellectual development and the material interests of the entire monarchy swayed by your sceptre, in conformity with the principles of justice and the exigencies of the age.

16. Taking into consideration the numerous and important measures that will

have to be submitted to us, it appears to us an object of paramount necessity that a Diet should be held annually in the city of Pesth.

17. We have to beg that your majesty may be graciously pleased to give the nation the assurance beforehand that its wishes in this respect may be complied with.

18. We trust that in this manner, and with the aid of the infinite goodness of the Almighty, some steps may be taken toward the end we have in view.

Note No. 16.

ACTS PASSED BY THE HUNGARIAN DIET IN THE SESSION OF 1847-8.

Act 1.

Is a mere record of services of the late Palatine.

Act 2.

Records the election of the Archduke Stephen as Palatine, and the fact that the letter of candidature was returned unopened.

Act 3.

It was this act that gave rise to such frequent conferences at Vienna. It is regarded by the Hungarians as a second "Golden Bull" or "Magna Charta," as it has rendered Hungary, to all intents and purposes, an independent kingdom, merely connected with Austria by the circumstance of the two countries being still under the sceptre of a common sovereign. (See Appendix, note No. 27, for Article Third in full.)

Act 4.

A Diet is to be held annually at Pesth. The members of the Lower House, who, of course, will no longer be bound by instructions, to be triennially elected.

The king has the right to prorogue the Diet, and may dissolve it before the expiration of the three years; but, in the latter case, he is obliged to summon another Diet within three months after the dissolution of the former one.

This right is, however, virtually annulled by the next clause, which expressly states that the annual session of the Diet can not be closed, nor the Diet dissolved, before the accounts of the past year and the budget for the ensuing year have been laid before the Diet, and a decision thereon been taken by that Assembly.

The president and vice-president of the Upper House are appointed by the king, the other officers by the House. The Lower House elects by ballot its president, vice-presidents, and all its officers. The presidents of both Houses are appointed for the whole duration of the Diet, three years, the other officers only for a session.

Act 5.

As this is a mere provisional law, it was deemed expedient to leave the so-called half-spurred nobles in possession of the elective franchise.

Thus, § 1 states that the Diet, not feeling itself authorized to deprive any one of a political right, leaves all who have hitherto enjoyed the elective franchise in possession of it. It is needless to observe that this class of nobles will be disfranchised by the next Diet.

The qualifications for electors are,

§ 2. To have attained the age of twenty years; Hungarians by birth or naturalized; not under guardianship, nor in domestic service, nor convicted of fraud, theft, murder, &c.

a. To possess, in towns, real property in houses or lands to the value of £30; in the country, real property equal in value to a quarter session of the former urbarial laws; *i. e.*, property equal in value to a plot of ground varying in extent in the different counties, but, in general, from eight to ten English acres.

b. The elective franchise is also given to manufacturers and tradesmen who have a manufactory, work-shop, or shop; also to artisans domiciled in a place, and who have a fixed employment, and work with at least one assistant.

c. Also to those who, not possessing any of the above qualifications, have a fixed income of £10 yearly, derived from land or investments.

d. And unconditionally, or irrespective of their income, to all physicians, surgeons, lawyers, engineers, academical artists, professors, members of the Hungarian academy, apothecaries, clergymen, chaplains, public notaries, and schoolmasters.

Burgesses of free towns not having any of the above qualifications, but who have hitherto enjoyed the elective franchise, are still to retain it (*i. e.*, until the next Diet).

Every one who is an elector may be elected; or, in other words, the qualification for a deputy is the same as that for the enjoyment of the elective franchise, except that the deputy must have attained the age of twenty-four years, and be conversant with the Hungarian (Magyar) language.

There are to be in all four hundred and forty-six deputies; viz., three hundred and seventy-seven for Hungary and the annexed territories, and sixty-nine for Transylvania, when the union is effected. Buda and Pesth will return seven deputies; the county of Pesth, ten; the three Croatian counties, eighteen; the Croatian, Slavonic, and Banat military frontiers, fifteen.

A deputy is to receive a daily allowance of 10*s.*, besides £40 annually to pay for his lodgings in Pesth.

Act 6.

An act for the *de facto* reincorporation of the three Transylvanian counties.

Act 7.

Decrees the union of Hungary and Transylvania; for the purpose of effecting which a Transylvanian Diet is to be summoned as soon as possible. Transylvania to send sixty-nine deputies to the Lower House, and a certain number of Transylvanian nobles to be members of the Upper House. But it is expressly stated that the act is provisional; and that an equitable adjustment of the interests of both countries, and other ulterior measures, are left for the consideration of the first united Diet of Hungary and Transylvania.

Act 8.

Establishes the principle of general taxation for all classes without distinction. The minister to lay before the next Diet a plan of equitably adjusting the rates to be levied, which are to commence from the 1st of November, 1848; the amount of taxation to be of course decided by the next Diet.

Act 9.

Abolishes the roboth, tne tithe of one ninth of the produce to the landlord, and all other urbarial services whatsoever, from the day on which the Act is published (April 11). Manorial courts are also abolished. The landlords are to receive an indemnification—rather vaguely expressed by a high-flown Magyar phrase, viz., " The Legislature places the indemnification of the landed proprietors under the protecting shield of the national public honor." (A nemzeti Közbestilet véd-paizsa ala helyezi.)

Acts 10, 11, and 12.

Acts passed as supplementary to the preceding act, respecting certain urbarial rights enjoyed by the peasants—such as that of cutting wood in the manorial forests, etc.; also respecting urbarial lawsuits, and suits brought before the manorial courts.

Act 13.

Abolishes tithes to the clergy without compensation, or, according to the words made use of, simply records the fact of the clergy having voluntarily renounced taking tithes without claiming a compensation.

The poorer clergy, whose incomes were principally derived from tithes, to be duly provided for.

Lay persons, who have acquired possession of tithes by contracts, etc., to receive a compensation

Act 14.

Respects the establishment of a bank of credit, particularly with a view to afford pecuniary assistance to the landed proprietors, a bill respecting which is to be prepared by the ministry, and submitted to the next Diet.

Act 15.

Virtually abolishes the Aviticity laws, the ministers being empowered to make the necessary modifications in the civil code, to be submitted to the next Diet for their complete and final abolition; all Aviticity lawsuits to be meanwhile suspended.

Acts 16 and 17.

The so-called autonomic rights, hitherto enjoyed by the counties, being incompatible with the present Constitution, and with an executive power exercised by a responsible ministry; these acts place the management of county affairs in the hands of permanent comitat committees, for the turbulent county congregations.

Act 18.

Provisional law on the press, which has been severely criticised, and caused great dissatisfaction, especially III., § 30, 2, which requires the proprietor of a daily paper to deposit £1000 as caution money. (The sum was originally fixed at £2000; but after the bill had passed both Houses, it was again taken into consideration, in consequence of the remonstrances of the Committee of Public Safety of Pesth, and the sum reduced to £1000). Also IV., § 37, which requires a person establishing a printing or lithographic press to deposit £400 as caution money.

ACT 19.

Places the university under the jurisdiction of the Minister of Public Instruction; the said university to be henceforward conducted on what are generally termed liberal principles.

ACT 20.

Reorganizes the Unitarian religion; that is to say, Unitarianism is declared to be in Hungary what it has long been in Transylvania, one of the legally recognized Christian sects.

§ 2. Places all the legally recognized religions (Roman Catholic, Greek Church, Calvinist, Lutheran, and Unitarian) on a footing of perfect equality. The money required for ecclesiastical and educational purposes to be furnished by the state, which implies that the clergy of all the recognized religions are to be paid by the state. None of the schools to be exclusively confined to any particular sect, but open to all without distinction. Bills for carrying out these principles to be prepared by the ministers, and submitted to the next Diet.

ACT 21.

Respects the national colors; Hungarian vessels to bear the Hungarian flag. The Hungarian flag has three horizontal stripes of the same colors as the Italian, only in a reversed order; the Hungarian being red, white, and green; the Italian green, white, and red.

ACT 22.

Respects the organization of the National Guard, the most important clauses of the act are:

§ 1. All persons, from the age of twenty to fifty, are to serve in the National Guard, who are: 1st, not in domestic service; 2d, who possess real property— in towns, of the value of £20; in the country, of the value of half a session (equivalent to from sixteen to twenty English acres). Thus, by a strange anomaly or oversight, the qualification of a National Guard is higher than that for an elector (see Act 5); also those who possess an annual income of the value of £10.

§ 3. Magistrates are empowered to admit persons not possessing these qualifications, but who are otherwise worthy of the honor, into the ranks of the National Guard, whenever they may deem it expedient.

§ 8. Optional for a person to serve in the cavalry or infantry; but those who do not choose the former must serve in the latter.

§ 9. The National Guard elect their officers up to the rank of captain. The field officers, i. e., all above the rank of captain, are appointed, in Hungary, by the Palatine-vicegerent, on the proposal of the Minister of War; in the annexed territories, by the Ban (of Croatia).

§ 11. The commander-in-chief of the National Guard is, in Hungary, the Palatine; in the annexed territories, the Ban; in the Hungarian Littoral, the governor.

ACTS 23, 24, 25, 26, AND 27.

Provisional acts—until the next Diet—for the co-ordination (municipal reform) of the free towns and free districts.

ACT 28.

The Palatine was *ex-officio* Lord Lieutenant of the county of Pesth, and Captain General of the Jászygians and Cumanians; but these offices being under the control of the Minister of the Interior, are not deemed compatible with his present high functions as vicegerent of the kingdom. The present act was, therefore, framed to place the county of Pesth under the authority of an administrator, and the free districts Jászygia and Cumania under that of a Palatinal captain general; the said administrator and captain general to have the rank of lords lieutenant, and, as such, seats and votes in the Upper House.

Act 29.

Declares judges to be the only officers of the crown that are not removable.

Act 30.

Empowers the ministry to raise £1,000,000; of which sum £800,000 is to be employed for rail-roads, and £200,000 for the regulation of rivers.

Act 31.

A provisional act respecting theatres.

Note No. 17.

(*Translation from the Illyrian.*)

DEMANDS OF THE CROATIANS.

DEMANDS OF THE NATION WHICH WERE UNANIMOUSLY RESOLVED UPON AT A NATIONAL MEETING OF THE THREE KINGDOMS, DALMATIA, CROATIA, AND SLAVONIA, CALLED TOGETHER BY THE PROVISIONAL COMMITTEE, AND HELD AT THE CAPITAL, AGRAM, IN THE TOWN-HALL, ON THE $\frac{12}{23}$TH OF MARCH, AND WHICH HAVE BEEN TRANSMITTED, THROUGH AN INFLUENTIAL DEPUTATION, TO THE IMPERIAL THRONE FOR SANCTION.

The nations of the United Kingdoms, animated by the desire of continuing, as heretofore, under the Hungarian crown, with which the free crown of Croatia, Slavonia, and Dalmatia was voluntarily united by their ancestors; animated by the desire of remaining true to the reigning dynasty, which at present rules the land according to the Pragmatic Sanction; and, finally, animated by the desire of maintaining the integrity of the Austrian monarchy, and that of the kingdom of Hungary, while they at the same time are anxious to uphold those great boons which were obtained for the whole Austrian empire during the three bloody and important days of the 12th, 13th, and 14th of March, make the following demands upon the king's sense of justice:

1. The extraordinary position in which the nation finds itself, as well as the restoration of its legal order, requires an authorized head; and with this view it has unanimously elected Baron Joseph Jellacic principal magistrate of the three united kingdoms, a man who possesses the confidence of the whole nation, and wishes that the command of the frontier troops, and the right of calling together the Diet, may also be granted to him.

2. That the Diet of these kingdoms be summoned to meet at Agram by May the 1st of this year at latest.

3. A strong and new union, in every respect of the kingdom of Dalmatia, which by tradition and by law belongs to us, with the kingdoms of Croatia and Slavonia, as well as the annexation of the military frontiers, as regards their political administration, and the incorporation of all other parts of our country, which in the

course of time have become lost to us and united with the Hungarian counties and Austrian provinces.

4. Their national independence.

5. Their own independent ministry, responsible to the Diet of these kingdoms, whose members shall consist of men of popular opinions, and devoted to the more modern tendencies toward freedom and progress.

6. The introduction of the national language into the interior and exterior administration of these kingdoms, as well as into all establishments for public instruction.

7. The foundation of a university at Agram.

8. Political and intellectual development on the principles of a free national spirit.

9. Freedom of press, creeds, instruction, and speech.

10. A yearly Diet at Agram, Eszeg, Zara, and Fiume, in turns.

11. The representation of the people on the principle of equality, without reference to rank, for the approaching as well as all future Croatian, Dalmatian, and Slavonian Diets.

12. Equality of all in the sight of the law, as well as publicity in law proceedings, together with a jury and responsibility of the judges.

13. Proportionate taxation upon all classes, without regard to rank.

14. Exemption from all compulsory labor and "corvée."

15. Establishment of a national bank.

16. Restoration of our national funds, which hitherto have been under Hungarian management, as well as of all properties and funds belonging to the finance department. The above to be managed by a responsible finance minister.

17. A National Guard, the command of which to be vested in the "lands captain," chosen by the Diet, according to the old custom.

18. The national troops of every description, in times of peace, to remain in the country; the officers to be natives, and the word of command to be given in the national language; in times of war, or of observation of a foreign enemy, viz., upon frontier duty, the troops to receive food, pay, and clothing. All foreign troops to leave the country, and the "military colonists" who are now in Italy to be sent home.

19. The national troops to swear fidelity to the common Constitution, their king, and the freedom of their nation, and of all other free nations composing the Austrian monarchy, according to the principles of humanity.

20. All political prisoners, whether in the United Kingdoms or in other free provinces of Austria, and especially our distinguished author and worthy fellow-countryman, Tomasseo, to be set at liberty.

21. Right of association, assembly and petition.

22. Abolition of all custom-houses upon the frontiers of our country, and Slavonic-Italian-Austrian states, and proclamation of reciprocal free trade.

23. Free entry of sea salt, according to our old rights.

24. The abolition of all imperial and public "corvée" on the military frontier, as is proposed in case of private individuals in the provinces, and a restoration to the communes of their forest and pasturage rights.

25. The frontier funds shall be managed by our own ministry, instead of the War Department, as heretofore.

26. Every frontier man to enjoy equal rights and liberties with the other inhabitants of the United Kingdoms.

27. The town and country communes of the country to be organized upon the principles of liberty, with the right of self-government and freedom of speech.

28. The old names for the lieutenants of counties, "zupanie," to be resumed, and they themselves to be organized according to old customs, but in the spirit of modern freedom.

29. All offices, without exception, temporal as well as spiritual, to be vested exclusively in natives of the United Kingdoms.

30. Abolition of celibacy in the Church, and the use of the native language in Church service, according to the old Croatian rights and customs.

Note No. 18.

IMPERIAL MANIFESTO ANNOUNCING TO THE CROATIANS AND SLAVONIANS THAT THE BAN, BARON JOSEPH JELLACIC, IS SUSPENDED FROM ALL HIS DIGNITIES AND OFFICES.

We, Ferdinand I., Emperor of Austria, King of Hungary, Croatia, Dalmatia, Slavonia, the Fifth of that name, &c., assure you, inhabitants of our kingdoms Croatia and Slavonia, of our sovereign grace, and issue the following manifesto, viz. :

Croatians and Slavonians!

Our paternal heart found great satisfaction in the hope that, while complying with the wishes of our faithful nations, we extended the benefits of constitutional freedom to all our subjects, we thus bound the nations which Providence intrusted to our care, in gratitude to ourselves and our throne. We trusted, at the same time, that an equalization of rights and liberties would urge our people to brotherly union in the effort for a general improvement, for which we had opened the widest field. Relying as we did on these our intentions, we were painfully struck by the sad discovery that by *you*, in particular, our expectations were frustrated.

You, Croatians and Slavonians! who, united to the crown of Hungary for eight centuries, shared all the fates of this country; you, Croatians and Slavonians! who owe to this very union the constitutional freedom which alone among all Slavonic nations you have been enabled to preserve; you disappointed our hopes —*you*, who not only have shared in all the rights and liberties of the Hungarian Constitution, but who besides—in just recompense of your loyalty, until now stainlessly preserved—were lawfully endowed with peculiar rights, privileges, and liberties, by the grace of our illustrious ancestors, and who, therefore, possess greater privileges than any of the subjects of our sacred Hungarian crown. You disappointed our hopes, to whom the last Diet of the kingdom of Hungary and its dependencies, according to our own sovereign will, granted full part in all the benefits of the enlarged constitutional liberties, and equality of rights. The legislation of the crown of Hungary has abolished feudal servitude in Croatia as well as in Hungary; and those among you who were subjected to *roboth*, have, without any sacrifice on their part, become free proprietors. The landed proprietors receive for their loss an indemnification, which your own means could never provide. That indemnification will be entailed on our Hungarian crown estates with our sovereign ratification, and without any charge to you.

The right also of constitutional representation was extended to the people in your case no less than in Hungary; in consequence of which no longer the nobility alone, but likewise other inhabitants and the military frontier, take part by their representatives in the legislation common to all, as much as in the municipal congregations. Thus you may improve your welfare by your immediate co-operation. Until now, the nobility contributed but little to the public expenses; henceforward the proportional repartition of the taxes among all inhabitants is lawfully established, whereby you have been delivered from a great burden. Your nationality and municipal rights, relative to which vain and malicious reports have been spread, with the aim of exciting your distrust, are by no means in danger. On the contrary, both your nationality and your municipal rights are enlarged, and secured against all encroachments; not only is the use of your native language lawfully guaranteed to you forever in your schools and churches, but it is likewise introduced in the public assemblies, where the Latin language has been until now in use.

Calumniators sought to make you believe that the Hungarian nation desired to suppress your language, or at least to prevent its further development. We ourselves assure you that such reports are totally false, and that we see with pleasure that you exert yourselves to develop and establish your own mother tongue, in preference to the dead Latin language. The Legislature is willing to support you in your efforts, by providing livings for your priests, to whom the spiritual care of the soul and the education of your children is intrusted. For eight centuries you have been united to Hungary. During the whole of that time the Legislature has always had due regard for your nationality. How could you, therefore, believe that the Legislature, which has guarded your mother tongue for eight centuries, should now be opposed to it?

And notwithstanding all this, whereas the guarantee of your nationality, and the enlargement of your constitutional liberties, ought to have been greeted with ready acknowledgment, persons have been found among you who, instead of the thankfulness, love, and loyalty which they owe to ourselves, have hoisted the standard of fanatical distrust; who represent the Hungarians as your enemies, and who use every means to sever the two nations, namely, the very same who persecuted your fellow-citizens, and by intimidation which endangered personal safety forced them to leave their country, because they had attempted to enlighten you as to the real truth. Our deep concern respecting these troubles was heightened by our anxiety, lest perhaps the very man had given up himself to this criminal sedition whom we have overwhelmed with tokens of our royal bounty, and whom we appointed as guardian of the law and security in your country. Our deep concern was heightened by the apprehension lest this man, abusing the position to which our bounty raised him, had not corrected the notions of the falsely-informed citizens, as he ought to have done; but, animated by party hatred, had still more inflamed their fanaticism; yes, lest, unmindful of his oath as subject, he dared to conspire against the union of Croatia with Hungary, and hereby against the integrity of our holy crown and our royal dignity.

Formerly, in Hungary and its dependencies, we administered the executive powers by our Hungarian Chancery and Home Office, and in military concerns by our Council of War. To the orders issued in this way, the Bans of Croatia, Dalmatia, and Slavonia were obedient, just as they were bound, in more remote times, to obey the orders of our Hungarian authorities, issued in a different manner and in different forms, according to the mode of administering our executive power arranged by the Parliament with our ratification.

In consequence of the request addressed to us by our faithful states, and guided by our own free will, in the last Hungarian Parliament we graciously sanctioned a law, according to which our beloved cousin, His Imperial Highness the Archduke Stephen, Palatine of Hungary, was, during our absence from Hungary, declared our royal lieutenant, who, as such, had to administer the executive power by the hands of our Hungarian ministers, whom we simultaneously appointed, intrusting them with all authority, which before was vested in the Royal Chancery, the Home Office, the Treasury, and the Council of War.

In spite of this, Baron Joseph Jellacic, whom we graciously favored with the appointment of Ban of our kingdoms of Croatia, Dalmatia, and Slavonia, is accused of having the temerity to refuse this due obedience.

We, the King of Hungary, Croatia, Slavonia, and Dalmatia, we, whose person is sacred to you, we tell you, Croatians and Slavonians, the law too is sacred, and must be considered so! *We have sworn to the Eternal King of all kings, that we ourselves will preserve the integrity of our Hungarian crown, and of our Constitution, and that we will no less ourselves obey the law than we will have it obeyed by others.*

We will keep our royal oath. We are gracious to our loyal subjects, forbearing to the guilty who repent, but inexorably severe toward obstinate traitors. And we mean to give over to avenging justice those who presume to trifle with our royal oath. He who revolts against the law revolts against our royal throne, which rests upon the law, and Baron Jellacic is accused, with his notorious adherents, of not only opposing the law, but of persisting in his disobedience, regardless of the paternal exhortations which we have addressed to him.

The first care of our beloved cousin, the Archduke Palatine, and of our Hungarian ministry, was, to call upon Baron Jellacic to explain himself in respect to your nationality, your rights, and your liberties; so that, as soon as possible—besides other measures—the Croatian Congress might be assembled, and those laws might thus be published, whose blessings we never intended to withhold from you, and that after this the Ban should be publicly invested with his dignity; since before this installation, he could not be considered as a legitimate dignitary.

Notwithstanding our repeated orders, the baron is accused of having disobeyed, and of having by this disobedience exposed you to the dangers of anarchy. But as though it were not enough that the Ban himself did not obey, he is accused of having seduced the lawful authorities to the same disobedience, and of having *forced* them, no less than the people themselves, *by violent means*, to hostile demonstrations against Hungary.

All of you must have witnessed the acts of which he is accused; all of you must have seen whether he persecuted those who wished to preserve the union of Croatia with Hungary, whether he deposed them arbitrarily from their offices, whether he brought a trial by court-martial upon all those who refused to do homage to his political views, and by this means compelled many to flight and emigration; all of you must have seen whether the Ban prevented the legally-appointed lord lieutenants from entering upon their duties; whether he violently seized the funds belonging to the treasury, and even employed our own troops to perpetrate such arbitrary actions.

You must know whether he arbitrarily charged you with new taxes, *and without any authority* forced the people to take up arms—an act which we ourselves can not authorize without the consent of the legislative power. You must be able to bear witness too, if he allowed, that his notorious adherents incited the populace by false reports relative to the Hungarians, as if they threatened your nationality; if he allowed, that sedition was preached in illegal assemblies; that arbitrary appointments were made; and that in consequence of the excitement occasioned by these proceedings, bloody conflicts, and plunder, and murder have taken place in Hungary. You know the personal affront which has been offered, under the very eyes of the Ban, to an illustrious member of our royal house, viz., our lord lieutenant, the Archduke Palatine, in the public square of Agram,* a town which of late has repeatedly been the scene of riots. You must know it, if the Ban punished the perpetrators of such deeds. It can not be unknown to you, if he really refused obedience to our royal commissioner, Baron Hrabowszky,† our privy counselor and field-marshal lieutenant, who has been appointed to re-establish public order and security.

Moved by paternal care for the welfare of our perhaps misled subjects, we tried the last means—to grant opportunity of personal defense to the accused, before we listened to the complaints against him. We summoned Baron Jellacic to dis-solve the Croatian Congress, which, without our sanction, and therefore in defi-ance of the law, he illegally convoked for the 5th of June of this year; and we ordered him to appear personally before us, in order to effect the conciliation which is needed for re-establishing order in Croatia.

But Jellacic has as little obeyed this our present command as our former reg-ulations, and has neither dissolved the Congress, nor has he appeared before us at the appointed time. Thus, obstinate contempt of our own sovereign command was added to so many complaints against Baron Jellacic. No other means was left, to protect our royal authority against the injury of such conduct, and to up-hold the laws, than to send our faithful privy counselor, L. F. M. Hrabowszky, as our royal commissioner, to inquire into those unlawful proceedings, and to indict the Baron Jellacic and his accomplices; and, lastly, *to deprive the Baron Jellacic of his dignity as Ban, and of all his military offices.* I sternly exhort you to renounce all participation in seditions, which aim at a separation from our Hun-garian crown; and under the same penalty, I command all authorities to break off immediately all intercourse with Baron Jellacic, and those who may be im-plicated in the accusations against him, and to comply unconditionally with the orders of our royal commissioner.

Croatians and Slavonians! We guarantee your nationality and your liberties, and the fulfillment of your just requests, with our royal word; do not, therefore, credit any seducing insinuations, by which your country is to be given up to op-pression and infinite misery.

Listen to the voice of your king addressing you, as many as still are his faithful Croats and Slavonians.

Herewith we summon every one to publish and spread this manifesto, accord-ing to his loyalty to our sovereign authority.

Given in our town of Innspruck this day, the 10th day of June, 1848.

FERDINAND.

Note No. 19.

LOUIS KOSSUTH'S SPEECH OF THE 11TH JULY, 1848.

Gentlemen,—In ascending the tribune to demand of you to save our country, the greatness of the moment weighs oppressively on my soul. I feel as if God had placed into my hands the trumpet to arouse the dead, that—if still sinners and weak —they may not relapse into death! but that they may wake for eternity, if any vigor of life be yet in them. Thus, at this moment, stands the fate of the nation!

---

* The portrait of the Archduke Palatine was, in the spring of 1848, publicly burned in Agram, under the windows of the Ban Jellacic, who did nothing to prevent or to punish this disorder.

† Baron Hrabowszky was arrested by the Austrian authorities at the entrance of Windisch-grätz into Pesth.

Gentlemen, with the decision on my motion, God has confided to your hands the decision affecting the life or the death of our people. But it is because this moment is most important, that I am determined not to have recourse to the weapons of rhetoric; for, however opinions in this house may differ, I find it impossible not to believe—impossible not to feel the conviction—that the sacred love of our country, and such a feeling for her honor, independence, and liberty, as to render this assembly ready to sacrifice its last drop of blood, are common to us all in an equal degree. But where such a feeling is common, there no stimulus is required: cool reason alone has to choose among the remedies. Gentlemen, the country is in danger! Perhaps it would suffice to say thus much; for, with the dawn of liberty, the dark vail has dropped from the nation. You know what the condition of our country is; you know that besides the troops of the line, a militia of about twelve thousand men has been organized; you know that the authorities have been empowered to place corps of the National Guard on a war footing, in order to establish an effective force to defend the country, and to punish sedition, which is rife on our frontiers. This command found an echo in the nation. How could this have been, unless the nation felt that there is danger? This in itself is an evident proof that the presentiment of danger is general. Nevertheless, gentlemen, I think I ought to give you a general, if not a detailed sketch of the state of our country.

At the dissolution of the last Parliament, and when the first responsible cabinet entered on its functions with an empty exchequer—without arms, without means of defense—it was impossible not to see, and to grieve in seeing, the terrible neglect which the interests of the country had suffered. I myself was one of the many who for years have called upon the executive power and the nation to be just at length to the people, for the day would come when it would be too late for justice. The feeling for justice, of patriotism perhaps, and general enthusiasm, may yet avert from our heads the full force of the fatal word, " Too late !" Thus much is certain, that the nation and the executive power have retarded justice; and that by this very delay, the moment when first they became just to the people caused the overthrow of all existing institutions.

Under such circumstances we took the reins of government, menaced by treachery, rebellion, reactionary movements, and by all those passions which the policy of Metternich leagued to us as a cursed inheritance. Scarcely had we assumed the government—nay, not all of us had even assembled—when we already received the most authentic information that the Pansclavonic agitation had no other object than to excite the whole of the upper provinces to open rebellion, and that even the day had been fixed when the outbreak should take place in Schemnitz. But I would only furnish outlines—I desist therefore, and will only add, that for the present the upper province is tranquil. This quiet, however, is by no means a safe tranquillity; it is a fire that smoulders under the ashes. In the heart of the country, even among the Hungarian race itself—which on the banks of the Drave, and in the vicinity of the O-Kérer camp, gives proofs of its vitality with such soul-elating readiness for sacrifices—it was by no means an easy task, after so long a slavery, to familiarize the people with the idea of liberty, and to lay down its first principles; for agitators were not sparing in their efforts to excite the people's fears concerning those—I can not find words—gifts, but rights, which the last Parliament had granted them. Nine weeks have since elapsed. In the interior prevails quiet, and the Hungarian race is prepared for sacrifice, and voluntarily—not from compulsion—it carries its life where it is needed.

Croatia is in open rebellion! Many years have elapsed, gentlemen, when not

II. B B

only one or the other, but numbers, called the attention of the government to the fact, that in encouraging—I say not forgiving, but *encouraging*—the Illyric agitation, it would nourish a serpent in its bosom which would compass the ruin of the dynasty. And since the revolutionary state in which we find Europe shaking on her foundations, the gentlemen in those parts fancied they might with impunity break out in open rebellion. Had Hungary given any cause whatever for this rebellion, she would, without considering the fact that there is a revolution, ask you to be just to Croatia, and to subdue the revolt, not with the force of arms, but with the sacred name of justice.

Entertaining as I do such sentiments, I am obliged to throw a transient glance on the relations between Hungary and Croatia. Gentlemen, you are aware that the nation has granted all its rights and privileges to Croatia, and that already at a time when it only conferred its own rights on the most favored nationalities. Since Arpad, Hungary possessed no right whatever in which Croatia, from the date of her alliance with us, did not participate. But besides having shared with us every right, Croatia obtained in addition, and at our expense too, particular privileges. I find in history, that the large parts of great empires have reserved for themselves certain rights—that Ireland, for instance, possesses less than England; but that the greater part of a whole nation should deny itself rights in favor of a small minority, is a fact which stands isolated, but not the less glorious, in the relations of Hungary with Croatia. Where is a reason to be found that, even if we take up arms to quell the disturbance, we should feel in our own hearts the conviction of having ourselves provoked the disturbance? In the past no such reason exists; nor has, perhaps, the last Parliament, which opened a new epoch in the life of the nation, caused any change whatever in the late and so particularly favorable circumstances of Croatia. I say, no! The rights we have acquired for ourselves, we have likewise acquired for Croatia; the liberty that was granted to the people, was likewise granted to the Croats; we extended the indemnity allowed by us to our nobility, at our own expense, to Croatia—for that country is too small and powerless to raise herself the indemnity.

With regard to nationality, Croatia entertained apprehensions—though produced by various conceptions and by erroneous ideas—for the Parliament has expressly decreed that in public life the Croats should have the fullest right to make use of their own language in accordance with their own statutes; and thus their nationality has been sanctioned, by this public recognition. Their municipal rights the Parliament has not only not impaired, but extended and augmented.

Is there a greater privilege than that of regulating the election of representatives, which representatives are convoked to frame laws, to grant and to protect liberty? And the Parliament has said: "You, our Croatic brethren, shall decide among yourselves how to elect your representatives." By this measure, the last Parliament has consolidated the municipal independence of Croatia. If, therefore, in the past, no reason can be found to excuse this rebellion, surely the acts of the last Parliament offer none.

Or does the fault lie with the ministers? We have taken a step, gentlemen, for which we are responsible. Had we succeeded in pacifying the excited minds, I should feel glad indeed to mention it; as it is, I must refer to it with the confession, that the cabinet in this instance has somewhat exceeded the limits of the law; it exceeded the limits, for it deemed it impossible to allow the natural consequences of the law to prevail. If the Parliament has recognized the right of the Croats to conduct their own affairs in their own language, the cabinet, on account of such circumstances, believed itself justified to extend this recognition of their nationality likewise to their relations with the government, and decreed to correspond with Croatia in the Hungarian language, with the addition of a Croatian translation, and in this manner to issue all decrees. The Croats attach much importance to the power of their Ban: the last Parliament has not only preserved this Ban's power inviolate, but at the same time insured his influence upon the whole government, by framing a law for the Ban to take part in the councils of the state. The cabinet, therefore, considered nothing of greater importance than immediately to invite the Ban (whom the power that has fallen under the lash of truth and liberty, in the last moment of its existence, forced upon us like a curse, that he might essay whether the demon of diabolical reaction could not again be raised!) to take his seat in the councils of state of the Palatine Stephen, and to confer with the cabinet how tranquillity, peace, and order might best be re-established in Croatia, and to state the just demands of the Croats, to a compliance with which the cabinet expressed its ready assent, provided it should be in its power to obtain their sanction; if not, it would bring before you, the representatives of the nation, a motion, and stake its own existence on the carrying of the measure. The Ban did not appear: obstinately he refused the invitation, confiding not in the law, but in a rebellion, at the head of which he has placed himself, while he pronounced his secession from the Hungarian crown.

I will not deny that Croatia has to complain of special grievances which, up to this day, remained without redress; but neither the cabinet nor the nation have occasioned them—they are simply an heir-loom which the old government left behind. The nation, however, has always made these grievances its own, and left nothing untried to amend them, as it would have done if they had indeed been its own. And this was certainly one of the causes why we invited the Ban, on his nomination by his majesty, to co-operate with the cabinet in accomplishing the speedy removal of the grievances, for we were conscious not only of our authority, but of our duty to re-establish the law where it is injured. But by his revolt the Ban has prevented the cabinet from communicating its decree to the Croats respecting their petition laid before his majesty in the Provincial Diet, in 1845. Under all these circumstances, the cabinet, nevertheless, has not omitted to do what it considered necessary to pacify Croatia and its fellow-citizens. The past Parliament conferred the franchise on the military frontier, and thus gave them a right which they never had possessed. To effect its realization, the cabinet has not only made such arrangements as were in its power, but has left no means whatever untried by which the population of the frontiers might be gained. It authorized and empowered the commander, Baron Hrabowsky, as royal commissioner, to make the land of the inhabitants of the frontiers their own property, in the same manner as the Hungarian urbarial subjects have received theirs, and to cause the crown-socage there to be abolished; it authorized him to confer on them the new privilege of exerting themselves in commerce, trade, and arts; it empowered him to facilitate in every possible way the free choice of domicile; it empowered him to introduce into the so-called free communities the communal system which exists in the localities, provided with a regular magistracy, on a civic basis, and with free power of the people of electing their own authorities. At the same time, it decreed that the people themselves should elect, according to communities and districts, men to come to this house, and impart and explain to the cabinet the wishes of the people, that we might, without delay, grant whatever could lawfully be granted. But they—these unfortunate, deluded men—replied with sedition, with rebellion, so that no further opportunity offered itself to realize the benefits which, weeks ago, we felt inclined to bestow.

Of their nationality I have already spoken. Concerning its official duties, the cabinet, from the very outset, selected a number of individuals from the provinces, without making any party distinction—nay, for the Croatian affairs it has, in various branches of the administration, formed distinct sections, which are not yet filled up, because the tie between us has been forcibly torn. One of the loudest complaints was, that in the Litorate, which supplies Croatia up to the Save with sea salt, the importation of common salt is prohibited. We have allowed the importation of common salt, and lowered the price considerably.

In one word, we have not neglected any thing whatever which, within the limits of integrity, of liberty, and of the rights of the people, we could do to pacify their minds. We, gentlemen, can not, therefore, admit that on the part of the cabinet the slightest cause has been given to provoke the Croatian rebellion.

If a people think the liberty they possess too limited, and take up arms to conquer more, they certainly play a doubtful game—for a sword has two edges. Still I can understand it. But if a people say, Your liberty is too much for us, we will not have it if you give it us, but we will go and bow under the old yoke of Absolutism—that is a thing which I endeavor in vain to understand.

The case, however, stands nearly thus: In the so-called petition which was sent to his majesty by the Conventicle of Agram, they pray that they may be allowed to separate from Hungary—not to be a self-consistent, independent nation, but to submit to the Austrian ministry. This, gentlemen, is the part of the old Vendée, which no terrorism on our side has provoked, and which, under the mask of sham loyalty, spins reactionary intrigues. Or is it loyalty, I ask, that they refuse to belong to the Hungarian crown, which, as the symbol of the people of these realms, is not only the most powerful, but also the sole reliance of his majesty and the dynasty? Or is it a proof of fidelity, not to obey the Hungarian, but the Austrian ministry, which receives its commands from the whims of the Aula,* and which possessed not even the power to protect its lord and king, who was compelled to flee from the house of his ancestors? Or do they, perhaps, give proof of greater fidelity by expressing the will of depending of the Viennese ministry, which, if it were a ministry (for at present it is no such thing), and if it were to be asked, "Who is your master—whose orders do you obey?—the emperor's, the Aula's, the Diet's at Vienna, or the regent's at Frankfort?" would be unable to make a reply; a ministry which not even knows whether its prince will be subject to the Frankfort Assembly, whether Austria will be drowned in great Germany, or whether the small Vienna will swallow Germany? But they allege that from a sentiment of loyalty they oppose King Ferdinand V.! I do not, indeed, ascribe to the sentiment of freedom so great an influence on the masses, as not to be persuaded that even this sham loyalty, in its awkward affectation, is but an empty pretext under which other purposes are concealed. On the part of the leaders it covers the reactionary tendency; but on the other hand, this idea is connected with the plan of erecting an Austro-Slavonian monarchy. They say: "Let us send deputies to Vienna; let us procure the majority for the Slavonian element, and Austria will cease to be a German empire; and what with the Bohemians, and our people down here, a new Slavonian empire will rise." This is a rather hazardous game, and Europe will probably soon decide on the question; for if we should not master these affairs, they will become a European question. Thus much is certain, that this combination (if of any consequence at all) will doubtless involve the ruin of the Austrian dynasty. There can be no doubt about it.

---

* *Viz.*, the Academic Legion of Vienna.

His highness the Archduke John, named Regent of Germany, took his departure for Germany the day before yesterday. In a few days he returns, and then we shall see whether there is any hope of an arrangement. That insane demand, however, of the Croats, that, on the part of Hungary, if an arrangement is contemplated, all preparations for war shall cease, we have "*indignato pectore*" rejected; and we have considered it to be our duty to declare that the Hungarians, come what may, will arm! that the government will concentrate all its power, and has, therefore, convoked the Parliament, to be enabled to make more mighty preparations. It would not be advisable, and you will not, indeed, demand that I should demonstrate by figures those forces which are concentrated on the Drave by the energy of our commissioner, Czányi. But thus much I can say, that of the importance of those forces sufficient proof is afforded by the circumstance that up to this moment the Croats, though long since desirous of the bread and the wine of our beautiful Hungarian land, have not dared to enter our territory; they could not have attempted it without being repulsed, although they were prepared, while we had to make our preparations.

Another affair is the Servian rebellion in the lower countries. Words can not trace its motives! Croatia, although a land bound to the Hungarian crown, which can not loose the binding tie without committing high treason, is nevertheless a distinct land. But he that wishes to establish on the territory of Hungary a distinct power, is so great a traitor, so arrant a rebel, that he can only be answered with the rope of the "Statarium." But, gentlemen, the shedding of blood is, even in case of guilt, a matter of great importance. While the government, therefore, took into consideration that to force the misguided masses into the horrors of a civil war, merely on account of the faults of some ambitious criminals, would, in these excited and revolutionary times, be an act for the omission of which we should deserve the approbation of God and man—we have, even in this respect, left nothing untried. We have, therefore, made preparations for the realization of all those wishes which in this case could possibly present themselves. But I believe that, without an injury to the integrity of the country, no other wish could here transpire except the convocation of the congress for the benefit of the religious creed of the Hungaro-Servians, which the old government had not convoked for many years.

This decree has been issued, but the Archbishop Rajacic has thought proper to convene at Karlowitz a meeting of the people, and to proclaim it as the Servian National Assembly, upon which the assembled multitude, amounting, with the hordes of robbers who had intruded from adjoining Servia, to several thousands, usurped a national position, declared the Banat, the Batska, Syrmia, and Baranya their property, and elected for themselves a patriarch and vayvode.

Upon the first signs of these disturbances we dispatched royal commissioners, while we endeavored to collect our armies. But, under existing circumstances, to collect troops on which we can rely, is by no means an easy task. It is therefore, I believe, to be considered a great advantage for the country that we have obstructed this rebellious insurrection in its upward progress; that we have repulsed it from the frontier, and have thus preserved the country from an inundation up to the moment when we shall have collected a sufficient force to swoop down like eagles, and to crush the robber-hordes.

While we were concentrating our forces, the royal commissioner, P. Czernovics, deemed it prudent to try peaceful negotiations, and, after having opened a correspondence with the leaders of the rebellion, concluded an armistice of ten days, in which time the leaders have to dismiss their hordes, and they are not only themselves to return to their allegiance, but they have likewise to lead back to obedience the unfortunate and deluded people. This armistice expires on the 4th of July, and the royal commissioner has concluded it on his own responsibili'y, without being specially authorized thereto; but having been empowered, as royal commissioner, by all requisite means to re-establish peace, he was of opinion that this measure would have that effect; and this, then, is one of those measures the approbation or condemnation of which depends on its result. At this moment a considerable military force stands under the command of a general, as expert, and as great a tactician, as he is courageous and brave. His plan of operation has been drawn on the spot, and has been communicated to the Minister of War, who approves of it. The actions of a general on the field of battle, being purely strategetic, ought, in my opinion, to be exempt from publicity—for we will not go back to the time when the Imperial War Council in Vienna directed from its easy chair the Hungaro-Turkish field-battles, and in consequence of which we were either defeated, or, if such was not the case, it only originated in the fact of a commander being present who pocketed the order of battle, and thus beat the Turks. (Cheers.)

I will only allude to one topic more. Since yesterday a rumor is current that a renewed armistice had been concluded with the Servian rebels. I and the whole of the cabinet know nothing of this. Our last reports, up to the 6th, contain not the remotest intelligence respecting it, nor do they warrant any such conclusions; on the contrary, instead of an armistice, we look hourly forward to reports of battle and victory. I will not say how many soldiers we have in those parts, or how great our power is; but I rejoice in being able to state that the readiness of the Hungarian nation for the defense of the country has by far exceeded my hopes and confidence. A few years ago I said despondingly, I wished God would vouchsafe to give me one point only, relying on which I could say, this nation knews to feel for liberty, and I would not despair of its future. The Almighty has granted me life to see that day, and I doubt no longer the future of the nation! (Loud cheers.)

The third of the circumstances, gentlemen, which exhort us to place the country in a state of defense, is the position of the countries on the Lower Danube. As I exact from every nation, with regard to Hungary, not to interfere with her internal affairs, so the Hungarian will not meddle with the internal affairs of those nations. I only mention that on the banks of the Pruth a mighty Russian army has appeared, which can turn to the right and to the left, which can act as a friend and as an enemy; but even because either one and the other is possible, the nation must be prepared.

The fourth circumstance is the Bosnian frontier, where, according to the latest intelligence, the Bosnian vizier establishes a camp of from forty to fifty thousand men, to observe with attention the disturbances in Servia, and to be enabled to act in the interest of his government as his duty commands. It has happened that Bosnian rajahs, in great numbers, and armed, entered Croatia, and pleaded for so doing, persecution by the Turks and a desire of finding an asylum. According to Turkish custom, some oppressive acts have certainly taken place; but this much I can say, that on the part of the Sublime Porte no new hostile steps have been taken against the Christian rajahs, who, therefore, have only arrived for the purpose of participating in the robberies and disturbances here in the country. To prevent the passing of the frontiers is the second cause of the Bosnian vizier's armament; and at present we have no reason to doubt that the position of the Seraskier of Bosnia is friendly toward us.

Finally, gentlemen, I must allude to our relations with Austria. I will be just, and therefore I find it but natural that the government of Vienna feels aggrieved at its inability further to dispose over Hungary. But even if natural, grief is nevertheless not always just; still less does it follow, that from sympathy with grief, the nation should incline to permit any of its rights to be alienated. (Cheers.)

Yes, gentlemen, most undoubtedly such movements take place, which have for their objects to restore to the Viennese government, if not all, at least the departments of War and Finance; the rest will soon follow. If, then, they once have the power of the purse and sword, they will soon have power over the whole nation. The Croatian movement is evidently connected with this scheme, for Jellacic has declared that he cares not for liberty, and that it is all the same to him whether or not the government at Vienna again obtains possession of the departments of War and Finance. And in the last days the vail of these public secrets has been lifted without reserve. The Viennese ministers have thought proper, in the name of the Austrian emperor, to declare to the cabinet of the King of Hungary, that, unless we make peace with the Croats at any price, they will act in opposition to us. This is as much as to say, that the Austrian emperor declares war to the King of Hungary, or to his own self. Whatever opinion you, gentlemen, may have formed of the cabinet, I believe you may so far rely on our patriotic feelings and on our honor, as to render it superfluous on my part to tell you that we have replied to this menace in a manner becoming the dignity of the nation. But just when our reply was on its way, a second note arrived, which clearly stated what a horrible man the Minister of Finance must be to refuse a grant of money to the rebel Jellacic; for, since Croatia has broken out into open rebellion, I have of course suspended the remittance of money to the commander-general at Agram. I should not be worthy to breathe the free air of heaven—nay, the nation ought to spit me in the face—had I given money to our enemy. But the gentlemen of Vienna hold a different opinion; they considered my refusal as a disgusting desire to undermine the monarchy. They have put their shoulders to the wheel, and transmitted to the dear rebel one hundred thousand, so they say, but in reality one hundred and fifty thousand florins in silver. This act, gentlemen, might excite the whole House to an angry spirit—to national indignation; but be not indignant, gentlemen, for the ministry, which by adopting such a miserable policy believed for a time to prolong its precarious existence, exists no longer. The Aula has crushed it. And I hope, whoever the men may be that compose the next ministry, they will understand that, without breaking their oath of allegiance to the Austrian emperor, who is likewise King of Hungary, and without siding with the rebels against their lord and master, they can not in future adopt that policy without bidding also defiance to Hungary, which, in that case, would throw the broken alliance at the feet of Austria, which feeds rebellion in our own country, and that we would look for friends in other quarters!

Gentlemen, I have no cause to complain of the Austrian nation; I wish they had power and a leader, both of which have hitherto been wanting. What I have said refers to the Austrian ministry. I hope that my words have also been heard at Vienna, and that they will exert some influence on the policy of the new ministers.

The Austrian relations, the affairs of the countries on the Lower Danube, the Servian disturbances, the Croatian rebellion, Pansclavonian agitators, and the reactionary movements—all these circumstances, taken together, cause me to say the nation is in danger, or rather, that it will be in danger unless our resolution be firm! And in this danger, where and with whom are we to look for protec-

tion? Are we to look to foreign alliances? I will not form too low an estimate
of the importance of relations with foreign countries, and I think that the cabinet
would be guilty of a dereliction of duty, if, in this respect, we were not to exert
ourselves to the utmost of our power.

In the first moments of our assuming office, we entered into correspondence
with the British government, and explained that Hungary has not, as many have
attempted to promulgate, extorted rights and liberties from her king, but that we
stand on common ground; with our lord and king we have further entered into
an explanation of the interests we have in common on the Lower Danube. On
the part of the British government we have received a reply, such as we might
have expected from the liberal views and from the policy of that nation. In the
mean while, we may rest convinced that England will only assist us if, and as far
as she finds it consistent with her own interests.

As for France, I entertain for the French, as the champions of liberty, the most
lively sympathy, but I am, nevertheless, not inclined to see the life of my nation
dependent upon their protection and their alliance. France has just seen a second
18th Brumaire. France stands on the threshold of a dictatorship; perhaps the
world may see a second Washington: it is most likely that we shall see a second
Napoleon rising out of the ashes of the past. This much is certain: France can
give us a lesson that not every revolution is for the interest of liberty, and that a
nation *striving for liberty can be placed under the yoke of tyranny most easily
when that liberty exceeds proper limits.* It is, indeed, a most lamentable event for
such a nation as the glorious French nation undoubtedly is, that in the streets of
Paris the blood of twelve thousand citizens has been shed by the hand of their
fellow-citizens. May God preserve us from such a fury in our own country! But
whatever form the affairs of France may assume—whether that man whom Providence has placed at the head of that nation becomes a second Washington, who
knows how to reject the crown, or a second Napoleon, who, on the ruins of the
people's liberty, erects the temple of his sanguinary glory, one thing is certain—
that France is far from us. Poland relied on French sympathy; that sympathy
existed, but Poland is no more!

The third is the German empire. Gentlemen, I say it openly, I feel that Hungary is destined to live with the free German nation, and that the free German
nation is destined to live with the free Hungarian nation, in sincere and friendly
intercourse, and that the two must superintend the civilization of the German
East. From this point of view, then, we have thought of a German alliance, and
as soon as Germany made the first step toward her unity, by convoking the
Frankfort Parliament, we considered it to be one of our first duties to send two
of our countrymen (one of whom has now been elected president by this House)
to Frankfort, where they have been received with the respect which is due to the
Hungarian nation. But just because the Frankfort Assembly was still struggling
for existence, and because that body had not developed itself, with which negotiations could have been brought to a result (this can only be done with the ministry to be constituted after the election of the regent); there is even now one of
our embassadors in Frankfort to negotiate, as soon as official relations can with
propriety be opened, respecting the league which we desire to enter into with
Germany—though with the proviso that we will not abate a hair's-breadth from
our rights, from our consistency, from our national freedom, for the sake either of
liberty or of menaces, from whomsoever they may proceed. The danger, therefore,
is great, or rather, a danger threatening to become great gathers on the horizon of
our country, and we ought, above all, to find in ourselves the strength for its re-

moval. *That nation alone will live which in itself has sufficient vital power; that which knows not to save itself by its own strength, but only by the aid of others, has no future.** I therefore demand of you, gentlemen, a great resolution. Proclaim that, in just appreciation of the extraordinary circumstances on account of which the Parliament has assembled, the nation is determined to bring the greatest sacrifices for the defense of its crown, of its liberty, and of its independence, and that, in this respect, it will at no price enter with any one into a transaction which even in the least might injure the national independence and liberty, but that it will be always ready to grant all reasonable wishes of every one. But in order to realize this important resolution, either by mediating, if possible, an honorable peace, or by fighting a victorious battle, the government is to be authorized by the nation to raise the effective strength of the army to two hundred thousand men, and for this purpose to equip immediately forty thousand men, and the rest as the protection of the country and the honor of the nation may demand. The expense of raising an army of two hundred thousand men, its armament, and its support for one year, will amount to forty-two millions of florins; but that of raising forty thousand men from eight to ten millions of florins. Gentlemen, if you assent to my motion, I propose within a few days to lay before the House a detailed financial plan; but I here mention beforehand, that nothing is further from my thoughts than to ask of the nation a taxation of forty-two millions of florins; on the contrary, my plan is that every one shall contribute according to his means, and if that will not cover the expense, we shall be obliged to let our credit make up the deficiency. I rejoice at being able to declare that the plan which I mean to propose is based upon an estimate which agrees with the rates of taxation, as fixed a century ago by Maria Theresa for Transylvania, and which in reality is much more moderate. Should my plan be adopted, and should the House make an especial proviso that the readiness for the sacrifice on the part of the representatives of the nation shall not dwindle away without result, the nation will be able to bear the burden, and to save the country. In case the imposed taxation should not suffice for the establishment of a military power, such as circumstances urgently demand, I claim the power for the executive to open a credit to any amount which the representatives may deem necessary. This credit shall supply the deficiency either as a loan, or by the issue of paper-money, or by some other financial operation.

These are my proposals. (Cheers.) Gentlemen, I am of opinion that the future of the nation depends on the resolution of the House on my motion; and not alone on that resolution, but in a great measure on the manner in which we form it. And this is the reason, gentlemen, why I refrained from mixing this question with the debate on the address. I believe, if a nation is threatened on every side, and if it feels in itself the will and the power to repel the danger, that the question of the preservation of the country ought not to be tacked to any other question.

This day we are the ministers of the nation; to-morrow, others may take our place: no matter! The cabinet may change, but thou, O my country! thou must forever remain, and the nation, with this or any other cabinet, must save the country. But in order that this or any other set of men may be able to save it, the nation must develop its strength. To avoid all misunderstanding, I declare solemnly and expressly, that I demand of the House two hundred thousand soldiers, and the necessary pecuniary grants. (Cheers.)

---

* These words of 1848 are a prophecy and a condemnation of what Austria did in 1849.

Gentlemen, what I meant to say is, that this request on the part of the government ought not to be considered as a vote of confidence. No; we ask for your vote for the preservation of the country! And I would ask you, gentlemen, if any where in our country a breast sighs for liberation, or a wish waits for its fulfillment, let that breast suffer yet a while, let that wish have a little patience, until we have saved the country. (Cheers.) This is my request! You all have risen to a man, and I bow before the nation's greatness! If your energy equals your patriotism, I will make bold to say, that even the gates of hell shall not prevail against Hungary!

Note No. 20.

ADDRESS MADE TO THE EMPEROR BY THE HUNGARIAN DEPUTATION, WITH HIS REPLY.

"May it please your majesty to order: 1. That all the Hungarian regiments who are not actually before the enemy may return immediately into Hungary, to receive the orders of the Hungarian ministry. 2. To order the army which is in Hungary, under pain of punishment, to act against the insurgents, whatever name or whatever standard they may usurp, and to do its duty for the defense of the country and the maintenance of the integrity of Hungary. 3. The Hungarian nation wishes to regulate the question of nationality and administration between it and the Croatian nation, according to the basis of liberty, equality, and fraternity. Croatia is now under military despotism, and its inhabitants can not express their wishes or their desires to the Hungarian Legislature. Your majesty is, in consequence, entreated to order that the Croatian nation may be delivered from this despotism, in order that they may freely manifest their wishes, and that Fiume, which has been occupied in a perfidious manner, and the Slavonian consulate, may be immediately given up. 4. The Hungarian nation feels no doubt but that your majesty will not only oppose the efforts of the reactionists, who have only their own interests in view, but will punish them. 5. The Hungarian nation demands, in fine, that your majesty will sanction the laws voted by the Hungarian Diet, will come to Pesth, and support by your royal presence the authority of the Legislature and of the constitutional government. We the more anxiously desire that your majesty should accede to our prayer, as a refusal would shake the confidence, and make it impossible for the ministry to maintain internal tranquillity and public order."

His majesty replied in the following terms:

"It is painful to me not to be able to respond to the desire expressed by the deputation of Hungary relative to my journey, in consequence of the delicate state of my health. I will carefully examine the laws presented, as it can not be imagined that I can have any intention to infringe on existing ones. I repeat that it is my firm wish to maintain the laws, the integrity, and the rights of the kingdom of my Hungarian crown, conformably to my royal oath. As to the other points mentioned, they are in part settled, conformably to the wish of the nation; with regard to those which are not so, I will make known my decision, through the medium of my ministry, as promptly as possible."

Note No. 21.

Dear Cousin Archduke Stephen!—My ministry in Vienna have explained to me in a writing, which I communicate to you herewith, the disasters which seem to have come upon the whole monarchy by obedience to the direction of the Hungarian ministry since the last Diet in Pressburg; and that it is of the greatest necessity to come to a mutual explanation, to prevent dissension, and to cause the Pragmatic Sanction to be considered on all sides as of full force and efficacy. My Austrian ministry addressed itself, on the 10th of May, 1848, as you know from my writing directed to you on the 12th of May, 1848, with the offer to the Hungarian ministry to enter into negotiation upon some questions concerning the whole monarchy. My ministry propose to you again the same mode of uniting yourselves, on one hand, upon the definitive Constitution, which may assure the union of the governments on this and on the side of the Seitha; but, on the other hand, to come soon to a decision as to the differences between Hungary and the states belonging to it.

As to the last point, I had the hope that my uncle, the Archduke John, would carry into successful operation the function of mediator, granted to him on the 19th of June, 1848; but the dignity granted to him as Regent of the German Empire has not only interrupted the negotiations between Hungary and Croatia, but rendered the recommencement of them difficult. On the alarming increase of the civil war on the Lower Theiss and Danube, I can not longer delay to recommend the peaceful efforts of my ministry at Vienna to the immediate consideration and reflection of the Hungarian ministry, to stop by that, this bloody fight. According to the proposals presented to me, and to which I can not refuse my approbation, some members of the Hungarian ministry should come to Vienna as soon as possible, to enter into negotiation upon the above-mentioned objects with the Austrian-German ministry. But as it is to be hoped that the pacification of the Hungarian questions will only take place if the Hungarian ministry must expect that the Austrian-German ministry will enter into negotiations only under the following conditions:

1st. The Ban Jellacic, or a plenipotentiary sent by him and by the respective counties, will assist at the negotiations at Vienna.

2d. All attacks and hostilities of Hungary against Croatia, Slavonia, and the military frontier against Hungary are immediately to cease.

3d. The personal measures taken against the Ban are to be stopped.

4th. The provisional superintendence of the military frontier will be undertaken by the Minister of War in Vienna.

As I promise myself the utmost readiness on the part of my Hungarian ministry to assist in stopping as soon as possible the cruelties of a civil war, I hope that it will come to Vienna in the course of eight or fourteen days, for the above-mentioned negotiation. In order that no time may be lost, I advise Baron Jellacic to make the necessary preparations for his journey, and to take precaution that the negotiations of my ministry may not be delayed by his neglecting to fulfill the above-mentioned conditions. FERDINAND, M. P.

Schönbrunn, August 31, 1848.

Note No. 22.

THE PALATINE'S LETTER TO THE EMPEROR.

Your Majesty,—The state of Hungary is at this moment so critical that the most violent outbreak is to be expected daily. Anarchy reigns in Pesth. The authorities are displaced from their sphere of action by a Committee of Public Safety; and while the Council of the Lieutenancy, under the strong guidance of Count Zichy, maintains, at least outwardly, its consideration, the Hofkammer (Exchequer) is almost a nullity. The nobles also have risen in masses to secure rights *de facto*.

In this anomalous and critical state of things, every one expects preservation by the immediate formation of a responsible ministry.

Even if we consider this plan as a calamity, yet the question must be put in this shape, "Which is the least calamity?"

I shall at present attempt, in a few words, to bring forward the three measures by which alone I hope to be able to attain any result in Hungary. The first measure would be to withdraw the whole armed force from the country, and to leave it a prey to total devastation; to look passively upon the disorders and fire-raisings, and also the struggle between nobles and peasants, &c.

The second measure would be to recall the Palatine and send a royal commissary to Pressburg, invested with extraordinary power, and accompanied by a considerable military force, who, after dissolving the Diet there, should proceed to Pesth, and carry on the government there with an iron hand, as long as circumstances should permit.

From the first measure, I openly confess, I myself shrink. It is immoral, and it is, perhaps, not becoming in a government utterly to desert subjects, of whom a part, at least, are well disposed, and to allow them to fall a sacrifice to all the cruelties of an insurrection. Besides, this would have a most prejudicial effect in the other provinces, from the example given by it to the ungovernable, uncultivated masses.

The second measure, on the contrary, is a good one; and although it has, at the first moment, the appearance of a separation, it is nevertheless, for the present period, the only measure to preserve this province, supposing always that the gentlemen now to be appointed are able to exercise full influence upon the interior defense, which certainly can not be asserted with full confidence beforehand. With the arrival of a more favorable time, much can be arranged otherwise, which at present might seem to occasion a separation.

I do not know whether something might be gained by negotiation with Batthyányi and Deak, but I know that the negotiation can be carried only through them, for if things come to debate at Pressburg, every thing is to be apprehended. Relative to this, however, as a faithful official of the state, I take the liberty to call your majesty's attention to a highly important circumstance. What will happen if Count Batthyányi, in case of the negotiation's not coming to a successful termination, should be ready to risk every thing, and resign his office? Here I consider it to be my duty, without exaggeration, but only in conformity with truth, to observe that we ought to be prepared, in such an event, with an armed force along the Danube, and on the road leading from Pressburg to Pesth, to oppose a demonstration likely to be called forth by the young men of Pressburg, and by a part of the nobles. In this case, the third measure would remain.

Supposing that the means are not wanting for its execution, this third measure would have to be carried into execution with great haste.

But here arise some questions.

(*a*) Is there not a want of sufficient money? Consequently, is it not impossible to send to Hungary a large military force, by which I understand at least forty or fifty thousand men?

(*b*) Is this force at hand, and ready to be employed quickly?

Is there, further,

(*c*) A commissary to be found who is willing and qualified to undertake this employment? But, lastly,

(*d*) Is there no doubt as to whether this measure would be sufficient to obtain the wished-for end? Will there not be a necessity for a greater force in Galicia or Italy?

If a favorable answer can be given to these questions, which, in my position, I am unable to answer myself—such an answer that the execution is possible without delusion, and without calculations which may afterward prove inaccurate—I have no further remarks to the former observations; supposing that a compromise is attempted with Count Batthyányi, and that, moreover, the opinion is taken of the great officers of the realm, who, in any case, are to be summoned to Vienna.

I confess openly that, in the present state of affairs, I should pronounce myself in favor of the second measure; and I doubt not that all the great dignitaries (although I have not yet consulted them) would be of the same opinion. I have only certainty as to the views of the Judex Curiæ (Chief Justice) Mailath.

If, however, your majesty, according to your wise insight, should consider the first or third measure more suitable, your majesty will doubtless issue your commands in conformity with the existing laws and the usage hitherto observed, and give me notice whether I am at present to remain in Vienna, or whether I may set off in any other direction.   STEPHEN.

March 24, 1848.

Note No. 23.

RESCRIPT OF THE EMPEROR FERDINAND TO THE BAN OF CROATIA.

My dear Baron Jellacic,—The unquestionable proofs of fidelity and attachment to my dynasty, and to the interests of the collective monarchy, which, since your appointment as Ban, you have repeatedly given, as well as the readiness with which you endeavored to carry out the recommendations I issued respecting an understanding with my Hungarian ministry, assured me that it could never have been your intention to oppose yourself in a treasonable way to my commands, or to endeavor to bring about a dissolution of that connection which has united the dependencies of Hungary for centuries with my Hungarian crown, and which will also hereafter tend more firmly to consolidate and promote their common welfare. It is with peculiar satisfaction to my paternal heart to revoke the judgment pronounced in my manifesto of the 10th of June last—that an investigation should take place with regard to your conduct, and that in the mean time you should be suspended from your dignity of Ban, and from all your military offices and functions, in consequence of representations which find the most entire contradiction in your faithful devotion, attested by deeds. Having transmitted to my cousin, the Archduke Palatine of Hungary, all that is necessary in this respect, I expect further from your sense of duty and loyalty that, in the position to which my confidence has raised you, you will always and solely labor to promote the welfare of the collective monarchy, to maintain the integrity of the Hungarian crown, and aid the beneficial development of the Hungarian dependencies.　　　　　　　　　　　　　　　　　　　　　Ferdinand.

Schönbrunn, September 4th, 1848.

Note No. 24.

MANIFESTO OF THE EMPEROR OF AUSTRIA TO THE PEOPLE OF HUNGARY.

A few days ago I made known to my faithful Hungarian subjects how much I have at heart the prompt and complete re-establishment of peace and legal order in the country. Unhappily, the state of things has become worse, and civil war threatens every part of Hungary. The danger of this state of things, and my desire to prevent an effusion of blood, and the propagation of anarchy and terror, have induced me to confide to Field-marshal Lieutenant Count Francis Lamberg the command of all my troops in Hungary. I have ordered him to take upon himself, in my name, this command, and that he make it his first task to bring about the pacification of all parts of the country. I have a firm confidence that all the authorities, civil and military, will promptly and implicitly follow his orders, and render him every efficacious support. I have taken all the necessary measures for suppressing the disturbances which have broken out in the north of Hungary, by sending a military force from Moravia. I expect from my people of Hungary a concurrence full of confidence in the extraordinary commissioners invested with my powers; the more so as I have already adopted means for reconciling their internal divisions to the satisfaction of all parties, and to establish between the Hungarian and non-Hungarian states of my empire that complete unity which existed for ages to the general safety, and which is guaranteed by the Pragmatic Sanction. Given at my capital and residence of Vienna this 25th of September, 1848.　　　　　　　　　　　　　　　　　　　　Ferdinand.

Note No. 25.

PROCLAMATION OF THE EMPEROR OF AUSTRIA TO HIS HUNGARIAN ARMY.

As I determined to suffer, under no circumstances, a conflict between my troops under the command of the Hungarian ministry, and those commanded by the Ban of Croatia, I have ordered my F. M. L. Count von Lamberg, in the quality of an imperial plenipotentiary commissioner, to repair without delay to the headquarters of the Hungarian army-corps, and to stop all hostilities, which order I sent at the same time to the Ban. I expect from the commanders of both forces, as also from the troops commanded by the former, that they will obey immediately my royal orders, and conclude this unnatural contest between troops who have sworn allegiance to the same flag, and who have to fight only for a mutual purpose, that is, the defense of the fatherland. I hope, at the same time, that those soldiers who have been seduced to desert their standards, will follow my royal call and return to them, to fulfill, under their lawful officers, in accordance with their oath, their duties to their king and country. Given at my capital, Vienna, 25th of September, 1848.　　　　　　　　　　　　　　　　Ferdinand.

Note No. 26.

ADDRESS OF THE EMPEROR OF AUSTRIA TO THE HUNGARIAN DIET.

Ferdinand I., constituted Emperor of Austria, salutation to the representatives and magnates of Hungary, Transylvania, etc., etc., assembled in the Diet at Pesth. To our profound grief and indignation, the Chamber of Representatives has allowed itself to be led by Louis Kossuth and his partisans into great illegalities; it has even put into execution, against our royal will, several illegal resolutions, and very recently has adopted, against the mission of our royal commissioner, Count von Lamberg, charged to restore peace, and before he had even shown his full powers, a resolution of the 27th ult., in consequence of which our royal commissioner was attacked by a furious populace, and assassinated in the most cruel manner. Under these circumstances our royal duty forces us to adopt the following measures for the maintenance of security and the laws: 1. We dissolve the Diet. In consequence, as soon as our royal rescript shall have been published, it is to close its sittings. 2. We declare illegal and without effect, all the resolutions and decrees of the present Diet, which have not been sanctioned by us. 3. We submit all the troops and armed corps in Hungary, in the annexed countries, and in Transylvania, to the command in chief of our Ban of Croatia, Slavonia, and Dalmatia, the Lieutenant Field-marshal Baron Jellacic. 4. Until tranquillity and order shall be established in the country, the kingdom of Hungary is subjected to the law of war, and in consequence the authorities can not convoke assemblies of comitats, towns, and districts. 5. Our Ban of Croatia, Slavonia, and Dalmatia, Baron de Jellacic, is sent, by the present decree, as commissioner plenipotentiary of our royal majesty. In consequence of these full powers, we declare that all that the Ban of Croatia may order, decree, or resolve, must be considered as having been ordered and resolved in virtue of our royal power. For that reason, we order all civil and military authorities of our kingdom of Hungary and Transylvania, and the annexed countries, to obey all the orders of the Baron de Jellacic, our royal commissioner, as they are bound to obey ourselves. 6. We particularly recommend our royal commissary to see that the aggressors and murderers of our royal commissary, Count Lamberg, and the authors and accomplices of that revolting act of cowardice shall be punished, in conformity with the laws. 7. The other current affairs of the civil administration shall be treated in conformity with the laws of the *employés* of the different ministries. Representatives of all parts shall deliberate and settle, in a legal way, how the unity of conversation and direction of the common interests of all the monarchy, and the guarantee of all nationalities, shall be re-established in a lasting manner, and to fix on that basis the relation of all countries and nations united under our crown. Given at Schönbrunn, 3d of October, 1848.   (Signed)   FERDINAND.

(Countersigned)   RECSEY.

Note No. 27.

ARTICLE III. OF THE HUNGARIAN DIET, IN THE SESSION OF 1847–8.

ON THE FORMATION OF THE RESPONSIBLE HUNGARIAN MINISTRY.

§ 1. The person of the king is sacred and inviolable.

§ 2. In the absence of the king, the executive power, limited by the laws and by the Constitution, is administered in the kingdom and its dependencies by the

Palatine-viceroy, with full powers, save the unity of the crown and the maintenance of its alliance with monarchy; and under these circumstances, the person of his royal highness, the Archduke Palatine Stephen, is equally inviolable.

§ 3. His majesty, and in his absence the Palatine-viceroy, are to exercise the executive power, in accordance with the laws, through the organ of the independent Hungarian ministry; and their decrees, orders, and judgments, whatever they may be, shall not be valid, until they have been countersigned by one of the ministers residing at Buda-Pesth.

§ 4. Each member of the ministry is responsible for his official acts.

§ 5. The ministry resides at Buda-Pesth.

§ 6. Whatever has been, or ought to have been, up to the present time, under the jurisdiction of the Hungarian Chancery, the Council of Lieutenancy, the Aulic Chamber (including the mines), and all affairs civil, military, and ecclesiastic, as well as every thing that concerns the finances and defense of the country, shall for the future be regulated and directed by the Hungarian ministry; and his majesty shall exercise the executive power exclusively through his ministry.

§ 7. The appointments of archbishops, bishops, priors, abbés, as well as those of barons of the kingdom, the right of pardon, the granting of titles of nobility and orders of knighthood, are reserved directly to his majesty.

§ 8. The employment of the Hungarian army beyond the frontiers of the kingdom, as well as the appointment to military offices, shall also be ordered by his majesty, under the counter-signature of a responsible Hungarian minister, who, according to § 13, shall be always in communication with the king.

§ 9. All those matters which, before the proclamation of the present law, ought to have been submitted to the decision of his majesty, by the high administrative courts hereinbefore mentioned, shall henceforth depend, in the absence of his majesty, on the decision of the Palatine-viceroy, with the exceptions of the cases pointed out in § 6, 7, 8.

§ 10. The ministry shall be composed of a president and, if he does not hold a portfolio, of eight other members.

§ 11. The prime minister shall be named, in the absence of his majesty, by the Palatine-viceroy, reserving to his majesty the power to ratify or annul the appointment.

§ 12. The other ministers shall be presented for the approval of the king by the prime minister.

§ 13. One of the ministers shall always reside near the person of the king, and charged to take part in those affairs which concern at the same time his own country and the hereditary states; he shall be the responsible representative of his kingdom.

§ 14. In addition to the minister residing near the king's person, according to § 13, to watch over interests hereinbefore mentioned, the ministry shall be composed of the following departments:

A. The Home Department.

B. Finance.

C. Public Works, Roads, Canals, and Navigation.

D. Agriculture, Industry, and Commerce.

E. Public Worship and Instruction.

F. Justice and Grace.

G. Defense of the Country (War).

§ 15. The ministry presides over the affairs of each department. Each department is divided into several sections, each section under the direction of a chief.

§ 16. The administration of the affairs of each department shall be regulated by the ministry itself.

§ 17. In the absence of his majesty, or the Palatine-viceroy, the prime minister presides over the cabinet council; having the right to convoke the council whenever he thinks it necessary.

§ 18. Each minister is responsible for the ordinances that he has countersigned.

§ 19. To protect the public interests of the kingdom, a Council of State shall be established at Buda-Pesth, under the presidence of the king, the Palatine-viceroy, or the prime minister: the definite organization of this council shall be settled at the next session.

§ 20. To the usual members of the ministry of foreign affairs attached to his majesty's person shall be added two counselors of the Royal Hungarian Chancery, upon the proposition of the minister.

§ 21. The affairs mentioned in § 7, and reserved to the king, shall be intrusted to the responsible Hungarian minister residing near the person of the king, together with the state counselors and heads of sections.

§ 22. The other referendary counselors of the Royal Aulic Chancery shall be transferred to the before-mentioned Council of State.

§ 23. The members of the Royal Council of Lieutenancy and of the Aulic Chamber shall be placed in the sections of the ministerial departments; conforming in this respect, as well also as to the Council of State, to Article 58, of the year 1791.

§ 24. The presidents of the high courts, mentioned in § 6, shall be members of the Council of State established by § 19; and they shall preside in the absence of the king, the Palatine-viceroy, and the ministers.

§ 25. All the functionaries and officers of the high courts of administration and of the councils of government before mentioned in § 6, consequently not only those who have obtained a new office, but those who shall not have been able to be placed in the ministerial sections, shall receive their salaries.

§ 26. The permanent organization of the tribunals' jurisdiction (counties, towns, etc.), shall henceforward be preserved in its full extent.

§ 27. The tribunals shall be maintained in their legal independence, and according to their present system, until further decisions.

§ 28. The ministers have seats in both Chambers of the Diet, and are to be heard whenever they think proper.

§ 29. The ministers are to obey the summons of each of the Chambers, and are obliged to give all the information asked of them.

§ 30. The ministers are obliged, on the demand of each of the Chambers, to produce all their official documents, either to the Chamber itself, or to the committee charged by the Chamber with the investigation of them.

§ 31. The ministers have no vote in the Diet, unless they be members of the Upper Chamber, or have been elected deputies in the Chamber of Representatives.

§ 32. The ministers may be impeached:

A. For any acts or decrees prejudicial to the independence of the country, to her constitutional guarantees, to existing laws, to individual liberty, or to private property, which may have been published by them in their capacity of ministers.

B. For dereliction of duty, fraud, or misapplication of the money which may be intrusted to them.

C. For neglect in the execution of the laws, or in the maintenance of the public tranquillity and security, as far as the powers which have been intrusted to them are sufficient.

II.   C c

§ 33. The impeachment of ministers shall be tried by a committee of the Upper Chamber of Representatives.

§ 34. The ministers shall be tried by a committee of the Upper Chamber, elected by scrutiny by the Chamber itself, the committee determining the punishment in proportion to the crime. For this purpose, thirty-six members shall be chosen, among whom twelve may be refused by the commission of the Chamber of Representatives, charged with the conduct of the trial, and twelve others by the accused ministers. The court formed of the twelve remaining members shall judge the ministers.

§ 35. The right of pardon can not be exercised relative to condemned ministers, but in case of a general amnesty.

§ 36. The ministers are subject to the common law, with regard to crimes committed by them not in their official capacity.

§ 37. The ministers are obliged to present annually, for the discussion and decision of the Diet, the budget of the receipts and expenditure of the kingdom, and to give an account of all the public funds intrusted to their administration.

§ 38. The salaries of the ministers shall be provisionally fixed by the Palatine-viceroy, until the final decision of the next session.

Note No. 28.

CORRESPONDENCE BETWEEN KOSSUTH AND W. H. STILES, AND THE REPORT OF THE SAME BY THE LATTER TO THE UNITED STATES GOVERNMENT, AS PUBLISHED IN EXECUTIVE DOCUMENT NO. 43, 31ST CONGRESS, 1ST SESSION.

Mr. Stiles to the Secretary of State.

Legation of the United States, Vienna, December 12, 1848.

Sir,—A short time since, a personal application was made to me by a friend of Mr. Kossuth, formerly Minister of Finance, but of late chief of the government of Hungary, inquiring, on behalf of that gentleman, whether I would undertake an intervention for the settlement of the differences now existing between the imperial government and the kingdom of Hungary. I frankly stated, on that occasion, the difficulties which such a step suggested to my mind, arising from the fact that it was a domestic quarrel between the government of the Austrian empire and one of its dependencies, and with which no foreign power could properly have any concern; that it was a subject which the United States had ever regarded with peculiar jealousy, and that I could not, therefore, reconcile it to myself to be in any manner instrumental in committing her; that, besides, so extensive, as I understood, had been the preparations made by the imperial government for the subjugation of Hungary, that it was scarcely to be expected that it would, at this eleventh hour, listen to any proposals of settlement short of the unconditional submission to imperial authority. To this it was answered, that commissioners had repeatedly been sent to apprise the imperial government of the anxiety which the Hungarians felt for a settlement of their differences, but that, as these commissioners had never returned, or even made a report of their proceedings, they had reason to apprehend that the imperial government was still unadvised of the desire which the Hungarians entertained for reconciliation; that, as at present all intercourse was cut off between the two countries, there seemed no other means of bringing their views to the knowledge of the imperial authorities except through the aid of some foreign representative at this court; and, further, that the armies now arrayed against each other, upon their respective frontiers, amounted to at least two hundred thousand men on either side, and it was only to be concluded, from the spirit which animated them, that great bloodshed must ensue unless some arrangement could be effected. I then inquired whether the object for which the interposition was sought was the separation of Hungary from Austria; or, if not, whether it was to gain time in order to make a more successful resistance; that if either of these objects were in contemplation, I could not listen for one moment to the application. On being solemnly assured to the contrary, and that no other end was in view but an amicable adjustment of the impending difficulties, I stated that the only ground upon which I could consent to interfere was that of humanity, and to save the useless effusion of blood; that such an appeal I should not consider myself justified in resisting; but that even in that event, my interference, if approved by the imperial government, would simply go to the extent of opening the door of reconciliation between the opposing parties, and by which the unhappy differences which distract the two countries might be, between themselves and through the instrumentality of their respective authorities, peaceably and satisfactorily arranged. Immediately after this interview, I called upon Prince Schwartzenberg, Minister of Foreign Affairs, and communicated to him frankly all that occurred, the application which had been made to me, and the reply which I had given; that I had no disposition to interfere between the Austrian government and one of its provinces, and that I would only take such action or pursue such a course in the matter as might be agreeable to the imperial government. He appreciated my motives, commended the consideration with which I had acted, and advised that, in case I should receive any communication from that quarter, I would have an interview with Prince Windischgrätz upon the subject, who was fully charged by the emperor with the proceedings determined on in relation to Hungary; but at the same time expressed the opinion that matters had progressed too far—that they could enter into no negotiation with rebels, and that nothing short of unconditional surrender could now be submitted to by the government. A week after these occurrences had transpired, I received, by means of a stratagem which enabled it to pass through the lines of the Austrian army, the communication herewith inclosed, marked document A, signed by L. Kossuth, president of the Committee of Defense, and countersigned by Francis Pulszky, the state secretary. Upon the receipt of this communication, I called, as directed by Prince Schwartzenberg, on Prince Windischgrätz, and found that he was absent from the city. On his return the next day, however, I had an unofficial interview with his highness; explained to him fully, as I had done previously to Prince Schwartzenberg, the motives by which I was prompted, and the views which I entertained in the matter, and the manner in which I was received by him. His answer to the application, and, in short, all that occurred on that occasion, you will find detailed in my replies to Mr. Kossuth, copies of which are inclosed, marked documents B and C. Since then I have heard nothing from either side, and presume the matter of intervention, as well as all hopes of reconciliation, are at an end. The imperial forces have proceeded to Hungary, and the affair will be decided on the battle-field—a conclusion to be deplored, not only from motives of humanity, but policy; since, if Hungary is subdued (which will most certainly be the case, from the superior strength and discipline of the imperial army), such a result will only aggravate the feelings of hostility which now exist; and as a country determined to be free can not, in these days, be held in subjection for any length of time by mere military force, this very conclusion may lead eventually to the liberation of Hungary and its total separation from the Austrian empire. Before closing this communication, I have only to add, sir, that as in this (to me) entirely novel situation, I have endeavored to act with all the circumspection which the delicate nature of the subject so imperiously required; as I have studiously avoided the least step which I thought could in any manner compromise my country; and as, if any error has been committed, it has been done for the sake and in the cause of humanity, I trust that the course which, without time for special instruction, I have thought proper to pursue in this matter, will not meet the disapprobation of my government.

I have the honor to be your obedient servant,

WILLIAM H. STILES.

Hon. JAMES BUCHANAN, Secretary of State.

Document A, accompanying W. H. Stiles's Dispatch No. 40.

Pesth, November 29, 1848.

Informed of your not being unwilling to negotiate a truce between Austria and Hungary in the interest of humanity, we gladly avail ourselves of this opportunity to call upon the feelings of justice of the representant of the United States, inviting you to initiate the negotiation of an armistice for this winter between the two armies standing on the frontiers of Austria and Hungary, and so to stop the calamities of a war so fatal to the interests of both countries.

Accept, likewise, the sincere assurance of our feeling most happy at every occasion which brings us in friendly intercourse with the United States, those natural supporters of freedom and civilization.

The President of Committee of Defense,

L. KOSSUTH, M. P.

The State Secretary,

FRANCIS PULSZKY, M. P.

To Mr. STILES, Embassador of the United States.

Document B, accompanying W. H. Stiles's Dispatch No. 46.

Vienna, December 2, 1848.

Sir,—Your communication bearing date Pesth, November 29, 1848, and desiring me, for the interest of "humanity," and "to stop the calamities of a war so fatal to both countries," to endeavor "to negotiate a truce between Austria and Hungary," was this evening received.

Aware of the importance of time in the matter, I proceeded, immediately after perusing your note, to the residence of Prince Schwartzenberg, Imperial Minister of Foreign Affairs, but found that he was absent at Olmütz. I then drove out to Schönbrunn, the head-quarters of Prince Windischgrätz, and was informed that he, also, had gone to Olmütz. I shall at once address Prince Schwartzenberg upon the subject of your communication, and, upon the return of Prince Windischgrätz (who is hourly expected here), shall seek, at the earliest moment, a personal interview with him; but, in the mean time, as the matter is attended with great difficulties arising from the facts, first, that the controversy is a domestic one, and Austria may, consequently, be unwilling to permit of any foreign interference; and, second, that as the preparations for the attack of Hungary on the part of the imperial government are said to be very extensive, and any delay in their operations they may conceive detrimental to their interests, I can hold out to you but little hopes of success in obtaining the desired armistice. For the cause of humanity, however, and to prevent the useless effusion of blood, the only grounds upon which I can consent to take any step toward opening the door of reconciliation between Austria and Hungary, and by which the difficulties which now unhappily distract the two countries may be adjusted between themselves, you may rest assured that no exertion on my part shall be spared which may be calculated to effect so desirable an object.

I have the honor to be your obedient servant,

William H. Stiles,

Chargé d'affaires of the United States of America.

Mons. L. Kossuth, President of the Committee of Defense, Hungary.

Document C, accompanying W. H. Stiles's Dispatch No. 46.

Vienna, December 3, 1848.

Sir,—In my note of last evening, I advised you that Prince Windischgrätz was absent from Vienna, but that I would embrace the earliest opportunity, after his return, of having an interview with him upon the subject of your communication. Informed this morning of the arrival of the prince, I immediately repaired to Schönbrunn, had an interview with his highness, and have just returned. I opened to him the subject of your communication; stated the difficulty which I understood the Hungarians had labored under in bringing their views to the knowledge of the government, now that all communication between the two countries was cut off, and the ground upon which you had appealed to me for my interference. He received me with the utmost kindness, thanked me for my efforts toward reconciling the existing difficulties; but replied, in substance, as follows: "I can do nothing in the matter;" "I must obey the orders of the emperor." "Hungary must submit." "I will occupy Pesth with my troops, and then the emperor will decide what is to be done." "I have received orders to occupy Hungary, and I hope to accomplish this end—I can not, therefore, enter into any negotiations." "I can not consent to treat with those who are in a state of rebellion." He deplored the necessity which compelled him to move against Hungary; recited the forbearance which had distinguished his course in the recapture of Vienna, and added that similar motives would govern his future conduct. Nothing further of importance occurred during the interview, except that, in reply to a statement which I made to the effect that the Hungarians had attempted previously, as I had understood, an arrangement of their differences with the imperial government, he replied that it was the first application of the kind which had come to his knowledge.

Unwilling to detain longer the person who awaits this answer, and begging you to be assured of the deep regret which I feel at the unsuccessful result of my efforts to bring about the pacification of the two countries,

I have the honor to be your obedient servant,

William H. Stiles,

Chargé d'affaires of the United States of America.

Mons. L. Kossuth, President of the Committee of Defense, Hungary.

P. S.—It will not be uninteresting to you to learn that the Emperor Ferdinand has abdicated the throne in favor of his nephew; that the Archduke Francis Charles has renounced his right of succession; and that the Archduke Francis Joseph has been proclaimed Emperor of Austria, under the name of Francis Joseph I.

W. H. Stiles.

Secretary of State to Mr. Stiles.

Department of State, Washington, February 2, 1849.

Sir,—I have the honor to acknowledge the receipt of your dispatch No. 46, which reached the department on the 15th ultimo.

You were placed in a novel and embarrassing position by the application made to you in behalf of Mr. Kossuth, to "undertake an intervention for the settlement of the differences existing between the imperial government and the kingdom of Hungary;" and I am gratified that your prudence and ability were equal to the occasion. In our foreign policy, we must ever be governed by the wise maxim not to interfere with the domestic concerns of foreign nations; and from this you have not departed. You have done no more, in your own language, than to attempt to open the door of reconciliation between the opposing parties, leaving them to adjust their differences without your intervention. Considering there was reason to believe that the previous offers of the Hungarian government for a reconciliation had never reached the imperial government, and that no other practicable mode of communicating these offers existed, except through your agency, you acted wisely in becoming an intermediary for this purpose alone. Had you refused thus to act upon the request of Mr. Kossuth, you might have been charged with a want of humanity, and been held, in some degree, responsible for the blood which has since been so profusely shed in the war. The president entirely approves your conduct.

It may be remarked that the request of Mr. Kossuth to yourself, in his letter of the 29th of November, 1848, does not seem to be confined to the single object which alone you had informed his friend you would attempt to accomplish.

I am, sir, respectfully, your obedient servant,

JAMES BUCHANAN.

WM. H. STILES, Esq., &c., &c., Vienna.

Note No. 29.

GÖRGEY'S DECLARATION TO HIS ARMY.

The Hungarian army of the Upper Danube, of which the essentials once formed part of the Austrian military establishment (that is to say, before the sanction of the Hungarian War Office placed the Hungarian regiments under the sole and exclusive direction of that office), took, obedient to the will of the constitutional king of Hungary, their oaths to the Constitution of that country. In the first instance, this corps was placed under the command of the Archduke Palatine, and opposed to the imperial and royal* troops under Jellacic.

Notwithstanding the most melancholy political troubles, they have since remained faithful to their oaths, by yielding their obedience only to the commands of the Hungarian responsible Secretary at War, or of the Committee of Defense, whose legality has received that secretary's recognition and sanction.

Leaning on this incontrovertible fact, the corps of the Upper Danube makes the most decided protest against any insinuations of its having served to promote the private interests of any party in Hungary, and the corps brands all such rumors as disgraceful calumnies. But this very incontrovertible fact of the unshaken loyalty with which the corps on the Upper Danube has, in the combat for the maintenance of the Hungarian Constitution, cheerfully submitted to all orders of the Committee of Defense, in spite of the most unspeakable deprivations and disappointments, justifies this corps in its expectation that the Committee of Defense will conscientiously avoid one thing—to wit, the placing this corps in any equivocal position.

After the corps of the Upper Danube, obedient to the orders of the Committee

---

* Imperialist troops.

of Defense, had, with the rarest self-denial, and by a most fatiguing outpost service, protected the frontier of the country; after having, in the battle of Wieselburg, prevailed against the superior numbers of the enemy; after dauntlessly maintaining its hopeless position at Raab, until, outflanked by the enemy's superior power, they had to make their retreat (which was necessary for the protection of the capital), by an obstinate fight with the enemy's flanking column; after this corps, without having found among the population of the country on the other side of the Danube the promised sympathies, and without having been assisted by any preparations of the Committee of Defense for preventing the enemy's advance on the highways and lines of Dotis, Banhida, Neszmély, Csakvar, Zamoly, Ondod, and Sarkany, remained partly in front and partly in the rear of the said places in battle array, until the victorious advance by more of the enemy's right wing caused us, in our turn, to take the offensive by way of Mártonvásar; and having, at the express command of the Committee of Defense, exchanged this offensive attitude for a defensive position in front of Buda, the corps has but one comforting prospect left to it, viz., the prospect of a decisive contest in the immediate vicinity of and in the capitals of Hungary.

The peremptory tone of the orders of the Committee of Defense, and the proclamations which that body addressed to the people, justified the expectation that, in the long-wished-for and at length approaching decisive moment, an enthusiastic energy would be displayed by it.

Instead of all that ought and might have been done, dispatches were on the 1st of January, 1849, received at the head-quarters at Promontorium, containing,

Firstly. The news that the Committee of Defense had left the capital.

Secondly. An order from the committee instructing us to accept a decisive battle on the so-called first line—Buda, on the height of Zeteny, Bia, &c.—without, however, sacrificing the corps, or exposing the two capitals to a bombardment; that is to say, in case of a defeat, the corps was instructed, regardless of the sole safe transit, and of the pursuing enemy, to make its escape to the left bank of the Danube, without defending the town.

Thirdly. An order to allow a deputation to pass to the chief commander of the hostile army.

Each of these three facts would alone suffice to shake the confidence of the corps in the members of the Committee of Defense; but coming together as they did, they were calculated to create a suspicion of the corps having hitherto been (to use the most lenient expression) a useful but a dangerous instrument in an unpracticed hand.

In order, therefore, amid the political intrigues which are likely to prey upon our unfortunate country, to maintain an unshaken and legal position, the corps of the Upper Danube makes the following public declarative profession:

Firstly. The corps of the Upper Danube, faithful to its oath for the maintenance of the Constitution of Hungary, as sanctioned by King Ferdinand the Fifth, intends to defend that Constitution against all foreign enemies.

Secondly. But the corps of the Upper Danube intends likewise to oppose all those who, by untimely republican agitations in the interior of the country, would endeavor to overthrow the constitutional kingdom.

Thirdly. The terms Constitutional Monarchy, which the corps on the Upper Danube proposes to defend to the last man, imply in themselves that the corps can not and will not obey any orders, except those which reach it in a legal form from the responsible Secretary at War, or from the deputy appointed by that functionary (at present General Vetter).

Fourthly. The corps of the Upper Danube, mindful of its oath to the Constitution of Hungary, and mindful of its honor, has a perfect consciousness of its duties and its intentions; and it declares, in conclusion, that it will not submit to the results of any negotiations with the enemy, unless such negotiations guarantee the Hungarian Constitution on the one side, and the military honor of the corps on the other. GÖRGEY, Major General.

Waitzen, January 5, 1849.

Note No. 30.

TEXT OF THE CIRCULAR OF THE RUSSIAN GOVERNMENT TO ITS FOREIGN AGENTS, ON THE ENTRANCE OF ITS TROOPS INTO TRANSYLVANIA, FEB. 9, 1849.

The news of the entrance of our troops into Transylvania being likely to give rise to false interpretations, we send you some explanations on the matter. It is notorious that great cruelties were committed in Transylvania by the Hungarian insurgents, who, headed by the Polish refugee Bem, have been recently repulsed by the Austrian army. The terror which, in consequence of such revolting excesses, was occasioned in the environs of Hermanstadt and Kronstadt, and the temporary absence of military forces, which rendered the Austrian generals unable to defend from pillage those towns (placed, as it were, before the eyes of our advanced posts), caused the inhabitants to invoke, through the authorities, the assistance of the general-in-chief of our troops. The Austrian generals on their part had, for the same reason, expressed a desire to ascertain to what extent they could calculate, if necessary, on support from us. General Lüders, who referred the matter to the emperor, received, by order of his majesty, the reply, that in case the towns of Hermanstadt and Kronstadt should be seriously threatened by an invasion of the Hungarian insurgents, at a time at which the Austrian government should not possess the means of protecting them against such great disorder, he was authorized to send a sufficient force into these two towns; that, however, he ought only to do that in the event of inevitable necessity, and only on the express demand of the Austrian military authorities. When, after the granting of this authorization, the danger of the towns became more imminent, in consequence of an advantage obtained by the insurgents at Mediafels, and when the inhabitants had renewed their earnest prayers to our general, with an invitation in due form from the Austrian generals Puchner and Schurter, General Lüders did not think it right to leave long unaccomplished wishes so expressed. He consequently caused the two towns to be occupied by detachments of troops, the effective of which had been previously indicated by the Austrian generals. The inhabitants, especially the Germans, who justly feared the barbarous cruelty of the Szeklers, saluted the arrival of these troops with the liveliest marks of joy. Our soldiers were received with open arms, the population went out to meet them, and gave them bread and salt; and a number of German and Wallachian families, who had been preparing to cross the frontier, abandoned their intention as soon as they saw that their lives and properties were assured. Such are the facts in all their simple truth; they prove that the emperor, in authorizing the entrance of some troops into Transylvania, was only influenced by motives of humanity, and that the matter was exclusively local, without any sort of connection with armed intervention in the interior affairs of the empire of Austria. This empire has gloriously and recently proved, by the energy with which it has crushed four successive insurrections, that it is too powerful to require our material assistance in Transyl-

vania   Austria is already victorious in Hungary, and the insurrectional domination will soon be at an end.   Even if Bem, owing to the insufficiency of the Austrian forces, had succeeded in taking Hermanstadt and Kronstadt, that would not
have saved the insurrection from the complete defeat which awaits it.   But, however brief such an occupation might have been, it would have sufficed to give up
those two flourishing towns to pillage and murder, and it was this misfortune that,
in accordance with the Austrian authorities, we were desirous to prevent.   Such
was the object of the entrance of our troops ; it must, consequently, be well understood, that their presence will be only temporary.   Already, indeed, have our
generals received orders to recross the frontier as soon as the dangers which threatened the country shall have ceased to exist.

Note No. 31.

DECLARATION OF INDEPENDENCE BY THE HUNGARIAN NATION.

We, the legally-constituted representatives of the Hungarian nation assembled
in Diet, do by these presents solemnly proclaim, in maintenance of the inalienable
natural rights of Hungary, with all its appurtenances and dependencies, to occupy
the position of an independent European state; that the house of Lorraine-Habsburg, as perjured in the sight of God and man, has forfeited its right to the Hungarian throne.   At the same time, we feel ourselves bound in duty to make known
the motives and reasons which have impelled us to this decision, that the civilized
world may learn we have taken this step out of overweening confidence in our
own wisdom, or out of revolutionary excitement, but that it is an act of the last
necessity, adopted to preserve from utter destruction a nation persecuted to the
limit of the most enduring patience.

Three hundred years have passed since the Hungarian nation, by free election,
placed the house of Austria upon its throne, in accordance with stipulations made
on both sides, and ratified by treaty.   These three hundred years have been, for
the country, a period of uninterrupted suffering.

The Creator has blessed this country with all the elements of wealth and happiness.   Its area of one hundred and ten thousand square miles presents, in varied
profusion, innumerable sources of prosperity.   Its population, numbering nearly
fifteen millions, feels the glow of youthful strength within its veins, and has shown
temper and docility which warrant its proving at once the main organ of civilization in Eastern Europe, and the guardian of that civilization when attacked.   Never was a more grateful task appointed to a reigning dynasty by the dispensation
of Providence than that which devolved upon the house of Lorraine-Habsburg.
It would have sufficed to do nothing to impede the development of the country.
Had this been the rule observed, Hungary would now rank among the most prosperous nations.   It was only necessary that it should not envy the Hungarians
the moderate share of constitutional liberty which they timidly maintained during
the difficulties of a thousand years with rare fidelity to their sovereigns, so that
the house of Habsburg might long have counted this nation among the most faithful adherents of the throne.

This dynasty, however, which can at no epoch point to a ruler who based his
power on the freedom of the people, adopted a course toward this nation, from
father to son, which deserves the appellation of perjury.

The house of Austria has publicly used every effort to deprive the country of
its legitimate independence and Constitution, designing to reduce it to a level

with the other provinces long since deprived of all freedom, and to unite all in a common sink of slavery. Foiled in this effort by the untiring vigilance of the nation, it directed its endeavor to lame the power, to check the progress of Hungary, causing it to minister to the gain of the provinces of Austria, but only to the extent which enabled those provinces to bear the load of taxation with which the prodigality of the imperial house weighed them down; having first deprived those provinces of all constitutional means of remonstrating against a policy which was not based upon the welfare of the subject, but solely tended to maintain despotism and crush liberty in every country of Europe.

It has frequently happened that the Hungarian nation, in despite of this systematized tyranny, has been obliged to take up arms in self-defense. Although constantly victorious in these constitutional struggles, yet so moderate has the nation ever been in its use of the victory, so strongly has it confided in the king's plighted word, that it has ever laid down arms as soon as the king, by new compacts and fresh oaths, has guaranteed the duration of its rights and liberty. But every new compact was as futile as those which preceded it; each oath which fell from the royal lips was but a renewal of previous perjuries. The policy of the house of Austria, which aimed at destroying the independence of Hungary as a state, has been pursued unaltered for three hundred years.

It was in vain that the Hungarian nation shed its blood for the deliverance of Austria whenever it was in danger; vain were all the sacrifices which it made to serve the interests of the reigning house; in vain did it, on the renewal of the royal promises, forget the wounds which the past had inflicted; vain was the fidelity cherished by the Hungarians for their king, and which, in moments of danger, assumed a character of devotion; they were in vain, because the history of the government of that dynasty in Hungary presents but an unbroken series of perjured deeds from generation to generation.

In spite of such treatment, the Hungarian nation has all along respected the tie by which it was united to this dynasty; and in now decreeing its expulsion from the throne, it acts under the natural law of self-preservation, being driven to pronounce this sentence by the full conviction that the house of Lorraine-Habsburg is compassing the destruction of Hungary as an independent state; so that this dynasty has been the first to tear the bands by which it was united to the Hungarian nation, and to confess that it had torn them in the face of Europe. For many causes a nation is justified, before God and man, in expelling a reigning dynasty. Among such are the following:

When it forms alliances with the enemies of the country, with robbers, or partisan chieftains to oppress the nation. When it attempts to annihilate the independence of the country and its Constitution, supplied by oaths, attacking with an armed force the people who have committed no act of revolt. When the integrity of a country, which the sovereign has sworn to maintain, is violated, and its power diminished. When foreign armies are employed to murder the people, and to oppress their liberties.

Each of the grounds here enumerated would justify the exclusion of a dynasty from the throne. But the house of Lorraine-Habsburg is unexampled in the compass of its perjuries, and has committed every one of these crimes against the nation; and its determination to extinguish the independence of Hungary has been accompanied with a succession of criminal acts, comprising robbery, destruction of property by fire, murder, maiming, and personal ill treatment of all kinds, besides setting the laws of the country at defiance, so that humanity will shudder when reading this disgraceful page of history.

The main impulse to this recent unjustifiable course was the passing of the laws adopted in the spring of 1848, for the better protection of the Constitution of the country. These laws provided reforms in the internal government of the country, by which the commutation of servile services and of the tithe were decreed; a fair representation guaranteed to the people in the Diet, whose Constitution was before that exclusively aristocratical; equality before the law proclaimed; the privilege of exemption from taxation abolished; freedom of the press pronounced; and, to stem the torrent of abuses, trial by jury established, with other improvements. Notwithstanding that, as a consequence of the French February Revolution, troubles broke out in every province of the Austrian empire, and the reigning dynasty was left without support, the Hungarian nation was too generous at such a moment to demand more privileges, and contented itself with enforcing the administration of its old rights upon a system of ministerial responsibility, and with maintaining them and the independence of the country against the often renewed and perjured attempts of the crown. These rights, and the independence sought to be maintained, were, however, no new acquisition, but were what the king, by his oath, and according to law, was bound to keep up, and which had not in the slightest degree been affected by the relation in which Hungary stood to the provinces of the empire.

In point of fact, Hungary and Transylvania, with all their possessions and dependencies, never were incorporated into the Austrian empire, but formed a separate independent kingdom, even after the adoption of the Pragmatic Sanction, by which the same law of succession was adopted for Hungary which obtained in the other countries and provinces.

The clearest proof of this legal fact is furnished by the law incorporated into the act of the Pragmatic Sanction, and which stipulates that the territory of Hungary and its dependencies, as well as its independence, self-dependence, Constitution, and privileges, shall remain inviolate and specially guaranteed.

Another proof is contained in the stipulation of the Pragmatic Sanction, according to which the heir of the crown only becomes legally King of Hungary upon the conclusion of a coronation treaty with the nation, and upon his swearing to maintain the Constitution and the laws of the country, whereupon he is to be crowned with the crown of St. Stephen. The act signed at the coronation contains the stipulation that all laws, privileges, and the entire Constitution, shall be observed, together with the order of succession. But one sovereign, since the adoption of the Pragmatic Sanction, refused to enter into the coronation compact, and swear to the Constitution. This was Joseph II., who died without being crowned; but for that reason his name is not recorded among the kings of Hungary, and all his acts are considered illegal, null, and void. His successor, Leopold II., was obliged, before ascending the Hungarian throne, to enter into the coronation compact, to take the oath, and to let himself be crowned. On this occasion, it was distinctly declared, in Art. 10, 1790, sanctioned upon oath by the king, that Hungary was a free and independent country with regard to its government, and not subordinate to any other state or people whatever; consequently, that it was to be governed by its own customs and laws.

The same oath was taken by Francis I., who came to the throne in the same year, 1790. On the extinction of the imperial dignity in Germany, and the foundation of the Austrian empire, this emperor, who allowed himself to violate the law in innumerable instances, had still sufficient respect for his oath publicly to avow that Hungary formed no portion of the Austrian empire. For this reason, Hungary was separated from the rest of the Austrian states by a chain of customs' guards along the whole frontier, which still continues.

The same oath was taken on his accession to the throne by Ferdinand V., who, at the Diet held at Pressburg last year, of his own free will sanctioned the laws that were passed, but who, soon after breaking that oath, entered into a conspiracy with the other members of his family, with the intent of erasing Hungary from the list of independent nations.

Still the Hungarian nation preserved with useless piety its loyalty to its perjured sovereign, and during March last year, while the empire was on the brink of destruction, while its armies in Italy suffered one defeat after another, and he, in his imperial palace, had to fear at any moment that he might be driven from it, Hungary did not take advantage of so favorable a moment to make increased demands; it asked only that its Constitution might be guaranteed, and those abuses rectified—a Constitution to maintain which fourteen kings of the Austrian dynasty had sworn a solemn oath, which every one of them had broken.

When the king undertook to guarantee those ancient rights, and gave his sanction to the establishment of a responsible ministry, the Hungarian nation flew enthusiastically to his support, and rallied its might around his tottering throne. At that eventful crisis, as at so many others, the house of Austria was saved by the fidelity of the Hungarians.

Scarcely, however, had this oath fallen from his lips, when he conspired anew with his family, the accomplices of his crime, to compass the destruction of the Hungarian nation. This conspiracy did not take place on the ground that any new privileges were conceded by the recent laws which diminished the royal authority. From what has been said, it is clear that no such demands were made. The conspiracy was founded to get rid of the responsible ministry, which made it impossible for the Vienna cabinet to treat the Hungarian cabinet any longer as a nullity.

In former times, a governing council, under the name of the Royal Hungarian Stadtholdership, the president of which was the Palatine, held its seat at Buda, whose sacred duty it was to watch over the integrity of the state, the inviolability of the Constitution, and the sanctity of the laws; but this collegiate authority not presenting any element of personal responsibility, the Vienna cabinet gradually degraded this council to the position of an administrative organ of court absolutism. In this manner, while Hungary had ostensibly an independent government, the despotic Vienna cabinet disposed at will of the money and blood of the people for foreign purposes, postponing its trading interests to the success of courtly cabals, injurious to the welfare of the people, so that we were excluded from all connection with the other countries of the world, and were degraded to the position of a colony. The mode of governing by a ministry was intended to put a stop to these proceedings, which caused the rights of the country to molder uselessly in its parchments; by the change, these rights and the royal oath were both to become a reality. It was the apprehension of this, and especially the fear of losing its control over the money and blood of the country, which caused the house of Austria to resolve the involving of Hungary, by the foulest intrigues, in the horrors of fire and slaughter, that, having plunged the country in a civil war, it might seize the opportunity to dismember the lands, and to blot out the name of Hungary from the list of independent nations, and unite its plundered and bleeding limbs with the Austrian monarchy.

The beginning of this course was by issuing orders during the existence of the ministry, directing an Austrian general to rise in rebellion against the laws of the country, and by nominating the same general Ban of Croatia, a kingdom belonging to the kingdom of Hungary. Croatia and Slavonia were chosen as the seat of military operations in this rebellion, because the military organization of those countries promised to present the greatest number of disposable troops; it was also thought that, since those countries had for centuries been excluded from the enjoyment of constitutional rights, and subjected to a military organization in the name of the emperor, they would easily be induced to rise at his bidding.

Croatia and Slavonia were chosen to begin this rebellion, because in those countries the inhuman policy of Prince Metternich Had, with a view to the weakening of all parties, for years cherished hatred against the Hungarian nation. By exciting in every possible manner the most unfounded national jealousies, and by employing the most disgraceful means, he had succeeded in inflaming a party with rage, although the Hungarians, far from desiring to oppress the Croatians, allowed the most unrestrained development to the provincial institutions of Croatia, and shared with their Croatian and Slavonian brethren their political rights, even going the length of sacrificing some of their own rights, by acknowledging special privileges and immunities in those dependencies.

The Ban revolted, therefore, in the name of the emperor, and rebelled openly against the King of Hungary, who is, however, one and the same person; and he went so far as to decree the separation of Croatia and Slavonia from Hungary, with which they had been united for eight hundred years, as well as to incorporate them with the Austrian empire. Public opinion and undoubted facts threw the blame of these proceedings on the Archduke Louis, uncle to the emperor, on his brother, the Archduke Francis Charles, and especially on the consort of the last-named prince, the Archduchess Sophia; and since the Ban, in this act of rebellion, openly alleged that he acted as a faithful subject of the emperor, the ministry of Hungary requested their sovereign, by a public declaration, to wipe off the stigma which these proceedings threw upon the family. At that moment affairs were not prosperous for Austria in Italy; the emperor, therefore, did proclaim that the Ban and his associates were guilty of high treason, and of exciting to rebellion. But while publishing this edict, the Ban and his accomplices were covered with favors at court, and supplied for their enterprise with money, arms, and ammunition. The Hungarians, confiding in the royal proclamation, and not wishing to provoke a civil conflict, did not hunt out those proscribed traitors in their lair, and only adopted measures for checking any extension of the rebellion. But soon afterward the inhabitants of South Hungary, of Servian race, were excited to rebellion by precisely the same means.

These were also declared by the king to be rebels, but were nevertheless, like the others, supplied with money, arms, and ammunition. The king's commissioned officers and civil servants enlisted bands of robbers in the principality of Servia to strengthen the rebels, and aid them in massacring the peaceable Hungarian and German inhabitants of the Banat. The command of these rebellious bodies was further intrusted to the rebel leaders of the Croatians.

During this rebellion of the Hungarian Servians, scenes of cruelty were witnessed at which the heart shudders; the peaceable inhabitants were tortured with a cruelty which makes the hair stand on end. Whole towns and villages, once flourishing, were laid waste. Hungarians fleeing before these murderers were reduced to the condition of vagrants and beggars in their own country; the most lovely districts were converted into a wilderness.

Thus were the Hungarians driven to self defense, but the Austrian cabinet had dispatched some time previously the bravest portion of the national troops to Italy, to oppress the kingdoms of Lombardy and Venice, notwithstanding that our country was at home bleeding from a thousand wounds, still she had allowed them to leave for the defense of Austria. The greater part of the Hungarian regiments were, according to the old system of government, scattered through the other provinces of the empire. In Hungary itself, the troops quartered were mostly Austrian; and they afforded more protection to the rebels than to the laws, or to the internal peace of the country.

The withdrawal of these troops, and the return of the national militia, was demanded of the government, but was either refused, or its fulfillment delayed; and when our brave comrades, on hearing the distress of the country, returned in masses, they were persecuted, and such as were obliged to yield to superior force were disarmed, and sentenced to death for having defended their country against rebels.

The Hungarian ministry begged the king earnestly to issue orders to all troops and commanders of fortresses in Hungary, enjoining fidelity to the Constitution, and obedience to the ministers of Hungary. Such a proclamation was sent to the Palatine, the viceroy of Hungary, Archduke Stephen, at Buda. The necessary letters were written and sent to the post-office. But this nephew of the king, the Archduke Palatine, shamelessly caused these letters to be smuggled back from the post-office, although they had been countersigned by the responsible ministers, and they were afterward found among his papers when he treacherously departed from the country.

The rebel Ban menaced the Hungarian coast with an attack, and the government, with the king's consent, ordered an armed corps to march into Styria for the defense of Fiume; but this whole force received orders to march into Italy. Yet such abominable treachery was declared by the Vienna cabinet.

The rebel force occupied Fiume, and disunited it from the kingdom of Hungary, and this abominable deception was disavowed by the Vienna cabinet as having been a misunderstanding; the furnishing of arms, ammunition, and money to the rebels of Croatia was also declared to have been a misunderstanding. Finally, instructions were issued to the effect that, until special orders were given, the army and the commanders of fortresses were not to follow the orders of the Hungarian ministers, but were to execute those of the Austrian cabinet.

Finally, to reap the fruit of so much perfidy, the Emperor Francis Joseph dared to call himself King of Hungary, in the manifesto of the 9th of March, wherein he openly declares that he erases the Hungarian nation from the list of the independent nations of Europe, and that he divides its territory into five parts, dividing Transylvania, Croatia, Slavonia, and Fiume from Hungary, creating at the same time a principality (vayvodeschaft) for the Servian rebels, and having paralyzed the political existence of the country, declared it incorporated into the Austrian monarchy.

Never was so disgraceful a line of policy followed toward a nation. Hungary, unprepared with money, arms, and troops, and not expecting to be called on to make resistance, was entangled in a net of treachery, and was obliged to defend itself against this threatened annihilation with the aid of volunteers, National Guards, and an undisciplined army levy *en masse*, aided by the few regular troops which remained in the country. In open battles, the Hungarians have, however, been successful; but they could not rapidly enough put down the Servian rebels, and those of the military frontier, who were led by officers devoted to Austria, and were enabled to take refuge behind intrenched positions.

It was necessary to provide a new armed force. The king, still pretending to yield to the undeniably lawful demands of the nation, had summoned a new Diet for the 2d of July, 1848, and had called upon the representatives of the nation to provide soldiers and money for the suppression of the Servian and Croatian rebellion, and the re-establishment of public peace. He, at the same time, issued a solemn proclamation in his own name, and in that of his family, condemning and denouncing the Croatian and Servian rebellion. The necessary steps were taken by the Diet. A levy of two hundred thousand men, and a subsidy of forty millions of florins, were voted as the necessary force, and the bills were laid before the king for the royal sanction. At the same moment, the Hungarians gave an unexampled proof of their loyalty, by inviting the king, who had fled to Innspruck, to go to Pesth, and by his presence tranquillize the people, trusting to the loyalty of the Hungarians, who had shown themselves at all times the best supporters of the throne.

This request was proffered in vain, for Radetzky had in the mean time been victorious in Italy. The house of Lorraine-Habsburg, restored to confidence by that victory, thought the time come to take off the mask and to involve Hungary, still bleeding from past wounds, in the horrors of a fresh war of oppression. The king from that moment began to address the man whom he himself had branded as a rebel, as "dear and loyal" (Lieber Getreuer); he praised him for having revolted, and encouraged him to proceed in the path he had entered upon.

He expressed a like sympathy for the Servian rebels, whose hands yet reeked from the massacres they had perpetrated. It was under this command that the Ban of Croatia, after being proclaimed as a rebel, assembled an army, and announced his commission from the king to carry fire and sword into Hungary, upon which the Austrian troops stationed in the country united with him. The commandants of the fortresses, Eszek and Temesvar Gynlaschervar, and the commanders of the forces in the Banat and in Transylvania, breaking their oaths taken to the country, treacherously surrendered their trusts; a Slovack clergyman with the commission of colonel, who had fraternized at Vienna with the revolted Czecks, broke into Hungary, and the rebel Croat leader advanced with confidence, through an unprepared country, to occupy its capital, expecting that the army in Hungary would not oppose him.

Even then the Diet did not give up all confidence in the power of the royal oath, and the king was once more requested to order the rebels to quit the country. The answer given was a reference to a manifesto of the Austrian ministry, declaring it to be their determination to deprive the Hungarian nation of the independent management of their financial, commercial, and war affairs. The king at the same time refused his assent to the laws submitted for approval respecting the troops and the subsidy for covering the expenditure.

Upon this the Hungarian ministers resigned, but the names submitted by the president of the council, at the demand of the king, were not approved of for successors. The Diet then, bound by its duty to secure the interests of the country, voted the supplies, and ordered the troops to be levied. The nation obeyed the summons with readiness.

The representatives of the people then summoned the nephew of the emperor to join the camp, and as Palatine to lead the troops against the rebels. He not only obeyed the summons, but made public professions of his devotion to the cause. As soon, however, as an engagement threatened, he fled secretly from the camp and the country, like a coward traitor. Among his papers a plan, formed by him some time previously, was found, according to which Hungary was to be simultaneously attacked on nine sides at once—from Styria, Austria, Moravia, Silesia, Galicia, and Transylvania.

From a correspondence with the Minister of War, seized at the same time, it was discovered that the commanding generals in the military frontier and the Austrian provinces adjoining Hungary had received orders to enter Hungary, and to support the rebels with their united forces.

This attack from nine points at once really began. The most painful aggression took place in Transylvania, for the traitorous commander in that district did not content himself with the practices considered lawful in war by disciplined troops. He stirred up the Wallachian peasants to take up arms against their own constitutional rights, and, aided by the rebellious Servian hordes, commenced a course of Vandalism and extinction, sparing neither women, children, nor aged men; murdering and torturing the defenseless Hungarian inhabitants; burning the most flourishing villages and towns, among which, Nagy-Igmand, the seat of learning for Transylvania, was reduced to a heap of ruins.

But the Hungarian nation, although taken by surprise, unarmed and unprepared, did not abandon its future prospects in any agony of despair.

Measures were immediately taken to increase the small standing army by volunteers and the levy of the people. These troops, supplying the want of experience by the enthusiasm arising from the feeling that they had right on their side, defeated the Croatian armaments, and drove them out of the country. One of the leaders abused the generosity of the victors, after a battle in which the rebels were defeated, and a truce was granted to them to decamp by night. Another body of ten thousand men were surrounded, and the whole, to a man, taken prisoners

The defeated army fled in the direction of Vienna, where the emperor continued his demoralizing policy, and nominated the beaten and flying rebel as his plenipotentiary and substitute in Hungary, suspending by this act the constitution and institutions of the country, all its authorities, courts of justice, and tribunals, laying the kingdom under martial law, and placing in the hand of, and under the unlimited authority of, a rebel, the honor, the property, and the lives of the people; in the hand of a man who, with armed bands, had braved the laws, and attacked the Constitution of the country.

But the house of Austria was not contented with this unjustifiable violation of oaths taken by its head.

The rebellious Ban was taken under the protection of the troops stationed near Vienna, and commanded by Prince Windischgrätz. These troops, after taking Vienna by storm, were led as an imperial Austrian army to conquer Hungary. But the Hungarian nation, persisting in its loyalty, sent an envoy to the advancing enemy. This envoy, coming under a flag of truce, was treated as a prisoner, and thrown into prison. No heed was paid to the remonstrances and the demands of the Hungarian nation for justice. The threat of the gallows was, on the contrary, thundered against all who had taken arms in defense of a wretched and oppressed country. But before the army had time to enter Hungary, a family revolution in the tyrannical reigning house was perpetrated at Olmütz. Ferdinand V. was forced to resign a throne which had been polluted with so much blood and perjury, and the son of Francis Charles, who also abdicated his claim to the inheritance, the youthful Archduke Francis Joseph, caused himself to be proclaimed Emperor of Austria and King of Hungary. But, according to the family compact, no one can dispose of the constitutional throne but the Hungarian nation.

At this critical moment the Hungarian nation demanded nothing more than the maintenance of its laws and institutions, and peace guaranteed by their integrity. Had the assent of the nation to this change in the occupant of the throne been asked in a legal manner, and the young prince offered to take the customary oath that he would preserve the Constitution, the Hungarian nation would not have refused to elect him king in accordance with the treaties extant, and to crown him with St. Stephen's crown, before he had dipped his hand in the blood of the people.

He, however, refusing to perform an act so sacred in the eyes of God and man, and in strange contrast to the innocence natural to youthful breasts, declared in his first words his intention of conquering Hungary, which he dared to call a rebellious country, although he himself had raised rebellion there, and of depriving it of that independence which it had maintained for a thousand years, to incorporate it into the Austrian monarchy.

And he has but too well labored to keep his word. He ordered the army under Windischgrätz to enter Hungary, and, at the same time, directed several corps of troops to attack the country from Galicia and Styria. Hungary resisted the projected invasion, but being unable to make head against so many countries at once, on account of the devastation carried on in several parts of the interior by the excited rebels, and being thus prevented from displaying its whole power of defense, the troops were, in the first instance, obliged to retire. To save the capital from the horrors of a storm like that to which Prague and Vienna had mercilessly been exposed, and not to place the fortunes of a nation—which deserved better—on the die of a pitched battle, for which there had not been sufficient preparation, the capital was abandoned, and the Diet and national government removed in January last to Debreczin, trusting to the help of a just God, and to the energies of the nation, to prevent the cause from being lost, even when it should be seen that the capital was given up. Thanks be to Heaven, the cause was not lost!

But even then an attempt was made to bring about a peaceful arrangement, and a deputation was sent to the generals of the perjured dynasty. This house, in its blind self-confidence, refused to enter into any negotiation, and dared to demand an unconditional submission from the nation. The deputation was further detained, and one of the number, the former president of the ministry, was even thrown into prison. The deserted capital was occupied, and was turned into a place of execution; a part of the prisoners of war were there consigned to the ax, another part were thrown into dungeons, while the remainder were exposed to fearful sufferings from hunger, and were thus forced to enter the ranks of the army in Italy.

The measure of the crimes of the Austrian house was, however, filled up, when, after its defeat, it applied for help to the Emperor of Russia; and, in spite of the remonstrances and protestations of the Porte, and of the consuls of the European powers at Bucharest, in defiance of international rights, and to the endangering of the balance of power in Europe, caused the Russian troops, stationed at Wallachia, to be led into Transylvania, for the destruction of the Hungarian nation.

Three months ago we were driven back upon the Theiss; our just arms have already recovered all Transylvania; Klausenburg, Hermanstadt, and Kronstadt are taken; one portion of the troops of Austria is driven into the Bukowina; another, together with the Russian force sent to aid them, is totally defeated, and to the last man obliged to evacuate Transylvania, and to flee into Wallachia. Upper Hungary is cleared of foes.

The Servian rebellion is further suppressed; the forts of St. Thomas and the Roman intrenchment have been taken by storm, and the whole country between the Danube and the Theiss, including the county of Bacs, has been recovered for the nation.

II.   D d

The commander-in-chief of the perjured house of Austria has himself been defeated in five consecutive battles, and has with his whole army been driven back upon and even over the Danube.

Founding a line of conduct upon all these occurrences, and confiding in the justice of an eternal God, we, in the face of the civilized world, in reliance upon the natural rights of the Hungarian nation, and upon the power it has developed to maintain them, further impelled by that sense of duty which urges every nation to defend its existence, do hereby declare and proclaim, in the name of the nation legally represented by us, the following :

1st. Hungary, with Transylvania, as legally united with it, and the possessions and dependencies, are hereby declared to constitute a free, independent sovereign state. The territorial unity of this state is declared to be inviolable, and its territory to be indivisible.

2d. The house of Habsburg-Lorraine—having, by treachery, perjury, and levying of war against the Hungarian nation, as well as by its outrageous violation of all compacts, in breaking up the integral territory of the kingdom, in the separation of Transylvania, Croatia, Slavonia, Fiume, and its districts, from Hungary—further, by compassing the destruction of the independence of the country by arms, and by calling in the disciplined army of a foreign power, for the purpose of annihilating its nationality, by violation both of the Pragmatic Sanction and of treaties concluded between Austria and Hungary, on which the alliance between the two countries depended—is, as treacherous and perjured, forever excluded from the throne of the united states of Hungary and Transylvania, and all their possessions and dependencies, and are hereby deprived of the style and title, as well as of the armorial bearings belonging to the crown of Hungary, and declared to be banished forever from the united countries and their dependencies and possessions. They are, therefore, declared to be deposed, degraded, and banished forever from the Hungarian territory.

3d. The Hungarian nation, in the exercise of its rights and sovereign will, being determined to assume the position of a free and independent state among the nations of Europe, declares it to be its intention to establish and maintain friendly and neighborly relations with those states with which it was formerly united under the same sovereign, as well as to contract alliances with all other nations.

4th. The form of government to be adopted for the future will be fixed by the Diet of the nation.

But until this point shall be decided, on the basis of the foregoing and received principles which have been recognized for ages, the government of the united countries, their possessions and dependencies, shall be conducted on personal responsibility, and under the obligation to render an account of all acts, by Louis Kossuth, who has by acclamation, and with the unanimous approbation of the Diet of the nation, been named Governing President (Gubernator), and the ministers whom he shall appoint.

And this resolution of ours we proclaim to make known to all the nations of the civilized world, with the conviction that the Hungarian nation will be received by them among the free and independent nations of the world, with the same friendship and free acknowledgment of its rights which the Hungarians proffer to other countries.

We also hereby proclaim and make known to all the inhabitants of the united states of Hungary and Transylvania, their possessions and dependencies, that all authorities, communes, towns, and the civil officers, both in the counties and cities, are completely set free and released from all the obligations under which they stood, by oath or otherwise, to the said house of Habsburg; and that any individual daring to contravene this decree, and by word or deed in any way to aid or abet any one violating it, shall be treated and punished as guilty of high treason. And by the publication of this decree, we hereby bind and oblige all the inhabitants of these countries to obedience to the government, now instituted formally, and endowed with all necessary legal powers.

Debreczin, April 14, 1849.

Note No. 32.

ARMISTICE ENTERED INTO AFTER THE BATTLE OF NOVARA, BETWEEN THE KING OF PIEDMONT AND FIELD-MARSHAL RADETZKY.

The King of Sardinia gives his positive and solemn assurance to cause to be concluded, so far as depends upon his honor, a treaty of peace, on the basis of the following articles:

Art. 1. The King of Sardinia will disband the Hungarian, Polish, and Lombard corps, reserving to himself the right of retaining certain officers of other corps as he may think fit.

Art. 2. Count Radetzky will interpose with the emperor, in order to obtain a complete amnesty for the Hungarian, Polish, and Lombard soldiers subjects of his said majesty.

Art. 3. The King of Sardinia admits that eighteen thousand Austrian infantry and two thousand cavalry may occupy the territory which lies between the Po, the Ticino, and the Sesia; and that one half the garrison of the citadel of Alexandria shall be composed of Austrian troops. This occupation shall not exercise any influence over the civil and judicial administration of the division of Novara. One half of the garrison of the town and citadel of Alexandria to be composed of three thousand Austrians, and the other half of the troops of his Sardinian majesty. The Austrians shall have free communication between Alexandria and Lonellina, by Valenza. A mixed military commission shall be named for regulating the conduct of the Austrian troops. The Duchies of Modena, Piacenza, and Tuscany, that is to say, the territories which did not belong to Piedmont before the war, shall be evacuated by the Sardinian troops.

Art. 4. The entrance of the Austrian moiety of the garrison of the citadel of Alexandria not being capable of taking place for three or four days, it is guaranteed by the Sardinian government.

Art. 5. The Sardinian fleet shall retire from the Adriatic, with all the steamers, within a fortnight, and return to their own ports, and the Piedmontese who shall be in Venice shall receive orders to return to their own states within the same period.

Art. 6. King Victor Emmanuel engages to conclude promptly a durable peace, and reduce his army to the peace footing.

Art. 7. The King of Sardinia holds as inviolable all the conditions above stipulated.

Art. 8. Plenipotentiaries from both parties shall be sent to some town, to be hereafter named, for the purpose of concluding a definitive peace.

Art. 9. The peace shall be made independently of the stipulations of this armistice.

Art. 10. Should not a peace be concluded, the renunciation of the armistic shall be made ten days before the recommencement of hostilities.

Art. 11. All prisoners of war shall be promptly and reciprocally delivered up.

Art. 12. All the Austrians who have already passed the Sesia shall be bound to return within the limits above traced.

(Signed)

CHRZANOWSKY,
RADETZKY.

March 24, 1849.

Note No. 33.

LETTER OF GÖRGEY TO GENERAL RÜDIGER.

General,—I presume you are familiar with the melancholy history of my country. I will not, therefore, enter into a detail of events which are so ominously connected, and which involved us in a desperate struggle for our legal liberties, in the first instance, and for our existence in the second. The better—indeed, I may say, the larger part of the nation, did by no means carelessly brave the chances of such a contest; but once engaged (and enjoying the support of many honorable men, who, though not Hungarians by birth, came, by the force of circumstances, to be parties in the conflict), they have honestly, manfully, and victoriously held out to the last.

But the policy of Europe compelled his majesty, the Czar of Russia, to league with Austria for our overthrow, and for the termination of our war for the Hungarian Constitution. Many of our true patriots had foreseen and prophesied the event. History will one day unfold what it was which induced a majority in the Provisional Government to close their ears against the voices of our patriots.

The Provisional Government exists no more. The hour of danger found them most weak. I, who am a man of action (though not of a vain action), I saw that all further effusion of blood was useless—that it was fatal to Hungary. I knew this from the commencement of the Russian invasion.

I have this day called upon the Provisional Government to make an unconditional resignation; for their continuing in office can not fail still further to cloud and to jeopardize the fortunes of my country. The Provisional Government became convinced of this truth; they resigned, and gave the power of the state into my hands.

I make use of this circumstance for the purpose of preventing a further sacrifice of human life; and since I am too weak to defend my peaceable fellow-citizens, I will, at least, liberate them from the miseries of war. I make an unconditional surrender. This act of mine will, perhaps, induce the leaders of other Hungarian armies to follow my example. I place my reliance on the notorious generosity of his majesty the Czar, trusting that he will consider the case of numbers of my brave comrades, who, as former officers in the Austrian army, are seriously compromised; and that he will not sacrifice them to a melancholy and uncertain fate. I trust that his majesty will consider the case of the unfortunate people of Hungary, who rely on his love of justice; and that he will not hand them over, helpless and unarmed, to the blind thirst of their enemies. Perhaps it is enough, if it is *I* who am the only victim.

General! I address this letter to you, because it was you who gave me marks of respect which have gained my confidence.

If you wish to put a stop to further and useless sacrifice of human life, I entreat you to take measures that the melancholy act of surrender may take place at your earliest convenience, but in such a manner that our arms be surrendered *only* to the troops of his majesty the Czar of Russia. For most solemnly do I protest, I would rather see my corps engaged and annihilated in a desperate battle, no matter against what odds, than make an unconditional surrender to Austrian troops!

To-morrow, on the 12th of August, I intend to march my troops to Vilagos. On the 13th, I proceed to Boros Jenö; and on the 14th, to Béd. I inform you of these movements, because I wish that you should lead your force between the Austrian troops and mine—that you should surround me, and cut me off from the Austrians.

In case this maneuver were to prove unsuccessful, and in case the Austrian troops were to pursue ours, I mean to oppose an effective resistance to their attacks, to turn upon Great Warasdin, for the purpose of meeting the army of his majesty the Czar; for it is to his army alone that my troops are prepared to make a voluntary surrender.

I expect your reply at your earliest convenience: and I remain, with my assurances of unlimited respect,   ARTHUR GÖRGEY.

Old Arad, August 11, 1849—9 o'clock, P.M.

Note No. 34.

LETTERS OF HUNGARIAN MINISTERS ON THE ABDICATION OF KOSSUTH.

Esterhazy on the Hungarian Revolution.

The following letter from Prince Esterhazy, member of the Hungarian cabinet, was published in the London Times of the 1st of December last:

My dear Lord,—I sincerely regret my absence from town and other unavoidable causes have delayed forwarding the present letter.

I am principally induced to address you these lines by the report of what takes place in England relative to Hungary, and the strange confusion of ideas which seems to prevail there at this moment in several quarters, mixing up actions of an essentially revolutionary character with constitutional and patriotic principles.

Before entering more fully on the subject, a retrospective glance at the crisis of the spring of 1848 becomes necessary.

It is impossible to deny that, owing to the overwhelming circumstances of that period, the political existence of the Austrian empire was exposed to the greatest danger, and that the maintaining of the Hungarian crown on the head of the Emperor Ferdinand was a condition of absolute necessity to the salvation of the empire.

But the different concessions consecutively extorted from the government in a moment of surprise and feebleness had already lessened the power of resistance in its hands. Underhand dealings had succeeded in blinding and corrupting public opinion in general, and particularly that of the Hungarian Diet, which, notwithstanding the benevolent and constitutional intentions of the government, set forth in the royal propositions of the Diet of 1847, and the respect constantly shown, since the Diet of 1825, to the fundamental principles of the Hungarian Constitution, had taken a direction of a most dangerous character, heightened by the general excitement of Europe after the events in France, in February, 1848.

A virtual separation was fast approaching. Under such circumstances, nothing could be of higher importance than to maintain the principle of the union and the rights of the crown. I may fairly state, that a pure and simple refusal of the petitions presented by the deputation which arrived here shortly after the sad scene in March would have seriously compromised this first-rate interest.

The only way to avoid complications of a dangerous character for the monarchy and pernicious for Hungary itself, was to consider the concessions already obtained from the emperor in a legal form, although by violent pressure from without, as the *final term*, but not as the *starting-point* for renewed agitation.

It was the false view taken of this important point, and the tendency of a violent party to employ these concessions, not for the legal consolidation of the rights of their country, but for the annihilation of the royal power and of the union, which hastened the untoward development of the Hungarian disturbances.

One of the petitions of the aforesaid deputation was the creation of a Hungarian ministry, from which Count Batthiányi and M. Kossuth could not be excluded, exercising as they did a preponderating influence over public opinion in Hungary; and such was the calamity of that epoch, that the value of their influence was in reverse proportion to the value of their principles. With the former I had, up to that period, but a slight, with the latter no social relation whatever.

The formation of such a ministry, granted by his majesty, was perhaps at that moment, and among different other combinations, not the most prejudicial step for supporting monarchical interests and the principle of the union, because the absolute maintenance of the Pragmatic Sanction was thus formally confirmed, and a positive engagement taken to that effect.

The insuring of this vital interest induced me to put aside every personal consideration. In consequence of urgent and reiterated solicitations from persons whose loyalty and devotedness to the reigning dynasty were above all doubt, having besides powerful motives to believe that my accepting the place especially designated by a recent law as that of *a minister to reside near the person of the emperor*, would be as conducive to smooth the difficulties in the transaction of affairs of so delicate a nature, as to suit the personal convenience of his majesty the emperor, I yielded at last, and accepted the proposed office.

In order to form an opinion of this administration, it is not only necessary to replace one's self in the period and in the peculiar circumstances of its formation, but also to enter into an analysis of the nature of its composition.

If, on one side, it contained undoubtedly elements, which by their precedents gave rise to mistrust and repugnance, there were in it, on the other hand, elements of a less alarming character, men of pure reputation, who in their opposition never went beyond the line of parliamentary decency and privilege.

Under this head, I put in the first rank the Count Stephen Széchényi, a man equally well known in England, with whom I am connected by the ties of old-standing friendship, whose loyalty could not more be doubted than his patriotic feelings, and whose exertions for the material welfare of Hungary are as meritorious as the political impulse, of which he was almost the first to give the signal, proved to be calamitous.

There were at the head of several departments, as I mentioned before, men of trustworthy character, who labored under no illusion as to the political tendency and the clandestine plans of their colleague, and endeavored, although unsuccessfully, to counteract them.

I may dispense with pointing him out. His name is but too much heard in England, where the would-be friends of Hungary have prepared for him a reception, showing a striking contrast to the evidence of high treason, and to the calamities and misfortune which, by subversive schemes, he brought on his country, as well as to the state in which he left it at the moment of his flight.

It is evident that two ways were open to the pursuit of those patriotic views which he boasted of. One of them was the path of legality, in devoting his undeniable ability to the task of effacing the means employed in extorting concessions from the crown.

But the secret motives which guided him, his vanity, and the party to which he was devoted, drove him into the opposite path, and, following this direction, he brought on the catastrophes of which his country has been the theatre, and was himself led to acts of treason, with their just consequences. This result of the proceedings, of which he was at once the moving power and the instrument, the frequent difference between his words and his deeds, and his reluctance to act manfully in case of need, by courageously exposing his life, have now, I think, blotted out, among the majority of the nation, the phantasmagoria of his unpropitious influence. To that the last blow was given, when, seeing the end of his ephemeral power fast approaching, he resorted to republican utopias, more in tended, I apprehend, for exportation to foreign markets than for home consumption in our own, as I can hardly think him capable of such an egregious mistake as really to indulge in the hope of making such a scheme palatable to a population, whose genius, traditional history, feelings, and habits, are so eminently monarchical and aristocratic.

It was for the purpose of guiding the destinies of the kingdom of Hungary in so desirable a direction as the first of the above-mentioned two roads was leading to, that I devoted all possible efforts of my co-operation, opening thus the door for an honorable retreat to those who had already seriously committed themselves in following the opposite direction.

The affording to Louis Kossuth the opportunity of carrying out, in the capacity of a minister of the emperor as King of Hungary, the patriotic intention he pretended to profess, was to offer him a sphere of activity, and a situation which he could hardly ever have dreamed of obtaining, and which would have been thought glorious enough, had not the violence of his passion carried him away.

Nothing appeared, therefore, more urgent than to support the loyal fraction of the administration in exercising a salutary influence over the spirit of the Diet, and the nation in general; for I maintain that the majority of both was corrupted and paralyzed by the system of subordination, seduction, and terrorism practiced by a fanatical minority, which considered all means to be lawful, and gave itself up to the dictates of agitation and its leader.

The events of the month of May, 1848, brought on the departure of the imperial family to Innspruck. I followed there with so much the more zeal, as the circumstances afforded me an opportunity for demonstrating my feelings of loyalty, respect, and devotedness. During the four weeks I remained there, the affairs relating to Hungary were brought forward in conference under protocols. I never placed before his majesty any subject not previously discussed in this way. If I mention here the complication between Hungary and Croatia, it is only to allege the motives for the delay in giving my resignation; for I felt the strongest desire to contribute to the success of a reconciliation which, although possible, was from the first moment surrounded with difficulties, owing to the signal want of good faith on the part of the extreme fraction of the Hungarian ministry, residing at Pesth, in publishing a document (the manifesto of the emperor against the Ban of Croatia), which, according to an agreement solemnly entered into by their president at Innspruck, in open conference, ought not to have been published but on a certain eventuality, which, not having taken place, could give no right whatsoever to break so solemn an engagement.

Following the successive periods, we arrive at the untoward one when the revolutionary faction began to lift the mask, yet without openly throwing it off.

One part of the ministry, which was still honest in its intentions, was paralyzed and counteracted by the decisions of the Hungarian Diet, contrary to the intentions of its real majority, and of the country itself.

This situation became more and more dangerous as the hope of seeing the financial regulations and those concerning the army carried out in a spirit less at variance with the fundamental principles of the union and the royal prerogative faded away; and as the intended solution of these questions, in vain opposed by my strongest efforts, was contrary to those principles, and equivalent in its results to a total separation (as the troops levied and the money raised were to be applied exclusively to Hungarian purposes), I could no longer hesitate in my determination to resign.

If any circumstance could have added more weight to this resolution, it was the shameful and treasonable attempt to shake the fidelity of the army. In the state of moral and physical intoxication in which the deluded instruments of treason were previously placed, all sorts of means were resorted to, from inducements held out to ambitious pretensions down even to the most contemptible pecuniary bribes. On my arrival at Vienna, I tried once more to tender my good offices in the affairs of Croatia, the Ban being at that time present, as likewise the Count Batthiányi, and the Archduke John acting as mediator. Seeing, however, that this negotiation would not lead to a satisfactory result, I only awaited the arrival of the Emperor Ferdinand, in order to tender my final resignation.

Among the sad and shameful events which have at a later period branded the Hungarian insurrection, the atrocious and cowardly murder of Count Lamburg was the first dreadful scene. This bloody termination of a mission of peace and conciliation gave the last stamp to the increasing revolutionary character of the Hungarian events. It was rendered the more infamous by the false and hypocritical pretenses under which the fury of the mob had been excited against the unhappy victim of his loyal and patriotic zeal, and by the criminal impunity of the principal perpetrators of that revolting act, who remained unpunished by the authorities, while the perpetrator of it, far from hiding himself, openly boasted of the bloody deed.

At the end of September, I left Vienna and its environs, which for the moment had become uninhabitable through the excesses of the revolted mob, and a state of things bordering upon anarchy.

Having retired to my castle of Eisenstadt, situated only two miles from the frontiers, calculating thus on my personal freedom, I found myself, the very day after the battle of Schwechat, surrounded and watched by a set of spies, and a turbulent body of armed peasants called "Landsturm," and thus prevented from leaving the place without endangering the safety of my family. It was at that time confidentially stated to me that I should be transported by violent means into the interior of the country upon the least attempt to leave my residence. This was the way in which the principle of personal liberty and independence was practically carried out.

At last, in December, the imperial troops relieved me from so painful a position.

To sum up: I feel it to be a duty toward my sovereign, my country, and myself, to point out the difference which exists between the period of fruitless efforts, made by upright and honorable men, to stop the revolutionary torrent, and to reconcile the constitutional changes introduced into our ancient Hungarian Constitution with the fundamental principle of the Pragmatic Sanction, and that period during which the extreme party succeeded in exercising an exclusive and pernicious influence over the country.

Whatever faults may have been committed in the course of events so momentous, whatever may be the opinions entertained and the judgment passed on that head, of one thing you may rest assured, and take my word for it, that if the sympathies of the revolutionary and subversive party can not assuredly be denied to its Hungarian leader, he is by no means entitled to the sympathy of the friends of order and of real constitutional liberty, for of these he had undermined the basis in Hungary by inflaming the public mind instead of promoting that gradual progress, the country would else undoubtedly have made the improvements in its moral and material interests which it stands so much in need of.

P. Esterhazy.

Vienna, Nov. 13, 1851.

Casimir Batthiányi on Kossuth and the Fall of Hungary.

The following communication from Casimir Batthiányi, in comment upon the preceding, appeared in the London Times of the 30th ult.

Sir,—In *The Times* of the 1st of December appeared a letter from Prince Paul Esterhazy, and shortly afterward an answer, or, rather, echo to it, which has only the relative importance to myself of having the name of Batthiányi appended to it. The Batthiányi family is, as you are probably aware, a not less numerous one than the Esterhazy and several other Hungarian families. No member of these families has an exclusive right to the family name; but, for the sake of distinction, it is customary for each member to place his Christian name to his signature, or at least such distinctive name or title as he alone has a right to claim. Having been literally assailed by questions on the subject, I beg leave, in order to prevent all further mistakes, to declare, once for all, that I am not the writer of that letter; and in making this declaration, I trust that your sense of justice will induce you to find space in your columns for some further observations which I should wish to make, not on the letter in question, but on that of Prince Esterhazy.

The prince's letter, clouded as it is in a sort of diplomatic halo, seems more adapted to involve the events of the Hungarian Revolution in obscurity than to throw any light on "the strange confusion of ideas" of which the prince complains, and which certainly do prevail. Although it presents a clear view of the feelings and impressions under which the prince entered the Hungarian ministry, and remained in it up to its dissolution, we look in vain in it for a clew to the motives which, consistently with the high character of a statesman, induced the prince to enter a ministry from the majority of whose members he differed so materially, as he himself admits, both in opinions and principles. What could have been his object in coalescing with men "the value of whose influence was in reverse proportion to the value of their principles?" For what purpose could he have associated himself with men for whom he entertained so little consideration? How are we to understand his meaning when he informs us that his principal motive for doing so was not owing to any sympathy he felt for those men, or any political or social connection he had with them, but to the "reiterated solicitations" of other men "whose loyalty and devotedness to the reigning dynasty were above all doubt?" How, under such circumstances, could he hope to counteract the policy of those who had such "a preponderating influence over public opinion in Hungary?" What result could he have anticipated from such a delicate and important mission, when he disagreed with and stood aloof from his fellow-ministers? Was it fair to intrude into the secrets of a council that trusted to his honor and discretion when he did not mean to identify himself with its policy? What would you say in England of a statesman who entered a ministry under such conditions,

and with the express design of following a totally different policy from his colleagues ?   What would you say of the member of an administration who, years
after the death of its chief—in whose general policy he must, ostensibly at least,
in accepting his offer of a seat in the cabinet, have acquiesced—should apologize
for the share he had taken in that administration, and whitewash himself before
another party in office by alleging that he had remained inactive, or steered a different course than his colleagues, slandering, at the same time, the memory of one
who rests in his grave, accusing of misdemeanors and want of loyalty one whose
voice can no longer indignantly repel such aspersions ?

It was not thus that the late Count Louis Batthiányi acted when he asked
Prince Esterhazy to enter the administration of which he was the head.   It was
owing to his high station—to the respect in which his character, though but little
known in Hungary at that period, was generally held—to his long diplomatic career, which it was supposed had afforded him the best opportunities of studying
constitutional life in all its intricacies and in its most perfect state of development,
that Prince Esterhazy was deemed peculiarly adapted for the important but delicate mission of the minister of the Hungarian crown, who had to remain near the
person of the sovereign, and thus form the link between the Hungarian and Austrian governments; and on whom, therefore, chiefly devolved the task of maintaining the rights of the nation, of smoothing any difficulties that might arise, and
of maintaining, in conformity with the Pragmatic Sanction, the connection between Hungary and the Austrian hereditary states.

The principal motives, however, that induced Louis Batthiányi to select such
men as Prince Esterhazy for his colleagues, were precisely those put forward by
the prince himself, viz. : 1st. The firm determination of " maintaining the Hungarian crown on the head of the Emperor Ferdinand, as well as the laws which had
received the royal sanction." 2d. The conviction that the formation of a Hungarian ministry " was not the most prejudicial step for supporting monarchical interests and the principle of the union, because the absolute maintenance of the
Pragmatic Sanction was thus formally confirmed;" and, 3d. The impression that
" the concessions already obtained from the emperor in a legal form," whatever
may have been the " pressure" under which they were obtained, should be regarded " as the final term, but not as the starting-point for renewed agitation."

In following up these very principles, Louis Batthiányi called into his administration not only Prince Esterhazy, but Count Stephen Széchényi, and other equally enlightened, patriotic, and honorable men, whom the prince slurs over in his
letter, but who have acquired a well-merited reputation in their own country,
either as practical statesmen, equally distinguished for firmness of principle and
for wisdom and moderation in their views, like Mr. Francis Deaki; or as men of
highly-cultivated minds and profound knowledge, like Baron Joseph Eötvös and
Mr. Bartholomew Szemere; or as independent men and brilliant orators, with
liberal, though moderate tendencies, like Mr. Gabriel Klauzal; or, finally, as the
representatives of military honor and bravery, like General Meszaros.   Their
combined influence secured a large majority in the Diet, as well as in the municipal corporations throughout the country, and this influence was entirely and exclusively exercised in the maintenance of the *status quo*, that would unquestionably have settled down into a permanent order of things had it not been for the
events that intervened.   I am not going to recapitulate these events.   They are
historical facts which can not be denied.   Suffice it to say, 1st. That the financial
regulations, and those concerning the army, to which the prince alludes, were
clearly designated by the acts of the Diet of 1847–8, as belonging exclusively to

the functions of the Hungarian government; 2d. That Kossuth was appointed Hungarian Minister of Finance with the express consent of his majesty; and, 3d. That the Hungarian troops were placed by a royal decree under the orders of the Hungarian Minister of War, who was empowered to administer to them the oath on the Constitution. It was no wonder, therefore, that "the troops levied and the money raised" were "applied exclusively to Hungarian purposes," at a period, too, when rebellion had broken out, which, supported as it was by a power at first unknown and scarcely suspected, but soon divined and fully unmasked, threatened to engulf the country and sweep away its Constitution, which, old and time-honored in its origin and practice, had, in the opinion of all honest men, been invigorated by the recent reforms. And it was this reformed Constitution that had been guaranteed by the oath of the king—a king who was no longer under the trammels of an insurgent mob at Vienna, but who had repaired a month afterward, of his own free will, to his good city of Pressburg, where he was surrounded by a loyal nation full of gratitude and reverence for the throne.

The statement of Hungarian troops and money being reserved exclusively for Hungarian purposes is not, moreover, strictly correct. The grant of troops for Italy was made conditionally, it is true, because Hungary had then no troops to spare; but was made with the view of keeping up the integrity of the Austrian empire, according to the spirit of the Pragmatic Sanction, and, at the same time, of conferring the blessing of constitutional liberty on the Italian subjects of his majesty, and thus consolidating the empire upon the only principle that could thenceforward secure its existence—that of a confederation of autonomic states.

This grant, which has lately been the subject of discussion in the English press, is the best proof of the loyal policy of Louis Batthiányi's ministry, as well as of the conciliatory spirit that pervaded the majority of the Diet. And this same policy was pursued by Louis Batthiányi until the last moment, notwithstanding all the disappointments and deceptions he was doomed to experience. To this policy he sacrificed even his popularity; and while he spurned on one hand the threats of the inconstant masses, and on the other braved death itself in the consciousness of his integrity and patriotism, he was subjected to the taunts of detractors during his life, was executed by those he had faithfully served, and now disavowed after his death, and mixed up with the scum of unprincipled demagogues and political *condottieri*, by one of those whom he had selected to stand honorably by his side, and aid him in his efforts to save the crown and extricate the Austrian empire from the abyss into which it had been plunged by the temporizing and wavering policy which this government had so long pursued. And Louis Batthiányi followed this policy until the atrocious murder of Count Lamburg. This foul deed so disgusted him, that he went to Vienna and resigned his office into the hands of his majesty, showing thereby his disapprobation of popular justice exercised in a summary manner, as well as his dissent from a measure which, whatever may be its ultimate result, was illegal both in its form and its principle.

How Prince Esterhazy during this interval fulfilled the duties he had assumed, what part he acted, what share he took in furthering the patriotic endeavors of the premier, in what direction he used his authority and influence, are facts which probably lie concealed in his letter. Hungary knows very little of his doings. Neither does he give us himself the least information on this point, nor offer any explanation of the principal, and the only special accusation which he brings against the prime minister, under whom he consented to take office, and to remain in office long after the fact alluded to was accomplished. The accusation is, that Louis Batthiányi published the decree of the emperor, by which the Ban of Croatia was deprived, as a traitor, of all honors, titles, and dignities before a certain eventuality took place; whereas, according to the prince, a solemn agreement was entered into, at a conference at Innspruck, that the decree should not be published until this eventuality had actually occurred. Strange as this story sounds, and trifling as the circumstance is in itself, even on the supposition that Louis Batthiányi had, in the interest of his own country, taken such a liberty toward a set of men whose influence predominated at court, and who had already, in several instances, shown their want of good faith, and had moreover constantly exercised a direct, and therefore illegal influence on the internal affairs of Hungary; still, in order to give it the least semblance of truth, the public had a right to expect that his highness would have shown what the eventuality alluded to really was. Then, and then only, would the public have been able to form a correct judgment respecting the statement, and to examine whether the eventuality had not actually taken place, or whether the Hungarian premier had not also, on his part, laid down certain conditions before he consented to receive the royal decree—such as, for instance, the quiet removal of the Ban, or a severe rebuke from the king, with a peremptory order to desist from his military preparations. What is certain, is the historical fact of the brilliant reception which the Ban met with immediately afterward, and before Louis Batthiányi could have ever had time to publish the document at that same court of Innspruck, whither he had been summoned to appear *ad audiendum verbum regium.* It is also certain, that at the same time as this decree was drawn up, manifestoes were addressed by the emperor to the Croatians themselves, warning them not to suffer themselves to be led astray by the maneuvers of the Ban, but to adhere steadily to the Hungarian ministry.

That the Ban, in despite of these proceedings, continued his preparations, and soon invaded Hungary in the name of the emperor, and that, at the very moment he was doing so, the decree in question was not only revoked, but fresh honors showered on him; that he was successively made lieutenant field-marshal, commander-in-chief of all the forces in Hungary, and royal plenipotentiary commissary, are so many proofs that Louis Batthiányi regarded the king's word and signature as sacred and irrevocable, and acted in conformity with this conviction, while the counselors of his majesty at Vienna and Innspruck did not scruple to compromise the dignity of the sovereign, by persuading his majesty to affix his signature first to one document, and then to another of a totally opposite tendency. The whole transaction was, in fact, a trick practiced on the good nature and faith of Louis Batthiányi and the Hungarian nation, in order that the nation might be lulled into a fatal security, and the way smoothed for the Ban, that he might be enabled quietly to proceed to Pesth, and there place himself in possession of power and full executive authority. Is not such a proceeding in itself sufficient to justify—nay, even command such an indiscretion on the part of Louis Batthiányi as is here imputed to him? There is, moreover, one circumstance that must always be borne in mind when these events are made the subject of discussion, which is, that this proceeding, as well as every other of the same kind, was not taken, and could not have been taken by Louis Batthiányi, without the consent and authorization of his imperial highness the Archduke Stephen, the Palatine and vicegerent of the kingdom. It will thus appear that the decree in question was published, and sent in the name of the Palatine to all the authorities under his jurisdiction. It was the same in respect to the indictment issued against the Ban, in virtue of the royal decree, and to the commission by which General Wrabowsky and two royal attorneys were empowered to institute legal proceedings against the Ban, if he persisted in his refusal to obey the royal commands. All these documents I repeat, were issued in the name of, and signed by the Palatine.

It can not be denied that there was a faction in the country, and even in the Diet, that was daily increasing in numbers, and that Kossuth was weak enough to countenance, whose object was to keep up a perpetual agitation, not for the purposes of maintaining the laws and liberties of the country, but with the view of hurrying the country into revolution. This faction was kept down by Louis Batthiányi so long as he was able to maintain his position. If, without getting precisely the upper hand, this faction finally succeeded in spreading terror in the ranks of all other parties, and forcing the country into extreme measures, it was merely because it was enabled to gain a firm footing through the policy pursued by the Austrian ministers. The urgent necessity of placing Hungary in a state of defense against the machination of the Austrian cabinet served as a good pretext to cloak the real designs of the faction. The tortuous policy pursued toward Hungary from the very beginning, and the strange spectacle of his majesty's Hungarian and Austrian troops fighting on both sides during the Servian insurrection and the Croatian inroad, first shook the confidence which the nation had so long placed in the throne, and eventually forced the Batthiányi ministry to resign. The manifesto of the Austrian ministers against the Hungarian Constitution; the rehabilitation of the Ban; the manifestoes of September, October, and December, by which the Diet was dissolved, the Constitution destroyed, and the country placed under martial law; the abdication of Ferdinand, and the assumption of the crown of Hungary by the Emperor Francis Joseph, in contempt of legal forms, and the compact by which all his predecessors had ascended the Hungarian throne, which stood open to him in a legal way, if he had chosen to avail himself of it; and, finally, the dogged and stubborn refusals of Prince Windischgrätz to listen to any compromise with "rebels"—all these circumstances combined drove the nation to have recourse to arms, and to rely exclusively on its own resources. The Austrian Constitution of March the 4th, 1849, by which the political existence of Hungary was blotted out, and Hungary treated as a mere province of the Austrian empire, gave the strongest hold to that insatiate party, and served as a welcome argument for breaking the ties that attached Hungary to the Habsburg dynasty. The blind and unscrupulous policy of the faction that had seized the reins of government in Austria soon made the most moderate men in Hungary regret that the defense of the country had been so long neglected, and obliged even those (and they formed a majority in the country) who were averse to the extreme measure of the deposition of the Habsburg dynasty and the declaration of complete independence, to acquiesce in this measure, when it was accomplished, rather than to withdraw from the service of the country.

And in asserting that, with the exception of a contemptible faction, it was, at the commencement, the loyal intention of every one in Hungary to maintain the union with Austria, I do not—whatever he may have done since—exclude Kossuth himself.

The very versatility of his mind and temper, which makes him embrace every novelty with so much ardor and such sanguine expectations, is the best proof that, although stamped by nature for an agitator, he was honest and sincere in this respect, and would have remained so had Austria kept her side of the bargain. Besides, what could have induced any man of common sense in Hungary, at that period, to overstep the bounds of constitutional legality, the attainment of which had been the constant aim of so many Diets, and which was for the first time fully sanctioned and supported by guarantees by which, it was fondly hoped, would render such a desirable state permanent; at a time, too, when he who had provoked a struggle would have been left alone, because the country had every thing to lose and nothing to gain by it? Yes, I repeat, Kossuth himself was sincerely desirous of keeping up the connection with Austria on the terms that had been agreed to. But when the underhand practices that had been constantly carried on could no longer be concealed; when unexpected blows were dealt in the dark, with the intention of wearing Hungary out, and exhausting her strength and patience in fruitless struggles, then it was that Kossuth's impetuous and restless temper, and the inherent weakness of his character and laxity of principle, predominated over his better feelings. Ambition, and a hankering after notoriety, and the suppleness with which he always yielded the most pressing and least scrupulous, placed him first in contradiction with himself, and then involved him —and it may be said, also, the other ministers—in an inconsistent policy, and finally led him to the self-willed and arbitrary measures which accelerated the fall of the Batthiányi ministry. It is unnecessary to charge a man with more failings and follies than he has been guilty of. Kossuth has already enough to answer for before the tribunal of public opinion respecting his political conduct, which was unquestionably the main cause of the ruin and downfall of his country.

Deficient in the knowledge of men and things, in the steadfast bearing, cool judgment, and comprehensive mind of a statesman, and without the firm hand of a ruler; setting at naught all sound calculation, while he played a game of chance, and staked the fate of the nation on the cast of a die; encountering danger with hair-brained temerity when distant, but shrinking from it when near; elated and overbearing in prosperity, but utterly prostrate in adversity; wanting that strength and intrepidity of character that alone commands homage and obedience from others, while he suffered himself to be made the tool of every intriguer he came in connection with; mistaking his manifold accomplishments and natural genius for an aptitude to govern a country in times of trouble; and setting, in the flights of fancy, no bounds to the scope of his ambition, Kossuth hurried away the nation into a course of the most impolitic measures, and grasped the highest power in the realm by dubious means; but, when scarcely in possession of it, suffered it to be wrested from his hands by the man whom he had himself most injudiciously raised to a high station, and against whom, although he had received repeated warnings, as well as proofs of his treachery and worthlessness, he never dared openly and boldly to proceed; by the man whom he had hoped to ensnare, while he crouched beneath him in abject fear, but by whom he was finally outwitted.

The generous sympathy of the English nation can not be quashed by being told that Austria was the benefactor of Hungary, while the Hungarian Diet was a factious assembly, and the majority of the Hungarian ministers a set of rebels In doing honor to Kossuth, the English people have shown their sympathy for the cause of an unfortunate country that has been bereaved of its chartered rights and liberties; and in fomenting this sympathy, Kossuth has been obliged to pay a tribute to the feelings of legality that animates even the humblest classes in England, by eschewing in his speeches the demagogical rant in which he had indulged only a week before at Marseilles. The applause of the English people was not given to the revolutionary character of the man, but to the able manner in which he brought the grievances of his country before them. Several unprejudiced and impartial English journals have already begun to inquire how far Kossuth has a right to the distinction that has been accorded to him, and the *Examiner*, in particular has cast a sharp glance on his past career, and on the presumption with which he launches into his new one. It is not, however, for the English people to settle his right as to the position he is to hold among his own countrymen. The right belongs exclusively to the latter, and not to those who are scattered over the world in exile, but to those in whom reposes the will of the nation at home.

Meanwhile, my own decided opinion on the subject is this, that Kossuth has not the least right to set himself up as the sole and exclusive representative of his country—not the least right to reassume the title of governor and the functions of dictator, as he does in his address from Brussa to the citizens of the United States; and that it is a most unwarrantable, as well as most illogical, proceeding on his part, to contend, as he does in the same document, that the Hungarian nation could not legally enter into any engagement, or adopt any measure that would be incompatible with the act by which he was raised to the dignity of governor; it being obvious, even if he had not resigned this dignity, that when the nation was reconstituted on its former constitutional basis, its legal representatives in Diet assembled would have the right to act in whatever way they might deem the most conducive to the welfare of the country. I am also of opinion that, so far from following a sound policy in wishing, as he does, to remodel the reformed Constitution of 1848, and ingraft on it principles of republicanism and unleavened democracy—principles which are at variance with our national laws and institutions, as well as with the manners, customs, and genius of the people—he would have acted more wisely, and rendered a more essential service to his country, if, after his liberation from the thralldom of detention, he had appeared before the world in the simple character of a private individual. The conspicuous part which he took in the affairs of his country, and his subsequent misfortunes, would have secured him general respect, while the modesty of his demeanor, by effacing from the minds of his countrymen the recollection of the faults and errors he committed, and through which Hungary has been brought to her present state of misery and servitude, would have given him a precedence by courtesy among his companions in exile, and placed him in a position to receive that useful advice and assistance which they would have gladly offered him, for the purpose of hereafter repairing by a course of sound and moderate policy the injuries inflicted on the land of their birth. But instead of acting in this manner, he has set himself up as the dictator of his countrymen. It is, therefore, the sacred duty of those who, although far from wishing to fetter his activity, are not disposed to admit his claims, publicly to protest against his proceedings. Without dwelling any longer on the weighty motives for caution which may be deduced from his past career, I will merely observe that his pretension to be still regarded as governor is the more barefaced from the circumstances attending his resignation. The circumstances are these: He was summoned by Görgey and three members of the ministry to resign. He instantly complied, and resigned the governorship without convening the Council of State, that he was bound by law to consult on every important occasion. He resigned without intimating his intention of doing so to the three other ministers (of which I was one), and who were, consequently, quite unaware of the fact. He did not resign his authority into the hands of the ministers, as under such circumstances he was bound to do, but into the hands of Görgey. He even invested Görgey with a power and authority with which he had not been invested himself, viz., the dictatorship. He delegated a power which he only held himself personally, and, in fact, provisionally, by a direct mandate of the Diet. He resigned in the name of the ministry, which he had no right whatever to do.

Although it may be safely affirmed that he was in a state of moral and physical coercion when he gave in his resignation, it must be borne in mind that he voluntarily confirmed this act when he was free from all restraint, and could never be persuaded to reassume his abandoned power, neither at Lugos, in the midst of General Bem's army, nor subsequently at Mehadia, when Bem urgently requested him to do so, and try the last chance that remained of success, to which request he again returned a negative answer in writing. By thus acting, he abandoned Hungary to her fate, and exposed all those who had taken a part in the war to the vengeance of Austria. He confirmed his avowed intention of retiring into private life, by crossing the frontier and entering the Turkish dominions before the capitulation of Vilagos could possibly be known to him, and while there were still fortresses and armies in Hungary by which the national cause could have been sustained. In his letter of refusal to General Bem, he in fact suggested the expediency of calling together some eminent men in order to form a Provisional Government. On his arrival at Widdin, he again publicly declared (in a letter since published) his resolution of retiring into private life—a resolution which for a short time he acted upon.

Leaving the public to judge how far those facts are reconcilable with his present pretensions, I have the honor to remain your obedient, humble servant.

COUNT CASIMIR BATTHIANYI.

Paris, Hôtel de Ville, Place Ville l'Evêque, Dec. 10.

Letter of Count Casimir Batthiányi to the Editors of the Allgemeine Zeitung.

Respected Editors,—I have read, in a number of the Allgemeine Zeitung, an article signed by M. M. Vukovics and Horvath, concerning the act of abdication of Louis Kossuth, late Governor of Hungary, which had originally appeared in the Cologne Gazette. Against the truth of that article I have nothing to say in general; although, to avoid any misconstruction, I deem it necessary to make some remarks concerning myself. I must observe, in the first place, that, even according to the statements of both those gentlemen in the last Ministerial Council, there was no question about the dissolution of the government. Görgey merely received the commission to treat with Russia on the conditions that the legal autonomy of Hungary be maintained, and a general amnesty be granted.

At Arad, also, the government was threatened on all sides by enemies; not only by external, but even more by internal ones. There was no possibility of its existing then. But no cabinet meeting had been appointed in advance, and it was scarcely necessary to do so, as the posts of the ministers were properly at the side of the governor. It was by accident that I heard of a meeting of a Ministerial Council. While I was about to go to Csanyi's dwelling, in order to satisfy myself of the truth of the information, the council, or, rather, a private conference of ministers (for no summons had come either from the governor or from the president of the ministry) had already terminated. I met M. Vukovics under the gate, who told me what had taken place as an accomplished fact. Both the above-mentioned gentlemen (Vukovics and Horvath) venture to apply to me the maxim *qui tacet consentire videtur*, since I then made no strenuous objection to the steps that had been taken. One reason of my not doing this is, that I considered that step as being merely personal in reference to the ministers who signed it. In the second place, my objections would not have availed effectively, in being made in the street, in a private conversation. Thirdly, I wished to hasten home, feeling fully convinced that I would be probably called by the governor to a regular Ministerial Council without delay, as he could not properly effectuate, either for himself or for the government, the act of abdication without the assent of the members of the government

When I at last learned that the governor was no more in the fortress, and that he had probably already departed, I repaired, in company with Szemere, chairman of the ministry, to Lugos. We found the governor at Radna, where he showed us the document, signed by the three ministers. To our inquiry as to his reply to them, he answered us, " Well, I said they might have their will ;" without, however, reading to us his written answer to them.

After reaching Lugos, we learned that General Bem cared so little about the fracture of his shoulder that he had gone to Arad, where the troops, scattered near Temesvar, were reassembling, and amounted already to the number of thirty thousand men.

Had I been present, even accidentally, in the conference held at Csanyi's house, I should in no case have signed that document addressed to the governor by the three ministers, as I had then already the full conviction of Görgey's being at heart a traitor; but I had still a hope that he would save his army, if nothing else. Moreover, Görgey was at this time all-powerful at Arad. Wherefore the propriety of increasing his power ? At Lugos I imparted to Governor Kossuth my views of the irregularity and invalidity of his act of abdication, and I sought to induce him to await the return of General Bem, which was expected every moment. I had not the least doubt of his (General Bem's) intention to break through into Transylvania, in order to maintain himself there. When General Bem returned, Governor Kossuth had already fled to Turkey, and refused to return, though the general dispatched a request to him to do so.

On the flight of the governor becoming known, the army of Bem dissolved itself. He himself was forced to fly over the Transylvanian mountains and through Wallachia to Widdin, where I arrived about the same time, with several thousand of the troops, which had held the passes of Mehadia, Aravitza, and Arsova, as long as it was possible to do so, and who left those positions only when they saw there was no doubt our cause was utterly lost.

In requesting the respected editors to give a kind insertion in their paper, I sign myself, respectfully, COUNT CASIMIR BATTHIANYI,
Late Minister of Foreign Affairs of Hungary.

Kuttahia, April 27, 1850.

Letter from B. Szemere to Messrs. Vucovics and Horvath.

I have heretofore but said what I did not do, namely, that I took no part in the surrender of the dictatorship to Görgey, and given my motives for my course. You, not being able to deny your signatures, and feeling yourselves touched by the disclosure of my motives, ought to have given the grounds for your action. The question stood simply historical, and not personal. You, however, instead of stating the motives for your action, deemed it better to make me a partaker in it, which of course could not be accomplished. Not being able on such basis to argue from facts, you used mere suspicions against me. This I have not done toward you, and never shall do. Read attentively my article of the 24th of March, and you will not find in it one word casting suspicion merely upon you. It was written with that feeling excited by the unexpected and unjust attack upon me, and which I had a right to repel without making unnecessary accusation And behold there appears your second reply in Nos. 117 and 118 of the Cologne Gazette of this year, in which I find trifling word-pickings and lawyerlike special pleading, instead of the views of statesmen, who look to what is im-

II. E E

portant and general. I see in it a dark ground on which you have embroidered offensive allusions and phrases of suspicion. Frankly, I must say that I regret having given you an opportunity for writing that offensive article. I had a higher conception of your love of justice and impartiality; and it is probable that I am not the only person who has been deceived. I will not follow you into that field of petty and trifling lawyer-like word-fencing, nor am I inclined to imitate your arrow shooting of suspicions. Nay, your conduct in writing that reply will not even influence my judgment as to your former political course. Your mode of treating me can not release me from the obligation I owe to truth. Nor do I desire to prolong this contest, which, by this trifling imparted to it by your reply, has become unpalatable to the public. I regret that you have not endeavored to clear up the chief point, i. e., to point out the motives for the surrender of the dictatorship; for, though you always believed Görgey to be disposed to treachery, I will not doubt that you might assign plausible motives for your conduct. Nay, I will express myself more explicitly, and say that I do not think that those three ministers said to have agreed to it (out of the seven comprising the ministry) were guilty of having originated the proposal, but that the governor of the country (Kossuth) was the guilty one, and who, without asking the concurrence of those three, though they were present, gave the decision. Gentlemen, he who loves the fatherland more than persons can not now or ever justify that conduct. How strange is man! While we were yet fighting the battles of freedom in the fatherland, many of us thought our cause was badly conducted, and that we should perish. But it was urged, union is paramount—let there be no discord, and we were consequently silent. Now in exile, it would be well to clear up fully the Hungarian question, not so much for the sake of the past as for the sake of the present, and still more for the future. It is a vital question to ascertain the errors of the past, but yet it is now urged that particular individuals and certain errors, though these errors can be proved to have been fatal, should be spared. As for me, I say, " the country, liberty, and the future before all." Nations need not hereafter certain names—that time is passed by. What patriot in this era clings to any name but the holy name of liberty? He who does is an idol worshiper. I do not belong to that class. BARTH. SZEMERE.

Paris, May 21, 1850.

The Public Letter of M. Szemere.

Mr. Editor,—In the number of the 20th of December, 1851, of your journal, *The Semi-weekly Courier and New York Enquirer*, in its morning edition, an article is inserted, with the heading " Governor Kossuth." In it is embodied the authentic act of abdication of the government by Kossuth, and among the names of the subscribers thereto, I find also my own.

I did indeed, take part in the business of the war, which we were compelled to wage, for our constitutional liberty and independence, against the Austrian dynasty. I have, indeed, participated in that holy war, but, in so doing, I only fulfilled my duties as a citizen and man, and consequently I have done nothing which could entitle me to lay claim to any particular glory ; yet, on the other hand, I must insist that I have done nothing which could, by any means, bring shame upon me, or soil a clear conscience.

I feel myself therefore constrained, for the sake of truth, for my own honor and political character, to make the following declarations:

1. That I never subscribed that act of abdication.

2. That I never saw the same.

3. That neither my sense of duty as a citizen nor as a patriot would ever have allowed me to put my signature to that act, had I ever seen it, or had its existence ever been made known to me, which never was the fact.

Since it is undoubtedly the fact, that Mr. Kossuth neither was, nor could have been compelled to that abdication by any moral or physical force whatever, and, as besides Mr. Kossuth himself had for weeks, or even months before, spoken of General Görgey as a traitor, I can not see how his abdication and transfer of the supreme power into the hands of a traitor, can be consistent with his so-much-praised heroism and love of country. In war and in revolutions, the hero and superior mind is manifested not by words, but by deeds. In the controversy between Kossuth and Görgey in Arad, on the 11th of August, 1849, one or the other must have sunk, and we see that neither of them appears to have been a hair the worse. Görgey caused Kossuth to be *requested* to abdicate, and Kossuth *hastened* to do it, and immediately thereafter *fled across the Turkish boundary.*

It is important to remark here, that at this moment there were still in the hands of the nation *four* fortresses, and two of these the strongest in the whole country, namely, Komorn and Peterwardein, as well as an army of one hundred and thirty-five thousand men, and three hundred field officers. I believe that never before in the history of the world has the head of a nation turned his back on so powerful a military force.

Görgey laid down his arms only with twenty-six thousand men. The rest of the army surrendered only because they heard, not only that Mr. Kossuth had abdicated, and, by so doing, had declared the hopes of the nation as forever lost, but that he had himself fled the country, giving himself no thought for the fate of his party, his friends, the army, the fortresses, and the nation. He went over the boundaries entirely alone; he avoided carefully his friends and acquaintances, especially all those who assembled on the boundaries, in order that he might the more certainly secure his own safety.

Mr. Kossuth was chosen governor on the 14th of April, 1849, not directly by the people, but by the National Assembly, *provisionally*, and not by votes, but by acclamation, and under the condition of ruling in connection with the ministry, which was also made responsible for every thing.

It is true that Mr. Kossuth could resign his office. In this case, if the National Assembly were in session, new dispositions of authority could have been made; in the absence of the Assembly, the government must of necessity remain in the hands of the ministers.

It is not necessary to remark that the nation had the sovereign right to delegate executive power, but that the person to whom the same had been delegated could never transfer his right to a third party.

Mr. Kossuth, however, on the 11th of August, 1849, in Arad, not only resigned, which he had the power to do, but not only did not assemble the ministry, which had received powers of government contemporaneously with himself, but he transferred to another the power which had been intrusted to his own person.

He did more, he appointed a dictator, which he was not himself.

Mr. Kossuth can no longer consider himself, either in law or in right, as the Governor of Hungary,

Because he *voluntarily* surrendered this power:

Because he transferred this power to another, which he had no right to do:

Because he also abdicated in the name of the whole ministry, without having previously consulted them:

Because he immediately transferred the power of the state to Görgey, a man whom he, and he more than all others, had long before considered a traitor.

Finally, because he did all this without consulting with, and without the knowledge of, that ministry, which had been appointed with him, and consequently even, so far as mere form is considered, acted contrary to the law.

It is not my intention to dissect the unfortunate and ever fluctuating policy of Mr. Kossuth; yet as I am obliged to exculpate myself from any inferences to be drawn from that act, which, nevertheless, though done *in my name*, was done *without my knowledge* and *without my consent*, it is impossible for me on this occasion not to declare, that Mr. Kossuth has no claim, either in law or of right, to the character of Governor of Hungary. *Not in law*, because he so hastily surrendered the office, without even observing the legal forms; *not of right*, because, while on the 14th of April, 1849, when our troops were every where victorious, we saw him stand forward as governor, yet afterward, on the 11th of August, 1849, when we were suffering continual defeat, we saw him hastily and precipitately free himself from the same office; that is to say, in the day of victory and glory he accepted the office; in the day of danger, *he surrendered it* to the first who demanded it of him.

And now he steps forward, weakly and unconsciously forgetting all this, before the world as the Governor of Hungary, and as the dictator among his fellow-exiles, demanding from us unconditional obedience, and asks a second time for a power for which he showed himself before partly incapable, and part of which he misused.

However much I pity the political want of conscience shown in his public character, however much we may rejoice, if he should succeed by his rhetorical agitation to obtain money and sympathy for the cause of Hungary, in order that he may in some measure restore what he has injured by his uncalculating, feverish, vacillating, unprincipled policy; yet, on the other hand, every sensible-minded Hungarian must be convinced, that to recognize Mr. Kossuth as governor, or, as he earnestly claims to be acknowledged, the absolute dictator, would be equivalent to devoting the cause of Hungary for a second time to a severe downfall. We welcome him, therefore, to our ranks, only as a single gifted patriot, perhaps even the first among his equals; but as governor we can not acknowledge him, we who know his past career, and we value divine liberty and our beloved fatherland above every personal consideration.

While I respectfully request you, Mr. Editor, to receive these lines, I take, at the same time, the liberty to make the following remarks: Criticise, examine, condemn, as much as you will, the actions of those persons who have appeared in the late Hungarian War of Independence, we deserve it all; each of us has more or less been wanting; only touch not with contemptuous hand the cause itself, for that cause was, at least, as pure and holy as the war of the American Revolution; in a word, we were the defenders of right and law against the efforts of faithlessness and anarchy; we were the heroes, the apostles, the martyrs of freedom under the persecutions of tyranny. Consider Mr. Kossuth as a rhetorical advocate of the Hungarian cause; he may be its pleader, he never was its *hero*, because at the *first* approach of danger he was the *first* to shrink. In forming an opinion upon his career and his political character, this is all the more important and decisive test, since he (who is beyond all doubt a man the most avaricious of glory that ever lived) always, in every way, by every possible means, endeavored to concentrate confidence in his own person; and hence it was natural enough, that by his weakness in the day of danger the cause of the nation fell with him.

The people, however, remained steadfast, while he had become a fugitive, and, with his crossing the boundaries of Hungary, he filled no longer that high place to which the confidence of a brave people had elevated him.

BARTHOLOMÆUS SZEMERE,
Formerly President of the Hungarian Ministerial Council.
Paris, 4th Jan., 1852, No. 12 Rue Boursault.

Letter of S. Vucovics, late Minister of Justice of Hungary.

Sir,—In *The Times* of December 30, 1851, appeared a letter from Count Casimir Batthiányi, which met, I do not doubt, with the unanimous approbation of our countrymen in that part of it which vindicates the first Hungarian ministry, and more particularly that immortal patriot, Count Louis Batthiányi, against the unpatriotic and groundless aspersions of Prince Esterhazy. The noble count, however, in the latter part of his letter, turns suddenly to another subject, and undertakes to discuss some principles and events of our Revolution in a manner which has placed him in direct antagonism to the advocates of the cause of Hungary. I must confess that it is with great regret that I feel myself compelled to combat the assertions of a man who, by his patriotism, his intelligence, and his great sacrifices on the altar of his native country, has taken so distinguished a place in our ranks.

It is true that, after the close of the Diet of 1847–8, and after the royal sanction given to the reforms carried by it, the whole country, with scarcely the exception of a small faction, was sincerely attached to the maintenance of the union with the house of Austria. This circumstance is of paramount importance, because Hungary, with its constitutional and independent ministries of war and finance, was then thoroughly in a condition in a short time to have created a power sufficient to cope with, and even to overturn the house of Austria, shackled as it then was by the critical state of Vienna and Italy. The nation, however, held to the unhappy delusion that the lately sworn oath of the king was taken in good faith. The more, therefore, I agree with the noble count as to the prevailing sentiment and opinion of the country at the close of the Diet on the 11th of April, 1848, the more decidedly must I combat his assertions that the nation, after so many clandestine and open attacks of the court on the ancient Constitution, and even after the imposition of the Austrian Constitution of the 4th of March, 1849, which annihilated the autonomy and independence of Hungary, felt compelled to have an ultimate recourse to the force of arms; but, nevertheless, remained permanently averse to a deposition of the dynasty, and that it accepted the resolution of the Diet to that effect—stated to have been carried by a minority—merely as a *fait accompli*.

I shall disprove this assertion by a simple narrative of those events which widened the chasm between the people and the dynasty.

So early as the commencement of the Serbian insurrection, the popular suspicion gained ground that the insurrection had been stirred up by the secret intrigues of the court, and confidence in the truth and good faith of the king disappeared accordingly. The nation, however, still indulged the hope that a weak king, though betrayed into ambiguous proceedings, would not permit himself to be carried away into a flagrant breach of the Constitution. This was the time when the king, in the opinion of the people, was kept distinct from the Camarilla. But when the Austrian ministry openly attempted to deprive Hungary of its ministries of war and finance, when the base game of the degradation and restoration of Jellacic was played, and when the Hungarian army, fighting in the name of the king against the insurrections of the Servians and Croats, became aware that the balls of that same king thinned their ranks from the hostile camp, the nation arrived at the universal conviction that the Habsburg dynasty were only pursuing their old absolute tendencies, and that they wanted to force Hungary into self-defense, in order, under the pretext of rebellion, to deprive it of all its constitutional rights and guarantees. It needs no proof that a loud indignation and even hatred of the dynasty spread far and wide in the country in consequence of these intrigues and proceedings. In spite of this natural excitement, and of the war itself carried on by the nation with an increasing enthusiasm of hatred of the house of Austria, no party in the country urged a declaration of *déchéance* or forfeiture against the dynasty. Even all the faithless acts recorded in the letter of Count Casimir Batthiányi, and the cruelties committed in the name of that court in Lower Hungary and Transylvania, did not turn the scales in this direction. The Pragmatic Sanction was still considered as good in law; and the many precedents of our history, when the nation and its kings went to war with each other, and ultimately settled their disputes by solemn pacts confirming the Constitution of the land, conveyed the notion that a reconciliation was even then not impossible.

Without these precedents and reminiscences of history, and only guided by the universal feeling of the country against the dynasty, the Hungarian Parliament would have pronounced the forfeiture of the house of Austria so far back as October, 1848, when Jellacic was appointed absolute plenipotentiary of the king in Hungary, with discretionary power of life and death; or in December, 1848, when, in Olmütz, the succession to the Hungarian throne was changed and determined, without the concurrence of the nation, through the Diet. To force the nation and its Parliament to the last step in its momentous crisis, the court itself broke the dynastic tie.

This was done by the imposition of the Constitution of the 4th of March, 1849, by which the house of Austria itself annihilated the Pragmatic Sanction, treating free and independent Hungary with the arrogance of a conqueror. The nation, more irritated by this act than by any preceding event, saw that the hour was come, beyond which further to defer the dethronement of the dynasty would be alike incompatible with the laws and the honor of Hungary. All the channels of public opinion, the public press, the popular meetings, and even the head-quarters of the army, resounded with emphatic declarations of the impossibility of reconciliation with the dynasty. The garrison of Komorn, the most important fortress of the country, petitioned the government for the declaration of forfeiture. Most assuredly no party maneuvers were wanted in this universal excitement, caused by the Constitution of the 4th of March, to carry a parliamentary resolution of forfeiture.

When the proposition of forfeiture was made, on the 14th of April, 1849, in the House of Representatives, only eight members voted against it, in a house never attended by less than from two hundred and twenty to two hundred and forty members. The House of Magnates adopted this resolution without opposition. The press, of all shades of opinion, though enjoying the most unlimited freedom, also declared for the resolution of the Diet. It was, moreover, received throughout the whole country with patriotic assent and determination. If there was a party opposed to the forfeiture, how came it that it did not hold it to be a duty to declare its opposition in the Diet or through the Press?

What were the views of that party? What measures would they have desired to be taken in consequence of the Constitution of the fourth of March? I find nothing to meet these questions in the letter of Count Casimir Batthiányi

Still less can the act of forfeiture be considered as the work of a party, because the so-called Madaraz party, to which, perhaps, the noble count alludes, was at that very moment vanquished, and the elected governor, in consequence, chose his ministry from the ranks of its opponents.

I must also differ from the noble count with regard to the actual legality of the act of forfeiture and Declaration of Independence of the 14th of April, 1849. I consider this act completely valid in every respect. The noble count supports his view by remarking on the subsequent transfer of power to Görgey. It is necessary, therefore, that I should narrate the whole circumstances of that event.

When the intelligence of the unfortunate battle of Temesvar reached Governor Kossuth, who was then in the fortress of Arad, he immediately summoned a council of the ministry to deliberate on measures of public safety still possible. At this council, in which all the ministers took part, it was resolved to invest Görgey, who stood alone at the head of an unconquered army, with full powers for negotiating a peace. It was, moreover, resolved to dissolve the government, which could not be carried on in any fixed place of safety under the existing circumstances. We did not, however, insert in the instrument investing Görgey with full power (and dispatched to him immediately) the abdication of the government. On the same day (it was the 11th of August, 1849), Görgey declared, in the presence of some of the ministers who had assembled at Csanyi's (who was one of them), that he could not accept the commission because the resignation of the government was not contained in it, while he was sure that the enemy would enter into no negotiations with him so long as Kossuth and his ministry were thought to be behind him. The ministers who were present, after a short deliberation, considering it to be their duty not to stand in the way of the negotiation which had been resolved on as necessary, accordingly sent their resignation to the governor, whom they requested to resign as well. The governor soon after sent his abdication for counter-signature by those members of the ministry, and accordingly the government formally dissolved itself, after having done so *de facto* in the previous council of ministers. I must mention the circumstance that in the governor's instrument of abdication conditions were prescribed by Görgey which were not inserted in the original instrument of authorization issued by the full council. These conditions were the preservation of the nationality and the autonomy of Hungary. Four ministers took part in this resignation of the governor, as above stated—Aulick, Csanyi, Horvath, and I. Two of the ministers, Szemere and Batthiányi, were absent when the formal declaration of the abdication was discussed at Csanyi's residence. I have not mentioned among the ministers our late colleague, the finance minister Dushek, because his treachery, which was afterward brought to light, excludes him from our ranks. From all these circumstances, it will be manifest how unjust the reproaches of Count Casimir Batthiányi are, that no new cabinet council was held.

It is notorious that Görgey abused the full powers with which he was intrusted, instead of procuring the preservation of Hungary by a negotiation for peace, by an ignominious treachery to his native country. From that very moment the power conferred on him by the above-mentioned instrument, and the conditional abdication of the government consequently and legally reverted to him who had invested him with it. To deny this would be to recognize, in the foreign rule which crushed Hungary in consequence of that treachery, legitimate right and lawful power.

The noble count himself answers the question why Kossuth, before crossing the Turkish frontier, did not resume power again. He states that Kossuth could not know, before crossing the frontier, the catastrophe of Vilagos, and therefore left the country in the belief that Görgey would faithfully fulfill his commission; a belief which was the more natural because Görgey had an unconquered army under him, and almost all the fortresses at his disposition—a power more than sufficient to carry on the negotiations, and even to menace the enemy with a continuation of the war. The noble count did not take his present view of this question when, after the treachery of Görgey became known, he countersigned the order written at Widdin by Kossuth, as Governor of Hungary, to the fortress of Komorn.

I, however, perfectly agree with the noble count, that the nation, once more restored to its constitutional existence, and free from foreign yoke, will have the unlimited right to dispose of all the affairs of the country, and consequently of the executive power. To assert a contrary opinion would be a crime against the nation. Not of a liberated nation, which, of course, would have the right to choose whom it will, but of a nation crushed by a usurping power, the claims of Kossuth as elected Governor of Hungary are, I submit, lawful.

I also concur with the noble count, that Kossuth is not the exclusive representative of our native country, and of our war of liberty and independence. Hungary is historically represented by all those who took part in the constitutional and military vindication of its rights, and more especially, and side by side with the governor, by the constitutionally chosen members of the House of Representatives. I consider, however, Kossuth to be the chief representative of the interests of our native country, on account of his deeds as well as his position; but I am far, indeed, from seeing in him a dictator. A dictatorship would find in all those who, like me, hold firmly to the republican principles pronounced by him, the most determined opposition.

Republican principles have not been proclaimed at Kossuth's dictation, as the aim of our national exertions. They were, during our struggle, the well-ascertained and deep-rooted sentiment of the country, and Kossuth could only faithfully represent the proclaimed will and feeling of the nation by inscribing them on his banner. Immediately after the Declaration of Independence, all the manifestations of the national will were unanimous in the desire for a republic. The ministry, which was nominated by the governor as a consequence of that legislative act, declared in both Houses of the Diet that its efforts would be directed to the establishment of a republic. Both Houses joined in this declaration, and in the government no opposition whatever was manifested against it. One of the first acts of the new government was to remove the crown from all national escutcheons, and from the great seal of Hungary. The press, in all its shades, developed republican principles. The new semi-official paper bore the name of *The Republic.* It is true that the government was only provisional, for the war continued, and the definitive decision of this question depended on unforeseen circumstances. We should have preferred almost any settlement to the necessity of a subjection to the Austrian dynasty; and at the price of emancipation from that detested power, the nation would ever have been prepared, for the sake of aid, to choose a king from another race; but certainly, if it had been the unaided victor in the struggle, never. Monarchical government would have been for us the mere resort of expediency. The government of our wishes and principles was the republic.

I do not feel at all convinced, as the noble count asserts, that the institutions and habits of Hungary are incompatible with a democratic republic. I find, on the contrary, traits in them which lead me to an opposite conclusion. The aggregate character of the numerous nobility which resigned its privileges in the Diet of 1847–48, of its own accord, and which was in its nature more a democratic than an aristocratic body, because neither territorial wealth nor rank interfered with or disturbed the equality of its rights; the national antipathy to the system of an Upper House, which was considered as a foreign institution, because it had been introduced under the Austrian dynasty; the immemorial custom of periodically electing all officials, and even the judges; the detestation in which bureaucracy and all the instruments of centralization were held in all ages, while the attachment to the municipal self-government was irradicable; the fact that, in consequence of the laws which had been sanctioned in April, 1848, the county authorities, formerly only elected from the nobility, were democratically re-constituted, and exercised their functions in this form till the catastrophe of Vilagos, without the slightest collision between the different classes of society—the peaceful election of the representatives of the last Diet, conducted almost on the principle of universal suffrage—all these facts unmistakably prove that the germ of democracy lay in our institutions, and that these could receive a democratic development without any concussion. Those characteristic traits of our nation which have been so often misrepresented as signs of an aversion to a republic, and which may be more properly called civic virtues; as, for example, our respect for law, our antipathy to untried political theories, our attachment to traditional customs, and our pride in the history of our country, are no obstacles to, but rather guarantees, and even conditions of a republic, which is to be national and enduring. It would be, indeed, an unprecedented event in history, if staunch royalism could be the characteristic of a country which, like Hungary, has found in its kings, for three hundred years, the inexorable foes of its liberties, and which in that time, for its defense, had to wage six bloody wars against its dynasty.

As to the criticisms by the noble count of the personal character of Kossuth, I take leave to assert that a great majority of the Hungarian nation do not share his opinion. It is not my task to appear as a personal advocate, and I wish, therefore, to advert only to one point of his attack, which may seem to be based on facts. The noble count asserts that Kossuth has attained to power by doubtful means. I am amazed at this assertion, knowing, as I do, that Kossuth was proposed by Count Louis Batthiányi, and nominated by the king, with the universal applause of the nation, to the Ministry of Finance. After the resignation of the first Hungarian ministry, he was freely and unanimously elected by the Diet to the presidency of the Committee of Defense, and, after the declared forfeiture of the dynasty, to the governorship of the country. I know no more honorable means by which a man can be raised to power.

I am unable to guess at the motives of the patriotic count which have prevailed on him to publish the latter part of his letter, and I must believe that its consequences will be pernicious to our common cause, if an irreconcilable division between our countrymen should be the unhappy result.

I trust, sir, that your friendly sentiments for the welfare of Hungary will prevail on you to give these lines a place in your esteemed journal, and I remain, sir, your obedient servant, S. VUCOVICS,

Late Minister of Justice in Hungary.

London, January 17, 1852.

Note No. 35.

Eleven Generals and two Staff-officers shot or hanged at Arad, on the 6th of October, 1849.

1. Lous Aulick.
2. Charles, Count Leiningen-Wessenberg.
3. Ernest Kiss, of Ellemer and Ittebe, shot.
4. John Damjanic.
5. Joseph Nagy-Shandor.
6. Ignatz Török, shot.
7. George Löhner.
8. Charles, Count Vécsey.
9. Charles Knezick.
10. Ernest Pölt von Pöltenberg.
11. Joseph Schweidel, shot.
12. Aristides Dessewffy, shot.
13. William Lazar.
    Colonel Kazintsky, shot a few days after.

Ministers and other Civil Officials.

Louis Batthiányi, President of the Ministry.

Ladislaus Czanyi, Minister of Public Works.

Baron Perenyi, late Septemvir, Lord Lieutenant and President of the Upper House.

Prince Woroniscki, } Aides-de-camps of Dembinski.
Charles Abancourt, }

Peter Gisoro, Commander of the German Legion.

Emerick Szacsvay, Secretary of the Diet.

Baron Jessenak, Government Commissioner in Upper Hungary.

Csernys, Member of the Treasury Board.

Fékéte, the Guerilla leader

An immense number of inferior officers were sent to fortresses to be imprisoned for life or a term of years; and about seventy thousand Hungarians, who had taken part in the combat, were forcibly enlisted in Austrian regiments.

On the 6th of October, thirteen generals and staff-officers were executed. Four of these heroic men met their end at daybreak, the commutation of their sentence to " powder and lead" exempting them from the anguish of witnessing the death of their companions in arms. Among the rest was Ernest Kiss. His brother had become insane after Görgey's treachery; his cousin had fallen, a second Leonidas, in the defense of the Rothenthurm Pass; he himself, the richest landed proprietor in the Banat, whose hospitable castle was all the year round filled with Austrian cavaliers and officers, was on the 6th of October sentenced to death by the Austrian court-martial, on which sat many of the partakers of his hospitality. His friends at Vienna had interceded to save his life, but in vain. He died a painful death: the Austrian soldiers who were ordered to carry the sentence into effect, and who for a whole year had faced the fire of the Hungarian artillery, trembled before their defenseless victim; three separate volleys were fired before Kiss fell: his death-struggles lasted full ten minutes.

The report of the firing was heard in the castle, where those officers sentenced to be hung were preparing for death. Pöltenberg had been in a profound sleep, and startled, as he told the Austrian officer, by the first volley, he had jumped out of bed. The unhappy man had been dreaming that he was in the face of the enemy, and heard the firing of alarm signals at his outposts: it was the summons from the grave.

At six o'clock in the morning the condemned officers were led to the place of execution. Old Aulick died first; he was the most advanced in years, and the court-martial seemed thus to respect the natural privilege of age. Distinguished by his zeal and efforts in the cause of his country, more than by the success which attended them, Aulick was inferior to many of his comrades in point of talent, but in uprightness and strength of character none surpassed him.

Count Leiningen was the third in succession, and the youngest. An opportunity had been offered him, late on the preceding evening, of escaping by flight; but he would not separate his fate from that of his brother-in-law, who was a prisoner in the fortress. His youth, perhaps, inspired him with a desire of giving to his elder companions in sorrow around him an example of heroic stoicism in death; and, on reaching the place of execution, he exclaimed, with melancholy humor, "They ought at least to have treated us to a breakfast." One of the guard of soldiers compassionately handed him his wine-flask. "Thank you, my friend," said the young general; "I want no wine to give me courage; bring me a glass of water." He then wrote on his knees, with a pencil, the following farewell words to his brother-in-law:

"The shots which this morning laid my poor comrades low, still resound in my ears, and before me hangs the body of Aulick on the gallows. In this solemn moment, when I must prepare to appear before my Creator, I once more protest against the charges of Kmetty, at the taking of Buda, which an infamous slanderer has raised against me. On the contrary, I have on all occasions protected the Austrian prisoners. I commend to you my poor Liska and my two children. I die for a cause which always appeared to me just and holy. If, in happier days, my friends ever desire to avenge my death, let them reflect that humanity is the best political wisdom. As for"—Here the hangman interrupted him: it was time to die.

Török, Lahner, Pöltenberg, Nagy-Shandor, Knezick, died one after the other; Vécsey was the last. Perhaps they wished, by this nine-fold aggravation of his torment, to make him suffer for the destruction caused by his cannon at Temesvar. Damjanic preceded him. The usual dark color of his large features was heightened by rage and impatience. His view had never extended further than the glittering point of his sabre; this was the star which he had followed through life; but now he saw whither it had conducted him, and impatiently he exclaimed, when limping up to the gallows, "Why is it that I, who have always been foremost to face the enemy's fire, must here be the last?" The deliberate slowness of the work of butchery seemed to disconcert him more than the approach of death, which he had defied in a hundred battles.

This terrible scene lasted from six until nine o'clock. Nine gibbets stood in a line; for all there was only one hangman and two assistants. All the victims died with the calmness and composure worthy of brave but conquered soldiers, without a trace of cowardice, without a sign of that enthusiasm which they had sufficiently manifested in life; they could well afford to disdain any outward expression of it in the face of death.

Many miles distant from Arad, on the morning of this day—one rendered forever memorable for infamy in the annals of Austria—the sun dawned upon a silent circle of spectators who had been disappointed of an exhibition. Count Louis Batthiányi, the former president of the Hungarian ministry, had been sentenced to terminate his career on the gallows, and in the very centre of the metropolis that had idolized him. The count had wounded himself slightly with a small poniard, and, "from considerations of humanity," he was shot at sunset, on the spot where, according to the express orders of Haynau, he was to have suffered the most ignominious of all deaths. His execution had been determined on for five weeks, but there was a dread at Vienna of the desperate feeling which such horrifying intelligence might strike into the garrison at Komorn. This fortress had capitulated on the 27th of September; on the 3d of October, the Austrians took possession of it with the usual formalities; that very same day Haynau hurried to Pesth, signed the death-warrant of Count Batthiányi, and returned the next morning. His task was accomplished. Within the same hour the sentence of death was announced to the unhappy nobleman.

"To be hung! Was this their mercy in mitigating my imprisonment? To be hung! Oh, base and dastardly revenge! Yes, the person who has sworn to my death—my death—" These were the words Batthiányi spoke, at short pauses, when he heard his sentence. At the last word he broke off abruptly, bearing with him to the grave a secret which had long found its interpretation in the aristocratic circles of Vienna.—*Schlessinger.*

THE END.